final PASSAGES

final
PASSAGES

The Intercolonial
....
Slave Trade of British
....
America, 1619–1807
....

GREGORY E. O'MALLEY

Published for the OMOHUNDRO INSTITUTE OF
EARLY AMERICAN HISTORY AND CULTURE,
Williamsburg, Virginia, by the UNIVERSITY OF
NORTH CAROLINA PRESS, Chapel Hill

The Omohundro Institute

of Early American History

and Culture is sponsored jointly

by the College of William and

Mary and the Colonial

Williamsburg Foundation.

On November 15, 1996, the

Institute adopted the present

name in honor of a bequest from

Malvern H. Omohundro, Jr.

Set in Minion by Tseng Information Systems, Inc.
Manufactured in the United States of America

Library of Congress Cataloging-in-Publication Data
O'Malley, Gregory E.
Final passages : the intercolonial slave trade of British
America, 1619–1807 / Gregory E. O'Malley.
pages cm
Includes bibliographical references and index.
ISBN 978-1-4696-1534-9 (cloth : alk. paper)
ISBN 978-1-4696-2984-1 (pbk.: alk. paper)
ISBN 978-1-4696-1535-6 (ebook)
1. Slave trade — Great Britain — History. 2. Slave trade —
Great Britain — Colonies — America — History. 3. Great
Britain — Colonies — History. I. Title.
HT1162.O58 2014
306.3′620941 — dc23
2014008432

The paper in this book meets the guidelines for
permanence and durability of the Committee on
Production Guidelines for Book Longevity of the
Council on Library Resources. The University of
North Carolina Press has been a member of the
Green Press Initiative since 2003.

For my parents,

Jim and Kim,

for everything.

acknowledgments

This project, in various incarnations, has been in the works for just more than a decade—time enough to accumulate many debts and a legion of creditors. Generally, these are not debts one can repay. Hopefully the many people and institutions who assisted this endeavor see something in the book to make the aid worthwhile, beyond just their names on this page. The results would have been far inferior without so much support and encouragement.

In the dissertation phase, first and foremost, I benefited from a model advisor. Phil Morgan challenged, encouraged, and criticized in the right measures. The time and energy he commits to students is admirable. He remains a great mentor and friend. Jack Greene also critiqued and shepherded the project, teaching me an enormous amount about the archive as well as history. Others made Johns Hopkins a great place to study. My dissertation committee—Michael Johnson, Ron Walters, Simon During, Jane Guyer—offered sage advice. Sara Berry and the late John Russell-Wood were wonderful teachers. And all the members of the Early American Seminar at Hopkins taught me a great deal, both from their wonderful examples and their suggestions and criticisms for my drafts; I thank Toby Ditz, Kate Murphy, Catherine Molineux, Rich Bond, Andrew Miller, Carl Keyes, Molly Warsh, Jessica Stern, Jessica Roney, Eran Shalev, Justin Roberts, James Roberts, Joe Adelman, Katie Jorgensen Gray, Alec Haskell, Mark Thompson, and Tom Foster. Non–early Americanists in my cohort, most notably Caleb McDaniel, Ethan Miller, and Clare Monagle, also exchanged drafts, coffees, ideas, and good cheer.

Beyond Hopkins, numerous scholars shared insights, sources, and constructive criticisms. Stephen Behrendt and Trevor Burnard read a dissertation proposal and helped me avoid starting on the wrong foot. Lorena Walsh offered comments (and shared data) at that stage and then kept returning with more assistance—as a not-so-anonymous reviewer and as a recommender. David Eltis has been an incredible help; he offered guidance on building a database of slave-trading voyages, shared data on intra-American trafficking, wrote recommendations, and read drafts of several dissertation chapters. Peter Mancall read drafts, wrote recommendations, and gave me a hard time about anything he could think of. Paul Lachance shared data as well, and Brad Wood shared his forthcoming edition of James Murray's letters.

I have also benefited from presenting work-in-progress before sharp, thoughtful audiences that pushed me in good directions (and away from some bad ones). Appearances at the Omohundro Institute of Early American History and Culture, the Rocky Mountain Seminar in Early American History, the Caltech Early Modern Group, the USC-Huntington American Origins Seminar, the Bay Area Seminar in Early American History and Culture, the UCSC Cultural Studies Seminar, and a "next generation" of the Hopkins Early American Seminar were all extremely helpful. Great colleagues at my academic postings have also offered valuable input in less formal settings. Morgan Kousser, Jean-Laurent Rosenthal, and Tracy Dennison at Caltech deserve special mention, as do Roy Ritchie at the Huntington, and Kate Jones, Gail Hershatter, Terry Burke, and Lynn Westerkamp at the University of California, Santa Cruz. The reviewers of the entire manuscript for the University of North Carolina Press—Barbara Solow, Patrick Manning, and Jennifer Morgan—were incredible, saving me from errors, alerting me to sources, and helping to develop key arguments. I hope they see results from their careful reading and insightful criticisms. Much of Chapter 7 appeared previously in David Gleeson and Simon Keith Lewis, eds., *Ambiguous Anniversary: The Bicentenary of the International Slave Trade Bans* (Columbia, S.C., 2012); much smaller segments herein were published in "Beyond the Middle Passage: Slave Migration from the Caribbean to North America, 1619–1807," *William and Mary Quarterly*, 3d Ser., LXI (2009), 125–172. I thank both publishers for allowing me to repurpose that material here.

The staff at many libraries and archives shared a wealth of knowledge and, of course, the collections—most notably at Johns Hopkins' Milton S. Eisenhower Library (especially Jeannette Pierce and Lynne Stuart); the South Caroliniana Library (Graham Duncan and Brian Cuthrell); the South Carolina Department of Archives and History (Charles Lesser); the Library Company of Philadelphia (Jim Green); the Historical Society of Pennsylvania; France's Archives Nationales d'Outre Mer; the British Library; Britain's National Archives; the Bristol Central Library, the Bristol Record Office, and the Bristol University Library; the Devon Record Office; the Liverpool Record Office, the University of Liverpool Library, and the Merseyside Maritime Museum; the Virginia Historical Society; the South Carolina Historical Society; the Georgia Historical Society; and the John D. Rockefeller, Jr. Library of Colonial Williamsburg.

Financial support came from many corners. The History Department at Hopkins funded the dissertation stage. The Harvard Atlantic History Seminar's predoctoral travel fellowship funded research in England in 2004. A grant from the Johns Hopkins Center for Africana Studies also supported that trip. An Andrew W. Mellon Fellowship from the Virginia Historical Society supported research there. A Singleton Fellowship from Johns Hopkins supported a semester writing in Florence in 2005. A National Endowment for the Humanities Post-Doctoral Fellowship at the Library Company of Philadelphia facilitated my research there in 2006 (and next door at the Historical Society of Pennsylvania). A Mellon Caltech Huntington Postdoctoral faculty appointment employed me for two years, while funding research at the Huntington, as well as in South Carolina and France. A Gilder Lehrman Fellowship supported research at Colonial Williamsburg's Rockefeller Library in 2009. Finally the American Council of Learned Societies' Oscar Handlin Fellowship and the Omohundro Institute's Andrew W. Mellon Postdoctoral Fellowship bought me a year and a half to finish writing (and a temporary reprieve from the long-distance phase of my academic marriage). The University of California, Santa Cruz, kindly supported me in taking these last two fellowships.

Many at the Omohundro Institute have played a major role in the project's late stages. During my time as fellow, the Institute sent me to numerous conferences and brought me to Williamsburg several times, where Ron Hoffman put me up in his home. Fredrika Teute's insights on morphing a dissertation into a book have been invaluable; she sharpened many arguments while taking me on lovely walks with her dogs. Kathy Burdette's editing has been incredible; trust me, dear reader, you owe her your thanks. (She even promised to tell no one about my five-*however* paragraph.) All the staff, scholars, and fellows of the Institute really made it a home away from home; long live "ye Olde!"

Finally, I need to thank family and friends more than I can ever say. Thanks to the entire O'Malley and Sullivan clans. Craig Jaffe, always a great friend, came through at an especially tough time. Too many other friends to name have let me bore them with archival discoveries and academic angst; my thanks to all for the encouragement and love. My parents, Kim and Jim, opened endless doors of opportunity, cheered me on, and dusted me off when I stumbled. Brian O'Malley and Krishna Upadhya kept their door open when we enjoyed the same city and stayed great friends at other times. And Elaine Sullivan entered my life when this project did; even if she can't wait to know me without it, she helped it reach completion more than she will ever realize. I thank a graduate student softball league for bringing us together, and I thank Elaine for a million things, big and small, with all my heart.

contents

illustrations

TABLES

final PASSAGES

introduction

In November 1755, more than three hundred Angolan men, women, and children sailed into the Caribbean Sea, crowded aboard the French ship *l'Aimable*. They were bound for the French sugar colony of Saint-Domingue but never got there. As *l'Aimable* traversed the Lesser Antilles, she ran across "his [British] majesty's ship" *Fowler*, armed to the teeth and cruising for prizes. Though official declaration had yet to arrive, the *Fowler* signaled war's descent on the Caribbean. At its helm, Admiral Thomas Frankland led a naval squadron that was getting a head start on privateering. *L'Aimable* was among the first victims. The African captives on board likely heard a warning shot from the *Fowler's* cannon but were probably spared the terror of a significant battle, as a slave ship was no match for a naval fleet. What capture by British privateers meant for the enslaved cargo of *l'Aimable* was a change of ownership and itinerary. Instead of heading to Saint-Domingue, *l'Aimable* set a new course for Barbados, where the Middle Passage ended for these 327 survivors of the Atlantic crossing. For some, all that remained of their voyage to American slavery was a short, overland trip within the island. For others, however, much of the journey was still to come.[1]

Under British naval custom, Admiral Frankland was entitled to one-eighth of his fleet's prizes, so he claimed 146 of *l'Aimable's* captives—his share from not only that ship but also two other French slavers captured and sent to Antigua around the same time. Frankland did not sell his prizes locally. Instead, he partnered with a Bridgetown merchant, Gedney Clarke, in transshipping the Angolan people to South Carolina. Clarke maintained steady correspondence with traders in other colonies, and Charleston merchant Henry Laurens had informed Clarke of exceptionally high demand for enslaved Africans in South Carolina in recent months. Furthermore, Laurens had reported that the only expected slave shipments to South Carolina that year were from the Gambia River region, and the first ships to arrive from Gambia had reported that such vessels "are not likely to get half their Compliment of Slaves . . . [because]

1. "Antigua, December 9," *South-Carolina Gazette*, Dec. 25, 1755–Jan. 1, 1756. For more on *l'Aimable's* transatlantic voyage, see *Voyages: The Trans-Atlantic Slave Trade Database*, accessed August 2011, www.slavevoyages.org (hereafter cited as *Voyages*), Voyage ID no. 31523.

the small Pox is very rife in every part of that River." From this intelligence, Laurens deduced that South Carolina would be undersupplied with African laborers, driving up prices relative to other American markets. Since ventures to Africa took months to plan and even longer to execute, Laurens recognized that traders from across the Atlantic would be slow to react to the rising prices. Sensing opportunity, he had proposed to numerous West Indian merchants that "there is a chance of making Money on a parcell of Slaves purchas'd with you to come down here in the Fall." Gedney Clarke and Thomas Frankland responded readily to Laurens's intelligence.[2]

Thus, the convergence of smallpox in the Gambia River, the Seven Years' War between Britain and France, relative demand in South Carolina and Barbados, and the mercantile ambitions of Frankland, Clarke, and Laurens forced 146 weary Angolan travelers back to sea after just three or four weeks of recovery from the Middle Passage in Barbados. For this next journey, they boarded a brig named—in bitter irony—*Relief*. Conditions were grim. Once at sea, the *Relief* proved "much out of kilter, [with] her Decks and all her upper works in want of Caulking." It was late December, so the temperature would have dropped considerably during the northbound voyage, but with "the Water that came down through the Deck," the Angolans were shivering before they even left the Caribbean. "Capt. Moses," who was not actually the ship's captain but rather the mate overseeing the captives, "was oblig'd to put their Cloaths on a few days after he left Barbadoes to preserve them." Moses likely delegated this task to the "three Negroes . . . put on board to take care of the rest." Unfortunately, the rough cotton garb typically given to captives simply soaked up the dripping water, offering little comfort. To fix the ship's problems, the *Relief*'s captain, William Lightbourn, sailed the ship only as far as Anguilla before halting for nine days of stopgap repairs. The *Relief* then pushed on to South Carolina and colder weather. Not surprisingly, "the Slaves . . . suffer'd very greatly." Six of the Angolans died at sea, and when the *Relief* finally reached Charles-

2. Frankland's squadron also captured the ship *Alcion* and the snow *Partein*, both bound for Saint-Domingue with enslaved Angolans; see "Antigua, November 4," *South-Carolina Gazette*, Dec. 4–11, 1755; "St. John's in Antigua, November 4," *Maryland Gazette*, Dec. 26, 1755. On "the Commodore's eighth share of prizes," see Richard Pares, *War and Trade in the West Indies, 1739–1763* (Oxford, 1936), 282–283. It is also possible that Frankland purchased more slaves than his share alone entitled him. Quoted material from Henry Laurens to Smith and Clifton, Jul. 17, 1755, in Philip M. Hamer et al., eds., *The Papers of Henry Laurens*, 16 vols. (Columbia, S.C., 1968–2002), I, 294–295 (hereafter cited as *Laurens Papers*); for similar information sent to Gedney Clarke, see ibid., 316–318, 324–325, 331–332. For more on Clarke's business selling prizes from privateering, see S. D. Smith, *Slavery, Family, and Gentry Capitalism in the British Atlantic: The World of the Lascelles, 1648–1834* (New York, 2006), 113–116.

ton's harbor on January 12, 1756, "six or seven more [were] very low and weak." A month had passed since their departure from Bridgetown.[3]

Still, the suffering captives did not land in Charleston immediately. South Carolina law required the *Relief* to spend ten days quarantined on Sullivan's Island in the harbor, where Laurens sent "a Doctor on board to visit and a carefull Woman as to nurse" the ailing captives. Laurens insisted that "Our Pest House where the Slaves are to be placed during their Quarentine is in good order and they have a plenty of Wood at hand," but surely for the Angolans, encountering their first winter outside the tropics, the fire was inadequate to chase away the chill. Even Laurens lacked confidence, adding, "We hope the Cloathing they have will be sufficient." At least on land they could stay dry. It was cold, but the unwilling immigrants "found the most favourable Weather that could be wish'd for at that Season of the Year or their mortallity must have been much more considerable."[4]

Laurens did not wait for his captives to survive quarantine before publicizing their availability. In the first issue of the *South-Carolina Gazette* after their arrival, Austin and Laurens announced the sale of "a Cargo of prime ANGOLA Men and Women SLAVES, Chiefly young People and healthy," scheduled for January 22, their first day out of quarantine. Charleston slave merchants advertised arriving Africans as soon as possible, a week or more in advance of a sale, hoping to attract distant buyers, and Laurens was confident the *Relief*'s enslaved men and women would draw planters to Charleston "from the remote parts of the Country." Austin and Laurens distorted the truth, however, when marketing the Angolan captives as "healthy." Despite "plenty of wood" and the visits of doctors and nurses, survivors of the *Relief*'s leaky intercolonial voyage (not to mention the Middle Passage before that) struggled to recover. "The Flux"—probably dysentery—was rampant among them. Even "Capt. Moses was in a low poor state of health." By the time January 22 came around, thirteen survivors of the seaborne passage had perished in South Carolina, and there were "several more in great danger." Of the 127 surviving Angolans, Austin and Laurens "could only bring into the Yard 105" to be viewed by potential buyers. "[T]he rest that remain'd alive were in a bad condition with the Flux," with 11 of them "sick in the Hospital." The additional voyage after surviving the Middle Passage had been too much.[5]

3. Laurens to Gidney [Gedney] Clarke, Jan. 12, 1756, in *Laurens Papers,* II, 62–65.

4. Laurens to Clarke, Jan. 12, 1756, Feb. 21, 1756, ibid., 62–64, 100–101, esp. 100.

5. *South-Carolina Gazette,* Jan. 15, 1756; Laurens to Law, Satterthwaite, and Jones, Barbados, Jan. 12, 1756, and Laurens to Clarke, Jan. 31, 1756, both in *Laurens Papers,* II, 64–66, 82–84.

From the merchants' perspective, the problems went beyond the dead and ailing human commodities. The event did not attract as many buyers as Laurens had hoped because "it unluckily happen'd that a Pereparamina [pneumonia] prevail'd . . . in many parts of the Province" at the time. Buyers still snatched up most of the enslaved people "that were able to appear in the Yard," but Laurens felt that the poor turnout had dampened prices. The sale was probably a "scramble," in which merchants allowed buyers to enter their "yard," or board a ship, only at a designated time, with the Africans arranged according to predetermined prices. Buyers could then rush in and literally grab individuals on a first-come, first-served basis. Traders hoped that in the frenzy buyers would overlook blemishes and maladies that would otherwise drive down prices. But if few buyers turned out and the captives lacked the appearance of strength and health, the strategy could fall flat. Laurens reported that most prospective buyers deemed the Angolan people from the *Relief* "a very indifferent parcell, that they were much too small a People for the business of this Country and on this Account many went away empty handed that would otherways have purchas'd." Laurens eventually "put off all [but] about ten" of those healthy enough to appear for the sale, but not before reducing prices. Another problem for the traders was that other speculators in the American slave market had noticed the high prices in Charleston. With Frankland's fleet delivering numerous French prize vessels to Barbados and Antigua, many intercolonial traders had bought up the twice-captured Africans and shipped them to Charleston. Intercolonial trade had glutted the market. "The monstrous prices given for a few Slaves in the month of October has produced all this Evil," Laurens explained. Traders "brought down parcell after parcell from the West Indias incessantly all this Winter." [6]

Of course, such market conditions only mattered to the Angolan captives in terms of their personal situations and forced migrations. Those who were sold departed the yard of the Austin and Laurens mercantile house quickly, perhaps bidding a hasty farewell to fellow captives with whom they shared ties of kinship or bonds forged in the crucible of the slave ships. They faced yet another journey—this time overland to the home or plantation of their buyer. For some, this trip was mercifully short, just across town, but if Laurens was correct in predicting that the sale would draw planters "from the remote parts of the Country," some of the Angolans faced marches of more than one hundred miles over several days. Meanwhile, others from the *Relief* remained un-

6. Laurens to Law, Satterthwaite, and Jones, Jan. 31, 1756, Laurens to Clarke, Jan. 31, 1756, in *Laurens Papers,* II, 81–82, 82–84.

sold; a final plantation journey had to wait. Laurens found buyers for some of them over the following weeks, so they filed out of the merchants' yard one and two at a time. After a month, just ten of the sickest remained. With the Charleston market glutted, Laurens figured that these stragglers "could not sell . . . in Town at any tolerable price being much reduced and ordinary." He decided to transship them once more. These last unsold survivors returned to sea. Only one woman was spared this move, "being very much swell'd and having Impostume on her Knee." [7]

Thankfully, this last passage was just "round to George Town, a Port to the Northward" of Charleston by sixty miles but still within the colony. During the first month in George Town, six of the Angolans found themselves sold by Laurens's agents, fetching, in Laurens's words, "more than the whole Nine would have brought" in Charleston. Meanwhile, back in the entrepôt, Laurens sold the woman he described as "the Wench that remain'd with us in Town." Sometime in April or May, one of the three Angolans who remained unsold in George Town finally succumbed to the hardships of the journey. The other two survived, however. They finally sold more than six months after (and more than two thousand miles away from) their first arrival in the Americas. [8]

■ The Angolan men and women from *l'Aimable* who rode the *Relief* to South Carolina before dispersing across the colony endured a particularly convoluted journey to American slavery, but they were just a few among hundreds of thousands of enslaved people who faced final passages after surviving an Atlantic crossing to British America. Time and again, African captives climbed off the vessels that carried them from Africa to Jamaica or Dominica or South Carolina, only to be forced aboard a schooner that whisked them away again to North Carolina or Martinique or Cartagena. Studies of the Atlantic slave trade highlight the infamous Middle Passage, the forced crossing of the Atlantic, concluding the story with a sale of captives in the American port where the ocean crossing ended. Implicit in that choice of endpoint is an assumption that plantation owners—and others eager to exploit enslaved labor— were the buyers of enslaved people after the Atlantic crossing. But another type of buyer prowled the sales of recently arrived Africans in early America: one seeking captives to exploit, not as laborers, but as commodities. Trading

7. Laurens to Law, Satterthwaite, and Jones, Jan. 12, 1756, Laurens to Clarke, Mar. 3, 1756, both ibid., 65, 123–124.

8. Laurens to Clarke, Mar. 3, Apr. 5, 1756, ibid., 123, 140–141. On the fates of the last three Angolans, see Laurens to Thomas Frankland, June 4, 1756, 208–210.

between American colonies, these speculators monitored the prices for people in various ports and forged commercial connections across imperial borders. When opportunities arose, they pounced, buying newly arrived captives in one port, forcing them back aboard ships to another colony, and selling them all over again. For the traders, such dealings opened myriad economic possibilities because enslaved workers were among the most coveted assets in the colonial Americas. For the captives, such speculative endeavors meant that their forced migrations often continued after the transatlantic voyage. This intercolonial trafficking—its scale and reasons for existence, the strategies of the traders, its importance to imperial rivalries, its connections to broader commerce, and the final passages it entailed for African captives—is the subject of this book.

The scope of *Final Passages* reaches from the major ports of African arrival in British America (or the United States) to any destinations to which Africans continued their migrations. These disembarkation ports—such as Bridgetown, Barbados; Kingston, Jamaica; Charleston, South Carolina; and Roseau, Dominica—were not just end points of the transatlantic slave trade. They were entrepôts, gateways through which African captives passed en route to a host of colonies throughout the British, Spanish, and French Empires (and occasionally others) in the Americas. There are several reasons for focusing on the intercolonial trade from British entrepôts in particular. First, British merchants were among the most active transatlantic slave traders. Roughly 12.5 million African people entered the transatlantic slave trade, and British (and U.S.) traders carried more than one-quarter of them, more than 3.5 million. Only Portuguese, including Brazilian, traders carried more Africans across the Atlantic, and British deliveries outstripped even them during the slave trade's peak years in the eighteenth century. Furthermore, British intercolonial traders engaged in a diverse range of slave transshipment activities. The outposts of British America—spread across the Caribbean, North America, and occasionally South America—adopted varied economic regimes and labor systems. In some regions, slave plantations anchored economies; in others, enslaved people toiled in more marginal tasks and professions. Not only did the labor demands of British colonies differ considerably over time and space, but so did the relationships of various colonies to Atlantic trading patterns. This diversity fostered a range of slave-trading activities within the empire. Transimperial commerce further bolstered the trade. British transatlantic traders delivered Africans to entrepôts in British America, and then British colonists or foreign settlers navigated the transshipment of the human commodities across imperial lines—legally or otherwise. Study of the intercolonial slave trade from British American entrepôts thus allows for analysis of trade and forced migration both within and beyond the British Empire. Exploring the range of routes African people traveled after the Middle Passage exposes many political and economic reasons for intercolonial trading activities, revealing many layers of profit from the further migrations that enslaved people endured.[9]

Final Passages develops five main, interrelated arguments about this traffic in human beings. First, and most simply, the intercolonial slave trade was robust in scale. Of the roughly 2.7 million Africans forced across the Atlantic to British American ports from the mid-seventeenth to the early nineteenth century, approximately 15 percent—well over 300,000 people—promptly boarded new ships bound for other parts of the Americas. More than 200,000 of them departed the British Empire, bound primarily for French and Spanish settlements. Over 70,000 African people endured transshipment from the Caribbean to North America. Another 50,000 captives faced final passages from one British Caribbean territory to another. Many more were purchased by speculators who moved people within their colony of arrival for resale. This extensive intercolonial slave trading occurred for a variety of reasons. Colonists in many American regions wanted enslaved Africans but rarely saw vessels arrive directly from Africa, owing to both economics and geopolitics. In the broadest sense, demand exceeded supply. Europeans struggled to obtain as many captives on the African coast as they desired, and not all colonies could prevail in drawing shipments. Those settlements that lacked large numbers of potential buyers, sufficient capital, or well-connected merchants often failed to attract shippers directly from Africa who typically carried two or three hundred Africans per voyage. The need to sell all of these captives quickly, without deflating prices or offering extensive credit, steered transatlantic slave ships away from small, underdeveloped British colonies—such as the Bahamas or North Carolina—and also from larger, more prosperous ones where the exploitation of African labor nonetheless remained marginal, such as Pennsylvania or Massachusetts. Slave trading to these colonies could only be profitable on a smaller scale, a niche intercolonial slavers were keen to fill.[10]

Trafficking between colonies was also robust because geopolitical and mercantile factors left many colonists outside British territory struggling to ac-

9. For estimates of the volume of the transatlantic slave trade and the share carried by merchants of various nations and empires, see *Voyages,* accessed August 2011, http://slavevoyages .org/tast/assessment/estimates.faces?yearFrom=1501&yearTo=1866.

10. David Eltis, *The Rise of African Slavery in the Americas* (New York, 2000), chap. 7.

quire enslaved laborers from merchants of their own empire. Most notably, the colonies of Spanish America relied on foreigners for slave shipments owing to treaties dating back to the fifteenth century, which barred Spanish merchants from Africa. In the sixteenth and seventeenth centuries, the Spanish turned chiefly to Portuguese and Dutch suppliers, but from 1660 onward, British slavers became increasingly important for providing Spanish America's African immigrants. Likewise, from the late seventeenth through the eighteenth century, French colonists looked to British traders to supplement insufficient deliveries from their own traders. The resulting British trade to foreign colonies often involved intercolonial shipments because relations between Britain and both France and Spain were tense. At times, commerce between the colonies of these powers was illegal in the eyes of one government or another, and even when condoned, it was complicated and perilous. Large vessels carrying hundreds of ailing African captives and out-of-date diplomatic information across the ocean typically avoided the risk of entering foreign harbors. Merchants trading people across imperial borders had to proceed with caution, so more nimble intercolonial traders possessed a great advantage due to their proximity to foreign markets. They could forge personal connections in foreign colonies and keep abreast of changes in policy or policing.

A second key claim of *Final Passages* is that the extensive scale of intercolonial slave trading powerfully shaped enslaved people's experiences. Study of the forced migrations between American colonies reminds us that the Middle Passage across the Atlantic was, for all its horrors, but one part of a long and multifaceted journey to American slavery. For most twenty-first-century readers, "Middle Passage" conjures thoughts of the plight of African people in their Atlantic crossings, but the voyage was actually termed "middle" to reflect European, not African, experience. For many European traders, the transatlantic voyage formed the second leg of a three-part journey: a first passage, from Europe to Africa with trade goods; a "middle" passage, from Africa to America with slaves; and a third voyage, from America back to Europe with colonial staples. There were certainly deviations from this "triangle" trade, but it was such three-legged journeys that gave the Middle Passage its name. The irony is that, despite these Eurocentric origins, the term "Middle Passage" fits the experiences of many African migrants in ways that historians often fail to recognize. Their journeys did not usually begin at ports of embarkation for the ocean crossing, nor did they necessarily end when transatlantic vessels first reached the Americas. Instead, people fell into slavery both in African coastal regions and deep in the interior, with extended journeys to port cities increasingly common (especially for men) as the slave trade expanded in the eighteenth century. Stops to toil for African owners along the way, for a harvest season or even a few years, sometimes punctuated these trips. Only upon reaching the Atlantic coast were such people sold to Europeans for a further voyage to the New World.[11]

Just as enslaved people funneled into the Atlantic slave trade from wide regions in West Africa, many spread outward from their ports of arrival in the New World. It is useful to think of the Atlantic slave trade as analogous to a major river system, such as the Nile. Like the tributaries of a river, slave traders within Africa channeled people from wide catchment areas to ports of embarkation, and from these ports, transatlantic vessels flowed into a metaphorical torrent, propelled across the Atlantic by the actual watercourse forged by the trade winds and equatorial currents. From the major American entrepôts, forced migrants then branched out again, like the bifurcating streams of a

---

11. On the journeys of slaves within Africa, see Paul E. Lovejoy, *Transformations in Slavery: A History of Slavery in Africa*, 3d ed. (New York, 2011), 53–62, 73–83; Patrick Manning, *The African Diaspora: A History through Culture* (New York, 2009), 101–113, 123; Vincent Brown, *The Reaper's Garden: Death and Power in the World of Atlantic Slavery* (Cambridge, Mass., 2008), 32–38; Paul E. Lovejoy and David Richardson, "Competing Markets for Male and Female Slaves: Prices in the Interior of West Africa, 1780–1850," *International Journal of African Historical Studies*, XXVIII (1995), 261–293; Femi J. Kolapo, "The Igbo and Their Neighbours during the Era of the Atlantic Slave-Trade," *Slavery and Abolition*, XXV (2004), 114–133; Robin Law, *The Slave Coast of West Africa, 1550–1750: The Impact of the Atlantic Slave Trade on an African Society* (Oxford, 1991), 182–191; Law, *The Oyo Empire, c. 1600–c. 1836: A West African Imperialism in the Era of the Atlantic Slave Trade* (Oxford, 1977), esp. 207–236; Phyllis M. Martin, *The External Trade of the Loango Coast, 1576–1870: The Effects of Changing Commercial Relations on the Vili Kingdom of Loango* (Oxford, 1972), esp. chap. 4; Joseph C. Miller, *Way of Death: Merchant Capitalism and the Angolan Slave Trade, 1730–1830* (Madison, Wis., 1988), 105–126; Jan Hogendorn, "Economic Modelling of Price Differences in the Slave Trade between the Central Sudan and the Coast," *Slavery and Abolition*, XVII, no. 3 (December 1996), 209–222; G. Ugo Nwokeji, "African Conceptions of Gender and the Slave Traffic," *William and Mary Quarterly*, 3d. Ser., LVIII (2001), 47–68; Douglas B. Chambers, "Ethnicity in the Diaspora: The Slave-Trade and the Creation of African 'Nations' in the Americas," *Slavery and Abolition*, XX, no. 3 (December 2001), 25–26; David Northrup, "Igbo and Myth Igbo: Culture and Ethnicity in the Atlantic World, 1600–1850," ibid., XXI, no. 3 (December 2000), 1–20; Jerome S. Handler, "Survivors of the Middle Passage: Life Histories of Enslaved Africans in British America," ibid., XXIII, no. 1 (April 2002), 37–38; Robert A. Sargent, *Economics, Politics, and Social Change in the Benue Basin, c. 1300–1700: A Regional Approach to Pre-colonial West African History* (Enugu, Nigeria, 1999), 190–195; John Thornton, "The African Experience of the '20. and Odd Negroes' Arriving in Virginia in 1619," *WMQ*, 3d Ser., LV (1998), 432; Thornton, *Africa and Africans in the Making of the Atlantic World, 1400–1680* (New York, 1992), 194; Charles Piot, "Of Slaves and the Gift: Kabre Sale of Kin during the Era of the Slave Trade," *Journal of African History*, XXXVII (1996), 34, 47; Alexander X. Byrd, *Captives and Voyagers: Black Migrants across the Eighteenth-Century British Atlantic World* (Baton Rouge, 2008), 17–31.

river's delta—some great and some small. The routes of the intra-American phase of the slave trade meandered through time, with some channels flowing heavily for a few years, only to dry up in the next. Cumulatively, however, such intercolonial channels comprised an ongoing forced migration of hundreds of thousands of people. Only by analyzing this intercolonial phase after the Atlantic crossing does the full scope of the slave trade and the African migration experience become evident.[12]

The final passage added risks in ways both obvious and subtle. Of course, intercolonial trade prolonged the journeys of African people to American slavery, so it added to the mortality of the slave trade as ill and debilitated survivors of the Atlantic crossing reboarded ships and returned to sea. Such dispersal also increased cultural and linguistic isolation for captives as traders parceled out shipmates from single African regions; local buyers purchased some, whereas others were selected for transshipment. Owing to patterns in the transatlantic slave trade that linked some American locales with particular African source regions for enslaved people, those transshipped faced a likelihood of settling in a colony where most other enslaved people hailed from foreign parts of Africa. Intercolonial dispersals thus caused social alienation for many captives while diversifying the colonies' enslaved populations.

This study's third core argument is that intercolonial trade was not just incidental to the British transatlantic slave trade but vital to its growth and to the growth of American slavery more generally. Traders venturing from Africa to America in the seventeenth and eighteenth centuries tended to specialize in slave trading, so they usually transported hundreds of captives per shipment. As such, they concentrated deliveries on the largest, most established American markets for enslaved labor where demand was consistently strong. Intercolonial traders, by contrast, could operate on a smaller scale because they incorporated slave trading into a mixed commerce. As a result, they targeted a wider range of colonial markets. Many British colonies, in their early decades of experimenting with forced African labor, relied on intercolonial sources of enslaved workers. Likewise, some small British colonies—or larger ones where slavery remained marginal to the economy—continued to rely on intercolonial supplies through most of their histories with slavery. The

12. Philip D. Morgan presents one of the few arguments for viewing the slave trade in this way, arguing, "Ports on either side of the Atlantic were funnels for large slaving hinterlands that fanned out across the land"; see Morgan, "The Cultural Implications of the Atlantic Slave Trade: African Regional Origins, American Destinations, and New World Developments," in David Eltis and David Richardson, eds., *Routes to Slavery: Direction, Ethnicity, and Mortality in the Transatlantic Slave Trade* (London, 1997), 122–145, esp. 133–134.

intra-American trade was instrumental to the institution's spread from Barbados (England's first sugar-producing island), initially to the Chesapeake and Jamaica, and eventually to all the British colonies of North America and the Caribbean. Furthermore, the trade abetted slavery's growth outside the British Empire by connecting British transatlantic traders to French and Spanish colonial markets, where demand exceeded the supply of exploitable African laborers. Meanwhile, all of this intercolonial trafficking—foreign and domestic—spurred the African trade. As British American ports such as Bridgetown and Kingston became hubs of transshipment, British traders contemplating ventures to Africa came to rely on these entrepôts as stable markets where hundreds of enslaved captives would sell quickly at almost any time. Robust intercolonial trade made the transatlantic slave trade a more reliable—and more expansive—business.

A fourth, and related, argument of *Final Passages* is that the economic significance of this intercolonial commerce in human beings extended well beyond the profits from buying African people at one price and selling them at a higher one. For many merchants in the Americas, the intercolonial slave trade facilitated other branches of commerce, entangling the profits of many traditional trades with the buying and selling of people. As colonies on the North American mainland carved out an economic niche as provisioners to the sugar colonies of the Caribbean—exporting wheat, fish, pork, and timber to the tropical heart of Britain's colonial enterprise—traders sometimes struggled to find lucrative commodities for the return voyage from the Caribbean. North American markets often saw gluts of sugar and rum, but the British Caribbean produced little else. Enslaved people arriving from Africa, however, offered another commodity in which to take returns for North American produce, helping to complete a trade circuit that made North America the breadbasket of the Caribbean. Traders looking to export North American staples to Europe also found intercolonial slave trading useful. Chesapeake and Lowcountry planters often preferred to sell their rice, indigo, or tobacco to traders who offered enslaved workers in exchange. As a result, some merchants acquired enslaved people in the Caribbean with the principal aim of securing trade partners in North America.[13]

13. On the importance of exports to the Caribbean to North American colonial economies, see Jack P. Greene, *Pursuits of Happiness: The Social Development of Early Modern British Colonies and the Formation of American Culture* (Chapel Hill, N.C., 1988), 51, 62, 67, 126, 144–145; John J. McCusker and Russell R. Menard, *The Economy of British America, 1607–1789* (Chapel Hill, N.C., 1991), 78–80, 92–110, 174, 198–203; Richard Pares, *Yankees and Creoles: The Trade between North America and the West Indies before the American Revolution* (Cambridge, Mass., 1956).

In a similar fashion, British traders and imperial policy makers used the intercolonial slave trade to open other branches of commerce with French and especially Spanish America. Until the late eighteenth century, both France and Spain officially barred foreign traders from their American colonies, but high demand for enslaved Africans in both empires led to exceptions—sometimes official, sometimes ad hoc—for foreign merchants selling African people. From the 1660s through the eighteenth century, Britain pursued this trans-imperial slave trade relentlessly, gradually asserting themselves as the primary slave suppliers to Spanish America and as important traders (rivaling the French themselves) to French colonies. To be sure, the British hoped to profit from the sale of enslaved people in foreign colonies, but such hopes were always entangled with dreams of opening foreign territories to the export of British manufactured goods. Because intercolonial slave trading enmeshed with other mercantile activities and geopolitical objectives, the profits derived from enslaved Africans in the Americas were not solely from their labor but arose out of this nexus of functions. Compared to other commodities, enslaved Africans were unique not only in their humanity but also for their ability to bring myriad trade partners to the table. The exploitation of enslaved Africans as laborers produced massive amounts of affordable staples from American soils; the exploitation of Africans as goods facilitated a bustling trade that aided Britain's rise to commercial supremacy in the Atlantic world.[14]

14. This argument for an economic significance to the slave trade that extends beyond the profits from buying and selling enslaved people alone resonates with Eric Williams's thesis and with the work of more recent scholars who have refined his argument. Williams himself seemed to shift at times from arguing that the slave trade funded industrialization to the more general claim that slavery (and the plantation system) funded industrialization; my interpretation of the intercolonial slave trade fits better with the latter claim. See Williams, *Capitalism and Slavery* (Chapel Hill, N.C., 1944). The literature debating the economic importance of the slave trade is vast. This list is not exhaustive but provides an entry to this literature. My interpretation of the economic importance of the intercolonial slave trade is especially resonant with Barbara L. Solow, "Caribbean Slavery and British Growth: The Eric Williams Hypothesis," *Journal of Developmental Economics,* XVII (1985), 99–115; Kenneth Morgan, *Slavery, Atlantic Trade, and the British Economy, 1660–1800* (New York, 2000); David Richardson, "The Slave Trade, Sugar, and British Economic Growth, 1748–1776," in Barbara L. Solow and Stanley L. Engerman, eds., *British Capitalism and Caribbean Slavery: The Legacy of Eric Williams* (Cambridge, 1987), 103–133; Eltis, *Rise of African Slavery,* chap. 10; Daron Acemoglu, Simon Johnson, and James Robinson, "The Rise of Europe: Atlantic Trade, Institutional Change, and Economic Growth," *American Economic Review,* XCV (2005), 546–579. See also Henry A. Gemery and Jan Hogendorn, eds., *The Uncommon Market: Essays in the Economic History of the Atlantic Slave Trade* (New York, 1979); Stanley L. Engerman, "The Slave Trade and British Capital Formation in the Eighteenth Century: A Comment on the Williams Thesis," *Business History Review,* XLVI (1972), 430–443; Roger An-

Given this strategic and economic importance, this study's fifth and last main argument is that the intercolonial slave trade influenced imperial policy, gradually pushing Britain, France, and Spain away from mercantilism and toward policies of freer trade. By the late sixteenth century, Spain was exempting the slave trade from the empire's prohibition on foreign trade in the colonies in order to secure a labor supply. Spain's *asiento de negros* opened Spanish America exclusively to a series of merchants who contracted to supply enslaved Africans. By the mid-seventeenth and eighteenth centuries, much of the asiento commerce became intercolonial as the Dutch and then the British used their own Caribbean Islands as trade hubs to target Spanish America with shipments of captives. Even outside this asiento policy, Spanish officials occasionally dropped their trade barriers in times of acute labor shortage, allowing Spanish colonists to secure captives by venturing elsewhere. Likewise, starting in the 1660s, England granted exceptions to its own prohibitions against foreign trade with its colonies, allowing the export of enslaved people from the English Caribbean to rival colonies. Over the course of the eighteenth century, Britain pursued such commerce with increasing intensity, culminating in the 1760s with the creation of Caribbean "free ports" that welcomed foreign subjects to British territory to buy enslaved people and British manufactured goods. France's shift to freer trade came later and more suddenly. The French disapproved of any exceptions to trade barriers throughout the seventeenth and most of the eighteenth centuries, even to overcome labor shortages. But by the late eighteenth century, France, too, dropped prohibitions in order to secure supplies of enslaved Africans from the British. For all these powers, some of their first experiments with free trade were designed to facilitate intercolonial commerce in unfree people.

■ Despite the intercolonial slave trade's significance—to the institution of slavery, to the African Diaspora, and to the economies and empires of the Atlantic world—historians have paid scant attention to such final passages. In recent decades, scholars have made remarkable strides in understanding and quantifying the transatlantic portion of the slave trade, identifying its principal routes and carriers and recovering African captive experiences of the Atlantic crossing. Following Philip Curtin's groundbreaking census of the trans-

stey, "The Volume and Profitability of the British Slave Trade, 1761–1807," in Stanley L. Engerman and Eugene D. Genovese, eds., *Race and Slavery in the Western Hemisphere: Quantitative Studies* (Princeton, N.J., 1975), 3–31; David Eltis, *Economic Growth and the Ending of the Transatlantic Slave Trade* (New York, 1987); McCusker and Menard, *Economy of British America,* 39–46.

atlantic trade in 1969, dozens of scholars scoured archives to refine understandings of various branches of the trade from Africa to the Americas. This research culminated in the *Trans-Atlantic Slave Trade Database*—released on CD-ROM in 1999 and placed on the Internet in 2008—which made data from dozens of scholars accessible, facilitating new insights not only on the scale of the transatlantic slave trade but also on mortality, instances of rebellion, the ethnic makeup of enslaved populations, and the mercantile organization of the trade.[15] Dozens of other studies shed light on the transatlantic trade's economic significance, its cultural import, and the shipboard experience itself. Yet all this work has focused almost exclusively on transatlantic shipments and migrations, largely ignoring, or only mentioning in passing, the continued migrations of Africans surviving the Middle Passage.[16] Although historians of

15. Philip D. Curtin, *The Atlantic Slave Trade: A Census* (Madison, Wis., 1969); David Eltis et al., *The Trans-Atlantic Slave Trade: A Database on CD-ROM* (Cambridge, 1999); *Voyages,* accessed August 2011, www.slavevoyages.org.

16. David Eltis and David Richardson give greater attention to intra-American movements than most slave trade historians, estimating that as many as 25 percent of Africans arriving in the Americas quickly entered the intercolonial traffic. They do not analyze such movements, however. See Eltis and Richardson, *Atlas of the Transatlantic Slave Trade* (New Haven, Conn., 2010), 198–199. In an earlier essay, Eltis estimated that only 5 to 10 percent of Africans arriving in the Americas "quickly moved to other parts of the Americas, as part of an intra-American slave trade"; see Eltis, "The Volume and Structure of the Transatlantic Slave Trade: A Reassessment," *WMQ,* 3d Ser., LVIII (2001), 35; see also Eltis, *Rise of African Slavery.* Joseph C. Miller also gives intra-American movements greater attention than most, arguing, "The ships [from Africa] headed to a single Brazilian captaincy must, finally, be understood as moving through no more than an intermediate stage in a complex redistribution to further destinations" down the Brazilian coast or in the interior. See Miller, "The Numbers, Origins, and Destinations of Slaves in the Eighteenth-Century Angolan Slave Trade," in Joseph E. Inikori and Stanley L. Engerman, eds., *The Atlantic Slave Trade: Effects on Economies, Societies, and Peoples in Africa, the Americas, and Europe* (Durham, N.C., 1992), 77–115, esp. 89; see also Miller, *Way of Death;* Thornton, *Africa and Africans,* 159–160. Manning notes that further migrations after the Atlantic crossing led to "additional fatalities" beyond those that occurred on the Middle Passage alone (*African Diaspora,* 121). Studies focusing exclusively on the transatlantic slave trade are abundant; see Herbert S. Klein, *The Atlantic Slave Trade* (New York, 1999); James A. Rawley, *The Transatlantic Slave Trade: A History* (New York, 1981); Joseph E. Inikori, "The Volume of the British Slave Trade, 1655–1807," *Cahiers d'études africaines,* XXXII (1992), 643–688; Jay Coughtry, *The Notorious Triangle: Rhode Island and the African Slave Trade, 1700–1807* (Philadelphia, 1981); Edward Reynolds, *Stand the Storm: A History of the Atlantic Slave Trade* (Chicago, 1993); Paul E. Lovejoy, "The Volume of the Atlantic Slave Trade: A Synthesis," *Journal of African History,* XXIII (1982), 473–501; Daniel P. Mannix, *Black Cargoes: A History of the Atlantic Slave Trade, 1518–1865* (New York, 1962); Robert Louis Stein, *The French Slave Trade in the Eighteenth Century: An Old Regime Business* (Madison, Wis., 1979); Steven Deyle, "'By Farr the Most Profitable Trade': Slave Trading in British Colonial North America," *Slavery and Abolition,* X (1989), 107–125; Richardson,

slavery in regions poorly supplied by direct African trade often note their region's reliance on intercolonial sources, scholars have not investigated such routes thoroughly, and studies of Britain's transatlantic slave trade have been particularly prone to omitting analysis of intercolonial movements.[17]

Most historical attention to intercolonial slave trading has been outside the British Empire. Scholars of the Dutch and Danish slave trades, for example, have highlighted transshipments of Africans because Dutch and Danish colonies drew many people from Africa but exploited few enslaved laborers. These settlements served primarily as trade emporiums rather than plantation settlements, so scholars have recognized that most arriving Africans were imported, not for labor, but for exploitation as commodities in trade to for-

---

"Slave Trade, Sugar, and British Economic Growth," in Solow and Engerman, eds., *British Capitalism and Caribbean Slavery,* 103–133; Emma Christopher, *Slave Ship Sailors and Their Captive Cargoes, 1730–1807* (New York, 2006); Marcus Rediker, *The Slave Ship: A Human History* (New York, 2007); Stephanie E. Smallwood, *Saltwater Slavery: A Middle Passage from Africa to American Diaspora* (Cambridge, Mass., 2007).

17. For examples of local studies considering the intercolonial slave trade, see Lorena S. Walsh, "The Chesapeake Slave Trade: Regional Patterns, African Origins, and Some Implications," *WMQ,* 3d Ser., LVIII (2001), 139–170; Susan Westbury, "Analysing a Regional Slave Trade: The West Indies and Virginia, 1698–1775," *Slavery and Abolition,* VII (1986), 241–256; Allan Kulikoff, "A 'Prolifick' People: Black Population Growth in the Chesapeake Colonies, 1700–1790," *Southern Studies,* XVI (1977), 392; Kenneth Morgan, "Slave Sales in Colonial Charleston," *English Historical Review,* CXIII (1998), 905–927; Daniel C. Littlefield, "Charleston and Internal Slave Redistribution," *South Carolina Historical Magazine,* LXXXVII (1986), 93–105; Walter E. Minchinton, "The Seaborne Slave Trade of North Carolina," *North Carolina Historical Review,* LXXI (1994), 1–61; Darold D. Wax, "'New Negroes Are Always in Demand': The Slave Trade in Eighteenth-Century Georgia," *Georgia Historical Quarterly,* LXVIII (1984), 193–220; James G. Lydon, "New York and the Slave Trade, 1700 to 1774," *WMQ,* 3d Ser., XXXV (1978), 375–394. Jean-Pierre Leglaunec shows that transshipment from the Caribbean was actually the most important source of Louisiana's slaves during the period of Spanish control. See Leglaunec, "Slave Migrations in Spanish and Early American Louisiana: New Sources and New Estimates," *Louisiana History,* XLI (2005), 185–209. On forced migration in the British Caribbean after abolition, see D. Eltis, "The Traffic in Slaves between the British West Indian Colonies, 1807–1833," *Economic History Review,* XXV (1972), 55–64; Hilary McD. Beckles, "'An Unfeeling Traffick': The Intercolonial Movement of Slaves in the British Caribbean, 1807–1833," in Walter Johnson, ed., *The Chattel Principle: Internal Slave Trades in the Americas* (New Haven, Conn., 2004), 256–274. Scholars of nineteenth-century slavery place more emphasis on intra-American slave movements than historians of the colonial period because, after 1807, the transatlantic slave trade was outlawed in the British and U.S. contexts. Thereafter, the institution's westward migration can only be explained by intra-American trade; see Johnson, ed., *Chattel Principle;* Johnson, *Soul by Soul: Life Inside the Antebellum Slave Market* (Cambridge, Mass., 1999); Michael Tadman, *Speculators and Slaves: Masters, Traders, and Slaves in the Old South* (Madison, Wis., 1989); Steven Deyle, *Carry Me Back: The Domestic Slave Trade in American Life* (New York, 2005).

eign plantations. Likewise, the intercolonial slave trade has garnered attention from scholars of Spanish America because few Spanish slave traders ventured to Africa before the nineteenth century, leaving Spanish colonies reliant on foreign traders. Perhaps because the British both engaged in African trade and exploited African labor extensively, scholars of the British slave trade have overlooked the intercolonial traffic.[18]

■ The sources available for the study of the British intercolonial slave trade fall into four principal categories. Assessment of the scale of the traffic (and many other conclusions in the book) derives from a database I compiled of individual shipments carrying enslaved people between colonies. This database draws information primarily from the Naval Office Shipping Lists, records kept by British officials stationed in the major ports of British America. The shipping lists document the names of vessels and captains, the dates of each ship's arrival and departure, its cargo, and often additional information about the vessel—such as size, owners' names, ports of registration, and crew size. The lists for twenty-six individual British colonies were mined in their entirety for this study. Supplemented with newspapers and other trade records—including some from French and Spanish American colonies—the resulting database documents more than 7,600 intra-American slave-trading voyages and under-

18. On the importance of intercolonial transshipment to the Dutch slave trade, see Johannes Postma, "A Reassessment of the Dutch Atlantic Slave Trade," in Postma and Victor Enthoven, eds., *Riches from Atlantic Commerce: Dutch Transatlantic Trade and Shipping, 1585–1817* (Boston, 2003), 115–138; Han Jordaan, "The Curaçao Slave Market: From *Asiento* Trade to Free Trade, 1700–1730," ibid., 219–257; Wim Klooster, "Curaçao and the Caribbean Transit Trade," ibid., 203–218; Postma, *The Dutch in the Atlantic Slave Trade, 1600–1815* (New York, 1990); Postma, "The Dispersal of African Slaves in the West by Dutch Slave Traders, 1630–1803," in Inikori and Engerman, eds., *Atlantic Slave Trade,* 283–299. For the smaller Danish trade, see Sv. E. Green-Pedersen, "The Scope and Structure of the Danish Negro Slave Trade," *Scandinavian Economic History Review,* XIX (1971), 149–197. For studies emphasizing the importance of intercolonial trade to peopling Spanish America with Africans, see António de Almeida Mendes, "The Foundations of the System: A Reassessment of the Slave Trade to the Spanish Americas in the Sixteenth and Seventeenth Centuries," in David Eltis and David Richardson, eds., *Extending the Frontiers: Essays on the New Transatlantic Slave Trade Database* (New Haven, Conn., 2008), 63–94; Colin Palmer, *Human Cargoes: The British Slave Trade to Spanish America, 1700–1739* (Urbana, Ill., 1981); Palmer, "The Company Trade and the Numerical Distribution of Slaves to Spanish America, 1703–1739," in Paul E. Lovejoy, ed., *Africans in Bondage: Studies in Slavery and the Slave Trade* (Madison, Wis., 1986), 27–42. Linda A. Newson and Susie Minchin also use the phrase "final passage" to refer to the extensive intra-American journeys of Africans within Spanish America; see Newson and Minchin, *From Capture to Sale: The Portuguese Slave Trade to Spanish South America in the Early Seventeenth Century* (Boston, 2007), chap. 6; see also Frederick P. Bowser, *The African Slave in Colonial Peru, 1524–1650* (Stanford, Calif., 1974), chaps. 2, 3.

lies the principal findings of this study, especially with regard to quantifying the scale of forced African migration along various routes of the trade.[19]

Of course, the records underlying this database are far from perfect, so it is worth commenting on the shortcomings and the steps taken to overcome them. To avoid redundancies with extant scholarship and to enhance compatibility with such work, I modeled the intercolonial database on *Voyages: The*

19. For the estimate of arrivals from Africa in British colonies, see *Voyages*, accessed August 2011, http://slavevoyages.org/tast/assessment/estimates.faces?yearFrom=1501&yearTo=1808& disembarkation=205.305.204.304.307.306.309.201.308.311.203.310.202.301.302.303. Because the intercolonial database I compiled includes more than seven thousand voyages, with dozens of data points collected for each shipment, it is not feasible to print the database in the present work. I intend to publish the database in a searchable, sortable online format, but that project is ongoing. The methodology used in compiling the database is discussed in greater detail in the Appendix, which also presents and explains detailed estimates of the scale of trafficking along many routes. For the principal records consulted in compiling the database, see the Naval Office Shipping Lists in Britain's National Archives, most of which are also available in microfilm editions (Walter E. Minchinton, ed., *The Naval Office Shipping Lists, in the Public Record Office, London* [Wakefield, 1966-1981]): for Antigua, T 1/498, CO 10/2, T 1/502, T 1/512; for the Bahamas, CO 27/12-15; for Barbados, CO 33/13-23, T 64/47-49; for Bermuda, CO 41/6-8; for Demerara, CO 116/17; for Dominica, CO 76/4-8; for Florida, CO 5/573; for Georgia, CO 5/709-710; for Grenada, CO 106/1-5; for Jamaica, CO 142/13-29, T 1/507, T 1/512; for Martinique, CO 166/6-7; for Maryland, CO 5/749-750; for Massachusetts, CO 5/848-851; for Montserrat, T 1/489, T 1/498, T 1/507, T 1/512; for Nevis, CO 187/1-2, T 1/489, T 1/498, T 1/507, T 1/512; for New Hampshire, CO 5/967-969; for New Jersey, CO 5/1035-1036; for New York, CO 5/1222-1228; for Saint Kitts, CO 33/18, CO 243/1, T 1/489, T 1/498; for Saint Vincent, CO 265/1-2; for South Carolina, CO 5/508-510; for Surinam, CO 278/8-9; for Tobago, CO 290/1-3; for Tortola, CO 317/1; for Trinidad, CO 300/16; for Virginia, CO 5/1441-1450. The generosity of scholars researching other aspects of the slave trade supplemented my research to compile this database. Most vitally, David Eltis shared a wealth of information gathered for *Voyages* (www.slavevoyages.org). Despite omitting intercolonial movements from *Voyages*, the research for that database yielded information about such movements. The most important additions in this regard came from import records for Spanish colonies housed in the Archivo General de Indias. Philip D. Morgan also provided information, primarily from South Carolina import tax records that he studied in research for *Slave Counterpoint: Black Culture in the Eighteenth-Century Chesapeake and Lowcountry* (Chapel Hill, N.C., 1998). Lorena Walsh shared a database of slave-trading voyages to the Chesapeake, which she compiled for her article "Chesapeake Slave Trade," *WMQ*, 3d Ser., LVIII (2001), 139-170. Several published sources also present datasets of slave-trading voyages that were incorporated into my database: Minchinton, "Seaborne Slave Trade of North Carolina," *North Carolina Historical Review*, LXXI (1994), 1-61; Herbert S. Klein, comp., "Slave Trade to Havana, Cuba, 1790-1820" (a dataset of slave imports on file at the University of Wisconsin Data and Program Library Service, Madison, Wis.); Elizabeth Donnan, ed., *Documents Illustrative of the History of the Slave Trade to America*, 4 vols. (Washington, D.C., 1930-1935); James A. McMillin, *The Final Victims: Foreign Slave Trade to North America, 1783-1810* (Columbia, S.C., 2004). For McMillin's database, see Appendix B on a CD-ROM that accompanies the book.

Trans-Atlantic Slave Trade Database (www.slavevoyages.org) and tailored its coverage to shipments not documented on the *Voyages* Web site. I defined an intra-American or intercolonial slave-trading voyage as a shipment between two American locales for which the enslaved people on board changed vessels or owners (usually both) after their arrival in the Americas. In other words, I did not include slave-trading voyages that acquired captives in Africa, even if the vessel continued from a first American port of disembarkation to a second one. Such journeys are discussed in the literature on the transatlantic slave trade and are documented in *Voyages,* so counting them again here would cause redundancy for scholars comparing data on the intercolonial trade to published transatlantic data. To avoid overlap between the datasets, I checked every journey in the intercolonial database against *Voyages* to ensure that such shipments were not continuations of transatlantic ventures. Where newspapers or other sources supplemented the Naval Office Shipping Lists (or even when shipping lists from multiple colonies were consulted), double-counting of voyages was a concern, so I searched in the extant intercolonial database for each voyage discovered before adding it as new. In fact, just over 30 percent of the voyages in the intercolonial database have been documented in more than one source.

If dangers of double-counting were mitigated through tedious cross-checking of the database against itself and other datasets, other problems proved more vexing. For one, the records underlying the database offer fairly thorough coverage for the mid- to late eighteenth century but only spotty coverage for earlier periods. Even where seventeenth- and early-eighteenth-century lists survive, they often fail to document whether ships carried enslaved people because they focused on tracking certain "enumerated" trade goods specified by British trade legislation. Enslaved African people were not so enumerated. Their movements entered the records haphazardly, according to the whims of particular record keepers. Only in the 1720s did officials shift to consistently recording all trade goods on board the vessels entering and clearing their ports. Surviving shipping lists also tend to be more complete for British mainland colonies than for the Caribbean, although coverage for Jamaica is quite good. As a result, the intercolonial movements of Africans can be quantified more accurately for some colonies and eras than others. For places and times where port records are lacking, other sources allow more qualitative assessments of the traffic: statements from colonial officials, newspapers, or comments in merchant correspondence. Further discussion of gaps in the database—and efforts to fill them—is located in the Appendix. Another limitation of the database is that the port records underlying it typically say little about the captives carried. Most often, the records identify enslaved people only as "Negroes," saying nothing about age, sex, or background. As such, conclusions about gender- or age-specific patterns in the intercolonial trade are less definitive than would be ideal. Nonetheless, other types of sources—again, newspaper advertisements for slave sales and mercantile correspondence—provide some qualitative information about age and gender trends. Those are discussed where evidence permits in the pages that follow. One last caveat is that the intercolonial database is restricted to seaborne voyages because officials only carefully monitored ports. Yet many enslaved migrants to early America underwent significant overland journeys to interior regions far removed from their initial ports of arrival in the Americas. Such transits are omitted from the intercolonial database (but are discussed from other sources, primarily in Chapter 7).

The second key body of sources for this study is the correspondence (and, occasionally, accounts) of merchants engaged in the trade. Their papers include material from the major British slave-trading companies—the South Sea Company and, to a lesser extent, the Royal African Company—but also from numerous independent traders engaged in the traffic throughout the Caribbean and North America. Merchants' documents offer crucial insights on why intercolonial slave trading was so prevalent, how such ventures were organized, and how traders incorporated slave trading into other commercial activities. Although port records reveal a great deal about where enslaved people moved and in what numbers, merchant papers reveal more about the reasons behind such movements and give glimpses of what African captives endured in the process.

A third corpus of primary material is the correspondence of colonial officials. Exchanges between British colonial governors or officeholders and the British Board of Trade, which oversaw colonial policies, include summary views of slave trading in certain colonies. Such information is especially useful where port records are unavailable. Statements and reports from colonial officials suggest general patterns of trade that assist in estimating the trade's volume when a shortage of statistical sources prevents more rigorous quantitative analysis. The lack of port records is a particular problem for the seventeenth and early eighteenth centuries, so government correspondence is invaluable for that period. Throughout the colonial era, similar correspondence between officials in France and their governors in America also sheds light on the illegal trade between British and French possessions in the Caribbean, which rarely appeared in port records, owing to its clandestine nature.

The final category of source material is testimony from people who witnessed or survived the slave trade. Rare firsthand accounts from African captives who endured the trade provide glimpses of lived experience in the forced migration, but unfortunately, precious few such documents exist. Even when written, stories from slave trade survivors typically focus more on life under slavery in the Americas than on the details of the slave trade itself. Nonetheless, these scant sources offer valuable perspectives, supplemented by occasional accounts left by travelers and abolitionists who witnessed the slave trade and recorded their impressions. These testimonies offer a vital alternative to the port records and merchant accounts that define enslaved people as commodities rather than as people.[20]

■ The paucity of firsthand accounts from captives in the slave trade raises the issue of the words and labels we use to refer to them. Slave traders and government officials seldom recorded much about the backgrounds of groups of captives, let alone individuals' names, stories, or personalities. Records usually label people simply as "Negroes" or "Slaves," offering the historian little to work with in the quest for more humanizing descriptors. To avoid endless repetition of the commodified term *slave,* I will often refer to those carried in the slave trade as *Africans* or simply as *people.* Holding (and moving) people in bondage was a willful practice rooted in violence and coercion. In recognition of this, I also regularly refer to traded people as *captives, forced migrants,* or *enslaved people.* Where surviving evidence reveals that a group or individual is from a particular African region, I employ ethnic, linguistic, or regional labels, such as *Angolan, Igbo, Gambian,* or *Akan,* but with trepidation. Knowing that a group of captives departed Africa from a particular port or region does not equate to knowing their ethnicity, sense of identity, or lan-

20. Handler identifies just fifteen surviving firsthand accounts of the slave trade to British America ("Survivors of the Middle Passage," *Slavery and Abolition,* XXIII, no. 1 [April 2002]). The most useful for information on the intercolonial trade are "The Interesting Narrative of the Life of Olaudah Equiano, or Gustavus Vassa, the African, Written by Himself," in Vincent Carretta, ed., *The Interesting Narrative and Other Writings* (New York, 2003); James Albert Ukawsaw Gronniosaw, "A Narrative of the Most Remarkable Particulars in the Life of James Albert Ukawsaw Gronniosaw, an African Prince, as Related by Himself" (1772), rpt. in William L. Andrews and Henry Louis Gates, Jr., eds., *Slave Narratives* (New York, 2000), 1–34; Venture Smith, "A Narrative of the Life and Adventures of Venture, a Native of Africa: But Resident above Sixty Years in the United States of America; Related by Himself" (1798), in Vincent Carretta, ed., *Unchained Voices: An Anthology of Black Authors in the English-Speaking World of the Eighteenth Century* (Lexington, Ky., 2004), 369–387; and Abduhl Rahhahman, "Abduhl Rah[h]ahman's History," in John W. Blassingame, ed., *Slave Testimony: Two Centuries of Letters, Speeches, Interviews, and Autobiographies* (Baton Rouge, 1977), 684–685.

guage with precision. The routes people traveled to African ports were complex and evolving. Furthermore, even when we can be fairly sure that a group of captives was Aja or Igbo with regard to language or regional background, all we have really recovered—as Ian Baucom so eloquently points out—is a general "type," not individuals. Where possible in the pages that follow, I will refer to such African regional "types" because they are more specific than labels of *slave* or *African,* but such labeling falls short of rendering people in their full and complex humanity. The slave trade's abstraction of people as commodities pervades the surviving documentation and taunts the historian seeking to recover more fully formed individuals.[21]

Whatever their personal experiences, one thing the vast majority of captives in the British intercolonial trade shared was that they were Africans who had recently arrived in the Americas. Of the 26,830 people whose background is noted in the intercolonial database, 24,713 of them (more than 92 percent) were described as "New Negroes," "Africans," or a more specific African ethnicity. Fewer than 8 percent of people were described as "Seasoned" or as otherwise having spent substantial time in the Americas. Furthermore, these statistics actually overstate the significance of American-born, or creolized, slaves to the traffic. Many port records labeled most captives simply as "negroes," only adding occasional qualifiers for particular groups as "seasoned," implying that the typical group of "negroes" was not acculturated to the American slave regime. But without more definitive proof of their background, such groups labeled only as "negroes" are not counted either way in calculating the statistics above. Additionally, port records documenting voyages that exported enslaved people from British colonies to foreign territories—the branch of the trade carrying the greatest numbers of people—rarely specified the origins of the "negroes" departing (so they are not counted in the statistics above, either), yet anecdotal descriptions of such ventures in merchant and government accounts virtually never mention movements of seasoned people. Traders consistently describe the traffic as a transshipment within a matter of days or weeks of Africans' disembarking from the Middle Passage.[22]

21. Ian Baucom, *Specters of the Atlantic: Finance Capital, Slavery, and the Philosophy of History* (Durham, N.C., 2005), 11, 43–48.

22. Several studies of North American slave importation critique the notion that most slaves arriving in British North America from the West Indies were seasoned, but the assumption persists in North American slave historiography. For arguments against seasoned hands in the trade, see John C. Coombs, "Building 'the Machine': The Development of Slavery and Slave Society in Early Colonial Virginia" (Ph.D. diss., College of William and Mary, 2003), 103; Walsh, "Chesapeake Slave Trade," *WMQ,* 3d Ser., LVIII (2001), 139–170; Susan Alice Westbury, "Colonial Vir-

Two principal factors account for the predominance of recently arrived Africans in the intercolonial trade. First, Caribbean planters had little reason to sell acclimatized slaves. The biggest risk in slave investment was mortality, and this danger was greatest in an African's first year in the new disease environment of the Americas, while recovering from the slave trade. Enslaved workers also became more valuable to an owner after adapting to the plantation regime. The exceptions to this rule of increasing value after seasoning were recalcitrant or rebellious slaves, which gave rise to the second factor limiting the presence of acclimatized or American-born people in the intercolonial trade: most buyers preferred recently arrived Africans. Plantation owners and other prospective buyers questioned the motives of anyone offering acclimatized people for sale, wary that prior owners were seeking to unload problems. This fear of importing strong-willed or rebellious people pushed many colonies to enact prohibitive import duties on enslaved people who had resided in another colony for any considerable amount of time.[23]

---

ginia and the Atlantic Slave Trade" (Ph.D. diss., University of Illinois at Urbana-Champaign, 1981), 94; Westbury, "Slaves of Colonial Virginia: Where They Came From," *WMQ*, 3d Ser., XLII (1985), 228–237; W. Robert Higgins, "Charles Town Merchants and Factors Dealing in the External Negro Trade, 1735–1775," *South Carolina Historical Magazine*, LXV (1964), 205–217; Darold D. Wax, "Preferences for Slaves in Colonial America," *Journal of Negro History*, LVIII (1973), 371–401; William D. Piersen, *Black Yankees: The Development of an Afro-American Subculture in Eighteenth-Century New England* (Amherst, Mass., 1988), 6–7. Likewise, Walsh argues that very little evidence exists for the presence of seasoned slaves on the ground in the seventeenth-century Chesapeake; see "The Differential Cultural Impact of Free and Coerced Migration to Colonial America," in David Eltis, ed., *Coerced and Free Migration: Global Perspectives* (Stanford, Calif., 2002), 117–151. Other studies assume that slaves arriving in North America from the West Indies were either born there or had at least spent considerable time in the islands; see Lorenzo Johnston Greene, *The Negro in Colonial New England, 1620–1776*, 4th ed. (New York, 1942), 36; John Hope Franklin, *From Slavery to Freedom: A History of Negro Americans* (New York, 1974), 54; Edgar J. McManus, *Black Bondage in the North* (Syracuse, N.Y., 1973), 20; Melville J. Herskovits, *The Myth of the Negro Past* (Boston, 1958), 45; Kulikoff, "A 'Prolifick' People," *Southern Studies*, XVI (1977), 392; T. H. Breen and Stephen Innes, *"Myne Owne Ground": Race and Freedom on Virginia's Eastern Shore, 1640–1676* (New York, 2005), 70; Robert E. Desrochers, Jr., "Slave-for-Sale Advertisements and Slavery in Massachusetts, 1704–1781," *WMQ*, 3d. Ser, LIX (2002), 623–664. Ira Berlin comes down somewhere in between, arguing that seventeenth-century arrivals from the Caribbean should not be viewed as Africans but as "Atlantic creoles." But referring to the eighteenth century, he states, "Transshipment of African slaves from the Caribbean was so swift as to make the West Indian layover little more than a short stop in the voyage" (Berlin, *Many Thousands Gone: The First Two Centuries of Slavery in North America* [Cambridge, Mass., 1998], 17–63, 183). Because most of my quantitative data on slave origins is from the eighteenth century, it does not directly refute Berlin's interpretation, but there is little reason to believe that slave traders and purchasers applied different logic in the seventeenth century.

23. In 1693, South Carolina barred the immigration of slaves who had participated in a recent

When traders did transship seasoned people, planters avoided them, a lesson James Burnett of Jamaica learned the hard way. In 1772, he sent a group of enslaved Jamaicans to South Carolina for sale, where his agent John Hopton "tried to barter [them] away for Produce and at private Sale but could not succeed." Hopton eventually resorted to an auction that netted low prices. When Burnett criticized Hopton for the cut-rate sales, the agent fired back that he had tried to warn Burnett. "Were they my own property I could not have done more in the disposal of them," Hopton argued, "for the people here as I mentioned to you before seem prejudiced against West India Negroes, that, with the heavy Duty laid on all season'd Slaves imported into this Province, have been a means of lessening the Value of them prodigiously." Indeed, the previous year, Hopton had cautioned Burnett that "People here in general object to the West India negroes as there are a great many of them sent here for their Roguery." Virginia trader Charles Steuart agreed, when he explained to Anthony Fahie why two enslaved men whom Fahie sent from Saint Kitts fetched low prices in 1751. As Steuart put it, "New Negroe Boys of 3 f't high will sell considerably better than the best West India Negroes, for it is generally supposed that they are ship'd off for great Crimes." Despite the linguistic and cultural barriers, most slaveholders preferred to buy recent African immigrants, taking solace in the knowledge that no prior European master had sold them owing to a rebellious streak or some unseen malady. When Charleston merchant Levinius Clarkson courted transshipments of Africans in 1773, during a moment of high demand in his province, the instructions he offered to would-be partners were standard: "Should you meet with any new Negroes who have not been Six Months in any of his Majesty's Colonies . . . you may purchase ten or twelve on our joint Account." [24]

-----

revolt in Barbados, and in 1703 it passed a more general prohibitive duty on all seasoned slaves, which it renewed several times; see W. Robert Higgins, "The Geographical Origins of Negro Slaves in Colonial South Carolina," *South Atlantic Quarterly*, LXX (1971), 37–38; Donnan, ed., *Documents*, IV, 257 nn. 2, 4, 315 n. 2. Rhode Island legislated against importing seasoned slaves in 1708 and renewed in 1715: see Berlin, *Many Thousands Gone*, 48; "Act of the General Assembly, July 15, 1715," in Donnan, ed., *Documents*, III, 114. New York followed suit by 1731, and, despite a crown-ordered repeal in 1735, the duty reappeared in later decades (ibid., 446–447, 447–449, 456). Georgia also passed such a law (Wax, "'New Negroes Are Always in Demand,'" *Georgia Historical Quarterly*, LXVIII [1984], 203–204).

24. John Hopton to James Burnett, 1772, in Donnan, ed., *Documents*, IV, 443–444; Hopton to Burnett, Sept. 7, 1771, in Henry Laurens Papers, 1747–1860, South Carolina Historical Society, Charleston; Charles Steuart to Anthony Fahie, July 13, 1751, in Charles Steuart Letter Book, 1751–1763, microfilm, M–32, John D. Rockefeller, Jr. Library, Williamsburg, Virginia. Clarkson: Levinius Clarkson to David van Horne, Charleston, Feb. 23, 1773, in Donnan, ed., *Documents*, IV,

The possible exception to this widespread preference for newly arrived Africans occurred in some northern colonies, especially during the seventeenth and early eighteenth centuries and in towns where Africans were employed as domestic servants. For instance, in 1715, Philadelphia merchant Jonathan Dickinson cautioned a correspondent in Jamaica against transshipping slaves to his port, saying that Philadelphians did not want slaves, "save those that Live in other P'vinces." But Dickinson himself was not requesting seasoned slaves from Jamaica; he preferred that none be sent to him at all. And the prohibitive duties on seasoned slaves in Rhode Island and New York suggest that preferences for American-born or acculturated people were unusual, even in the North, at least by the mid-eighteenth century. Responding to both trade laws and market demand, intercolonial traders ensured that African captives fresh off of transatlantic vessels predominated in the slave trade between American colonies.[25]

■ Taken together, the facets of the intercolonial slave trade highlighted in *Final Passages*—the trade's considerable scale, the experiences of captives, the practices of traders, and the policies of empires—compel us to reckon with colonial societies' view of Africans as commodities. In many respects, Africans moved through the Atlantic world not as migrants but as trade goods, and that idea—so perverse to modern sensibilities—is important to confront. Historians are, of course, aware that African people were bought, shipped, and

---

456–457. On the prohibitive duty against seasoned slaves from other colonies, which had been in place since the 1720s, see Peter H. Wood, "'More Like a Negro Country': Demographic Patterns in Colonial South Carolina, 1700–1740," in Engerman and Genovese, eds., *Race and Slavery in the Western Hemisphere*, 145–146, esp. n. 44.

25. Jonathan Dickinson to John Lewis, May 2, 1715, Jonathan Dickinson Letter Book, 1715–1721, Yi 2 /1628, alcove 4, shelf 12, Library Company of Philadelphia. For contrasting views emphasizing northern colonists' preference for seasoned slaves, see Greene, *Negro in Colonial New England*, 36; McManus, *Black Bondage in the North*, 20. This belief that North American settlers preferred seasoned slaves stems at least partly from the mistaken assumption that all slaves delivered to North America from the Caribbean were seasoned. For instance, Franklin asserts that mainland settlers exhibited "a decided preference for slaves seasoned in the islands," but as evidence, he cites abundant imports to South Carolina from the islands in the 1760s. At that very time, South Carolina enforced a prohibitive duty on slaves who had spent more than a few months in the islands, so clearly a preference for seasoned slaves was not driving the intercolonial trade (*From Slavery to Freedom*, 54). Herskovits states that only 930 of 4,551 slaves reaching New York and New Jersey between 1715 and 1765 were "native Africans," when in actuality the records he cites show only that few slaves arrived in New York and New Jersey directly from Africa; the records do not describe the nativity of the slaves arriving from the West Indies. Herskovits simply assumed they were not "native Africans" (*Myth of the Negro Past*, 45).

sold, but the implications of that commodification run deeper. Indeed, one reason historians have not studied intercolonial dispersals of African people in detail may be that other migrations do not tend to share a similar distribution phase because voluntary migrants are less beholden to commodity flows. Perhaps because the slave trade moved people rather than inanimate goods, scholars have been less inclined to look for wholesalers and retailers, bulk traders and distributors. But the intercolonial trade, which mixed slave trading with more general commerce, reveals ways in which colonial merchants did not view the slave trade as distinctive. In their eyes, enslaved people were just another product. Understanding this helps explain the convoluted journeys of enslaved people, as they were swept into commodity flows alongside crops and trade goods. Furthermore, the experience of sale, transshipment, and resale in America must have conveyed to many arriving Africans their new status as chattel. Enslaved people who recorded their stories often fixated on their sale—having their monetary worth publicly negotiated—as a defining moment, and slaves transshipped within the Americas confronted this commodification multiple times. As Africans of diverse backgrounds encountered views of themselves as property and found themselves commingled in ships dispersing them from major American entrepôts, the trade might have been one site where new, collective identities as Africans—rather than Mandingos, Akans, or Igbos—began to form.[26]

This conflict between traders treating the enslaved as commodities and the enslaved reacting as people highlights one of the biggest challenges of writing about the slave trade: the dual nature of all events. While traders exchanged slaves as goods, African people traveled as captives—breathing, thinking, observing their surroundings, hoping to escape or at least to survive. The archival

26. Byrd argues powerfully for the slave trade journey itself as a shaper of the new ethnicities that Africans and their descendants would forge in the Americas (*Captives and Voyagers*, 32–56). For the best discussion of slaves' reactions to being bought and sold, see Johnson, *Soul by Soul*. His work deals with nineteenth-century experiences, so most of the slaves involved were born in the Americas, yet the availability of numerous firsthand accounts for that period yields greater insight on the experience. Newly arrived Africans might have reacted differently, but, given the public physical examination of their bodies and their understanding of slavery from their experiences within Africa, it seems likely that they understood their sale, and hence value, was being negotiated. For discussion of the evolution of African identities in the Americas, see Michael A. Gomez, *Exchanging Our Country Marks: The Transformation of African Identities in the Colonial and Antebellum South* (Chapel Hill, N.C., 1998). For some of the best treatments of commodification as a process increasingly affecting enslaved Africans as they moved through the trade from Africa to the Americas, see Smallwood, *Saltwater Slavery*, 5–6, 35–36; Baucom, *Specters of the Atlantic;* Brown, *Reaper's Garden*, 28–32.

record complicates the challenge of maintaining both of these perspectives, for it is composed almost entirely of documents from the European perspective. This problem hit home for me one day late in a research trip in London, as I paged through the account book of a slave ship. Trading for slaves on the African coast, the compiler had documented each transaction, one or two people at a time. For the trader, the accounting must have seemed monotonous, with page after page of repetitive transactions—purchased a woman for one gun, one barrel powder, two barrels brandy; purchased a man for two guns, and so on. My eyes glazed over, and I began to skim ahead until, with a start, I realized I had gotten dangerously numb to the bias of the archive. These transactions were only repetitive to the merchant who recorded them. For enslaved Africans arriving at the Atlantic coast, these were singular events. A captive in the slave trade only experienced being sold from an African merchant to a European trader once, shortly before she was ferried by canoe to an enormous ship—a hollow island—anchored in the harbor. Few people who endured that side of such an exchange would ever set foot in Africa again. Being traded for some cloth and a gun was a defining event of enslaved people's lives. From that viewpoint, page upon page of transactions in a European slave trader's account book acquires a whole new meaning.

Thus, one goal of this project is to maintain perspective on the captives' humanity while still presenting an unflinching account of traders' exploitation of them as commodities. Both viewpoints are essential. Since twenty-first-century people share widespread agreement that human trafficking is not just immoral but exceptionally so, writing off traders as simply wicked and barbaric, as unfit for study or empathy, comes too easily. But regarding traders as one-dimensional villains obscures some of the most important lessons to be learned from the study of slavery. Merchants trading slaves were representative figures of their time and place. Understanding them helps us understand the economy and worldview of a slaveholding society, including the dehumanization that some people faced and resisted. If one is concerned with moral lessons to be drawn from this traffic, vilifying slave traders as savage and sadistic offers little insight. The more useful and truly troubling lesson in studying the slave trade is that the traders were "normal" in other aspects of their lives, unexceptional to most contemporaries. Slave traders trafficked in people without interrogating their actions. Merchants could, and did, write to each other to plan slave trade ventures and then, in following paragraphs, send updates about their wives and children. Recognizing their mix of ordinary human behavior with slave trading illustrates the pervasive demeaning of Africans in the minds of slaveholding and slave-trading societies in colonial America. Ordinary people participated without moral qualms. Furthermore, confronting the traders' view of people as commodities forces a reckoning with the profits colonial societies gained through their dehumanization of people: the slave trade both depended on it and reinforced it.[27]

Scholars of race often argue that in the era of the slave trade, Europeans held inchoate notions of Africans as racially distinct. If so, exploiting Africans as commodities offers a crucial arena in which European attitudes toward Africans developed. Slave sales were public spectacles. Buyers and sellers negotiated the monetary value of people at waterfronts, marketplaces, and stores, with Africans on display as marketable goods. Nowhere else was the treatment of one category of people as property so clearly visible. By exposing the colonial public to human commodification, the slave markets of the seventeenth and eighteenth centuries were constructing race. Newspaper advertisements routinely announced Africans for sale alongside rum and textiles. Port records had columns documenting the importation of goods called "Negroes" alongside columns for other imports like butter, timber, cloth, or pork. In 1772, shipping lists for Barbados for the first time lumped a column for "New Negroes" alongside those for "Horses" and "Cattle" under the heading "Live Stock." With racialized classification of Africans' supposed inferiority on the rise in colonial America, the buying, shipping, and selling of African people surely advanced their debasement in European eyes.[28]

<hr>

27. For an example of studying the trade from only the African perspective, Clarence J. Munford explicitly "views the ocean traverse strictly from the perspective of its African victims . . . rejecting much recent historiography on the Middle Passage as bigoted and apologetic" (*The Black Ordeal of Slavery and Slave Trading in the French West Indies, 1625–1715* [Lewiston, N.Y., 1991], ix). By contrast, Johnson analyzes the behavior of buyers and sellers in the slave market for great insights on the worldview of a slaveholding society; see *Soul by Soul*.

28. Writing about the domestic slave trade in the nineteenth-century United States, Johnson argues, "At no site was race more readily given daily shape than in the slave market" (*Soul by Soul*, 136). "New Negroes" and "Live Stock": Naval Office Shipping Lists for Barbados, Records of the Treasury 64/48, National Archives, Kew. The literature on the origins of racism is vast and contested, but most scholars agree that Euro-Americans' racialized views of Africans became more systematic and articulated toward the late eighteenth century. For a range of viewpoints, see Williams, *Capitalism and Slavery;* Oscar Handlin and Mary F. Handlin, "Origins of the Southern Labor System," *WMQ*, VII (1950), 199–222; Carl N. Degler, "Slavery and the Genesis of American Race Prejudice," *Comparative Studies in Society and History*, II (1959), 49–66; Winthrop D. Jordan, *White over Black: American Attitudes toward the Negro, 1550–1812* (Chapel Hill, N.C., 1968); Edmund S. Morgan, *American Slavery, American Freedom: The Ordeal of Colonial Virginia* (New York, 1975), 316–337; Ivan Hannaford, *Race: The History of an Idea in the West* (Baltimore, 1996); Robin Blackburn, "The Old World Background to European Colonial Slavery," *WMQ*, LIV (1997), 65–102; Alden T. Vaughan and Virginia Mason Vaughan, "Before

Scholars of slavery often describe a paradox of human property—slaveholders sought to define Africans as property, but managing them as slaves required confronting their humanity. Other forms of property did not run away, sabotage tools, fall ill, feign sickness, get pregnant, rise up in rebellion, negotiate perquisites, steal livestock, practice religions, or seek education. The list goes on and on. Enslaved people could be bought and sold, loaned and rented, mortgaged and financed like other forms of property, but ultimately they were human beings with all the virtues and vices, complexities and dramas, that humanity everywhere entails. Slaveholders constantly reckoned with that humanity; enslaved people made sure of it. Slave traders, however, confronted the human-property paradox to a lesser degree. They feared shipboard rebellion and mortality, but needing captives *not* to do something required much less human interaction than needing slaves *to* do something. Slave traders only needed captives not to rebel or die, whereas slaveholders had to cajole enslaved people to work. As a result, merchants in the slave trade were remarkably successful—disturbingly so—in downplaying Africans' humanity. In fact, many traders in Europe or New England only encountered the people they traded as numbers in ledgers, since the captives were both bought and sold by their employees and agents in faraway ports. As the emerging global capitalist system rendered economic relationships more impersonal, the tallying of slaves in merchants' account books was among the most extreme examples of the new order.

Study of the intercolonial slave trade renders this human commoditization more starkly than even the transatlantic trade. Focusing on the intercolonial trade makes it hard to see the commerce in human beings as defenders of the trade publicly portrayed it—as less of a business transaction than as a migration of laborers (albeit forced) to help colonize the New World. When merchants moved enslaved people from one American colony to another for profit, they moved captives between two regions that both desired slave labor. Intercolonial merchants concerned themselves with where slave prices were low or high, not with where the empire needed African labor most. This distinction was not lost on (and was quite galling to) British planters, especially when British merchants exported enslaved Africans from British colonies to foreign ones. In exporting African laborers from the empire, intercolonial traders—and the British officials who encouraged and supported them—implicitly prioritized a

Othello: Elizabethan Representations of Sub-Saharan Africans," ibid., 19–44; Joyce E. Chaplin, "Race," in David Armitage and Michael J. Braddick, eds., *The British Atlantic World, 1500–1800* (New York, 2002), 154–172.

view of Africans as items to be sold for profit over a view of them as workers to be exploited for labor. Ironically, this would leave outraged British colonial planters in the position of demanding that their government take the humanity, or at least the labor capacity, of enslaved Africans more seriously. Valuing enslaved Africans as potential workers, British planters struggled to fathom their empire's tolerance of a trade that supplied such workers to their rivals. Imperial officials, on the other hand, categorized Africans as assets to exchange in an imperial political economy. A recent exploration of the development of plantation slavery emphasizes that British imperialists abstracted African people into units of work—part of the worker's alienation from his or her labor under the emerging, impersonal capitalist economy. "To Britons . . . it was the labor of the enslaved that defined them." But this abstraction as depersonalized laborers was not the only manner of subsuming Africans' humanity to an economic understanding of their value. In pursuing the intercolonial trade, the value of the enslaved as assets for trade could overshadow even their labor value.[29]

The economic logic of slave trading pushed people toward such a dehumanizing view, and the intercolonial trade pulled multitudes of colonists across the Americas into complicity. The final passage's thousands of small shipments and exchanges familiarized far more buyers and sellers, port officials and dock workers, printers and readers with the commerce in people than the transatlantic trade alone would have. Merchants trading Africans (and printers advertising sales, and port officials tallying comings and goings) offered public and disseminated performances of Africans treated as goods. And the step from witnessing and abiding such treatment to seeing Africans as something less than human, or as a lesser type of human, was a small one. The regular and visible exchange of enslaved people as property in the markets of early America offered one important site where colonists learned to see African men and women as economic units with their humanity obscured.[30]

29. Simon P. Newman, *A New World of Labor: The Development of Plantation Slavery in the British Atlantic* (Philadelphia, 2013), 13.

30. Karen Ordahl Kupperman shows that, in the early decades of British settlement in North America, many colonists formed positive impressions of native Americans because of their "presentment of civility," especially as reflected in the respect that community leaders commanded from common people (Kupperman, "Presentment of Civility: English Reading of American Self-Presentation in the Early Years of Colonization," *WMQ*, LIV [1997], 193–228). This offers an instructive contrast to the manner in which most European settlers first encountered African people—toiling on plantations as slaves or being shipped as commodities in the slave trade. It may help account for why some colonists deemed Africans less capable of assimilation or civilization than native Americans. American settlers encountered no powerful African leaders—only beleaguered survivors of the slave trade.

1. Final Passages

CAPTIVES IN THE INTERCOLONIAL SLAVE TRADE

*They took me to the Island of Dominica. After that I was taken to
New Orleans. Then they took me to Natchez. —Abduhl Rahhahman*

In both popular portrayals, like that of Kunta Kinte in *Roots,* and
scholarly studies, the story of the slave trade typically ends (and the story of
slavery in America begins) with a vessel reaching the Americas after the Atlantic crossing. Traders sold captives in port, and the journey was over. The enslaved presumably marched to a nearby plantation to begin their struggle to
adapt to a new world and to assert their humanity despite the system of chattel slavery. For many survivors of the Middle Passage, this depiction is accurate enough, but hundreds of thousands of other captives found themselves
purchased by colonial merchants. Rather than march inland to a plantation,
these survivors of the Middle Passage—weary, debilitated, angry, and con-
fused—boarded new vessels and returned to sea within days or weeks of their
first arrival in America.[1]

Telling stories of captives' final passages between American colonies is a
crucial part of understanding the slave trade, but the stories are difficult to
recover. Owing to the power imbalance of slavery, few accounts from African perspectives survive to document the intercolonial traffic. Often, we can
only infer enslaved experiences by reading between the lines of traders' documents. One of the many tragedies of the slave trade is this relegation of captives to anonymity. The gap in time between the abolition of the transatlantic
slave trade and the abolition of slavery itself ensured that only a few survivors

1. Alex Haley, *Roots* (Garden City, N.Y., 1976), 192–201. Tellingly, the most famous popular
portrayal of the slave trade in the last twenty years—Steven Spielberg's *Amistad*—takes events
that actually occurred aboard an intercolonial slaver and sets them aboard a transatlantic vessel
to avoid confusing an audience familiar only with slave ships crossing the Atlantic. See David
Franzoni, *Amistad,* directed by Steven Spielberg (Universal City, Calif., 1997). For rich historical
accounts that focus on captive experiences of the Middle Passage but that end the journeys at
a first American port, see Marcus Rediker, *The Slave Ship: A Human History* (New York, 2007);
Stephanie E. Smallwood, *Saltwater Slavery: A Middle Passage from Africa to American Diaspora*
(Cambridge, Mass., 2007).

of the traffic lived to experience freedom and, just perhaps, to document their stories for posterity. The recording and publishing of a few firsthand accounts arose out of the movement to end the slave trade, but that campaign generated little interest or support until the late eighteenth century. And even then, abolitionism—and the publishing of African and African American authors—was confined almost entirely to the British Isles and British North America. In the previous hundreds of years of migration, stories were never recorded, and for most parts of the Americas, no firsthand accounts from Africans survive at all.[2]

The narratives that we do possess from slave trade survivors are treasures for their rarity, but most offer few details. Abduhl Rahhahman typified autobiographers by describing his survival of the transatlantic and intercolonial slave trades in three terse sentences: "They took me to the Island of Dominica. After that I was taken to New Orleans. Then they took me to Natchez." Rahhahman's use of the passive voice and a depersonalized "they" evokes powerlessness and anger. His omission of detail hints at suppressed traumas, but the account offers little description of shipboard conditions or experiences. James Albert Ukawsaw Gronniosaw offered a similarly spare recollection of the final passage, explaining that, after he survived an Atlantic crossing to Barbados, a man purchased him who lived "in the City of New-York; to which place he took me with him." The sparseness of such narratives intimates captives' disheartened experiences, but recovering more detail about their actual journeys requires supplementing survivors' laconic stories by reading between the lines of European sources—accounts of merchants and ship captains, quantitative data derived from port records, and documents produced by both sides in the abolition debates.[3]

2. On the limited geographic and temporal scope of the literature generated by survivors of the slave trade, see Moira Ferguson, "The Literature of Slavery and Abolition," in F. Abiola Irele and Simon Gikandi, eds., *The Cambridge History of African and Caribbean Literature*, I (New York, 2004), 238–254.

3. "Abduhl Rah[h]ahman's History," in John W. Blassingame, ed., *Slave Testimony: Two Centuries of Letters, Speeches, Interviews, and Autobiographies* (Baton Rouge, 1977), 684–685, esp. 685; "A Narrative of the Most Remarkable Particulars in the Life of James Albert Ukawsaw Gronniosaw, an African Prince, as Related by Himself (1772)," rpt. in William L. Andrews and Henry Louis Gates, Jr., eds., *Slave Narratives* (New York, 2002), 12. Katherine Faull Eze describes another, similar account left by a man known as Andrew the Moor, or Ofodobenda Wooma, who did not offer any details about his voyages in the slave trade but who noted crossing the Atlantic to Antigua followed by a subsequent sale in New York; see Eze, "Self-Encounters: Two Eighteenth-Century African Memoirs from Moravian Bethlehem," in David McBride, Leroy Hopkins, and C. Aisha Blackshire-Belay, eds., *Crosscurrents: African Americans, Africa, and Germany in the Modern World* (Columbia, S.C., 1998), 29–52.

The major exception to this absence of survivors' descriptions (and to the pattern of traders' and sailors' leaving only unsympathetic reports) is Olaudah Equiano's famous—and famously problematic—autobiography. Equiano offers the most detailed narrative of the slave trade that survives from the captive perspective, and his account includes more than just the oft-quoted segments on the Middle Passage from the Bight of Biafra to Barbados. Equiano also describes, in at least some detail, a voyage to Virginia that occurred shortly thereafter. The trick for historians of the slave trade is that the authenticity of this portion of Equiano's autobiography is questioned from two angles. First, although historians have corroborated later events in Equiano's narrative with archival research, two documents challenge his claim of surviving the slave trade as a boy: a record of his baptism as an adult in England and a ship register from a vessel on which he worked as a free man, both of which list Equiano's birthplace as South Carolina. The second challenge to Equiano's authenticity comes from scholars who argue that his engagement in the abolitionist cause renders him suspect as an accurate portrayer of lived experience.[4]

Both cautions have merit, but they do not negate the usefulness of Equiano's observations for studying the intercolonial slave trade. Equiano was indeed an abolitionist seeking to outrage and galvanize the British public, so his descriptions of the horrors of the slave trade must be tempered with skepticism and evaluated against other information. But all sources are fraught with bias and are products of their genre; the job of the historian is to seek insight despite such limitations. Perhaps more critical is the question of whether Equiano actually endured the slave trade. On one hand, two documents explicitly label Equiano's place of birth as South Carolina, and one can imagine an abolitionist of African descent fabricating a story of surviving a traumatic Middle Passage to give his story more punch. On the other hand, concocting a plausible narrative of childhood in an Igbo community and abduction into the slave trade and its associated traumas would have been no simple task for an

4. Vincent Carretta, who uncovered the documents suggesting Equiano's American birth, describes the "circumstantial evidence that Equiano was . . . African American by birth" as "compelling but not absolutely conclusive." See Carretta, *Equiano, the African: Biography of a Self-Made Man* (Athens, Ga., 2005), xvi, 3–5. For treatments suggesting that Equiano wrote something of a fiction for abolitionist purposes, see S. E. Ogude, "Facts into Fiction: Equiano's Narrative Reconsidered," *Research in African Literatures*, XIII (1982), 31–43; Frank Kelleter, "Ethnic Self-Dramatization and Technologies of Travel in *The Interesting Narrative of the Life of Olaudah Equiano, or Gustavus Vassa, the African, Written by Himself* (1789)," *Early American Literature*, XXXIX (2004), 67–84.

American-born man living in England in the late eighteenth century. Equiano knew a remarkable amount about cultural practices specific to the region in which he claimed he was born, and his account of his Igbo village fits well with modern scholarly understanding of the region's history. In the European world of Equiano's day, ethnographic accounts of the region were unavailable, so either he developed his understanding of the region from firsthand knowledge, or, if Equiano was not born in the Biafran interior, he surely interviewed survivors of the slave trade from that region. Furthermore, Equiano showed a remarkable sensitivity and insight on the psychological traumas and challenges to self-identification that a captive from this particular region would have experienced. As such, even if one chooses to believe the baptismal record and ship's manifest over Equiano's autobiography, his account is still useful as a "biography of a people" or a "composite of the actual memory of others he encountered." If treated as a fictional tale based on interviews with survivors, Equiano's narrative is uniquely valuable for documenting the slave trade (Plate 1).[5]

There are additional reasons to value Equiano's insights. Beyond claiming to have endured a journey from Barbados to Virginia as a captive, Equiano described working aboard numerous slavers as a sailor. As a young man, Equiano was owned by a Caribbean merchant who put him to work aboard several ships engaged in intercolonial trade—including the trade in African people— both within the Caribbean and between the Caribbean and the North American mainland. In fact, many of Equiano's observations about captive experiences are from descriptions of his life as a sailor, and other historical sources corroborate Equiano's presence on such vessels. The ships he mentions can be found in colonial port records with details, such as vessel name, captain's name, owner's name, and ports of call—not to mention enslaved people in the cargo—all matching Equiano's memory as portrayed in his *Interesting Narra-*

5. A persuasive argument for Equiano's African birth based on his knowledge of Igbo culture appears in Paul E. Lovejoy, "Autobiography and Memory: Gustavus Vassa, alias Olaudah Equiano, the African," *Slavery and Abolition*, XXVII (2006), 317–347. For a similar argument based on Equiano's sensitivity to the adaptation of an individual's identity as he or she moved from the Biafran interior into the diaspora, see Alexander X. Byrd, "Eboe, Country, Nation, and Gustavus Vassa's *Interesting Narrative*," *William and Mary Quarterly*, 3d Ser., LXIII (2006), 142– 144. "Biography of a people": Carretta, *Equiano, the African*, 7. "Composite of the actual memory of others": G. Michelle Collins-Sibley, "Who Can Speak? Authority and Authenticity in Olaudah Equiano and Phillis Wheatley," *Journal of Colonialism and Colonial History*, V, no. 3 (Winter 2004), 6. For a thoughtful reflection on the importance of making the most of "voices of blacks from that era [which] are so few and so faint," see Annette Gordon-Reed, *Thomas Jefferson and Sally Hemings: An American Controversy* (Charlottesville, Va., 1997), 227.

PLATE 1. Portrait of Olaudah Equiano (also know as Gustavus Vassa). Frontispiece from *The Interesting Narrative of the Life of Olaudah Equiano, or Gustavus Vassa, the African, Written by Himself* (London, 1789). Image courtesy of Documenting the American South, The University of North Carolina at Chapel Hill Libraries

tive. Given Equiano's presence aboard such vessels, even his possibly fictitious account of captivity in the trade comes from an unusually informed and sympathetic source. In a sense, the question of his authenticity is moot. Even if we reject Equiano's claim of being traded, he offers rare eyewitness testimony to the experiences of others caught in the intercolonial slave trade.[6]

6. Carretta, who discovered the evidence that Equiano might have been born in America rather than Africa, nonetheless argues, "Once Equiano entered the literate society of the Royal Navy his account of his subsequent life is remarkably consistent with the historical record" (*Equiano, the African*, xvi, 3–5). My work suggests that Equiano's record of consistency extends back into his enslaved life on merchant vessels. For example, Equiano states that he was owned for several years by a Montserrat merchant named Robert King and that he worked aboard King's vessel *Prudence* in 1765, under a Captain Farmer, when the vessel transshipped Africans from Montserrat to Charleston ("The Interesting Narrative of the Life of Olaudah Equiano, or Gustavus Vassa, the African, Written by Himself," in Vincent Carretta, ed., *The Interesting Nar-*

■ The first stage of the final passage was transfer from a transatlantic slaving vessel. Africans reaching British America typically made their first landfall (or at least anchorage) at one of a few entrepôts where both planters and merchants frequented sales of arriving African people. In 1647, upon sailing to Bridgetown, Barbados—the oldest English entrepôt of the slave trade—settler Richard Ligon described one such bustling port. Ligon's ship "put into *Carlile Bay*, . . . where we found riding at Anchor, 22 good ships, with boates plying to and fro, with Sayles and Oares, which carried commodities from place to place; so quick stirring, and numerous, as I have seen it below the bridge at *London*." Arriving Africans must have witnessed similar scenes all across the Americas, and if the hubbub of the harbor impressed a traveler from the English capital, most captives from West Africa, where seafaring was not commonplace, had surely seen nothing like it. Colonial ports were familiar with arriving slave ships and feared the "Contagious or Malignant Distempers" often on board, so arriving Africans—at least in the eighteenth century—generally spent a week to ten days in quarantine aboard ship before being offered for sale. If officials perceived communicable diseases among them, the quarantine could extend for weeks.[7]

Contagion was poorly understood, however, so during this period, arriving Africans frequently saw strangers board their ships. Merchants inspected their human commodities, doctors visited to treat ill captives, and workers—often

---

rative and Other Writings [New York, 2003], 99–101 [hereafter cited as Equiano, *Interesting Narrative*]). South Carolina port and duty records corroborate this account, noting the arrival of a sloop *Prudence*, under Captain Thomas Farmer, owned by Robert King, delivering seventy enslaved Africans from Montserrat in February 1765; see "Negroes Imported into South Carolina, 1765," in Elizabeth Donnan, ed., *Documents Illustrative of the History of the Slave Trade to America*, 4 vols. (Washington, D.C., 1930–1935), IV, 411; *Records of the Public Treasurers of South Carolina, 1725–1776* (Columbia, S.C., 1969), reel 2, 420 (microfilm).

7. Richard Ligon, *A True and Exact History of the Island of Barbados* (London, 1657), 21. For a sample quarantine law, see Charleston's (designed to stop the spread of "Contagious or Malignant Distempers"), passed in 1744 ("Act for Establishing Quarantine, 1744," in Donnan, ed., *Documents*, IV, 298–300, esp. 298). In the early eighteenth century, Jamaica required a quarantine period of eight days; see Colin Palmer, *Human Cargoes: The British Slave Trade to Spanish America, 1700–1739* (Urbana, Ill., 1981), 113. In 1789, Jamaican port official Stephen Fuller estimated "on an average, fifteen days between the days of reports [of vessels' arrival in port] and the days of the sales" of the slaves imported, presumably owing to quarantine; see Fuller, *Notes on the Two Reports from the Committee of the Honourable House of Assembly of Jamaica . . .* (London, 1789), 38. Governor James Wright of Georgia recommended the construction of a facility at Savannah for the quarantine of arriving slaves in 1766, but it is unclear whether the policy was ever enacted; see Darold D. Wax, "'New Negroes Are Always in Demand': The Slave Trade in Eighteenth-Century Georgia," *Georgia Historical Quarterly*, LXVIII (1984), 204–206.

enslaved—carried fresh water and provisions aboard. Equiano wrote that, on the day his vessel reached Barbados from the Bight of Biafra, "many merchants and planters now came on board ... [and] made us jump" in order to test the captives' health. Likewise, Charleston merchant John Guerard reported that when one of his slaving vessels arrived in 1752, he was "on Board just for a few minutes in the evening of the day he arrived," even though the vessel had to wait ten days in quarantine. Captives surely resented the inspections, but such visits also brought welcome improvements. In defending the slave trade, Robert Bisset cited a report that "fresh provisions, fruit, and vegetables, ... are immediately sent on board for the Slaves," and despite his proslavery bias, there is little reason to doubt the account. Merchants often noted the importance of refreshing debilitated captives. Among the visitors to many ships were also earlier survivors of the Middle Passage. Equiano reported widespread fear among captives upon arrival in Barbados, but "the white people got some old slaves from the land to pacify us. They told us we were not to be eaten, but to work, and were soon to go on land, where we should see many of our country people." One wonders what other information passed between veterans of the slave regime and new arrivals on such occasions.[8]

After the quarantine period, many groups of captives disembarked. Ashore, they usually resided in walled compounds, often at the homes of merchants. In fact, Jamaica's "Code Noir"—which compiled the colony's extant slave laws as of 1788—included a requirement that merchants selling slaves "procure or hire ... a proper place or enclosure ashore" rather than conduct sales aboard ship. Similarly, in Barbados, Equiano alleged that upon disembarkation, the merchants took him and his fellow captives to the "merchant's yard, where we were all pent up together like so many sheep in a fold" while awaiting sale. This wait in the yard lasted for "a few days; I believe it could not be above a fortnight." Equiano was not alone in using a livestock metaphor to describe such accommodations; employees of the British South Sea Company referred to their facility for holding captives awaiting transshipment from Jamaica to Spanish America as a "Penn." These "Penns" or "yards" were presumably

8. John Guerard to William Jolliff, May 4, 1752, John Guerard Letter Book, 1752-1754, 34/0321 OvrSz, fols. 22–23, South Carolina Historical Society, Charleston; Robert Bisset, *The History of the Negro Slave Trade, in Its Connection with the Commerce and Prosperity of the West Indies, and the Wealth and Power of the British Empire*, 2 vols. (London, 1805), I, 79 (in the same passage, Bisset also notes that arriving Africans "meet with their countrymen" already living in the colony); Equiano, *Interesting Narrative*, 60–61. Smallwood emphasizes that merchants gave arriving Africans abundant fresh food and water to improve their appearance for market (*Saltwater Slavery*, 158–160).

crowded. In 1688, Jamaican officials confiscated the property of a Spanish trader, Iago del Castillo, resident in Kingston. His assets included "70 or 80 Negroes in his Yard." They would have endured cramped conditions and exposure to the elements, as implied by the terms "yard" and "pen." Detailed descriptions of such facilities in British colonies do not survive, but accounts from Spanish American port cities note walled yards or interior patios designed to accommodate enslaved Africans awaiting sale. Some captives might not have been entirely exposed to elements; abolitionist Thomas Clarkson did interview one sailor who noted that "a shed had been built" for slaves temporarily housed at an open-air compound at the Barbados wharf, "in order that the slaves in wet weather might get under it and be dry." Nonetheless, such shelter was rudimentary at best, and clothing was minimal. British traveler Nicholas Cresswell described witnessing "a Cargo of Slaves land" on his first day in Barbados. It was "one of the most shocking sights I ever saw. About 400 Men, Women, and Children, . . . all naked, except a small piece of blue cloth about a foot broad to cover their nakedness." [9]

Other captives waited for transshipment on the ships in which they crossed the Atlantic. In fact, many survivors of the Middle Passage apparently never set foot on land in their first British American port. Kingston merchant John Jones noted that, at times of high demand, traders looking for slaves to transship sometimes purchased captives before they disembarked. In 1728, he wrote to a partner in Bristol: "Demand for Negroes still Continues; there is now 500 in [the] harbour and all bought up by the traders to So. Keys [in Cuba] where of late they have made very great Voyages." Equiano described a similar transaction. In 1776, by then a free man, Equiano engaged to serve as an overseer on

9. Additional Manuscripts, 12432, fol. 51, British Library, London (hereafter cited as BL, Add. MSS); Equiano, *Interesting Narrative*, 62 (if Equiano fabricated his own experience of being traded in this way, his duties in later years included having "different cargoes of new negroes in [his] care for sale," so he had often observed the conditions arriving Africans faced before sale or transshipment [104]); Directors of the South Sea Company to Rigby and Pratter, Apr. 21, 1725, in South Sea Company Records, 1711–1846, microfilm, Add. MSS, 25564, 215, Milton S. Eisenhower Library, Johns Hopkins University, Baltimore, Md. (hereafter cited as SSC Records); "The Case of Mr. Smith Kelly Deputy to John Mournsteven[?] Esq'r Provost Marshall Generall of Jamaica," CO 1/65, fols. 380–382, National Archives, Kew; Thomas Clarkson, *The Substance of the Evidence of Sundry Persons on the Slave-Trade, Collected in the Course of a Tour Made in the Autumn of the Year 1788* (London, 1789), 41 (Colin Palmer also notes "rudely constructed houses and huts" within the pens [*Human Cargoes*, 61]); *The Journal of Nicholas Cresswell, 1774–1777* (New York, 1928), 35–36. For merchant properties accommodating slaves in Spanish American cities, see David L. Chandler, "Health Conditions in the Slave Trade of Colonial New Granada," in Robert Brent Toplin, ed., *Slavery and Race Relations in Latin America* (Westport, Conn., 1974), 58–59, 65–66.

a new plantation to be established on the Mosquito Shore of British Honduras. En route, Equiano and the owner of the new plantation, Dr. Charles Irving, stopped in Kingston for supplies. Once other necessary plans and purchases had been made, "our vessel being ready to sail for the Musquito shore, I went with the Doctor on board a Guinea-man, to purchase some slaves to carry with us." Apparently, these people spent little time, if any, on Jamaican soil.[10]

Regardless of whether captives disembarked or remained on ship while they waited, it comes as little surprise that they suffered greatly, physically and emotionally. Cresswell remarked that arriving people "appear much dejected." They also fought all manner of illnesses, making medical attention a crucial part of their interval in the entrepôts. To some degree, captives benefited from the need for slaves to appear healthy because traders paid medical experts to treat captives for smallpox, dysentery, yaws, and the other common ailments of the slave trade. But dealers paying for treatment prioritized the appearance of health over actual cures. Clarkson noted that for people suffering from yaws, which caused pustules to break out on the skin, "Caustick is. . . applied to the yaw spots, to burn them off." Such treatment gave captives the guise of healthy skin, but the underlying infection would cause new "yaw spots" to emerge. For example, Jamaica slaveholder Henry Coor testified to the House of Commons in 1790 that he had purchased Africans whose skin appeared "very clean and black; but in 6 weeks or two months, they all broke out violently with the yaws." Once these men and women were conversant in English, they explained that their condition had been masked by the traders "on board [who] rubbed them with something that made their skin clean," at least temporarily. Then again, considering that Europeans' preferred treatment for yaws in the period was drinking mercury, captives who had their yaws masked instead of "cured" might have been better off.[11]

On the appointed day for sale, captives saw buyers swarm among them,

---

10. John Jones to Isaac Hobhouse, Kingston, Mar. 2, 1728, XIII, fol. 129, Jeffries Collection, Bristol Central Library, Bristol, U.K. (hereafter cited as Jeffries Coll.); Equiano, *Interesting Narrative*, 205.

11. *Journal of Nicholas Cresswell*, 36; Clarkson, *Evidence on the Slave-Trade*, 45. Smallwood emphasizes that survivors of the Atlantic crossing reached American ports exhausted, depressed, and ill (*Saltwater Slavery*, 60, 157–162, 178–179). "Very clean and black": House of Commons of Great Britain, *Abridgment of the Minutes of the Evidence, Taken before a Committee of the Whole House, to Whom It Was Referred to Consider of the Slave-Trade*, 4 vols. (London, 1789–1791), IV, 38–50, esp. 48. For more on the diseases typically afflicting captives in the slave trade, see Richard B. Sheridan, *Doctors and Slaves: A Medical and Demographic History of Slavery in the British West Indies, 1680–1834* (New York, 1985), 113–120.

choosing slaves. As Hercules Ross, a twenty-year resident of Jamaica, remembered such occasions, "On the day advertised by the agent, buyers attend aboard; at a given hour the sale is declared open, when each exerts himself to get first among the slaves to have a good choice, and the whole of the healthy and likely ones, are often sold that day." Here also, captives might have encountered veteran slaves from their African region. In his House of Commons testimony, Henry Coor recalled that, when purchasing newly arrived African people, "He took a slave with him to interpret," presumably someone from the same African region. Coor sought to question prospective slaves about illnesses that traders might have concealed. Through such dialogue with enslaved translators, captives might have gleaned information about slaveholders, but probably not enough to discern between two types of buyers in the crowd—planters and speculators. One wonders what the translators felt, as they facilitated the sale of more men and women of their linguistic background into American slavery.[12]

In most ports, at most times, the majority found themselves purchased by local planters, but perhaps a quarter arriving in British America ended up in the possession of colonial merchants intending to send them elsewhere for resale. Hercules Ross recalled that when he lived in Jamaica, "There used to be in Kingston many people who bought on speculation" from transatlantic slave vessels. Such traders invested in human commodities "to carry them to the country, and retail them, or to ship them off." From the late seventeenth through the eighteenth century, these merchants became increasingly prominent, particularly in the most active ports of slave importation.[13]

Most captives purchased by such speculators did not wait long before boarding an intercolonial vessel. Some simply transferred from one ship to another in the harbor, but even for those who reached land in an entrepôt, the sojourn before heading back to sea was usually brief. Equiano claimed not to have waited "above a fortnight" in Barbados before transshipment to Virginia. Other slave trade stories corroborate the impression of short layovers before intercolonial journeys. Of fourteen known slave trade survivors to leave narratives of their arrival in British America, six describe additional movements within three weeks of completing the Atlantic crossing. (In at least one case, however, this further movement came aboard the same vessel in which the

---

12. House of Commons, *Evidence of the Slave-Trade,* IV, 47, 143. Equiano also recalled, "Soon after we were landed [but before the sale], there came to us Africans of all languages" (*Interesting Narrative,* 60).

13. House of Commons, *Evidence of the Slave-Trade,* IV, 143.

author endured the Middle Passage, and in several cases it is unclear whether the individual changed ships.) When merchant letters or port records indicate the dates of a captive's transatlantic arrival and intercolonial departure, such accounts support the conclusion that most Africans spent little time waiting in between. Export records for Barbados noted six captives aboard the vessel *Hard Times* when it departed for Bermuda on November 19, 1785. These people from the Windward Coast of Africa had reached Barbados on the *Endeavour* just twenty days earlier. Others reembarked more quickly. In 1787, twenty-two men, women, and children arrived in Barbados from Sierra Leone as part of a larger group on the *Knight*. They spent thirteen days at the island before boarding the *Fanfan* for Trinidad. Likewise, in 1801, the thirty mostly Igbo people boarding the *Escape* in Tobago had spent just sixteen days on the island since their arrival from Africa aboard the *Nanny*. They were bound for Saint Vincent.[14]

The notable exception to this trend of fairly short waits was the South Sea Company's practice, in Barbados and Jamaica, of sometimes stockpiling people for transshipment to Spanish America. Company agents in Barbados held orders to keep "50 good, sound, and Healthy Negroes" on hand in case company agents in Spanish America should request them. Jamaica was an even bigger company hub, and agents there also had orders that "a Stock in hand will be always necessary" so that "as Demands arise from the Several Factorys [in Spanish colonies] You may not be at a Loss to give them immediate Supplys." This policy suggests that some prisoners waited many weeks, if not months, before the company deemed transshipment necessary.[15]

Despite its usual brevity, the layover offered benefits to some forced migrants. For one, time on land offered better chances for flight. In 1725, South Sea Company officials scolded managers in Jamaica upon receiving their report that "a considerable Number" of African captives awaiting transshipment to Spanish America "were missing." Flight or theft by other traders or planters

14. Equiano, *Interesting Narrative*, 62. Jerome S. Handler identified and analyzed the fourteen African accounts of the slave trade to British America (Handler, "Survivors of the Middle Passage: Life Histories of Enslaved Africans in British America," *Slavery and Abolition*, XXIII, no. 1 [April 2002], 27). All these narratives were consulted for the present work, but most provide little detail on transatlantic or intra-American journeys. *Hard Times:* CO 33/19, fol. 54, 106/2, fols. 10, 15. For these captives' transatlantic vessel *Endeavour*, see *Voyages*, accessed July 2011, Voyage ID no. 81279. *Knight:* CO 33/20, fol. 22a; *Voyages*, accessed July 2011, Voyage ID no. 82204. *Escape:* CO 290/1, fol. 21; for these captives' transatlantic journey on the *Nanny*, see *Voyages*, accessed July 2011, Voyage ID no. 82870.

15. SSC instructions for Dudley Woodbridge, Jan. 17, 1718, SSC Records, Add. MSS, 25563, 236; SSC to Rigby and Pratter, Nov. 12, 1724, ibid., 25564, 136–137.

is the probable explanation. Less mysterious was the disappearance of an Igbo man from traders in Dominica. In 1786, Liverpool merchant Thomas Leyland inquired of his agents on the island about "a Negro man that [had] run away from the *Enterprize*" upon that ship's arrival the previous year. Apparently, the fugitive had managed to leave the island before being recaptured, because Leyland's agents reported that a vessel called *Vulture* had returned the man to Dominica from an unnamed location. Most escapees probably met similar fates, but time in an entrepôt at least offered better prospects for flight than time at sea.[16]

The more common benefit of layovers was a chance to recuperate after the Middle Passage, especially when such Atlantic crossings had been particularly grueling. In October 1762, Kingston merchant Jasper Hall saw his ship *Africa* limp into port "Leaky, and unfit to Proceed further without Repair . . . [with] many sickly Negroes" from an unspecified part of West Africa. Hall had planned to send the vessel on to Havana, but after seeing the rickety ship and its ailing prisoners, he postponed the onward journey. Hall's crew disembarked the captives,

> to the Number of 630, many of whom being taken with the small Pox, and 400 Innoculated, they necessarily continued in the Island until the January following, when all that remained alive, being but 521, were . . . reshipped on Board the *Affrica,* and cleared out for the Havannah their Original and real Destination.

This was not a true transshipment, since the captives continued to Cuba on the same vessel that ferried them across the Atlantic, but their stopover nonetheless underscores a potential benefit of an interlude between transatlantic and intercolonial journeys. From Hall's perspective, the pause was as much about the "Repair of the Vessell, as refreshment of the many sickly Negroes," but for the imprisoned people suffering smallpox and other ailments, it offered an opportunity to recover. That more than one hundred fewer people reembarked suggests that for many captives, this respite was too little, too late.[17]

Unlike Jasper Hall, who claimed ownership of all captives aboard the *Africa,* most traders forcing enslaved people from one colony to another selected

16. SSC to Rigby and Pratter, Apr. 21, 1725, ibid., 25564, 215; Thomas Leyland to Captain Charles Wilson, Liverpool, Dec. 9, 1786, Letter Book of Thomas Leyland, 387 MD 59, 199, Liverpool Record Office, U.K. For the 1785 voyage of the *Enterprize* from Bonny, on the Bight of Biafra, to Dominica, see *Voyages,* accessed July 2011, Voyage ID no. 81287.

17. "The Case of the *Africa,*" Mar. 27, 1769, in Donnan, ed., *Documents,* II, 533–536. For more on the *Africa,* see *Voyages,* accessed July 2011, Voyage ID no. 75031.

only some captives from a transatlantic vessel. As a result, who endured subsequent journeys was not random. One deciding factor was health. Speculating merchants avoided purchasing captives they considered too frail to survive another voyage or to garner a higher price elsewhere. At times, Africans from particular regions faced increased odds of transshipment. During the British monopoly of the slave trade to Spanish America, Jamaican merchants Tyndall and Assheton insisted that Kingston offered a good market "Especially for Gold Coast's and Pappaw's which the South Sea [Company] Factors buy before any others" for transshipment to Spanish America. Some intercolonial traders exhibited gender and age biases, as well.[18]

In other cases, paradoxically, the people transshipped were precisely those *not* chosen. Rather than lower prices, some slave dealers opted to move slow-selling captives to smaller markets in hopes of finding less discriminating buyers. Equiano described transshipment from Barbados this way: "I and some few more slaves, that were not saleable among the rest . . . were shipped off in a sloop for North America." Likewise, Thomas Clarkson reported a sailor's recollection that, upon arriving in the Americas, "slaves that are sickly . . . are in general bought upon speculation." In particular, the sailor remembered an instance when the "surgeon" of a vessel on which the sailor worked purchased some survivors of the Middle Passage "at Barbadoes, who were in a very weak and disordered state. Having recovered them a little, he sold them afterwards at Jamaica." Sometimes, those least fit for extended journeys after the Middle Passage were precisely those selected to endure yet another voyage.[19]

Regardless of such patterns, from the captives' standpoint, the vagaries of who went where after reaching the New World were capricious, especially when the sorting severed emotional and cultural ties. All sorts of bonds — not just shackles — linked prisoners aboard slave ships to one another. With some regularity, family members withstood the Middle Passage together,

18. Tyndall and Assheton to Isaac Hobhouse, Jamaica, Mar. 13, 1729, Jeffries Coll., XIII, fol. 96. "Pappaw," often spelled "papaw," was an "ethnic" designation that British traders used for some slaves from the Gold Coast region. Tyndall and Assheton later clarified the company's ethnic preferences even further, stating, "They prefer Angolas to Callibarrs but Pappaws before any" (fol. 117). Thirty years earlier, the owners of the slave ship *Blessing* also noted the preference for Angolans in the transshipment trade to Spanish America, advising the captain to sell his slaves in the eastern Caribbean unless he ended up acquiring the slaves in Angola, in which case he should proceed directly to Jamaica to sell the slaves to transshipment traders. See owners of the *Blessing* to Thomas Brownbill, Oct. 10, 1700, Norris Papers, II, 920 NOR 2, fol. 179, Liverpool Record Office.

19. Equiano, *Interesting Narrative*, 62; Clarkson, *Evidence on the Slave-Trade*, 88.

probably having been kidnapped in the same village raid or captured in the same war. The most famous family members to cross the Atlantic were the "two princes of Calabar," Little Ephraim Robin John and Ancona Robin Robin John, brothers from a prominent slave-trading family on the Bight of Biafra. Captured and sold into slavery in 1767 by rival traders on the African coast, the Robin Johns eventually exploited Atlantic connections to make their way home again—and resume slave trading. Most families sucked into the slave trade were not so lucky.[20]

Clarkson alleged that a ship captain he interviewed acknowledged having "seen relations on board the same ship." The captain recalled one particular

> young woman [who] had been complaining, that her father had been brought on board at the same time, but that she had never seen him since. This was occasioned by the large bulk-head across the ship [dividing captives by sex]. . . . On coming however into St. Kitt's, when all the slaves were upon deck, she looked about for her father, and espied him first. Her sensations on this occasion were not easy to be described.

Another trader whom Clarkson interviewed recalled seeing a "husband, wife, and two children, in one ship, and those who called themselves and appeared to be brothers and sisters in another." Slave trader–turned-abolitionist Reverend John Newton shared similar recollections with the House of Commons in 1790, insisting that, during the slave sales in which he participated, "Relations were separated as sheep and lambs are separated by the butcher." Not only abolitionists reported that family members jointly survived the Atlantic crossing; in the same hearings at which Newton testified, ship captain Clement Noble defended the slave trade (including his own nine voyages to Africa and America), but acknowledged "the slaves being in great distress, and making grievous outcries on the sale" because the captives "think they are going to be parted from their husbands, wives, mothers, children, etc." Noble went on to defend the trade's morality with the dubious argument that purchasers were "very particular in making exchanges, so that husbands, wives, mothers, and children, and even acquaintances, shall go together," but he did not refute the existence of families, nor did he claim to have avoided separating them; he left it to the kind hearts of buyers to avoid severing such ties.[21]

20. On the journey of the Robin Johns, see Randy J. Sparks, *The Two Princes of Calabar: An Eighteenth-Century Atlantic Odyssey* (Cambridge, Mass., 2004).

21. Clarkson, *Evidence on the Slave-Trade*, 15, 23; House of Commons, *Evidence of the Slave-*

Familial connections were not the only ones in jeopardy at sales. Many Africans who shared a language or some culture but who had not shared an ethnic identity in Africa began to forge cohesive identities during the journey. The diverse people who spoke Igbo dialects (in what is now Nigeria) had little sense of a collective Igbo identity within Africa, but they developed one as they bridged differences of dialect when thrust together in the slave trade and when encountering people more foreign to them. By the time captives reached America, those who had been strangers beforehand had spent several traumatic months together aboard ship—and perhaps together before that in a slave-trading caravan or a castle on the African coast. Tensions could emerge in such trying circumstances, but so could strong bonds.[22]

Given such ties among prisoners disembarking from the Atlantic crossing, the parsing of people for transshipment or local sale inevitably caused painful separations. After the "traumatic alienation" from family and homeland, many Africans faced additional goodbyes in American entrepôts. Intercolonial dispersal marked another phase of the slave trade's "serial displacement." Clarkson reported that the same ship captain who recalled a young woman reconnecting with her father in Saint Kitts also remembered, "When slaves are brought to market, it is never considered whether relations are separated or not: the only consideration is, how those who have the disposal of them shall sell them best." Former Jamaican overseer Robert Ross agreed, telling the House of Commons that he had often purchased arriving Africans for the plantation he managed, "but was never forced to buy any one he did not like, with a view of not separating relatives." In private correspondence about a sale of American-born slaves in 1765, Charleston trader Henry Laurens presented

Trade, III, 51–52, 58. For more examples of families crossing the Atlantic together, see Audra A. Diptee, "African Children in the British Slave Trade during the Late Eighteenth Century," *Slavery and Abolition*, XXVII (2006), 189–190.

22. On the forging of Igbo ethnicity during the slave trade journey, see Alexander X. Byrd, *Captives and Voyagers: Black Migrants across the Eighteenth-Century British Atlantic World* (Baton Rouge, 2008), chaps. 1, 2. On the importance of shipmate bonds, see Smallwood, *Saltwater Slavery*, 189–190, 196, 203–205; Vincent Brown, *The Reaper's Garden: Death and Power in the World of Atlantic Slavery* (Cambridge, Mass., 2008), 44–46 (Brown notes dispersal within Jamaica as a threat to arriving Africans' family and shipmate bonds but does not mention the added danger of dispersal beyond the island [49]); Orlando Patterson, *The Sociology of Slavery: An Analysis of the Origins, Development, and Structure of Negro Slave Society in Jamaica* (Rutherford, N.J., 1969), 150; Michael Craton, *Empire, Enslavement, and Freedom in the Caribbean* (Princeton, N.J., 1997), 154; Philip D. Curtin, *Two Jamaicas: The Role of Ideas in a Tropical Colony, 1830–1865* (Cambridge, Mass., 1955), 23; Michael A. Gomez, *Exchanging Our Country Marks: The Transformation of African Identities in the Colonial and Antebellum South* (Chapel Hill, N.C., 1998), 165–166.

a contrary perspective, insisting that he made it a priority "to avoid that inconvenience and I will say inhumanity of separating and tareing assunder my Negroe's several families"—but he added the caveat, "in case of irresistable necessity." Laurens suggested that his concern for preserving families applied "even in the Sale of New Negroes" from Africa, but his use of "even" suggests that he knew his concern for African families was unusual. Regardless, one wonders how much difference in price constituted "irresistable necessity" to a man in the business of selling people.[23]

Equiano described witnessing such divisions when he worked as a sailor in the Caribbean. "At or after a sale," he noted, "it was not uncommon to see negroes taken from their wives . . . and children from their parents, and sent off to other islands. . . . Oftentimes my heart has bled at these partings; when the friends of the departed have been at the water side, and, with sighs and tears, have kept their eyes fixed on the vessel till it went out of sight." A Barbadian woman named 'Sibell also recalled heartbreaking separations when, in 1799, she told an Englishman named John Ford her tale of enduring the slave trade. According to Ford, 'Sibell boarded a European ship on the African coast, where she "find my Country woman Mimbo, my Country man Dublin (etc. so named by the English), My Country woman Sally, and some more," but she was unable to keep track of these people after crossing the Atlantic. 'Sibell could only say, "Dey sell dem all about and me no savvy where now," after which, Ford reported, "she burst into tears and could say no more." The dispersal of captives "all about" after the Atlantic crossing severed many communal ties. Desperate as they were to preserve families and friendships, African people just arriving in the Americas—not yet proficient in English nor familiar with American slaveholders—had few tools with which to resist separation.[24]

23. Smallwood, *Saltwater Slavery*, 121; Clarkson, *Evidence on the Slave-Trade*, 16; House of Commons, *Evidence of the Slave-Trade*, IV, 28 (see also 12, 124–125, 127); Henry Laurens to Elias Ball, Apr. 1, 1765, in Philip M. Hamer et al., eds., *The Papers of Henry Laurens*, 16 vols. (Columbia, S.C., 1968–2002) (hereafter cited as *Laurens Papers)*, IV, 595. Laurens is the only merchant I have documented expressing concern about preserving Africans' families in private correspondence, but when testifying in public hearings about the morality of the slave trade, many people claimed to have preserved families; see House of Commons, *Evidence of the Slave-Trade*, II, 117, 131. Byrd describes the slave trade within Africa as involving "serial displacement" for captives, and the concept can also be applied across the Atlantic (*Captives and Voyagers*, 17).

24. "The Interesting Narrative of the Life of Olaudah Equiano, or Gustavus Vassa, the African (1789)," in Andrews and Gates, eds., *Slave Narratives*, 126 (this version is based on a different eighteenth-century edition of Equiano's text than the one cited elsewhere in the present work; all other citations refer to Carretta's 2003 edition). In some editions, this passage referred explicitly

The sorting and mixing of Africans in the American entrepôts of the slave trade also disrupted cultural continuities between Old World and New. Most captives aboard vessels crossing the Atlantic shared cultural traits with many shipmates, having come from the same general region (though it is important to recognize that all people from a region like the Gold Coast or the Bight of Biafra did not share a single language, faith, or culture). When such a group was divided in an American entrepôt, its members faced an increasing likelihood that wherever they ended up, many of their fellow slaves would speak foreign languages and practice different cultures. This made companionship difficult for newly arrived Africans; it also impaired their ability to cooperate, perhaps hindering rebellion, and encouraged the creation of pidgin languages and hybrid cultures (Map 1).

■ On January 9, 1786, thirty-five "Men, Women, boys and Girls" from Angola climbed aboard a small brig in Kingston's busy harbor and returned to sea. They had recently survived a crossing of the Atlantic from their ancestral land with hundreds of other captives, but the vagaries of the Atlantic market for laborers split them off for transshipment. Embarking on their second ocean voyage, they found the sea a little less foreign, but aspects of the new journey differed from the Atlantic crossing. They were a smaller group now, and they crowded into a much smaller space. Their new vessel, the *Mars,* measured only forty tons—whereas transatlantic slavers averaged two hundred tons. The crew had also packed the *Mars* with goods besides enslaved people; in addition to sharing space with each other, the Angolans aboard the *Mars* maneuvered around barrels of rum, sugar, and pimento. The observant among

---

to American-born slaves as well as recent arrivals: "At or after a sale, even [of] those negroes born in the islands, it is not uncommon to see [them] taken from their wives"; see Equiano, *Interesting Narrative,* 110. On 'Sibell, see Smallwood, *Saltwater Slavery,* 204. Smallwood shows that most arriving Africans were passive during sale, owing to fatigue, illness, and depression (ibid., 179). Such reticence contrasts with American-born slaves, who made emotional or strategic appeals during sales. For instance, a German traveler in 1784 described an American-born, or creolized, father in North Carolina imploring a crowd, "Who buys me must buy my son too." See Johann David Schoepf, *Travels in the Confederation (1783-1784),* ed. and trans. Alfred J. Morrison, 2 vols. (Philadelphia, 1911), II, 148; see also Bradford J. Wood, *This Remote Part of the World: Regional Formation in Lower Cape Fear, North Carolina, 1725-1775* (Columbia, S.C., 2004), 100-101. In 1859, an enslaved man pointed out his wife's strong arms and healthy teeth from the auction block, encouraging a buyer that he "better buy us" together and adding, "We'm fus' rate bargain." Quoted in Daina Ramey Berry, "'We'm Fus' Rate Bargain': Value, Labor, and Price in a Georgia Slave Community," in Walter Johnson, ed., *The Chattel Principle: Internal Slave Trades in the Americas* (New Haven, Conn., 2004), 55. See also Walter Johnson, *Soul by Soul: Life Inside the Antebellum Slave Market* (Cambridge, Mass., 1999), esp. chap. 6.

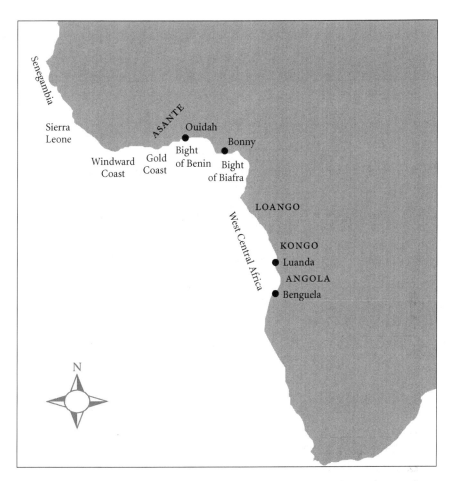

MAP 1. Major African Coastal Regions of Embarkation in the Transatlantic Slave Trade. Drawn by the author

these captives probably gleaned from the sun or stars that this new voyage no longer carried them west. Instead, the *Mars* cruised primarily eastward in the early days of the journey, followed by a northward turn. Whether the captives perceived this direction or not, they surely noticed its effect on the weather as they sailed out of the Caribbean and up the North American coast. Winter gripped North America, and even in Georgia that January and February, locals remarked at "the severity of it." Given the equatorial climate from which they came, the Angolan captives had probably experienced nothing like the winter weather into which they sailed. The *Mars* rocked and thrashed in violent waves whipped up by storms out of the northeast. Frigid rains and high seas drenched the deck with water that dripped and sloshed into the hold of the little vessel. The storms also battered the *Mars* with contrary winds, causing an unexpectedly "long passage." Provisions ran low. The crew headed for the nearest harbor, but one of the Angolan women succumbed to some combination of cold and hunger and "died two days before [the *Mars*] got into port." Her shipmates saw her body dragged away without ceremony to a watery grave. Mercifully, the other thirty-four prisoners survived to reach Savannah, Georgia—probably unaware that their intended destination had been a place called Charleston, farther up the coast. The harsh weather and shortage of provisions had interrupted the journey, but the captives nonetheless suffered ill effects. The merchant in charge of their sale perceived them as "a very slight made People" compared to most Angolans. Perhaps their passage from Jamaica on short rations made them appear so. One man died "a few days after they arrived." The others recovered their health in Savannah, though it took quite some time. It would be summer in this new land—eight months since they had sailed from Jamaica—before the last survivors of this group of Angolans were sold.[25]

■ For most African captives in the slave trade, the experience of an intercolonial voyage differed significantly from the voyage across the Atlantic, but not all intercolonial journeys were alike. Whether a vessel was bound from one British American port to another or to a French or Spanish colony had major implications for captives' shipboard experiences. Voyages that transshipped people within the British Empire differed from those to foreign colonies, not only in the routes they traveled but also with regard to the number of people typically carried and the composition of the nonhuman cargo. As a result, survivors of the Middle Passage who embarked on an intercolonial journey within the British Empire faced a different kind of final passage than their fellow prisoners selected for voyages across imperial lines.

For intercolonial journeys within the British Empire, most captives trav-

---

25. This account of the captives aboard the *Mars* is drawn from the Naval Office Shipping Lists for Jamaica, CO 142/19, fol. 19; and from the letters of Savannah merchant Joseph Clay in three collections at the Georgia Historical Society, Savannah: Clay and Telfair to Daniel Bordeaux, July 19, 1784, Clay, Telfair, and Co. Letter Book, 3 vols. (unpaginated), I; Clay, Telfair, and Co. to Roebuck and Merckle, Feb. 14, 1784, ibid.; Clay to Thomas Wallace and Joseph Donaldson, Apr. 22, 1784, in Joseph Clay Papers, 5 vols., III, 318–320. For the completion of sales of this group of captives, see Clay, Telfair, and Co. to John Coppells and William Coppells, August 1784, Clay, Telfair, and Co. Letter Book, I. For average vessel tonnages in the transatlantic slave trade, see vessels listed on *Voyages*, accessed July 2011, http://slavevoyages.org/tast/database/search.faces?yearFrom=1514&yearTo=1866.

eled in significantly smaller groups than those in which they had crossed the Atlantic. The average slaving voyage within the empire carried just over twenty captives, and half of such voyages carried eight enslaved people or fewer. In fact, a quarter of these ventures carried just one or two people. (Such voyages obviously moved a small fraction of all people transshipped, since a single shipment with fifty captives moved as many enslaved people as fifty vessels carrying one person at a time.) Given the small size of such intercolonial ventures, captives forced aboard faced a high risk of separation from shipmates from the Atlantic crossing. Returning to sea shortly after surviving the Middle Passage must have been distressing in any case, but captives who had just lost track of companions must have sailed with a particular sense of despondency. Indeed, Henry Laurens noticed that "a Cargo is often injured by turning their back on the Islands," adding, "The Slaves grow dispirited and pine away for want of knowing the reasons why they don't stop there." If such despair was common for groups of slaves, individuals sent as the only captive on a ship surely suffered a traumatic isolation.[26]

With their shrunken cohort, captives aboard transshipments within the British Empire typically had to adjust to close quarters on smaller vessels. Nearly half sailed aboard sloops, with schooners and brigantines accounting for most of the remainder (Table 1). Types of sails and rigging—not size of ship—determined designations of vessel type in the seventeenth and eighteenth centuries, but sloops generally had only one mast and schooners just two. Whereas the average transatlantic slave-trading vessel measured 158 tons, the average craft for slave transshipments between British colonies measured just 48 tons—and even that figure is skewed upward by a small number of very large ships. Sixty percent of intercolonial slavers measured 40 tons or fewer, and vessels under 20 tons were not uncommon. Measurements of tonnage are not directly proportional to the space available aboard ship, but the dramatically lower tonnage measurements of intercolonial slavers would have immediately impressed confined circumstances on African captives.[27]

26. Laurens to John Knight, Dec. 31, 1756, in *Laurens Papers*, II, 389. The average number of enslaved people was calculated from 2,985 known voyages between British colonies (or U.S. states) for which the number of captives carried was recorded.

27. By the nineteenth century, sloops and schooners with more than two masts were common, but in eighteenth-century usage, a sloop was a single-masted vessel (rigged fore-and-aft) and schooners had two masts. See William A. Baker, *Sloops and Shallops* (Barre, Mass., 1966), 59–70; Alan McGowan, *The Ship*, IV, *The Century before Steam: The Development of the Sailing Ship, 1700–1820* (London, 1980), 36–40; Colin Munro, *Sailing Ships* (London, 1973), 170. The average for tonnage was calculated from 2,636 voyages for which the vessel's tonnage is known.

TABLE 1. Vessel Types in the Slave Trade between British Colonies
(or U.S. States) to 1808

Vessel type	Number of shipments with documented vessel type	% of shipments with documented vessel types
Sloop	1,159	47.0
Schooner	511	20.7
Brig	443	18.0
Other	353	14.3
TOTAL	2,466	100.0

Source: Database of 7,685 intercolonial slave shipments, compiled by the author.
For a detailed discussion of sources consulted, see Appendix, below.

Such little ships had several implications for enslaved passengers. First, de-spite the decreased numbers of people carried, these voyages were often ter-ribly cramped. Sloops and schooners tended to be shallow, so regardless of the number of people on board, there was not much space. Such vessels were humble craft, and few models or plans of them survive in maritime archives and museums, but one plan for a sloop of a little over one hundred tons shows a hold depth of just nine feet at its tallest. And this modeled sloop would have been larger (by tonnage) than 97 percent of the ships carrying slaves between British colonies. Furthermore, such holds would often have been divided with intermediate decks. When Virginia trader Charles Steuart wrote to a partner on the Caribbean island of Saint Kitts about potential vessels for their inter-colonial trade—in African people and other commodities—he explained that he preferred "a double Deck'd Brig'a[ntine] or Snow about 100 Tons," to "a Sloop or Schooner." He described the "Vessel [he had] in view" as having a "9 ft hold clear, and 3 ft. 3 Inch's clear between Decks." Steuart also specified that such a vessel "could bring Slaves here between Decks," so captives in the intercolonial trade might well have crawled into a space just over three feet high for most or all of such journeys. Since Steuart promoted this "double

For summaries of the sizes of vessels employed in the transatlantic portion of the slave trade, see *Voyages,* accessed July 2011, http://slavevoyages.org/tast/database/search.faces?yearFrom= 1514&yearTo=1866; see also David Eltis, *The Rise of African Slavery in the Americas* (New York, 2000), 125–128; Herbert S. Klein, *The Atlantic Slave Trade* (New York, 1999), 84, 142–144; James A. Rawley, *The Transatlantic Slave Trade: A History* (New York, 1981), 252–258.

Deck'd" vessel for its ability to cram more enslaved people into small spaces than "a single Deck'd Vessel" could accommodate, there is at least some reason to hope that most vessels in the intercolonial trade were "single Deck'd," affording a bit more space for captives.[28]

Regardless of the arrangement of decks, captives forced aboard intercolonial slavers typically competed for space with trade goods. Of 3,511 intercolonial slave shipments within the British Empire for which the vessel's complete cargo is known, 3,120 of them (about 90 percent) carried goods for trade alongside people. Barrels of rum and sugar were most common, but enslaved people wedged in among all manner of items—bread, nails, livestock, deerskins, textiles, and anything else carried on ships of the era (Plate 2). North Carolina merchant James Murray hinted at the cramped quarters for captives when he referred friends who planned to buy slaves in Charleston to a Captain Mace for the trip back to North Carolina. Captain Mace, according to Murray, "promised them the refusal of any passages he could spare, but" Mace urged the slave buyers not to delay in claiming the spots they needed because "the boat was so little and would be so crammed that that would be their last shift for negroes if they got any." Profitable trading voyages demanded that ships be stuffed to the rafters, so enslaved captives occupied little spaces, leaning against barrels or sitting on crates. If captives were too numerous and the hold especially crowded, enslaved passengers might even have remained on deck for entire journeys.[29]

When the voyagers returned to sea, ensconced in whatever nooks they found, they learned that small vessels posed challenges besides the tight quarters. Because sloops and schooners were shallow, they proved particularly vulnerable to dripping (or sloshing) water penetrating the hold. A pervasive damp plagued all ships, which made sailing for days aboard any vessel unpleasant, even for voluntary passengers. As an Age of Sail proverb put it, he who would go to sea for pleasure would go to hell for a pastime. And vessels that rose only a short height above the water were even more damp than

28. Baker, *Sloops and Shallops*, 111–113; Steuart, McKenzie, and Co. to Thomas Ogilvie, July 13, 1751, Charles Steuart Letter Book, I, 1751–1753, microfilm, M-32, John D. Rockefeller, Jr. Library, Williamsburg, Va.

29. Murray to Ribton Hutchison and Frederick Grimké, July 21, 1736, in Bradford J. Wood, ed., *James Murray in North Carolina: Letters, 1732–1781*, vol. XIII of *The Colonial Records of North Carolina*, 2d Ser. (forthcoming). N. A. M. Rodger notes that passengers and crews on merchant vessels struggled more with crowding than their counterparts on military ships because merchant vessels were so thoroughly packed with goods; see Rodger, *The Wooden World: An Anatomy of the Georgian Navy* (London, 1986), 63.

PLATE 2. "Slave deck of the *Albaroz*, Prize to the *Albatross*, 1845," watercolor by Francis Meynell. This image portrays a transatlantic slaver bound for Brazil, but the people perched on and between barrels of goods or provisions may evoke something of the experience of captives in the intercolonial slave trade, since vessels typically carried mixed cargoes of goods and enslaved people. © National Maritime Museum, Greenwich, London

most. In normal seas, spray rained over the sides, and in rougher seas, waves splashed on the deck and water sloshed below. Such conditions made for enough discomfort that the British navy experienced higher rates of desertion on smaller vessels in the eighteenth century. Even worse, some of the smallest ships of the intercolonial slave trade might even have lacked decks altogether. In the seventeenth century, most sloops were open, and the convention of enclosing them only spread gradually from northern North America southward, from the late seventeenth to the early eighteenth centuries. Unenclosed vessels would have been especially common for short voyages that did not cross large stretches of open water.[30]

30. On higher rates of desertion owing to moisture in the hold on the British navy's small ships, see Rodger, *Wooden World*, 62–63. Colin Munro agrees, saying that sloops "provided very little accommodation for the crews, who lived in extreme discomfort" (*Sailing Ships*, 170). Worse yet, the cramped naval sloops that Rodger and Munro describe were actually much larger, by

Despite the hardships, some enslaved passengers discovered advantages to transshipment with a smaller group for the final passage. Most notably, shorter voyages with fewer people reduced the filth that plagued slaving vessels. For instance, the mostly Igbo men, women, and children who reached Barbados aboard the Royal African Company's vessel *Marigold* in 1679 must have greeted transshipment with some relief. More than 100 of their shipmates had died during an excruciating three-and-a-half-month crossing of the Atlantic. Upon their arrival in Barbados, company factors Edwyn Stede and Stephen Gascoigne exclaimed, "Wee never saw soe stinking foule and nasty [a] Ship in our Lives." Stede and Gascoigne had planned to send the *Marigold* on to Nevis, but to preserve the health of the ship's surviving captives, they transferred 115 of them to a different vessel. Surely these prisoners would have preferred an end to their journey, but release from the "foule and nasty"—not to mention deadly—*Marigold* would have offered at least some comfort.[31]

Slave trade survivor Venture Smith was less specific about the difference between his Atlantic crossing and a subsequent intercolonial voyage, but he found the second voyage less onerous. In the 1730s, Smith reached Barbados with about two hundred other captives from the Gold Coast but was not sold there (unlike the vast majority of them). As it turned out, the merchants who owned his ship and his shipmates did not claim ownership of him. The steward of the vessel had purchased Smith in Africa as a private venture—hence, his given name. This steward preferred to carry Smith onward to the vessel's next port of call, in Rhode Island. Since Smith remained aboard the same ship for the whole journey, technically he was not transshipped in the intercolonial trade, but his insights contrasting the transatlantic and intra-American phases of his journey are revealing. Neither account is detailed, but for the Middle Passage, Smith focused on high mortality. By contrast, he called the trip from Barbados to Rhode Island "a comfortable passage." For some captives, sharing a ship with fewer people, in perhaps calmer coastal waters, improved conditions.[32]

tonnage, than the sloops of the intercolonial slave trade. Baker argues that by 1700, most northern sloops had decks, but most in the South did not (*Sloops and Shallops*, 61).

31. Edwyn Stede and Stephen Gascoigne to the Royal African Company, Barbados, June 10, 1679, in Donnan, ed., *Documents,* I, 249–250. For more on the *Marigold*'s transatlantic journey, see *Voyages,* accessed July 2011, Voyage ID no. 15060.

32. Venture Smith, "A Narrative of the Life and Adventures of Venture, a Native of Africa: But Resident above Sixty Years in the United States of America, Related by Himself (1798)," in Vincent Carretta, ed., *Unchained Voices: An Anthology of Black Authors in the English-Speaking*

Improved food might also have contributed to more comfortable intercolonial voyages for some. Equiano asserted that "on the passage [from Barbados to Virginia] we were better treated than we were coming from Africa, and we had plenty of rice and fat pork." Indeed, there are several plausible explanations for better food on some final passages. Most simply, the lengthy crossing of the Atlantic restricted offerings in the Middle Passage to food that would keep for weeks at sea. Rations were limited, unsatisfying, and unhealthy—and if barrels leaked and food spoiled, provisions ran short. After weeks at sea, captives and ship crews alike would welcome the possibility of fresh food in American ports. Since intercolonial voyages were generally shorter than the Atlantic crossing, keeping food edible on a final passage was also less difficult. The mercenary explanation for improved fare in the intercolonial trade was the proximity of captives to market. Traders wanted captives to appear robust and healthy for sale; offering better food on the final passage aided human commodities in their recovery from the Atlantic crossing. As the Barbados firm of Lascelles and Maxwell put it when discussing a scheme for buying Africans in Barbados for transshipment to Jamaica, "The Negroes must improve in a fair weather passage that seldom exceeds a run of 10 or 12 days." Lascelles and Maxwell did not specify how additional time at sea would "improve" their captives, but presumably they referred to captives' recuperating from the Middle Passage thanks to the availability of fresher food, or other improved conditions, on the relatively short intercolonial voyage. Of course, any group of captives' chance of an improved diet depended on the traders who organized their journeys. Philadelphia merchant Robert Ellis complained to his partners that, when their shipment arrived from Charleston, "The Negros Prov'd to be very weak, wanting Provisions enough aboard of the Ship." Despite their financial interest in keeping slaves well fed, some traders neglected captives' conditions on the final passage.[33]

Prisoners on such intercolonial voyages might have enjoyed some relief from surveillance because security could be lax compared to the Atlantic crossing; intercolonial traders discussed it infrequently. In a rare exception,

World of the Eighteenth Century (Lexington, Ky., 2004), 375. For Smith's transatlantic voyage, see *Voyages*, accessed July 2011, Voyage ID no. 36067.

33. Equiano, *Interesting Narrative*, 62; Lascelles and Maxwell to J. and A. Harvie, Sept. 23, 1752, Lascelles and Maxwell Letter Books, 1739–1769, microfilm, V, 97601/2, fol. 16, Eisenhower Library (all but one of the original Lascelles and Maxwell Letter Books were destroyed in the bombing of London during the Blitz in World War II, so only these transcriptions survive); Robert Ellis to Cleland and Wallace, July 1, 1738, Robert Ellis Letter Book, 1736–1748, Am 9251, 104, Historical Society of Pennsylvania, Philadelphia.

in 1769, Henry Laurens warned a young, inexperienced ship captain that if he "should Ship Negroes on board your Sloop" from Jamaica to South Carolina, he must "be very careful to guard against insurrection. Never put your Life in their power a moment. For a moment is sufficient to deprive you of it and make way for the destruction of all your Men." Other intercolonial merchants and captains probably shared such concerns about slave resistance, but they wrote about it far less often than transatlantic slave traders did, and apparently their vigilance often stopped short of shackling their captives. Even Laurens rarely mentioned security in the rest of his voluminous correspondence about the intercolonial trade. In the transatlantic trade, the use of restraints varied from voyage to voyage, imposed more often on men than on women or children and more likely for all captives at night. Some transatlantic traders only shackled captives while vessels remained on the African coast, whereas others removed shackles selectively to reward cooperative behavior. By contrast, most intercolonial traders between British colonies appear to have done without restraints altogether. Charleston trader John Guerard repeatedly organized transshipments of enslaved people from Barbados to South Carolina on his sloop *Molly*, under Captain Richard Watts, but his letters about these voyages never mentioned security logistics. When Guerard contemplated sending the ship to Africa for slaves, however, his attitude toward confining captives changed. Writing to a co-owner of the *Molly*, Guerard noted, "If the Scheme I have hinted for Watts going . . . to Gambia is . . . Carried into Execution, he would require . . . the implements for Secureing the Negroes." In the previous year, Watts had delivered one hundred enslaved captives from Barbados, so sometimes even sizable groups apparently avoided shackling for the final passage. Such restraints not only hampered movement but also wore away flesh, causing sores that made even tiny motions excruciating and often led to infection. For captives recovering from such sores, relief from such constraint for the final passage was no minor improvement.[34]

34. Laurens to Hinson Todd, Apr. 14, 1769, in *Laurens Papers*, VI, 437–438; see also Michael J. Jarvis, *In the Eye of All Trade: Bermuda, Bermudians, and the Maritime Atlantic World, 1680–1783* (Chapel Hill, N.C., 2010), 155; Guerard to William Jolliff, Nov. 14, 1753, Guerard Letter Book, fol. 192. Robert Harms argues that some transatlantic traders kept enslaved people shackled throughout voyages, others removed shackles once out to sea, and still others used the removal of shackles as an incentive for compliant behavior (Harms, *The Diligent: A Voyage through the Worlds of the Slave Trade* [New York, 2002], 314–315). Smallwood argues that Royal African Company slavers often stopped using shackles once out to sea and occasionally did without them altogether when supplies were a problem (*Saltwater Slavery*, 40–41, 143). A century after the Royal African Company's monopoly, other traders testified to the same practice, believing that slaves would not revolt without a feasible means of returning to the region from which they had

In addition to avoiding shackles for the final passage, most captives faced less oversight from crew members than they had for the Atlantic crossing. Transatlantic ships typically carried unusually large crews due to concerns about security, but the same was not true aboard intercolonial slavers. Of 3,343 intercolonial slave trading voyages for which the number of crew members is known, more than 80 percent carried 10 sailors or fewer, and nearly half carried 6 or fewer. These small crews were not simply a reflection of fewer captives on board; crews were often minimal even on vessels carrying large numbers of slaves. Although the overall ratio of captives to sailors was quite low in the intercolonial trade—fewer than 4 enslaved people for every sailor—this number is skewed by numerous voyages carrying just 1 or 2 African captives. In such cases, the crew outnumbered their prisoners. By contrast, on many voyages, captives heavily outnumbered crewmen. In 1765, the sloop *Henry* sailed from Jamaica to Georgia, carrying just 6 sailors to manage 250 Africans—a ratio of more than 41 slaves per sailor. The same year, the little schooner *Susquehanna* employed just 3 crewmen to supervise 70 captives from Jamaica to Maryland—a ratio of 23 slaves per sailor. In 1784, the schooner *Polly* transported 150 enslaved people from Dominica to Antigua with a crew of only 4, or about 38 slaves for each sailor. (Such skewed ratios also appeared on voyages that left the British Empire, such as the sloop *America,* departing Jamaica for Cuba in 1765 with only 4 sailors to oversee 196 Africans—49 slaves per sailor.) These cases are extreme but not isolated. Intercolonial vessels that carried 100 or more captives averaged more than 11 slaves per sailor. Vessels in the transatlantic trade, on the other hand, averaged fewer than 10 captives per sailor at their peak in the late eighteenth century, and in earlier periods, transatlantic traders carried even fewer slaves per sailor. If large crews in the transatlantic trade reflected merchants' concerns about controlling African prisoners, smaller crews aboard intercolonial slavers indicate that security was less of a concern. Along with some relief from scrutiny and abuse for captives, however, might have come neglect. It is hard to imagine how a crew of 6 sailors fed and nursed 196 ailing captives, for example, while also sailing their ship.

---

embarked. James Frazier, a captain on ten transatlantic slave-trading voyages, told the House of Commons in 1790, "So soon as the ship was out of sight of land, he usually took off their handcuffs, and soon after their leg-irons" (House of Commons, *Evidence of the Slave-Trade,* II, 16; see also ibid., I, 76–77). Rediker notes that some traders shackled only men (*Slave Ship,* 72, 234, 267–268). The absence of references to shackling in the papers of intercolonial traders is no guarantee that restraints were not used, but the contrast with correspondence about the transatlantic trade asserting the need for security is suggestive.

As on some transatlantic slavers, a few captives might have been tasked with feeding or tending their fellow forced migrants.[35]

If captives enjoyed some improved conditions over the Middle Passage, other aspects of the final passage added new hardships. For many forced migrants aboard intercolonial voyages, one shock was a change in climate, since one common route was from the Caribbean to North America. Virtually all captives dragged into the Atlantic slave trade hailed from the tropics, so the journey northward from the islands carried most to temperate climes for the first time. When such ventures occurred outside the summer months, it was an abrupt and dangerous change, especially when combined with the damp, unsanitary conditions of a slave ship. North American agents for Caribbean (or British) slave traders sometimes noted charging their clients for clothes and blankets purchased only after the captives' arrival in North American ports, suggesting that the captives' last days aboard ship were bitterly cold. Anticipating this problem in 1664, Governor Stuyvesant of New Amsterdam cautioned Governor Beck of Curaçao that, when he organized transshipments of Africans, he needed to remember to provide some form of protection against the cold. A century later, Henry Laurens stipulated that Africans sent his way needed to "be clad with Linnen woolen and a Blanket" for the voyage, fearing that some Caribbean traders would forget to outfit their captives for colder climes. The Virginia firm of Aitchison and Parker preferred to avoid nonsummer months altogether when they planned transshipments from the islands to the mainland, insisting that enslaved people would turn a profit if "they can be here by the End of July or August, but after [that time] the mornings and Evenings begin to turn Cool they frequently grow Sickly." Not all traders had such foresight. In 1719, Antigua merchant Benjamin Bullard sent five Africans to William Pepperell of Kittery Point (in modern Maine), but four of the captives died in the northward passage, and

---

35. For the large crew carried by transatlantic slavers relative to other merchant vessels and particularly low slave-to-sailor ratios at early dates, see Eltis, *Rise of African Slavery*, 119, 157–160; for peak slave-to-sailor ratios in the transatlantic trade during the late eighteenth century, see Klein, *Atlantic Slave Trade*, 83–85. In the intercolonial trade, aboard the 3,304 voyages for which both the number of crew and the number of captives are documented, a total of 101,995 enslaved people were managed by a total of 27,872 sailors for an overall ratio of 3.66 to 1. For the 297 of these voyages carrying 100 or more captives, 4,032 sailors supervised 44,794 captives for a ratio of 11 to 1. For the *Henry, Susquehanna,* and *America,* see CO 142/18, fols. 110, 151–152; for the *Polly,* CO 76/4, 43. On captives charged with feeding others on slave ships, see Sparks, *Two Princes of Calabar,* 84.

the lone survivor—a young woman—died after three weeks on land. As Pepperell explained to Bullard, "It may have resulted from deficient clothing so early in the spring." [36]

For those who survived transshipment, arrival at another American port brought a second sales cycle. Possibly less shocking than the initial landing in the Americas, resale still brought additional indignities. When Thomas Riche sent a group from Philadelphia to North Carolina in 1765, he instructed ship captain John Burroughs, "If you have easey weather take care of the slaves and get them shaved and greased before you [arrive] . . . lest they discover old age by their heads." We can only guess what enslaved Africans made of such treatments. American-born slaves often commented on the degradation of the auction block, and surely arriving Africans felt similarly. Their rare accounts omit detailed discussion of sales, perhaps reflecting suppression of the experience. The preparations for sale were similar to those in the transatlantic trade, but other aspects of arrival in the intercolonial traffic were more distinct. Many transshipped people reached smaller ports where African arrivals were less frequent and policies and infrastructure for handling them less developed. A less populous Caribbean island or a North American port where slavery was less prevalent might lack a mandated quarantine, and merchants there often lacked enclosed yards for imprisoning large numbers of people awaiting sale. Instead, enslaved Africans often found themselves offered for sale individually or in small groups at a merchant's home, where they resided until sold. In 1761, about twenty African men, women, and children disembarked from a short, upriver transshipment from Philadelphia to Trenton, New Jersey, where they apparently took up residence at the home of merchant Samuel Tucker. Three months later, Tucker's partner, Thomas Riche, implied this when he encouraged Tucker, "Pray advertise the remainder of them Negros for Sale at Vendue if you think they will sell as I Am Assured they must be in your way." The following year, Riche again sent Africans to Tucker—this time, people from

36. "Director Stuyvesant to Vice-Director Beck, 1664," in Donnan, ed., *Documents,* III, 431–433; Laurens to John Haslin, Nov. 19, 1764, in *Laurens Papers,* IV, 507 (see also 540); Aitchison and Parker to Charles Steuart, Apr. 2, 1770, Charles Steuart Papers, MS 5040, 1747–1784, microfilm, M-68, reel 9, Rockefeller Library. Pepperell quoted in Joseph Williamson, "Slavery in Maine," *Collections of the Maine Historical Society,* VII (1876), 213; see also William D. Piersen, *Black Yankees: The Development of an Afro-American Subculture in Eighteenth-Century New England* (Amherst, Mass., 1988), 5. For examples of North American traders' outfitting captives with cloth or blankets after they arrived and awaited sale, see "Account of Sale, Charles Town, July 17, 1756," in *Laurens Papers,* II, 259; Robert Raper to Thomas Boone, January 1761, Robert Raper Letter Book, 1759–1770, doc. 34/511, fol. 65, South Carolina Historical Society.

the Senegal River area—but Tucker again struggled to sell them. After about a month, Tucker complained of the difficulty of keeping the slaves so long, and Riche instructed him to board them out if necessary. Likewise, advertisements from Boston often offered small numbers of people for sale along with West Indian produce at the homes of merchants or ship captains or even at homes where they boarded temporarily. The *Boston Weekly News-Letter* in 1734 included an advertisement for imports "To be Sold by Joseph Lindsay, just arrived from Barbados likely young Negro Boys and Girls; Also Barbados Rum . . . Sugar and cotton Wool. Inquire at Mrs. Barnsdell's." The scene at such small sales must have been far less chaotic than at an auction or scramble after the Middle Passage.[37]

Because some smaller markets of the slave trade saw inconsistent demand, and because some people faced transshipment when merchants had difficulty in finding buyers for them, some survivors of the intercolonial slave trade endured protracted delays before sale. When finding buyers proved particularly challenging, an unfortunate few experienced yet another transshipment. In early 1764, a group of fifty men, women, and children boarded a sloop in Saint Kitts bound for Charleston, South Carolina. Their African background is unknown, but merchants described them as "New Negroes," meaning that on one ship or another they had recently arrived from Africa—perhaps together, perhaps not. They all survived the springtime passage to Charleston but were "extreamly meagre and thin." The Charleston slave market was a pitiless place, and no one would offer prices to satisfy the weary travelers' latest captor, Henry Laurens. As such, Laurens looked beyond Charleston for a market. After several weeks, they boarded a third slave ship, bound back southward, for a short journey to Beaufort, South Carolina, where trader Francis Stuart hoped to have better luck. In a similar incident, one woman survived transshipment from the Caribbean to Georgia, only to have traders there reject her. "The old Wench," Savannah merchant Joseph Clay scoffed, "we dare say we shall be obliged to return you again." Part of the problem was apparently that the Caribbean trader who sent her north, John Nugent, had neglected to

37. Thomas Riche to Captain John Burroughs, [October 1765], Thomas Riche Letter Book, II, 1764–1771 (unpaginated), Am 9261, Historical Society of Pennsylvania; Riche to Samuel Tucker, Nov. 12, 1761, and Oct. 18, 1762, ibid. Unfortunately, only Riche's responses survive, not the details of Tucker's complaints. For sample advertisements of slaves at merchants' homes, see Donnan, ed., *Documents*, III, 25–26, 28–29, 38–40 (quotation on 39), 116–117. Wood notes North Carolina ports' occasionally ordering vessels carrying slaves into quarantine if authorities suspected contagious illness on board, suggesting that quarantine was not standard policy (*Remote Part of the World*, 39, 256 n. 78).

consider that it would be winter in North America when she arrived. "She has suffered very much with the Cold," Clay continued. "Indeed we imagine from her complaints that her Legs and feet are frost Bitten add to which she is Blind . . . [so] we Cannot offer her to any one." Clay sent the frostbitten woman back, like any other commodity deemed defective. Sadly, the people typically caught in this limbo between the Middle Passage and American slavery were those least apt to endure the experience. The sick, the very young, and the old attracted the least interest from slaveholders, damning them to a sort of purgatory—not fully drawn into American slavery, but not released from it, either.[38]

■ On October 21, 1722, 150 mostly Akan-speaking men, women, and children felt their vessel enter a harbor after the long Atlantic crossing. The majority— confined to the dark, muggy hold, rank with human waste—perceived the change only as a waning of their prison's rocking on the open waves. The people ranged from those merely weary, cramped, and irritable to those suffering dangerous illnesses, perhaps scurvy, yaws, or dysentery. Though not all the captives came from the same community or polity, many had likely been captured together in battle, others kidnapped together in village raids. For many, such ties would shortly be cut.[39]

Upon dropping anchor, the ship, a snow called *Judith*, received new faces on board, bringing fresh food and water. Among these newcomers were likely previous survivors of the Atlantic crossing from the Gold Coast to tell the captives they had reached Jamaica, an island where people like themselves toiled. Regardless of what the new arrivals heard about this new land, most would not be staying. Among the visitors to the vessel was a European man who scrutinized the human cargo in embarrassing detail, just as the men who purchased them in Africa had done. He peeled back lips to examine teeth. He looked closely at breasts and genitals for signs of age or disease. He barked orders and gestured for captives to jump up and down or turn around. He touched

38. Laurens to Smith and Baillies, Apr. 30, 1764, in *Laurens Papers*, IV, 255–258 (see also Austin and Laurens to Gedney Clarke, Mar. 3, 1756, ibid., II, 123–124); Clay to John Nugent, Mar. 9, 1775, Joseph Clay and Co. Letter Books, II. Nugent moved between Caribbean islands in this period, so it is unclear from which island the woman traveled.

39. This sketch of the experience of 150 Akan people who survived the Atlantic crossing aboard a vessel called *Judith* is derived from Basnett, Miller, and Mill to Humphry Morice, Nov. 9, 1722, BL, Add. MSS, 48590, fols. 29–31. Basnett, Miller, and Mill were the Jamaica agents for the vessel's owners. The background of the people on board is known from *Voyages*, accessed July 2011, Voyage ID no. 76444.

bodies without warmth, intimacy, or permission. As this strange newcomer made his way through the assembled people from the Gold Coast, he selected about one-third of them. Most were young men and teenaged boys, though a few young women and teenaged girls also joined this group. All of them were fairly healthy, at least by the standards of a transatlantic crossing. The fifty-seven selected were dragged away from the others and marched off the ship, never again to see any shipmates or kinsmen in the group that remained.

The first group of Akan-speaking prisoners to leave the *Judith* found themselves forced aboard a slightly smaller, two-masted craft that did not rise quite as high out of the water. On board, crewmen cajoled the fifty-seven young men and women into the shallow hold (probably separated by sex), where they discovered other Africans waiting. It was terribly crowded, and only some of the others on board were Akan-speaking peoples. Many of the new shipmates were strange, with unfamiliar country marks (scars or tattoos) and incomprehensible languages. The new assemblage of people in this sloop had arrived in Kingston on at least four different ships from Africa. Jumbled together, they now sailed back to sea. Unbeknownst to them, the South Sea Company's agent in Jamaica had purchased them for transshipment to the Spanish American mainland.[40]

Back aboard the *Judith,* nearly one hundred people from the Gold Coast remained. With the healthiest men and women removed, the quarters were less cramped, but a wait of several days ensued, and many suffered from illness. Finally, one morning, the sailors brought the captives on deck a few at a time, washing them roughly, rubbing them down with a liquid, and then shackling them at one end of the deck. After a few hours, more European strangers boarded the ship. They looked over the captives a bit, but this time, none were whisked away. The leaders of the sailors looked frustrated. Though the captives probably knew nothing of it, a hurricane had visited Jamaica shortly before their arrival, suppressing local planters' usual enthusiasm for a slave sale.

The morning after the failed sale, the European man who had selected the first group of captives returned to the vessel. He examined the remaining Akan-speaking men, women, and children again, with another man follow-

40. Details on the African origins of all the captives aboard this South Sea Company transshipment from Jamaica to Spanish America are lacking, but since they came from four different transatlantic vessels, diversity was very likely. The *Griffin,* like the *Judith,* was from the Gold Coast; see *Voyages,* accessed July 2011, Voyage ID no. 75575. The other two vessels, *Delight* and *May Flower,* do not appear in the *Voyages* database, however, and no information on the African region where they acquired slaves survives.

ing behind him making notations. This time, sailors took thirty-three people from the vessel. Like the first separation, this sorting sundered ties between individual captives, but now it was the feeblest people forced off the ship: the ill, the youngest, and the oldest. Many of them dazed with fevers or weak from nausea, these thirty-three people struggled down ladders or were lowered by ropes into small open boats, which ferried them to shore. Rejected a second time by the South Sea Company's agent, these suffering captives were slated for auction, the last resort of transatlantic slave traders, after a few more days of recovery from the Middle Passage. Many in this group probably lived out their remaining days on Jamaica, but smugglers in the slave trade to Spanish America frequented slave auctions, so some of the captives—if their health recovered—eventually boarded sloops or schooners bound to the Spanish Caribbean or smaller ports of the Spanish Main.

Just 60 of the original Gold Coast people remained on the *Judith*—21 men, 8 women, 27 boys, and 4 girls. They must have wondered at the implications of the separations and why they remained aboard, but before long, other captives began to join them. In a few groups, 90 people boarded their vessel and were forced into the hold among them. Most of the new companions were fellow Akan-speakers from another Gold Coast vessel, but others probably seemed strange to the original prisoners. These newcomers had reached Jamaica on yet another vessel from an unspecified part of Africa. The *Judith* was now as crowded as ever, with 150 prisoners on board again, but in a new configuration. Eventually, the vessel hoisted its sails once more, fired a cannon in salute to the town, and glided back to sea. The South Sea Company had hired it to deliver people to Portobelo, on the Isthmus of Panama.

■ Africans exported from British colonies to foreign territories faced quite different conditions from their counterparts on intercolonial vessels that remained in the empire. Among the most noticeable variances was the mix of goods and people. Whereas intercolonial voyages between British colonies carried small numbers of captives among mixed cargoes for general trade, vessels headed to foreign territory made slave trading a bigger part of their business. Nearly one-third of voyages exporting enslaved people from British colonies specialized in the slave trade, carrying no other goods. On such vessels, as on the Middle Passage, captives jostled for space with one another, not with barrels of rum. Accordingly, voyages leaving the British Empire carried three times the number of people—sixty-eight on average—than the typical intercolonial venture within the empire. A quarter of the voyages to foreign

TABLE 2. Vessel Types in the Slave Trade from British to Foreign
Colonies to 1808

Vessel type	Number of shipments with documented vessel type	% of shipments with documented vessel types
Sloop (or *balandra*)	654	35.3
Schooner (or *goleta*)	644	34.7
Brig (or *bergantin*)	230	12.4
Paquete	150	8.1
Other	176	9.5
TOTAL	1,854	100.0

Source: Database of 7,685 intercolonial slave shipments, compiled by the author.
For a detailed discussion of sources consulted, see Appendix, below.

colonies carried one hundred or more slaves. As a result, Africans exported
from British colonies were more likely to share the final passage with many of
their shipmates from the Middle Passage. As the mixing of people from the
Judith with Africans from other vessels indicates, however, there were exceptions. Groups of people sharing intercolonial voyages had not always endured
the Atlantic crossing together.

Similar to people transshipped within the empire, groups of captives departing British territory found themselves boarding smaller vessels than the
ones that carried them across the Atlantic. Sloops and schooners also dominated this foreign branch of the intercolonial slave trade, each accounting
for more than one-third of all voyages (Table 2). Schooners probably appeared more often in this foreign branch of the trade due to their reputation
for speed, which appealed to merchants hoping to avoid Caribbean pirates
and, perhaps, foreign imperial officials on illicit ventures to French or Spanish
colonies. In fact, the *paquetes* (packets) mentioned in Spanish records, which
accounted for 8 percent of voyages, might also have been schooners or similar small, fast vessels. The British referred to some ships as "packets," but the
term referred more to a function—parcel, or packet, delivery—than to a type
of vessel. Schooners and cutters (which were similar to schooners but added
more sails for speed) often served as packets. Thus, if *paquetes* was another
term for schooners or kindred vessels, such small craft accounted for more
than three-quarters of ships carrying slaves from British to foreign colonies.

On voyages for which vessel tonnage is known, the average was fifty-five tons, reinforcing the impression of smaller craft in the intercolonial trade. Fewer than 15 percent of vessels topped one hundred tons.[41]

These smaller ships suggest that conditions remained cramped during the final passage out of the British Empire despite smaller groups of captives. In fact, some endured conditions even more congested than aboard their Middle Passage vessel. The most common measurement for crowding aboard slave ships is a ratio of people carried to vessel tonnage. Generally, ships in the intercolonial slave trade leaving British territory carried fewer slaves per ton (0.89 on average) than vessels in the British transatlantic trade (1.60). Even Dolben's Act of 1788, designed to make the slave trade more humane, only limited traders to one captive per ton, so on average, intercolonial vessels departing British territory met that standard. However, these figures may be misleading because many vessels in the intercolonial trade to French and Spanish colonies carried trade goods as well. Vessels in the transatlantic trade, by contrast, tended to specialize. Relative to the size of the entire ship, captives in the intercolonial trade to foreign colonies appeared to enjoy more room, but when trade goods filled the bulk of a ship's hold, a small number of slaves could be confined to a proportionally tiny space, just as they were in the domestic trade. Given the varied composition of intercolonial slaving ventures, averages of captives per ton do not fully reflect the range of experiences.[42]

Examining individual shipments reveals that some African people faced much more crowded conditions. In 1746, British traders in Jamaica packed 280 Africans aboard a twenty-three-ton sloop called *Relief* for a voyage to Spanish America, crowding more than 12 slaves per ton. In 1788, 100 Africans crammed aboard the little ten-ton schooner *Sorcière* for the short passage from Dominica to Martinique. Likewise, the *Batchellor*'s fifteen tons somehow ferried 150 African captives from Jamaica to Río de la Hacha in 1743. (Such crowding occasionally occurred on voyages within the British Empire as well. In 1763, 252 Africans piled into the fifteen-ton schooner *Hawk* in Kingston for a final passage to New Providence in the Bahamas—a ratio of nearly 17 slaves per ton.) Merchants in the transatlantic slave trade certainly confined

41. David R. MacGregor, *Merchant Sailing Ships, 1775–1815: Sovereignty of Sail* (Annapolis, Md., 1985), 91; McGowan, *The Ship*, IV, 9–10; Munro, *Sailing Ships*, 170.

42. The estimate of crowding in the intercolonial trade is derived from the database of intercolonial voyages compiled by the author; 1,125 shipments from British to foreign territory in the database document both the vessel's tonnage and the number of captives. The estimate of crowding in the British transatlantic trade is from Klein, *Atlantic Slave Trade*, 133; his figure is for the period before the passage of Dolben's Act.

captives to cramped conditions, but they considered such extreme crowding poor strategy because it bred disease, and mortality cut profits. Crowding was no simple mistake of the inexperienced in the intercolonial trade, however. Between 1745 and 1748, Captain Peter Bedlow made six slaving voyages from Jamaica to various ports of Spanish America in his twenty-ton sloop *May Flower*. The numbers of prisoners on these voyages were 220, 180, 220, 200, 210, and 50, with the last voyage carrying fewer slaves only to make room for a shipment of dry goods. Apparently Bedlow, and many others in the intercolonial trade out of the British Empire, considered crowding aboard ship less of a mortality risk during shorter, intra-American voyages.[43]

Nevertheless, intercolonial traders could not ignore mortality, given the high cost of buying African people in an American entrepôt. Indeed, traders' fear of deaths among their human commodities was exemplified by South Sea Company factor John Merewether in 1738. He described being "under a good deal of care about the negroes" in Jamaica awaiting transshipment to Spanish territory because an outbreak of "small pox increases greatly" in Kingston. To prevent the disease from spreading among his captives, Merewether ordered that the *"Clara* was smoakt with brimston and tar before the Negroes were put on board" for a voyage to Cuba. He further "ordred a double q'ty of provisions on board," being willing to incur extra cost to avoid mortality among his charges. Increased rations, he hoped, would keep the captives healthy—or at least appearing so—until they could be sold. Unfortunately, the extra food proved little comfort to them, as smallpox still broke out aboard the *Clara* before departure.[44]

Upon arrival in Spanish or French American ports, captives in the intercolonial trade faced different conditions than people disembarking in a second British colony. For much of the slave trade era, French and Spanish officials deemed commerce with the British illegal, so many captives were smuggled in. Instead of landing in a busy entrepôt on a bustling afternoon, many captives reaching French or Spanish territory climbed into harbor dinghies in the dead

---

43. *Relief:* CO 142/15, fol. 60. *Sorcière:* CO 76/5, fol. 10. *Batchellor:* CO 142/15, 88. *Hawk:* CO 142/18, fol. 48. *May Flower:* CO 142/15, fols. 56–57, 60, 77–78a, 80a, 97, 101, 103. Like Bedlow, Thomas Hindeman captained four extremely crowded voyages to various Spanish American ports between 1745 and 1747. His twenty-five-ton sloop *Peachy* carried 160 and 200 captives on each of these ventures, or between 6 and 8 prisoners per ton (CO 142/15, fols. 56–57, 61, 77, 80, 95). Klein notes that in the transatlantic trade the number of slaves carried relative to a ship's capacity declined over time as traders learned to limit crowding and as some governments regulated the traffic (*Atlantic Slave Trade,* 148–149).

44. John Merewether to SSC, Jan. 29, 1738, in Donnan, ed., *Documents,* II, 461–462.

of night. Others landed in hidden bays in sparsely populated areas, away from the prying eyes of officials. Little is known about the transit of these contraband peoples from the water's edge into French or Spanish colonial society.

Thousands of other captives entered Spanish America through the proverbial front door, but their experiences still differed from those of people transshipped between British territories. During the British asiento, sloops from Barbados and Jamaica regularly ferried captives to Spanish American entrepôts legally; even when British traders did not control the asiento, they often contracted with foreign holders of the monopoly for legal deliveries. British smugglers from Jamaica and elsewhere also bribed their way into both French and Spanish territories, meaning that captives still entered through the main ports in broad daylight while imperial officials simply pretended not to notice. Despite the public arrival of such captives, their experiences differed from arrivals in British colonies, owing to the bureaucratized system of slave importation to Spanish America involving a series of inspections and imprisonments.[45]

First, a health inspector boarded arriving vessels to examine enslaved people for signs of contagious illness. If he recognized smallpox or measles among the captives, they spent weeks in quarantine, usually landing a few miles from the port town to undergo this holding period on land. Once given a clean bill of health, African men, women, and children filed into town, likely bound for a merchant's enclosed compound. At the main ports of the Spanish slave trade—Cartagena, Portobelo, and Veracruz—such facilities were common sites, known as *"casas negrerias,"* or "negrories." These prisons presented high walls for security and offered little shelter from the weather. Captives bided their time, recuperating from the convoluted journey. Many suffered from dysentery, fevers, scurvy (especially in the seventeenth century), yaws, and other deleterious effects of living on ships and in prisons for most of the past year. Merchants, and the doctors they hired, tended to captives regularly, treating some ailments and masking others, deciding who was ready for sale and who needed more time to recover from the journey. Peter d'Oyle took the position of "surgeon" for the South Sea Company's Portobelo factory in 1724, with instructions to "Visit the Negroes daily and take Particular Care of the Sick to preserve them the best you can." Despite such attention, deaths were expected, as the company also told d'Oyle to "lay before the Council a Weekly

45. A detailed study of African arrivals, inspections, and sales in Spanish America is available in Chandler, "Slave Trade of New Granada," in Toplin, ed., *Slavery and Race Relations in Latin America*, esp. 52–67.

or Monthly Account . . . of the Negroes and how many have died . . . and of what Distempers." He surely had much to report; mortality was frighteningly high in the negrories of Spanish America. In 1725, the South Sea Company received reports that "the Negrory at Portobelo . . . by Reason of Dampness . . . [was] destructive to the Negroes." Some dying captives apparently received visits from priests, since the South Sea Company complained about their Havana agent's "being obliged to Baptize the negroes before they die that they may be buried in the Church." The service cost the company seven pesos, which executives deemed an exorbitant waste on dying commodities. Whether ailing Africans welcomed the comfort offered by Spanish holy men or viewed it as another intrusion with uncertain ramifications is unknown.[46]

If arriving in Spanish America under the asiento contract, the enslaved, once merchants deemed them ready for sale, appeared before Spanish customs officials for yet another inspection. Individuals stood before inspectors naked, or perhaps with a loincloth, while the strangers looked them over and measured their height. The inspectors assessed whether each captive would be counted as a whole person or some fraction thereof for the traders' quota. When finished, the inspectors branded the new arrivals on the right breast with the symbol of a crown over the letter R, marking them as legal entries (and as property) in the eyes of the crown — another step in the process of commodification. Only after this bureaucratic evaluation could traders offer enslaved people for sale, which of course meant further inspections from prospective buyers.

Regardless of whether an individual departed British territory as part of the highly regulated asiento trade, arrival in a foreign colony brought another chaotic sale and new separations from shipmates — although, in Spanish America, enslaved people often sold in fairly large groups first to middlemen. These imprisoned travelers also encountered new foreign languages and perhaps new foreign customs. After several weeks aboard a British vessel and an interval in a British colony awaiting transshipment, some enslaved people probably acquired some rudimentary English — at least the limited vocabulary required to avoid abuse by following simple instructions. Transshipment to Spanish or French territory forced captives to start that adaptive process

---

46. Ibid., 58; instructions to Peter d'Oyle, June 18, 1724, SSC Records, Add. MSS, 25564, 110; SSC to Rigby and Pratter, Apr. 21, 1725, ibid., 25564, 213; SSC to Mr. Farril, June 5, 1718, ibid., 25563, 343–344. South Sea Company officials similarly referred to facilities in Spanish America for holding enslaved people awaiting sale as "negrories"; see, for example, SSC to Gilbert Grimes, Oct. 26, 1717, SSC Records, Add. MSS, 25563, 157–158.

over again. In addition, arrival in a Spanish or French colony likely meant a Catholic baptism.[47]

Another peculiarity of the slave trade to Spanish America was that, for many African men, women, and children, long and strenuous journeys still awaited. People who landed in Cartagena marched hundreds of rugged miles into the populous highlands to the south, forced to make the journeys on foot because Spanish regulations severely limited river travel to control the movement of specie within the empire. Likewise, people sold in Veracruz marched inland for sale in the Valley of Mexico—a journey of about two hundred miles, not to mention an elevation gain of more than seven thousand feet. Most dramatically, enslaved people sold at Portobelo faced overland voyages across the Isthmus of Panama to the Pacific. Despite the debilitating journey just to reach Portobelo, many intrepid people seized the march across Panama as a chance to flee, eventually creating a sizable maroon community in the Panamanian jungle. The majority of captives crossing the isthmus, however, reached the Pacific with their captors for yet another sea voyage, this time down the South American coast. Most would disembark after two or three weeks at Callao, the main port of entry for Lima. Other travelers landed at Trujillo, farther north, to march the rest of the way to Lima, with traders selling some of them in smaller towns along the way (Map 2). All told, the South American portion of the voyage to Peru probably added four or five months to an African's journey, with the additional voyages adding 10 percent to the risk of mortality en route from Africa.[48]

47. The South Sea Company had a policy of "Selling in Parcels" in Spanish America; see SSC to James Pym, Dec. 12, 1723, SSC Records, 25564, 10. Other foreign traders in Spanish America likely had similar practices, since Spanish merchants then transported most captives over long distances to central Mexico, Peru, and other population centers far from the Caribbean ports. The Iberians were particularly scrupulous about baptizing Africans sent to American colonies; see Joseph C. Miller, *Way of Death: Merchant Capitalism and the Angolan Slave Trade, 1730–1830* (Madison, Wis., 1988), 402–404; Frederick P. Bowser, *The African Slave in Colonial Peru, 1524–1650* (Stanford, Calif., 1974), 3, 28, 47–48, 234–242.

48. On voyages inland from Cartagena, see Chandler, "Slave Trade of New Granada," in Toplin, ed., *Slavery and Race Relations in Latin America*, 73–78. Linda A. Newson and Susie Minchin also document mortality after the Middle Passage among slaves reaching Cartagena, but their study focuses on arrivals directly from Africa during the period of the Portuguese asiento: see Newson and Minchin, "Slave Mortality and African Origins: A View from Cartagena, Colombia, in the Early Seventeenth Century," *Slavery and Abolition*, XXV, no. 3 (December 2004), 32–35. On the Valley of Mexico as the main destination for captives disembarking in Veracruz, see Colin A. Palmer, *Slaves of the White God: Blacks in Mexico, 1570–1650* (Cambridge, Mass., 1976), 27–33, 43–50. The best information on the Pacific slave trade from Panama to Peru is in two sources: Bowser, *African Slave in Colonial Peru*, 26–87; Newson and Minchin, *From*

MAP 2. Entrepôts and Major Slaveholding Regions of South America.
Drawn by the author

■ On May 13, 1729, 360 African men, women, and children reached Kingston, Jamaica, having survived the Atlantic crossing aboard the *Freke Galley*. Their African region of origin is unknown. Unlike most arrivals, the people from the

---

Capture to Sale: The Portuguese Slave Trade to Spanish South America in the Early Seventeenth Century (Boston, 2007), chap. 6; see also Klein, *Atlantic Slave Trade*, 23–25. Bowser and Newson and Minchin focus on the period before the British transshipped slaves to Spanish America regularly, but Panama continued to be the slave trade's gateway to Peru in the British period, as evidenced by the South Sea Company's giving permission to their factors in Panama to travel to Lima to collect debts in 1723 (SSC to factors at Portobelo and Panama, [1723], SSC Records, Add. MSS, 25564, 37).

Freke Galley were not exposed to public sale but rather were inspected by just one group of men. Probably unbeknownst to the captives, the agents in charge of their sale sold them all to a group of Jewish merchants from Jamaica and a Cuban trader visiting the island. This mercantile cabal planned to smuggle the African prisoners into Cuba by landing them at the "South Keys," sandy shoals off the Cuban coast. To that end, just two weeks after the enslaved people arrived in Jamaica, they returned to the harbor. Their captors split them into equal groups to board two smaller vessels for the final passage.

One sloop was called *Ruby*. Despite merchants' describing her as "well fitted," she would not get far. Shortly after crowding aboard, the African captives heard three loud cannon booms, followed by a massive explosion that ruptured the ship around them. "Just as [the *Ruby* had] hoisted Sale," she had fired her "Guns by Way of Saluting the Town," and "a Spark of fire gott into the Powder Room and instantly blew her up." The explosion was so powerful that it "blew some of the Men who were Aft over the Gaff" — sailors at the back of the ship flew over a spar that supported the *top* of the mainsail. Many, crew and captives alike, died instantly. Bodies hit the water with fragments of the ruptured sloop crashing down around them. Meanwhile, the main husk of the vessel "hoisted up and then immediately sunk." Captives and crew trapped in the wreck were dragged to the deep, but people blown free fared little better. Those in shackles had little hope of treading water or swimming, and those injured in the blast struggled to cling to floating debris. Miraculously, "13 White Men and about 40 Negroes were taken up alive," having managed to escape both the explosion and drowning, but they were "in a miserable Condition," many "with their Limbs sadly broken and maimed." All told, "above Sixty white men perrish'd and out of One hundred and eighty Negroes not above forty odd [were] Saved." [49]

■ By extending already perilous journeys in the slave trade, the intercolonial branch of the traffic exposed enslaved Africans to myriad risks. Sea travel could be dangerous, sailors vicious, and individuals wrenched from all that was familiar subject to despair. These hazards plagued the Atlantic crossing as

49. Tyndall and Assheton to Isaac Hobhouse, June 8, 1729, Jeffries Coll., XIII, fols. 103, 105 (there are two copies of the letter, each damaged, but together they reveal the entire document); *American Weekly Mercury*, Oct. 30–Nov. 6, 1729; *New-England Weekly Journal*, July 28, 1729. See also *Pennsylvania Gazette*, July 24, 1729. The *Gazette* also published an uncannily similar report two weeks later with a different captain's name given, which almost certainly referred to this incident despite the name change (Aug. 7, 1729). On the *Freke Galley*'s arrival from Africa, see *Voyages*, accessed July 2011, Voyage ID no. 16517.

well, but an intercolonial journey added extra hardship for enslaved people swept into a final passage by market forces. The most serious danger was, of course, disease. The crowded conditions, exposure to the elements, and limited availability of fresh food and drink all combined to make the slave trade rife with illness, and the people embarking on intercolonial journeys had usually only begun to recover from the privations of the Atlantic crossing. One blunt measure of these unhealthy conditions is death. Mortality rates are undocumented for most known intercolonial shipments, but enough data survive to suggest broad patterns. Of 237 intercolonial voyages for which mortality can be computed from traders' reports or port records, 89 shipments (38 percent) saw people die. These 237 ventures carried a total of 14,374 enslaved people and lost 562 of them, suggesting a mortality rate of just less than 4 percent.[50]

This estimate of the proportion of captives who died on intercolonial voyages is significantly lower than estimates for the Atlantic crossing, but that is largely a function of the shorter voyages in the intercolonial trade rather than healthier conditions. Scholars of the transatlantic portion of the slave trade posit average mortality of about 12 percent—ranging from about 20 percent in the seventeenth century down to just under 10 percent by the late eighteenth century. (Unfortunately, data for the intercolonial trade do not allow for a similar assessment of trends over time. Most available data is from the second half of the eighteenth century.) Although a higher proportion of enslaved people lost their lives aboard transatlantic voyages, calculation of a rate of mortality requires factoring in the variable of time—conventionally

50. There are several reasons why data on mortality are difficult to find for the intercolonial branch of the slave trade. Most intercolonial slave-trading voyages were smaller in scale than transatlantic ventures, so they were not documented as thoroughly by merchants engaged in the trade or by the insurance companies often engaged to underwrite transatlantic shipments. Furthermore, colonial port records are spotty—especially for the Caribbean. The port records document many slave-trading shipments, but only in cases where port records survive from both ends of an intercolonial journey do they reveal anything about mortality. Even where such records do survive, there are possible explanations besides mortality for discrepancies in the number of captives recorded at a vessel's departure and arrival, such as smuggling to evade duties. That mortality does not explain all discrepancies in slave import and export figures is underscored by occasional cases in which the number of slaves reported aboard a vessel at the end of its journey exceeds the number of people recorded at the beginning. (Such cases are ignored in the mortality calculations herein. If, instead of ignoring them, one assumes they reflect a lack of mortality on the voyage, the effect on the overall mortality rate is negligible, lowering it by a small fraction of a percent.) Nonetheless, it is useful to compare the import and export figures for a given voyage where both are available to assess the overall trends, even if the numbers reached do not offer definitive evidence of mortality.

calculated as deaths per thousand individuals per month. This computation for the intercolonial trade shows a higher rate of mortality than in the transatlantic trade. Captives enduring final passages died at a rate of about 80 individuals per 1,000 per month. That is a significantly higher rate than experienced in the transatlantic trade, which averaged about 60 fatalities per 1,000 individuals per month. When one considers that most captives aboard intercolonial slavers had only recently survived the debilitating Middle Passage, the increased mortality risk for the next stage of the journey comes as little surprise.[51]

Mortality was not spread evenly. Of the voyages for which mortality is known, more than 60 percent experienced none at all. Meanwhile, the deadliest 10 percent of voyages accounted for more than two-thirds of the mortality in the sample. This concentration of death on a relatively small number of horrific voyages meshes well with trends in the transatlantic trade. Scholars of the Middle Passage note a similar "wide distribution of mortality rates by voyage." Two key factors caused this tendency and almost certainly explain the deadliest shipments in the intercolonial traffic as well. First, some voyages languished at sea for days or weeks longer than expected due to calm winds, storm damage, or equipment failures, leading to shortages of food and water. Such delays and privations fostered diseases such as dysentery and yaws. Outbreaks of highly communicable diseases were even more liable to cause high-mortality voyages. If smallpox or measles erupted, a voyage could see devastating mortality among both the enslaved and the crew. In March 1773, for example, forty enslaved people—an unusual mix of recently arrived Africans and seasoned plantation workers—departed Antigua for Georgia aboard the brig *Ann*. The passage dragged on for more than a month, and in the meantime, "both the Measles and small Pox" broke out. Two of the captives died at sea, unceremoniously tossed overboard. The others survived to see the waters off Savannah, but the government there quickly issued a "proclamation," ordering the vessel into quarantine and demanding "the inoculating [of] the Negroes." As traders awaited permission to sell their human cargo,

51. For calculating the mortality rate in the intercolonial trade, there are 113 voyages in the database for which both mortality data and the length of the voyage in days are known. Those voyages carried a total of 3,397 people for a total of 75,136 person-days, or an average voyage duration of 22.12 days. Of the 3,397 people in the sample, 200 died, or 58.9 people per thousand. Projected out to a full month, those 58.9 deaths per thousand per 22.12 days become 79.88 deaths per thousand per month. For the mortality rate in the transatlantic trade, see Herbert S. Klein et al., "Transoceanic Mortality: The Slave Trade in Comparative Perspective," *WMQ*, 3d Ser., LVIII (2001), 93–118; Klein, *Atlantic Slave Trade*, 132–142.

the captives struggled to survive in the floating pesthouse. "Four or five more withered two or three days after their Arrival." Soon thereafter, a doctor visited to perform the inoculations and to oversee the "attending and Care of them." Several shipments of "Beef . . . Greens and . . . Rice" arrived, as well, but the care was too late for many. Ten people died during a two-month quarantine. All told, only twenty-eight of the forty captives who left Antigua ever set foot in Savannah. Such deadly outbreaks were particularly likely aboard voyages in which merchants shipped the so-called "refuse" slaves they purchased at cheap prices owing to their debilitated condition after the Middle Passage. Already ailing, such affordable enslaved people carried germs into the final passage, which endangered their own lives and others around them.[52]

One sobering aspect of the intercolonial trade's high mortality is that merchants who planned transshipments often examined people arriving from Africa and purchased only those who seemed healthy enough for another voyage. In 1733, Captain John Sheffield of the *Orange Tree* planned to buy slaves in Bridgetown, Barbados, for a trading venture to Boston. But when smallpox surfaced among recent African arrivals whom Bridgetown merchants were trying to sell, Sheffield decided to forego his plan. Instead, he sailed to Speight's Town, a smaller port on the island, to acquire twenty people in better health. Thankfully, all survived the journey to Boston. Even where outbreaks of smallpox did not intervene, intercolonial traders generally selected Afri-

---

52. Of 237 voyages for which mortality is known, 148 saw no fatalities. For calculating the concentration of mortality aboard the deadliest voyages, I omitted the tragic explosion aboard the *Ruby* from the sample since that catastrophe was so large that it skews the data. Nonetheless, of the 427 enslaved people who lost their lives on the 236 remaining voyages in the sample, 290 of them died aboard just the 24 deadliest shipments. Another possible explanation for this small number of voyages accounting for most of the lost people is that factors other than mortality — such as smuggling, clerical errors in port records (or by the historian), or a vessel's unreported stops — contributed to the lower number of enslaved people recorded at the end of a vessel's journey. Such factors cannot be dismissed, but given that transatlantic slave-trading vessels saw a similar concentration of mortality on disease-ridden voyages, it seems likely that the data here reflect actual mortality fairly well. "Wide distribution of mortality rates by voyage": Klein, *Atlantic Slave Trade*, 136; see also Klein et al., "Transoceanic Mortality," *WMQ*, 3d Ser., LVIII (2001), 93–118. The smallpox outbreak aboard the brig *Ann* is documented in the Clay and Co. Letter Books, I: Clay and Co. to Scott, Mackie, and Dover, Apr. 22, 1773 (see also another to them May 8, 1773); Clay and Co. to Doctor Frazier, Mar. 16, 1773; Clay and Co. to Captain Wetherden, Mar. 29, 1773; and see also letters to Captain Wetherden, Mar. 15, 16, 24, Apr. 8, 1773; Clay and Co. to John Lightenstone, Apr. 6, 7, 1773. For more on yaws affecting slaves, see Todd L. Savitt, *Medicine and Slavery: The Diseases and Health Care of Blacks in Antebellum Virginia* (Urbana, Ill., 1978), 73–77; for treatment with mercury, see James Walvin, *Black Ivory: A History of British Slavery* (London, 1992), 122.

cans for transshipment who appeared healthy and avoided those who did not. The South Sea Company employed such practices in Jamaica. In 1717, for example, when the *John Galley* delivered 242 men, women, and children from the Gold Coast, a company factor planned to send the people on to Spanish America, but after he had "carefully looked over [the] Negroes" reported that he "shall be obliged to take out 32," who were too unhealthy. Likewise, when Barbados merchants Stede and Gascoigne transshipped most of the Africans from the "stinking foule and nasty" *Marigold* in 1679, they "tooke 7 [people] a Shoare w'ch were not fitt to be sent not being able to stand." Despite being spared transshipment, all seven of these people died in Barbados. In other words, the ability of traders to screen for healthy slaves actually curtailed shipboard mortality on intercolonial voyages by leaving behind the people most likely to die. And still people died at a higher rate aboard intercolonial slave ships than on the Middle Passage. Furthermore, comparison in the intercolonial and transatlantic slave trades should not obscure the fact that the risk of death for individuals was cumulative. The mortality of the intercolonial trade was an added risk to the African people lucky and strong enough to survive the Atlantic crossing.[53]

Shipboard mortality tells only part of the story of illness in the trade. Even captives who survived were affected by the mortality around them. Deaths among shipmates could be heartbreaking, and they could also be dehumanizing moments, as sailors discarded the dead, unmourned and without rites or ceremonies. Survivors could also disembark alive—and be counted as such in port records—but still be sick from the journey. Some would recover, such as a woman who disembarked in Philadelphia from Jamaica with "the yaws upon her w'ch seems terrible," but from which she recovered. Others carried illnesses that lingered more dangerously. One man survived a final passage to Charleston, but weeks later, he still appeared "extreamly low in flesh." A girl who arrived in Charleston looked "very meagre and in a dangerous way." These migrants stepped off ships alive, but the slave trade still might have killed them. A Philadelphia merchant summed up this ambiguity around mortality in the slave trade in harrowing terms by describing two people sent to him from Saint Croix as "half dead" on arrival. Whether or not they succumbed, such people suffered grievously, serving as reminders that death is not the only measure of health risks or hardship. And, of course, many did die after the voyage ended, so port records often failed to capture the full story

---

53. Donnan, ed., *Documents*, I, 249, II, 225, III, 41. For this transatlantic journey of the *John Galley*, see *Voyages*, accessed July 2011, Voyage ID no. 75697.

of the slave trade's mortality. When Virginia trader Charles Steuart received a group of 48 captives transshipped from Barbados in 1751, all of the prisoners reached land alive, but "one of the Women came ashore very sick and is since dead." Furthermore, "four of the rest complain'd a little, and two of them had the same symptoms with what the Woman was taken . . . , viz. a swelling about the Eyes." The woman was a casualty of the slave trade; whether her companions recovered is unknown. In a sales account for a group of people transshipped from Barbados to an unknown location in 1727, the ledger had separate rows tabulating those who "Dyed at Sea," totaling four, and those who perished "After Landing," two.[54]

Diseases might have been the biggest threat to captives in the intercolonial trade, but as the explosion of the *Ruby* indicates, there were other dangers. Sea travel was fraught with peril, and enslaved people faced all the usual risks. An enslaved man named Lucy—presumably born in America or somewhat acculturated—"was drownded on the passage" from Saint Croix to Georgia in 1773. Though the circumstances of his death are unclear, merchants describing the incident to Lucy's owner stated that, upon inquiry, "it appeared to us to be quite an Accident." What compounded such maritime hazards was the treatment of enslaved people as expendable, even if valuable. In 1772, two enslaved boys shipped from Saint Christopher to the North American mainland felt their vessel collide with another and saw it quickly flood with water. The captain of their ship escaped but abandoned the terrified boys to drown with the sinking ship. He then manifested his sense of loss in quantifiable terms by suing the owner of the other vessel for damages resulting from lost property. Applying this economic logic to the deaths of people and suing for reparations rather than saving lives evokes the infamous intentional drowning of captives from the transatlantic slave ship *Zong*. In that 1781 incident, Captain Luke Collingwood ordered 132 people thrown overboard because the ship ran low on water after accidentally sailing past Jamaica. The case eventually went to court, but not to determine whether the crew was guilty of murder. The

54. Jonathan Dickinson to John Lewis, Aug. 15, 1716, in Jonathan Dickinson Letter Book, 1715–1721, Yi 2/1628, alcove 4, shelf 12, fol. 92, Library Company of Philadelphia; Laurens to Law, Satterthwaite, and Jones, Jan. 31, 1756, in *Laurens Papers*, II, 81–82; Laurens to Haslin, Nov. 19, 1764, ibid., IV, 506–508, esp. 506; Riche to Thomas Shute, Jan. 1, 1763, Riche Letter Book, I; Charles Steuart to Mess'rs Menvielle, William Moore, Jr., Isaac DePiza, and Benj'a Massiah, July 5, 1751, in Charles Steuart Letter Book, I; "Miscellaneous Letters and Papers," BL, Add. MSS, 48590, fol. 31 (most of the relevant papers in this set comprise letters and papers to Humphry Morice on the West Indies slave trade, especially to the Spanish). For a rich discussion of captive perceptions of the deaths of shipmates at sea, see Smallwood, *Saltwater Slavery*, 137–152.

Zong's owners filed suit against their insurer to demand compensation for the people killed by their own employees. Both of these cases evince the slave trade's dynamic of reducing people, as one historian of the *Zong* puts it, "to a monetary equivalent."[55]

Equiano captured the dangers of sea travel for captives viewed as commodities in recounting his adventure aboard the *Nancy*. He worked on the sloop as a sailor, shortly after purchasing his own freedom with money saved from private trade. Equiano and his fellow crewmen had "taken several slaves on board" in Montserrat and "steered for Georgia," but disaster struck as they worked their way north out of the Caribbean. In the dark of night, several miles off the shore of a small, uninhabited island of the Bahamas, the *Nancy* got caught in a calm wind with a current pushing the sloop toward a cluster of rocks that barely breached the surface. The crew was helpless to steer the vessel to safety without wind, and the captives in the hold must have felt the jolt as their prison "struck against the rocks." Water gushed in as the rocky shoal "pierced and transfixed" the *Nancy* (Plate 3). According to Equiano, because the sloop's boat did not have enough room for both crew and captives, "the captain [William Phillips] immediately ordered the hatches to be nailed down on the slaves in the hold, where there were above twenty." Portraying himself as the hero, Equiano related convincing the crew that everyone could be saved by making several trips ferrying people from the immovable sloop to the small island a few miles off. Regardless of whether Equiano was truly so instrumental, both captives and crew appear to have survived the disaster after suffering several days with little food or water on the deserted island. Equiano's portrayal of Captain Phillips nailing shut the hold points to an important truth about captivity in the slave trade. When problems at sea arose— whether a ship was sinking or provisions ran short because a storm severed the mast—enslaved people were at greater risk than anyone else aboard ship.[56]

This vulnerability ran deeper than exposure to maritime accidents. Captives in all branches of the slave trade were subject to traders and crews in positions of absolute authority, and captors' attitudes ranged from humane to indifferent to sadistic. Merchants' economic interest in keeping enslaved

55. George Reese, ed., *Proceedings in the Court of Vice-Admiralty of Virginia, 1698–1775* (Richmond, Va., 1983), 95–96; Clay and Co. to Nugent, Dec. 21, 1773, Clay and Co. Letter Books, 1772–1776, I; James Walvin, *The Zong: A Massacre, the Law and the End of Slavery* (New Haven, Conn., 2011); Ian Baucom, *Specters of the Atlantic: Finance Capital, Slavery, and the Philosophy of History* (Durham, N.C., 2005), 7.

56. Equiano, *Interesting Narrative*, 147–157, esp. 147, 149. See also Carretta, *Equiano, the African*, 127–131.

BAHAMA BANKS. 1707.

Sus God speaketh once, yea twice, yet Man perceiveth it not In a Dream in a Vision of the Night, when deep sleep falleth upon Men in slumbrings upon the Bed. Then he openeth the Ears of Men & sealeth their instruction Job Ch.33 Ver 14 15. 16. & 29. & 30

PLATE 3. Engraving from the 1789 edition of Equiano's *Interesting Narrative,* showing the intercolonial slave ship *Nancy* wrecked in the Bahamas. Image courtesy of Documenting the American South, The University of North Carolina at Chapel Hill Libraries

people healthy tempered mistreatments by crews and traders, but abuses still occurred. Some violence was systematic, such as the branding of enslaved people, which was practiced by some traders, governments, and individual slaveholders. Other violence was less routine, and the line blurred between crews' using harsh measures to control their charges and simply to enjoy their power. Equiano described one enslaved man locked "in irons for some trifling misdemeanor." Charleston trader Henry Laurens might also have alluded to shipboard violence in 1764 when he reported the arrival of "twenty poor New Negroes" to the Barbados merchant who had sent them. "One Man was maim'd by a Shot in his ancle," Laurens wrote. The injury might have preceded the intercolonial voyage, but if so, Laurens had little reason to inform the letter's recipient of the condition, unless he was just complaining about the human merchandise he was being asked to sell. A similar hint of abuse came to Philadelphia trader Thomas Riche when he received word that an African man he had transshipped to North Carolina had suffered "much damage by falling in the fire" before he could be sold. Riche relayed the incident with a vague connection implied between the injury and a report the man was "Subject to Fitts," but how he actually fell in the fire went unstated. Since a sailor or overseer would have little reason to acknowledge that his corrections or abuses damaged a valuable human commodity, the injuries inflicted upon enslaved people are often shrouded in historical records.[57]

Other violence against enslaved people had no connection to merchants' and sailors' need to impose order. Sexual abuse in the slave trade was a clear expression of enslaved people's vulnerability to the whims of captors and of the captors' reveling in their own empowerment. Describing his years as a sailor aboard intercolonial slave ships and overseeing captives at the merchant's house while awaiting transshipment, Equiano insisted that the rape of African women and girls was commonplace. "It was almost a constant practice with our clerks, and other whites," Equiano charged,

> to commit violent depredations on the chastity of the female slaves; and these I was, though with reluctance, obliged to submit to at all times, being unable to help them. When we have had some of these slaves on board my master's vessels to carry them to other islands, or to America, I have known our mates to commit these acts most shamefully, to the disgrace, not of Christians only, but of men. I have even known them to gratify their brutal passion with females not ten years old; and these abominations some of them practised to such scandalous excess, that one of our captains discharged the mate and others on that account.

Equiano's abolitionist motives call for some circumspection, but his depiction of sexual abuse as commonplace and accepted receives somewhat veiled corroboration in the correspondence of trader Henry Laurens. In December 1764, Laurens reported to Barbados merchants John and Thomas Tipping on the sale of "three poor wretched human creatures" whom the Tippings had transshipped to Charleston aboard the *Austin*, skippered by Matthias Holme. Despite the beleaguered condition of these people and the death of a fourth man "on the passage," Laurens sold the survivors profitably, lamenting that much more money could have been made if the Tippings had ventured to send "fourscore or an hundred prime Negroes." Such a venture would have reaped great rewards, Laurens added, "especially if you had avail'd yourselves of that

---

57. Equiano, *Interesting Narrative*, 107; Laurens to Haslin, Nov. 19, 1764, in *Laurens Papers*, IV, 506–507; Riche to Samuel Cornell, June 10, 1766, Riche Letter Book, II. The South Sea Company routinely branded captives in Barbados and Jamaica before shipping them to Spanish America; see George Peele to Peter Burrell, [Havana], in Donnan, ed., *Documents*, II, 462; see also Chapter 6, below. As noted above, Spanish colonial officials also branded enslaved people arriving in their territory to mark them as legally entered.

Skill which you think so peculiar to Capt. Holme in the choice of Females."
Holme's sexual interest in female slaves was insinuated by his response to this
suggestion, as described by Laurens: "He smiles at this, and says you would
not trust him with a commodity worth his care." Whether or not this account
alludes to sexual domination of enslaved women, given the regular sexual exploitation on slave plantations and the sexual bravado of nineteenth-century
American slave traders, Equiano's allegation of similar abuses in the intercolonial trade is credible.[58]

Equiano's presence as a dissenting voice, however muted, bearing witness
to rapes and abuses in the slave trade connotes the element of chance in the
treatment enslaved people received. Depending on which vessel one traveled
aboard—and under what crew—conditions could vary considerably. Sometimes the presence of African (or African American) sailors, such as Equiano,
in the crew of a slave ship might have helped some captives secure slightly
more humane treatment. Sailors of African descent, slave or free, were certainly not rare in the eighteenth-century British Atlantic. In fact, at least one
man of African descent captained an intercolonial slaver. In 1784, when the
sloop *Pelican* cleared Saint George's, Grenada, bound for Saint Martin with
fifteen "New Negroes," a naval officer documenting the departure listed the
captain as "Maglois, free negroe." Maglois's role in the slave trade raises questions about identity in the era of the intercolonial slave trade. Did Maglois harbor abolitionist sympathies, like Equiano, but follow orders from the owner of
his vessel to carry slaves in order to earn his living? Or did Maglois, as a free
man who had risen to some standing in colonial society, simply not identify
with enslaved people? Self-interest, opportunism, humanity, or ethnic identi-
fication could determine the attitudes of Maglois and other people in similar

58. Equiano, *Interesting Narrative,* 104; Laurens to John and Thomas Tipping, Dec. 4, 1764,
in *Laurens Papers,* IV, 513–514. For more on rape in the transatlantic slave trade, see Wilma King,
"African Children and the Transatlantic Slave Trade across Time and Place," in David T. Gleeson and Simon Lewis, eds., *Ambiguous Anniversary: The Bicentennial of the International Slave
Trade Bans* (Columbia, S.C., 2012), 61–62. On boasts made by nineteenth-century domestic slave
traders in the United States regarding their sexual exploits with enslaved people, see Edward E.
Baptist, "'Cuffy,' 'Fancy Maids,' and 'One-Eyed Men': Rape, Commodification, and the Domestic
Slave Trade in the United States," in Johnson, ed., *Chattel Principle,* 165–202. On sexual exploi-
tation in plantation societies, for a good start, see Trevor Burnard, *Mastery, Tyranny, and Desire:
Thomas Thistlewood and His Slaves in the Anglo-Jamaican World* (Chapel Hill, N.C., 2004);
Barbara Bush, *Slave Women in Caribbean Society, 1650–1838* (Bloomington, Ind., 1990), 110–118;
Philip D. Morgan, *Slave Counterpoint: Black Culture in the Eighteenth-Century Chesapeake and
Lowcountry* (Chapel Hill, N.C., 1998), 398–412; Bernard Moitt, *Women and Slavery in the French
Antilles, 1635–1848* (Bloomington, Ind., 2001), 99–100.

circumstances. The presence of a captain or crew member of African descent on an intercolonial slave ship was no guarantee of kind treatment for captive voyagers. Nonetheless, some sailors of color harbored antislavery sympathies and might have had an ameliorating effect.[59]

Considering the rampant abuses, dire illnesses, and traumatic dislocations of the slave trade, some captive men and women sought escape through suicide. Equiano recalled one man who, after facing abuse from the sailors, grew

> weary of life, [and] took an opportunity of jumping overboard into the sea; however, he was picked up without being drowned. Another, whose life was also a burden to him, resolved to starve himself to death, and refused to eat any victuals; this procured him a severe flogging; and he also, on the first occasion which offered, jumped overboard at Charles Town, but was saved.

Although a minor contributor to overall mortality in the forced migration, suicide, just as in the transatlantic branch of the trade, offered enslaved people an extreme option for defying their commodification and oppression. It also serves as a dramatic expression of the hopelessness that many enslaved people felt. Such traumas, however, could also forge strong bonds among survivors.[60]

Captives in the intercolonial trade found precious few opportunities to resist their enslavement—at least overtly. Only one known revolt occurred aboard a British intercolonial slave ship. This lack of open rebellion is a

59. CO 106/3, fol. 50. Emma Christopher argues for complex, overlapping identities for sailors of African descent who worked on slave ships, suggesting that American-born sailors might have been more likely to identify with captives along racial lines because of the discrimination they faced in colonial societies based on skin color. African-born sailors, however, might have absorbed less of the color-line logic of the Americas. See Christopher, *Slave Ship Sailors and Their Captive Cargoes, 1730–1807* (New York, 2006), 51–90. On the other hand, individuals of African descent who attained positions that afforded freedoms or privileges—within slavery or as free people—often took pride in their status, identified with colonial society or their employers, and sought to maintain distinctions between themselves and enslaved people in more debased positions. See Jarvis, *In the Eye of All Trade,* 104–107, 148–156, 334–335. For more on sailors of African descent, see W. Jeffrey Bolster, *Black Jacks: African American Seamen in the Age of Sail* (Cambridge, Mass., 1997).

60. Equiano, *Interesting Narrative,* 107–108. On suicide in the slave trade more generally, see Harms, *The Diligent,* 261–262; Miller, *Way of Death,* 413, 420, 427; Eltis, *Rise of African Slavery,* 171. Although suicide occurred, Eltis also shows that it contributed only a small part to overall mortality in the trade (157–159). Byrd argues that the terror and trauma of the slave trade was crucial for the forging of new identities for enslaved people that tied them to one another ("Eboe, Country, Nation," *WMQ,* 3d Ser., LXIII [2006], 146–147).

marked contrast to the transatlantic branch of the slave trade, in which about 10 percent of vessels saw an uprising of the enslaved, most of which met brutal repression. At first glance, the lack of comparable rebellion aboard intercolonial slavers seems surprising, especially given the smaller crews overseeing captives, but the lack of forceful resistance in the final passage becomes less surprising when one considers the captives' situation. Weakened by months of uncomfortable and unsanitary conditions, bewildered and disheartened by a convoluted journey that had carried them thousands of miles from home, and faced by gun-toting overseers, enslaved men and women must have found daunting the prospect of organizing a successful revolt once embarked in the intercolonial trade. Without knowledge of American geography or the skills to maneuver a sailing ship, envisioning a successful outcome—even if the captives managed to overpower their captors—must have been difficult. For precisely this reason, revolts in the transatlantic slave trade usually occurred while a vessel remained in sight of the African coast. At that stage of the journey, captives suffered less illness and fatigue and saw better odds of returning home (or someplace habitable) if rebellion led to escape. Tellingly, the one known case of violent resistance in the intercolonial trade did not involve debilitated and disconcerted recent survivors of the Middle Passage but rather a solitary enslaved man from Spanish America on a ship hailing from Bermuda. He had endured much less travel and presumably better understood his circumstances. He killed several white sailors, including the captain of the vessel, before two enslaved Bermudian sailors working on board killed him.[61]

The famous case of revolt aboard the schooner *Amistad* in 1839 offers an instructive exception to the lack of violent rebellions on the final passage. The *Amistad* was neither a British vessel nor sailing from a British port, and, in fact, the insurrection occurred after British and U.S. abolition of the slave trade. Nonetheless, the contrast of this partly successful revolt with the lack of

61. Eltis, *Rise of African Slavery*, 157, 170–173, 180–181; Miller, *Way of Death*, 409–410; Harms, *The Diligent*, 261, 314–315. David Richardson argues that, when one factors in the amount of time slaving vessels spent on the African coast, the number of revolts that occurred there was not disproportionate; revolts during the Atlantic crossing were still considerable, with Africans exploiting opportunities to rise up in rebellion, especially when ships' crews experienced high mortality due to disease. See Richardson, "Shipboard Revolts, African Authority, and the Atlantic Slave Trade," *WMQ*, 3d Ser., VIII (2001), 69–92. Considering that in the early stages of acquiring slaves on the African coast, however, relatively few would have been present aboard the ship, the data still seem to suggest that large groups of Africans who significantly outnumbered their captors were more inclined to revolt when in sight of the African coast. The act of rebellion aboard a Bermudian intercolonial vessel is described in Jarvis, *In the Eye of All Trade*, 156.

rebellions in the British intercolonial trade is revealing. In June 1839, the *Amistad* departed Havana, Cuba, carrying 53 enslaved men, women, and children from the Mende country—in modern Sierra Leone—who had disembarked from the Atlantic crossing about ten days earlier. They were headed to the smaller Cuban port of Puerto Príncipe (now Camagüey), typically about three days' sail away. The schooner had a small crew—a captain, a cook, a cabin boy, and two sailors. In addition, the two traders who had purchased the Mende people rode as passengers. On the third day of the voyage, delayed by contrary winds, the Spanish cook, Celestino, taunted the captives that they would be cooked and eaten when they arrived. His jest was a huge mistake.

Believing Celestino's threat, the Africans—led by the charismatic Sengbe Pieh, called Cinqué by the Spanish—decided they would rather die fighting than suffer cannibalism. That night they managed to break loose of their bonds to rise up against their captors. In the fighting, the Mendes killed the captain and Celestino, whereas the Spanish killed two of the rebels. The two Spanish seamen escaped the *Amistad* in the schooner's boat, leaving only the slaves' former owners and the cabin boy in captivity aboard the vessel. The Mende rebels spared their lives to have them sail for Africa.

During the day, former slaveholders Pedro Montes and Jose Ruiz complied, sailing the vessel east, toward Africa. At night, however, they duped their captives-turned-captors by turning the vessel to the north and west. The *Amistad* meandered about for days and ran out of provisions. Eight of the self-liberated people died before the U.S. brig *Washington* rescued the remainder, guiding the *Amistad* to New York. After a lengthy and dramatic series of court cases eventually reaching the Supreme Court, the United States government affirmed the freedom of the surviving Mende rebels and sent them to Sierra Leone. For some of the captives, at least, rebellion led to escape.[62]

Despite this success, the inability of the Mende people to sail the *Amistad* to Africa once they had seized control reveals one of the enormous obstacles to rebellion that Africans faced in the intercolonial trade. Enslaved people who commandeered a ship they could not sail in dangerous seas near foreign lands put themselves in a very precarious position. Furthermore, in 1839, the rebels aboard the *Amistad* enjoyed an advantage that earlier captives did not.

---

62. This synopsis of the *Amistad* revolt draws heavily on Iyunolu Folayan Osagie, *The Amistad Revolt: Memory, Slavery, and the Politics of Identity in the United States and Sierra Leone* (Athens, Ga., 2000), 3–18; and Howard Jones, *Mutiny on the Amistad: The Saga of a Slave Revolt and Its Impact on American Abolition, Law, and Diplomacy* (New York, 1987), 14–30.

Because the slave trade to the United States was illegal after 1807, the Mende men, women, and children from the *Amistad* eventually gained their freedom through the American courts—and even then, the decision was fiercely contested. Earlier rebels would have found no such assistance anywhere in the Americas, except perhaps in Haiti after its independence. If the revolt on the *Amistad* had occurred before 1807, the rebels would only have managed to transfer themselves into enslavement in North America. It is well worth noting that the captives on the *Amistad* only mutinied once they became convinced that it was their last hope of avoiding cannibalization. Most captives, having suffered months of captivity and dislocation, bided their time.

Undoubtedly, African migrants resented captivity and longed for escape, so the lack of shipboard rebellions offers a window on their physical and mental condition by the time they embarked on final passages. Weary from months of forced migration in horrid conditions, the prisoners in the intercolonial slave trade were cautious of their foreign surroundings and captors. The captives' declining rebelliousness with distance from Africa suggests that they found it increasingly difficult to envision successful revolts as they progressed through the slave trade. This is not to suggest that captives were psychologically defeated but to highlight the adversity. Disoriented by foreign geography, languages, and customs, unfamiliar with the operation of large sailing vessels, and exhausted or ill from months of grueling travel, most captives in the intercolonial slave trade resigned themselves to awaiting better opportunities to resist enslavement on land. Such opportunities would be rare at their final destinations, but the determined would find them.

■ The final passages that many Africans endured after their journeys across the Atlantic added considerable hardship. Experiences varied widely, depending on where an individual was headed, on the size of the shipment, and on an individual's gender, ethnicity, age, and state of health. But for all Africans transshipped after their arrival in British America, the final passage meant another lengthy slog after an already exhausting Atlantic voyage. The further time in transit increased the likelihood of illness and death. Transshipment also caused separations from countrymen and companions. Perhaps most important, the experience of transshipment and resale in America must have inculcated people with their new status. Africans purchased by merchants after the Middle Passage experienced sequential cycles of being bought and sold, sweeping them into commodity flows alongside trade goods like sugar, rum, dry goods, and naval stores. People who had the chance to record their stories of enduring slavery often fixated on the auction block—on the experience of being purchased, of having a price for their worth publicly negotiated—as a defining moment. Slaves in the intercolonial slave trade confronted this commodification repeatedly. They never accepted their status as property, but the experience conveyed their new society's view of them as chattels.[63]

63. For the best discussion of slaves' reactions to being bought and sold, see Johnson, *Soul by Soul*. His work deals with nineteenth-century experiences, so most of the enslaved people involved were born in the Americas, but nonetheless, the more extensive primary sources in slaves' own words for that time period allow for a deeper appreciation of the humiliation of the experience.

2. Black Markets for Black Labor

PIRATES, PRIVATEERS, AND INTERLOPERS IN THE ORIGINS OF THE INTERCOLONIAL SLAVE TRADE, CA. 1619–1720

> The 3d of *June [1722]*, they met with a small *New-England* Ship,
> bound home from *Barbadoes*, which . . . yielded herself a Prey to the
> Booters: The Pyrates took out of her fourteen Hogsheads of Rum, six
> Barrels of Sugar, a large Box of *English* Goods . . . , [and] six Negroes,
> besides a Sum of Money and Plate, and then let her go on her Voyage.
> —Capt. Charles Johnson, *General History of the Pyrates*[1]

By the mid-eighteenth century, networks of intercolonial trade would link the many European colonies of the Americas, facilitating a dispersal trade in the enslaved African people arriving from across the Atlantic. But during the early decades of English colonization in the Americas, such regular intercolonial trade circuits lay in the distant future. Instead, in the foundational decades of slavery in English America (ca. 1619–1700), the dispersal of Africans was more haphazard, often taking place, not on merchant ships, but rather on the vessels of pirates and privateers. Even where pillaging was not involved,

---

1. Captain Charles Johnson [Daniel Defoe], *A General History of the Pyrates,* ed. Manuel Schonhorn (Mineola, N.Y., 1999), 314. The current consensus among literary scholars is that Defoe was not actually the author of the *General History,* but this edition (which attributes authorship to Defoe) is still the best scholarly edition in many regards, including its tracing of primary sources the author used to compile the accounts. Most scholars now accept the interpretation of P. N. Furbank and W. R. Owens that Defoe did not write the book under the pseudonym of Captain Charles Johnson (Furbank and Owens, *The Canonisation of Daniel Defoe* [New Haven, Conn., 1988], 100–109; see also C. R. Pennell, "Introduction: Brought to Book; Reading about Pirates," in Pennell, ed., *Bandits at Sea: A Pirates Reader* [New York, 2001], 4, 20 n. 3). Either Captain Johnson actually existed or was the pseudonym of some other well-informed author. In any case, the *General History* is a tricky source for historians because, at times, it presents excellent research from newspapers, published trial accounts, and correspondence with seamen, whereas at other times, it presents outright fictions. I have relied upon it below only where it presents information on pirates known to have been real historical figures and where other sources corroborate the general outline of the story. The quotation presented here is from Johnson's recounting of the career of George Lowther, which is historical.

dispersals by merchants often violated trade laws protecting monopolies. As a result, many Africans arriving in the Americas found themselves distributed by illicit traders.

■ Given that early English forays to the New World aimed more at raiding Spanish America than establishing agricultural settlements, it comes as little surprise that the early English slave trade was entangled with privateering and piracy. Theft offered a way for other European powers to catch up with the Spanish and Portuguese, who were many decades ahead in both colonization and the enslavement of Africans. The English established their first American colonies in the context of privateering campaigns against Spain, and that predatory, parasitical character colored the early English slave trade. The primary hope of English (and Dutch and French) privateers was always to snare a Spanish treasure ship ferrying Peruvian silver to Europe, but the corsairs and buccaneers rarely hesitated to prey upon the Spanish American economy in other ways as opportunities presented themselves. Of these secondary opportunities, slavery and the slave trade were among the most profitable. Because enslaved people sold for high prices relative to the amount of space they required aboard a ship, a vessel full of them carried two or three times the cash value as that same vessel transporting colonial produce or other vendible commodities, excepting only gold or silver. In the labor-starved Americas, exploitable workers were the next best thing to coin.

In the resulting illicit commerce, the captives were twice stolen—enslaved in Africa for sale to Atlantic traders and then seized in American waters by pirates who viewed African people as loot. Such appropriation could be perilous and terrifying for those treated as property if their traders resisted pirates at sea or if marauders attacked settlements. Once taken, the enslaved could face extended journeys. Pirates and privateers delivered enslaved people to a range of colonies, often seeking developing markets that were eager enough for commerce to overlook suspicions about arriving traders. As such, illicit dealers introduced some of the first enslaved Africans to many colonies and, in the process, helped disseminate the logic of people treated as property across the Americas.[2]

2. For an overview of the link between privateering and early English settlement in the Americas, see Mark Hanna, *Pirate Nests and the Rise of the British Empire, 1570–1740* (forthcoming); Kenneth R. Andrews, *Elizabethan Privateering: English Privateering during the Spanish War, 1585–1603* (Cambridge, 1964); Kris E. Lane, *Pillaging the Empire: Piracy in the Americas, 1500–1750* (Armonk, N.Y., 1998), chaps. 2, 4; C. M. Senior, *A Nation of Pirates: English Piracy in Its Heyday*

English pirates and privateers began seizing Africans from the Spanish and Portuguese even before England possessed colonies in which to exploit slaves. Christopher Newport's privateering voyage of 1592 hijacked a Portuguese slaving vessel in the Caribbean, en route to the Spanish Main. As valuable as the stolen laborers were in theory, Newport's crew struggled to profit from the capture since the English privateers were enemies of the only colonial powers (and slave exploiters) in the Americas at the time—the Spanish and Portuguese. A Portuguese merchant from the captured slaver offered to help sell the captives at Spanish Puerto Rico if Newport released him, but once the corsairs let him disembark at San Juan, he simply never returned. Unable to manage a sale, Newport's crew gave up: "Passing along to the Westernmost ende of the sayd Island, about some 9. or 10. leagues from the towne wee landed the Negros, and sunke their ship." Another English privateer, William King, repeated an almost identical debacle the same year, capturing a Portuguese slaver with 270 captives off Dominica and then releasing the slaves on Puerto Rico after failing to convince the Spanish to buy them.[3]

A year later, privateer John Burgh found an inventive solution to the problem of fencing stolen slaves in enemy territory. In 1593, Burgh's crew plundered a Spanish pearl fishery off modern-day Venezuela, stealing not only the jewels but also one hundred Africans whom the Spanish exploited as divers and laborers. Burgh's crew kept the pearls for their return to England, but lacking a safe market to sell the kidnapped Africans, Burgh ransomed them back to the Spanish slaveholders instead. On such a remote outpost, the settlers preferred to pay to get their laborers back rather than wait for another shipment of slaves from Africa. Future privateers would follow Burgh's example. The next year, James Langton's privateering crew managed a similar scam at Santo Domingo. After raiding a village and stealing numerous slaves, the corsairs extorted their victims "for the Ransome of their houses from burneing, and to restore them their *Negroes* againe, by whose Labour and Industry they had their great profitt." That English privateers such as King and Burgh snatched Africans from the Spanish even before English plantations created an alternate market for enslaved people underscores their exchange value in the colonial marketplace. The allure of slave stealing would only increase for privateers

<hr />

(New York, 1976). On relative value of slave cargoes, see James A. McMillin, *The Final Victims: Foreign Slave Trade to North America, 1783–1810* (Columbia, S.C., 2004), 73.

3. Kenneth R. Andrews, *English Privateering Voyages to the West Indies, 1588–1595: Documents Relating to English Voyages to the West Indies from the Defeat of the Armada to the Last Voyage of Sir Francis Drake* (Cambridge, 1959), 189, 213–214.

and pirates in the seventeenth century as venues for exploitable workers blossomed across the Americas.[4]

In the early years, England's fledgling colonies did not immediately embrace enslaved Africans as their main source of labor, but the rampant piracy and privateering of the era nudged them in that direction. Well before English merchants followed Portuguese (and later, Dutch) merchants into the slave trade on the West African coast in significant numbers, brigands of various nationalities sailed into English colonial ports looking to sell African people stolen from, or en route to, Spanish America. Most famously, in 1619, English North America's first Africans reached Virginia in this way. Off the Yucatán coast, Dutch privateers stole roughly two hundred Angolan captives from the Portuguese slave ship *São João Bautista*, which was bound for Campeche. So these stolen migrants, who had survived an especially long transatlantic voyage—from Angola across the Equator and through the entire Caribbean to Mexico—now found themselves forcibly rerouted. The Dutch brigands stopped first clandestinely at (Spanish) Jamaica to refresh the unhealthy survivors of the Atlantic crossing and to sell 24 boys to Spanish colonists who did not mind dealing with the Protestant enemy. Then, after another unknown stop, the corsairs delivered "20. and Odd Negroes" at Point Comfort, Virginia. At this foundational moment in the history of North American slavery, the arrival of African captives had less to do with planters' demand for enslaved laborers than with the privateers' desire for a market in which to vend stolen Africans. That Virginians accepted proffered people rather than actively sought a supply of slaves from the outset may go some way toward explaining the slow development of codified slave law and strict enforcement of a color line in seventeenth-century Virginia. In the 1620s, some of the first Africans in Dutch New Amsterdam also arrived owing to Dutch privateering expeditions against the Spanish and Portuguese. Similar ventures continued over the following decades, with a French privateering ship, *La Garce*, delivering a stolen cargo to New Amsterdam in 1642 and privateers forcing the captured Spanish ship *St. Anthoni* to deliver another 44 slaves ten years later.[5]

4. Ibid., 234, 249.

5. Linda M. Heywood and John K. Thornton argue for the role of privateers in settling the first generation of Africans—mostly Angolans—in English and Dutch American colonies: see Heywood and Thornton, *Central Africans, Atlantic Creoles, and the Foundation of the Americas, 1585–1660* (New York, 2007), ix–48. On the first African arrivals in Virginia, see Engel Sluiter, "New Light on the '20. and Odd Negroes' Arriving in Virginia, August 1619," *William and Mary Quarterly*, 3d Ser., LIV (1997), 395–398; Thornton, "The African Experience of the '20. and Odd Negroes' Arriving in Virginia in 1619," ibid., LV (1998), 421–434. Sluiter and Thornton helped

As slavery caught on as a primary source of labor across English America in the seventeenth century—first in the sugar-producing Caribbean islands, and later on the North American mainland—privateers played a crucial role in supplying African laborers, seizing them both on land and at sea. Barbados was the first English colony to commit fully to enslaved labor and likely received its first Africans via theft from the Spanish or Portuguese. Some of the first settlers in Barbados in 1627 arrived with Africans whom, in the words of one historian, "Captain Henry Powell had obtained . . . at some point between Guiana and Barbados." Unless these black founders of Barbados were canoe fishermen swept across the Atlantic and into Powell's path by the equatorial currents, piracy or privateering was the likely cause of their enslavement by these English settlers in the Caribbean. Up until 1670, Spain refused to recognize any French, Dutch, or English claims in the Americas as legitimate, so even at times of official peace within Europe, the Americas (and especially the multinational Caribbean) remained a lawless zone. As the saying went, there was "no peace beyond the line," an imagined line in the Atlantic beyond which European peace treaties did not apply because European powers refused to recognize each other's claims. Convoys and heavily armed merchant ships were standard, and privateers pillaged in the Caribbean with the blessing of their monarchs. Even after the Treaty of Madrid brought the Americas under the jurisdiction of European peace deals in 1670, pirates and privateers still found plenty of room to operate, and they often stole slaves.[6]

———

debunk earlier assumptions that the Dutch had shipped these first African Virginians from the Dutch West Indian colonies; for those incorrect assumptions, see Wesley Frank Craven, *White, Red, and Black: The Seventeenth-Century Virginian* (Charlottesville, Va., 1971), 76–82; Daniel P. Mannix in collaboration with Malcolm Cowley, *Black Cargoes: A History of the Atlantic Slave Trade, 1518–1865* (New York, 1962), 54–55; Johannes Menne Postma, *The Dutch in the Atlantic Slave Trade, 1600–1815* (New York, 1990), 12. Since many of the two hundred captured Angolans from the *São João Bautista* are unaccounted for, the privateers likely made an intervening stop between Jamaica and Virginia, but where is unknown. For more on the slow development of slave law and rigid racial hierarchy in seventeenth-century Virginia, see T. H. Breen and Stephen Innes, *"Myne Owne Ground": Race and Freedom on Virginia's Eastern Shore, 1640–1676* (1980; New York, 2005); J. Douglas Deal, *Race and Class in Colonial Virginia: Indians, Englishmen, and Africans on the Eastern Shore during the Seventeenth Century* (New York, 1993). On privateers' delivering Africans to New Netherland, see Joyce D. Goodfriend, "Burghers and Blacks: The Evolution of a Slave Society at New Amsterdam," *New York History*, LIX (1978), 128–129. In addition to the cases noted above, a "Captain Ax" was also documented selling three slaves in New Netherland in 1636, and Goodfriend speculates plausibly that this was the Providence privateer Samuel Axe. See also Heywood and Thornton, *Central Africans*, 36.

6. For the first Africans to Barbados, see Hilary McD Beckles, *A History of Barbados: From Amerindian Settlement to Caribbean Single Market* (New York, 2006), 20. For discussion of

In 1628, English privateer Arthur Guy and his crew aboard the *Fortune* captured a Portuguese slaver bound from Angola to Spanish America. Guy rerouted these stolen west central Africans, already survivors of the Middle Passage, hundreds of miles north to Virginia. Thereafter, such pillaging of the Spanish American slave trade only increased. Records for the period are spotty, but Spanish sources document at least sixteen cases of English privateers' capturing slavers bound for Spanish America in the 1630s alone. These hijackings redirected about 2,400 Africans—mostly Angolans—to English colonies. Given the nascent state of the slave regime in English territories, such an influx was a major contribution to the African population. Many of these English marauders probably worked from the short-lived Providence Island colony (off the Mosquito Coast of modern Nicaragua), which was founded in 1629 and acquired "many [of its] negroes" from English privateers, according to John Winthrop. Providence leaders ordered one of the first privateering ventures from the settlement to seize enslaved Africans who were experienced in diving for pearls. By 1641, when the Spanish conquered Providence Island, more than half the colony's population of about seven hundred was of African descent.[7]

Foreign privateers also delivered enslaved people to English colonies. Of course, the Dutch brought the first Africans to Virginia. Likewise, a shipwrecked Spaniard stranded in Bermuda in 1639 reported that the few Africans in those islands came from two sources: "Some of them have landed from vessels wrecked here, others have been left here by the Dutch who captured them," presumably from Portuguese slave traders bound to Spanish America. French privateers might also have delivered stolen slaves to English colonists in smaller numbers. Dutch New Amsterdam officials reported the arrival of French privateer Guert Tyssen in 1652, "having with him a Spanish prize." Tyssen "purchased and trucked provisions and other necessaries, with divers persons, both English and Dutch, in exchange for negroes and other commodities." As these colonial officials observed, Tyssen and other buccaneers were at the forefront of treating African people as goods for exchange.[8]

---

the "Lines of Amity" in the Atlantic beyond which European peace treaties had no force, see Roland D. Hussey, "Spanish Reaction to Foreign Aggression in the Caribbean to about 1680," *Hispanic American Historical Review*, IX (1929), 291; Richard S. Dunn, *Sugar and Slaves: The Rise of the Planter Class in the English West Indies, 1624–1713* (1972; rpt. Chapel Hill, N.C., 2000).

7. Heywood and Thornton, *Central Africans*, 40–42. Karen Ordahl Kupperman, *Providence Island, 1630–1641: The Other Puritan Colony* (New York, 1993), 106, 170–171.

8. For Bermuda, see Vernon A. Ives, ed., *The Rich Papers: Letters from Bermuda, 1615–1646; Eyewitness Accounts Sent by the Early Colonists to Sir Nathaniel Rich* (Toronto, 1984), 382; J. Henry

Not content with snaring ships at sea, English privateers also raided Spanish settlements to steal, among other things, African people. When Governor Thomas Modyford of Jamaica ordered privateer Henry Morgan to raid Saint Jago de Cuba in 1670, he clearly expected slave snatching as part of the operation. Modyford instructed that any "Women-slaves Prisoners" from the raid "be brought hither, and sold for account of your Fleet and Army," along with "such of the men also that cannot speak *Spanish*." ("Men-Slaves" who could speak Spanish were to be put "to the Sword," a chilling reminder of the dangers to the enslaved of being caught between competing empires.) Modyford also gave Morgan permission, "if Ships present, to carry them [the stolen slaves] for *New-England* or *Virginia*" to sell there. Perhaps some captives taken in Morgan's raid of Saint Jago were among the 109 enslaved people on his Jamaican estate when he died there in 1688.[9]

Morgan's expedition was not unique, for when word of the Treaty of Madrid reached the Caribbean later in 1670, one of the sticking points for the English and Spanish officials there was how to handle stolen slaves. In the treaty, Spain acknowledged England's claim to Jamaica and several other American possessions, bringing the first official peace to the Caribbean, but the negotiators in Europe had left many details vague. So colonial officials from Jamaica ventured to Cartagena to treat with their Spanish counterparts. Prisoners of war of European descent were immediately exchanged, but the English did not put captured Africans in that category. "To pacifie in some measure" the Spanish complaints about slaves stolen in raids, the English agreed

> That all *Spanish Negroes,* of the Provinces of *Carthagena* and *Panama,* which had been taken and could be found in *Jamaica,* and that could prove they were free in their own Country, should be set at liberty: And that all *Negroes* of the said Provinces, which were Slaves should be redeemed by their Masters, if they would come for them, at eighteen or twenty pounds *per* head.

In other words, free people from Spanish America who had been enslaved by the English were entitled to freedom, but the burden of proof was on them to establish that they had been free in Spanish America. Enslaved blacks stolen

Lefroy, ed., *The Historye of the Bermudaes or Summer Islands* (London, 1882), 84, 144–145. For New Amsterdam, see E. B. O'Callaghan, ed., *Documents relative to the Colonial History of the State of New York . . .* (Albany, N.Y., 1858), II, 24.

9. Joel H. Baer, ed., *British Piracy in the Golden Age: History and Interpretation, 1660–1730* (London, 2007), I, 70–71; David Cordingly, *Under the Black Flag: The Romance and the Reality of Life among the Pirates* (San Diego, Calif., 1997), 16.

from Spanish America were, in essence, legitimated as lawful prizes, since the only concession to the Spanish was that former owners had the right to buy them back from the English. Regardless of the terms, that the negotiators addressed kidnapped slaves at all attests to the frequency of slave raiding in the preceding years. The English also consented, under the treaty terms, to suppressing such piracy in the future, another indication that it had been rampant.[10]

Such raiding did not cease once the Spanish recognized Northern European claims to New World territories. If anything, the treaty simply contributed to a gradual shift from privateering to more frequent occurrences of outright piracy. In fact, continued English interest in plundering Spanish America was given powerful voice just a few years after the Treaty of Madrid, when England appointed privateer Henry Morgan as lieutenant governor (and acting governor) of Jamaica in 1675. Clearly, pillagers of the Spanish remained in the crown's good graces. Piracy without crown blessing was also on the rise over the ensuing decades, at times reaching an impressive scale. In 1683, a polyglot crew of thirteen Dutch, French, and English ships besieged Veracruz, the primary port city of Spanish Mexico. One of the French captains had a license for privateering from the colonial governor at Petit-Goâve, Saint-Domingue, but the other twelve ships' claims to be under his command were dubious, so the line between privateering and piracy was blurry at best. In any case, the crew plundered Veracruz, kidnapped and ransomed Spanish colonial officials, and appropriated enslaved Africans. After dividing the loot, as Jamaica governor Thomas Lynch put it, "away they went, carrying also with them about a thousand Negroes and Mulatos." The pillagers scattered the captured slaves (and formerly free people of color) across the Caribbean and beyond, severing whatever family, cultural, and emotional ties they had managed to establish in Veracruz. Lynch reported that the French carried some to Petit-Goâve. Others, the pirates sold illegally at Spanish Cuba. Some captives landed in Jamaica, where Lynch sought their confiscation as pirate booty. Still other captives from the Veracruz raid probably contributed to the early black population of South Carolina. English merchants and imperial officials of the period often accused South Carolina of harboring pirates and offering markets for what they stole, and in 1683, South Carolina reportedly received about two hundred enslaved people—either from the pirate raid on Veracruz or some other raid of Spanish America. Similarly, in 1688, a Virginia court investigated several masters

10. Baer, *British Piracy*, I, 274–275.

on suspicion of having taken their slaves in illegal raids of Spanish colonies. One of the accused, Edward Davis, denied acquiring his slave in such a raid, "And saith the Negro is his, and that he bought him at Sea from a Vessel belonging to Barbados about Twelve months since, and says he was not on board any Privateer." The unnamed enslaved man in question contradicted this testimony, insisting he "first Lived Amongst the Spanish and was taken away from them by one Edward Davis." Considering the frequency of English privateering raids in the period, the man's testimony is plausible.[11]

By the 1670s and 1680s, English privateers were not only targeting the Spanish and Portuguese. The Dutch had become major players in the transatlantic slave trade, and (especially when Anglo-Dutch relations periodically turned hostile) English privateers went after Dutch slave traders bound for Curaçao. Preying upon Dutch slavers was particularly vital in supplying African workers to England's newly acquired colony of Jamaica. It is little wonder that, when colonist Richard Ligon described the Africans living in Barbados in the 1650s, he made passing reference to the particular skills of those African slaves who had been "bred up amongst the *Portuguese*." Whether such people had lived among the Portuguese in their outposts in west central Africa or in Brazil, Africans with knowledge of Portuguese ways ended up residing in Barbados owing to the prevalence of privateering in English America's first decades with slavery.[12]

Of course, the English not only acquired but also lost enslaved Africans through piracy and privateering. As English slavery and the slave trade grew, pirates and foreign privateers targeted English captives, in turn. Contemporaries estimated that French raids of Montserrat, Antigua, and the English half of Saint Christopher in 1666 succeeded in carrying off 15,000 Africans

11. For Lynch's account of the Veracruz raid, see ibid., 228. On the arrivals in South Carolina, see Peter H. Wood, *Black Majority: Negroes in Colonial South Carolina from 1670 through the Stono Rebellion* (New York, 1974), 44. On South Carolina's general harboring of pirates, see Mark Gillies Hanna, "The Pirate Nest: The Impact of Piracy on Newport, Rhode Island, and Charles Town, South Carolina, 1670-1730" (Ph.D. diss., Harvard University, 2006), esp. 114-116; Shirley Carter Hughson, *The Carolina Pirates and Colonial Commerce, 1670-1740* (1894; rpt. New York, 1973), esp. 13-21. For the Virginia case, see CO 1/65, fols. 100-101, National Archives, Kew. Other mainland colonies also likely imported slaves from Caribbean pirates; see, for example, Edgar J. McManus, *Black Bondage in the North* (Syracuse, N.Y., 1973), 19-20.

12. Richard Ligon, *A True and Exact History of the Island of Barbados,* ed. Karen Ordahl Kupperman (1657; Indianapolis, 2011), 103. On the importance of raids on Dutch slavers to Jamaica, see Carl Bridenbaugh and Roberta Bridenbaugh, *No Peace beyond the Line: The English in the Caribbean, 1624-1690* (New York, 1972), 259.

for "their own sugar plantations." This was undoubtedly an enormous exaggeration, since that figure topped the African population of those islands at the time, but the raid was significant enough to hamper the growth of the English economy in the region. A French raid on the British island of Nevis during Queen Anne's War (1702–1713) yielded people among the plunder, six of whom ended up in Louisiana. In 1706, Governor John Johnson of Antigua feared similar raids by the French on his fledgling colony, believing the French would then use the stolen Africans to help fulfill a contract for slave deliveries to Spanish America. Governor Nicholas Laws of Jamaica also complained of incursions. In 1724, he wrote to Spanish officials in Cuba, accusing them of sheltering "a Parcel of Banditti, who pretend to have Commissions from you." Laws demanded "ample Restitution to Captain *Chamberlain* of all the Negroes . . . lately taken off from the North-Side of this Island, and also of such Sloops and other Effects."[13]

One group of Africans kidnapped more than once highlights both the scale of Caribbean slave raiding and the dislocation it triggered for the people treated as loot. In 1687, Captain George Lenham of the English sloop *Ruby* delivered "foure Negroe Men and a Negroe boy" to Kingston. According to naval officers there, Lenham had taken the slaves in a raid "from on Shoare at the Isle of Thera and Providence from Rebells and Piratts." Presumably, the "Rebells and Piratts" had previously seized these serially displaced people somewhere else. For these Africans and many others, the lawlessness of the early Caribbean made their journey to American plantations a particularly violent, prolonged, and disruptive transition to new lives in the Americas. As valued commodities, enslaved people became coveted prizes in the contest for wealth and empire in the early Americas.[14]

13. James Pritchard, David Eltis, and David Richardson, "The Significance of the French Slave Trade to the Evolution of the French Atlantic World before 1716," in Eltis and Richardson, eds., *Extending the Frontiers: Essays on the New Transatlantic Slave Trade Database* (New Haven, Conn., 2008), 212; Natalie A Zacek, *Settler Society in the English Leewards, 1670–1776* (New York, 2010), 42–43; Daniel H. Usner, Jr., *Indians, Settlers, and Slaves in a Frontier Exchange Economy: The Lower Mississippi Valley before 1783* (Chapel Hill, N.C., 1992), 25; Governor John Johnson to Secretary of State Charles Hedges, Jr., Antigua, May 28, 1706, CO 7/1; Colin A. Palmer, "The Company Trade and the Numerical Distribution of Slaves to Spanish America, 1703–1739," in Paul E. Lovejoy, ed., *Africans in Bondage: Studies in Slavery and the Slave Trade* (Madison, Wis., 1986), 27–42; Nicholas Laws to the Alcaldes of Trinidado de Cuba, Jan. 26, 1722, rpt. in Johnson, *General History of the Pyrates*, 45–46.

14. Naval Office Shipping List for South Carolina (hereafter cited as NOSL), CO 142/13, fol. 34. "Isle of Thera and Providence" probably refers to the Bahamas, since "Isle of Thera" presumably refers to Eleuthera, a Bahamian port. The Bahamas were haunts of pirates in the period.

■ As much as pirates and privateers contributed to enslaved populations in English, Dutch, and French America in the seventeenth century, theft was not the only source of African people for these empires; each increasingly traded for slaves in West Africa, as well. Still, the rise of the northern Europeans' transatlantic slave trades put only a small percentage of Caribbean and North American slave importation on a solid legal footing. Black- and gray-market slave trading in America increased alongside such legal trading for two key reasons. First, each empire established a monopoly company with the exclusive right to the transatlantic slave trade in its territory. Second, each empire forbade its colonists to purchase African people from (or trade most goods with) foreign traders. Colonists seeking slaves and traders seeking profits routinely violated these strictures, so even where piracy and pillaging were not involved, early slave trading often operated outside the law, giving rise to surreptitious intercolonial trading.

Interlopers on the Royal African Company's monopoly on slave deliveries to English America, for example, resorted to additional movements of their captives after the Atlantic crossing to avoid confiscation by company officials or imperial authorities. Africans delivered to Jamaica by the interloper *Hawke* in 1686 traveled overland for the last stage of their clandestine journey. To avoid detection by Royal African Company factors, Captain Thompson disembarked his "somewhat under a hundred" African prisoners on the sparsely populated north side of the island. The merchants in charge of their sale— Josiah Barry and a Mr. Waterhouse—then sorted the healthy Africans from the unhealthy, leaving the ill slaves on nearby plantations. Those fit to march moved south. Barry and Waterhouse hired a local hunter to guide them over the mountains to the more populous southern coast of Jamaica, near Kingston, where they planned to sell the people to area plantations. The Royal African Company caught wind of their activities and initiated an investigation, but by the time authorities gathered depositions from various witnesses, Barry and Waterhouse had distributed the Africans throughout the island. In such cases, attempts to circumvent regulated markets led to convoluted voyages in the intra-American slave trade.[15]

By the last third of the seventeenth century, the Royal African Company supplied enough Africans to satisfy English demand in the most established colonies—notably Barbados—but colonies toward the margins of the English slave trade often felt overlooked and sought to sidestep the company's

15. See depositions regarding the interloper Hawke, various dates in late 1686 and early 1687, CO 1/61, fols. 75–88, 1/62, fols. 10–13.

monopoly. Some English planters and merchants in these fledgling colonies traveled illegally to foreign territory to acquire Africans and transship them home. Planters on the less populous English Leeward Islands—such as Saint Christopher, Nevis, and Montserrat—sought transshipments from neighboring Dutch and Danish islands (Map 3).[16] In 1687, the Royal African Company complained to the English Committee for Trade and Plantations that settlers "of Nevis and St. Christophers are setting upp a Trade of bringing Negroes and other goods in English shipping from a Dutch Island called Statia [Saint Eustatius]." According to the company's agent at Nevis, the colonists hardly disguised their illegal trading: "Some of the chiefs of this Island and St. Christopher's often discourse of the greater convenience of buying Negroes from the Dutch on St. Eustatius than from the Company."[17] In 1688, Governor Nathaniel Johnson of the English Leeward Islands suggested that the scale of such trading was significant, noting that he faced local opposition to the establishment of a court of exchequer in Saint Christopher due to this illegal slave-trading interest. Johnson attributed the heel-dragging primarily to

16. Some scholars have argued for the Dutch slave trade's pivotal role in supplying the English and French Caribbean with slaves during the foundational years of their sugar cultivation in the mid-seventeenth century, but others suggest this Dutch role has been exaggerated, especially regarding the English. English slave traders supplied their own colonies in this period more than previously thought, and most Dutch deliveries targeted more lucrative Spanish American markets. However, studies focused solely on the transatlantic slave trade underestimate the number of captives delivered from Africa to the Dutch Caribbean, who were later smuggled to French or British territory. For the upward revision of English deliveries to their own colonies in the mid-seventeenth century, see Jelmer Vos, David Eltis, and David Richardson, "The Dutch in the Atlantic World: New Perspectives from the Slave Trade with Particular Reference to the African Origins of the Traffic," in Eltis and Richardson, eds., *Extending the Frontiers*, 237–239; Eltis, "The British Transatlantic Slave Trade before 1714: Annual Estimates of Volume and Direction," in Robert L. Paquette and Stanley L. Engerman, eds., *The Lesser Antilles in the Age of European Expansion* (Gainesville, Fla., 1996), 182–205; Larry Gragg, "'To Procure Negroes': The English Slave Trade to Barbados, 1627–60," *Slavery and Abolition*, XVI (1995), 65–84. On the prior understanding that Dutch slave deliveries dominated early British and French slave imports, see Bridenbaugh, *No Peace beyond the Line*, 33, 66; Dunn, *Sugar and Slaves*, 59–67; David W. Galenson, *Traders, Planters, and Slaves: Market Behavior in Early English America* (New York, 1986), 13.

17. Petition of the RAC to the Committee for Trade and Plantations, July 19, 1687, CO 1/62, fol. 130. The crown also received reports that its finances were hurt by the export of sugar from the English Leeward Islands to Saint Eustatius in this trade, though the goods or slaves that English colonists received in exchange went unmentioned; see "An Account of How His Majesty Is Deprived of Revenues in the Leewards, 19 July 1687," CO 1/62, fols. 224–225. See also Elizabeth Donnan, ed., *Documents Illustrative of the History of the Slave Trade to America*, 4 vols. (Washington D.C., 1930–1935), II, 241–242, 336–337. RAC agent at Nevis quoted in Bridenbaugh, *No Peace beyond the Line*, 260.

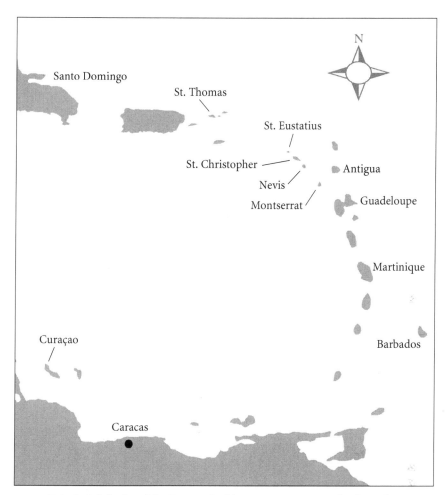

MAP 3. Principal Colonies of the Eastern Caribbean, ca. 1700. Drawn by the author

Joseph Crisp, a member of the colony's council, who also served as escheator (an overseer of crown-owned lands). According to Johnson, "the Royall African Company represent him [Crisp] . . . as a great trader to the Dutch Islands, by the Sugars sent thither by stealth and Negro Slaves brought in return in the same manner." Crisp's connections and influence within Saint Christopher likely facilitated his contraband activities.[18]

Governor Johnson also alleged that English interlopers on the Royal African Company's monopoly relied on transshipment of Africans from one colony to

18. Nathaniel Johnson to the Committee for Trade and Plantations, Nevis, June 2, 1688, CO 1/64, fol. 331B.

another to smuggle slaves into his territory without detection. Expressing concern about Danish efforts to settle islands in his jurisdiction, Johnson insisted, "Whatever Islands are setled by the Danes will, as [Dutch] St. Thomas and St. Eustace are, be free ports of trade." This would, Johnson warned, "much encourage our English Interlopers to trade to Africa having the liberty of such ports as receptacles untill they can have a convenient oppertunity of dispersing their Slaves in the Islands of this Government. . . . If they faile in that," the interlopers could join "in with the Danes for a Spanish trade." Some of these illicit merchants might have carried their captive Africans from Dutch or Danish islands to the English Leewards in the same ship that brought them across the Atlantic, but typically they were transshipped in smaller vessels. It was easier for English planters or colonial merchants to venture to the Dutch and Danish "free ports of trade" in small ships. Such purchasers could buy a few people and smuggle them back in small numbers, either avoiding detection by English authorities altogether or passing such Africans off as slaves purchased legally at some earlier date. Although they recognized such illegal trading, imperial officials in smaller English colonies lacked the naval power to enforce trade regulations. When Johnson wrote to the Board of Trade about allegations of settlers' smuggling Africans from Dutch colonies into the Leeward Islands, he asked for orders but pointed out that "the attendance of a Man of Warr will be absolutely necessary for execution of them, and will in divers other respects be very usefull to His Maj'ties Service; [and for halting] the violation of the acts of trade and of the Royall Affrican Companies Charter." In the absence of law enforcement, transshipments from foreign colonies continued.[19]

Interlopers on the Royal African Company's monopoly were not alone in such clandestine intercolonial trade. The company's own employees occasionally defrauded the company through illegal transshipments, as well. In 1703, the company charged Captain Daniel Johnson, Jr., of the company's ship *St. Christopher,* with landing a cargo of African people at the sparsely inhabited Turks Islands to sell some of them to smaller vessels headed to other English settlements. Johnson's intention was, allegedly, to sell some of the Africans on his own account without informing the company that the people had ever reached the Americas. To aid the investigation, Governor Nathaniel Johnson (now of South Carolina) sent a report to the Board of Trade based on testimony from sailors resident in his colony. He reported that, at the Turks Islands, the *St. Christopher* transferred captives to one vessel bound for Ber-

19. Ibid., fol. 333.

muda and to another bound for South Carolina, though he discovered no proof that Captain Johnson had sold the Africans for his own profit rather than the company's. Given that the Turks Islands were virtually uninhabited, it is hard to imagine another reason for Captain Johnson to deliver Africans there, unless the *St. Christopher* had been forced to stop for repairs. Colonies such as Bermuda and South Carolina in 1704 were precisely the type of backwaters where slaveholders looked to the black market to obtain workers, since neither colony received direct shipments from Africa at that date.[20]

■ These same decades of the late seventeenth century, during which northern Europeans entered the transatlantic slave trade in ever greater numbers and Caribbean privateering declined outside times of declared war, also ushered in the so-called "golden age" of Caribbean piracy. A burgeoning slave trade, declining privateering, and growing piracy were not unrelated. The line between piracy and privateering was always blurry, and many a privateer crossed it when European diplomats formally declared peace. Profiting greatly from the capture of foreign merchant ships during wars, many privateers continued their pillaging after peace was declared, losing their state's blessing and becoming pirates. The growth of the transatlantic slave trade contributed to the rise of piracy less directly but no less significantly. Slave trading vessels carried some of the largest crews of any ships plying the Atlantic for the simple reason that they were floating prisons as well as ships of trade. Perhaps as many as one in ten transatlantic voyages faced violent resistance from their African prisoners, and merchants paid for large crews to control them. For the next stage of these ships' voyages, these large crews were unnecessary. Sugar and tobacco shipped from the Americas back to Europe were far less prone to rebellion. From the merchants' perspective, once their sailors had survived the hazards of trade on the African coast and the Middle Passage, most of them had outlived their usefulness. As a result, many a sailor lost his job in the Caribbean after the Middle Passage, gradually giving rise to a large body of unemployed seamen in Caribbean ports. They often had few prospects and a grudge against merchants. It was a recipe for piracy.[21]

20. "Case of the *St. Christopher, 1703–1704,*" in Donnan, ed., *Documents,* IV, 250–253.

21. For the estimate that 10 percent of transatlantic voyages experienced insurrection, see David Richardson, "Shipboard Revolts, African Authority, and the Atlantic Slave Trade," *WMQ,* 3d Ser., LVIII (2001), 72. On privateers transitioning to piracy, see Marcus Rediker, *Villains of All Nations: Atlantic Pirates in the Golden Age* (Boston, 2004), 6–8. With the decline of piracy by the 1720s, merchant ships in general started sailing with smaller crews; see Rediker, *Between the Devil and the Deep Blue Sea: Merchant Seamen, Pirates, and the Anglo-American Maritime World,*

Regardless of where they came from, the Caribbean pirates of the golden age — roughly 1670 to 1720 — often stole people. The infamous pirate William Kidd delivered Africans to New York in 1699. Likewise, in 1704, a "Vendue Master" in Boston announced the sale by auction of "A Negro Boy named Jack, Alias Emannuel who was a slaive Taken from the Portuguese by the Pirate Sen'r Quares and his crew in the Brigt. *Anna* and brought into this port." [22] Since the Portuguese mainly delivered Africans to Brazil and Spanish America, the *Anna* probably seized Jack in the Caribbean. In November 1716, *HMS Scarborough,* stationed at Barbados, heard reports of a pirate vessel under a Captain Kennedy using Saint Croix as a base for numerous attacks on Caribbean shipping. Among others, Kennedy's crew captured the *Greyhound Galley* of London en route to Jamaica from the Gold Coast. The pirates stole forty presumably Akan captives and some gold from the *Greyhound* before allowing her to continue. Setting out in pursuit, the *Scarborough* surprised and cornered the pirates in a sheltered cove at Saint Croix and "cannonaded for several Hours." Desperate, the pirates "run a-ground" trying to slip past their pursuers out to sea. They then decided to escape in their ship's small boats but struggled with how to manage their African captives in flight. After putting half of the captives in one boat, the pirates "quitted their Ship, and set her on Fire, with 20 Negroes in her, who were all burnt; 19 of the Pyrates made their Escape in a small Sloop, but the Captain and the rest, with 20 Negroes, betook to the Woods, where 'twas probable they might starve, for we never heard what became of them afterwards." Tragically, enslaved Africans who fell into the hands of pirates were often treated not only as commodities but also as liabilities in the desperate moments when the law intervened.[23]

1700–1750 (New York, 1987), 74–75. On transatlantic slave ships' legally and illegally discharging sailors upon reaching the Caribbean, see Rediker, *The Slave Ship: A Human History* (New York, 2007), 251–253; Emma Christopher, *Slave Ship Sailors and Their Captive Cargoes, 1730–1807* (New York, 2006), 202–211.

22. McManus, *Black Bondage in the North,* 20; "Notices of Sales, 1704–1705," in Donnan, ed., *Documents,* III, 19.

23. Johnson, *General History of the Pyrates,* 66–67. *Voyages: The Trans-Atlantic Slave Trade Database,* accessed August 2010 (www.slavevoyages.org), lists a John Evans as captain of a vessel called *Greyhound* that delivered captives from the Gold Coast to Jamaica in late 1716 or early 1717 (Voyage ID no. 78305), and again from an unknown African port to Jamaica in 1718 (Voyage ID no. 76593), lending credibility to this letter. It is certainly interesting to note that, according to the *Voyages* website, the *Greyhound* left Africa in 1716 with 273 captives but delivered only 236 to Kingston. Although losing 37 captives to disease on the Middle Passage was by no means unheard-of, losing them to pirates remains a distinct possibility and meshes quite well with Johnson and Evans's estimate that the pirates stole 40 captives.

Edward Teach—Blackbeard—also plundered Africans from slave traders. Teach served aboard several privateers during Queen Anne's War, then initiated his pirate career as a lieutenant under Captain Benjamin Hornigold. Teach took charge of his own ship in 1717, when Hornigold's crew captured a French slave-trading vessel near Martinique. The fate of the Africans from that vessel is unknown, but Teach converted the "Guinea-man" into a pirate ship, renaming her *Queen Anne's Revenge*. Blackbeard's *Queen Anne* took her "revenge" on Englishmen as well as their enemies. Over the next year, Blackbeard captured dozens of vessels in various parts of the Caribbean before moving northeast along the coast of North America. Teach and his crew plundered several ships bound for Charleston in 1718, including "a Brigantine with 14 Negroes aboard; all which being done in the Face of the Town, struck a great Terror to the whole Province of *Carolina.*" Shortly thereafter, Teach's crew "Robbed an English Brigantine comeing from Guinea," bound for Virginia. Like many pirates, Teach carried his contraband to more remote parts, sailing for relatively undeveloped North Carolina, where he hoped to sell the African captives away from prying eyes. His vessel ran aground, however, and Teach "Surrendered himself upon the King's pardon to the Governour of North Carolina," Charles Eden. The British crown spearheaded a campaign to end piracy at that time, offering pirates clemency from colonial governors if they surrendered and swore to mend their evil ways. Teach—at least nominally—seized that opportunity, but the surrender proved controversial. Virginia's governor, Alexander Spotswood, objected to the terms, accusing Eden of harboring pirates and profiting from their trade.[24]

The controversy is illustrative of pirates' role in the slave trade of the late seventeenth and early eighteenth centuries. Not all colonies had equal access to Atlantic trade in general or to shipments of enslaved Africans in particular. Those colonies underserved by legal trade often proved willing to deal with pirates. Various colonies found themselves in that position at different stages in their development, and North Carolina certainly struggled to attract slave traders in the first half of the eighteenth century. As former governor George Burrington would complain in a 1736 report on North Carolina's ports, a lack

24. Donald G. Shomette notes pirates under Benjamin Hornigold capturing a French slaver near Saint Vincent, but where they took the Africans on board is unclear; see Shomette, *Pirates on the Chesapeake: Being a True History of Pirates, Picaroons, and Raiders on Chesapeake Bay, 1610–1807* (Centreville, Md., 1985), 194. For the vessel off Charleston, see Johnson, *General History of the Pyrates,* 74. For the vessel off Virginia, see Alexander Spotswood to Charles Eden, Nov. 7, 1718, Lee Family Papers, 1638–1867, section 76, folder 1, MSS 1 L51, fol. 109, Virginia Historical Society, Richmond.

of overseas trade prevented the delivery of exploitable Africans on any meaningful scale, despite strong demand. "It is a great misfortune to the people of North Carolina," Burrington moaned, "that they buy and sell at the second hand" in virtually all branches of commerce. This was especially problematic in the slave trade because "the planters are obliged to go into Virginia and South Carolina to purchase [slaves] where they pay a Duty on each Negroe, or buy the refuse, distemper'd or refractory Negroes brought into the Country from New England and the Islands, which are Sold at excessive Rates." It was precisely such underdeveloped trade that made colonists in many colonial backwaters willing to deal with and harbor pirates. It was no accident that Blackbeard appealed to the governor of such a colony for his pardon.[25]

Regardless of Eden's motives in granting the pardon, within months, reports reached Virginia of Teach's continued depredations despite his pledge to reform, spurring Spotswood to take matters into his own hands. According to a complaint filed by North Carolina officials, Spotswood ordered several naval vessels "to Surprize and kill the men [Teach's crew] within the Country of Carolina, and to Seize the goods [including African people], and to bring them away to Virginia, where he had them condemned as Pyrat's goods." Blackbeard's crew put up a spirited resistance but were outgunned by the Virginians. Blackbeard himself fell in the fighting, and the Virginia fleet reportedly sailed home in triumph with numerous prisoners to stand trial and "*Black-beard's* Head still hanging at the Bolt-sprit End." Suggesting a self-interested economic motive for Spotswood's actions, the North Carolina protest alleged that the contraband (both goods and enslaved people) was "not put into the hands of the Kings Officers as it ought to be, but imediately into his own [Spotswood's] hands." Regardless of the veracity of such allegations—or Spotswood's countercharge that Eden was soft on piracy—the

25. George Burrington to the Commissioners of His Majesty's Customs, July 27, 1736, CO 5/295, fols. 29–35. Burrington noted the role of New England in supplying slaves because merchants from that region controlled the trade between North Carolina and the West Indies until the mid-eighteenth century. See also Donnan, ed., *Documents*, IV, 236. Numerous North American colonies were accused of harboring and trading with pirates in the late seventeenth century, but by the time of the English crown's crackdown on piracy in the 1710s and 1720s, it tended to be the more economically marginal colonies that were most willing to trade with pirates; see Hughson, *Carolina Pirates*, 39, 52–59. David J. Starkey argues that piracy "tended to emerge and thrive at the junctures when disequilibria were evident between demand and supply," which accurately describes the situation of most English colonies (besides Barbados and eventually Jamaica) vis-à-vis the slave trade until the eighteenth century. The discrepancy between supply and demand for slaves persisted for many colonies well into the eighteenth century; see Starkey, "Pirates and Markets," in Pennell, ed., *Bandits at Sea*, 107.

Africans in the case experienced a disorienting, terrifying series of moves in the Americas. Their forced migrations were dictated not only by supply and demand in the various colonies but by piracy, armed skirmishes, and political squabbles.[26]

Teach's grisly demise was part of a dramatic end to the golden age of piracy, as concerted military efforts to protect Atlantic shipping decimated pirates' numbers by the 1720s. But continued incidents of slave theft on the high seas in these waning years attest to the brigands' interest in profiting from the slave trade. In the year of Teach's death, the pirate crew of Captain Charles Vane also captured a slaver bound for Charleston, with more than ninety captive Africans on board. Vane ordered several of his pirates aboard the slaver to take control of her, but these men simply used the opportunity to escape Vane's crew and claim the same pardon that Blackbeard had disingenuously sought earlier in the year. This subset of Vane's crew sailed the slave ship into a nearby South Carolina harbor, where they "sent an Express to the Governor, to know if [they] might have the Benefit of his Majesty's Pardon, and they would surrender themselves to his Mercy, with the Sloops and Negroes." The pardon was granted, and the African prisoners returned to the merchants who claimed the right to sell them to area planters.[27]

Likewise, Captain John Rackham and his crew—which included the famous women pirates Anne Bonny and Mary Read—faced trial in 1720 for numerous acts of piracy, including a charge that they "did, Piratically, and feloniously, set upon, board, break, and enter, a certain Merchant Scooner, called *Neptune*" bound from Jamaica to an unknown destination. From the *Neptune,* they allegedly "did Steal . . . her Tackle, Apparel, and Furniture, of the Value of Fifty Pounds of Current Money of Jamaica, and also Ten Negroe Slaves, of the value of Three hundred Pounds of like current Money." The value of the enslaved people relative to the goods in this case speaks to their attraction for pirates. Finally, in 1724, unnamed pirates stopped the *Princess Galley* as she entered Barbados from Africa, stealing ten captives and several cannon before allowing the ship to continue.[28]

26. Johnson, *General History of the Pyrates,* 83; Philip Ludwell, "Animadversion on a Paper Entituled, 'Virginia Addresses,' Printed in Philadelphia," 1719, Lee Family Papers, section 61, MSS 1 L51, fol. 81.

27. Johnson, *General History of the Pyrates,* 137; Hughson, *Carolina Pirates,* 91-93; Rediker, *Villains of all Nations,* 127-147; Robert C. Ritchie, *Captain Kidd and the War against the Pirates* (Cambridge, Mass, 1986).

28. Baer, *British Piracy,* III, 21-26; Cordingly, *Under the Black Flag,* 104-105. Other pirates documented stealing slaves include Captain John Quelch on the coast of Brazil in 1704 (Baer,

Some scholars have suggested that pirates avoided stealing and selling enslaved Africans due to a sense of shared working-class interest with the captives of the slave trade, but the evidence, especially from the Caribbean, contradicts that claim. Pirates operating on the West African coast did sometimes eschew enslaved people as prizes, preferring to steal the rum, textiles, firearms, and metals that Europeans sold to African merchants in exchange for people. The enthusiasm of pirates in the Caribbean for stealing slaves, however, suggests that any reluctance to steal people on the African coast was probably more logistical than moral. Enslaved Africans simply carried more monetary value after they had survived the Atlantic crossing. Pirates on the African coast would need to manage these captives across the ocean for the most advantageous sale, a task they would have preferred to avoid.[29]

Managing enslaved Africans to market was no minor consideration, as the pirate Francis Spriggs learned in 1725. Spriggs and his crew captured the "Sloop Humber," a South Sea Company vessel commanded by Captain Dursey, on which the company "had Ship'd 60 Neg's for the Havana" from Jamaica. Spriggs and his cohort transferred the captive Africans to their own vessel as prizes (along with Dursey as a prisoner, possibly intended for ran-

---

British Piracy, II, 267–268); and Walter Kennedy, whose crew split up in 1721 and reportedly set their pirate ship *Rover* adrift. It was later found with nine Africans alone on board (Johnson, *General History of the Pyrates*, 210).

29. Cordingly counters the notion that pirates did not trade in slaves, stating that the "the typical plunder" was less likely to be gold or silver than "bales of silk and cotton, some barrels of tobacco, an anchor cable, some spare sails, the carpenter's tools, and half a dozen black slaves" (*Under the Black Flag*, xiv). Peter Earle emphasizes pirates' important role in the slave trade of southeast Africa (Earle, *The Pirate Wars* [London, 2003], 113–115). Rediker notes that pirates sometimes rejected many types of goods (and enslaved people) if they lacked a way to fence them, but at other times, they would seize and sell slaves (*Villains of All Nations*, 34, 54, 88, 189 n. 31). For the argument that pirates preferred not to deal in slaves, see Kenneth J. Kinkor, "Black Men under the Black Flag," in Pennell, ed., *Bandits at Sea*, esp. 198. Peter Linebaugh and Rediker cast the egalitarianism of pirate crews ("hydrarchy," in their telling) as a "danger . . . to the increasingly valuable slave trade," highlighting piracy's disruption of African trade while de-emphasizing pirates' interest in seizing slaves as loot (Linebaugh and Rediker, *The Many-Headed Hydra: Sailors, Slaves, Commoners, and the Hidden History of the Revolutionary Atlantic* (Boston, 2000), 168–169. Charles Johnson likely contributed to the view that pirates opposed the slave trade with his creation of the fictional French pirate Captain Misson, who captured vessels on the coast of Africa but refused to take slaves. Misson gave rousing speeches to his men about the immorality of slavery. Most of Johnson's accounts of pirates were pieced together (and romantically embellished) from newspaper reports, trial transcripts, and correspondence with seamen, but the Misson story was apparently pure invention that the author "gave the illusion of history" (Johnson, *General History of the Pyrates*, 383–418; for the editor's interpretation that Misson was fictional, see 683).

som). Unfortunately for all involved, Spriggs lacked the foresight to anticipate the abundance of provisions required to sustain both pirates and prizes until they reached a safe port. Eventually their plight became so dire that when Spriggs's crew pillaged another vessel, they forced the captured ship to take 10 of the hungry African captives. Soon thereafter, Spriggs's band captured "the Brigantine Friendship of Boston," and after looting it, the pirates sent Captain Dursey aboard with permission to take "as many of the Negroes as he would." Dursey only "took 28 . . . because the Pyrate would allow him no more than 2 Barrels of Flower for Supporting them to Boston (to w'ch place the Brigantine was bound)." With 29 new passengers and few additional supplies to support them, the *Friendship* cut short its voyage at Charleston, but "bringing in [only] 25 of the Negroes, the other 3 dying in the passage." Starving captives serve as another reminder of the particular vulnerability of enslaved people to supply shortages and other dangers at sea. It also explains why wiser pirates than Spriggs were wary of stealing enslaved people if they lacked nearby opportunities to sell them.[30]

For pirates on the African coast, stealing people was a problematic business, given the brigands' lack of welcome at European trade forts and their distance from American markets where slaves held most value. The goods Europeans traded to acquire Africans, by contrast, were easily portable and could be fenced to a wider range of customers right there in Africa. None of this should suggest that pirates never cooperated with African people or accepted men of African descent into their crews. Pirates were nothing if not opportunistic. But the evidence from the Caribbean suggests that pirates simply preferred to steal slave cargoes close to their intended ports of sale. The case of Bartholomew Roberts (Black Bart, the most successful of the golden age pirates in terms of number of captured ships) illustrates that pirates' minimal theft of slaves in African waters reflected their distance from markets rather than antislavery sentiments. In January 1722, Roberts's fleet entered the harbor at Ouidah, in the Bight of Benin, cornering a dozen slavers nearly ready to embark on the Middle Passage. Rather than flee with this valuable but problematic quarry or free the slaves out of some sense of solidarity, Roberts mimicked the English Caribbean privateers of the sixteenth century: he ransomed the slaves (and ships) back to the merchants. Roberts held no sympa-

30. Directors of the South Sea Company to Rigby and Pratter, Apr. 21, 1725, in South Sea Company Records, 1711–1846, microfilm, Add. MSS, 25564, 216, Milton S. Eisenhower Library, Johns Hopkins University, Baltimore, Md.; see also Johnson, *General History of the Pyrates*, 356–357.

thy for the captive Africans. When one of the slave traders, Captain Fletcher of the *Porcupine,* refused to pay the ransom to which the other slave traders had agreed, the pirates covered the deck of the *Porcupine* with tar and set her ablaze—with 80 African people still in the hold, "chained together in pairs. The wretched captives were 'under the miserable choice of perishing by fire or water: those who jumped over-board were seized by sharks, a voracious fish plenty in this Road, and in their sight, torn limb from limb alive.'" [31]

The rampant thefts of enslaved Africans in American waters raise questions about the scale of this black market for black laborers, but the traffic is difficult to quantify, owing to the illegality of piracy and interloping and also the paucity of reliable port records for the seventeenth century. Anecdotal reports, however, suggest that such activity was considerable. Certainly by the late seventeenth century, piracy and privateering had reached a significant scale. As the governor of Jamaica noted in 1687, when beseeching the crown to station two naval frigates at his island to protect merchant vessels, "The South Seas are now more than ever infested with Pirates and Privatiers." [32]

Furthermore, the growth of the black population in many English colonies before 1700 or 1720 is difficult to explain without giving weight to the importance of plundered slaves. A comparison of the growth of enslaved populations with data on direct deliveries of enslaved people from Africa is striking. In 1672, Governor William Stapleton of the English Leewards reported that in recent years, the monopoly company had delivered no slaves to Nevis, Montserrat, or Antigua, and that each island had received only about 300 slaves from independent traders who had purchased licenses from the company. Yet these colonies were home to nearly 4,000 African people. Likewise, the first known vessel delivering slaves directly from Africa to South Carolina arrived in 1710, but by then, the colony was home to more than 4,000 people of African descent. Documented deliveries from Africa account for only three-quarters of New York's more than 2,000 slaves by 1700. Pennsylvania housed

31. Cordingly, *Under the Black Flag,* 212; see also *Voyages,* accessed August 2011, Voyage ID no. 75996. Howell Davis offers another example of a pirate who did steal slaves on the African coast (Johnson, *General History of the Pyrates,* 175). On the multiethnic composition of many pirate crews, see Rediker, *Villains of All Nations,* 9; Linebaugh and Rediker, *Many-Headed Hydra,* 164–167. On the more fluid race relations that prevailed in the maritime world of the Atlantic compared to land-based society, see W. Jeffrey Bolster, *Black Jacks: African American Seamen in the Age of Sail* (Cambridge, Mass., 1997), esp. chap. 4.

32. Proposal of the duke of Albemarle, governor of Jamaica, Apr. 15, 1687, CO 1/62, fols. 99–100. In the seventeenth and eighteenth centuries, Europeans often referred to the Caribbean as the "South Sea," although the phrase is more commonly applied to the southern Pacific Ocean.

approximately 2,000 black people by 1720, but no known vessels from Africa had reached the colony except perhaps a 1684 vessel of unknown origin that delivered 150 enslaved people. New Jersey was also home to more than 2,000 Africans by 1720 without having received a single African shipment. Finally, more than 1,500 people of African descent resided in New England by 1700, yet known direct African shipments had delivered fewer than 300 slaves. Legal transshipments of enslaved people from English colonies that received captives directly from Africa in the seventeenth century, most notably Barbados, account for some of this black population growth, but pirates and privateers also played a sizable role.[33]

■ What were the implications of these black- and gray-market trades—piracy, privateering, interloping—to the development of slavery and the slave trade in English America? Most obviously, these illegal activities diverted thousands of African people from the normal routes of the slave trade, serving as an unconventional distribution network to a broader range of American destinations. Often, the voyages themselves were violent and chaotic, as Africans were forcibly moved from ship to ship and their captors struggled to evade authorities and enemies. Haphazard captures and the security concerns of black-market sellers mitigated against a routinized trade along well-worn paths, but within the randomness were patterns. One key attribute that often determined whether colonists were willing to deal with pirates or interlopers was a lack of access to more regular or legitimate trade. Where slave trading was concerned,

33. For population estimates, see Robert V. Wells, *The Population of the British Colonies in America before 1776: A Survey of Census Data* (Princeton, N.J., 1975), 112, 135, 143; John J. McCusker, *Rum and the American Revolution: The Rum Trade and the Balance of Payments of the Thirteen Continental Colonies* (New York, 1989), II, 566, 568; Ira Berlin, *Many Thousands Gone: The First Two Centuries of Slavery in North America* (Cambridge, Mass., 1998), 369. On the discrepancy between slave trade data and population growth in the English Leewards, Carl and Roberta Bridenbaugh note the numbers gap, asking rhetorically, "Who can question that they [the Africans] were procured from nearby Statia in Dutch sloops? How else can this phenomenon be explained?" (*No Peace beyond the Line*, 254.) In addition to Dutch interlopers, I would add English interlopers buying slaves at Dutch islands and pirates and privateers as parts of the explanation. On South Carolina, see *Voyages*, accessed August 2010, http://www.slavevoyages.org/tast/database/search.faces?yearFrom=1601&yearTo=1701&mjslptimp =21300. Wood states unequivocally that the 1,000 Africans in South Carolina by 1695 "came from the West Indies" (*Black Majority*, 131, 143–145). For the 1684 shipment to Pennsylvania, see Gary B. Nash, "Slaves and Slaveowners in Colonial Philadelphia," *WMQ*, XXX (1973), 223–256, esp. 225. For transatlantic deliveries to northern colonies before 1720, see *Voyages*, http://www.slavevoyages.org/tast/database/search.faces?yearFrom=1514&yearTo=1720&mjslptimp =20100.20300.20400.20500.20600.20800.20900.

especially in the seventeenth and early eighteenth centuries, this meant that black-market sellers often headed to mainland North America or to the minor English Caribbean islands to offload slaves. Settlers in the colonies that clamored against the Royal African Company's monopoly opened their harbors to illicit slave sellers, asking few questions about where these dealers or their captives came from. Some historians argue that such planters, starved for coercible labor, "regarded the interlopers as the Robin Hoods of the Caribbean," and the same might also be said of pirates and privateers in some quarters. Hence, Blackbeard appeared in the backwater of North Carolina, and reports circulated in 1698 of unnamed pirates, who "delivered slaves to the Hudson Valley estate of Frederick Philipse." In other words, piracy and privateering were particularly important to the growth of slavery in those colonies that were not important centers of the slave trade. Many English colonies got their first tastes of slavery, not because they requested shipments of Africans, but because pirates or privateers turned up with plundered people. Though difficult to assess, this was an important factor contributing to individual colonies' decisions to adopt slavery.[34]

From the captives' perspective, capture by pirates or privateers complicated their migrations, threatening them with additional dangers and cultural isolation. On one hand, corsairs and privateers often captured whole shiploads of Africans together, so the rerouting of their journeys did not necessarily add to the risk of separation from shipmates, kinsmen, or people of shared language and background. On the other hand, transshipment via pirate or privateer added to culture shock. In many cases, the new captors would have spoken different languages than the slave traders who had ferried captives across the Atlantic. More important, European traders usually purchased slaves at African ports frequented by their countrymen, so Africans captured by privateers of a rival crown found themselves sent in a different direction than the one traveled by most captives from their region. Transfer from one empire's domain to another increased the likelihood of settling among people from unfamiliar parts of Africa, with whom they shared less in terms of culture, language, and religion. For instance, English traders in the mid-seventeenth century supplied England's Caribbean colonies with people primarily from the Bight of Biafra, with the Gold Coast and Bight of Benin as the most important supplementary regions. Meanwhile, slave traders of other nationalities

34. William A. Pettigrew, *Freedom's Debt: The Royal African Company and the Politics of the Atlantic Slave Trade, 1672–1752* (Chapel Hill, N.C., 2013); Bridenbaugh, *No Peace beyond the Line*, 260; McManus, *Black Bondage in the North*, 20.

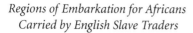

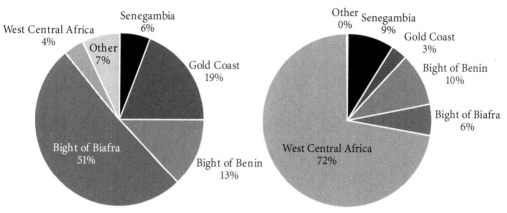

Regions of Embarkation for Africans Carried by English Slave Traders

Senegambia 6%
West Central Africa 4%
Other 7%
Gold Coast 19%
Bight of Biafra 51%
Bight of Benin 13%

Regions of Embarkation for Africans Carried by Non-English Slave Traders

Other 0%
Senegambia 9%
Gold Coast 3%
Bight of Benin 10%
Bight of Biafra 6%
West Central Africa 72%

FIGURE 1. Comparison of Captive Origins in the English and Non-English Transatlantic Slave Trades, 1641–1680

Source: On English slave traders supplying England's Caribbean colonies in the mid-seventeenth century, see *Voyages: The Trans-Atlantic Slave Trade Database,* accessed September 2012, http:// slavevoyages.org/tast/assessment/estimates.faces?yearFrom=1641&yearTo=1680&flag=3.5& disembarkation=305.304.307.306.309.308.311.310.301.302.303; on slave traders of other nationalities in the same time period, see *Voyages,* accessed January 2013, http://slavevoyages.org/tast/assessment /estimates.faces?yearFrom=1641&yearTo=1680&flag=1.2.4.6.7. If slave-trading voyages to Brazil are excluded as less likely to fall victim to English pirates or privateers, the proportion of west central Africans declines significantly but remains larger than the proportion of the migration from any other African region.

focused on different parts of the African coast in the period. West central Africans from the Congo-Angola region accounted for nearly three out of every four captives in the non-English trade. As a result, pirates and privateers who stole slaves from non-English traders for sale in the English Caribbean were likely to carry west central Africans to colonies where people of other backgrounds predominated, diversifying the slave quarters and placing the west central Africans at particular risk of isolation (Figure 1). For the mainland North American colonies, the contrast between the populations arriving in the English slave trade and via piracy and privateering would have been especially stark. In the decades of the late seventeenth and early eighteenth centuries, when North America's enslaved population began to grow rapidly, English slave traders brought almost no west central Africans to the mainland, instead drawing chiefly from the Bight of Biafra and Senegambia. By contrast, west central Africans accounted for well over 40 percent of the total captive popu-

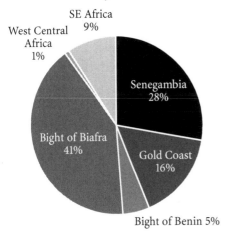

Regions of Embarkation for Africans Carried Directly to North America

SE Africa 9%

West Central Africa 1%

Senegambia 28%

Bight of Biafra 41%

Gold Coast 16%

Bight of Benin 5%

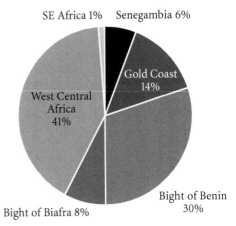

Regions of Embarkation for Africans Carried to Other American Regions

SE Africa 1%   Senegambia 6%

Gold Coast 14%

West Central Africa 41%

Bight of Biafra 8%

Bight of Benin 30%

FIGURE 2. Comparison of Captive Origins in the Transatlantic Slave Trades to North America and Other American Regions, 1671–1710

Source: On the composition of the English slave trade to North America, 1671 to 1710, see *Voyages: The Trans-Atlantic Slave Trade Database,* accessed September 2012, http://slavevoyages.org/tast /assessment/estimates.faces?yearFrom=1671&yearTo=1710&flag=3.5&disembarkation=205.204.201 .203.202; and for the composition of the overall slave trade, 1671 to 1710, see *Voyages,* accessed January 2013, http://slavevoyages.org/tast/assessment/estimates.faces?yearFrom=1671&yearTo=1710 &disembarkation=402.403.401.404.405.804.702.805.703.701.801.802.803.305.304.307.100.306.309 .308.311.310.705.501.704.502.600.900.301.302.303.

lation forced across the Atlantic in this period by slave traders of all nations, so Congolese and Angolan people likely appeared more frequently among the captives delivered by pirates and privateers (Figure 2).[35]

Capture in the dangerous world of piracy and privateering also increased the risks of bodily harm for those caught in the crossfire of battle. As the burning of the *Porcupine* and the shortage of food under Captain Spriggs attest, theft on the high seas created volatile situations in which pirates or traders might deem human commodities expendable. African men, women, and children could be sacrificed as pawns in power plays or abandoned when flight and survival trumped anticipated profits. Enslaved people seized by corsairs might also have faced increased risk of sexual exploitation. Charles Johnson's

35. For more on the significance of the large number of west central Africans in the overall slave trade during the prime era for privateering and piracy, see Heywood and Thornton, *Central Africans,* ix, 8–48.

rendition of the adventures of pirate captain Edward England notes that when England's crew plagued the West African coast near Cape Coast Castle in 1719, "they liv'd there very wantonly for several Weeks, making free with the Negroe Women, and committing such outragious Acts, that they came to an open Rupture with the Natives." A slave ship captain taken over by England's crew offered a similar account, reporting that the pirates "diverted themselves" with the enslaved women on board before abandoning the ship. One historian of pirates argues that such sexual abuse was status- or race-specific, observing that most enslaved Africans seized by pirates were "sold as booty, . . . [and] female slaves were often abused and raped, a fate shared only rarely by white female captives." Of course, violations also occurred aboard nonpiratical slave-trading vessels, but the transfer to captivity aboard a new ship under a crew that already operated outside the law might have escalated the danger of abuse.[36]

■ In the summer of 1717, a group of about twenty Africans who had recently survived the Atlantic crossing to Barbados found themselves purchased by a merchant who loaded them aboard a sloop called *Mary* that ferried them back out to sea, headed north. The captives shared space in their new vessel with barrels of rum and sugar. After about a fortnight at sail, the sloop steered these captives toward a second New World landfall, aiming for the harbor of Charleston, South Carolina, but they never made it. Nearing the inlet, the *Mary*'s sailors suddenly erupted in commotion as another, larger vessel rapidly approached. The captives heard a blast of cannon fire from this other ship—a warning shot—and then the *Mary* dropped her sails and slowed to a crawl. Soon a boat from this second vessel carried a crew to board the *Mary*. These new arrivals took control of the *Mary*, sailed her some distance off, and dropped anchor.

Eventually, after the pirates had plundered another vessel bound into Charleston, the *Mary* put to sea again, carrying her captives farther north. The Africans had new captors, but their vessel remained the same, and they shared the same cramped space with barrels of trade goods. After a short passage, the *Mary* glided into a small inlet in North Carolina. This was no bustling port like the one they had entered at Bridgetown, Barbados, or Charleston, but rather a remote, unpopulated cove. Here they boarded small boats that ferried them to shore, along with the rum and sugar. Then, strangely, their captors "carren'd"

36. Johnson, *General History of the Pyrates*, 117; Rediker, *Villains of All Nations*, 138; Earle, *Pirate Wars*, 172.

the sloop "and then burnt her." After a convoluted journey, the weary prisoners had finally disembarked in North America.[37]

Unfortunately, the fate of these African travelers after touching land is uncertain, but presumably their pirate captor, Stede Bonnet, sold them to area planters or merchants willing to trade with outlaws. These migrants' experience illustrated the patterns in the black market and the changes afoot in the slave-trading economy by the end of the golden age of piracy. For one thing, their erratic route through the slave trade was typical of the black market. Changes of ownership at sea via theft and the need of black-market dealers to move away from the prying eyes of colonial officials led to unusual itineraries. These stolen captives endured a similar fate to many others taken by pirates: their change of ownership steered them onto a new course—away from a major port and toward a backwater of the slave economy.

That Bonnet's crew stole these Africans from an intercolonial slave trader bound from Barbados to South Carolina, however, was a sign of changing times. By the early eighteenth century, several elements converged to minimize the role of pirates, privateers, and interlopers in slave distribution in the Americas. As colonial societies matured, governments and merchants seeking law and order promoted (and funded) crackdowns on piracy; the reason we know about the African migrants aboard the *Mary* is that Bonnet was captured not long after landing these people in North Carolina. He hanged at Charleston in 1718. Interlopers were rendered obsolete less violently. In 1698, England rescinded the Royal African Company's monopoly, opening the transatlantic slave trade to all subjects of the empire. Thereafter, only foreign traders had to worry about smuggling slaves into English colonial ports. In addition, the black-market slave trade became less important, owing to the growth of British Atlantic trade. The *Mary* represented this trend in two ways. First, by 1717, Barbados was importing enough slaves from Africa that such captives could be purchased at reasonable prices for reexport to other colonies. In fact,

37. This narration of these slaves' "final passage" is pieced together from three primary sources: *The Tryals of Major Stede Bonnet* (London, 1719), rpt. in Baer, *British Piracy*, II, 327; Johnson, *General History of the Pyrates*, 96; and NOSL, CO 5/508. The quoted material appears identically in both *Tryals* and the *General History* (Johnson borrowed liberally from many published accounts of piracy). Those sources do not name the captured slave-trading vessel *Mary* but simply identify her as "a Sloop with Negroes, Rum, and Sugar, Capt. Joseph Palmer from Barbadoes." South Carolina import records for 1717, however, show an arrival earlier that same year of a Captain Joseph Palmer with a sloop called *Mary*, full of rum, sugar, and nineteen slaves from Barbados. Since all the other details of vessel type, route, and cargo match, I have assumed that the same Joseph Palmer repeated the voyage in the same ship later that year, when he, his crew, and their captives fell prey to the pirates.

slave prices fell considerably in Barbados from the mid-seventeenth century to 1700 due to the increased supply. Second, commerce between various colonies gradually became regularized, and the slave trade was incorporated in the general intercolonial traffic. As this trading network grew and distributed enslaved Africans between colonies more efficiently, fewer colonists would look to the black market for black workers. As the eighteenth century wore on, the transshipment of slaves would increasingly become the role of merchants, not pirates.[38]

38. For another example of pirates' seizing an intercolonial slaver, see the account of pirate George Lowther's theft of Africans bound from Barbados to New England in 1722 (Johnson, *General History of the Pyrates,* 314). On falling prices in Barbados, see Larry Gragg, *Englishmen Transplanted: The English Colonization of Barbados, 1627–1660* (New York, 2003), 103.

3. Captive Markets for Captive People

LEGAL DISPERSALS OF AFRICANS IN
A PERIPHERAL ECONOMY, CA. 1640–1700

The way this plantation has been supplyed with negroes hath
been from Barbados. —Benjamin Bennett, 1708

These following Goods may be sent on my particular account;
viz. 4 Negros, 2 men and 2 women, not to exceed 25 years old
and to bee likely. —William Byrd, 1685

These . . . Children were not worth the Money. —David Jeffries, 1707

Although the first several decades of the intercolonial slave trade saw
a significant role for the black (or gray) markets of piracy, privateering, and
interloping, most trafficking in African people was not illegal. Trading African
slaves was perfectly permissible in the seventeenth-century English empire, as
long as one respected royally sanctioned monopolies and mercantilist trade
laws. From the mid-seventeenth century onward, the English transatlantic
trade grew steadily, delivering captives directly from Africa to some American colonies, especially in the Caribbean. As this trade developed, intercolonial slave trading emerged haltingly alongside it. Early ventures took experi-
mental form: traders often organized shipments along routes not soon to be
repeated as they responded to particular trade problems or fulfilled requests
from remote buyers. Only gradually would a routinized commerce distribute African people from the entrepôts of English America to the numerous
secondary ports. This slow development of slave trading between colonies
reflected the state of commerce more generally. With a few notable exceptions, seventeenth-century English America (mainland and Caribbean) was
a peripheral world. Colonial trade, in slaves or otherwise, was irregular and
focused primarily on the mother country.

This chapter examines the tentative beginnings of the legal intercolonial
slave trade. It highlights a wide range of transshipment strategies in this ex-
perimental period—from the least routinized ventures to the emergence of

more regular distributions along consistent paths. One impetus for such dispersals was the monopoly system in the English transatlantic trade. Because the Royal African Company concentrated deliveries on the wealthiest colonies with the most established slave systems, other colonies, eager for labor but cut out of African trade, looked either to the black market or to these entrepôts for access to enslaved Africans. In this disadvantaged market position, the colonies overlooked by the Royal African Company became captive markets for slave dealers in the entrepôts. Buyers in these captive markets were frustrated by—but willing to accept—shipments of captive people deemed unsellable in the major ports of African arrival in the Americas.

Over the course of the century, such intercolonial movements gradually shifted from singular, reactive shipments toward a more systematic, speculative trade. Initially, transatlantic agents for the Royal African Company resorted to transshipment primarily to solve sales problems, but ever more merchants and planters recognized that such ventures could be quite profitable in their own right, especially when incorporated with other intercolonial trade. Traders between Barbados and the Chesapeake might have recognized the potential profits earliest. In the late seventeenth century, that branch of the trade developed on a model that foreshadowed the evolution of the trade between other colonial regions in the following century. This intercolonial trafficking would work best for traders when enmeshed with other commerce. Trading enslaved people both enhanced and was enhanced by the trade in nonhuman goods, playing an important role in the elaboration of commercial networks between colonies.

■ In the early decades, several factors inhibited the development of more regular intercolonial trade. Fundamentally, seventeenth-century English America housed fewer markets for slave traders to supply than would later be the case. Even in the late seventeenth century, English settlement in North America clustered along just a few major bays and rivers of the eastern seaboard. In the Caribbean, English settlement was confined to Barbados, a few of the small Leeward Islands, and the southeastern coast of Jamaica around Kingston. English settlement in Jamaica, South Carolina, and Pennsylvania was just beginning; Georgia did not yet exist; islands such as Grenada, Dominica, and Tobago were not yet English possessions. In addition to the smaller number and size of the markets, commerce between these fledgling colonies (in slaves or goods) developed only slowly. "As the seventeenth century drew to a close, [colonial trade and communication] routes were still largely independent of each other, like the bent spokes of some giant rimless wheel," one scholar explains. If England was the hub of this metaphorical wheel, colonial outposts were the points at the end of the spokes, and that missing rim of the wheel was intercolonial trade. As these ports grew, however, connections between them would emerge.[1]

The primitive state of seventeenth-century markets did not entirely stifle intercolonial slave trading. Because so few English colonies could support purchases of hundreds of African captives at a time, transatlantic slave traders confined deliveries to a small number of ports, even though a broader range of colonies sought exploitable labor. Barbados was the oldest and most populous Caribbean possession as the English slave trade emerged. In the early 1640s, sugar cultivation took root on the island, and settlers looked to African labor to replace indentured servants who loathed the backbreaking work. Emulating sugar planters in Brazil, Barbados colonists became the first English Americans to invest in African labor on a large scale. As a result of this head start and the ensuing rapid growth of the sugar economy, Barbados received more than 80 percent of English America's direct emigrants from Africa before 1665. Thereafter, Jamaica—recently conquered from the Spanish—emerged as a second important destination for transatlantic slavers, but other colonies were largely ignored. Even by 1700, well over 80 percent of Africans who had survived the Middle Passage to English America had landed in one of these two colonies. Although Barbados and Jamaica exploited more slaves than other English territories, the transatlantic trade's concentration on the two was out of proportion with their enslaved populations. By 1700, they were home to fewer than 60 percent of English America's enslaved people (Table 3).[2]

Virtually all other English American colonies housed higher proportions of the empire's slaves than their share of African arrivals would lead one to suspect. The Chesapeake was home to more than 12 percent of English America's Africans by 1700, yet fewer than 4 percent of Africans disembarking from the Middle Passage in English colonies had done so in the region. Likewise, An-

1. Ian K. Steele, *The English Atlantic, 1675–1740: An Exploration of Communication and Community* (New York, 1986) 17, 27. See also Nuala Zahedieh, "Economy," in David Armitage and Michael J. Braddick, eds., *The British Atlantic World, 1500–1800* (Basingstoke, Hampshire, U.K., 2002), 60; John J. McCusker and Russell R. Menard, *The Economy of British America, 1607–1789: Needs and Opportunities for Study* (Chapel Hill, N.C., 1991), 78–80, 108.

2. On Barbados's early predominance in the English slave trade, see David Eltis, "The British Transatlantic Slave Trade before 1714: Annual Estimates of Volume and Direction," in Robert L. Paquette and Stanley L. Engerman, eds., *The Lesser Antilles in the Age of European Expansion* (Gainesville, Fla., 1996), 182–205.

TABLE 3. A Comparison of English Colonies' Shares of the Empire's Enslaved Population in 1700 with Their Shares of Direct African Arrivals by 1700

Colony/Region	Proportion of the total black population of English America in 1700 (N = 154,100)	Proportion of the total direct migration from Africa to English America by 1700 (N = 319,148)
The "North" (i.e., Pennsylvania to Maine)	3.4%	0.9%
The Chesapeake	12.7%	3.8%
The Carolinas	1.8%	0.0%
Antigua	6.6%	1.9%
St. Christopher (French and English sides)	9.5%	1.1%
British Virgin Islands	0.3%	0.0%
Barbados	32.5%	56.9%
Jamaica	27.3%	28.5%
Nevis & Montserrat	5.8%	6.9%
TOTAL	100.0%	100.0%

Sources: Estimates of direct arrivals from Africa calculated from *Voyages: The Trans-Atlantic Slave Trade Database,* accessed December 2013 (http://slavevoyages.org/tast/assessment/estimates.faces ?yearFrom=1501&yearTo=1700&disembarkation=304.309.201.308.203.202.301.302.303); population figures calculated from John J. McCusker, *Rum and the American Revolution: The Rum Trade and the Balance of Payments of the Thirteen Continental Colonies* (New York, 1989), II, 555–712.

Note: Bermuda has been excluded from this analysis because the *Voyages* database does not offer estimates for the colony; Nevis and Montserrat are treated together because *Voyages* presents estimates for them together. The total number of Africans arriving in the colonies collectively was much higher than the resulting total population, owing to both the transshipment of captives outside the empire and, especially, high mortality among the first African settlers.

tigua housed more than 6 percent of Africans toiling in English America in 1700, but fewer than 2 percent of African migrants had disembarked from the Middle Passage at the island. The story was similar elsewhere.[3]

Differential rates of mortality are very unlikely to explain these wide discrepancies, especially since mortality was high for African settlers in all English colonies during the seventeenth century. Furthermore, most of the African immigration to such colonies was too recent for natural reproduction to contribute much. Instead, Barbados and eventually Jamaica served as entrepôts for most of English America in the period. Before about 1660, even Jamaica imported African captives from Barbados, only transitioning thereafter to become an entrepôt in its own right. Thus one can think of Barbados as a seventeenth-century Ellis Island for African immigrants to English America.[4]

3. For population estimates, see John J. McCusker, *Rum and the American Revolution: The Rum Trade and the Balance of Payments of the Thirteen Continental Colonies*, II (New York, 1989), 555–573, 694. Estimates of the Chesapeake's African population in particular by 1700 range widely. Ira Berlin suggests 20,752 (Berlin, *Many Thousands Gone: The First Two Centuries of Slavery in North America* [Cambridge, Mass., 1998], 369); Robert V. Wells offers the low-end estimate of 12,000 (Wells, *The Population of the British Colonies in America before 1776: A Survey of Census Data* [Princeton, N.J., 1975], 112, 135, 143, 147, 161–162); Allan Kulikoff puts the figure at 16,500 (and argues that natural increase only contributed significantly after 1710; see Kulikoff, "A 'Prolifick' People: Black Population Growth in the Chesapeake Colonies, 1700–1790," *Southern Studies*, XVI [1977], 391, 393, 415–416). Regardless of which estimate one prefers, transatlantic deliveries do not account for the population, especially since most immigration occurred in the last decades of the century, leaving little time for natural reproduction to contribute. Both Lorena S. Walsh and David W. Galenson have pointed out that current data on the transatlantic slave trade cannot account for the Chesapeake slave population by 1700; see Walsh, "The Differential Cultural Impact of Free and Coerced Migration to Colonial America," in David Eltis, ed., *Coerced and Free Migration: Global Perspectives* (Stanford, Calif., 2002), 123; Galenson, *White Servitude in Colonial America: An Economic Analysis* (New York, 1981), 212–217. To give a few more examples, documented deliveries from Africa account for only three-quarters of New York's approximately 2,300 slaves by 1700. By 1720, Pennsylvania housed approximately 2,000 slaves, but no known vessels from Africa had reached the colony—excepting perhaps a 1684 vessel of unknown origin that delivered 150 captives. New Jersey by 1720 was also home to more than 2,000 Africans without having received an African shipment. Finally, more than 1,500 people of African descent resided in New England by 1700, but direct African shipments had delivered fewer than 300 slaves. For the 1685 shipment to Pennsylvania, see Gary B. Nash, "Slaves and Slaveowners in Colonial Philadelphia," *William and Mary Quarterly*, 3d Ser., XXX (1973), 225. For transatlantic deliveries to northern colonies before 1720, see *Voyages: The Trans-Atlantic Slave Trade Database*, accessed December 2010, http://www.slavevoyages.org/tast/database/search.faces?yearFrom=1514&yearTo=1720&mjslptimp=20100.20300.20400.20500.20600.20800.20900.

4. Beyond just slave trading, Barbados engaged in more intercolonial commerce than any other English American colony in the seventeenth century; see Larry Gragg, *Englishmen Trans-*

Anecdotal reports reinforce the impression that Barbados and Jamaica served as gateways for the slave trade to English America in the seventeenth century. When Lieutenant Governor Benjamin Bennett of Bermuda reported to England in 1708, "The way this plantation has been supplyed with negroes hath been from Barbados," he could just as well have been describing any other colony. In 1680, Governor Bradstreet of Massachusetts offered a similar account. "Now and then," he reported, "two or three Negro's are brought hither from Barbados and other of his Majesties plantations." One of Bradstreet's successors, Governor Dudley, stated in 1708 that little had changed for the Massachusetts slave trade, though he did note that one direct African shipment arrived in 1700. In 1680, Governor William Leete of Connecticut noted, "For Blacks, there comes sometimes 3 or 4 in a year from Barbadoes." Another Connecticut governor a generation later, Gurdon Saltonstall, followed suit, insisting, "Their hath not been one vessell either of the Royall Affrican Company's or of separate traders, that hath imported any negroes" to Connecticut from Africa in the preceding ten years. Instead, "Sometimes half a dozen in a year may be imported from the West Indies." Governor Samuel Cranston of Rhode Island related that "the whole and only supply of negroes to this colony, is from the island of Barbadoes; from whence is imported one year with another, betwixt twenty and thirty." [5]

New York also relied on West Indian transshipments. The Royal African Company neglected the colony, and in 1676, New York's duty collector, William Dyer, explored the legality of settlers' obtaining slaves from other colonies, suggesting that such behavior was already occurring. Dyer's superi-

planted: The English Colonization of Barbados, 1627–1660 (New York, 2003), especially 1, 106–110; Gragg, "An Ambiguous Response to the Market: The Early New England–Barbados Trade," Historical Journal of Massachusetts, XVII (1989), 177–178. On slave transshipment from Barbados to Jamaica, Philip D. Curtin estimates that Jamaica imported roughly 16,000 slaves from the eastern Caribbean between 1655 and 1701; see Curtin, The Atlantic Slave Trade: A Census (Madison, Wis., 1969), 57–58. His estimate draws primarily on Orlando Patterson, The Sociology of Slavery: An Analysis of the Origins, Development and Structure of Negro Slave Society in Jamaica (Rutherford, N.J., 1969). Improved data on Jamaica's direct imports from Africa, however, suggests that 16,000 was a substantial overestimate of this intercolonial trade; see Eltis, "British Transatlantic Slave Trade before 1714," in Paquette and Engerman, eds., Lesser Antilles in the Age of European Expansion, 195, 196.

5. Benjamin Bennett to Board of Trade, in Elizabeth Donnan, ed., Documents Illustrative of the History of the Slave Trade to America, 4 vols. (Washington, D.C., 1930–1935), II, 48; Governor Bradstreet to the Committee of Trade and Plantations, Boston, May 18, 1680, ibid., III, 15 (Bradstreet estimated the total number of Africans in the colony at that date to be only "about one hundred or one hundred and twenty"); Governor Dudley to Board of Trade, 1708, ibid., 23–25; William Leete quoted ibid., 2; Samuel Cranston to Board of Trade, 1708, ibid., 110.

ors reassured him that he need not prosecute intercolonial traders as inter-lopers because the Royal African Company only claimed exclusive right "to the first . . . transportacion of Negroes out of Guiny, and when they are once sold in Barbadoes, Jamaica etc. . . . they care not whither they are transported from thence; . . . therefore you need not suspect the Company will oppose the introduceing of black Slaves into New Yorke from any place (except from Guiny)."[6]

Such dependence on Barbados and Jamaica was not confined to the North. South Carolina also relied on Caribbean shipments. The colony was founded in 1670, and the first settlers brought enslaved people with them from Barba-dos, some of whom had resided in Barbados long enough to establish families that were partly disrupted by the journey. But even with slavery part of the plan in Carolina from day one, the first documented vessel delivering cap-tives directly from Africa did not arrive until 1710. Yet the colony was home to roughly one thousand slaves by 1695, and by 1710, to more than four thou-sand. A few undocumented vessels from Africa probably contributed, but Caribbean sources provided most of these early Africans. Barbados was the most likely supplier. Some call South Carolina the "colony of a colony" be-cause many of its early settlers came from Barbados, which was running out of available land, and because some planned to make their livings by raising provisions to export to the crowded island from whence they came. The links with Barbados—social, economic, and cultural—were not quickly severed, so South Carolina's reliance on the island for Africans continued after the initial colonizers arrived. In 1709, the governor and council of South Caro-lina reported that, in addition to direct African shipments, "Wee are allso often furnished with negros from the American Islands, chiefly from Barba-dos and Jamaica." South Carolina's import records do not document arrivals before 1710, but Barbados certainly supplied the majority of Africans arriving in the seventeenth century, given the island's prominence in England's early slave trade and its extensive links with South Carolina. By the early eighteenth century, Jamaica also transshipped several dozen Africans annually to South Carolina, sometimes in exchange for enslaved native Americans.[7]

6. Ibid., III, 435.

7. Governor and Council of South Carolina to Board of Trade, Sept. 17, 1709, in Donnan, ed., *Documents*, IV, 256. On South Carolina's founding and the links to Barbados, see Justin Roberts and Ian Beamish, "Venturing Out: The Barbadian Diaspora and the Carolina Colony, 1650–1685," in Michelle LeMaster and Bradford J. Wood, eds., *Creating and Contesting Carolina: Proprietary Era Histories* (Columbia, S.C., 2013); W. Robert Higgins, "The Geographical Origins

TABLE 4. Estimates of Africans Reaching North American Colonies
from the Caribbean, 1651–1710

South Carolina	2,900
North Carolina	25
Virginia	2,650
Maryland	1,200
Pennsylvania / New Jersey	1,725
New York	1,025
New England	1,100
TOTAL	10,625

Source: Gregory E. O'Malley, "Beyond the Middle Passage: Slave Migration from the Caribbean
to North America, 1619–1807," William and Mary Quarterly, 3d Ser., LXVI (2009), 141–142, 146,
149, 160–161, 163.

North America was not the only destination. In fact, the earliest routes
of dispersal from Barbados likely developed to other islands of the English

_____

of Negro Slaves in Colonial South Carolina," South Atlantic Quarterly, LXX (1971), 34; Jennifer L.
Morgan, Laboring Women: Reproduction and Gender in New World Slavery (Philadelphia, 2004),
123–126; Peter H. Wood, Black Majority: Negroes in Colonial South Carolina from 1670 through
the Stono Rebellion (New York, 1974), especially chap. 1, "The Colony of a Colony." Since most
Barbadian planters purchased slaves from the Royal African Company on credit and such debts
were often long outstanding, some might have faced legal difficulty leaving the island with liens
on their slaves, but whether the company managed to prevent such departures is unclear; see
David W. Galenson, Traders, Planters, and Slaves: Market Behavior in Early English America (New
York, 1986), 35, 54, 84, 149. On the lack of direct African deliveries to South Carolina before 1710,
see Voyages, accessed December 2010, http://www.slavevoyages.org/tast/database/search.faces
?yearFrom=1601&yearTo=1710&mjslptimp=21300. Wood asserts that the 1,000 Africans in South
Carolina by 1695 "came from the West Indies" (Black Majority, 131, 143–145). Surviving Jamaican export records from mid-1709 to mid-1711 show fifteen vessels carrying 237 slaves departing
for South Carolina in the two-year period (Naval Office Shipping Lists for Jamaica, CO 142/14,
National Archives, Kew). Barbados shipping lists also survive for much of this early period, and
other lists for Jamaica are available, as well, but they document only the exports of "enumerated
goods" from the British Navigation Acts; slaves were not "enumerated." For a sample shipment
from Barbados, see reference to the sloop Turtle, which carried an unspecified number of slaves
from Barbados to South Carolina in 1697 ("Case of the Turtle, 1697," in Donnan, ed., Documents,
IV, 249–250). On South Carolina's exchanging native Americans for African slaves, see Higgins,
"Geographical Origins of Negro Slaves in South Carolina," South Atlantic Quarterly, LXX (1971),
35; Alan Gallay, The Indian Slave Trade: The Rise of the English Empire in the American South,
1670–1717 (New Haven, Conn., 2002).

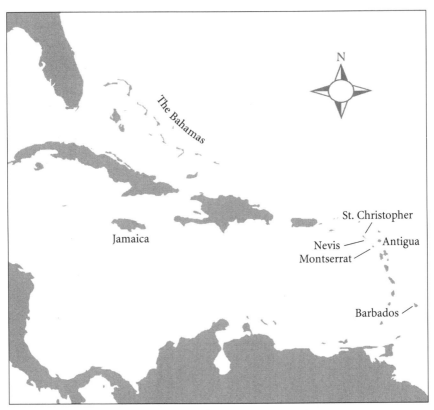

MAP 4. Principal English Colonies in the Caribbean, ca. 1700. Drawn by the author

Caribbean. Before the 1670s, several of England's Lesser Antilles—most notably Antigua, Saint Christopher, and Montserrat—received virtually no direct shipments of African people, yet they still developed African populations. Presumably, they relied primarily on transshipment from Barbados, though they also smuggled Africans from Dutch sources. Barbados probably exported about 1,200 slaves to the other Lesser Antilles, from the date of its first imports to 1675 (see Map 4). Nevis might have been a minor source of slave transshipments, since that colony also imported a higher proportion of English America's Africans in the early decades than its population would lead one to expect. By the mid-1670s, islands other than Barbados received regular transatlantic shipments as the Royal African Company increased the volume of England's slave trade. Deliveries to Barbados grew even more rapidly, however, and the less populous islands continued to rely partly on Barbados, probably receiving more than 6,000 captives from there in the last quarter of the seventeenth century. Antigua also began to shift from recipient to supplier in the intercolonial trade in the century's final decades.[8]

A contributing factor to the predominance of one or two American entrepôts in England's seventeenth-century slave trade was limited supply. Restrained partly by the English crown's grant of monopoly to the Royal African Company (and several less significant precursors), English merchants had not risen to primacy in Europe's African trade by the late seventeenth century. Furthermore, the structure (if not the nature) of the large, bureaucratic company encouraged the entrenchment of well-worn routes of transatlantic trade. The Royal African Company maintained fortified bases on the African coast, to which they sent ships repeatedly, and the company hired permanent agents in Barbados and Jamaica to manage the sales of the resilient captives who staggered off their vessels. This placement of company agents institutionalized the entrepôts, ensuring that Royal African Company ships would return year after year unless overwhelming market forces overcame the corporate inertia that confined trade to these markets. Inadvertently, by concentrating deliveries in just these two colonies, the Royal African Company created an impetus for intercolonial trade and relegated all other colonies to a disadvantageous position in that commerce. Other English colonies became captive markets for the captive people exported from Barbados and Jamaica. Desperate for labor, but too small or cash-strapped to attract direct African trade, these other colonies would be forced to settle for whichever people the entrepôt colonies chose to send onward.[9]

8. David Eltis, *The Rise of African Slavery in the Americas* (New York, 2000), 210–211. Stephanie E. Smallwood notes Antigua's sending Africans to some other islands in the late seventeenth century (Smallwood, *Saltwater Slavery: A Middle Passage from Africa to American Diaspora* [Cambridge, Mass., 2007], 173–174).

9. On the relative size of various empires' transatlantic trades, see *Voyages*, accessed November 2010, http://slavevoyages.org/tast/assessment/estimates.faces?yearFrom=1501&yearTo=1866. The Royal African Company was predated by earlier English joint-stock companies, including the Company of Royal Adventurers Trading to Africa, but these predecessors delivered few Africans to the Americas; see K. G. Davies, *The Royal African Company* (New York, 1957); George Frederick Zook, *The Company of Royal Adventurers Trading into Africa* (Lancaster, Pa., 1919). Geography was also a factor in Barbados's prominence in the early English slave trade (and England's decision to settle there in the first place). As the easternmost Caribbean island, Barbados made a logical first stop for vessels from Africa. And since the prevailing winds and currents travel from east to west in the region, the island was not easily reached from hostile Spanish settlements; see Richard S. Dunn, *Sugar and Slaves: The Rise of the Planter Class in the English West Indies, 1624–1713* (1972; rpt. Chapel Hill, N.C., 2000), 17–18.

■ With transatlantic slave traders concentrating deliveries in Barbados and Jamaica but without a robust intercolonial trade network to disperse the people they delivered, the result was haphazard, irregular African arrivals in the secondary ports of seventeenth-century English America, which frustrated aspiring slaveholders. The marketplace lacked enough intercolonial merchants to even out discrepancies between supply and demand in various colonies. Instead, individuals on both sides of the colonial slave market—sellers struggling to find buyers and buyers struggling to find workers—engineered isolated transshipments to solve their problems. The general trend was a dispersal of African people from the entrepôts of the transatlantic trade to colonies that lacked a direct link with Africa, but this dispersal operated intermittently, organized in a number of different ways, as prospective buyers and sellers of people sought to overcome the challenges of underdeveloped intercolonial trade.

On one side of this equation, sellers of African people in the entrepôts occasionally had difficulty selling some or all of their captives to local slaveholders. Markets glutted, and even in good times, buyers deemed individual Africans undesirable for enslavement. In the major markets, sellers had to meet high standards because preferable candidates for exploitation frequently sailed in from the Middle Passage. Planters in colonies lacking direct access to Africa could not afford to be so discriminating. They were clamoring for slaves—virtually any slaves. Sellers in the entrepôts, including the Royal African Company's agents, called "factors," capitalized on this demand elsewhere by rerouting captives they had a hard time selling. The company's ship *James* executed such a transshipment after delivering captives from Africa to Barbados. More than a year after leaving England, having spent over seven months acquiring people on the Gold Coast, Captain Peter Blake finally guided the *James* to Barbados in May 1676. But with his transatlantic voyage completed and his captives delivered to the company's agents, Blake did not sail for England. Instead, to his surprise, Blake received orders to take other Africans—different people from those he ferried across the Atlantic—on board his ship. Edwyn Stede and Stephen Gascoigne, the company factors in Barbados, commanded Blake "with all expedition to fitt my Shipp to take in Capt. Reckords Slaves [223 in number] to carry them downe to Nevis." A Captain Samuel Reckord had delivered Africans from the Bight of Biafra to Barbados around the same time that Blake delivered his from the Gold Coast, so these captives boarding Blake's ship in Barbados were almost certainly the survivors of Reckord's Atlantic crossing. In ordering Blake to ferry these presumably Igbo prisoners to Nevis, Stede and Gascoigne accomplished two goals. Most important, they dispersed African laborers to another English market with demand. But which captives faced transshipment was not merely chance. The company factors distributed people with their perceived marketability in mind, sending those deemed least desirable to a port receiving less frequent African arrivals. This strategy can be gleaned from the reaction in Nevis. When the *James* arrived there, the governor, General William Stapleton, complained that the trans-shipped captives were "Calabars"—a label Europeans applied to people who embarked for the Middle Passage from the Bight of Biafra, where the principal slave-trading town in the region was Old Calabar. Most "Calabars" were Igbo people, though smaller numbers of Efiks, Ibibios, and assorted others also embarked on the Middle Passage from the region. Regardless of their actual ethnolinguistic mix, English colonial planters judged the so-called "Calabars" the least suitable slaves—hence the Royal African Company's decision to have Blake carry "Calabars" away from Barbados, where buyers had other options once the *James* arrived with people from the Gold Coast (probably Akans), whom planters preferred. At least that was the interpretation of Governor Stapleton of Nevis, whom Blake reported protesting that "he did believe that I had on boord all the refuse of the Shipps that were att Barbadoes." What is remarkable, however, is that despite Stapleton's complaints, all the trans-shipped "Calabars" sold quickly in Nevis. Buyers in Nevis might grumble, but they lacked choices. And they wanted exploitable labor badly enough to be willing to settle.[10]

In 1679, Stede and Gascoigne organized a similar transshipment. When the "stinking foule and nasty" *Marigold* limped into Bridgetown's harbor from the Bight of Biafra, the factors chastised the ship's captain for letting such wretched conditions ravage his human cargo. More than one hundred of the *Marigold*'s prisoners had died before reaching the Caribbean, and many of

---

10. Captain Blake's journal of the "Voyage of the James, 1675–1676," in Donnan, ed., *Documents*, I, 205–206. For more on the voyage of the *James* from England to the Gold Coast to Barbados, see *Voyages*, accessed December 2010, Voyage ID no. 9968. The "Capt. Reckords Slaves" mentioned in Blake's letter, whom Stapleton described as "Calabars," almost certainly were captives from the transatlantic slave ship *John Alexander*, which was captained by a Samuel Reckord and which delivered captives from the Bight of Biafra to the English Caribbean that same spring of 1676. The *Voyages* database indicates that the *James Alexander* delivered the slaves directly to Nevis rather than Barbados, but given Blake's account of moving the captives from Barbados to Nevis in the *James*, it seems likely that the *John Alexander* delivered the people to Barbados from whence they were transshipped. See *Voyages*, accessed December 2010, Voyage ID no. 9971. On seventeenth-century planters' bias against Africans from the Bight of Biafra, see Eltis, *Rise of African Slavery*, 108. On the prominence of Old Calabar until at least 1750, see David Eltis and David Richardson, *Atlas of the Transatlantic Slave Trade* (New Haven, Conn., 2010), 126.

the survivors were sick. Yet rather than land the ailing Igbo captives for recuperation, the factors hired a vessel to transship 115 of them to Nevis. The company's motivation for the transshipment was partly just to supply Nevis with desired slaves—the *Marigold*'s original instructions had been to deliver to that island—but Stede and Gascoigne also considered Nevis a better market for selling people whom planters did not consider optimal.[11]

Such early transshipments were often afterthoughts for the shippers. Agents for transatlantic traders, especially for the Royal African Company, sold captives in their first American port, if possible. The people whom the agents managed to sell quickly fetched the highest prices, as early buyers selected those perceived as strong and healthy. As sales progressed, captives who did not sell right away often garnered only half the price of those sold first. The slow-selling people were often those suffering most—the sick, the very young, the aging, the crippled, the dying. Traders and planters had a name for these worst-off victims of the slave trade: "refuse." The logic of human commodification led merchants to see the sick, aged, and injured as trade problems rather than as people worthy of compassion.[12]

Such behavior from agents in the transatlantic trade was in marked contrast to intercolonial speculators' engagement in slave transshipment. Selling agents owned these ailing captives whether they liked it or not, but speculating intercolonial traders would only purchase people in an entrepôt if they had hopes of reselling them profitably. Speculators opted for those Africans most likely to command high prices in their destination market—namely, healthy and strong young adults. Selling agents for transatlantic traders, by contrast, typically transshipped people they deemed undesirable. In the underdeveloped economy of seventeenth-century English America, these dealers counted on the many bypassed colonies to serve as captive markets for captive Africans. This left planters in the Leeward Islands and other such neglected markets to complain of receiving the "refuse" after Barbados planters had their pick.[13]

11. Edwyn Stede and Stephen Gascoigne to the Royal African Company, Barbados, June 10, 1679, in Donnan, ed., *Documents*, I, 249–250. See also *Voyages*, accessed December 2010, Voyage ID no. 15060.

12. Galenson's study of the Royal African Company's slave sales in Barbados documents the trend of dramatically falling prices toward the end of sales (*Traders, Planters, and Slaves*, 55, 74–80). For nice discussions of Europeans' sense of difference from Africans as vital to the decision to enslave and trade people as commodities, see Eltis, *Rise of African Slavery*, chap. 3.

13. Dunn, *Sugar and Slaves*, 235. Also in British America, W. E. Minchinton notes that Virginians often received slaves not wanted in the South Carolina market; see Minchinton, "The Slave Trade of Bristol with the British Mainland Colonies in North America, 1699–1770," in Roger An-

On the rare occasions when traders from Africa did deliver captives to the smaller markets, the consequence was often more transshipment. Small markets easily glutted when transatlantic merchants, who generally carried several hundred captives, delivered to areas where too few colonists could afford enslaved labor. In 1708, when Lieutenant Governor Benjamin Bennett of Bermuda reported to the Board of Trade that his colony had "been supplyed with negroes . . . from Barbados," he also noted two incidents during the late seventeenth century—more than ten years apart—in which traders delivered Africans directly to Bermuda. In each instance, Bermuda lacked enough buyers locally to purchase all the arriving people: in the first case, Bennett reported, half of the Africans "were reshipt for Carolina and Virginia"; in the second, "most of them was carry'd to North Carolina, Virga, and placed on the Continent." Bennett does not specify who transshipped these Africans, but their arrival at a negligible port for the slave trade and their subsequent departure for more viable markets represent mistakes or experiments in the early decades of the commerce. Bermuda was so crowded that the colony barred further English immigration in 1658 and the importation of African American and native American slaves in 1675; the transatlantic shippers who delivered these captives to Bermuda erred in their assessment of local demand, bringing about intercolonial shipments along unusual routes.[14]

■ Whereas some seventeenth-century African immigrants to English America faced transshipment when agents struggled to unload them, others faced transshipment when frustrated slave buyers in outlying colonies solved problems of their own. In the first century of the English slave trade, many Africans endured a final passage, not on the initiative of merchants in the major entrepôts, but more directly at the behest of planters in regions inadequately supplied with African labor. Some labor-starved planters, disappointed with offers of slaves they considered "refuse" or unable to find people for sale at all, organized transshipments themselves. Edmund Scarborough personally ventured from his plantation on the Eastern Shore of Virginia to New Amsterdam

---

stey and P. E. H. Hair, eds., *Liverpool, the African Slave Trade, and Abolition: Essays to Illustrate Current Knowledge and Research* (Bristol, 1976), 46.

14. Benjamin Bennett to Board of Trade, Bermuda, Aug. 14, 1708, in Donnan, ed., *Documents*, II, 48; Michael J. Jarvis, *In the Eye of All Trade: Bermuda, Bermudians, and the Maritime Atlantic World, 1680–1783* (Chapel Hill, N.C., 2010), 56. Another possible explanation for the deliveries to Bermuda from Africa was some type of nautical problem that forced the slave-trading vessels to stop at the islands and prevented them from proceeding to more lucrative markets.

in 1655 to acquire slaves for himself, and possibly for neighbors as well. The first direct shipments from Africa to New Netherland had flooded the small market for slaves in that colony, and presumably Scarborough caught wind of it.[15]

If settlers from remote colonies lacked cash for such purchases, they needed to venture to entrepôts with something (or someone) to offer in exchange for enslaved Africans. Some hatched schemes equal parts callous and enterprising for this purpose. In 1645, Emanuel Downing proposed to John Winthrop that Massachusetts send Narragansett captives from an anticipated (hoped-for?) conflict to the West Indies in order to trade them for African slaves. "If upon a Just warre [with the Narragansetts] the Lord should deliver them into our hands," Downing wrote, "wee might easily have men, woemen, and children enough to exchange for Moores [Africans], which wil be more gaynefull pilladge for us then wee conceive, for I doe not see how wee can thrive untill wee get into a stock of slaves sufficient to doe all our buisiness [*sic*]." With his reference to women and children, Downing clearly indicates that soldiers were not the only enemies he considered fit for enslavement. Neither were such transactions merely hypothetical. Similar exchange of North American Indians for enslaved Africans in the West Indies may account for the earliest African arrivals in New England. Africans reached Massachusetts as early as 1638, when the Salem ship *Desire* returned from the West Indies, having exchanged captives from the Pequot War for both produce and African people.[16]

Such excursions to distant entrepôts by colonists seeking slaves were not typical, however. Most planters doubtless preferred to select slaves person-

15. For Scarborough in New Amsterdam, see "Order of the Council of New Netherland, 1655," in Donnan, ed., *Documents*, IV, 49–50; for more on Scarborough's place on Virginia's Eastern Shore, see T. H. Breen and Stephen Innes, *"Myne Owne Ground": Race and Freedom on Virginia's Eastern Shore, 1640–1676* (1980; rpt. New York, 2005), 11, 48–51. Officials in the Dutch West India Company encouraged sales of enslaved Africans from their colonies to neighboring English territories; see Joyce D. Goodfriend, "Burghers and Blacks: The Evolution of a Slave Society at New Amsterdam," *New York History*, LIX (1978), 136–137; see also Peter H. Wood, *Strange New Land: Africans in Colonial America* (New York, 2003), 20.

16. Emanuel Downing to John Winthrop, 1645, in Donnan, ed., *Documents*, III, 8. For more on the trade in native American slaves, see Gallay, *Indian Slave Trade*. Some suggest that the first Africans reached New England even earlier, with Chelsea, Mass., merchant Samuel Maverick possibly owning enslaved Africans by 1624, but the evidence is spotty; see Lorenzo Johnston Greene, *The Negro in Colonial New England, 1620–1776* (New York, 1942), 15–18; Edgar J. McManus, *Black Bondage in the North* (Syracuse, N.Y., 1973), 6; Wood, *Strange New Land*, 21. Linda M. Heywood and John K. Thornton suggest arrivals of slaves from Providence Island in the early 1630s (Heywood and Thornton, *Central Africans, Atlantic Creoles, and the Foundation of the Americas, 1585–1660* [New York, 2007], 32).

ally out of vessels arriving from Africa, but the sporadic timing of transatlantic shipments and the cost of travel to distant ports prevented most remote buyers from traveling to make purchases. Instead, aspiring slaveholders in neglected regions often courted shipments of Africans aggressively. For instance, frustrated by the Royal African Company's lack of deliveries to Virginia, the colony's assembly in 1660 encouraged Dutch shipments by exempting foreign vessels delivering Africans from paying export duties on tobacco. The law did not specify whether the anticipated Dutch shipments would come directly from Africa or from the Dutch Caribbean, but Virginians were clearly looking to attract shipments of enslaved people. Unfortunately for the labor-hungry Chesapeake planters, England's Navigation Act passed the same year made tobacco sales to foreign dealers illegal, and news of that law reached the colony less than a year later.[17]

As a result, the more common procedure of prospective buyers in secondary ports was to contact merchants or acquaintances in the entrepôts to request slave purchases—and transshipments—on their behalf. The merchants executing such orders placed themselves at considerably less risk than if they speculated on Africans, merely hoping to find buyers in a secondary port after transshipment. Instead, the buyer in the secondary port assumed the risk, trusting his correspondent in the entrepôt to choose slaves wisely and to negotiate good prices on his behalf. In 1685, William Byrd wrote to the merchants Sadler and Thomas of Barbados, requesting that when a Captain Wynne sailed from Barbados to Virginia, "These following Goods may be sent on my particular account; viz. 4 Negros, 2 men and 2 women, not to exceed 25 years old and to bee likely [i.e., desirable]." Beyond rough age and gender guidelines, Byrd left most of the details of price and selection to his Barbadian agents.[18]

Remote buyers like Byrd often felt that agents in the entrepôts abused their trust. In 1706, David Jeffries of Boston asked an agent in Jamaica to purchase several slaves for him, with a disappointing outcome. Jeffries complained, in a petition regarding import duties paid on the captives, that instead of people considered useful, he had received "a negro woman named Bilhah and four Small children one that Sucked at her Breast." Jeffries implored the colony to refund the import duty, insisting, "These sd Children were not worth the

17. Donnan, ed., *Documents*, IV, 5. For a more detailed discussion of the factors discouraging planters from traveling to the major entrepôts to purchase slaves, see Galenson, *Traders, Planters, and Slaves*, 119–120.

18. "William Byrd I to Messrs Sadler and Thomas, Merchants in Barbados, Virginia, 10 Feb., 1685," Letters of William Byrd I, Byrd Family Papers, MSS 1 B9968a, fols. 54–55, Virginia Historical Society, Richmond.

Money." His grievance illustrates the hazard of delegating purchases to a distant merchant, but with few or no ships arriving in a colony from Africa, many aspiring slaveholders continued to request that agents in an entrepôt buy and transship people on their behalf. Jeffries's experience also underscores yet again that African people deemed poor workers—in this case, children and a nursing mother—faced a likelihood of transshipment in this developmental period.[19]

■ Although many seventeenth-century slave merchants waited for buyers from more remote regions to come to them (in person or with written requests), a few traders saw promise in speculating on African people for transshipment. Recognizing that the Royal African Company failed to reach all potential markets—most notably in the Chesapeake—some early intercolonial dealers sensed opportunity. Virginia had been the first English American colony to import Africans, with people trickling in from 1619, but it was slow to become a major destination of African traders. Dutch privateers who captured Portuguese slavers supplied some of Virginia's early African settlers in exchange for tobacco and provisions, but especially after the 1660 Navigation Act barred Dutch shipping from English colonies, Barbados emerged as Virginia's key source of slaves. Around the same time, interest among Chesapeake planters for shifting from indentured English workers to enslaved African labor was waxing, but with sugar booming in the English Caribbean, the Royal African Company still ignored Virginia almost entirely. Transshipments from Barbados filled the void. Meanwhile, the Chesapeake also saw growing demand for sugar-related products from the Caribbean. Given these circumstances, some traders in the late seventeenth century believed that the most advantageous route from England to the Chesapeake was indirect, via Barbados. Merchant James Coates explained to Liverpool traders Benjamin Weston and Richard Norris in 1692, "To Send a Ship for Virginia his best way is to touch heare [Barbados], and . . . procure Rum, molasses, and Sug'r, w'ch with a very Small Cargo of Dry Course Goods properly Sorted for Virginia trade, will procure tobacco quicker and on better terms than any Europe Cargo alone doth or can." By the late seventeenth century, many traders to Virginia engaged in this alternate triangle trade, linking England, the Caribbean, and the Chesapeake.[20]

19. Petition of David Jeffries, June 12, 1707, in Donnan, ed., *Documents*, III, 23.

20. James Coates to Benjamin Weston and Richard Norris, Barbados, July 11, 1692, Norris Papers, II, 920 NOR 2/26, Liverpool Record Office, U.K. For discussion of the trade loop from En-

Coates did not designate Africans specifically as part of his suggested cargo, but other traders recognized that slave transshipment complemented such activities. In 1684, William Byrd reported to trading partners the arrival of a Captain Paggen from Barbados, delivering "34 negros, with a considerable quantity of Dry Goods, and 7 or 8 tun of Rum and Sugar." Byrd considered the shipment so well suited to the Virginia market that he anticipated a clamor for the goods and exploitable people that Paggen delivered to Virginia. "I fear [it] will bring our people much in debt," he insisted, "and occasion them to bee carelesse with the Tobacco they make." [21] Paggen repeated the voyage the following year, prompting Byrd to reiterate his impression of Virginians' enthusiasm for transshipments of Africans. He proposed to his partners that they send one of their own vessels on a similar voyage, under Captain Wynne. "The proposition abt negro's I hope will bee comply'd wth and Wynne dispatched, for Paggen's Concerne may justly glory in the trade of this River haveing been mighty Successful these two last years." Since the Royal African Company was failing to supply Virginia with enough captives to meet demand, Byrd, Paggen, and other merchants recognized that Africans could be purchased in Barbados for profitable resale in the Chesapeake. Slave transshipment was no afterthought for these traders, not just a way to dispose of people regarded as undesirable by the Barbados market. Instead, they speculated in African people as commodities, buying them in one American market with the sole intent of reselling them in another.[22]

Byrd even pushed the argument for this trade beyond the assertion that people could be sold for more in Virginia than in Barbados. Slave transshipments, he suggested, enhanced access to the profitable export trade in tobacco from the Chesapeake. In 1683, when discussing a proposed venture, Byrd cautioned his English partners, Perry and Lane, "If your designe by Barbadoes fails, we shall bee fairly disappointed, for without Servants or Slaves, no great Crop [of Virginia tobacco] is now to be purchased." In other words, Byrd considered labor one of the best commodities to exchange for a share of the tobacco export trade, especially in years when the tobacco harvest was small. Slave transshipment from Barbados to Virginia not only offered an opportu-

gland to the English Caribbean and to Virginia, see John C. Coombs, "Seventeenth-Century Chesapeake–West Indian Commerce and the Coastwise Trade in Slaves," unpublished paper, generously shared by the author. On transatlantic arrivals, see *Voyages,* accessed November 2010, http://www.slavevoyages.org/tast/database/search.faces?yearFrom=1601&yearTo=1700&mjslptimp=21000.21100.

21. William Byrd to Perry and Lane, Virginia, June 21, 1684, in Donnan, ed., *Documents,* IV, 59.
22. Byrd to Perry and Lane, Virginia, Mar. 29, 1685, ibid., 61 n. 2.

nity for profitable sales but also could facilitate other branches of Chesapeake trade.[23]

Meanwhile, alongside the triangle trade connecting England, Barbados, and Virginia, a bilateral Chesapeake-Caribbean trade emerged. As planters in the islands focused solely on sugar, some Virginia planters began producing provisions for the Caribbean. In exchange for feeding the islands, Virginians carried sugar products and enslaved people back to the Old Dominion. Even by the last decades of the seventeenth century, when direct African shipments gained ascendancy in Virginia's slave trade, transshipment from the Caribbean not only continued to supplement African deliveries but actually grew alongside the transatlantic trade. Colonial merchants regularly traded between the Chesapeake and Caribbean, and slave trading facilitated this commerce. Barbados shipping lists for the 1680s and 1690s show frequent trade with Virginia outside the years of King William's War (1688–1697). The 1680s' port records left the exact cargoes in such trade undocumented, but shipping lists from after the war show nearly one-quarter of voyages from Barbados to Virginia carrying slaves. It seems unlikely that fewer shipments in the 1680s included captives, since African arrivals in Barbados in that decade actually outpaced those of the 1690s.[24]

As ever more Chesapeake planters in the late seventeenth century shifted to exploiting enslaved labor, intercolonial trade from the Caribbean supplied a significant minority of the Africans reaching the region, especially until the Royal African Company's monopoly was repealed in 1698 (see Table 5). Transshipments reached significant enough volume, in fact, that interlopers in the

23. Byrd to Perry and Lane, Virginia, Mar. 26, 1683, MSS 1 B9968a, fols. 39–41.

24. Susan Westbury describes a "dividing line" in the 1670s between the period when Chesapeake slaves arrived from the West Indies and when they arrived from Africa, but that suggests too stark a contrast; arrivals from the West Indies never ceased. Proportionally, direct African shipments contributed most people after 1670, but intercolonial shipments actually grew in volume as well. See Westbury, "Slaves of Colonial Virginia: Where They Came From," *WMQ*, 3d Ser., XLII (1985), 229. On the rise of Barbados-Virginia trading in the seventeenth century, see John C. Coombs, "Building 'the Machine': The Development of Slavery and Slave Society in Early Colonial Virginia" (Ph.D. diss., College of William and Mary, 2003), chap. 2; Coombs, "The Phases of Conversion: A New Chronology for the Rise of Slavery in Early Virginia," *WMQ*, 3d Ser., LXVIII (2011), 343, 358. In the eighteenth century, the lower James River region continued to import more slaves from the Caribbean than did other parts of the colony, probably because that part of the colony focused on the provision trade with the islands; see Coombs, "Building 'the Machine,'" 93; and Lorena S. Walsh, "The Chesapeake Slave Trade: Regional Patterns, African Origins, and Some Implications," *WMQ*, 3d Ser., LVIII (2001), 146. On the likelihood of significant slave trading in the early Barbados-Virginia trade, see Coombs, "Seventeenth-Century Chesapeake–West Indian Commerce."

TABLE 5. Estimates of Enslaved People Arriving in the Chesapeake via Transatlantic and Intercolonial Trade, 1661–1710

Year	People imported directly from Africa	People imported from the Caribbean	Total	% from the Caribbean
1661–1665	1,600	150	1,750	9
1666–1670	0	150	150	100
1671–1675	625	225	850	26
1676–1680	1,775	225	2,000	11
1681–1685	100	625	725	86
1686–1690	2,125	500	2,625	19
1691–1695	1,925	400	2,325	17
1696–1700	3,300	500	3,800	13
1701–1705	5,575	525	6,100	9
1706–1710	7,225	500	7,725	6
TOTAL	24,250	3,800	28,050	14

Sources: For direct African shipments: *Voyages: The Trans-Atlantic Slave Trade Database,* accessed November 2010 (http://slavevoyages.org/tast/assessment/estimates.faces?yearFrom=1661&yearTo=1710&disembarkation=202). For Caribbean transshipments: Gregory E. O'Malley, "Beyond the Middle Passage: Slave Migration from the Caribbean to North America, 1619–1807," *William and Mary Quarterly,* 3d Ser., LXVI (2009), 141, 146. For an explanation of the five-year intervals, see Appendix, below.

transatlantic trade might have used the intercolonial traffic for cover. In 1688, the Royal African Company asserted that interlopers were acquiring slaves illegally in Africa and then sailing to Virginia, where they hoped to blend in with transshipments from Barbados. English authorities deemed this threat to the company's monopoly serious enough that the crown ordered its naval ketch *Deptford* to patrol the ports and coasts of the Chesapeake to enforce trade laws. At the company's urging, the crown instructed the *Deptford* to "take care all Shipps and vessels Importing Negroes from Guiney" have licenses from the Royal African Company and "that all Negroes Imported . . . from any of his Maj's Plantations in America be Certified under the hand of the Governor or Comander in Chief of such Plantations, that such negroes were Lawfully and fairely Shipt." Robust enough to cover illegal trafficking, the intercolonial trade had come into its own.[25]

25. "Orders and Instructions for Captain Thomas Perry Comander of his Ma'ty Ketch the Deptford," Dec. 31, 1688, CO 1/65, fols. 371–372.

TABLE 6. African Regional Background of Captives Delivered to Barbados
and Jamaica, 1601–1700

	Senegambia	Gold Coast	Bight of Benin	Bight of Biafra	West Central Africa	Other
Pre-1651	4,600	1,400	0	18,800	100	1,100
1651–1675	4,800	15,500	10,900	40,600	1,800	6,800
1676–1700	14,200	28,300	61,200	23,900	30,300	8,400
TOTAL	23,600	45,200	72,100	83,300	32,200	16,300
(N = 272,700)	9%	17%	26%	31%	12%	6%

Source: *Voyages: The Trans-Atlantic Slave Trade Database,* accessed August 2012 (http://slavevoyages
.org/tast/assessment/estimates.faces?yearFrom=1601&yearTo=1700&disembarkation=301.302).

■ The patterns of this nascent intercolonial slave trade had vital implications
for the captives it carried and for the communities they created in American
colonies. Because Barbados and, eventually, Jamaica were the main depots
from which Africans traveled to other English colonies, the African regional
backgrounds of captives arriving in both islands reveal something of the
ethnocultural makeup of the early African populations elsewhere. People who
departed Africa from the Bights of Benin and Biafra each accounted for between one-quarter and one-third of the forced migration to Barbados and
Jamaica, with captives from Senegambia, the Gold Coast, and west central
Africa also composing smaller but significant portions of the population (see
Table 6). Presumably, people from all of these regions entered the intercolonial slave trade, but the decisions traders made suggest that these people were
not all equally likely to face transshipment. If traders like Stede and Gascoigne
were typical in transshipping captives from the Bight of Biafra away from the
principal American markets, Igbos were probably overrepresented in colonies
that relied on intercolonial shipments of slaves. As such, the Igbos would have
been less prominent in seventeenth-century Barbados and Jamaica than the
data on the transatlantic trade alone suggests.[26]

26. For the ethnic backgrounds of captives from the Bights of Benin and Biafra, see Patrick
Manning, *Slavery, Colonialism, and Economic Growth in Dahomey, 1640–1960* (New York, 1982),
30; Paul E. Lovejoy, *Transformations in Slavery: A History of Slavery in Africa,* 3d ed. (New York,
2012), 79; Femi J. Kolapo, "The Igbo and Their Neighbours during the Era of the Atlantic Slave-
Trade," *Slavery and Abolition,* XXV, no. 1 (April 2004), 114–133; David Northrup, "Igbo and Myth
Igbo: Culture and Ethnicity in the Atlantic World, 1600–1850," *Slavery and Abolition,* XXI, no. 3

Ethnicity was not the only factor in captive sorting in the seventeenth-century entrepôts, however, and the biases of slave traders made the seventeenth century a particularly hazardous time to face a final passage between colonies. Since Jamaican and Barbadian factors sometimes took advantage of smaller markets to unload less desirable captives, sick and infirm Africans often boarded intercolonial voyages. The lack of surviving colonial port records from the seventeenth century does not allow for calculations of mortality in the traffic of the period, but there are two compelling reasons to presume that final passages were especially deadly before 1700. First, even the transatlantic trade suffered higher mortality in the seventeenth century than later, as traders exhibited less knowledge or concern of the importance of short voyages, shipboard sanitation, hydration, and provisioning. There is little reason to assume that intercolonial traders of the period knew better. Second, the practice of transshipping ailing captives—those most in danger of dying themselves and most likely to pass communicable diseases to shipmates—surely heightened the risks.[27]

Illness and mortality were only the most obvious perils facing Africans chosen for transshipment in the early decades of the traffic. Since most were bound for regions with less developed slave regimes, captives also faced isolation, especially if carried to the North American mainland. Whereas Africans toiling on large Barbadian and Jamaican sugar plantations would have lived among or near at least some people sharing their native language and culture, people transshipped to areas where slavery was not (or not yet) the dominant labor regime often lacked such company. If they survived the perilous journey, African settlers in seventeenth-century Massachusetts, Pennsylvania, or even Virginia faced a danger of settling among no one who spoke their language or understood their folkways, even if a few other Africans lived in their communities. However, a forced migration toward the margins of the English colonial slave system presented potential opportunities, as well, to those who survived the journey. Slavery in the sugar islands was notoriously harsh and deadly, and captives might have found less terrible circumstances after trans-

---

(December 2000), 1–20. For a more detailed analysis of intercolonial slave trading's impact on the ethnic makeup of enslaved populations in the Carolinas, see Gregory E. O'Malley, "Diversity in the Slave Trade to the Colonial Carolinas," in Michelle LeMaster and Bradford J. Wood, eds., *Creating and Contesting Carolina: Proprietary Era Histories* (Columbia, S.C., 2013), 234–255.

27. On the decline in shipboard mortality from the seventeenth to the eighteenth century, see Herbert S. Klein et al., "Transoceanic Mortality: The Slave Trade in Comparative Perspective," *WMQ*, 3d Ser., LVIII (2001), 100–101; Eltis and Richardson, *Atlas of the Transatlantic Slave Trade*, 169–179.

shipment, especially since social relations between blacks and whites were often more fluid in smaller households. Some African settlers in seventeenth-century North America would take advantage of relatively inchoate slave regimes to carve out a more advantageous existence—whether a less onerous brand of slavery or, by some combination of luck and pluck, emancipation.[28]

Furthermore, owing to patterns in the intercolonial trade, African settlers in North America who were not completely isolated might have benefited from slightly better prospects of family formation. When Byrd requested that the four Africans sent to him from Barbados in 1685 be "2 men and 2 women, not to exceed 25 years old," the gender balance of his preferred captives is striking—especially since males accounted for nearly 60 percent of Africans arriving in the Caribbean during the last third of the seventeenth century. Whereas slave buyers in the sugar islands typically exhibited a preference for males, Byrd's desire for an even sex ratio suggests an interest in seeing his slaves propagate. Though Byrd's interest in reproduction was likely economic—a desire to treat slaves like breeding livestock—for the captives, the consequence might have been a chance to form something like a normal family, even under the hardships of dislocation and enslavement. Sketchy seventeenth-century records make it impossible to calculate gender ratios in the intercolonial slave trade systematically, but anecdotal accounts such as Byrd's combined with traders' inclination to transship less economically valuable slaves (a category that included females) make it plausible that colonies receiving intercolonial shipments developed populations with more balanced sex ratios. The lack of choice for enslaved people should not be sugarcoated, but in some cases, gender parity could have provided solace and facilitated the sustenance of African traditions.[29]

28. For a good start on the less rigid slave regimes of seventeenth-century North America, see Breen and Innes, *"Myne Owne Ground"*; Berlin, *Many Thousands Gone*, 15–92; Douglas Deal, "A Constricted World: Free Blacks on Virginia's Eastern Shore, 1680–1750," in Lois Green Carr, Philip D. Morgan, and Jean B. Russo, eds., *Colonial Chesapeake Society* (Chapel Hill, N.C., 1988), 275–305.

29. Jennifer Morgan has demonstrated that planters—especially in developing slaveholding regions—often sought to acquire slave women for their combined value in agricultural work and reproduction. She also notes that gender ratios affected slave life far beyond the repercussions for reproduction; they "fundamentally shaped the experience of enslavement and carried with them complexities of identity, family formation, political culture, and emotional wholeness" (*Laboring Women*, 6, 77–92). On the proportion of males in the late-seventeenth-century slave trade to the Caribbean, see *Voyages*, accessed August 2012, http://slavevoyages.org/tast /database/search.faces?yearFrom=1663&yearTo=1700&mjslptimp=30000; Eltis, *Rise of African Slavery*, 95.

■ In 1698, the crown revoked the Royal African Company's monopoly on slave deliveries to English America, marking a turning point for the intercolonial slave trade. In the Chesapeake, for example, in preceding decades, the company's direct shipments from Africa had eclipsed transshipment by only a narrow margin, but after 1698, private traders would accelerate direct African shipments to the region. As Edmund Jennings, the president of the Virginia Council, reported to the Board of Trade in 1708, "before the year 1680 what negros were brought to Virginia were imported generally from Barbados." From 1680 to 1698, shipments from Africa became more common, "tho not in any proportion to what it hath been of late." With the transatlantic trade open to both the Royal African Company and independent traders, Jennings asserted that imports from Africa to Virginia boomed between 1699 and 1708, with the company delivering 679 Africans—and separate traders delivering 5,928 people.[30]

Virginia was not the only colony to see direct African trade blossom. Maryland's governor, John Seymour, offered a similar account. "Before the year 1698," he wrote, "this province has been supplyd by some small Quantitys of Negro's from Barbados and other her Ma'tys Islands and Plantations, as Jamaica and New England Seaven, eight, nine or ten in a Sloope." With the end of the monopoly, however, Seymour noted a dramatic change. The direct African "Trade seems to run high. . . . And the Planters owne themselves obliged to the separate Traders for these supplys, having never had any from the [Royal African] Company."[31]

Given this unshackling of the African trade from the company's nearly exclusive focus on Barbados and Jamaica, the other ports of English America ceased to be captive markets for captive Africans from the two entrepôts. One might expect intercolonial slave trading to have dwindled after 1698. As separate traders increased the direct supply of Africans to a wider range of colonies, one reason for the intercolonial slave trade seemed to disappear. But transshipments would only increase, even as formerly neglected colonies shifted to greater reliance on direct shipments. Across English America, demand for enslaved labor was surging and continuing to exceed transatlantic supply. Maryland's Act to Encourage the Importation of Negroes in 1704 recognized the continued importance of Caribbean sources by exempting Maryland vessels not only from import duties on slaves but also from duties on rum and sugar. Including these key Caribbean trade goods in a measure designed

30. Edmund Jennings to Board of Trade, Nov. 7, 1708, in Donnan, ed., *Documents*, IV, 89.
31. John Seymour to Board of Trade, 1708, ibid., 22.

to "Encourage the Importation of Negroes" shows that lawmakers considered the Caribbean a crucial source of slaves into the early eighteenth century. Furthermore, the sheer volume of intercolonial trade—in goods, not just in people—would increase dramatically over the century, offering a convenient platform for transshipments of African captives.[32]

Despite such continued reliance on intercolonial sources of slaves, the trade would need to evolve in the post-monopoly era. After 1698, intercolonial shipments would compete with ventures from Africa in most colonies, which required merchants to organize shipments in new ways. No longer would sellers in Barbados be able to foist ailing, unwanted Africans onto a host of other markets desperate for their labor. No longer would planters in Virginia have to write to acquaintances in the Caribbean to request purchases on their behalf. The captive markets for captive Africans would be harder and harder to find in the eighteenth century. The intercolonial slave commerce had previously been influenced by the shortage of supply in the English transatlantic trade, the restriction of that trade primarily to Barbados and Jamaica, and the nascent state of intercolonial trade in general. It was to become more sophisticated and more competitive, since buyers would have more routes to acquire enslaved Africans. More and more traders, like William Byrd before them, would become slave speculators, recognizing—and pouncing on—opportunities to traffic human cargoes between the colonies.

32. Act to Encourage the Importation of Negroes, 1704, ibid., 21.

4. To El Dorado via Slave Trade

OPENING COMMERCE WITH FOREIGN COLONIES, CA. 1660–1713

If we had negroes, the convenience of our ports . . . would certainly
draw all the trade [the Spanish] may have with strangers to us.
— Lt. Governor Thomas Lynch of Jamaica, 1682

Foreigners get the best of the negroes, and we only the refuse
at £22 a head. . . . Ready money has been refused because it was not
pieces-of-eight. — The Council and Assembly of Jamaica, 1686

In 1662, acting deputy governor of Jamaica Charles Lyttelton faced a
dilemma. Spanish American colonists kept arriving at his island with silver,
hoping to trade the mineral wealth of South America for African people delivered to Jamaica as slaves. Faced with these affluent outsiders, Lyttelton waffled
between chasing Spanish silver and upholding the law. On one hand, the English had spent the last century and a half pursuing Spanish American riches;
indeed, many English adventurers first sailed to the New World as pirates and
privateers, viewing Spanish treasure fleets as the ultimate prize. Now Spanish
colonists were sailing to English ports, begging for permission to leave their
silver behind when they departed. Surely, Lyttelton thought, this had to be a
good thing. On the other hand, Lyttelton's superiors had just laid down the
law against foreign trade. The Navigation Act of 1660 expressly forbade exports from all English colonies in foreign ships, so Spanish departures from
Jamaica with enslaved Africans would violate the act, since the law defined
African people as property. As a stand-in governor, Lyttelton faced a tricky
decision, and his choice reveals English imperial priorities in the second half
of the seventeenth century.

Although the letter of the law prohibited Spanish ships' trading at Jamaica,
Lyttelton concluded that the spirit of the law intended something different.
In his interpretation, when the Navigation Act discussed exports from England's colonies, the law's authors envisioned only colonial produce — sugar,
tobacco, timber — as likely exports. Under the reigning imperial philosophy

of the day, later dubbed "mercantilism," the utility of colonies rested in their gathering or cultivating such raw materials and exporting them to the mother country for manufacture or consumption. Furthermore, mercantilism dictated that colonies offered captive markets for the mother country's manufactured goods. When foreign vessels traded at English colonies, imperial policy makers feared the mother country would be cut out of both profitable aspects of holding colonies; New World produce slipped out of the empire, and foreign traders paid for it with European manufactured goods that competed with England's own exports.

Slave trading with Spanish American colonists did not fit neatly into this mercantilist conception of colonial trade. Africans' labor certainly helped cultivate the produce that made colonies profitable, but Lyttelton did not view selling some of these captive laborers to foreigners as cutting England out of its rightful colonial trade. The foreign slave trade lacked the problems of, say, a Dutch merchant in Virginia trading European manufactures for tobacco. No Jamaican sugar left the empire, and Spanish American buyers offered payment, not in European goods, but in silver or colonial produce. The only thing that pleased a mercantilist more than holding silver was taking it from his rivals. So Acting Deputy Governor Lyttelton boldly proclaimed that he considered fostering trade with Spanish colonists part of his mission for the king. Since Spanish officials refused to grant English slave traders access to their colonies, Lyttelton announced "that the Merchants and Inhabitants of the Island of Cuba, Hispagnola, or any other the King of Spain's Subjects in America shall receive free Trade and Comerce with the King my Majt's Subjects here."[1]

The crown quickly endorsed Lyttelton's actions. Upon hearing in 1663 that colonial officials in Barbados, unlike Lyttelton in Jamaica, had denied entrance to Spanish buyers seeking "a supply of Negro Slaves," the English Privy Council recognized the Navigation Act's potential to block opportunities to open Spanish American trade. In response, the council put Lyttelton's ad hoc policy on a more solid footing, announcing that allowing the trade

---

1. Charles Lyttelton, "A Proclamaçon," Sept. 21, 1662, HCA 49/59, fol. 12, National Archives, Kew. Lyttelton's predecessor in Jamaica had made a similar decision about prospective Spanish slave buyers in 1661. Since English merchants in the colony lacked slaves to offer at that moment, the governor purchased slaves from Dutch merchants to sell them to the Spanish buyers. The imports and exports canceled each other out, but the governor found Spanish slave buyers so tempting that he was less concerned with profiting from the immediate transaction than with establishing a more regular trade (George Frederick Zook, *The Company of Royal Adventurers Trading into Africa* [Lancaster, Pa., 1919], 84).

desired by the said Spaniards may redound not only to the increase of Our Revenue, but also to the signall Advantage of Our good Subjects both at home and abroad, . . . and judging that the cause doth not in any wise crosse the generall or speciall intention of the Act for Navigation,

. . . Wee do hereby give and graunt free licence and Warrant to any of the Spanish Subjects of America . . . to enter into any Road, Port or Haven, of Our said American Dominions . . . , and freely to sell, barter, and exchange . . . [for] Goods and Negroes.

This opening of trade was not without limits. The Spanish could only pay for Africans with the produce of their American colonies, including mining produce, not with European goods. The crown would not tolerate new competition for English merchants in supplying European goods to their own colonies. In addition, the Privy Council imposed a duty on each captive exported. That the council stipulated this duty as "Tenn peices [*sic*] of Eight for each Head"—pieces of eight being units of Spanish silver—reflects their powerful desire for Spanish specie.[2]

In the short term, this clarification of imperial policy in 1663 simply vindicated Lyttelton's opening of Jamaica to Spanish American traders, but the crown's endorsement of his move was also a harbinger of English policy toward Spanish America and the slave trade over a far lengthier span of time. For one thing, Lyttelton's choice and the subsequent Privy Council ruling reflected an important transition in English policy toward Spanish America. Where the first decades of English settlement in the Americas evinced overt hostility—most recently demonstrated by England's military seizure of Jamaica from the Spanish in 1655—the decision to welcome intercolonial trade with Spanish America in the 1660s exemplified a transition toward seeking a share of Span-

2. "The Privy Council to Francis Lord Willoughby," Whitehall, Mar. 11, 1663, in Elizabeth Donnan, ed., *Documents Illustrative of the History of the Slave Trade to America,* 4 vols. (Washington, D.C., 1930–1935), I, 161–164. English colonial officials continued to confiscate Spanish vessels for violating the Navigation Act if they failed to conduct trade according to the specific terms of the exemption to the law. One revealing example was the controversy over a Spanish sloop confiscated at Jamaica in 1688. The English seized the sloop for trading "contrary to the act of navegat'n" but later released it because the Spanish argued the "said sloop belongd to the assiento," and hence was legally acquiring slaves from the English (George Reid to a "Reverend Father," Jamaica, Dec. 14, 1688, CO 1/65, fols. 369–371, National Archives, Kew). On Spanish colonists' arriving in Jamaica to trade for enslaved Africans, see Zook, *Company of Royal Adventurers,* 84, 87; Nuala Zahedieh, "The Merchants of Port Royal, Jamaica, and the Spanish Contraband Trade, 1655–1692," *William and Mary Quarterly,* 3d Ser., XLIII (1986), 575.

ish wealth via trade rather than conquest. After the English Civil War, the restoration of Charles II to the throne in 1660 marked the end of the virulently anti-Catholic (and anti-Spanish) policies of the Interregnum, dominated by the Puritans. Charles II, and especially his successor, James II, struck a conciliatory tone with Spain, ensuring that the Privy Council's exception to the Navigation Act in 1663 was long lasting. The restored English monarchs also increased investment in the transatlantic slave trade, ensuring that a growing stream of forced African migrants would reach the English Caribbean. Under these policies, Spaniards sporadically ventured to Barbados and Jamaica for slaves through the remainder of the seventeenth century. The Africans who survived transshipment met a variety of fates: agricultural support of the mining industry in Peru; domestic service or artisanal trades in the bustling cities of the Spanish Main; or, for smaller numbers, ranching or diversified labor in the mixed economies of the Spanish Caribbean.[3]

The problem for England's hope of leveraging the slave trade to access Spanish America's silver mines was that the Spanish Empire still outlawed trade between its colonies and foreigners, with only occasional exceptions. As a result, from 1663 into the eighteenth century, English traders and imperial officials would seek a means of opening Spanish America to more extensive commerce. The English wanted to dominate the export of European manufactured goods to the whole of Spanish America, garnering silver in return. Unfortunately for these English dreams, the only exception to Spain's prohibition on its colonies' dealing with foreigners was the asiento de negros—the contract the Spanish crown granted to a foreign merchant to supply Spanish America with African laborers. The English never secured that contract in the seventeenth century, but since holders of the asiento often failed to satiate Spanish

3. For examples of Spanish settlers visiting Jamaica to buy slaves, see K. G. Davies, *The Royal African Company* (New York, 1957), 328–330. Spanish settlers in Peru preferred native Andean workers in the high-altitude mines and African labor in domestic service and in Peru's lowland agricultural sector (see Frederick P. Bowser, *The African Slave in Colonial Peru, 1524–1650* [Stanford, Calif., 1974]; James Lockhart, *Spanish Peru, 1532–1560: A Social History*, 2d ed. [1968; rpt. Madison, Wis., 1994], chap. 10). Enslaved people worked a range of jobs in colonial Mexico, but most were urban (see Colin A. Palmer, *Slaves of the White God: Blacks in Mexico, 1570–1650* [Cambridge, Mass., 1976], 43–45, 50). The Spanish Caribbean did not develop a plantation economy nor import numerous Africans until the mid-eighteenth century (Manuel Moreno Fraginals, *The Sugarmill: The Socioeconomic Complex of Sugar in Cuba, 1760–1860*, trans. Cedric Belfrage [New York, 1976], 15; Elena Andrea Schneider, "The Occupation of Havana: War, Trade, and Slavery in Eighteenth-Century Cuba" [Ph.D. diss., Princeton University, 2011]). In all regions, Spanish buyers were particularly interested in transshipments from English colonies when legal importation under the asiento faltered.

America's demand for slaves, the English did at least find a Spanish market for clandestine deliveries of human cargoes. Indeed, the desire for exploitable African people had brought Spanish settlers to Jamaica with silver in the early 1660s. From that point forward, many English traders and policy makers would view the slave trade as their best route to El Dorado—the mythical city of gold or silver rumored to lie somewhere in Spain's vast American claims.

The English appetite for Spanish silver (or cochineal, hides, or sugar) is not surprising, but their willingness to trade away African people to get Spanish American treasure highlights the pervasiveness of abstracting African people as commodities. Deputy Governor Lyttelton never argued that the Navigation Act did not apply to African people leaving the island because they were emigrants rather than exports. The slave trade rested on the thoroughgoing dehumanization and commodification of Africans in the minds of its practitioners and observers. Settlers in England's own American possessions clamored for laborers in the late seventeenth century, but policy makers, in focusing on African people's utility as commodities for bringing Spanish traders to the table, overlooked their value as laborers (to say nothing of their broader humanity). The policy of using the slave trade to open Spanish America to English commerce hinged on the abstraction of human commodification. Distant merchants and officials saw African people as just numbers tallied in ledgers and port records, commodities no different from others, leading English planters to complain that traders and policy makers had lost track of Africans' human value for labor.[4]

■ Involved in English plans to exploit the slave trade for access to Spanish America was the latter empire's unique limitations for African trade. From the fifteenth to the eighteenth centuries, alone among the European powers colonizing the Americas, Spain lacked an imperial or trading presence in West Africa. This predicament dated back to the Treaty of Tordesillas of 1494, in which the Papacy, Spain, and Portugal—with astonishing hubris—divided sovereignty over the entire non-European, non-Christian world between the two crowns. A simple north-south line running through the Atlantic separated their spheres: Spain got title to everything west of the line, comprising the Americas, whereas Portugal claimed the non-European Old World, including Africa and Asia. (Never mind that a portion of the Americas unexpectedly turned out to be east of the line—hence, Portuguese Brazil.) No one else in

---

4. On the violence of abstracting people as commodities, see Ian Baucom, *Specters of the Atlantic: Finance Capital, Slavery, and the Philosophy of History* (Durham, N.C., 2005), 5–14.

the world gave much credence to these grandiose claims, and other European powers colonized the Americas and established outposts on the African coast in spite of the Iberians. Seeking to bolster their ambitions, however, Spain and Portugal stuck largely to the terms of the agreement and stayed on their own sides of the line. By the time the Iberians acknowledged Tordesillas to be a dead letter, Spain lagged far behind her rivals in Africa and lacked the mercantile and naval wherewithal to remedy the predicament, leaving Spain without direct access to African sources of slaves for most of the colonial period.[5]

At first, this posed little problem for Spanish America's labor supply, as Spanish colonists relied on conquered native Americans for exploitable labor; but by the late sixteenth century, demographic catastrophe among the indigenous population caused a major labor shortage in Spanish America, giving rise to significant demand for enslaved Africans. Fortunately for Spanish colonists, the vast mineral wealth of their territories made them attractive buyers for those with slaves to sell. In general, Spanish bureaucrats (like their English counterparts) considered trade between their colonies and foreigners a breach of sound economic policy, but the desperation for labor in Spanish America encouraged exceptions to trade restrictions. To keep control over this foreign trade and to limit it to importations of people as much as possible, the Spanish crown negotiated a series of contracts with foreign merchants and nations for the right (the asiento de negros) to deliver prescribed numbers of Africans to specified Spanish American ports. Under such agreements, more than three-quarters of a million enslaved Africans reached Spanish America by the early nineteenth century, the vast majority of them carried by foreign traders. Between one-third and one-half of these slaves reached the Spanish colonies via transshipment, primarily from Dutch and British colonies.[6]

5. Geoffrey J. Walker, *Spanish Politics and Imperial Trade, 1700–1789* (Bloomington, Ind., 1979), 11–12; Bowser, *African Slave in Colonial Peru,* 29. For an overview of justifications that European powers asserted for their overseas territorial claims, see Anthony Pagden, *Lords of All the World: Ideologies of Empire in Spain, Britain and France, c. 1500–c. 1800* (New Haven, Conn., 1995).

6. On the demographic crisis for the native peoples of South and Central America, see Alfred W. Crosby, Jr., *The Columbian Exchange: Biological and Cultural Consequences of 1492* (Westport, Conn., 1972). On the links of the demographic crisis to Spanish America's demand for enslaved Africans, see Palmer, *Slaves of the White God,* 1–35. The first asiento contracts actually dated back to 1518, but the trade remained small until demand spiked in the late sixteenth century. By the late eighteenth century, some Spanish American traders entered the African trade, making direct shipments increasingly common; see Philip D. Curtin, *The Atlantic Slave Trade: A Census* (Madison, Wis., 1969), 25, 268. *Voyages: The Trans-Atlantic Slave Trade Database,* ac-

The asiento was distinct from other international trades because it involved large contracts between the Spanish crown and foreign crowns or merchants for the delivery of Africans. Owing to the long-term nature of such contracts, holders of the asiento (called *asientistas*) set up permanent bases (called "factories") on Spanish American soil, and imperial governments of the asientistas inevitably became embroiled in conflicts with the Spanish crown over the terms of the agreement. Initially, the Spanish relied on the Portuguese to supply Africans. Through mere coincidence, the low point in availability of indigenous labor in Spanish America coincided with a union of the Spanish and Portuguese crowns, from 1580 to 1640. Thus, it was a relatively simple matter for the Spanish to negotiate asiento contracts, beginning in 1595, with the Portuguese, who had more extensive outposts and connections on the African coast than other Europeans at the time. This trade largely involved direct shipments from Africa to Spanish America and brought most of the estimated 200,000 Africans who arrived from 1595 until 1640, at which date Portugal reclaimed independence from Spanish rule.[7]

Embittered by Portuguese independence, Spain looked elsewhere for slaves after 1640, but two decades passed before the asiento system thrived again. From 1640 to 1663, the slave trade to Spanish America slowed considerably, and it was in this context that Spanish American colonists ventured to English colonies in the early 1660s hoping to trade silver for slaves, touching off Lyttelton's dilemma about the Navigation Acts. In 1663, Spain partially solved its slave supply problem by negotiating a new asiento, signing the Genoese merchant house of Grillo and Lomelin to deliver 3,500 Africans annually to Spanish America for seven years. A series of similar contracts followed over

---

cessed January 2011, estimates that slave traders forced just over 600,000 African people directly to Spanish America from Africa by 1807 (http://slavevoyages.org/tast/assessment/estimates .faces?yearFrom=1501&yearTo=1807&disembarkation=702.703.701.705.704). Intercolonial deliveries added significantly to that figure after 1660, however. British colonies sent roughly 150,000 additional Africans, whereas Dutch and French colonies added perhaps 50,000 more. On direct arrivals in Spanish America from Africa before 1663 and the significant contributions of transshipments from foreign colonies thereafter, see António de Almeida Mendes, "The Foundations of the System: A Reassessment of the Slave Trade to the Spanish Americas in the Sixteenth and Seventeenth Centuries," in David Eltis and David Richardson, eds., *Extending the Frontiers: Essays on the New Transatlantic Slave Trade Database* (New Haven, Conn., 2008), 82; see also David Eltis, "The Volume and Structure of the Transatlantic Slave Trade: A Reassessment," *WMQ*, 3d Ser., LVIII (2001), 36, 45.

7. *Voyages,* accessed January 2011, http://slavevoyages.org/tast/assessment/estimates.faces ?yearFrom=1595&yearTo=1640&disembarkation=702.703.701.705.704.

the remainder of the century, with Dutch traders increasingly playing the central role.[8]

The restoration of the asiento seemed to undercut the need for transshipments of African captives from the English Caribbean to Spanish America, but English merchants vied for a share of the trade without holding the asiento itself because virtually all asientistas struggled to fulfill their quotas for slave deliveries. In 1663, the English Company of Royal Adventurers Trading to Africa inked a contract with Grillo and Lomelin to supply Africans to the asientistas in the Caribbean for transshipment to Spanish America. Grillo and Lomelin subcontracted the Royal Adventurers for delivery of 3,500 Africans per year—the full number they had promised to Spain—to Barbados or Jamaica, from whence the Genoese would purchase them for transshipment to Spanish America. The Royal Adventurers' eyes were bigger than their fleet. Only in a perfect year could the fledgling English company deliver so many Africans to Grillo and Lomelin, and then only if the company neglected English buyers entirely. The Adventurers managed to deliver only two or three thousand Africans over several years combined, so Grillo and Lomelin canceled the contract in 1671. Still, foolhardy as the Royal Adventurers' promises were, their overestimate of their slave-trading capacity speaks to English eagerness for Spanish American trade. And the Genoese asientistas' willingness to subcontract the inexperienced Royal Adventurers speaks to the convenience of English Caribbean entrepôts (especially Jamaica) for trade to Spanish America. Contemporaries estimated the costs of transshipment from Jamaica as 20 percent lower than from the Dutch Caribbean entrepôt of Curaçao.[9]

8. Almeida Mendes, "Foundations of the System," in Eltis and Richardson, eds., *Extending the Frontiers*, 76–77. For more on the Dutch asientos of the late seventeenth century, see Wim Klooster, "Curaçao and the Caribbean Transit Trade," in Johannes Postma and Victor Enthoven, eds., *Riches from Atlantic Commerce: Dutch Transatlantic Trade and Shipping, 1585–1817* (Boston, 2003), 203–218; Han Jordaan, "The Curaçao Slave Market: From *Asiento* Trade to Free Trade, 1700–1730," ibid., 219–257; Postma, *The Dutch in the Atlantic Slave Trade: 1600–1815* (New York, 1990), 26–55; Postma, "The Dispersal of African Slaves in the West by Dutch Slave Traders, 1630–1803," in Joseph E. Inikori and Stanley L. Engerman, eds., *The Atlantic Slave Trade: Effects on Economies, Societies, and Peoples in Africa, the Americas, and Europe* (Durham, N.C., 1992), 283–299.

9. Davies, *Royal African Company*, 43, 327; Zook, *Company of Royal Adventurers*, 93–95. Although the Royal Adventurers fell far short of their contract, they did sell some slaves to Grillo and Lomelin. In 1665, the Dutch governor of Curaçao—who was also selling to the Genoese asientistas—reported that Grillo and Lomelin made purchases in Jamaica. In the following year, the Adventurers' agent in Jamaica belatedly obtained crown permission for such sales; see Vice-Director Beck to Director Stuyvesant, Curaçao, Apr. 16, 1665, in Donnan, ed., *Documents*, I, 167–168. Almeida Mendes says of Grillo and Lomelin's asiento, "During this period the direct trade

English alacrity for Spanish trade climbed all the way up England's imperial ladder, influencing decisions of colonial management. For instance, in the Treaty of Madrid in 1670, England promised to curtail Caribbean piracy and privateering in exchange for Spain's acknowledgment of English claims to American colonies—a necessary first step to legitimizing intercolonial trade. The English also conveyed their intentions in appointments of colonial officials. Off and on between 1674 and 1682, former privateer Henry Morgan served as acting lieutenant governor of Jamaica, thanks in part to fame he earned from successful raids on Spanish colonies. Morgan's final term ended, however, when he neglected to embrace the new era of trading with, rather than pillaging, Spanish America. Noting Morgan's reluctance to promote the Spanish trade, particularly his endorsement of the Jamaica Assembly's nearly prohibitive £5 tax on slaves exported from the colony, English officials replaced him with Thomas Lynch, a man with ties to the Royal African Company.[10]

Lynch pursued the slave trade to Spanish America aggressively. The Dutch West India Company had succeeded Grillo and Lomelin as asientista, and the Dutch firm rarely looked to English sources for African people. Instead, Lynch promoted the sale of Africans by English slave traders to Spanish interlopers traveling to Jamaica in violation of the asiento. In 1682, Lynch reported to the Lords of Trade and Plantations on the arrival at Jamaica of "one Don Gaspar de Montesdoco from Havana to buy negroes." Montesdoco sought 150 Africans, and Lynch bemoaned Jamaica's inability to fulfill the request. Noting that the Dutch asiento was not running smoothly, Lynch pressed his superiors to secure this Spanish commerce for English merchants by promoting the transatlantic slave trade to Jamaica. "If we had negroes," Lynch argued, "the convenience of our ports that lie north and south of Carthagena and Portobello would certainly draw all the trade they [the Spanish] may have with strangers to us." Lynch's phrase "all the trade" suggested that the Spanish would pur-

<hr />

from Africa ended, and slaves began to arrive principally from other islands in the Caribbean, especially Curaçao, Barbados, and Jamaica (by now British)" ("Foundations of the System," in Eltis and Richardson, eds., *Extending the Frontiers,* 77); see also Zahedieh, "Merchants of Port Royal," *WMQ,* 3d Ser., XLIII (1986), 589. On the Treaty of Madrid and relative costs of transshipment from Jamaica and Curaçao, see Nuala Zahedieh, "Trade, Plunder, and Economic Development in Early English Jamaica, 1655–89," *Economic History Review,* 2d Ser., XXXIX (1986), 216, 219.

10. Frances Armytage argues that many privateers used knowledge of the Spanish coast to turn to illicit trade once England turned away from sponsoring raids; see Armytage, *The Free Port System in the British West Indies: A Study in Commercial Policy, 1766–1822* (New York, 1953), 16.

chase more than people in Jamaica if the colony were adequately supplied with African captives; having slaves to sell would open a broader Spanish commerce. Lynch's struggle to find Africans to offer the Spanish suitors, however, points out a significant obstacle to his plan. From the mid-seventeenth century, the English pursued opportunities to sell enslaved Africans abroad, but English merchants were not yet ascendant in the transatlantic portion of the trade. Exports of captives from English American colonies were necessarily limited.[11]

Still, Lynch encouraged Spanish trade in the following years. In 1684, he reported to the Lords of Trade that he had sent a man-of-war, the *Ruby*, to convoy the Spanish ship *St. Thomas* from Jamaica to Cartagena with three hundred enslaved Africans and their Spanish buyers on board. The Spaniards had purchased the Africans on credit, so Lynch sent the convoy to ensure the Spaniards would not fall prey to pirates and thus fail to pay. The Spaniards returned for more slaves, but the Royal African Company did not have captives available; Lynch allowed the Spanish to purchase from English interlopers who smuggled Africans to Jamaica in violation of the company's monopoly. Otherwise, Lynch cautioned, "this trade would be ended before it is well begun." The colonial governor expected the Lords of Trade to agree that trade with the Spanish was a higher priority than enforcing English law and the Royal African Company's monopoly. Reinforcing this priority, in 1685, the Lords of Trade sent instructions to all colonial governors, demanding they confiscate foreign vessels trading in their colonies, "excepting Spanish ships that are come to buy negroes." As a result of such encouragement, two subsequent asientistas in the mid-1680s maintained agents in residence in Port Royal, Jamaica, to purchase incoming Africans for transshipment to Spanish America. As many as half the African migrants whom the Royal African Company delivered to Jamaica in these years sold to buyers for the Spanish trade.[12]

Subsequent Jamaican governors followed Lynch's example, both in culti-

11. Curtis Nettels, "England and the Spanish-American Trade, 1680–1715," *Journal of Modern History*, III (1931), 9–11; Thomas Lynch to the Lords of Trade and Plantations, Jamaica, Sept. 29, 1682, in Donnan, ed., *Documents*, I, 279–281.

12. Lynch to the Lords of Trade, in Donnan, ed., *Documents*, I, 325–329. In this letter, Lynch also notes a recent Spanish purchase of 150 slaves from an interloper in Barbados (Lords of Trade to all governors, quoted in Nettels, "England and the Spanish-American Trade," *JMH*, III [1931], 14). On resident asiento factors in Jamaica, see Zahedieh, "Merchants of Port Royal," *WMQ*, 3d Ser., XLIII (1986), 590; Zahedieh also estimates that the Royal African Company "regularly sold between 25 and 50 percent of its slave cargoes to the Spaniards in the 1680s" (ibid.). See also Zahedieh, "Trade, Plunder, and Economic Development," *Economic History Review*, 2d Ser., XXXIX (1986), 219–221.

vating Spanish commerce and lamenting its refusal to fully flower. In 1685, Dutch merchants replaced a Spanish trader as holder of the asiento, and in 1687, Jamaica's lieutenant governor Hender Molesworth complained to English Treasury officials about decline: "Whilest the Assiento was in the hands of the Spanyards, we had a Spanish Trade for Negroes, . . . but [the asiento] coming into the hands of the Dutch they made use of us only until they could furnish themselves from Curasau." Indeed, the Dutch "made use" of Jamaica frequently as a source of African captives for a year or two but nearly cut off the trade thereafter. Molesworth described the loss as a tough economic blow for Jamaica. (No doubt his own considerable investment in the trade "as factor to the Royall Affrican Company" colored his opinion.) The following year, in a document cosigned by seventy-six colonists, Molesworth lobbied the crown to encourage the slave export trade from Jamaica, insisting that Spanish buyers paid with silver and also bought English goods.[13]

Despite Molesworth's complaints about trade languishing, exports of African people from Jamaica to Spanish America surged late in the century. In 1691, one of Molesworth's successors, Governor William O'Brien, earl of Inchiquin, claimed that an English fleet carried £100,000 of Spanish silver back to the mother country "thanks to the Assiento," by which he must have meant slave sales to Spanish traders or the Dutch holders of the asiento, since the English themselves did not possess the asiento contract. In 1698, Governor George Beeston reported to the Board of Trade that English merchants had arranged to sell three hundred Africans to Sir James Castillo, a factor for the Portuguese merchants who had recently taken the asiento, with payment to be made after the Portuguese delivered the captives to the Spanish. To encourage such trade and prompt payment, Beeston—like Lynch before him—ordered the military ship *Foresight* to convoy the Portuguese traders to Veracruz, "considering that it was upon the first settling of that trade, [and] that the money would go to England."[14]

13. Hender Molesworth to the Lords Councellors of the Treasury, Aug. 4, 1687, CO 1/63, fol. 2. Molesworth's mention of the asiento "in the hands of the Spanyards" probably refers to the years before 1663, when Spain did not award an asiento contract to a foreign merchant or company, but it may also refer to the tenure of Grillo and Lomelin, who were Genoese. On Molesworth's ties to the Royal African Company, see Zahedieh, "Merchants of Port Royal," *WMQ*, 3d Ser., XLIII (1986), 591. For Molesworth's petition, see Davies, *Royal African Company*, 332. Stephanie Smallwood also notes the prominence of Spanish buyers from the Royal African Company in Jamaica in the 1680s (Smallwood, *Saltwater Slavery: A Middle Passage from Africa to American Diaspora* [Cambridge, Mass., 2007], 172–173).

14. Inchiquin quoted in Nettels, "England and the Spanish-American Trade," *JMH*, III (1931), 8. Inchiquin also notably commented that it was "trade and the *asiento* which are the life of this

Other African departures from Jamaica occurred without government approval. Colonial official George Reid reported to the English secretary of state in 1688 that a large Dutch vessel had anchored off the island, which "pretends want of wood and water and some provisions," but since the ship was "bound for Curaçao for a thousand negros upon account of the Assiento," Reid suspected ulterior motives for the stop at Jamaica. He believed the vessel "defrauded the Roy'll Affrican Company's factors here." Reid did not explain his suspicions further but likely meant to insinuate that the Dutch vessel was buying slaves from English interlopers, who violated the Royal African Company's monopoly.[15]

Given the steadily growing English transatlantic slave trade and the enthusiasm of English traders for exchanging Africans for Spanish silver, Spanish buyers and foreign asientistas kept coming to Barbados and Jamaica through the late seventeenth and early eighteenth centuries. By 1708, some merchants estimated—probably overestimated—that English traders had exported six to seven thousand Africans to Spanish colonies in each of the previous three years. Whatever the actual number of Africans transshipped from Jamaica to Spanish America, the overall traffic contributed vitally to the capital accumulation that funded development of Jamaica's early sugar economy. Given the nascent state of Jamaica's agricultural sector, contemporary impressions that Port Royal was among the wealthiest English settlements in the period are difficult to explain without recognizing profits from Spanish trade. One typical observer described Port Royal merchants indulging "in the height of splendour." [16]

In addition to enriching Port Royal merchants, this rise of a slave trade from English to Spanish colonies diversified Spanish American slave quarters. Owing to Portugal's deep engagement in Kongo and Angola for supplies of captives, the majority of Africans reaching Spanish America by 1640 had come from west central Africa. To that date, the population of Africans in Spanish America was more homogeneous than the African community in other colonial settlements at any time. In the decades after 1640, as the asiento changed hands, African arrivals in Spanish America diversified somewhat. Direct African voyages reached Spanish America from Senegambia

---

place" (Zahedieh, "Merchants of Port Royal," *WMQ*, 3d Ser., XLIII [1986], 593). Beeston: see Sir William Beeston to Board of Trade, Jamaica, July 5, 1698, in Donnan, ed., *Documents*, I, 420.

15. Reid to secretary of state, Jamaica, Dec. 4, 1688, CO 1/65, fol. 368.

16. Zahedieh, "Trade, Plunder, and Economic Development," *Economic History Review*, 2d Ser., XXXIX (1986), 219–221; Colin Palmer, *Human Cargoes: The British Slave Trade to Spanish America, 1700–1739* (Urbana, Ill., 1981), 7.

TABLE 7. Estimates of Africans Shipped to Foreign Colonies, 1661–1715

Years	Estimate of Africans exported from Jamaica	Estimate of Africans exported from Barbados
1661–1665	2,000	820
1666–1670	1,200	1,110
1671–1675	130	330
1676–1680	350	330
1681–1685	3,500	1,150
1686–1690	3,500	1,150
1691–1695	2,100	570
1696–1700	2,910	1,560
1701–1705	1,810	1,750
1706–1710	3,840	1,750
1711–1715	7,210	2,050
TOTAL	28,550	12,570

Sources: For detailed discussion of the derivation of these estimates, see Appendix, below.
From Jamaica, the vast majority of enslaved people traveled to Spanish colonies; from Barbados, French colonies took a larger share, with Spanish colonies a secondary destination.

and the Bight of Benin, and the Dutch also transshipped Africans to Spanish America from Curaçao, an island that drew large numbers of captives from the Bight of Benin and west central Africa, as well as smaller streams from the Gold Coast, the Bight of Biafra, and Sierra Leone. Nonetheless, west central Africa remained the primary source for direct African migration until 1700. By contrast, the English Caribbean colonies transshipping captives to Spanish America drew few people from west central Africa. In the slave trade to Barbados and Jamaica from 1660 to 1710, the Bight of Benin was the most common African embarkation region, followed closely by the Gold Coast and the Bight of Biafra. None of these regions had been particularly prominent in direct African trade to Spanish America, so even if buyers for the Spanish American market exhibited a preference for west central Africans, they must have resorted to buying people of other, less familiar, backgrounds. Aja, Akan, and Igbo people would have predominated in vessels headed from English to Spanish America (Figure 3). Those who survived the journey landed in a world where most fellow slaves were west central Africans, heightening the risk of cultural isolation (a hazard perhaps partially offset by the more diversified

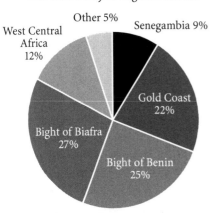

Regions of Embarkation for Africans Carried Directly to English America

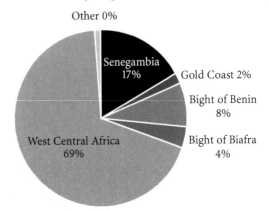

Regions of Embarkation for Africans Carried Directly to Spanish America

FIGURE 3. Comparison of Captive Origins in the Transatlantic Slave Trades to English and Spanish America, 1601–1710

Source: Voyages: The Trans-Atlantic Slave Trade Database, accessed January 2013, http://slavevoyages .org/tast/assessment/estimates.faces?yearFrom=1601&yearTo=1 710&disembarkation=702.703.701 .705.704, and http://slavevoyages.org/tast/assessment/estimates.faces?yearFrom=1601&yearTo=1710 &disembarkation=205.305.204.304.307.306.309.201.308.311.203.310.202.301.302.303.

work regimes of Spanish America, where plantation monoculture was rare before the mid-eighteenth century). As English slave traders branched out to Spanish markets, routes of migration from Africa overlapped, complicating the diaspora and the dissemination of African cultures and peoples across the New World.[17]

■ In addition to the budding slave trade connection between the English Caribbean and Spanish America, the last decades of the seventeenth century

17. On the regional origins of captives shipped from Africa to the Dutch Caribbean before 1700, see *Voyages,* accessed December 2011, http://slavevoyages.org/tast/database/search.faces ?yearFrom=1601&yearTo=1700&mjslptimp=32100. The literature on the ethnic backgrounds typical of captives from various African regions is vast; for good overviews, see Paul E. Love-joy, *Transformations in Slavery: A History of Slavery in Africa,* 3d ed. (New York, 2012), 52–79; Michael A. Gomez, *Exchanging Our Country Marks: The Transformation of African Identities in the Colonial and Antebellum South* (Chapel Hill, N.C., 1998). The implications of transfer from the British to Spanish colonial sphere extended well beyond the differing backgrounds of captives and varied work regimes. A different legal system, the influence of the Catholic Church, greater urban development, and the greater reliance on forced indigenous labor all combined to make African slavery in Spanish America quite different from its British American counterpart. Important as they were, such contrasts fall beyond the scope of this study.

also saw an emerging trade and migration of African people from the English Caribbean to nearby French islands. English merchants and imperial officials coveted Spanish markets most but were perfectly willing to be distracted by the French Caribbean when profitable opportunities presented themselves. From the French imperial perspective, all commerce between their colonies and foreigners was strictly forbidden—especially after 1664, when the French West Indies shifted from proprietary control to royal possessions. Nonetheless, throughout the colonial period, French traders failed to sate the demand for exploitable workers in Martinique, Guadeloupe, and eventually Saint-Domingue. Martinique and Guadeloupe, first settled in 1635, resorted to African labor within a few years, emerging as important sugar producers over the remainder of the century; Saint-Domingue, on the other hand, only developed a robust slave economy in the eighteenth century. The scale of France's own slave trade in the seventeenth century simply cannot account for the growth of the enslaved population of the French Caribbean, and the correspondence of French imperial officials is replete with laments and anxieties about where the extra Africans came from. Officials in France routinely exhorted their Caribbean underlings to curb colonial commerce with Dutch and English traders, and officials in French colonies alternated between defending their records on fighting foreign trade and decrying that fight as hopeless.[18]

In 1669, for example, Governor General Jean-Charles de Baas-Castelmore of the French West Indies responded to imperial demands that he block foreign trade in both goods and slaves by saying that such a policy sounded good in theory, but enforcement was probably not possible. De Baas ordered the policy registered in Martinique but informed his superiors, "I believe it will serve no purpose other than ceremony, since . . . [contraband traders] will not ask for pineapple." (In the colonial Atlantic world, pineapple was a well-known symbol of welcome; de Baas was suggesting that on his side of the ocean, foreign traders did not need the king's blessing to enter a French port.) Beyond the difficulty of enforcement, de Baas feared the implications of the foreign trade prohibition for the colonies' development: "I believe that it must not apply to the transport of Negroes, so that the revenue of the islands can

18. On the connection of policies against foreign trade and the shift from proprietary to royal colonies, and on French colonists' complaints about the shortage of Africans, see Kenneth J. Banks, "Official Duplicity: The Illicit Slave Trade of Martinique, 1713–1763," in Peter A. Coclanis, ed., *The Atlantic Economy during the Seventeenth and Eighteenth Centuries* (Columbia, S.C., 2005), 232–235. See also Bernard Moitt, *Women and Slavery in the French Antilles, 1635–1848* (Bloomington, Ind., 2001), chaps. 1 and 2; Michael J. Jarvis, *In the Eye of All Trade: Bermuda, Bermudians, and the Maritime Atlantic World, 1680–1783* (Chapel Hill, N.C., 2010), 161–165.

grow." Despite his protestations, the policy stayed in place, leaving him to report the following year that frustrated, undersupplied French colonists from Guadeloupe and Martinique often ventured to Barbados to trade.[19]

French officials continued to struggle with prohibiting such traffic over the ensuing decades. One chronic problem was the complicity of French governors and lower authorities in the Caribbean. Numerous administrators faced accusations of accepting bribes for toleration of the foreign slave trade; others faced charges of engaging in the trade themselves. In 1703, Governor General Charles-François de Machault wrote to France, insisting that "with regard to foreign trade, it did not happen. In times of war and peace it has remained my concern to stop the abuses." Whether guilty or not, Machault continued to fight allegations for months. Meanwhile, officials serving under Machault leveled similar charges at Governor Bouloc of Grenada: intendant François-Roger Robert of the French Windward Isles reported to France, "The inhabitants of Grenada continue to make serious complaints against M. de Bouloc." Most notably, Robert referred to allegations—which were echoed by other colonial officials—that Bouloc "sent completely publicly to [Danish] St. Thomas in search of Negroes, not making any defense of the foreign trade, which rules and ordinances of the king forbid." A decade later, Intendant Nicolas François Arnoul de Vaucresson of Martinique made accusations against the island's recently departed governor general, Raimond Balthazar Phélypeaux. Vaucresson stated that immediately after the War of the Spanish Succession (1701–1714), an English merchant from Antigua sailed to Martinique, proposing to "resume the old understanding" that had existed between the trader and Phélypeaux with regard to the importation of enslaved Africans. Presumably, Phélypeaux had either accepted bribes to allow the trade or set himself up as a middleman between the English trader and buyers in Martinique.[20]

19. Jean-Charles de Baas to council, Dec. 26, Jan. 15, 1669, Archives Nationales d'Outre-Mer, Aix-en-Provence (hereafter cited as ANOM), C8A, 1, fols. 13–23, esp. 13, 14, and fols. 25–31 ("je Croy qu'il n'y faudra point d'autre Ceremonie, puisque . . . [contraband traders] n'en demanderont pas d'anansas"; "Je crois qu'elle ne doit s'appliquer qu'au transport des Negres, affin que par ce secours elle puisse augmenter le revenu des Isles").

20. Banks, "Official Duplicity," in Coclanis, ed., *Atlantic Economy,* 231–232, esp. 238 (Banks argues that virtually all Martinique governors were complicit in the foreign slave trade); Charles-François de Machault to council, Oct. 2, 1703, ANOM, C8A, 15, fols. 49–52 ("qúa l'égard du commerce étranger, il ne se faissoit point. En temps de guerre et qu'en temps de paix restoit a moi a l'empêcher pour ce qui concerne les abus dont"). For a similar denial from Machault, see his letter of Apr. 9, 1704, fols. 216–220. For Robert's comments, see François-Roger Robert to council, Feb. 20, 1703, fols. 74–87 ("Les habitants de la Grenade continuent de faire de grandes plaints

Even when French governors upheld the prohibition on foreign trade, they faced a losing battle. At times, lower officials undermined them. In 1680, the comte de Blénac, governor general of the French West Indies, accused the governor of Saint Croix (then French) of welcoming foreign traders, especially those selling slaves. A generation later, Major Poulain de Guerville, stationed in the Caribbean, wrote to authorities in France to accuse a local official on Guadeloupe—described only as M. de Poullet—of permitting foreign trade, contrary to the orders of Governor General Malmaison, who resided in Martinique. When rebuked by French officials, Poullet acknowledged that "in the past four years some men of honor from England have visited this island, whom I received at my house" but insisted that he did so "for the honor of the nation," as the king's representative on the island.[21]

Such charges of complicity in foreign trade by officials outside the French Caribbean's administrative center of Martinique point to one of the key problems for those governors who sought to uphold the law. Barring foreign traders from the French Caribbean meant patrolling a vast territory with few naval vessels at one's disposal (see Map 3). Governor General de Baas demonstrated his zeal for enforcing French trade laws through several confiscations of foreign interlopers. Still, he often bemoaned his struggle to contain the problem. In 1674, de Baas caught wind of Dutch traders selling eighty Africans at Grenada, but he resided in Martinique; officials managed to arrive in Grenada in time to seize only seven of the Africans. De Baas's successor, Blénac, decried the same problem of foreign traders' heading to islands other than Martinique for trade away from his watchful eyes. He managed to catch two English vessels at Grenada in 1677, but two years later, he complained of his inability to curb contraband rumored at other French islands. Blénac wrote French officials that he had "received notice that Monsieur Hinselin," the governor of Guadeloupe, had "allowed ships and boats to leave his island," which Blénac specified as Grand Terre, one of the two islands comprising Guadeloupe, "without passports and that is the way to facilitate foreign trade." But the rest of Blénac's letter suggests that Hinselin's negligence (or complicity) was

---

contre M. de Bouloc. . . . Il a envoyé tout publiquement a St. Thomas chercher des negres, ne Faisant pas autrement de cas des defence de commerce étranger et des règlement et ordonnances du Roi qui le deffend"). For a similar charge against Bouloc, see Jean-Jacques Mithon de Senneville to council, Aug. 16, 1703, fols. 164–172.

21. Comte de Blénac to council, July 13, 1680, ibid., C8A, 2, fols. 334–350; Poulain de Guerville to council, C7A, 6, fols. 228–229; Poullet to council, Dec. 12, 1714, C7A, 6, fols. 237–239 ("depuis quatres années, il est venu en cetter isle bien des fois des anglois, et gens d'honneur, que j'ai reçu chez moy . . . le tout pour faire honneur a la nation").

just one of the ways to facilitate foreign trade. Blénac also reported writing to Marie-Galante—the other main island of Guadeloupe—to order a private citizen to cease and desist from "some commerce he had at Marigalande with the English." If anything, Blénac's problems containing foreign trade at Saint Christophe were even more daunting, since the French shared the island with the English (who called it Saint Christopher or Saint Kitts). "To prevent commerce at St. Cristophe between the French and the English," Blénac asserted a need for unprecedented powers. Since catching illicit traders in the act was extremely difficult, Blénac requested the authority to administer harsh punishments as a deterrent. He recommended paying a reward to "a sailor who will admit" to engaging in foreign trade. Blénac then hoped to "condemn the master of the vessel to the galleys" and to give "the merchant who will be charged a large fine for the first offense, and for the second, a corporal punishment." Without such powers at his disposal, Blénac feared the fight against illicit trade at Saint Christophe was hopeless.[22]

For imperial officials seeking to bar foreign trade, chronic shortages of slave labor and various trade goods in the French Caribbean exacerbated the problems of corrupt officials and a vast geography to police. Even colonial governors who sought to uphold trade restrictions routinely complained of French traders' failure to deliver enough exploitable Africans to ensure the economic growth of the islands. France's formal acquisition of Saint-Domingue in 1697 and securing of the asiento to supply slaves to the Spanish in 1701 only created more demand for captive Africans. This persistent undersupply in French Caribbean markets pushed up prices. (In addition, French transatlantic traders were less efficient in Africa than their English and Dutch counterparts, driving costs higher on the supply end of the slave trade.) Prices for Africans in the French Caribbean were sometimes twice the amount paid for similar people in English and Dutch colonies. This discrepancy made French colonial buyers attractive to Dutch and English slave traders, and vice versa. In other words, there was great incentive on both sides to ignore French law. Just as Gover-

---

22. De Baas to council, June 8, 1674, ibid., C8A, 1, fols. 279–289 (for an example of de Baas's confiscating an English vessel engaged in foreign trade in Martinique [with an unspecified cargo], see his letter to the king, June 23, 1676, fols. 373–377); Blénac to council, June 11, 1677, Jan. 1, 1679, C8A, 2, fols. 28–32, 147–155 ("Jay eu avis que Monsieur Hinselin, laissoit partir de son isle les barques, et Bateaux, sans passeporte. Et C'est La Le mojen de fasilitter le Commerse des Estrangers"; "quelque Commerse qu'il a fait à Marigalande avecq Les Anglois"; "pour Empecher le Commerse à St. Cristophe entre les françois Et Les Anglois"; "à un matelot qui le declarera, condemnant le maistre de la barque aux galeres, Le marchand quy aura chargé, a une grosse amande pour la premiere fois, Et pour la seconde a une peyne Corporelle").

nor General de Baas had proposed in 1669, many French governors exempted slave merchants from the foreign trade prohibition at times of acute need. In 1675, de Baas himself granted such an exemption at Martinique, reporting to French officials that a shortage of food forced him to allow four English vessels to deliver provisions — and a few enslaved Africans. In 1713, citing wartime shortages, the governor of Martinique allowed a more thoroughgoing opening to foreign traders, and English merchants estimated that they and Dutch traders carried 3,800 Africans to the colony in that year alone. French colonial officials saw a troubling tension between enforcing the law and facilitating economic growth.[23]

The problem was only more pronounced for other French colonies, since Martinique dominated the French Caribbean's transatlantic commerce in the late seventeenth and early eighteenth centuries. Indeed, in 1682, Guadeloupe planters implored the French Guinea Company to send more direct shipments from Africa "and not to send thither the refuse of the slaves of Martinico [Martinique]." Governor Hinselin of Guadeloupe, whom Governor General Blénac had accused of condoning foreign trade, stressed undersupply as critical to his colony's foreign trade problem. In 1684, having been rebuked by Blénac and French officials, Hinselin reported meeting with the "people assembled" to stress the importance of obeying the king's orders, but he also sent a rebuke of his own back to France, noting that "many lands are uncultivated because their owners do not have the Negroes they will need to make them worth something." He then remarked that the French monopoly company had failed to deliver to Guadeloupe in the preceding three years. Without consistent French trade, "the only good commerce there would be is made with our foreign neighbors," though he denied tolerating such activity. To compel his superiors to ensure that direct African shipments start arriving regularly

23. De Baas to council, Jan. 29, 1675, ibid., C8A, 1, fols. 316–321; for evidence of slaves on the English provision ships, see ibid., fols. 301–302, where a list of goods on one of the ships includes "une negresse"; unfortunately, similar lists for the other three ships do not survive. Banks notes constant slave shortages in the French Caribbean and their effect on prices, and he argues that securing Saint-Domingue and seizing the asiento only made the problem worse ("Official Duplicity," in Coclanis, ed., *Atlantic Economy*, 232–235); see also James Pritchard, *In Search of Empire: The French in the Americas, 1670–1730* (New York, 2004), 215–224. On the greater efficiency of British and Dutch traders leading to lower prices for slaves compared to the French transatlantic trade, see David Eltis, *The Rise of African Slavery in the Americas* (New York, 2000), 118–129. Martinique 1713: James Pritchard, David Eltis, and David Richardson, "The Significance of the French Slave Trade to the Evolution of the French Atlantic World before 1716," in Eltis and Richardson, eds., *Extending the Frontiers: Essays on the New Transatlantic Slave Trade Database* (New Haven, Conn., 2008), 213.

in Guadeloupe, Hinselin reminded them that one consequence of foreigners' supplying slaves was France's loss of "the sugar that they embark here for ports in foreign islands, in order to bring back negroes." [24]

Particularly galling to both planters and governors on Guadeloupe was the colony's dependence on transshipments from Martinique for virtually all legal trade. In 1711, Governor Malmaison of Guadeloupe suggested that France require its monopoly company to deliver slaves directly to Guadeloupe from Africa each year, adding immediately, "I will always be careful to prevent foreign trade with this island." In a subsequent letter, he clarified that the problem of relying on Martinique for transshipment went beyond the inadequate number of Africans arriving. Because Martinique planters had the first opportunity to buy, Malmaison also deemed the quality of Africans who reached Guadeloupe inadequate: merchants in Martinique only sent the "leftover and disabled." [25]

Early Saint-Domingue, which the French began settling even before securing title from Spain in 1697, saw the same connection between foreign trade and the failure of French traders to supply laborers. In 1694, Governor du Casse matter-of-factly reported the arrival at the colony of a vessel from Saint Thomas, which unloaded and sold one hundred weary Africans. When rebuked for permitting this, according to a contemporary abstract of his letter, du Casse wrote that "he would never have dreamed of allowing foreign trade [if] the colony had an abundance of all things," and he promised to block "any more Negroes from the Danish" if the king wished. But he reminded his superiors in France, "The colony has a need, and the French never bring a quarter of" what was required. In fact, du Casse's other letters suggest that most of the Africans Saint-Domingue obtained in accordance with French law came, not from trade at all, but rather from raids of Jamaica. Not surprisingly, he continued to lobby French officials to permit foreign slave traders into Saint-Domingue, at least until the colony got off the ground. Whether such trade was legal or not from the viewpoint of French leaders, the unmet demand for

24. "Voyages to Martinique, 1679, 1682," in Donnan, ed., *Documents,* I, 303; Governor Hinselin to council, Oct. 16, 1684, ANOM, C7A, 3, fols. 93–94 ("baucoup de terres sont incultes parce que les proprietaires n'ont pas les negres qu'il leur faudra pour les faire valloir"; "le seul bon commerce qu'il y auroit a faire avec les etrangers nos voisins"; "des sucres qu'ils embarqueroient icy pour les portes dans les isles etrangeres, donc ils raporteroient des negres").

25. Governor Malmaison to council, Jan. 29, Oct. 10, 1711, ANOM, C7A, 6, fols. 53–59, 82–85 ("Je serais toujours attentif a empercher le Commerce étranger en cete Isle"; "rebut et Infirmes"). For more on the Guadeloupe slave trade's reliance on Martinique, see David Geggus, "The French Slave Trade: An Overview," *WMQ,* 3d Ser., LVIII (2001), 119–138.

slaves in the French Caribbean—and the corresponding high prices—ensured that French colonists and foreign traders would work to make such trafficking a reality. By 1715, English colonies had probably shipped about nine thousand African people to the French Caribbean.[26]

The implications of such migration for captives are difficult to assess. On one hand, distances between the French and English colonies of the Lesser Antilles were quite short, mitigating the dangers of extra time at sea. A transshipment voyage, however unpleasant, might last only a day or two, greatly limiting the threat of disease outbreaks or provision shortages. On the other hand, captives illegally transshipped across imperial boundaries might have faced unique risks, hidden in secret compartments behind or below legal cargoes, or disembarked at night or in hidden coves lacking harbor facilities. Did people suffocate or overheat in claustrophobic hidden chambers? Were shipwrecks, injuries, abandonments, or drownings more common during nighttime disembarkations or evasions of authorities? The lack of records from smugglers leaves us to speculation, but illegal trades were probably hazardous for captives and crews alike. For those who survived, however, unlike the intercolonial traffic to Spanish America, this forced migration between English and French colonies in the seventeenth and early eighteenth centuries probably did not have profound cultural implications. Both the French transatlantic trade to Martinique and Guadeloupe and the English trade to its eastern Caribbean possessions drew on similar African regions for captives before

26. Governor du Casse to council, Oct. 1, 1694, ANOM, C9A, 3, fols. 55–61; abstract of du Casse to council, Dec. 15, 1696, fols. 246–250 ("Il n'a jamais songé au commerce estranger la colonie a abondance de toutes choses"; "plus de negres par les danois"; "la colonie en a besoin, et les françois n'en porteron jamais le quart de cequi"). For du Casse's reports of raiding Jamaica for slaves, see his letters of Mar. 16, 30, Apr. [? torn], 1694, fols. 4–30. For the request for toleration of foreign slave traders, see his letter of Feb. 2, 1697, fols. 266–278. Pritchard, Eltis, and Richardson argue that an array of sources were needed to populate the French Caribbean with Africans before 1713. Based on population data and estimated rates of mortality and natality, they suggest that the French islands must have imported more than 105,000 Africans by 1715, but direct African trade had supplied fewer than two-thirds of that number. French privateers' raids of foreign colonies contributed an additional 7,000 or 8,000 Africans, but intercolonial trade supplied most of the remainder. Given the volume of other empires' slave trades (and those empires' own African population growth), Pritchard, Eltis, and Richardson estimate that trade with Dutch colonies brought about 7,000 African people to the French Caribbean, Danish Caribbean sources contributed another 4,000, and commerce with the English Caribbean ferried in another 9,000. Even these estimates, they are careful to note, do not add up to enough people to account for the French Caribbean's population, so at least one of these sources likely contributed even more ("Significance of the French Slave Trade," in Eltis and Richardson, eds., *Extending the Frontiers*, 206–214).

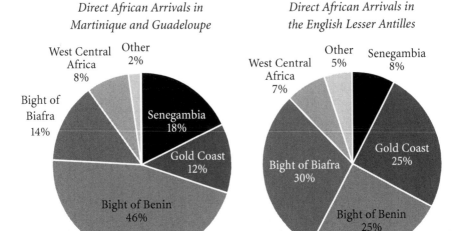

FIGURE 4. Comparison of Captive Origins in the Transatlantic Slave Trades to the French and English Lesser Antilles, 1641–1710

Source: Voyages: The Trans-Atlantic Slave Trade Database, accessed January 2013; for the French: http://slavevoyages.org/tast/assessment/estimates.faces?yearFrom=1641&yearTo=1710&disembarkation=402.403; and for the English: http://slavevoyages.org/tast/assessment/estimates.faces?yearFrom=1641&yearTo=1710&disembarkation=304.309.302.303.

1710. The French colonies drew nearly half of such captives from the Bight of Benin region, with Senegambia, the Bight of Biafra, and the Gold Coast (in descending order of importance) each providing significant supplemental streams of forced immigrants. The migration to the English Lesser Antilles was more balanced but drew largely from the same African regions. As a result, the mostly Igbo, Akan, and Aja captives transshipped from the English to the French Caribbean would not have found themselves among a profoundly different mix of people (Figure 4). They also transferred between two regimes largely committed to the same sugar monoculture.

■ Whereas English merchants, the English crown, and royally appointed colonial governors eagerly pursued this trade to foreign colonies, labor-hungry English plantation owners—especially in Jamaica—showed markedly less enthusiasm. In fact, by the 1680s, Jamaican planters lamented that the empire's desire to trade enslaved Africans for the riches of Spanish America prevented England's own colonies from receiving enough labor, kicking off a debate within the empire about the value of Spanish trade. The controversy raged, off and on, for more than a century. Jamaican planters ensured it was a war of more than just words with their control of the colony's assembly. A £5 tax on slaves exported from the island, levied by the Assembly in 1681, though quickly vetoed, was renewed on at least two more occasions in the 1680s and at numerous moments thereafter.[27]

And planters' efforts to curb the slave trade to Spanish America went beyond taxation. In 1688, the Royal African Company accused "the Government in Jamaica" of tampering with the exchange rate for Spanish silver in ways "much detrimentall to trade especially to such as have debts owing [to] them." (Colonies in the English Empire maintained their own currencies, so colonial officials had some purview over exchange rates.) Later that same year, a group of "Merchants Trading to Jamaica" made similar complaints about a "Declaration in the Court of Justice [of Jamaica] against the Importation of Mony [specie], to the great discouragem't of the Spanish Trade." Given the chronic scarcity of specie in English colonies, Jamaican officials had little reason to introduce a measure restricting the import of silver unless they desired a disruption of trade with Spanish America to prevent able-bodied Africans from leaving the colony.[28]

Jamaica planters also discouraged the Spanish slave trade by interfering with Spanish American colonists who ventured to their island. Although Spanish merchants on English colonial soil enjoyed sanction from the English crown, that was no guarantee of kind treatment from local officials whose sympathies lay with planters. Accordingly, in 1688, the Royal African Company stated that Jamaican administrators "forbid the Spaniards trading there which is of greate prejudice to the Royall Company." The company likely had in mind the plight of Señor Iago del Castillo, a Spanish trader in Jamaica. That same year, Castillo faced persecution from Jamaican authorities, who alleged that Castillo exploited his welcome in the colony to introduce "a forreigne Ecclesiasticall power." A minister in Jamaica reportedly claimed that Castillo was an ordained priest seeking to promote Catholicism under cover of trading for slaves. Rather than face investigation, Castillo fled the colony, leaving his

---

27. Richard S. Dunn argues that the plantation owners cemented their control of the Jamaican Assembly during the Glorious Revolution (*Sugar and Slaves: The Rise of the Planter Class in the English West Indies, 1624–1713* [1972; rpt. Chapel Hill, N.C., 2000], 162). On Morgan's support of the 1681 tax and further Assembly efforts to tax slave exports, see Nettels, "England and the Spanish-American Trade," *JMH*, III (1931), 11–13.

28. "Memorial of the Royal African Company, 1688," CO 1/65, fol. 50; "The Humble Peticon of Divers of the Planters and Merchants Trading to Jamaica," June 20, 1688, CO 1/65, fol. 363, ibid. For an introduction to colonial currencies, see John J. McCusker and Russell R. Menard, *The Economy of British America, 1607–1789* (Chapel Hill, N.C., 1991), 333–341.

possessions for confiscation by Jamaica officials. When a deputy proceeded to Castillo's residence to inventory and seize his belongings and trade goods, he found "about 70 or 80 Negroes in his Yard," awaiting transshipment to Spanish America. Valued at well over £1,000, the abandoned slaves were an enormous loss for Castillo. The authenticity of the charges against him is difficult to assess, but the Jamaican authorities' hostility to the export slave trade cannot have helped his case.[29]

In 1689, in response to the Royal African Company's allegations (and after another failed attempt to tax slave exports from the island), the Assembly of Jamaica explained to the crown why it opposed such trading. The planter-dominated legislature grumbled that "foreigners get the best of the negroes, and we only the refuse at £22 a head," a high price for the time. English slave merchants preferred to sell to "foreigners" because the Spanish—or those selling slaves to them—paid for Africans with Spanish silver. Jamaican planters' "ready money has been refused because it was not pieces-of-eight." Unfortunately for the Jamaicans, the crown craved Spanish silver as much as the traders did, and the Assembly's complaints fell on deaf ears. The controversy was far from over, however, given the plantation owners' power within the colony. The Jamaica Assembly continued to quarrel with imperial officials and merchants over this issue for decades to come, although Governor Beeston's consent, near the end of the century, to an export tax of twenty shillings per slave quieted the argument for a time.[30]

■ This debate over English colonies' trade to Spanish America reveals an important aspect of Britain's slave-trading activities. Discussions of the slave trade's reason for existence—in the colonial period and today—tend to emphasize supplying labor-starved colonies with workers, but English merchants', and even the English imperial government's, interest in supplying Spanish colonies with African workers (in exchange for silver) focused on exploiting Africans as commodities. English traders and policy makers considered African people especially useful for opening lucrative branches of commerce. The planters of Jamaica asserted other priorities for the empire. They insisted that the purpose of England's slave trade was, or at least should have

29. "Memorial of the Royal African Company, 1688," CO 1/65, fol. 50; "The Case of Mr. Smith Kelly Deputy to John Mournsteven, Esq'r, Provost Marshall Generall of Jamaica," ca. June 1688, CO 1/65, fols. 380–382, ibid.

30. Address of the Council and Assembly of Jamaica to the king and queen, July 26, 1689, in Donnan, ed., *Documents*, I, 370; Nettels, "England and the Spanish-American Trade," *JMH*, III (1931), 12.

been, to foster the development of England's own colonies. They fought a losing battle. English policy makers generally viewed the colonies' purpose as filling the homeland's coffers, and from the early days of English expansion to the New World, among the most popular schemes for generating revenue was siphoning off some of Spain's American silver. English privateers had plagued Spanish silver fleets, and English explorers had searched in vain for El Dorado. When English policy makers perceived that exporting Africans to the Spanish offered an alternate route to the mythical city, English policy supported the exchange regardless of planters' concerns. To English merchants and the English crown, enslaved Africans were not just laborers to be exploited on English plantations but also goods to be traded in the Atlantic marketplace.[31]

The mercantile value of Africans extended beyond the cash paid for them. English merchants and officials hoped to use the slave trade as a lever to pry open the gates of Spanish America to a broader commerce. Policy makers enthusiastically sought opportunities to increase exports of the mother country's manufactured goods, and many English leaders saw Spanish America as a promising market. Not only was it flush with silver, but Spain's colonies also suffered recurring shortages of European consumer goods—textiles, dishes, tools. The Spanish manufacturing and mercantile sectors were underdeveloped relative to their northern European rivals. Spain barred foreign traders from Spanish America, but demand for foreign manufactures remained high in these colonies.[32]

The question for English policy makers and traders was how to circumvent Spain's prohibitions to reach the unmet demand for manufactured goods. Here, the commerce in African people was key. The slave trade held promise because it was the one traffic for which Spain granted exceptions to their restrictions. The asiento was only the most obvious concession. Briefly in the 1670s, for example, officials in Spain recognized the acute labor shortage in their colonies by permitting colonists to venture to English colonies for pur-

31. On the importance of pillaging Spanish America to early English settlement plans, see Kenneth R. Andrews, *Trade, Plunder, and Settlement: Maritime Enterprise and the Genesis of the British Empire, 1480–1630* (New York, 1984), esp. 9.

32. On the failure of Spanish merchants to meet Spanish American demand for European manufactures, see Walker, *Spanish Politics and Imperial Trade*, 5, 11–14; J. H. Elliott, *Empires of the Atlantic World: Britain and Spain in America, 1492–1830* (New Haven, Conn., 2006), 109–114, esp. 224–226; Zahedieh, "Trade, Plunder, and Economic Development," *Economic History Review*, 2d Ser., XXXIX (1986), 216; John Lynch, *Spanish Colonial Administration, 1782–1810: The Intendant System in the Viceroyalty of Río de la Plata* (New York, 1958), esp. 1–10; Jonathan C. Brown, "Outpost to Entrepôt: Trade and Commerce at Colonial Buenos Aires," in Stanley R. Ross and Thomas F. McGann, eds., *Buenos Aires: 400 Years* (Austin, Tex., 1982), 3–17.

chases of Africans outside the asiento arrangement. Furthermore, even when such permission did not come from the top of the hierarchy, administrators in Spanish America often granted legal exceptions or turned a blind eye to smuggling to facilitate the entry of slaves. The English hoped to exploit this flexibility to open Spanish markets for manufactured goods, as well.[33]

In public statements about Spanish American commerce, English officials focused on the slave trade to avoid offending Spanish administrators who officially tolerated only that trade, but internal communication among English traders and officials shows that the slave trade was inextricably linked, from their perspective, with a more general commerce. Imperial official William Blathwayt hinted at this connection during the War of the League of Augsburg (1688–1697—King William's War, to the colonists) when he cautioned English leaders about the commercial importance of protecting Jamaica from invasion. "If it be lost to the French," Blathwayt warned, "all that profitable trade we now enjoy (though underhand) with the Spanish colonies, as well as the negro traffic, will be cut off." His distinction between "underhand" general trade and "the negro traffic" was something of a false dichotomy, since most vessels carried mixed cargoes of African captives and trade goods, but it does portray the slave trade as the commerce tolerated by the Spanish, giving cover to other trade. Looking back from 1728, a critic of Britain's South Sea Company, James Knight, also remembered Jamaica's Spanish American commerce developing as a combination of enslaved Africans and English manufactured goods:

> Within a few years after Jamaica was conquered . . . a Trade was opened with the Spaniards, and successfully carried on, for many Years, for Negroes, and other Merchandize; whereby great Quantities of the Manufactures of Great Britain were yearly vended.

In fact, Knight contended that when Jamaican traders ventured to Spanish America with African captives, "The Trade . . . carried on for Negroes, . . . was likewise the least Branch of their Commerce." In Knight's estimation, "a Sloop which carried out 120 Negroes" in the seventeenth-century trade to Spanish America "generally had on Board 7 or 8000 £ Value in other Merchandise,

33. On the general importance of slaves to opening Spanish American trade, see Zahedieh, "Trade, Plunder, and Economic Development," *Economic History Review*, 2d Ser., XXXIX (1986), 218–219. Bowser shows this exploitation of slave-trading privileges "as a blind to flood the area with contraband . . . merchandise" dating back to the Portuguese asientos of the sixteenth century (*African Slave in Colonial Peru*, 33–34). On Spanish permission for colonists to buy slaves in English colonies, see Nettels, "England and the Spanish-American Trade," *JMH*, III (1931), 13.

which they were not under any Difficulty of disposing; for the Necessity which the Spaniards were under for Negroes." So important was this mixed commerce that, in Knight's view, it spurred Jamaica's growth:

> The Reputation of the Riches brought in, by those Means, ocasioned the Island to be well supplied with all kind of Materials . . . and invited great Numbers of People to become Settlers there: So that this Commerce was a principle Mean of the Island's being so well settled.

Merchants in the Jamaica trade made similar arguments linking the slave trade with general Spanish American commerce during the War of the Spanish Succession (1701–1714). When the English crown announced an embargo on all foreign trade, Sir Gilbert Heathcote urged exempting the Spanish American trade from this policy, insisting, "We Exchange our Goods with 'em for nothing but Gold and Silver, and the Goods we traffick with are onely wearing Apparel and negroes for their mines." The crown agreed that the commerce was uniquely valuable, excepting it from the foreign trade closure in 1704.[34]

Although seventeenth-century participants in the Jamaica–Spanish America trade saw slave trading as facilitating the dry goods trade, many remained frustrated by the limits on the latter. At moments, English traders could convince a Spanish American "governor to Wink or looke through his fingers," as Heathcote put it, and some Spanish colonists ventured to English colonies to make additional purchases. Other enterprising English traders pushed the envelope further, sailing to Spanish America with hopes of eluding Spanish authorities and conducting illegal trade. One technique they used for avoiding Spanish privateers or officials was trading while at sea off the coast rather than actually entering a Spanish American harbor. As one observer explained it, Jamaican sloops approached the Spanish coast only at night, whereas "in the day they ply off and on as they call it to be out of sight." Spanish American merchants willing to engage in contraband trade knew to approach the English interlopers in small boats, "carrying ready money," since no credit was welcome in the illegal traffic. Of course, this was a risky business. If the lights on English vessels were visible to Spanish merchants at night, surely Spanish officials or privateers could spot them, as well. If caught, English interlopers tried flimsy excuses with mixed success. Typically, they blamed the weather.

34. Nettels, "England and the Spanish-American Trade," *JMH*, III (1931), 13, 17, 20; Zahedieh, "Merchants of Port Royal," *WMQ*, 3d Ser., XLIII (1986), 582; [James Knight], *Some Observations on the Assiento Trade, as It Has Been Exercised by the South-Sea Company: Proving the Damage, Which Will Accrue Thereby to the British Commerce and Plantations in America, and Particularly to Jamaica* (London, 1728), 2, 20.

When English ambassadors protested Spanish confiscation of a "New England Ketch . . . (Captain Ludbury Commander)" near Cartagena in the 1680s, they relayed Ludbury's excuse for his presence in Spanish waters. The vessel was "bound to Windward [i.e., to the east] . . . with Negroes, Goods, and Jewells" but "was driven by Stress of Weather to Carthagena and Seiz'd and Sold by the Spanyards." There was good reason for Spanish officials to doubt Ludbury's story. Not only was he claiming to be blown in the opposite direction he intended, but his uncontrollable vessel carrying African captives floundered conveniently toward the principal Spanish American port for the slave trade. When "Biscayan pirates" seized the sloop *Phoenix*, carrying twelve to fifteen Africans and an assortment of dry goods off the Spanish American coast in 1687, Captain John Jennings also maintained that his crew "was bound to windward, and by distress of weather were disabled . . . near the shoar of the [Spanish] main." It was a coincidence that his cargo was perfectly suited to Spanish trade.[35]

Spanish privateers were not the only challenge for slave traders crossing imperial boundaries. They also faced risks from their limited legal rights in foreign territory. An English colonial report on "Injuries Sustained by the English from the Spanyards" decried a 1686 incident in which Spanish colonial officials altered the exchange rate in their colonies, "raising the value of Pieces of Eight from Eight Ryalls to ten" while "English merchants [were] obliged to Sell their Goods at the same rate as formerly and those imprison'd who refuse." Since the Spanish crown officially barred English merchants from trading to Spanish colonies, they had little legal recourse to protest such treatment. Such perils made contraband trade operate differently from legal trades: insurance was

---

35. Nettels, "England and the Spanish-American Trade," *JMH*, III (1931), 20; "Notes on Illicit Trade Carried on by Sloops from Jamaica with the Spanish," n.d., MS 1049, Institute of Jamaica, Kingston, cited in Zahedieh, "Merchants of Port Royal," *WMQ*, 3d Ser., XLIII (1986), 582; "Injuries Sustained by the English from the Spaniards since the Treaty Concluded at Madrid the Year 1670," July 1687, CO 1/62, fols. 367–373. Sailing to windward means sailing toward the direction from which the wind blows, which, given the trade winds in the Caribbean, means sailing to the east. On imports to Cartagena, see Eltis, *Rise of African Slavery*, 206; Palmer, *Human Cargoes*, 103–105. *Phoenix*: "Deposition of John Jennings," CO 1/63, fols. 83–84, 86–87. For depositions from several among the *Phoenix*'s crew, see ibid., fols. 95–99; one of these depositions, from William Hodgson, included the claim "that he know not whither the said sloop [the *Phoenix*] was bound." This not only seems unlikely but also points out that neither Jennings nor any member of the crew gave a specific destination; they just noted that they intended to sail to "windward." Jennings estimated the value of the slaves at £230, and slave prices at the time averaged about £17 at Jamaica. On prices in the late-seventeenth-century Caribbean, see Davies, *Royal African Company*, 199.

unavailable for the Spanish American commerce; ships carried extra sailors, who earned hazard pay; and captives bore the brunt of the added danger.[36]

These threats also indicate the importance of intercolonial transshipment for deliveries across imperial boundaries. For one thing, transatlantic traders arriving directly from Africa generally carried several hundred captives, so the financial loss of confiscation in a foreign port was greater than for the much smaller, faster, more maneuverable sloops of the transshipment trade. In addition, knowledge of local geography, people, and laws (and the ways around them) gave intra-Caribbean traders an advantage for moving enslaved Africans between empires. Barbados governor Edwyn Stede alluded to the importance of such connections when reporting to the Privy Council on a Captain Howelson, who planned to transship people from Barbados to Spanish colonies in 1690. Stede noted that Howelson had "made or is making some agreem't w'th Sr. James Castello, the Cheife Administrator in those parts of the Affaires of the Assiento for Importing Negroes into the Spanish Indies." If one knew the man in charge of enforcing the rules, as Captain Howelson apparently did, one might just get around them. Intercolonial traders were more likely to forge such ties in neighboring foreign colonies than transatlantic traders arriving from Europe or Africa.[37]

■ Naturally, given the dangers and inconveniences of trade across borders and England's abiding enthusiasm for it, many English merchants and officials sought a more thoroughgoing opening of Spanish America to English commerce. One Jamaica merchant, George Kast, argued that England could best gain leverage from Spanish America's desire for exploitable Africans, not by encouraging the slave trade to Spanish colonies, but by outlawing it. Since the Spanish wanted slaves desperately, Kast argued, closing English ports to Spanish buyers would force Spain to open their ports to English slave traders, who could then more easily trade manufactured goods on the sly. Kast's counterintuitive plan never gained traction, but not for a lack of interest in cracking open Spanish America.[38]

Most English policy makers envisioned another strategy for gaining wider access to Spanish America. For all their illegal trade with Spain's colonies, and for all their commerce with various asientistas, seventeenth-century English-

36. "Injuries Sustained by the English from the Spanyards," ca. May 1687, CO 1/65, fols. 383–384; Zahedieh, "Merchants of Port Royal," WMQ, 3d Ser., XLIII (1986), 586.

37. Edwyn Stede to Council for Trade and Foreign Plantations, Barbados, Apr. 23, 1690, CO 28/1, fol. 45.

38. Nettels, "England and the Spanish American Trade," JMH, III (1931), 15–16.

men had never held the asiento itself, and by the early eighteenth century, English officials saw securing that contract as their best route to El Dorado. English colonial governors in the Caribbean could encourage individual transactions with the Spanish or the asientistas, and bold English merchants could risk ventures to Spanish American coasts, but such colonial actors were powerless to force a more thorough opening of Spanish markets. By the early eighteenth century, however, the English crown was not. As English naval and mercantile might increased in the Atlantic world, imperial policy makers grew ever more bold and bellicose while becoming no less interested in Spanish American trade. In fact, when France secured the coveted asiento in 1702, disappointed English leaders contemplated a naval blockade to bar French ships from Spanish ports. Ultimately, England rejected that strategy—in fact, English traders in the Caribbean sometimes sold slaves to the French asientistas—but English imperialists continued to covet the lion's share of Spanish American commerce.[39]

They found their opportunity to seize it during the War of the Spanish Succession. In that conflict, Britain fought for the ascendance of a Habsburg king to the Spanish throne, at least partly in exchange for a promise of exclusive trading rights in Spanish America. The course of the war, especially in its closing years, exposed the value British leaders attached to the Spanish American trade. As the war dragged on and the costs piled up, Whigs in Parliament countered peace advocates with a slogan of "No peace without Spain," as if to emphasize that commercial influence with a new Spanish monarch rather than gains against continental rivals was the goal of continuing the war. However, more war meant more debt. By 1710, the national debt from war expenditures had mounted to a staggering nine million pounds sterling, and the queen appointed Robert Harley chancellor of the exchequer with a mandate to solve the public credit crisis. A supporter of the Spanish trade himself, Harley did not allow the debt to become an argument for ending the war. Instead, he proposed an ingenious financial scheme to tie Britain's war debt to the promised commercial prize of trade with Spanish America: he created the South Sea Company. The company would have a monopoly on British trade with Spanish America once favorable terms of peace made access to such trade a reality, and holders of the public debt would trade their government bonds for shares

39. Palmer, *Human Cargoes*, 8. On French asientistas' buying from the English, see Colin A. Palmer, "The Company Trade and the Numerical Distribution of Slaves to Spanish America, 1703–1739," in Paul E. Lovejoy, ed., *Africans in Bondage: Studies in Slavery and the Slave Trade* (Madison, Wis., 1986), 28–34.

in the new company. Parliament quickly approved the plan, and the government's creditors became invested in the project of opening Spanish America to British trade. The very name of the company hinted at the expansion of Spanish trade, since "South Sea" referred to the Pacific Ocean, insinuating ambitions of direct trade with Peru.[40]

The public reaction to Harley's scheme was enthusiastic, but its success was a matter of perspective. Two-thirds of the bondholders traded public debt for shares in the company within weeks, and virtually all had accepted the deal within six months. The crown had found a useful way to manage its debt, earning Harley a knighthood. But in the peace negotiations of 1713, Britain failed to open Spanish America fully to British trade. Instead, Britain secured a more limited trading prize—the asiento de negros. The agreement was set to last for thirty years (an unprecedented duration), and it obligated the company to deliver 4,800 Africans per year to Spanish America. The company's directors and shareholders had hoped for broader mercantile privileges than just slave trading, but there was a silver lining. The Spanish granted a concession not included in prior asiento agreements: the South Sea Company could

40. This discussion of the end of the War of the Spanish Succession and the creation of the South Sea Company draws heavily on John Carswell, *The South Sea Bubble*, rev. ed. (London, 1993), esp. chap. 3 ("No peace without Spain": 39–40); and Carl Wennerlind, *Casualties of Credit: The English Financial Revolution, 1620–1720* (Cambridge, Mass., 2011), chaps. 5 and 6. Although I argue here that the creation of the South Sea Company and the push for peace on terms that opened Spanish America to British trade revealed the British government's enthusiasm, the rampant speculation that led to the famous South Sea Bubble of 1720 actually had little connection to the company's trading activities. The inflating (and bursting) of the bubble had roots in complicated finance schemes that involved the consolidation of additional government debt in exchange for rights to collect the interest and to sell more shares in the company. The bubble was also related to a broader wave of investment speculation in Britain and abroad, and neither that nor the problems of margin buying and illiquidity that produced the crash had anything to do with Spanish trade—although rumors of improved relations with Spain in late 1719 might have played a small part in the rising price of South Sea Company shares. See Peter M. Garber, *Famous First Bubbles: The Fundamentals of Early Manias* (Cambridge, Mass., 2000), 109–122; Julian Hoppit, "The Myths of the South Sea Bubble," Royal Historical Society, *Transactions*, XII (2002), 141–165; Carswell, *South Sea Bubble*, 91. On Dutch, British, and French interest in trade with Spanish America among the causes of the War of the Spanish Succession, see Walker, *Spanish Politics and Imperial Trade*, 19. On the linking of the "South Sea" with the trade to Peru in the era of the company's creation, see *The Considerable Advantages of a South-Sea Trade to Our English Nation . . .* (London, [1711?]); and Robert Allen, *An Essay on the Nature and Methods of Carrying on a Trade to the South-Sea* (London, 1712), both of which urge the British to pursue a direct trade to Peru; see also Paul W. Mapp, *The Elusive West and the Contest for Empire, 1713–1763* (Chapel Hill, N.C., 2011), 132–138.

send one annual ship laden with British manufactured goods directly to Spanish America.

The British insistence on this privilege in the peace negotiations underscores the link they saw between selling African people to Spanish America and selling British goods. Other provisions of the treaty seemed to facilitate smuggling of additional trade goods beyond what the annual shipment allowed. Britain demanded the right to send "necessaries" to their factors on Spanish American soil and even to send sloops from Jamaica with "refreshments" for the annual ship while it was anchored in a Spanish American harbor. As one British advocate for the asiento argued a few decades later, the terms of the contract were "so artfully contrived . . . that if rightly executed, would have fairly laid open all the Ports of the Spanish West Indies to the British Trade" despite explicitly limiting that commerce to enslaved Africans. These intentions surrounding the asiento reflect a mechanistic view of African people—and not just because the company traded them as slaves. In pursuing the slave trade to Spanish America, British merchants and policy makers valued Africans' worth in commodity exchange over their worth as potential laborers for British colonies—perhaps because many only encountered the people they traded as tally marks in ledgers and port records. Unfortunately for the South Sea Company and its investors, using the asiento to "lay open" Spanish America would prove more difficult than any of them imagined.[41]

41. "So artfully contrived": [James Houstoun], *A True and Impartial Account of the Rise and Progress of the South Sea Company: Wherein the Assiento Contract Is Particularly Considered . . .* (London, 1743), 11. Richard Pares also argues that "clauses of the [asiento] treaty were almost useless except as a pretext for [smuggling]" (*War and Trade in the West Indies, 1739–1763* [London, 1963], 11); see also Walker, *Spanish Politics and Imperial Trade*, chap. 4. On bondholders' enthusiasm for trading for shares of South Sea Company stock, see Wennerlind, *Casualties of Credit*, 201.

5. The North American Periphery of the Caribbean Slave Trade, ca. 1700–1763

Negroes may be said to be the Bait proper for catching a Carolina Planter, as certain as Beef to catch a Shark. — Anonymous, Charleston, 1738

We are under a Necessity to buy the refuse, refractory, and distemper'd Negros, brought from other Governments. — George Burrington, North Carolina, 1733

To be Sold for Cash or Jamaica Fish, Two likely Negro Boys — Advertisement, Boston, 1765

In the eighteenth century, the British slave trade reached its awful apogee, but North American colonies remained on the margins of a British colonial slave system centered in the Caribbean. From 1701 to 1775, British traders delivered just over 1.5 million African people to the Americas as slaves. More than 80 percent of them disembarked from the Atlantic crossing in the Caribbean, whereas only about 16 percent (~250,000) landed on the North American mainland. This discrepancy reflects the primacy of sugar in the British slave system but also overstates it. Far more Africans were indeed put to work on Britain's sugar islands than on the British mainland, but a significant portion of the people landing in the British Caribbean would not stay there. By the eighteenth century, a systematic, routinized network of intercolonial trade dispersed people outward from the British Caribbean. Some left the British Empire altogether, but within the empire, the most significant route of this intercolonial trade linked the Caribbean heart of the slave system with its North American periphery. From 1701 to 1775, thousands of intercolonial voyages carried nearly 50,000 enslaved African people from the Caribbean to North America—accounting for 1 in 6 African immigrants to the mainland. This robust intercolonial trade is somewhat surprising: with the British emerging as world leaders in the slave trade, why did transatlantic traders not supply all North American colonies with captives directly from Africa? Of course, many transatlantic traders did exactly that, with Virginia's James River and Charleston, South Carolina, becoming particularly important centers of direct importation. Nonetheless, direct African trade to North America did not fully meet demand, so the intercolonial trade from the Caribbean actually grew even as direct African arrivals increased.[1]

This continued importance of Caribbean sources for North America's African immigrants hinged upon the mainland's economic development as a periphery of the Caribbean sugar complex. With Britain's sugar islands generating staggering wealth and increasingly specializing on cultivating cane, many North American colonies found economic niches in selling provisions and supplies to the Caribbean. The New England colonies sent salted fish, livestock, and timber; mid-Atlantic settlements earned the name "bread colonies" for shipments of flour and other grains; Chesapeake planters outside the prime tobacco regions raised corn and livestock for the Caribbean; the Carolinas exported naval stores and livestock. All of these regions received sugar, rum, and tropical fruits in exchange. Including transshipments of African laborers in such commerce was no major leap. As William Byrd had done in the Chesapeake–West Indian trade of the late seventeenth century, other merchants in a wider range of British colonial ports would do in the eighteenth: monitor the prices of goods in various colonies, seek opportunities for profitable exchange, and trade African people when it seemed advantageous. Meanwhile, the presence of North American traders selling provisions and supplies in Caribbean ports only increased the allure of such markets for transatlantic slave traders. They could not only count on the sugar islands for the wealthiest plantation owners with the largest labor needs, but they could also count on the strong sugar economy (built upon slave labor) to draw North American traders to the islands.[2]

1. For estimates of the British transatlantic slave trade to the Caribbean and North America, see *Voyages: The Trans-Atlantic Slave Trade Database,* accessed August 2012, http://slavevoyages .org/tast/assessment/estimates.faces?yearFrom=1701&yearTo=1775&flag=3.5&disembarkation =205.204.201.203.202.402.403.401.404.405.804.702.805.703.701.801.802.803.305.304.307.306 .309.308.311.310.705.704.501.502.600.301.302.303. For estimates of the slave trade from the Caribbean to the North American mainland, see Gregory E. O'Malley, "Beyond the Middle Passage: Slave Migration from the Caribbean to North America, 1619–1807," *William and Mary Quarterly,* 3d Ser., LXVI (2009), tables I–X.

2. John C. Coombs notes that nonelite planters in the Virginia regions growing provisions for the Caribbean enjoyed more success in acquiring slaves than nonelite planters growing tobacco, owing to their connections to Caribbean sources of slave importation: "The Phases of Conversion: A New Chronology for the Rise of Slavery in Early Virginia," *WMQ,* 3d Ser., XLIII (2011), 343. David Richardson notes that, between 1768 and 1772, for example, the West Indies accounted for 64 percent of New England's total exports; he argues that New England's reliance on Caribbean markets for exports increased over the eighteenth century. See "Slavery, Trade, and Economic Growth in Eighteenth-Century New England," in Barbara L. Solow, ed., *Slavery and the Rise of the Atlantic System* (New York, 1991), 237–264, esp. 250. On the growth of intercolo-

Although most North American colonies provisioned the Caribbean, their connections to the islands, and to the trade in African people, were distinct. This chapter sketches three types of slave-trading relationships connecting the West Indies and North American colonies: deliveries from the islands to slave-trading entrepôts on the mainland, deliveries to northern colonies less dependent on enslaved labor, and deliveries to southern backwaters with burgeoning desire for slaves but little capital to pay for them. The organization of such commerce, and the ethnic and demographic mix of the captives it carried, varied in accordance with the type of North American market being targeted. An intercolonial trader incorporated slave trading into his business differently based on whether he targeted a place like Charleston, like Philadelphia, or like Edenton, North Carolina.

For African people arriving in the Caribbean, the patterns of this traffic had important implications. Centralization through hubs was efficient for traders and the economy—just as it is for modern passenger airlines and shipping companies—but for captives caught in the commercial migration, the complex network of Atlantic trade made for convoluted, multi-stage journeys with sorting and separations at each stage. The majority remained at the island where they arrived, especially young men, whom owners and overseers of sugar plantations preferred. Children faced higher odds of journeys to the northernmost British colonies; young women might be chosen for ventures to developing regions where planters valued fertility or lower prices; older captives were often sent to economically marginal colonies where prospective slaveholders had few options. All of this sorting increased the likelihood that kinship, cultural, and linguistic ties severed after the Atlantic crossing.[3]

---

nial trade and the mainland colonies' export of provisions and supplies to the Caribbean more generally, see John J. McCusker and Russell R. Menard, *The Economy of British America, 1607–1789* (Chapel Hill, N.C., 1991), 78–80, 92–110, 174, 198–203; Jack P. Greene, *Pursuits of Happiness: The Social Development of Early Modern British Colonies and the Formation of American Culture* (Chapel Hill, N.C., 1988), 62, 67, 126, 144–145, 184; Richard Pares, *Yankees and Creoles: The Trade between North America and the West Indies before the American Revolution* (Cambridge, Mass., 1956); Stephen Innes, *Creating the Commonwealth: The Economic Culture of Puritan New England* (New York, 1998), chap. 7; Herbert C. Bell, "The West India Trade before the American Revolution," *AHR*, XII (1917), 272–287. North America was so significant to the provisioning of Caribbean plantations that, when the American Revolution disrupted trade networks linking the regions, starvation was a major problem (mostly affecting enslaved people) in some Caribbean colonies; see Richard B. Sheridan, "The Crisis of Slave Subsistence in the British West Indies during and after the American Revolution," *WMQ*, 3d Ser., XXXIII (1976), 615–641.

3. On the sadness and anxiety of captives being separated after the Middle Passage, see "The Interesting Narrative of the Life of Olaudah Equiano, or Gustavus Vassa, the African, Written by Himself," in Vincent Carretta, ed., *The Interesting Narrative and Other Writings* (New York,

■ The least intuitive of the intercolonial slave trades linking the Caribbean and North America were the routes to colonies that also drew people directly from Africa—namely, Virginia, South Carolina, and Maryland. As these colonies became regular targets of traders from Africa in the eighteenth century, the transatlantic deliveries did not render intercolonial shipments obsolete. Intercolonial merchants showed remarkable willingness to compete against direct African trade. In fact, Virginia and South Carolina not only led the British mainland colonies in importing people directly from Africa but also continued to import the most captives from the Caribbean (Tables 8 and 9). Intercolonial deliveries did not keep pace with transatlantic arrivals, fluctuating in reaction to the transatlantic trade's volume and the state of local economies, but intercolonial arrival in Virginia and South Carolina remained considerable nonetheless. Maryland, meanwhile, occupied something of an intermediate position between the primary slave importing colonies of North America and the more marginal territories. The smaller Chesapeake colony drew captives from transatlantic traders with some regularity, but since traders from Africa targeted South Carolina and Virginia more frequently, Maryland supplemented the direct trade with a higher proportion of arrivals from the Caribbean (Table 10).

European traders in Africa acquired captives at vastly cheaper prices than intercolonial merchants could find in the Caribbean, so the persistence of intercolonial slave trading to Virginia, South Carolina, and Maryland in the eighteenth century involved factors other than cost. Nor can a dependence on exporting provisions to the Caribbean entirely explain the sustained transshipments because these colonies did not rely on that commerce to the same degree as their neighbors. Virginia, South Carolina, and Maryland led the British mainland in importing Africans because they also led in the production of staples for export to Europe. Three considerations, however, encouraged intercolonial traders to compete with the so-called "Guineamen" in North America's largest markets for enslaved laborers: First, intercolonial traders possessed an advantage in the proximity of their markets of supply and demand, which allowed timelier knowledge of market conditions. Second, although the Virginia, Maryland, and South Carolina economies depended less on the export of provisions to the Caribbean than some neighboring colonies, this provision trade still formed a considerable part of their commerce. Chesapeake planters grew wheat and corn and raised livestock on lands ill

2003), 126; Stephanie E. Smallwood, *Saltwater Slavery: A Middle Passage from Africa to American Diaspora* (Cambridge, Mass., 2007), 202–207.

TABLE 8. Estimated Numbers of African Captives Arriving in Virginia, 1701–1765

Year	Enslaved Africans directly from Africa	Enslaved Africans via the Caribbean	Total	% from the Caribbean
1701–1705	4,500	275	4,775	6
1706–1710	5,525	250	5,775	4
1711–1715	975	600	1,575	38
1716–1720	7,150	1,625	8,775	19
1721–1725	6,750	675	7,425	9
1726–1730	11,125	300	11,425	3
1731–1735	10,600	725	11,325	6
1736–1740	11,700	650	12,350	5
1741–1745	5,625	750	6,375	12
1746–1750	4,650	1,575	6,225	25
1751–1755	8,150	750	8,900	8
1756–1760	3,500	50	3,550	1
1761–1765	7,525	225	7,750	3
TOTAL	87,775	8,450	96,225	9

Sources: Figures for direct transatlantic migration derive from the Voyages website, but that site presents estimates of African arrivals by region (in this case, the Chesapeake) rather than by individual colony. To derive an estimate for Virginia alone, I analyzed the raw data in Voyages: The Trans-Atlantic Slave Trade Database on documented shipments to Virginia and Maryland (http://slavevoyages.org/tast/database/search.faces?yearFrom=1701&yearTo=1765&mjslptimp=21000.21100, accessed May 2011) to calculate Virginia's proportion of the documented arrivals in the Chesapeake for each five-year period. I then assumed that Virginia received the same proportion of the estimated total arrivals in the Chesapeake in the same period (http://slavevoyages.org/tast/assessment/estimates.faces?yearFrom=1701&yearTo=1765&disembarkation=202, accessed May 2011). Estimates of intercolonial trade derive from Gregory E. O'Malley, "Beyond the Middle Passage: Slave Migration from the Caribbean to North America, 1619–1807," William and Mary Quarterly, 3d Ser., LXVI (2009), 141.

TABLE 9. Estimated Numbers of African Captives Arriving in South Carolina, 1701–1765

Year	Enslaved Africans directly from Africa	Enslaved Africans via the Caribbean	Total	% from the Caribbean
1701–1705		625	625	100
1706–1710	225	625	850	74
1711–1715	775	625	1,400	45
1716–1720	1,450	875	2,325	38
1721–1725	3,025	425	3,450	12
1726–1730	4,825	500	5,325	9
1731–1735	13,825	875	14,700	6
1736–1740	14,050	225	14,275	2
1741–1745	875	125	1,000	13
1746–1750	2,125	300	2,425	12
1751–1755	7,675	2,275	9,950	23
1756–1760	14,450	1,275	15,725	8
1761–1765	18,100	2,500	20,600	12
TOTAL	81,400	11,250	92,650	12

Sources: Figures for direct transatlantic migration derive from the *Voyages* website, but that site presents estimates of African arrivals by region (in this case, the Carolinas / Georgia) rather than by individual colony. To derive an estimate for South Carolina alone, I analyzed the raw data on North Carolina, South Carolina, and Georgia (http://slavevoyages.org/tast/database/search.faces ?yearFrom=1701&yearTo=1765& mjslptimp=21200.21300.21400, accessed May 2011) to calculate South Carolina's proportion of documented arrivals in the region for each five-year period (100 percent, in most cases). I then assumed South Carolina received the same proportion of the estimated total arrivals in the region in the same period (http://slavevoyages.org/tast/assessment /estimates.faces?yearFrom=1701&yearTo=1765&disembarkation=203, accessed May 2011). Estimates of intercolonial trade derive from Gregory E. O'Malley, "Beyond the Middle Passage: Slave Migration from the Caribbean to North America, 1619–1807," *William and Mary Quarterly,* 3d Ser., LXVI (2009), 142.

TABLE 10. Estimated Numbers of African Captives Arriving in Maryland, 1701–1765

Year	Enslaved Africans directly from Africa	Enslaved Africans via the Caribbean	Total	% from the Caribbean
1701–1705	1,075	250	1,325	19
1706–1710	1,700	250	1,950	13
1711–1715	0	300	300	100
1716–1720	900	800	1,700	47
1721–1725	1,375	350	1,725	20
1726–1730	2,325	150	2,475	6
1731–1735	2,450	350	2,800	13
1736–1740	3,625	325	3,950	8
1741–1745	1,800	250	2,050	12
1746–1750	0	525	525	100
1751–1755	1,000	200	1,200	17
1756–1760	1,950	75	2,025	4
1761–1765	1,975	225	2,200	10
TOTAL	20,175	4,050	24,225	17

Sources: Figures for direct transatlantic migration derive from the *Voyages* website, but that site presents estimates of African arrivals by region (in this case, the Chesapeake) rather than by individual colony. To derive an estimate for Maryland alone, I analyzed the raw data in *Voyages: The Trans-Atlantic Slave Trade Database,* on Virginia and Maryland (http://slavevoyages.org/tast /database/search.faces?yearFrom=1701&yearTo=1765&mjslptimp=21000.21100, accessed May 2011) to calculate Maryland's proportion of documented arrivals in the Chesapeake for each five-year period. I then assumed Maryland received the same proportion of the estimated total arrivals in the Chesapeake in the same period (http://slavevoyages.org/tast/assessment/estimates.faces?yearFrom= 1701&yearTo=1765&disembarkation=202, accessed November 2011). Estimates of intercolonial trade derive from Gregory E. O'Malley, "Beyond the Middle Passage: Slave Migration from the Caribbean to North America, 1619–1807," *William and Mary Quarterly,* 3d Ser., LXVI (2009), 146.

suited to tobacco. South Carolina rice sold not only in Britain and southern Europe but also fed the enslaved populations of the Caribbean. Carolinians supplemented the grain with livestock. As a return trade from the Caribbean, enslaved people offered a logical choice. Third, intercolonial slave traders were rarely specialists; they were general merchants for whom the slave trade complemented other activities. They paid more for captives in American markets than their rivals paid for them in Africa, but they were willing to accept slimmer profit margins because selling African people facilitated other commerce. The trade in enslaved people, intercolonial merchants realized, opened other avenues of trade.[4]

To exploit their proximity to the American markets for enslaved laborers, intercolonial traders monitored variations in local economies and fluctuations in the transatlantic slave trade. In any given year, a colony might fail to receive its usual number of Africans or see local demand spike because of a great harvest. Sometimes the resulting price discrepancies lasted for years, as transatlantic traders adapted slowly to the economic emergence of a new colony (or a new staple within a colony). In 1738, an anonymous writer to the *South-Carolina Gazette* explained that merchants had delivered thousands of Africans annually to South Carolina over the previous decade owing to a "much greater Price here than in any other Part of America." These high prices attracted transatlantic traders, to be sure, but they also allowed for profitable intercolonial trade. "I have known many Slaves bought in Barbadoes, etc. and sent here for Sale," the letter to the *Gazette* continued, "which have been sold with good Profit." Apparently transatlantic traders did not always find or saturate the markets where prices were highest; their slow reaction to changed market conditions presented opportunities for their intercolonial counterparts.[5]

Charleston again offered such an opportunity in the 1750s and 1760s. The expansion of indigo to supplement rice cultivation pushed up demand (and prices) for African labor in South Carolina, and Governor James Glen noted in 1754 that intercolonial merchants seized the moment. "As Negroes are sold at higher Prices here than in any part of the King's Dominions," he reported, "we have them sent from Barbadoes, the Leeward Islands, Jamaica, Virginia and New York." Glen wrote partly to pat himself on the back by showing that "this Province is in a flourishing condition," but import records reveal the

4. On the export of provisions from the Chesapeake and Carolina to the West Indies, see McCusker and Menard, *Economy of British America*, 130, 174.

5. *South-Carolina Gazette*, Mar. 9, 1738.

surge of transshipments was no figment of his self-aggrandizing imagination. Throughout the 1740s, voyages transshipping Africans to Charleston had numbered in the single digits annually, with none at all in some years (even after the end of King George's War in 1748). In the 1750s, the high prices in South Carolina brought increased intercolonial deliveries alongside the transatlantic trade's acceleration.[6]

Sustained economic growth such as South Carolina experienced in the 1750s could create an opening for intercolonial trade over several years, but other market fluctuations had narrower windows, making them particularly suited to intercolonial traders operating over short distances. For example, intercolonial traders could time voyages for periods within the year when enslaved people sold to greatest advantage. The slave trade was more seasonal to North America than the Caribbean because northern ports could be obstructed by ice in the winter and because even mainland planters farther south avoided buying slaves in the colder months, fearing mortality among their investments. But once the spring growing season arrived, demand for new slaves in North American plantation colonies was strong. As such, South Carolina merchant John Guerard explained in 1754 that shipments arriving in the spring "come in at the best Time as the Planters have just Pitch'd their Crops and will give the more as the Negroes will be of Greater Service in hoeing thro' the whole Season."[7]

Traders to Africa faced many constraints on their ability to time arrivals in America with precision, such as irregular supplies in Africa and variable speeds crossing the Atlantic, so intercolonial traders from the Caribbean often achieved the coveted first delivery of the season. At the end of February 1757, South Carolina's first captives of the year arrived from Barbados rather than Africa, aboard the snow *Hannah,* prompting Charleston mer-

<hr />

6. James Glen to Board of Trade, Aug. 26, 1754, in Elizabeth Donnan, ed., *Documents Illustrative of the History of the Slave Trade to America,* 4 vols. (Washington, D.C., 1930–1935), IV, 313. Demand for slaves might also have spiked at this time owing to slow importation during the 1740s, thanks to King George's War (1744–1748), but this alone is an unsatisfactory explanation because shipments did not accelerate immediately following the war. Indigo production was introduced in South Carolina during the war, taking off as a secondary crop and buffering the region's economy against rice market fluctuations. See Greene, *Pursuits of Happiness,* 144; McCusker and Menard, *Economy of British America,* 186–188.

7. John Guerard to William Jolliff, May 6, 1754, John Guerard Letter Book, 1752–1754, 34/0321 OvrSz, fol. 258, South Carolina Historical Society, Charleston. Stephen Behrendt shows that demand for slaves in North American plantation colonies intensified in spring and summer, emphasizing crop cycles as the cause (Behrendt, "Markets, Transaction Cycles, and Profits: Merchant Decision Making in the British Slave Trade," *WMQ,* 3d Ser., LVIII [2001], 192–193).

chants Austin and Laurens to report with envy on the high prices this group of people fetched. The strong local economy and lack of African arrivals over the winter "has given such spirits to our Planters" that "when there was a sale of 200 Negroes from Barbados, mostly Calabars, they [buyers] were induced to give [£]280, [£]270, and £260 for the men that were tollerable." Such high prices for "Calabars"—captives from the Bight of Biafra, the African region South Carolina planters least preferred—led Austin and Laurens to predict, "The first Gambias that arrive we expect the prime Men will bring £300." In Carolina, Senegambia was the favored source of enslaved people. Regardless of ethnicity, timing was crucial. That the *Hannah* completed its venture from Barbados to South Carolina at precisely the moment when demand peaked in the Lowcountry was no coincidence. Intercolonial traders enjoyed greater control over their timing than transatlantic traders.[8]

In some years, the end of the season for deliveries also presented an opportunity. If transatlantic arrivals fell short of expectations, planters could get desperate toward harvest time. In May 1755, Austin and Laurens notified Caribbean correspondents that the only vessels to reach South Carolina from Africa that year had delivered "but a trifle to the number wanted." As a result, Austin and Laurens bemoaned a missed opportunity to transship captives at the beginning of the season but anticipated another chance toward the end of the year. They complained to partners in Saint Kitts that "Could you have sent 60 or 70 fine Slaves . . . as you propos'd We think we must have render'd an agreeable Account of them." Looking forward, however, "If we see two or three months hence that our Imports are but small, it may be worth while to take a share with you in One or two hundred to be here in the month of October and November." To compete with transatlantic traders, intercolonial merchants monitored markets carefully and rushed deliveries when prices spiked—or, better yet, when they anticipated such a peak.[9]

When timing was not ideal, traders to regions that also imported people directly from Africa simply opted out. John Guerard jumped in and out of the intercolonial slave trade between the Caribbean and South Carolina as the moment dictated. With various partners in England, Guerard invested in nu-

8. Austin and Laurens to Augustus and John Boyd and Co. [of London], [Charleston], Mar. 14, 1757, in Philip M. Hamer et al., eds., *The Papers of Henry Laurens*, 16 vols. (Columbia, S.C., 1968–2002), II, 493 (hereafter cited as *Laurens Papers*). For the *Hannah*'s arrival, see "Negroes Imported into South Carolina, 1757," in Donnan, ed., *Documents*, IV, 365. On the many factors limiting transatlantic slavers' control over the timing of their departure from Africa, see Behrendt, "Markets, Transaction Cycles, and Profits," *WMQ*, LVIII (2001), 171–204.

9. Austin and Laurens to Smith and Clifton, May 26, 1755, in *Laurens Papers*, I, 255–256.

merous trading ventures, including a number of transatlantic slaving voyages. One venture that Guerard financed repeatedly, with his partner William Jolliff of Poole, was a four-legged trade that sent English manufactures to Madeira, wine from Madeira to Barbados, enslaved Africans or Caribbean produce to Charleston, and Carolina produce back to England. The route remained the same whether the vessel carried Africans on the third leg or not. People became interchangeable commodities with rum or sugar. On such a four-legged journey in 1752, the captain of Guerard's ship *Molly,* Richard Watts, purchased one hundred captives from the ship *Africa* in Barbados for transshipment to South Carolina. But in 1754, when Captain Watts was completing the circuit again, Guerard wrote to him in Barbados with far less enthusiasm about slave transshipment to Charleston. Guerard pondered what

> might answer best from Barbados about which I am greatly at a Loss seeing we are so over Stockt with Rum . . . ; Muscovado Sugar Sells at [moderate prices] but I reckon it is Dear [expensive] at the Islands; Negroes I imagine will also fall in Price [in South Carolina] as the Planters Produce here is now Lower than has been for a few Years Past.

Befuddled, Guerard left the decision to Watts as the man on site, but his thinking illustrates that his primary consideration was just the relative prices of goods—including enslaved people—in Barbados and Charleston. Whether South Carolina planters wanted slaves was not the question; surely they did, but Guerard feared that low prices for Carolina's crops would keep planters from paying enough for Africans to make transshipment profitable. Since Guerard was not a slave-trading specialist, he bowed out. Virginia merchant Charles Steuart acted similarly, writing to correspondents in many colonies in 1752 and "advising that negroes are in great demand," only to report the following year, "The great number of Slaves imported last year . . . almost drained the Country of Cash, . . . [and prices] fell considerably." To these merchants, enslaved African people were one commodity among many to round out intercolonial cargoes.[10]

10. Guerard to Capt. Watts, Mar. 6, 1754, John Guerard Letter Book, fol. 235. Guerard and Jolliff were not alone in this "square" trade, linking England, Africa's Atlantic islands, the Caribbean, and the North American mainland. Shipping records for Virginia in 1732 note that two vessels transshipping slaves there from the Caribbean had come from Madeira before that. Such notation of previous stops is rare, though, so the frequency of such voyages is unclear; see "Negroes Imported into Virginia, 1727–1769," in Donnan, ed., *Documents,* IV, 189. On the symbiotic relationship of the trade in colonial staples from America to Europe and Madeira wine for the return back across the Atlantic, see David Hancock, *Oceans of Wine: Madeira and the*

But they were not quite like any other, because when market conditions were favorable, Guerard (and others) considered enslaved Africans the most advantageous of merchantable "goods." When Guerard organized Watts's venture in 1752, he pinned high hopes on the transshipment of people. The first two legs of that venture—from England to Madeira and from Madeira to Barbados—had not gone well, and Guerard explained to his partner that he saw only one way for the voyage to end profitably. "If he [Capt. Watts] does but ma[ke] choice of the right Sort of Negroes," Guerard prayed, "I may make some small Profit upon the Voyage and that is all the Chance I have." Discussing a similar proposed transshipment with Thomas Rock, a partner in Bristol, Guerard again attached high hopes to slaves. He suggested not only that African people could bring high prices but also that having them to sell facilitated the acquisition of crops for export, which avoided an unprofitable trip to England in ballast. When Rock's ship *Carolina* arrived from Antigua without the planned transshipment of people, Guerard complained that if the vessel had "brought Some [slaves] it would have been the most Likely means to have given her a Dispatch [i.e., to have quickly obtained a cargo for export], but now I shalle be under great Difficulty to Effect it." Merchants offering slaves in exchange for planters' crops had the advantage in reloading their vessels.[11]

Other merchants agreed that the high demand for labor in the colonies gave enslaved people a unique value for acquiring export cargoes. In 1749, James Murray of Cape Fear cautioned a ship captain in the West Indies against venturing to North Carolina as planned, reporting, "There . . . is now greater plenty of ships in the River than ever was known," which "occasions a great Scarcity of all the Produce of this Port fit for a forreign Markets." As a result, vessels in North Carolina that summer were forced to offer cut rates on shipping to avoid departing in ballast. If "necessity obliges you to come," Murray added, "I advise you to bring instead of Rum and Sugar some cheap Negroes but not old ones. If any thing brings a loading here they will." Similarly, in the

---

Emergence of American Trade and Taste (New Haven, Conn., 2009), 108–110. For Guerard's investments in the transatlantic slave trade, see *Voyages*, accessed May 2011, Voyage ID nos. 24010, 24011, 26018, and 26019. "Negroes are in great demand": Charles Steuart to Thomas Ogilvie, [Saint Kitts], Mar. 9, 1752, in Charles Steuart Letter Book, I, 1751–1753, microfilm, M-32, John D. Rockefeller, Jr. Library, Williamsburg, Virginia; see also Steuart to Mrs. Menvielle and Co., [Barbados], Mar. 26, 1752. "Great number of Slaves imported last year": Steuart to Susanna Menvielle and Elias Menvielle, [Barbados], Feb. 13, 1753, ibid.

11. Guerard to Jolliff, Mar. 26, 1752, John Guerard Letter Book, fol. 7; Guerard to Mr. Thomas Rock and Co., Mar. 17, 1752, ibid., fols. 3–4. In letters to Rock in the following weeks, Guerard continued to complain about the difficulty of obtaining a cargo for the *Carolina* (fols. 6–7, 11–12).

spring of 1755, Austin and Laurens discouraged vessels from coming to South Carolina: "Our Country is So well drayn'd of the Produce that we are Certain nothing Can be got on Freight for Europe worth Acceptance." If a vessel came despite this warning, they suggested, "the most Certain Article we can recommend to be Sent by her is a few fine Negro Men." There was no rice or indigo available for export unless a trader was selling Africans. In such cases, the discrepancy between the price paid and price received for captives was less important than using them to ensure an export cargo.[12]

For traders, a corollary to this was that buyers of slaves often paid with crops at the moment of a sale, minimizing the extension of credit. Charles Steuart and Alexander McKenzie of Virginia explained this advantage to prospective partners in the Caribbean when seeking to expand their intercolonial slave trading. Describing "our trade to the Islands," Steuart and McKenzie stated that Caribbean "produce generally sells higher here [in Virginia] than in any other part of the Continent, but" lamented, "One great misfortune attending our Trade is the long Credits we are obliged to give." One special commodity evaded this problem of waiting to collect debts: "Negroes are the only Article that will command ready money." As such, Steuart and McKenzie invited large transshipments, predicting that enslaved Africans "will continue in great Demand all this Season and a parcel of choice Slaves early in the Spring will come to a great Market. . . . Our Planters here have had great prices for their Tobacco . . . and are full of Cash, which nothing but Negroes will draw forth." To traders, who described them as an "Article" or "a parcel," African people stood out from other commodities only for their ability to convince planters to let go of their cash.[13]

Observing this phenomenon, an anonymous writer to the *South-Carolina Gazette* argued that high prices were not the only factor attracting slave shipments to his colony. In a 1738 editorial, he suggested,

Negroes may be said to be the Bait proper for catching a Carolina Planter, as certain as Beef to catch a Shark. How many under the Notion of 18 Months Credit, have been tempted to buy more Negroes

12. James Murray to David Hunter, Jul. 21, 1749, in Bradford J. Wood, ed., *James Murray in North Carolina: Letters, 1732–1781*, vol. XIII of *The Colonial Records of North Carolina*, 2d Ser. (forthcoming). For another example, see Austin and Laurens to Smith and Clifton, May 26, 1755, in *Laurens Papers*, I, 255–256.

13. Charles Steuart, Alexander McKenzie and Co. to Blackman and Adams, [Barbados?], Jul. 5, 1751, in Charles Steuart Letter Book, I. For another, similar example from Georgia, see Joseph Clay to William Fox, Junior, and Co., Sept. 1, 1774, Joseph Clay and Co. Letter Books, 1772–1776, II, Georgia Historical Society, Savannah.

than they could possibly expect to pay [for] in 3 Years! . . . Yet so great is the Infatuation, that the many Examples of their Neighbours Misfortunes and Danger by such Purchases do not hinder new Fools from bringing themselves into the same Difficulty.

The writer did not differentiate here between transatlantic and intercolonial arrivals of Africans, but the "bait" metaphor was equally applicable to both. From the planters' perspective, the "trap" was debt. Slaves were expensive, and if a planter purchased several African laborers from a merchant on credit, he was "caught." He had committed himself to paying that merchant at least a portion of future harvests. From the merchants' perspective, the quarry was, not the planter himself, but his produce. Shipping colonial staples back to Europe was a profitable branch of trade, and the sale of people helped traders "catch" a share of this commerce. Merchants preferred immediate payment but offered credit when necessary. In either case, they secured crops—present or future—for export. Merchants in the intercolonial trade could accept slim profit margins on slave sales if such transactions ensured them a share of staple exports to Europe.[14]

When carrying captives to a port where people also arrived directly from Africa, intercolonial traders' profits hinged on offering captives that suited planters' desires. Slaveholders in North American colonies that received people directly from Africa felt no compulsion to accept infirm, graying, or otherwise rejected people from other markets. As a result, intercolonial traders to major slaveholding colonies marketed the people they transshipped as only the best of who was available in the Caribbean. In 1750, Robert Pringle and Company of Charleston boasted in a newspaper advertisement of "About One Hundred choice healthy Negroes, most of them Gambia and Gold Coast Slaves, just imported from Barbadoes." Pringle did not elide these captives' transshipment; he announced it, hinting that purchasing captives in Barbados allowed him to select only people of the most desired African backgrounds. Another Charleston merchant, Joseph Pickering, extolled the advantages of transshipment more explicitly, emphasizing that his "seventy choice healthy Negroes from the West Indies [were] mostly of the Gold Coast and were the choice of two cargoes." Pickering implied that, unlike transatlantic traders, who inevitably reached the Americas with a number of captives suffering ill effects of the Middle Passage, transshipment traders made a "choice" of which people to transport a much shorter distance to market. Economic incentive

14. *South-Carolina Gazette*, Mar. 9, 1738.

encouraged intercolonial traders to exaggerate the quality of their wares, but private correspondence substantiates their intent to send only the healthiest captives, preferably young adult males, from Barbados to South Carolina. The perceived quality of captives was crucial in a competitive market.[15]

For the African migrants chosen for such journeys—and who survived the final passage—arrival in eighteenth-century Virginia or South Carolina held varied implications, depending on their African background and that of the people they joined. Between 1710 and 1724, when direct deliveries of enslaved people from Africa to South Carolina emerged, an inordinate number of them (nearly 60 percent) came from Senegambia. Another third of the direct arrivals came from the Gold Coast, and perhaps one in ten hailed from the Bight of Biafra. Complicating this fairly simple tripartite picture of transatlantic arrivals, however, was intercolonial trade from the Caribbean, which continued to supply about half of South Carolina's enslaved immigrants in this formative period. The ethno-linguistic composition of the intercolonial migration differed markedly. Although Senegambian people predominated in direct African trade to South Carolina, they composed only a small share of the forced migration from Africa to the British Caribbean in these years. Traders headed to the islands tended to acquire captives in African regions where larger cargoes of people could be assembled. Akan-speakers from the Gold Coast accounted for half of the captives disembarking in the British Caribbean, and another quarter of arrivals comprised people from the Bight of Benin (Figure 5). Peoples from a smattering of other African regions made up the remainder of the Caribbean migration. Assuming that the intercolonial trade from the British Caribbean to South Carolina reflected the ethnic composition of the transatlantic migration to the British Caribbean, this intercolonial trade must have diversified the enslaved population in South Carolina considerably. For captives from the Bight of Benin, in particular (mostly Aja in this period), transshipment to South Carolina was no doubt profoundly alienating. They composed more than a quarter of the slave trade to the British Caribbean, but no known voyages linked their home region and South Carolina directly. Transshipment for any of these people likely caused a traumatic severance from most countrymen and -women, and from heritage and history. For Senegambians, by contrast, such transshipment had the opposite

15. "Negroes Imported into South Carolina, 1749–1751," in Donnan, ed., *Documents*, IV, 301–302. Discussing Captain Watts's 1752 voyage, for example, John Guerard encouraged a partner that "if he [Watts] does but bring a good Sort I flatter my Self they [will] Sell well" (John Guerard Letter Book, fols. 17–18).

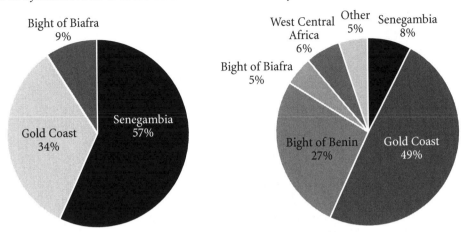

Direct African Arrivals in South Carolina   *Direct African Arrivals in the British Caribbean*

FIGURE 5. Comparison of Captive Origins in the Transatlantic Slave Trades to South Carolina and the British Caribbean, 1711–1725

Source: Voyages: The Trans-Atlantic Slave Trade Database, accessed September 2010, http://slavevoyages.org/tast/assessment/estimates.faces?yearFrom=1711&yearTo=1725&disembarkation =203; http://slavevoyages.org/tast/assessment/estimates.faces?yearFrom=1711&yearTo=1725 &disembarkation=305.304.307.306.309.308.311.310.301.302.303.

effect, carrying them away from a region where they would have been a tiny minority and toward a region where people of similar background predominated. After 1725, the intercolonial trade accounted for much less of the forced migration to South Carolina, and the contrast between the ethnic composition of each region's arriving Africans lessened, mitigating such effects. Nonetheless, South Carolina still received a much larger proportion of captives from Senegambia and far fewer from the Bight of Benin than was typical of the British Caribbean.[16]

16. On the Ajas' predominance among captives from the Bight of Benin, see Patrick Manning, *Slavery, Colonialism, and Economic Growth in Dahomey, 1640–1960* (New York, 1982), 30. On the preference of transatlantic slave traders to match the size of their enslaved cargo with the size of their American market, see Behrendt, "Markets, Transaction Cycles, and Profits," *WMQ,* LVIII (2001), 188–194; Lorena S. Walsh, "The Chesapeake Slave Trade: Regional Patterns, African Origins, and Some Implications," ibid., 155. For South Carolina's direct African trade from 1726–1775, see *Voyages,* accessed September 2012, http://slavevoyages.org/tast/database/search.faces?year From=1701&yearTo=1775&mjslptimp=21300; for the British Caribbean trade 1726–1775, see ibid., http://slavevoyages.org/tast/database/search.faces?yearFrom=1726&yearTo=1775&mjslptimp =33400.33500.33600.33700.33800.34200.34400.35100.35200.35500. In the most influential study of African cultures transferred to North American slave quarters, Michael A. Gomez emphasizes

The intercolonial slave trade to the Chesapeake held similar implications for captives. In the eighteenth century, the Chesapeake's direct African trade relied on the Bight of Biafra for about 35 percent of captives, far more than any other region, and west central Africa and Senegambia each accounted for a little less than half that proportion. Vessels from the Bight of Biafra were also prominent in trade to the British Caribbean, but for captives from other regions, the implications of transshipment from the Caribbean to the Chesapeake would have been profound. Any of the small number of Senegambians arriving in the Caribbean who were transshipped to the Chesapeake would have increased their odds of settling among people of shared backgrounds. Meanwhile, people from the Gold Coast—who composed one-quarter of the migration to the Caribbean—would have faced greatly decreased odds of settling near people who spoke their languages or shared their cultures. Those from the Bight of Benin faced similar risks, moving from a region where they accounted for about one in ten of arriving Africans, to a region where they made up only one of forty (Figure 6).

■ Looking beyond the largest North American slave markets, intercolonial traders' decision to include Africans in their cargoes is more intuitive because traders from Africa ignored many North American ports. The unmet demand for exploitable laborers elevated prices, enticing American speculators. What requires more explanation is why transatlantic traders did not target such markets themselves. Why leave some markets to intercolonial traders? The primary consideration was speed. Rapid sale was essential to the profitability of slaving voyages from Africa because longer trips (including stays in ports) meant increased payments to ship crews and higher captive mortality, not to mention the cost of provisions. With this in mind, most transatlantic slavers—whose average cargo in the eighteenth century exceeded three hundred people—sought ports capable of consuming an entire shipment quickly. This expectation required not only a region with strong demand for African laborers but also an economy robust enough to pay for them. In 1763, Henry Laurens (Plate 4) of Charleston explained the reasoning to merchant Joseph Brown of Georgetown, South Carolina, a much smaller port up the coast. Brown sought to attract a direct shipment from Africa, but Laurens insisted that transatlantic

the formation of "African ethnic enclaves" due to patterns in the slave trade that concentrated people of similar African backgrounds in the same American regions (Gomez, *Exchanging Our Country Marks: The Transformation of African Identities in the Colonial and Antebellum South* [Chapel Hill, N.C., 1998], 11, 38, 150); the intercolonial traffic complicated that picture by tangling the lines of transatlantic migration.

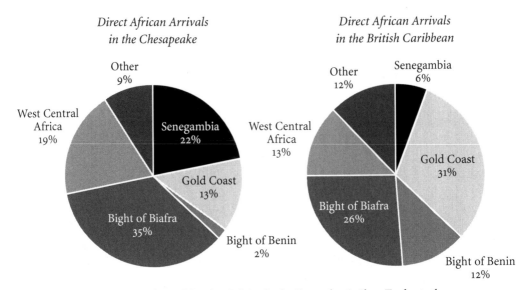

Direct African Arrivals
in the Chesapeake

Direct African Arrivals
in the British Caribbean

FIGURE 6. Comparison of Captive Origins in the Transatlantic Slave Trades to the Chesapeake and the British Caribbean, 1711–1725

Source: Voyages: The Trans-Atlantic Slave Trade Database, accessed January 2013, http://slavevoyages .org/tast/assessment/estimates.faces?yearFrom=1701&yearTo=1775&disembarkation=202 and http:// slavevoyages.org/tast/assessment/estimates.faces?yearFrom=1701&yearTo=1775&disembarkation =305.304.307.306.309.308.311.310.301.302.303.

traders would resist "sending a Vessel to your port without a warrantee both as to the price and remittances . . . especially while there is so fine a Markett for slaves in the Center of the province and in the old beaten Track. . . . The Affri-can Traders . . . allways seek for that Market where there is most money stir-ring and where there are men of Fortune who in Case of a Glutt will take of[f] a Cargo at some rate or other and pay for them." Even when prices were high at small ports, transatlantic traders feared being "forced to sell for long Credit in order to maintain the prices." Georgetown was a minor destination for the slave trade, and its situation relative to Charleston mirrored that of numerous other secondary ports throughout British America.[17]

A merchant such as Laurens had incentive, of course, to discourage Brown from directing African trade away from his established entrepôt, but data suggests that Laurens accurately described transatlantic traders' preferences. More than 97 percent of shipments from Africa to the Carolinas, for example, disembarked the captives in Charleston. For British America as a whole,

17. Laurens to Joseph Brown, Charleston, Dec. 24, 1763, in *Laurens Papers,* IV, 103–105.

HENRY LAURENS ESQ.

PLATE 4. Henry Laurens. By V. Green, based on a painting by J. S. Copley. Laurens (1724–1792) was one of the most prolific slave traders in mid-eighteenth-century Charleston before going on to play a major role in the American Revolution, including serving as president of the Continental Congress. Courtesy, Library of Congress

large markets also predominated. Between 1701 and 1765, well over half of all Africans surviving the Middle Passage landed in one of just two colonies—Barbados or Jamaica. Of those arriving in North America in the same period, nearly 80 percent landed in Virginia or South Carolina. In other words, most transatlantic slavers headed to big markets and ignored others. Prices in the overlooked colonies could rise quite high, however, so intercolonial traders capitalized by transshipping Africans from major entrepôts. To avoid glutting the limited markets of secondary ports, intercolonial traders just kept such ventures smaller than was viable for transatlantic traders. The average intercolonial voyage from the Caribbean to North America between 1701 and 1765 carried just twelve people. And, of the 808 of these voyages for which the complete cargo is known, 90 percent carried inanimate commodities—usually rum, sugar, molasses, or tropical fruits—alongside the human kind.[18]

18. On the proportion of arrivals in the Carolinas who disembarked at Charleston, see *Voyages*, accessed May 2011, http://slavevoyages.org/tast/database/search.faces?yearFrom=1514&

If the fear of glutting small markets warned transatlantic slavers off delivering full African cargoes to smaller American markets despite high prices, selling captives at multiple ports in the Americas offered a possible alternative, but it was not a popular choice. Hopping from port to port to find the highest prices rarely compensated for the higher operating costs, which merchants measured in increased port fees, seamen's wages, and mortality among their human cargo. Selling agents in the Americas railed against the practice. Such protests were self-serving, of course, since agents sought to garner more business themselves by encouraging transatlantic traders to ignore other ports, but the factors also saw the effects of prolonged voyages on African captives. Their beleaguered condition evoked little expression of sympathy, but the agents nonetheless wanted captives healthy on arrival out of concern for their salability.[19]

Perhaps none expressed their opposition to port hopping more forcefully than the Jamaican traders Tyndall and Assheton, who berated their partners in Bristol for the state in which a group of Africans from the port of Bonny, on the Bight of Biafra, reached them in 1729:

---

yearTo=1866&mjslptimp=21200.21300. Of the 466 shipments to the Carolinas documented in *Voyages* for which a specific port of disembarkation is listed, 453 went to Charleston. Another 369 voyages list only "South Carolina," not a specific port, as their point of disembarkation, so they were left out of this calculation. (The editors of *Voyages* assume that such ventures delivered slaves to Charleston, since merchants—not to mention the researchers reading their documents—used the name of a region and its major port interchangeably. If we accept that assumption, the proportion of vessels to the Carolinas that delivered to Charleston climbs to more than 98 percent.) On the proportion of Africans arriving in Barbados or Jamaica, see *Voyages,* accessed April 2011, http://slavevoyages.org/tast/assessment/estimates.faces?yearFrom=1701&yearTo=1765&disembarkation=205.305.204.304.307.306.309.201.308.311.203.310.202.301.302.303. On the proportion of North American arrivals in Virginia and South Carolina, see ibid., accessed May 2011, http://slavevoyages.org/tast/database/search.faces?yearFrom=1701&yearTo=1765&mjslptimp=20000. On slave traders' logic in choosing ports for sales, see Richard Nelson Bean, *The British Trans-Atlantic Slave Trade: 1650–1775* (New York, 1975), 63; Daniel C. Littlefield, "Charleston and Internal Slave Redistribution," *South Carolina Historical Magazine,* LXXXVII (1986), 93–105; Behrendt, "Markets, Transaction Cycles, and Profits," *WMQ,* LVIII (2001), 191–197; Kenneth Morgan, "Slave Sales in Colonial Charleston," *English Historical Review,* CXIII (1998), 905–927, esp. 908–909; Trevor Burnard and Kenneth Morgan, "The Dynamics of the Slave Market and Slave Purchasing Patterns in Jamaica, 1655–1788," *WMQ,* LVIII (2001), 205–228; John C. Coombs, "Building 'the Machine': The Development of Slavery and Slave Society in Early Colonial Virginia" (Ph.D. diss., College of William and Mary, 2003), 42–43, 52–54. On the average sizes of transatlantic cargoes, see Herbert S. Klein, *The Atlantic Slave Trade* (New York, 1999), 148–149.

19. Alexander X. Byrd notes the high mortality of captives aboard vessels that hopped between multiple American ports; see Byrd, *Captives and Voyagers: Black Migrants across the Eighteenth-Century British Atlantic World* (Baton Rouge, 2008), 52–55.

The *Aurora* is arrived with 270 Slaves: the worst cargoe of Bonny Slaves have been seen this long time, which You may guess by the ship's touching at every Place to Windward. . . . She was a month from B[arbadoes] hither, which Capt. Davis says was a great measure to Impare the Slaves.

Lest the Bristol owners suspect that the Jamaica traders hoped to monopolize commissions by diverting more business to their island, Tyndall and Assheton continued to emphasize the debilitating effects of a journey prolonged by port hopping in later letters. "[We] do assure you, the Owners of the *Aurora* suffer much by touching from Place [to] Place[;] there's not two thirds of her Cargoe now Living." In Tyndall and Assheton's eyes, the dangers of shipboard mortality during weeks of searching for higher prices outweighed the potential profits. Meanwhile, one can imagine the growing outrage and horror of the captives shackled aboard the *Aurora,* as each new harbor brought hope for release from the ship, but then despair, as the journey dragged on and disease spread. Heeding the lesson of disastrous voyages like this, fewer and fewer transatlantic traders sold enslaved Africans at multiple American ports as the eighteenth century wore on, perhaps contributing to the declining mortality in the slave trade.[20]

African slave traders' concentration on a limited number of American ports left openings for intercolonial exchanges elsewhere, but not all smaller Ameri-

20. Tyndall and Assheton to Hobhouse and Tyndall, Aug. 22, 1729, Jeffries Collection, XIII, fol. 111, Bristol Central Library, U.K.; Tyndall and Assheton to Isaac Hobhouse, Nov. 1, 1729, "Letters to Messrs. Isaac Hobhouse and Onesiphovous Tyndall, Merchants of Bristol from Their Agents in the West Indies," MSS 8029/16e, Bristol Record Office, U.K. For Tyndall and Assheton's earlier warnings about multiple stops, see Jeffries Coll., XIII, fol. 91, 97. In the seventeenth century, port hopping in search of high prices was somewhat more common. Ralph Davis, for example, notes the attraction of the Jamaican market for transatlantic traders in the late seventeenth century because of its size, but also shows that some investors in the trade instructed ship captains to island hop in search of the best prices (Davis, *The Rise of the English Shipping Industry in the Seventeenth and Eighteenth Centuries* [London, 1962], 294–296). Conversely, Richard S. Dunn notes the importance of a large economy to Royal African Company ships choosing American ports in the seventeenth century, noting that they often avoided smaller islands in part because they considered those buyers less likely to pay their debts (Dunn, *Sugar and Slaves: The Rise of the Planter Class in the English West Indies, 1624–1713* [1972; rpt. Chapel Hill, N.C., 2000], 235). Richard Pares states that port fees made port hopping for high prices (for any commodity) cost-prohibitive, at least by the early nineteenth century: *A West-India Fortune* (New York, 1950), 226. On the general decline in mortality in the transatlantic slave trade from the seventeenth to the eighteenth century, see Herbert S. Klein et al., "Transoceanic Mortality: The Slave Trade in Comparative Perspective," *WMQ,* 3d Ser., LVIII (2001), 93–118, esp. table II; see also Klein, *Atlantic Slave Trade,* 139–140.

can markets required the same strategies. Trading to colonies where enslaved people composed a major part of the labor force but where transatlantic arrivals were nonetheless lacking, intercolonial traders could rely on pent-up demand to make finding buyers fairly easy. The smaller economies of such colonies, however, meant currency was scarce, so that extending credit and collecting debts were problems. By contrast, targeting colonies with healthier economies but where slavery was a minor institution required aggressive marketing. Especially in the North, people had money to pay for slaves, but intercolonial traders had to convince prospective buyers to want them.

North Carolina and Georgia (after it legalized slavery in 1750) both fell into the former category, relying considerably upon enslaved labor, wishing to rely on it more, but struggling to steer African shipments away from larger, wealthier markets in South Carolina and Virginia. For Georgia, this problem was fleeting; after the Seven Years' War, the colony experienced an economic boom that attracted African traders. For North Carolina, the problem was chronic, with only nine known vessels—most of them much smaller than average ships in the transatlantic slave trade—ever delivering captives directly to the colony from Africa. The colony's hazardous coastline limited shipping, and development lagged without direct access to transatlantic trade or commerce with the Caribbean, which facilitated other colonies' starts with slavery. Settlers in North Carolina's Albemarle region complained in 1731 that a lack of access to Atlantic networks stymied the local economy, forcing them to rely on "the Merchants on James River in Virginia [to] Supply most of the Inhabitants . . . with Brittish Commodity's at unreasonable Rates . . . by Land or in Little Canoes." Planters at the more southerly, and newer, Cape Fear settlement hardly felt more connected. They often described living in a "remote part of the world." A deficit of trade and slave importation was central to this sense of isolation. The 1740 lament of Cape Fear planter John Watson was typical, when he said, "The want of the Negroes this Summer has been a Considerable Los[s]." Facing isolation, but still hoping to import Africans for forced labor, planters and merchants in such colonies had to be aggressive in courting (or organizing) deliveries of enslaved people.[21]

21. *Voyages*, accessed April 2011, http://slavevoyages.org/tast/database/search.faces?yearFrom =1514&yearTo=1776&mjslptimp=21200; petition from people of Albemarle, N.C., July 27, 1731, CO 5/293, fol. 24, National Archives, Kew. Bradford J. Wood not only uses the phrase "remote part of the world" as the title of his book on the colonial Cape Fear region; he also quotes many settlers' use of the word "remote" to describe their relative isolation from the broader Atlantic world. "This remote part of the world" was penned by leaders of a newly formed parish in the region (Wood, *This Remote Part of the World: Regional Formation in Lower Cape Fear, North Caro-*

TABLE 11. Estimates of Enslaved People Arriving in North Carolina from Various Sources, 1721–1765

Year	Arrivals directly from Africa	from the Caribbean	from mid-Atlantic colonies	from Virginia and South Carolina	Estimated enslaved population
					2,000 (as of 1720)
1721–1725	0	50	10	1,100	
					6,000 (as of 1730)
1726–1730	0	50	15	1,900	
1731–1735	0	50	20	700	
1736–1740	0	50	0	900	
1741–1745	0	125	5	1,100	
1746–1750	0	75	0	1,500	
					19,000 (as of 1755)
1751–1755	200	200	0	1,200	
1756–1760	450	100	0	3,900	
1761–1765	200	200	60	5,700	
TOTAL	850	900	110	18,000	41,000 (as of 1767)

Sources: For arrivals directly from Africa, see *Voyages: The Trans-Atlantic Slave Trade Database,* accessed May 2011, http://slavevoyages.org/tast/database/search.faces?yearFrom=1514&yearTo=1866 &mjslptimp=21200. For arrivals from the Caribbean, see Gregory E. O'Malley, "Beyond the Middle Passage: Slave Migration from the Caribbean to North America, 1619–1807," *William and Mary Quarterly,* 3d Ser., LXVI (2009), 147–151. Arrivals from the mid-Atlantic colonies were also calculated from my database of intercolonial voyages, but no estimates were added to the documented voyages since the traffic was so small. For arrivals from Virginia and South Carolina, quantifying migration is much more difficult, since much of this movement was overland and not within the purview of port officials. Even when seaborne, such traffic was often aboard small vessels that escaped official notice. To derive an estimate of the traffic from South Carolina and Virginia, population data for North Carolina was compared with the estimates of imports from other sources. Population data was derived from Marvin L. Michael Kay and Lorin Lee Cary, *Slavery in North Carolina, 1748–1775* (Chapel Hill, N.C., 1995), 19, including their estimate of natural population growth of 2.5 percent annually. There are numerous assumptions built into this calculation, so these estimates must be seen as quite tentative. Nonetheless, even if one modifies the estimate of natural population growth significantly, the overall picture changes little; the vast majority of enslaved Africans in North Carolina must have entered via Virginia and South Carolina.

The trials and travails of James Murray, a North Carolina merchant and planter, are illustrative of the colony's remoteness. Murray had lived a peripatetic life and maintained a broad mercantile correspondence but still had difficulty drawing African workers to North Carolina. And despite his desire to the see the colony prosper (which, in his mind, required enslaved Africans), he always recognized its shortcomings as a market for slave traders. Born in Scotland, Murray had worked in a London merchant house, and he made several return trips to Britain after settling in North Carolina in 1735. He also possessed contacts in the West Indies, since his London employers had engaged in Caribbean trade. If anyone could draw African workers to North Carolina—for toil on his own plantation or for sale to others—surely a man of Murray's connections could, especially since he arrived in the Americas with a cargo of English goods to sell, to get himself established. Yet Murray struggled. After twenty years in the province, Murray claimed ownership of just fourteen African people. By the 1760s, when he moved to Massachusetts, Murray had amassed a workforce of about thirty individuals and had imported others for fellow settlers, but he went to great lengths to accomplish this and saw many efforts rebuffed. The colony amassed an enslaved population of about 40,000 people by 1770—fifth among British North American colonies—but nonetheless failed ever to attract steady supplies of people directly from Africa. Most importations came in small shipments (overland or in small boats) from neighboring colonies, supplemented by occasional ventures from the Caribbean or more distant parts of the mainland.[22]

The key problem, Murray soon realized, was that his colony lacked wealthy merchants willing to speculate on shipments of Africans, largely because the colony was not producing enough to complete the circuits suited to the slave trade. Given his West Indian connections, Murray initially viewed the islands as his most promising option for acquiring Africans. Optimistic in his first weeks in America, Murray wrote to Antigua merchant David Tullideph, "In a little time with some cash and goods which (if I can get a vessel) shall send you in corn and pork to purchase Negroes." So many colonists desired African workers in his fledgling settlement that Murray regretted not having

lina, 1725–1775 [Columbia, S.C., 2004], 4–5, 226). "The want of the Negroes": Thomas Clark to John Watson and John Mackenzie, June 23, 1740, in Wood, ed., James Murray Letters.

22. On James Murray's life, see Wood's introduction to James Murray Letters. I thank Professor Wood for calling my attention to Murray and sharing the forthcoming edition of Murray's letters. Murray was not alone among North Carolina settlers in possessing connections around the Atlantic; see Wood, Remote Part of the World, 18. For the relative size of North Carolina's enslaved population by the late colonial period, see ibid., 6.

stopped at "the Islands in my way [to North Carolina] and sold all my goods for Negroes Rum and Sugar which are the best of Articles" for sale in Cape Fear. Instead, Murray's English goods "brought . . . a very good price" in Carolina" but required him to wait "for a year at least" for payments. In the ensuing weeks, Murray reiterated his impression that "quick remittance . . . could not be made for anything but Negros," but his confidence in North Carolinians' ability to pay even for coveted Africans waned quickly. Just months later, he was very cautious in encouraging London merchant Henry McCulloh to undertake a delivery of enslaved people to Cape Fear, presumably directly from Africa. "As to the consignment of negroes," Murray warned, "nothing could be of more service, to the country [Cape Fear] . . . but it is the Misfortune of the planters, on this river, to be much indebt'd to the traders." Many North Carolinians desired enslaved Africans, but their shortage of money or marketable staples made "it dangerous, for a man to undertake anything on their payments." Even though he was a merchant looking to spur North Carolina's commerce, Murray discouraged correspondents from the slave trade to North Carolina in the 1730s, only requesting a few small shipments of people for his own exploitation from South Carolina.[23]

By midcentury, the Cape Fear economy had grown, but Murray was only slightly more optimistic. In 1752, London merchant Richard Oswald contacted Murray to inquire about North Carolina's market. Because Oswald was one of the principal investors in the British slave-trading fort at Bunce Island, in modern Sierra Leone, his decision to contact Murray attested to the latter's Atlantic connections, and the letter offered a promising opportunity to draw exploitable labor to Cape Fear. But Murray's reply sent mixed messages. At first he seemed encouraging: "As to the Negroes you mention — the Prices are

23. Murray to David Tullideph, [Antigua], Brunswick, Feb. 21, 1735/6, Murray to William Dunbar, Brunswick, Feb. 23, 1735/6, Murray to Henry McCulloh, Brunswick, May 28 1736, and Murray and Samuel Johnston to Ribton Hutchison and Frederick Grimké, July 14, 1736 and July 4, 1739, all in Wood, ed., *James Murray Letters;* Wood, *Remote Part of the World*, 18, 226–228. On Virginia, South Carolina, and New York as sources of transshipment, see Marvin L. Michael Kay and Lorin Lee Cary, *Slavery in North Carolina, 1748–1775* (Chapel Hill, N.C., 1995), 21; Wood, *Remote Part of the World*, 38–40; Walter E. Minchinton, "The Seaborne Slave Trade of North Carolina," *North Carolina Historical Review*, LXXI (1994), 7. I have documented seventeen transshipments from New York to North Carolina, primarily from the Naval Office Shipping Lists for New York, CO 5/1222–1228. Arrivals from Virginia and South Carolina rarely appeared in port records (I have documented twenty-three shipments from Charleston and just six from various ports in Virginia), so most of that traffic likely occurred overland or in small boats that escaped the attention of customs officials. Anecdotal sources indicate that port records vastly underreport slave migration from neighboring colonies.

now high every where but highest here for we have no supply but from the West Indies or the Neighbouring Colonies." Pent-up demand left planters so eager that, "if the Negroes are healthy," North Carolinians would buy them "without great enquiry or distinction of Country" of origin. Beggars could not be choosers, Murray suggested, so North Carolina offered a seller's market. But then Murray struck a more cautionary tone. A reputation for honesty meant everything to an eighteenth-century merchant, and Murray refused to paint a rosy and incomplete picture. Murray warned Oswald that no North Carolina merchant was likely to "Contract for them [Africans]" in advance, "as there are few Men of Substance among us." Local traders could not afford to guarantee payments. They also rarely offered cash or even the most valuable American staples. Instead, Murray suggested selling any Africans delivered, "for Country produce (tar for Instance) to be shipt you in Six or 8 Months on Accot and risque of the buyer." If Oswald sent an African vessel to North Carolina, he could expect to sell the captives for tar—not a very lucrative staple— and to offer long credit. Not surprisingly, Oswald demurred.[24]

Murray's discouragement of slave trading to North Carolina despite a strong desire for slaves illustrates the vital role of speculators in dispersing captives on the American side of the Atlantic; aspiring slaveholders seeking exploitable people were not enough to ensure robust trafficking. Even high prices were not sufficient to attract speculators—transatlantic or intercolonial. The traders also needed to acquire commodities in exchange that would help them complete trade circuits. Since North Carolina produced little for export that excited merchants, few would speculate on deliveries of Africans to the province. Similar concerns about the reliability of payments also prevented most traders from targeting Georgia in the decade after that colony legalized slavery in 1750. When a small slave trade finally emerged from the Caribbean to North Carolina at midcentury, tellingly, many of the merchants who undertook such ventures were traders based in the colony, such as Richard Quince, Frederick Gregg, and Thomas Wright. Of 131 documented slave-trading voyages from the Caribbean to North Carolina in the eighteenth century for which the vessel's port of registration is known, more than 40 percent were registered in North Carolina, a remarkable number considering the colony's notoriously underdeveloped mercantile sector. Few others were willing to speculate on

24. Murray to Richard Oswald and Company, Nov. 16, 1752, in Wood, ed., *James Murray Letters*. For more on Oswald, see David Hancock, *Citizens of the World: London Merchants and the Integration of the British Atlantic Community, 1735–1785* (New York, 1995). Instead of North Carolina, Oswald directed most of his dealings to Austin and Laurens in Charleston; see *Laurens Papers*, esp. I–IV.

trade to the economically marginal colony, but North Carolinians were eager to export their naval stores, livestock, and other provisions to the wealthy markets of the Caribbean. Enslaved Africans offered one commodity among many in which (or in whom) such traders took their returns.[25]

Prospective buyers in colonial backwaters faced a disadvantage in the marketplace even when Africans arrived. Such neglected regions remained captive markets to which slave traders came only when they sought to unload captives they had trouble selling in markets with other options. As North Carolina governor George Burrington explained in 1733, "We are under a Necessity to buy the refuse, refractory, and distemper'd Negros, brought from other Governments." If aspiring North Carolina slaveholders hoped for better selection, they generally chose between two options for acquiring Africans. They could venture to entrepôts in other colonies to make purchases themselves, or they could place orders for slaves with merchants in the entrepôts, trusting those traders to make wise decisions on their behalf. Given his mercantile connections, James Murray often opted to trust merchants in other ports. In 1736, Murray and Samuel Johnston asked Charleston merchants Ribton Hutchison and Frederick Grimké, "If you can meet with four men and two women, or two men, two boys and two women, we desire you will buy them on our Joint accot: and send them by the first vessel," noting that they would pay the "freight" charges when the people arrived. Such an arrangement required buyers to grant significant authority to agents in the entrepôts. To facilitate their transaction, Murray clarified for Hutchison and Grimké, "We chuse not [to] confine you to any price nor to load you with Instructions about them being perswaded that you will do your best for our Interest." Desperate for labor, Murray made it clear that he was not picky.[26]

25. On the slow development of Georgia's slave markets due to a lack of capital after 1750, see Darold D. Wax, "'New Negroes Are Always in Demand': The Slave Trade in Eighteenth-Century Georgia," *Georgia Historical Quarterly,* LXVIII (1984), 197. Only a few hundred Africans reached Georgia via the Caribbean in the 1750s, but such trafficking accelerated dramatically as the Seven Years' War (1755–1763) waned, with nearly one thousand captives ferried between 1761 and 1765. Regular transatlantic deliveries quickly outcompeted such intercolonial deliveries thereafter. See O'Malley, "Beyond the Middle Passage," *WMQ,* 3d Ser., LXVI (2009), 150–152. Data on shipments from the Caribbean to North Carolina derives mainly from Naval Office Shipping Lists for Caribbean colonies since few colonial North Carolina port records survive. See Appendix, below; see also Minchinton, "Seaborne Slave Trade of North Carolina," *North Carolina Historical Review,* LXXI (1994), 7.

26. "Captain [Governor George] Burrington's Represent'n of the Present State and Condition of North Carolina," Jan. 1, 1733, CO 5/294, fols. 67–70; Murray and Johnston to Hutchison and Grimké, July 14, Aug. 27, Dec. 15, 1736, in Wood, ed., *James Murray Letters.* For similar ex-

To avoid handing over such power, other planters from bypassed colonies ventured to the entrepôts themselves to buy enslaved people. Murray noted neighbors' making several such trips from North Carolina to Charleston, reporting in 1739 that "Mr [Thomas?] Clark and Mr [Archibald?] Douglass has Set out for Sot Carolina in order to purchase Negroes." Cape Fear planter John Dalrymple apparently made similar excursions. In 1737, colony officials ordered Dalrymple to quarantine a group of Africans that he ferried from South to North Carolina when illness broke out among them, and other records suggest that this was not an isolated venture. Such journeys offered a planter the opportunity to choose captives for himself out of vessels arriving from Africa (or the Caribbean), but the travel would have been costly in terms of both time and money, ensuring that many planters resorted to agents for purchases, unless other business took them to a major slave market.[27]

Regardless of whether planters from the poorly capitalized provinces traveled to the entrepôts or relied on distant agents to acquire slaves, unique patterns emerged in the demographics of the enslaved population introduced to such backwaters. With limited buying power and often limited choices, planters at a distance from the entrepôts purchased more women and children than was typical of planters in regions importing Africans directly. James Murray's advice to traders on selling Africans in his province was that they send "cheap Negroes, but not old ones." These criteria excluded male captives of prime working age as too expensive, and, as ever, women and children (or the ill and disabled) were the alternatives, besides the aged, whom Murray explicitly rejected. The balance between eventual reproduction and immediate affordability in the decision making of remote planters who opted for women and children is unclear. Great efforts to acquire enslaved laborers might have made North Carolina planters particularly sensitive to encouraging natality. When Murray ordered slaves from James Rutherford in Jamaica in 1751, he specified a desire for significant numbers of women and children. He asked Rutherford to invest "two hundred pounds Sterling" in "a Cliver

<hr />

amples, see Murray to Rutherford, Jan. 19, 1750/1, and Murray to John Watson, Dec. 2, 1740, ibid. Minchinton also notes North Carolina planters' placing orders for slaves with merchants in other colonies, especially in the early eighteenth century ("Seaborne Slave Trade of North Carolina," *North Carolina Historical Review*, LXXI [1994], 23). Laurens also received requests from North Carolina planters; see Laurens to John Rutherford, Nov. 23, 1762, *Laurens Papers*, III, 168–169.

27. Murray to Andrew Bennet, Sept. 6, 1739, in Wood, ed., *James Murray Letters*; Mr. Clark was presumably Thomas Clark, Murray's brother-in-law, and Mr. Douglass was presumably Archibald Douglass. For mention of a similar trip, see Murray to McCulloch, June 23, 1740, ibid. For Dalrymple, see Wood, *Remote Part of the World*, 39.

boy of twelve years and one girl from twelve to fourteen, three Wenches from fifteen to twenty, and the Remainder in men from eighteen to twenty one." That "Remainder" left for purchasing men would not have been considerable. So-called "prime slaves" sold for as much as forty pounds sterling in the early 1750s, so even if Murray managed to purchase the two children specified for twenty pounds each and the three young women for thirty pounds each, he would have been lucky to have enough money remaining for the purchase of two men. In other words, Murray's age and gender specifications determined a group skewed female and young. He did not articulate reasons for choosing people of this description, but price might not have been the only consideration. Slaveholders throughout the Americas valued enslaved women for their combination of labor and fertility, and planters in less developed slaveholding regions exhibited a pronounced interest in acquiring enslaved females. To those developing slave regimes, women captives promised not only work — but also a next generation of workers.[28]

To captives, it made little difference whether price or fertility was foremost in the minds of planters like Murray, but the implications of the bias toward women and children had profound consequences for life in their strange, new land. In the slave trade to the Caribbean in the eighteenth century, males accounted for more than 60 percent of arriving captives. That meant there were fewer than two females for every three males who stepped off vessels arriving from Africa, profoundly limiting the possibilities for family formation, reproduction, and the maintenance of traditional gender roles. If planters in North Carolina — and other colonies on the margins of the Atlantic slave system — acquired disproportionate numbers of women, this tendency contributed to

28. Murray to James Rutherford, Jan. 19, 1750/1, in Wood, ed., *James Murray Letters*. Average colonial slave prices at that date are found in a 1753 report on the trade by John Pownal, secretary of the Board of Trade ("Mr. Pownal's Account of the Slave Trade," in Donnan, ed., *Documents*, II, 507). Bean estimates a slightly lower average price of £34 for enslaved adult males in Jamaica in 1751, but that price still suggests that Murray could have only purchased two men (*British Trans-Atlantic Slave Trade*, 202). Wood notes a preference among North Carolina settlers for enslaved women and suggests that might have been crucial to population growth (*Remote Part of the World*, 101–102). Philip D. Morgan and Michael L. Nicholls note a similar bias toward less expensive female and youthful slaves in the early decades of European settlement of the Chesapeake piedmont (Morgan and Nicholls, "Slaves in Piedmont Virginia, 1720–1790," *WMQ*, 3d Ser., XLVI [1989], 221–233). Likewise, Jennifer L. Morgan demonstrates that, when many slaveholders thought about enslaved women's work and value, "no rigid distinction between the procreative and the agricultural existed" (*Laboring Women: Reproduction and Gender in New World Slavery* [Philadelphia, 2004], 75). She also notes that, in developmental periods across many colonies and regions, slaveholders showed particular interest in acquiring slave women, presumably with an eye to procreation as well as field labor (77–92).

more balanced gender ratios and higher fertility among the enslaved population. (The pattern might also have further skewed Caribbean gender ratios toward males.) As a result, despite the hardship of transshipment, survivors of intercolonial voyages to North Carolina, Georgia, and other marginal regions of the slave system might have enjoyed greater prospects for family formation than their counterparts who remained in the Caribbean (or other centers of transatlantic importation).[29]

Less-developed colonies' preferences for relatively low-priced slaves had implications for African American populations beyond gender and age. When James Murray told his suppliers in other colonies, "I shall not confine you to any Country," he increased the odds of receiving captive people from backgrounds that buyers in the entrepôts preferred least. As such, Igbo people from the Bight of Biafra might have faced a particular likelihood of transshipment (or overland march) from an entrepôt of the slave trade—such as Charleston, the James River, or Bridgetown—to one of the marginal slaveholding colonies of the mainland, such as North Carolina or Georgia. This bias toward Igbos might have been most pronounced in the earliest decades of North Carolina slavery, when Virginia was an especially important source of captives. People from the Bight of Biafra accounted for nearly half of the Africans shipped directly from Africa to Virginia between 1660 and 1730; surely, they accounted for a major portion of the North Carolina trade. In addition to ethnicity, another factor that lowered the prices of some captives relative to others was health. Given Governor Burrington's complaints that North Carolina received the "refuse . . . and distemper'd Negros" from other colonies, ill or aged slaves might also have been likely to endure final passages from the centers of slave importation to developing slave societies, contributing to the risk of mortality in such migrations and at their destinations.[30]

29. On gender ratios in the slave trade to the Caribbean, see David Eltis, *The Rise of African Slavery in the Americas* (New York, 2000), 95–97. On the benefits to enslaved people of more balanced gender ratios and the unique memories and traditions carried by women and girls, see Morgan, *Laboring Women*, 6, 64–65.

30. For the African regional origins of captives shipped to Virginia from 1661 to 1730, see *Voyages*, accessed September 2012, http://slavevoyages.org/tast/database/search.faces?yearFrom=1661&yearTo=1730&mjslptimp=21100; see also Walsh, "Chesapeake Slave Trade," *WMQ*, LVIII (2001). Kay and Cary note some survival of Igbo (and other African) naming practices among enslaved North Carolinians in the eighteenth century (*Slavery in North Carolina*, 276–277). For more discussion of stages in the North Carolina slave trade and their implications for the captives' regional origins, see Gregory E. O'Malley, "Diversity in the Slave Trade to the Colonial Carolinas," in Bradford J. Wood and Michelle LeMaster, eds., *Creating and Contesting Carolina* (Columbia, S.C., 2013), 243–245, 247–248.

■ Colonies in the North also relied primarily on Caribbean transshipment for African immigration, although some northern colonies saw transatlantic trade briefly overtake Caribbean shipments in the mid-eighteenth century. For all of these colonies, African arrivals from the Caribbean played a complementary role to exports of provisions to the islands. For the mid-Atlantic bread colonies, a growing export trade in flour and other provisions facilitated captive transshipments in return. The cycle was evident in 1741, when Philadelphia merchant Robert Ellis sent turpentine, "Ship Bread," and pork to Barbados, instructing his correspondent there to "Bring the Net Proceeds in Good Likely young Negroes if cheap, or . . . bring me good Rum." From New England, traders shipped salted fish to the islands, incorporating enslaved Africans to the mixed cargoes of return voyages. A pithy Boston advertisement encapsulated the cycle of New England seafood for slaves: "To be Sold for Cash or Jamaica Fish, Two likely Negro Boys." The designation of a local catch as "Jamaica Fish" suggests the importance of Caribbean markets to New England fishermen, and accepting payments for slaves in only such fish or cash points to a return trip to the Caribbean to continue the cycle.[31]

Northern colonies' dependence upon the Caribbean for enslaved Africans over most of the eighteenth century is visible from many sources. Surviving port records from both the islands and some northern colonies allow fairly rigorous quantification of the traffic, and imperial correspondence, newspaper advertising, and merchant papers describe the commerce, as well. New York governor William Burnet prepared a report "of what Negro Slaves have been Imported" in the early eighteenth century, based on information "taken from the Custom House Books," and he noted more than four hundred Africans arriving from the islands between 1700 and 1715. From 1715 to 1741, surviving port records show that Caribbean transshipments outpaced transatlantic deliveries to New York almost two to one. For Pennsylvania, which included Delaware until 1776, no port records survive to document the traffic, but newspapers exist from 1720 onward and suggest a similar pattern. Caribbean sources supplied most captives, and Charleston sent numerous shipments, as well. Such deliveries peaked in the late 1730s, when several dozen Africans reached Pennsylvania annually from the West Indies. Spotty import records imply the same for New Jersey, whose slave trade was closely linked

31. Robert Ellis to Joseph Marks, May 12, 1741, Ellis Letter Book, 1736–1748, Am 9251, fol. 292, Historical Society of Pennsylvania (hereafter cited as HSP); *Boston-Gazette, and Country Journal,* Sept. 16, 23, 1765 (the advertiser specified that the enslaved boys "have been in the Country about three Months").

TABLE 12. Estimates of Enslaved People Arriving in Northern Colonies from the Caribbean, 1701–1770

Year	New York	Pennsylvania/ New Jersey	New England
1701–1705	225	275	250
1706–1710	25	275	250
1711–1715	200	200	250
1716–1720	725	150	250
1721–1725	450	75	250
1726–1730	825	150	375
1731–1735	600	200	375
1736–1740	250	600	375
1741–1745	20	125	125
1746–1750	9	200	200
1751–1755	4	375	125
1756–1760		125	125
1761–1765	17	225	125
1766–1770		100	75
TOTAL	3,350	3,075	3,150

Sources: Derivation of these estimates is discussed in Gregory E. O'Malley, "Beyond the Middle Passage: Slave Migration from the Caribbean to North America, 1619–1807," *William and Mary Quarterly,* 3d Ser., LXVI (2009), 157–165.

to Pennsylvania's, since both colonies bought people and merchandise from vessels sailing into the Delaware River. New Jersey saw extensive slave transshipments to the colony in the early 1730s, but then a decline.[32]

Given the marginality of slavery in New England, one might expect greater reliance on intercolonial deliveries there, but those colonies—especially

32. "Negroes Imported into New York, 1701–1726," in Donnan, ed., *Documents,* III, 444. James G. Lydon argues that West Indian deliveries for 1715 to 1741 outpaced direct African shipments by even more, but *Voyages* documents more direct African arrivals than Lydon found. See Lydon, "New York and the Slave Trade, 1700 to 1774," *WMQ,* 3d Ser., XXXV (1978), 382; *Voyages,* accessed April 2011, http://www.slavevoyages.org/tast/database/search.faces?yearFrom=1514& yearTo=1866&mjslptimp=20600. Edgar J. McManus notes the connection between northern exports of provision to the islands and the slave trade in return; see McManus, *Black Bondage in the North* (Syracuse, N.Y., 1973), 20. On the problems with newspapers for estimating the trade's volume, see the Appendix, below.

Rhode Island—stood out from their mid-Atlantic counterparts; several New England merchants plied the transatlantic slave trade in the first half of the eighteenth century, making direct African deliveries to the region feasible. These traders rarely consigned whole shipments from Africa to New England, but they often carried a few people home after selling most enslaved Africans in the plantation colonies. As Rhode Island merchant James Brown instructed his ship captain and brother, Obadiah, in 1717: "If you cannot sell all your slaves [in the West Indies] . . . bring some of them home; I believe they will sell well."[33] Autobiographer Venture Smith arrived in New England this way; he survived the Middle Passage to Barbados with two hundred fellow captives but was one of just four to remain on board to Rhode Island. Nevertheless, Caribbean transshipments supplemented this African trade to New England throughout the eighteenth century. The account book of ship captain Nathaniel Harris suggests that merchants or slaveholders in the entrepôts sometimes hired captains engaged in intercolonial trade to ship enslaved people to New England for sale. In 1712, "Mr. Nathanael Humphry of Antigua" paid Harris to deliver two captives from that island to Boston and to sell them on his behalf. Harris earned four pounds sterling for the "freight of 2 Negro's" from Antigua to Boston, reimbursement for the import duty on them, and a "Commission for Selling the Negro Man" of just less than two pounds. The other enslaved person apparently remained in Harris's possession at the time the account was recorded.[34]

Northern colonies resembled North Carolina and Georgia in their reliance on intercolonial deliveries of Africans, but the northern colonies did not lack the capital to attract merchants. Instead, transatlantic slavers ignored them

33. Quoted in William D. Piersen, *Black Yankees: The Development of an Afro-American Subculture in Eighteenth-Century New England* (Amherst, Mass., 1988), 4; see also Lorenzo Johnston Greene, *The Negro in Colonial New England, 1620–1776* (New York, 1942), 34–35.

34. "A Narrative of the Life and Adventures of Venture, a Native of Africa: But Resident above Sixty Years in the United States of America; Related by Himself" (1798), in Vincent Carretta, ed., *Unchained Voices: An Anthology of Black Authors in the English-Speaking World of the Eighteenth Century* (Lexington, Ky., 2004), 375; "Accounts of Nathaniel Harris, 1712," in Donnan, ed., *Documents*, III, 26. Voyages like Smith's are not included in the estimates of intercolonial slave movements in this book because it was a continuation of a transatlantic endeavor; Smith changed neither vessels nor ownership in Barbados. The *Voyages* database includes such movements in its statistics for the transatlantic slave trade, so omitting such shipments here makes this intercolonial data more complementary with the information available through *Voyages*. On the preponderance of arrivals from the Caribbean before the mid-eighteenth century, see Robert E. Desrochers, Jr., "Slave-for-Sale Advertisements and Slavery in Massachusetts, 1704–1781," *WMQ*, 3d Ser, LIX (2002), 623–664.

because they lacked a major reliance on slavery. This fundamental difference gave their branch of the intercolonial trade a different character. Most notably, merchants proved willing to speculate on small slaving ventures from the Caribbean to the North, and because demand was not pent up, they had to be aggressive in marketing. This offshoot of the intercolonial slave trade was especially appealing to merchants because the northern colonies' export of provisions to the Caribbean made a return trip with African people a viable corollary. As exports of flour, salted fish, and timber to the Caribbean grew increasingly important, return shipments brought rum, sugar, and tropical fruits. Especially at times when abundance limited the prices for such Caribbean commodities, transshipments of enslaved Africans offered a compelling alternative. Hence, advertisements for enslaved Africans in the North generally offered the people in small groups alongside Caribbean produce, at the home or store of a New England merchant or, less frequently, aboard the ship that carried them. In 1739, Philadelphia's *American Weekly Mercury* printed Captain Benjamin Christian's advertisement of "TWO verly [sic] likely Negroe Boys . . . [and] Also a Quantity of very good Lime-juice." Willing, Morris, and Company paid the Pennsylvania Gazette in 1761 to announce their offering of "A Negroe Man, and two New Negroe Boys" along with "Madeira, and an Assortment of other Wines, Rum, and Sugar, etc." In 1765, the *New-York Gazette; or, the Weekly Post-Boy* publicized the availability of "A Choice Parcel of Muscovado and Powder Sugars . . . and a Negro Wench and Negro Boy." To intercolonial traders between the Caribbean and northern North America, African people offered one among several commodities that suited their northward journeys, and such advertisements to the general public suggest speculative transshipments. In the eighteenth century, even smaller northern markets saw Africans delivered without special requests from prearranged buyers.[35]

In some cases, merchants boarded their captives awaiting sale with free people of African descent. For instance, in Philadelphia in 1751, John Strutton advertised "TO BE SOLD, A Parcel of likely Negroes, very reasonable." The advertisement then added that the "Said Negroes may be seen at a Free Negroe Woman's, in Chestnut-Street, opposite to Mr. Anthony Benezet's." In 1759, Strutton placed a similar ad for "A Parcel of likely strong Negroe Men and Women," some of whom possessed skills suggesting they were born in the Americas or had at least resided there for many years. In this case, Strutton informed buyers, "The said Negroes are to be seen at Emanuel Woodbe's

35. *American Weekly Mercury* (Philadelphia), June 14–21, 1739; *Pennsylvania Gazette*, Mar. 12, 1761; *New-York Gazette; or, the Weekly Post-Boy*, Mar. 21, Apr. 18, 25, 1765.

(Negroe) in Water street." Such involvement of free people of African descent in the slave trade raises questions about their attitudes toward slavery. Surely many free blacks sympathized with the plight of those caught up in the slave trade, especially given the wave of emancipations in Pennsylvania in the 1740s and 1750s, inspired by the Quakers' antislavery turn. Most of Philadelphia's free blacks in the 1750s had recently escaped enslavement themselves, and many attended churches with mixed congregations of the free and enslaved. In that atmosphere, slavery was unlikely to be treated as an unquestioned fact of life. For Emanuel Woodbe and the unnamed "Free Negroe Woman," housing Africans to be sold was likely an uncomfortable source of income, betokening the difficulty many free blacks faced in earning a living in societies that discriminated against them. That being said, since many Pennsylvania free blacks had embraced Christianity in the Great Awakening, they might have felt a considerable cultural distance from new Africans. From Strutton's perspective, the choice to board enslaved people with free black Philadelphians suggests a measure of trust. This willingness to lodge slaves with a free person of color is particularly interesting in the wake of New York's slave conspiracy scare of 1741, since that event saw New Yorkers suspicious of free black collusion in rebellion. In Strutton's mind, at least, enslaved people residing in the homes of free blacks were not feared to be dangerously unsupervised. African captives boarded in such a home might have been surprised at seeing free blacks assimilated into Euro-American society, but given their recent enslavement in Africa, black overseers would not have been a major departure from their experience. Regardless of skin color, they might have perceived these free blacks as simply part of a long line of captors, despised and feared, especially if language barriers separated them.[36]

Advertisements for such small groups of captives, in addition to exemplifying the intercolonial slave trade's integration with other branches of commerce, also show slave traders seeking to create a market for exploitable African workers. Traders to southern markets rarely bothered to advertise small groups of captives; they could rely on informal marketing and word of mouth to attract eager buyers. Only the importation of hundreds of Africans at once demanded that they advertise far and wide. Traders to northern markets, by contrast, worked harder to entice propertied men to become slaveholders and

36. *Pennsylvania Gazette*, Oct. 10, 1751, May 17, 1759; Gary B. Nash, *Forging Freedom: The Formation of Philadelphia's Black Community, 1720–1840* (Cambridge, Mass., 1988), 16–37. See also Shane White, *Somewhat More Independent: The End of Slavery in New York City, 1770–1810* (Athens, Ga., 1991), 182–183; Jill Lepore, *New York Burning: Liberty, Slavery, and Conspiracy in Eighteenth-Century Manhattan* (New York, 2005).

could not dump the enslaved Africans deemed undesirable elsewhere; the northern markets were not desperate for enslaved labor. When Saint Croix merchant Thomas Shute sent two captives to Thomas Riche in Philadelphia, Riche scolded him for sending "half dead negroes," reporting that "th[e]y fetch little more than paid the duty's and freight." Shute earned almost nothing. The problem was their perceived quality and not the Philadelphia market, as Riche pointed out: "At the same time good likely Slaves would fetch from 40 to 50 pounds." Despite the unwillingness to accept African people considered substandard commodities, northern markets attracted traders because they could expect timely payments. These colonies were marginal regarding the slave trade, but not in more general economic terms. Slavers were keen to siphon off this wealth.[37]

For instance, Philadelphia merchants in search of potential customers often dispersed Africans across the region. In the 1710s, when the slave trade to Pennsylvania was still minimal, trader Jonathan Dickinson somewhat reluctantly handled a number of sales of arriving Africans. Dickinson routinely discouraged merchants in other colonies from sending such captives, warning one correspondent about "a p[ar]cell of Negroes that lay on my hands a yeare," and lamenting to his brother-in-law in Jamaica, "The Negroes thou Sent mee have been on hand most of this Wint'r." Dickinson was more blunt to John Lewis of Jamaica. After selling people for him, Dickinson said, "I request Y'e not to Send any more, as . . . but few people Care to buy Negroes." To find buyers for those Africans who did arrive, Dickinson often looked well beyond Philadelphia. In the sale for Lewis, Dickinson reported selling "the three Negroes ye Sent" to some "Low'r Countey [Delaware] men at Thirty Pounds P head." Dickinson did not make clear whether he sent Lewis's captives to Delaware for sale or whether the "Low'r Countey men" had come to Philadelphia, but in other cases, Dickinson transshipped Africans within or even beyond his region in order to sell them. For one of his brother-in-law's enslaved women sent from Jamaica, Dickinson suggested that to find a buyer, he "must send her to Lower Countys or Maryland." Whether Dickinson would target the Chesapeake overland or by sea is unclear, but regardless he resorted to a broad hinterland to find markets for even small numbers of captives reaching Philadelphia.[38]

37. Thomas Riche to Thomas Shute, Jan. 1, 1763, Thomas Riche Letter Book, I, 1750–1764, Am 9261, HSP. Desrochers notes that eighteenth-century Boston received few captives deemed "refuse" by traders ("Slave-for-Sale Advertisements," *WMQ*, LIX [2002], 649).

38. Dickinson to John Beswick, Apr. 26, 1715, Jonathan Dickinson Letter Book, 1715–1721, Yi 2 / 1628, alcove 4, shelf 12, fol. 12, Library Company of Philadelphia; Dickinson to "Deare

In the 1730s and 1740s, Robert Ellis was the most prolific slave importer in Pennsylvania, acquiring Africans from Barbados, Antigua, Saint Kitts, and South Carolina. The market for enslaved workers in Pennsylvania was more developed during that era, so Ellis encouraged transshipments, but he still pursued buyers aggressively. Ellis advertised even small slave sales in Philadelphia newspapers, and he also distributed people throughout the region for sale by his agents on commission. In September 1736, Ellis informed a Mr. Shaw, who was either up or down the Delaware River from Philadelphia, of having "Sent [you] four Negros, Two Garls and Two Boys, which I Desire you will Dispose of them if you can, [for] not Less than Twenty Six Pounds Each." Ellis sold some of the other captives from the same shipment in Philadelphia but apparently spread the imported people around to avoid glutting the small Philadelphia market. Ellis again dispersed African captives for sale in January of 1739, when he handled two shipments, probably one from Charleston and the other from the Caribbean. He sent some Africans to Lewes, in what is now Delaware, for Jacob Kollock to sell on commission. Apparently Kollock succeeded, as Ellis's partner in Philadelphia, John Ryan, later complained about the high commission Kollock charged for his "Sales of 16 Negroes." Nor was Lewes the only destination for these Africans who disembarked at Philadelphia. To punctuate his complaint against Kollock, Ryan pointed out, "There are Others concern'd with us (Mr. Ellis and I) who have been at Vast Pains and Trouble in . . . Selling 'em up and down in Severall Parts of the Country . . . [who] can't pretend to Charge more than 5 P Cent Commission." For the African captives, this dispersal across the region presaged relative isolation from other African people. In the northern colonies, especially outside urban areas, most enslaved people resided with few other bondmen and -women, working on farms or at trades where they were vastly outnumbered by Europeans.[39]

Brother" [Isaac Gale?], May 2, 1715, ibid., fols. 13–14; Dickinson to John Lewis, May 2, 1715, ibid., fols. 21–22.

39. Ellis to "Mr. Shaw," Sept. 18, 1736, in Ellis Letter Book, fol. 8. The slaves Ellis was selling probably reached Philadelphia via transshipment from the Caribbean and from Charleston aboard the sloop *Elizabeth and Lavenia,* which delivered twenty-eight "Negroe Boys and Girls"; see *Pennsylvania Gazette,* Aug. 5–12, 1736; John Ryan to Jacob Kollock, Jan. 25, 1739, in Ellis Letter Book. For other examples of Ellis's acquiring Africans in South Carolina, see Ellis to Mess'rs Cleland and Wallace, July 1, 1738, and Ellis to Thomas Gadsden, July 1, 1738, ibid., 104–105; for the same in Antigua and Saint Kitts, see Ellis to David Hall, Apr. 22, 1740, 197–198; for the same in Barbados, see Ellis to Captain Meas, Apr. 1740, 203. For more on Ellis, see Darold D. Wax, "Robert Ellis, Philadelphia Merchant and Slave Trader," *Pennsylvania Magazine of History and Biography,* LXXXVIII (1964), 52–69. On the proportions of enslaved Africans in northern colonies and their concentration in urban areas, see McManus, *Black Bondage in the North,* 14–17; Ira

With the aggressive pursuit of buyers in the North came a decline of the seventeenth-century trend of sending special requests to an entrepôt for slaves. Rather than place themselves at the mercy of a distant merchant, more potential buyers in the North could count on a local market offering them a choice of captives for sale. This subtle power shift in the slave marketplace was illustrated by a small shipment in 1731. Walter Nugent of Antigua transshipped two Africans to Abraham Redwood, an absentee plantation owner living in Rhode Island. The delivery was apparently unsolicited, or at least the deal was not binding on Redwood, as Nugent informed him, "I send you two Negroes; if you like them, keep them, and give my Account credit for what you think they are worth. The Negroe man is a Peice [sic] of a Saylor and a fine Papa Slave [i.e., from near the modern nation of Ghana], [who] cost thirty pounds Sterling out of the Ship. The Negroe woman is a fine Slave." The discretion here was Redwood's. Rather than being at the mercy of his correspondent in the entrepôt, hoping that Nugent would buy Africans prudently on his behalf in Antigua, Redwood could assess the value of the people and decide for himself. In sending a man and a woman together, Nugent might have been hoping that Redwood would see the captives' potential as a breeding pair who would produce another generation of slaves for his family. Slaveholders, especially those buying their first slaves, often sought slaves in male-female pairs, regardless of whether the captives in question saw themselves as a couple or in any way connected.[40]

This decline in special orders in the North mirrored most of British America. Outside the most economically marginal markets, requests for merchants in the entrepôts to select and transship arriving Africans were increasingly rare in the eighteenth century. They were not obsolete, but potential buyers typically only solicited merchants with an unusual request—often, seeking a worker with specific skills. When John Frederick Pinney, an absentee plantation owner in England, noticed wages paid to a free white cooper in his account books, he scolded the manager of his Nevis plantation, James Browne. "For God's Sake, good Sr.," Pinney exclaimed, "buy me a negroe Cooper or two in any of the four Islands if you Can at any Price." Presumably,

---

Berlin, *Many Thousands Gone: The First Two Centuries of Slavery in North America* (Cambridge, Mass., 1998), 47–63; after about 1750, however, Berlin emphasizes that enslaved Africans grew as a proportion of northern populations (177–179).

40. Walter Nugent to Abraham Redwood, Antigua, Apr. 11, 1731, in Donnan, ed., *Documents*, III, 121–122. On slave buyers' interest in pairing male and female slaves, see Morgan, *Laboring Women*, 84–85.

Pinney expected Browne to write correspondents in the other Leeward Islands in search of such a cooper, not travel from island to island himself. Likewise, in 1760, Charleston merchant Robert Raper bought "a very quick, good [slave] boy" named Johnny at the request of Governor Thomas Boone of New Jersey, who sought a domestic servant. Raper also took the initiative of purchasing the boy's father, Sampson, on Boone's account, who, Raper suggested, "with a little instruction, will make a Gardiner." The liberty Raper took in purchasing this second captive for Boone suggests that those making requests for slaves remained somewhat beholden to the whims of their agents in the entrepôts, but a buyer could protest such charges unless he had granted the merchant permission to use such discretion.[41]

Unstated in Raper's account is what role Sampson played in preventing the shipment of Johnny to New Jersey without him. Did his son's skill or potential give him some leverage, or was he able to appeal to Raper's humanity to convince the trader to send father and son together? Nineteenth-century accounts of slave sales demonstrate that American-born slaves made pleas from the auction block, urging slaveholders to buy family members together, but it is crucial to consider that in the eighteenth century, such persuasion was often more difficult. To manipulate their own sales, nineteenth-century slaves capitalized on their command of English, growing sentimentality about family ties in American culture, and slaveholders' desire to imagine themselves as paternalistic. People disembarking from eighteenth-century slave ships were less likely to possess enough linguistic ability or understanding of their enslavers to appeal effectively. Perhaps skilled slaves chosen for intercolonial trade had such knowledge and influenced their own sales. In several ways, then, the market for skilled slaves differed from the one for recently arrived Africans (whose skills mostly went unrecognized by Europeans).[42]

41. John Frederick Pinney to James Browne, Bath, Oct. 27, 1755, Pinney Collection, Letter Book I, John Frederick Pinney, 1740–1742, 1754–1755, Special Collections, Bristol University Library, U.K.; Robert Raper to Governor Boone, Charleston, Feb. 24, 1761, Robert Raper Letter Book, 1759–1770, MSS 34/511, fol. 65, South Carolina Historical Society.

42. On the ability of American-born slaves in the nineteenth century to use subtle social cues in assessing potential new owners, see Walter Johnson, *Soul by Soul: Life inside the Antebellum Slave Market* (Cambridge, Mass., 1999), chap. 6. See also Johann David Schoepf, *Travels in the Confederation,* ed. and trans. Alfred J. Morrison, 2 vols. (Philadelphia, 1911), II, 148; Wood, *Remote Part of the World,* 100–101; Daina Ramey Berry, "'We'm Fus' Rate Bargain': Value, Labor, and Price in a Georgia Slave Community," in Walter Johnson, ed., *The Chattel Principle: Internal Slave Trades in the Americas* (New Haven, Conn., 2004), 55. On the contrasting silence of most arriving Africans at their sales, see Smallwood, *Saltwater Slavery,* 179.

Philadelphia merchant John Yeates regularly dealt in this market. In the early 1740s, numerous Caribbean merchants sent skilled people to Yeates—among them an unnamed sailor, "Sarah . . . a good Slave for House work," "Peter and Sambo . . . very Choice Brick makers," and "Margarett, a very Ingenious and Valueable Girl . . . [who] Can Work at her needle Very Well and Take Care of things in a house." The sellers in such cases usually paid freight charges and trusted Yeates to obtain high prices commensurate to the skills of the enslaved. Small, specialized transactions like these marked exceptions to intercolonial traders' usual avoidance of dealing in American-born slaves, and market considerations alone did not shape such transactions and migrations. In the case of Margarett, she was not only a skilled domestic worker but also the daughter of the man who sent her—Edward Polegreen—suggesting that his motives extended beyond profit and loss, especially since he acknowledged the family tie in his letter to Yeates. Was Polegreen sending Margarett north to remove her from the harsher regime of the Caribbean? Was he removing a reminder of his indiscretions with enslaved women from his own sight or from the sight of his wife? Was banishment a punishment for Margarett? Polegreen did not explain, only stating, "I humbly Begg the favour of you . . . to dispose of her . . . [to] a good Master or Mistress." Polegreen added that his daughter "is a very Carefull Girl and will make a very Good Slave to any Good Owner." Whatever the exact circumstances, Margarett's case marks a crucial difference in the market for skilled and American-born slaves versus that for recent African arrivals. American-born slaves were more encumbered with relations between enslavers and the enslaved. In most of the intercolonial slave trade—dealing in Africans—traders managed to keep captives more fully commodified in their own minds. Personal connections rarely bridged the sense of distance between slavers and the people they traded.[43]

Linked to this desire for skilled slaves and to the limited demand for plantation laborers in northern colonies was a preference in the North for enslaved children recently arrived from Africa. When Jonathan Dickinson discouraged shipments of enslaved people from the Caribbean in 1715, he qualified his

43. John Bayley to John Yeates, July 7, 1743, Urbin Strict to Yeates, July 26, 1743, John Francklin to Yeates, July 25, 1743, Edward Polegreen to Yeates, Aug. 13, 1742, and see also Stephen Butcher to Yeates, Sept. 1, 1743, all in John Yeates Correspondence, 1738–1749 (unpaginated), Yeates Papers, no. 740, HSP. For an example of the freight charges in such a case, see Ellis to Robert Horry, July 25, 1738, Ellis Letter Book, 114; Ellis mentions receiving forty shillings for the passage of an enslaved boy on one of his vessels. By contrast, "a passanger" paid £3 for travel aboard the same ship. Morgan highlights the importance to slave traders of an exaggerated sense of the differences between themselves and Africans (*Laboring Women*, chap. 1).

demurral, noting, "Our people Don't Care to buy Except boys and Girles." Courting transshipments a generation later, Robert Ellis routinely specified an interest in children. In 1748, he advised Charleston merchants, "If you shoud have a Ship w'th Negroes this Spring, you may send Twenty or Thirty Young Boys and Girls, and I shall Endeavour to dispose of them to Advantage." Likewise, newspaper advertisements often touted the availability of "likely young Negroes of about 10 or 12 Years of age" or "likely Negroe Boys and Girls" to entice buyers. Since northern slaveholders did not put their captives to the physically demanding toil associated with rice or sugar plantations, they had little incentive to pay the high prices that the market demanded for adults. Enslaved children cost less and could be trained for domestic service or artisanal trades.[44]

This predilection guided the invisible hand of the market that dragged a young James Albert Ukawsaw Gronniosaw into northern slavery. Born in Borno (in what is now northeastern Nigeria), Gronniosaw survived a Middle Passage from the Gold Coast to Barbados as a boy. Whereas most captives from his ship likely settled on sugar plantations, Gronniosaw's youth made him ill suited to cane work. Instead, he was purchased for transshipment:

> My new master's name was Vanhorn, a young Gentleman; his home was in New-England in the City of New-York; to which place he took me with him. He dress'd me in his livery, and was very good to me. My chief business was to wait at table, and tea, and clean knives, and I had a very easy place.

With the benefit of hindsight, Gronniosaw perceived his migration from Barbados to New York as advantageous—an escape from harder labor in the Caribbean cane fields—but his account gives no hint of how he experienced it as a child, separated from those with whom he had crossed the Atlantic, who perhaps had eased his fears at sea, told him stories of home, or ensured his

44. Dickinson to "Deare Brother," Apr. 30, 1715, Dickinson Letter Book, fol. 20; Ellis to Benjamin and John Savage, Apr. 25, 1740, Ellis Letter Book, 208 (Ellis's letters include many other examples of the preference for children: see, for instance, 197–198, 212, 213, 227, 253–255); *Pennsylvania Gazette*, June 14–21, 1733; *American Weekly Mercury*, July 5–12, 1733. On northerners' preference for children and training for artisanal trades, see McManus, *Black Bondage in the North*, 21, 36, 42–46; Darold D. Wax, "Preferences for Slaves in Colonial America," *Journal of Negro History*, LVIII (1973), 401; Desrochers, "Slave-for-Sale Advertisements," *WMQ*, 3d Ser, LIX (2002), 649; Wilma King, "African Children and the Transatlantic Slave Trade across Time and Place," in David T. Gleeson and Simon Lewis, eds., *Ambiguous Anniversary: The Bicentennial of the International Slave Trade Bans* (Columbia, S.C., 2012), 53.

share of the meager shipboard provisions. Selection of children for transship-ment must have separated young captives from older relatives or other adults who cared for them.[45]

For the development of African American cultures, the implications of chil-dren's prominence in this branch of the intercolonial trade were profound. Sold without their elders, young captives like Gronniosaw were more fully cut off from their origins. Furthermore, they typically took up residence as domestic servants in households with few, if any, other Africans. It is not sur-prising that some of the earliest African American Christian preachers (such as Gronniosaw) or English-language poets (such as Phillis Wheatley) emerged in northern colonies. Many such African-born children would grow up with more exposure to the English language and to Euro-American culture and values (and less connection to African ways) than was the case for enslaved people in plantation colonies.[46]

In the mid-eighteenth century, most northern colonies saw a brief period in which direct African shipments predominated, leaving intercolonial ship-ments in a subordinate role. Such transatlantic trade to northern colonies was small by the standards of the plantation settlements but still delivered unprecedented numbers of African people to the North. There were several reasons for its emergence. For one, the region experienced enormous popula-tion growth over the course of the eighteenth century, expanding its demand for all commodities—enslaved people included. Northern colonies also ex-panded their exports to Europe (of marine products, naval stores, and grain), making the region more attractive to transatlantic shippers. Finally, growing

45. "A Narrative of the Most Remarkable Particulars in the Life of James Albert Ukawsaw Gronniosaw, an African Prince, as Related by Himself" (1772), rpt. in William L. Andrews and Henry Louis Gates, Jr., eds., *Slave Narratives* (New York, 2002), 1–34. Gronniosaw does not spec-ify the age at which he crossed the Atlantic. Andrews and Gates suggest he was "still a boy" (1006), which fits with my reading. Adam Potkay and Sandra Burr estimate that Gronniosaw was born between 1710 and 1714 and note that, after living in New York with Van Horn, he was sold again around 1730. His age then would have been between sixteen and twenty, so he was younger when he crossed the Atlantic—but how much younger is unclear (Potkay and Burr, eds., *Black Atlantic Writers of the Eighteenth Century* [New York, 1995], 23). On English slaveholders' dress-ing enslaved Africans in livery as a marker of status, see Catherine Molineux, "Hogarth's Fash-ionable Slaves: Moral Corruption in Eighteenth-Century London," *ELH*, LXXII (2005), 497–499.

46. Paul Lovejoy notes that children surviving the slave trade to Cuba, especially those who settled in urban environments, tended to acculturate quickly and exploit their knowledge of local ways to purchase their freedom (Lovejoy, "The Children of Slavery: The Transatlantic Phase," *Slavery and Abolition*, XXVII, no. 2 [August 2006], 208–209). Children arriving in North Ameri-can cities probably acculturated with equal rapidity, especially when not living among African adults; see Peter H. Wood, *Strange New Land: Africans in Colonial America* (New York, 2003), 67.

numbers of those transoceanic carriers were northern colonists themselves as the region's merchant class expanded and diversified, enhancing northern colonies' connections to all Atlantic commercial networks. For New England, particularly Rhode Island, the transition to direct African imports came earliest, with the late 1730s heralding the shift. Thereafter, significant arrivals from the islands diminished (with the exception of seventy Africans in one apparently anomalous shipment from Barbados to Piscataqua—now Portsmouth, New Hampshire—in 1749). From the late 1730s through the early 1760s, voyages from Africa delivered close to five thousand captives to New England.[47]

In New York, intercolonial slave deliveries declined sharply after 1741. The slave conspiracy scare in Manhattan that year might have left colonists reluctant to import people from the West Indies, but the collapse of the British asiento and increasing competition from transatlantic traders were probably more significant factors. During the years when the British South Sea Company monopolized the slave trade to Spanish America, New York exported a great deal of flour to Jamaica, which the South Sea Company then smuggled to Spanish America under cover of the slave trade. Some of the proceeds were invested in enslaved Africans for return journeys to Manhattan. The outbreak of the War of Jenkins' Ear in 1739, and then King George's War (1744–1748), disrupted this flour trade as well as other Caribbean commerce, helping to explain the lull in importations. When peace returned, New Yorkers increased their imports of African people but no longer looked to the Caribbean. Instead, the colony's growing demand for slaves (and expanding exports) facilitated direct links with Africa, diminishing the need for transshipments. African trade to New York predominated for the remainder of the colonial period. New Jersey's experience mirrored New York's but involved more transshipments. As in New York, captive arrivals in New Jersey slowed to a trickle during King George's War and recovered in the late 1740s and early 1750s. In New Jersey, however, the postwar arrivals still came from the Caribbean. Only

47. McCusker and Menard, *Economy of British America*, 101–103, 107–109, 189–199, 203–205. *Voyages*, accessed April 2011, shows nearly five thousand captives reaching New England on vessels directly from Africa. This does not include the many small shipments in which slave traders delivered most captives farther south but kept some for delivery to New England (http://www.slavevoyages.org/tast/database/search.faces?yearFrom=1730&yearTo=1770&mjslptimp=20100.20300.20400.20500). McManus asserts that the rise in African shipments to northern colonies was linked to the rupture of the British asiento and the resulting close of Spanish markets to British slave traders. That northern merchants entered this trade in large numbers suggests that the driving force might have been increased northern demand rather than the closure of Spanish markets (*Black Bondage in the North*, 22–23).

in the late 1750s and early 1760s did the colony receive people directly from Africa, at which time transshipments ceased altogether.[48]

Pennsylvania's window of direct African trade came slightly later. The 1740s and 1750s saw sporadic and declining arrivals from the West Indies, but in the mid-1760s, such transshipments shot up again as employers replaced indentured servants who gained freedom in exchange for military service in the Seven Years' War. Broad participation in slave trafficking from the Caribbean among Pennsylvania merchants was suggested by a 1761 petition of "Divers Merchants of the City of Philadelphia, Trading to His Majesty's Coloneys in the West Indies." The twenty-four signers urged the colony's deputy governor to veto a bill taxing slave imports, suggesting that they viewed carrying Africans as a vital part of Caribbean trade. Still, enslaved people from the West Indies met only a portion of the demand created by departing indentured servants; direct African shipments also arrived during the five years after the Seven Years' War. The trade then halted abruptly; no known slave shipments—direct or intercolonial—entered Pennsylvania after 1767. The nonimportation pacts of the Revolutionary era surely contributed to the decline, along with the emergence of antislavery sentiment in the colony (and, to a lesser degree, across the North). The Quakers in Pennsylvania were among the first European settlers to vocalize antislavery arguments in the 1750s and 1760s, and such ideas gained currency in the years leading up to the Revolution.[49]

The rise of direct African shipments to the northern colonies undercut the transshipment trade from the Caribbean but triggered new routes of intercolonial trafficking. Although the transatlantic deliveries reflected increased demand in the North, slave traders still struggled to sell whole cargoes from

48. Lydon attributes New York's shifting trade patterns to lingering fear after the 1741 conspiracy scare ("New York Slave Trade," WMQ, 3d Ser., XXXV [1978], 387). For the South Sea Company's flour smuggling trade under the asiento, see Chapter 6, below; see also Elena Andrea Schneider, "The Occupation of Havana: War, Trade, and Slavery in Eighteenth-Century Cuba" (Ph.D. diss., Princeton University, 2011), 42–48. For New Jersey's African imports, see Voyages, accessed April 2011, http://www.slavevoyages.org/tast/database/search.faces?yearFrom=1514& yearTo=1866&mjslptimp=20800. One should note that these mid-eighteenth-century African deliveries to New York were not the first transatlantic slaving ventures to the colony. In the late seventeenth century, independent slave traders circumventing the Royal African Company's monopoly by acquiring slaves in East Africa occasionally delivered their captives to New York.

49. Darold D. Wax, "Negro Imports into Pennsylvania, 1720–1766," Pennsylvania History, XXXII (1965), 254–287; "Petition of the Merchants of Philadelphia," 1761, in Donnan, ed., Documents, III, 453–454. On the emergence of abolitionism in Pennsylvania, see Winthrop D. Jordan, White over Black: American Attitudes toward the Negro, 1550–1812 (Chapel Hill, N.C., 1968), 271–280.

Africa in northern ports. Africans surviving the Middle Passage to northern colonies thus often faced transshipment along the American coast. With the emergence of African deliveries to New York, for example, slave traders devised a number of strategies to disperse captives beyond the Manhattan market. When discussing a proposed African venture in 1762, New York merchant John Watts explained to his prospective partner in Barbados, "We cannot easily vend" an entire cargo, but "from fifty to a hundred would run high enough." In other words, Watts anticipated that one hundred captives was the maximum for his market before prices would fall considerably. To avoid a glut, Watts noted, "Virginia could take off a great many," suggesting that a vessel from Africa to New York should also sell people in another colony. Similarly, in 1765, New York traders advertised "A Parcel of likely Negro Men, Women, Boys, and Girls Slaves" who had recently arrived from Sierra Leone aboard the brigantine *Matty*. Some would be sold at "Coenties Pier" in New York, whereas others were available "at Second-River in the Province of New-Jersey." Whether the *Matty* stopped at both ports or whether another vessel transshipped captives from New York to New Jersey is unclear, but the dispersal from a northern port was typical. Boston shipping lists show a similar pattern. The first African vessel listed entering that harbor arrived in 1762, followed almost immediately by the first small shipments of enslaved Africans *out* of that harbor, bound to colonies as far away as Virginia and North Carolina.[50]

In the early 1760s, when Pennsylvania received its only regular direct African shipments, importer Thomas Riche dispersed arriving Africans within the Delaware River region as his predecessors had done but also targeted colonies further afield, commensurate with the larger groups of captives in the direct African trade. When Riche served as selling agent for the schooner *Hannah*, which delivered one hundred Africans directly to Philadelphia in 1761, he informed Samuel Tucker—up and across the Delaware River in Trenton, New

50. John Watts to Gedney Clarke, New York, Mar. 30, 1762, in Donnan, ed., *Documents*, III, 457; *New York Mercury*, Oct. 7, 1765; *New York Gazette or Weekly Post-Boy*, Oct. 3, 10, 1765; *Voyages*, accessed May 2011, http://slavevoyages.org/tast/database/search.faces?yearFrom=1765&yearTo= 1765&shipname=Mattey; Naval Office Shipping Lists for Massachusetts, 1686–1765, microfilm, CO 5/850, fol. 14. McManus also notes regular transshipments from New York to New Jersey after New York received slaves directly from Africa (*Black Bondage in the North*, 23). Several scholars have noted Rhode Island slave traders' transshipping captives down the coast; see Jay Coughtry, *The Notorious Triangle: Rhode Island and the African Slave Trade, 1700–1807* (Philadelphia, 1981); McManus, *Black Bondage in the North*, 21–22; Wax, "Preferences for Slaves," *Journal of Negro History*, LVIII (1973), 375; Piersen, *Black Yankees*, 4; see also "Instructions to Captain Pollipus Hammond," 1746, in Donnan, ed., *Documents*, III, 138–139.

Jersey—"I intend Sending 15 or 20 up to you for Sale, for which we shall Furnish you with advertisements by the Post on Monday." Two weeks later, hearing that Tucker had "sold most of the negros," Riche "Furnish'd [him] with a fresh Parcell." Presumably, Tucker earned commissions for his efforts. Riche also marched African captives about the countryside himself. After he received shipments, several days often passed without Riche's recording any letters in his letter book, and these gaps were typically followed by apologies for his delay in responding because of time spent "in the country." In most cases, Riche did not give reasons for such travel, but he suggested an explanation when a shipment of captives from Africa arrived during a cold spell in late 1763. Owing at least partly to the inclement weather, thirty-three captives from the small shipment had perished on the voyage to Pennsylvania, and many remained sick upon arrival. Riche reported that, because of the chill and the captives' ill health, "we Cannot move them about the Country for sale." [51]

Riche also looked farther afield for markets, regularly transshipping enslaved people to North Carolina, capitalizing on that market's limited supply of exploitable labor. Between 1761 and 1765, Riche transshipped recently arrived Africans on at least ten occasions to merchant Samuel Cornell, of New Bern, North Carolina, in groups ranging from a single person to twenty captives at once. Riche also occasionally sent people to Cape Fear. In addition to helping him avoid glutting Delaware River markets, such transshipment might have offered a way to vend captives deemed undesirable by buyers closer to home. For Captain John Burroughs's voyage from Philadelphia to New Bern aboard the schooner *Nelly,* Riche instructed the sailor, "If you have easey weather take care of the slaves and get them shaved and greased before you get up to Newburn lest they discover old age by their heads." For these nine enslaved people, uprooted from distant communities, graying hair about their temples brought subjection to further demeaning treatment (Plate 5). Meanwhile, slaves of advancing age might not have been the only people that Riche unloaded in the captive market of North Carolina. In a 1766 letter to Cornell, Riche defended himself against a complaint that one of the Africans he sent was "Subject to Fitts." These transshipments add to the impression that

51. Riche to Samuel Tucker, Aug. 1, Aug. 18, 1761, Riche Letter Book. For other transactions with Tucker, see ibid., letters dated Aug. 13, 16, Sept. 2, 14, 1762; Riche to Gampert and Heyman and Co., Oct. 21, 1763; and see also Riche to Gampert, Heyman, Hill, and Jacob Miller, Oct. 8, 1763. For an example where Riche refers to being in the country shortly after importing slaves, see Riche to Mr. Lewis, Aug. 6, 1761. See also *Pennsylvania Gazette,* June 3, 1762. For these captives' voyage from Africa to Pennsylvania, see *Voyages,* accessed February 2013, Voyage ID no. 28045.

PLATE 5. Frontispiece, *The Maroon*. The mid-nineteenth-century engraving depicts the demeaning preparation of human commodities for sale. Traders often oiled or greased the skin of captives and used dyes and makeups to mask signs of age or ill health. Mayne Reid, *The Maroon; or, Planter Life in Jamaica* (New York, 1864). The Library Company of Philadelphia

the enslaved migration to economically marginal colonies skewed away from people judged to be prime workers by traders and slaveholders. On the other hand, elders might have been a rare and welcome presence in communities of the enslaved, with their wisdom and rich knowledge of homelands left behind. Given the traders' emphasis on youthful vigor in choosing slaves, few elders endured the Atlantic crossing, and patterns in the intercolonial slave trade might have concentrated enslaved migrants of middle age or older in the more marginal colonies.[52]

The trend of coastal transshipments following direct African deliveries to northern ports possibly peaked in 1764, when Riche wrote to correspondents

52. Riche to Samuel Cornell, June 10, 1766, Riche Letter Book. For Riche's other shipments of Africans to North Carolina, see his letters to Cornell, dated Sept. 1, 1761, Sept. 29, Nov. 11, 1762, Aug. 23, Sept. 17, Dec. 13, 1763, Apr. 23, Aug. 18, Oct. 11, 1764, all ibid. For Cape Fear, see Riche to Anthony Mobson, Oct. 22, 1765, ibid. See also Riche's assorted bills of lading in Ports of Philadelphia and Barbados, Bills of Lading, 1716–1772 (unpaginated, loose sheets), no. 515, HSP. "Get them shaved and greased": Riche to John Burroughs, [October 1765], Riche Letter Book.

far and wide, panicking about reports that "five Sail of Guinea Men . . . Two of which are mine" were all bound for the Delaware River that summer. The result, he feared, would be that prices for "Slaves will Come Lower here then from the Islands." To prevent such a crash, in addition to his usual strategies for diffusing captives, Riche wrote to merchants about possibilities for transshipments from Philadelphia to the British Caribbean, Maryland, and even Cuba. Riche's adaptation to changing conditions and pursuit of new partners for dispersal underscore both the importance of intercolonial trade to making transatlantic slaving profitable and the role of such commerce in elaborating Atlantic commercial networks.[53]

■ These similar, yet distinct, intercolonial slave trades from the Caribbean to various North American regions highlight the varied ways in which American colonies connected to networks of Atlantic trade. Whether a colony's economy oriented toward producing staple crops for export to Europe or toward the export of provisions to the Caribbean; whether a region's commercial sector was highly capitalized or less developed; whether a colony exploited enslaved people as a primary or supplementary labor force—such local variations shaped patterns in the slave trade, not only with regard to whether enslaved Africans arrived directly or through intercolonial channels but also with regard to how the intercolonial slave trade sorted the African people trapped within it. As greater numbers of transatlantic slavers targeted ever more American ports, and as intercolonial traders linked the British mainland and Caribbean settlements ever more tightly to one another, they integrated a British American market for enslaved African people—and for many other goods, often produced by those Africans' labor. Captives were sorted according to desired or undesired attributes for various roles and swept into existing commodity flows. Here was a market for labor par excellence. Workers themselves were bought, sorted, moved, and sold wherever they would be most valued, with the only value that mattered calculated in pounds sterling.

53. Riche to Cornelius Coppinger, Apr. 2, 1764, ibid.; see also Riche to Henry White, Aug. 14, 24, 1764.

6. A for *Asiento*

THE SLAVE TRADE FROM BRITISH TO FOREIGN COLONIES, CA. 1713–1739

We have . . . determined That all the Factorys be made dependant on Jamaica where We Imagine it for the Comp's Service that all their Affairs . . . should Center. —Directors of the South Sea Company, 1725

In 1724, the heads of the South Sea Company wrote to their agents in Jamaica to commend their new plan for keeping tabs on African people at the island. The company sought a means to discourage theft of the company's captives awaiting transshipment and to differentiate those Africans the company delivered to Spanish America from the people introduced illegally. Keeping tabs on the company's deliveries was proving difficult because the outfit resorted to myriad methods of reaching its quota for deliveries of people to Spanish settlements—from direct African ventures, to purchases in the Caribbean for transshipment, to licensing independent traders in the islands for deliveries on the company's behalf. Since so much of this commerce centered in Jamaica, the company's agents on that island proposed a solution, and the company's Court of Directors wrote: "The Mark A with which you mark all the Negroes before they are sent out, we approve of, and hope it will Answer the ends proposed." As Africans passed through Jamaica en route to Spanish territory, in other words, the South Sea Company seared a brand into their flesh. The letter *A*, presumably, stood for *Asiento*. Captives would face another branding in Spanish America—the "Indulto Mark"—when Spanish officials recorded their legal entry, but South Sea Company officials wanted to mark their ownership at an earlier stage (Plate 6).[1]

---

1. South Sea Company to Rigby and Pratter, Nov. 12, 1724, in South Sea Company Records, 1711–1846, microfilm, Additional Manuscripts, 25564, 149, Milton S. Eisenhower Library, Johns Hopkins University, Baltimore, Md. (hereafter cited as SSC Records). The Spanish practice of branding of Africans with an "Indulto Mark" upon arrival was not new in 1724, and that practice likely continued. The agents at Jamaica introduced their own symbol to mark people as company property at an earlier stage in their journey to deter slave stealers and interlopers. For a prior reference to the company's branding slaves, see the company's 1718 instruction to Bar-

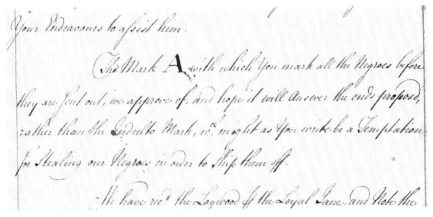

PLATE 6. A South Sea Company letter, illustrating the brand the company used to mark African people as their property at Jamaica. © The British Library Board, Add. MSS, 25564, 149

This practice highlights several aspects of Britain's intercolonial slave trade to foreign colonies in the era of the South Sea Company's asiento. Most obviously, branding was part of dehumanizing people as commodities for trade. Searing a mark of ownership into flesh not only calls to mind the treatment of livestock but, in the context of eighteenth-century shipping, a more direct parallel might be the standard practice of marking barrels and other shipping containers with the initials of an owner or a company's mark before goods jumbled in the holds of crowded ships. The *A* tagged African people not only as the property *of* the South Sea Company but also as property *in the eyes of* the company and all others engaged in such commerce. For captives, this introduced another painful indignity to a long line of them.[2]

The South Sea Company's branding of Africans also highlights other key points about Britain's slave trade to foreign colonies in the first half of the

---

bados agent Dudley Woodbridge to "take Care Negros be Mark'd w'th the Comp's Mark" (SSC Records, Add. MSS, 25563, 235).

2. One should bear in mind other contexts in which human branding occurred during the eighteenth century. In the European context, governments sometimes branded individuals as punishment, making their degraded status permanently visible to all. Habitual criminals might be branded with an "R" for "rogue," for example. Conversely, many West African cultures incorporated scarification into religious ceremonies and rites of passage. Thus, branding in and of itself might not have held the same negative connotations for the African victims as it did for the European perpetrators. The indignity would more likely have come from the coercion and from the practice's divergence from an accepted, celebrated, or sanctified community practice.

eighteenth century. Interlopers (English, French, Dutch, and others) routinely sold Africans in Spanish America despite the asiento contract, and South Sea Company factors in Spanish America complained incessantly of the difficulty of catching them. In response, the South Sea Company branded Africans to distinguish those legally introduced from those delivered by interlopers. Underlying this concern was the company's struggle to make the asiento yield the riches expected of it and its problem with enforcing restrictions on the slave trade between empires; interlopers seemed to slip easily across imperial boundaries.

That the company's new policy of branding Africans would be implemented in Jamaica—rather than on the African coast, on transatlantic slaving vessels, or at the company's bases in Spanish America—points to the central role of transshipment in the South Sea Company's trade. Company headquarters were in London, and its markets in Spanish America, but the heart of its slave-trading operation was in Jamaica. Just months after approving the branding policy, in fact, company executives in London announced that all other company employees in America would rank below the Jamaica agents in the company hierarchy. With Jamaica as the hub, the South Sea Company's commerce with Spanish America—like most slave trading between empires—was largely intercolonial. In its tenure as asientista, the South Sea Company delivered more than 60,000 African people to Spanish America, with more than 45,000 of them arriving in shipments from the British Caribbean rather than Africa (Table 13). The company's reliance on such transshipment only increased over the course of its asiento.[3]

The decision to operate the asiento as intercolonial trade complicated captives' journeys to New World slavery. Stopping at Jamaica instead of Cartagena, Portobelo, or Veracruz shortened the Middle Passage, but it added an uncomfortable sojourn, more inspections and sortings, and, of course, a final

3. On the number of Africans reaching Spanish America via transshipment, see the Appendix, below, esp. Tables 19 and 20. The columns for "Documented and Imputed Departures in Documented Shipments" offer a good approximation of the South Sea Company's transshipment trade. On estimates of the overall South Sea Company trade, see Colin Palmer, *Human Cargoes: The British Slave Trade to Spanish America, 1700–1739* (Urbana, Ill., 1981), 105–106. Palmer's study is the most thorough treatment of the South Sea Company's slave trading, but this chapter amends his portrayal in three main respects. One, Palmer notes the growing importance of Jamaica to the trade but still focuses on transatlantic voyages in describing captive experiences. Two, in focusing on "human cargoes," Palmer does not give much attention to how the company mixed slave trading with other commerce, which I see as central to their plans. Three, Palmer emphasizes recuperation as the reason for a Caribbean hub, downplaying the importance of Jamaica for assembling mixed cargoes of enslaved people and trade goods.

TABLE 13. Estimates of Africans Sent to Foreign Colonies, 1711–1740

Years	Estimated departures from Jamaica	Estimated departures from Britain's Lesser Antilles
1711–1715	7,210	2,050
1716–1720	5,610	3,200
1721–1725	13,960	2,050
1726–1730	8,010	2,530
1731–1735	19,660	2,730
1736–1740	4,830	2,390
TOTAL	59,280	14,950

Note: For discussion of the derivation of these estimates, see Appendix, below. Britain's Lesser Antilles included Barbados, Saint Kitts, Antigua, and Montserrat, but the majority of this traffic was from Barbados.

passage. For some ailing captives coming from Africa, the stop in Jamaica was life-saving, as escape from the ship and the availability of fresh food and water gave them the chance to recover from illnesses that plagued slave ships. But for many, the Jamaica hiatus prolonged the torture with new rounds of invasive inspections by merchants, new sortings that separated kin and shipmates, new uncertainty about the fate that awaited them, and the searing of the letter *A* into their flesh. Nor were the facilities in Jamaica especially healthy environments. If the layover saved some ailing captives from the Middle Passage, the prolonged journey killed others.

Despite the hardships for captives, the South Sea Company saw many reasons to emphasize intercolonial trade to fulfill the asiento. It simplified the company's role in the slave trade, allowing it to focus only on the final passage, leaving ventures to Africa largely to other merchants. This specialization was helpful because the company routinely fell short of its quota for African deliveries. Transshipment also allowed the company to use the slave trade as cover for contraband commerce, smuggling goods aboard slave trade vessels. British securing of the asiento was, after all, part of an effort to co-opt all European trade with Spanish America. The slave trade was entangled with other branches of commerce, and routing it through Jamaica (and sometimes other British colonies) was partly an effort to facilitate these related trades. Jamaica offered a convenient site for flows of African people, British manufactured goods, and North American provisions to converge for assembly as mixed cargoes for transshipment to Spanish America—with the legal trade in people covering the surreptitious deliveries of goods.

The South Sea Company's decision to transship Africans to Spanish America had larger ramifications than the simple effect on the company's slave trade business or on the journeys of the Africans caught up in the traffic. First, as the South Sea Company focused increasingly on intercolonial trade, it encouraged other British traders to engage in the transatlantic phase of the commerce in enslaved Africans. Especially in the 1720s and 1730s, as the transshipment strategy took hold, rather than compete with British transatlantic slavers, the South Sea Company became their greatest customer. Jamaica came to offer a thriving, stable market because the company's constant purchasing at the island minimized market volatility. Not coincidentally, the British transatlantic slave trade grew dramatically in this period: during the 1730s, British slave traders carried nearly twice as many African captives across the Atlantic as they had in the first decade of the century.[4]

Meanwhile, the South Sea Company's reliance on Jamaica as the hub spurred the colony's growth. The company offered commissions to merchants, rented facilities, purchased provisions, paid duties on goods and people imported and exported, and hired ship captains and sailors on the island. South Sea Company activities contributed to Jamaica's expansion in less obvious ways, as well. Especially as the company shifted to purchasing most of its African captives in Jamaica in the 1720s, such buying helped to ensure that a consistent supply of African laborers reached the island. Jamaican planters often complained that the South Sea Company took the most desirable slaves away, but considering that other British colonies regularly complained of slave traders' neglecting to bring Africans at all, the company likely fostered the growth of the island's population. Though self-interested, the company was not deceptive when claiming that traders from Africa flocked to Jamaica with "an expectation of a double market"—meaning both local planters and traders to Spanish America. Planters on the island might not have recognized this fringe benefit of the South Sea Company's presence, but the doubling of Jamaica's population of African descent between 1710 and 1740—from about 59,000 to nearly 118,000—suggests that the combination of local and South Sea Company demand attracted numerous transatlantic traders to the island.[5]

4. *Voyages: The Trans-Atlantic Slave Trade Database,* accessed April 2011, estimates that British (including colonial) merchants delivered about 126,000 Africans to the Americas from 1701 to 1710; 140,000 from 1711 to 1720; 190,000 from 1721 to 1730; and 216,000 from 1731 to 1740 (http://slavevoyages.org/tast/assessment/estimates.faces?yearFrom=1701&yearTo=1740&flag=3.5).

5. "Double market": quoted in Palmer, *Human Cargoes,* 67. For Jamaica population estimates,

Jamaica planters were not the only other buyers benefitting from this. Ironically, because of the company's presence, interlopers on its monopoly also worked from Jamaica. In fact, the South Sea Company sometimes unwittingly sold African people to the interlopers as the company sorted human cargoes at the island. Such interlopers contributed to the local economy as well, marking another way in which the company fostered Jamaica's growth, albeit unintentionally. It was no accident that the period of the company's asiento corresponded to the moment in which Jamaica and Barbados traded places as the sun and moon of the British Empire in America; Jamaica now shined brightest, having evolved from a backwater privateering base in the mid-seventeenth century to the bustling plantation and mercantile heart of Britain's American empire by the mid-eighteenth century. But given the smuggling of contraband goods aboard South Sea Company slave ships, the company's growing reliance on this Caribbean hub would also prove a source of friction with Spain, contributing to the ultimate downfall of the British asiento.[6]

■ One might expect Britain's securing of the asiento in 1713 to have undermined transshipment in the British slave trade to Spanish America. After all, one reason that earlier British traders transshipped Africans to foreign colonies (rather than trading directly from Africa) was the illegality of foreign trade in the eyes of Spanish officials. This clandestine trade before 1713 required personal connections, timely intelligence, and detailed geographic knowledge, all of which favored trading from neighboring provinces rather than Africa. But now that the asiento gave the South Sea Company legal access to Spanish American ports, why not sail straight from Africa to Spanish America? At times, the company did precisely that, but transatlantic trade was the company's preferred strategy only for deliveries to Buenos Aires, where no nearby British colony offered an alternative. Most company ships from Africa at least stopped at Jamaica or Barbados temporarily en route to Spanish territories, and many never continued. They left the final passage to company sloops that ferried African captives from Caribbean entrepôts.

In choosing indirect trade between Africa and Spanish America, the South Sea Company followed conventional wisdom. Their Dutch and French pre-

---

see John J. McCusker, Jr., "The Rum Trade and the Balance of Payments of the Thirteen Continental Colonies, 1650–1775" (Ph.D. diss., University of Pittsburgh, 1970), 692.

6. The operations of interlopers could be robust in scale; R. Assheton reported in 1729 that nineteen ships had recently returned from clandestine trade in Cuba (R. Assheton to Isaac Hobhouse, Kingston, Apr. 25, 1729, Jeffries Collection, XIII, fol. 100, Bristol Central Library, U.K.).

decessors had relied heavily on transshipment, partly because all asientistas had trouble fulfilling their quotas and resorted to acquiring Africans from any available sources. Dutch traders dominated the asiento from 1661 to the end of the seventeenth century, using Curaçao as their hub. Between 1658 and 1729, the Dutch carried nearly 100,000 Africans to Spanish America, the vast majority of them via Curaçao. The French Guinea Company took over the asiento from 1702 until 1712. The company ventured directly from Africa to Spanish territory regularly, but like the Dutch, they also relied at least partly on transshipment. The French asientistas undertook more direct African voyages because they had no Caribbean hub as close to Spanish America as Curaçao or Jamaica. Nonetheless, the company purchased Africans for transshipment from the Dutch in Curaçao, the Danish at Saint Thomas, the British on Barbados and Jamaica, and independent French traders in Martinique. Overall, the French Guinea Company delivered about 20,000 enslaved Africans to Spanish America, nearly half of them via transshipment.[7]

Drawing on these precedents, the South Sea Company incorporated transshipment from the British Caribbean as it planned its operations. In 1713, the company invited proposals from British traders to Africa "For Delivering healthful Sound Negroes of all Sizes at Carthagena, Porto bello, Vera Crus or Jamaica." The inclusion of Jamaica in the list of destinations illustrates the

7. A dizzying array of merchants held the asiento contract in the late seventeenth century—Genoese, Dutch, and later Portuguese—but the Dutch West India Company subcontracted to provide most of the slaves. On Curaçao as the Dutch entrepôt, see Wim Klooster, "Curaçao and the Caribbean Transit Trade," in Johannes Postma and Victor Enthoven, eds., *Riches from Atlantic Commerce: Dutch Transatlantic Trade and Shipping, 1585-1817* (Leiden, 2003), 203-218; Han Jordaan, "The Curaçao Slave Market: From *Asiento* Trade to Free Trade, 1700-1730," ibid., 219-257. For the estimate of nearly 100,000 Africans delivered by the Dutch, see Johannes Menne Postma, *The Dutch in the Atlantic Slave Trade, 1600-1815* (New York, 1990), 26-55. Meanwhile, *Voyages,* accessed March 2011, which incorporates Postma's data, shows just under 15,000 Africans arriving in Spanish America on Dutch ships from Africa in the same period (1658 and 1729), leaving roughly 80,000 to come from transshipment (http://slavevoyages.org/tast/database/search.faces ?yearFrom=1658&yearTo=1729&natinimp=8&mjslptimp=31100.31200.31300.31400.40000). In rough agreement, Klooster estimates that 42,000 Africans were shipped from Curaçao to Spanish America in the narrower time range between 1676 and 1716. On the French asiento, see Colin A. Palmer, "The Company Trade and the Numerical Distribution of Slaves to Spanish America, 1703-1739," in Paul E. Lovejoy, ed., *Africans in Bondage: Studies in Slavery and the Slave Trade* (Madison Wis., 1986), 27-42. On French purchases from Curaçao, see Jordaan, "Curaçao Slave Market," 224-225. The *Voyages* website documents forty-one French voyages directly from Africa to Spanish America during their asiento, carrying 10,618 people (http://slave voyages.org/tast/database/search.faces?yearFrom=1702&yearTo=1712&natinimp=10&mjslptimp =31100.31200.31300.31400.40000).

island's presence in the company's early considerations. Likewise, when the South Sea Company negotiated to buy captives on the African coast from Britain's other prominent slave-trading outfit, the Royal African Company, Jamaica again figured as a primary hub. The contract stipulated that the Royal African Company not only provide enslaved people to South Sea Company vessels on the African coast but also supply "the Usuall quantities of provisions allowed to Negroes from the Coast of Africa to Jamaica" or more, if going farther.[8]

Few, if any, of the South Sea Company's directors had experience in the slave trade to Spanish America, so in addition to following Dutch and French precedents, they relied heavily on advice from British slave traders in the Caribbean. Particularly influential were the recommendations sent by two Jamaican merchants, Mr. Kent and Mr. Thompson, in January 1714. Kent and Thompson, who would become two of the company's four initial agents in Jamaica, argued that transshipment from their island offered two primary advantages. First, it would allow the company to tailor its human cargoes to the Spanish market. Using Jamaica as a depot would allow the South Sea Company to withhold less desirable captives from shipments to the Spanish, who were notoriously finicky buyers. They also cautioned against recuperating these unhealthy Africans for later shipments. Instead, Kent and Thompson

> acquainted the Committee that by the Practice of picking out the Refuse Negros and recovering them much money had been lost. [T]herefore the best way is to take them out to sell 'em for what can be obtain'd for them there being several persons on the Island who drive that Trade.

With merchants in Jamaica willing to speculate on reviving the unfortunate Africans who ailed most after the Middle Passage—the "refuse"—Kent and Thompson urged the company simply to unload the unhealthy captives.[9]

8. "The South Sea Company: Minutes of the Court of Directors," in Elizabeth Donnan, ed., *Documents Illustrative of the History of the Slave Trade to America,* 4 vols. (Washington, D.C., 1930–1935), II, 156, 158–168.

9. "The South Sea Company: Minutes of the Committee of Correspondence," Jan. 5, 1713/14, in Donnan, ed., *Documents,* II, 173–174. Many of the South Sea Company directors were financiers who helped develop the plan to make the crown's creditors into a joint-stock company; the others were more likely appointed for reasons of patronage than experience. See John Carswell, *The South Sea Bubble,* rev. ed. (London, 1993), esp. chap. 3. On the high standards of Spanish slave buyers, see Palmer, *Human Cargoes,* 32, 63–64; Jordaan, "Curaçao Slave Market," in Postma and Enthoven, eds., *Riches from Atlantic Commerce,* 250. On Kent and Thompson's becoming factors, see "Minutes of the Court of Directors," Aug. 11, 1714, which refers to the Jamaican agents

Their second major argument in favor of a British Caribbean hub emphasized sensitivity to market fluctuations. Ships sailing from Africa with year-old information on Spanish demand would struggle to find favorable markets, Kent and Thompson insisted. Even if they were lucky enough to arrive at a Spanish port when slaves were most desired, whole cargoes of more than three hundred people could quickly saturate demand, forcing the company to lower prices or sell on credit. To avoid such problems, Kent and Thompson argued:

> The Compa. shou'd carry the Good Negr's over to the [Spanish]
> Coast in Sloops of their Own or hyred ones and not in the Ships that
> bring them [from Africa] for if they are Carried in Sloops [which
> were smaller than most transatlantic vessels] they may be Sold for
> ready money but otherwise for trust [i.e., credit] which has proved
> Hazerdous.

To ensure that these smaller ships found the ports with the highest prices, Kent and Thompson further recommended "that the Agents in Jamaica should keep a Correspondence with the Spanish Ports to know where Negroes are wanted." Only a base of operations in the British Caribbean, in other words, would allow the South Sea Company to respond effectively to Spanish market conditions. Notably, the health of captives was not a primary concern. In fact, the unspoken consequence of such a scheme would be periods of waiting in a merchant's yard in Jamaica for word from Spanish ports about "where Negroes are wanted." [10]

Of course, Kent and Thompson hoped for personal gain in routing the company's trade through their island, but company officials saw wisdom in their advice. As the South Sea Company put the asiento into practice over the following years, they adhered to many (though not all) of Kent and Thompson's recommendations. By the summer of 1714, before establishing any factories on Spanish soil, the company appointed agents in both Barbados and Jamaica. Transatlantic slaving vessels (whether owned by the company or fulfilling contracts for delivery to the company) carried orders to sail from Africa for one of those two islands. Until company officials got up and running in Spanish territories, the agents in Jamaica and Barbados gave "Certifi-

---

as Kent, Thompson, Morris, and Pratter. Kent did not retain the post long, but Thompson served the company in Jamaica until 1718; see SSC Records, Add. MSS, 25495, 397.

10. "Minutes of the Committee of Correspondence," in Donnan, ed., *Documents,* II, 173–174. For another example of the South Sea Company's advocating the use of small ships to avoid selling on credit, see 215–219.

cates," allowing independent traders "to go to the Spanish West Indies" and handle sales as temporary agents for the company. Even after settling factors in Spanish America in 1715, the company continued to order the vast majority of transatlantic slavers to Barbados or Jamaica as their first, if not only, stop in the Americas.[11]

As much as possible, the South Sea Company contracted British transatlantic traders (including the Royal African Company) for the delivery of Africans to their Caribbean hubs at predetermined prices, but to ensure steady supplies to Spanish America, the company also acquired Africans through other channels. The South Sea Company encouraged their Jamaica and Barbados agents to purchase Africans from independent slave traders if more were needed to meet their obligation to the Spanish. "We renew our Former Directions that you take Care to Supply our Several Factorys [in Spanish America] with Negros as they write for them," the company directors instructed in 1716, "and hope we shall be able from our Own ships to Furnish them, But if not We must leave it to you to Buy them, if to be Had at reasonable prices." Likewise, when Spain requested that the company deliver one hundred Africans to Santo Domingo in 1716, the directors assented and ordered "that the Comittee of Correspondence write to Barbadoes to procure the said Negroes." In fact, the company served many smaller Spanish American markets, such as Santo Domingo, exclusively via such transshipment. When company factor William Farril reported high demand at Havana in 1718—which was a minor port for the slave trade in the early eighteenth century—company officials in London replied, "We are well Pleased you have the prospect of selling 1000 Negroes yearly which We acquaint Mr. Woodbridge [in Barbados] with that he may supply you accordingly." Sending vessels from Africa to Spanish ports other than Veracruz, Cartagena, Portobelo, and Buenos Aires never seemed to be part of the plan.[12]

Some company vessels from Africa did continue from Jamaica or Barbados

11. "Minutes of the Court of Directors," Jul. 21, 1714, SSC to Thompson, Morice, and Pratter, Oct. 15, 1714, both in SSC Records, Add. MSS, 25495, 187–189, 429. For examples of early ships sent from Africa to Jamaica despite company agents in Spanish America, see "Minutes of the Court of Directors," Jun. 15, 1715, ibid., 25496, 79.

12. "Minutes of the Court of Directors," Apr. 28, 1714, SSC Records, Add. MSS, 25495, 295; SSC to Rigby and Pratter, Mar. 31, 1724, ibid., 25564, 85–86; "Minutes of the Court of Directors," May 16, 1716, ibid., 25496, 237; SSC to William Farril, Apr. 30, 1718, ibid., 25563, 313; "The South Sea Company to the Jamaica Factors," London, Feb. 6, 1716, in Donnan, ed., Documents, II, 204. For other examples of company instructions to buy slaves in Barbados or Jamaica if necessary, see SSC Records, 25495, 459; 25497, 164; 25563, 251; and 25564, 211–212.

to Spanish America, but even then, they often engaged in intercolonial trade. In 1718, company executives summed up the standard practice for managing vessels arriving from Africa in their instructions to their Barbados agent:

> Go on Board and View their respective Cargo of Negroes. . . . Take out and sell or Endeavour to Recover . . . Sick or Improper Negroes and in Lieu of them, . . . put on Board a like Number of good sound healthy and proper Negroes if they can be had at reasonable prices.

These orders were by no means unusual. In 1717, the company stressed to their factor at Panama, "We have given [the agents at Jamaica] repeated orders to let none go for your Parts but what are good and to pick out the Refuse and supply them with good ones." [13]

This sorting often thrust Africans of diverse backgrounds together in the holds of slave ships. In January 1718, for example, the *John Galley* sailed into Kingston "with 267 Slaves from Whidah [Ouidah, in modern Benin] in a bad condition, after burying 92 in the Voyage." Apparently smallpox or another highly communicable disease had erupted among these unfortunate, mostly Aja, captives. To prevent further loss of life—lost profits to the company— Jamaican agents Thompson, Pratter, and Haselwood brought ashore 102 ill survivors from the floating pesthouse. Rather than nurse these sufferers back to health, the agents sold them cheaply to speculators willing to bother. With the *John Galley*'s cargo now depleted through both death and sale, Thompson, Pratter, and Haselwood ordered the vessel to wait "in expectation of Our ship the Evelin," another transatlantic slaver. Three weeks later, the *Evelyn* sailed in from the Gold Coast according to plan, "with 159 Slaves out of which [Thompson, Pratter, and Haselwood] took 122 and put them on board the John Galley for Portobelo." So despite making its only purchases in Africa at Ouidah, the *John Galley*, ultimately delivered nearly as many Africans from the Gold Coast to Portobelo as it did from Ouidah. Even the company's transatlantic slavers engaged in intercolonial trade from Caribbean entrepôts. [14]

13. SSC to Dudley Woodbridge, Jan. 17, 1718, SSC Records, Add. MSS, 25563, 236–237; SSC to Gilbert Grimes, Oct. 26, 1717, ibid., 25563, 143. For a few of the many examples of the South Sea Company's ordering vessels from Africa to Jamaica or Barbados, and then on to Spanish America, see ibid., 25497, 52, 145, 155; ibid., 25563, 69–70.

14. For the *John Galley*, see SSC to Thompson, Pratter, and Haselwood, Apr. 30, 1718, ibid., 25563, 315. For more on the transatlantic voyages of the *John Galley* and the *Evelyn*, see *Voyages*, accessed February 2011, Voyage ID nos. 75696, 75433, but note that the sorting in Jamaica is not reflected in that database. For the likely ethnolinguistic backgrounds of the captives, see Patrick Manning, *Slavery, Colonialism and Economic Growth in Dahomey, 1640–1960* (New York, 1982),

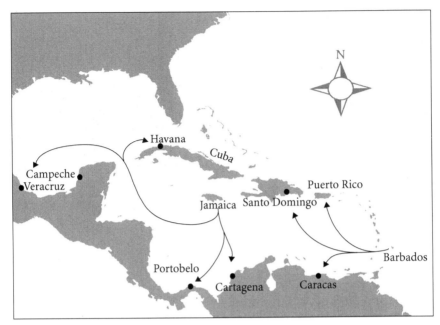

MAP 5. Entrepôts for the South Sea Company and Their Spanish American Destinations. Drawn by the author

Barbados and Jamaica served similar, but not identical, roles in the company's trade to Spanish America. For roughly the first decade of the British asiento, Barbados was the gateway to Puerto Rico, to the "Windward Coast," or "Wild Coast," of northern South America (modern Venezuela and adjacent lands and islands), and often to Santo Domingo and Cuba. Jamaica, meanwhile, supplied Veracruz (and thus all of Mexico), Cartagena and Portobelo (and thus Peru), and often Santo Domingo and Cuba (Map 5). Because Jamaica primarily transshipped to regions where the company established factories, while Barbados mainly sent Africans to regions where the company lacked employees, the two hubs employed different practices. In Jamaica, the company hired vessels to deliver Africans on freight or purchased sloops to

10–11, 30–34; Paul E. Lovejoy, *Transformations in Slavery: A History of Slavery in Africa,* 3d ed. (New York, 2012), 57, 79–80. If indeed contagious disease caused the mortality aboard the *John Galley,* then company agents showed either a poor understanding of contagion or a limited desire to minimize its effects by leaving healthier captives aboard the ship and embarking others on her for transshipment. Both factors are plausible. Vessels under quarantine in the period were routinely visited by merchants, doctors, and others bringing supplies, suggesting only partial understanding of contagion; meanwhile, all slave traders anticipated and accepted some mortality as part of the cost of buying, shipping, and selling people.

PLATE 7. Dudley Woodbridge, director general in Barbados of the South Sea Company (here referred to as the Royal Assiento Company). By John Smith, based on a portrait by Sir Godfrey Kneller. 1718. That Woodbridge sat for this portrait in London, labeled with his new South Sea Company title and clutching his new company commission in hand, speaks not only to the importance Woodbridge attached to the post, but also to Britain's grand vision of the riches that Spanish American trade would bring. © National Portrait Gallery, London

shuttle captives to Spanish America. Company factors in Spanish territory then managed sales and organized remittances. From Barbados, operations were complicated by the lack of factors to manage sales in the Spanish American ports served (with the exception of Cuba), so subcontracting private traders proved vital.

In the early years of the British asiento, Barbados appeared likely to rival or surpass Jamaica as the South Sea Company's primary Caribbean hub. Owing partly to problems at Jamaica and partly to the company's "special trust and Confidence" in their Barbados factor, Dudley Woodbridge, the role of Barbados expanded over the early years of the trade (Plate 7). In 1717, the company notified its agents in Jamaica that Cuba would no longer be part of their territory, having decided to "put Our Factory at the Havana under the Direction of Mr. Woodbridge, Our Agent at Barbadoes." The following year, after Woodbridge visited London, the company promoted him to "Agent and Director General at Barbados" and granted him extensive authority "to give out passes or grant Licenses to any person or persons to carry any Number of Negroes" from Barbados to Spanish America under company auspices, or even to take up such licenses himself if he desired to speculate in the market for exploitable Africans. Such subcontracting of the asiento via licenses was necessary because the company constantly struggled to fulfill its contract. The asiento not only gave the South Sea Company the right to sell slaves to Spanish America but also an obligation to do so. Regardless of the number of Africans actually delivered, the contract required the company to pay import duties for four thousand slaves annually. Failure to fulfill this quota promised to severely undermine profits, since the company still owed the taxes. (And the company would always struggle with the quota, just as prior asientistas had; a 1723 report showed "a deficiency of above ⅓" in fulfilling the asiento over the preceding two years.) To provide further incentive, the asiento waived any duty for the next eight hundred people imported after the quota of four thousand was met. As a result, the company was willing to sell licenses to independent traders. Granting such licenses in the Caribbean, rather than in London, fostered the growth of Caribbean markets and intercolonial merchant networks that traversed imperial boundaries. It also unwittingly helped create a cadre of independent traders with Spanish American connections that might later be exploited to circumvent the asiento monopoly.[15]

In any case, Barbados's prominence in the asiento trade proved short-lived. For one thing, Barbados primarily served the less robust markets of Spanish America. By late 1717, Woodbridge complained that weak demand and a lack of capital in "Windward" ports, such as Trinidad and Caracas, left many Africans from Barbados unsold. To manage the light demand, he suggested having single sloops stop briefly at several "Windward" ports on one journey, noting that those Africans not sold could "be Deliver'd to the Companys Factorys at Carthagena Puerto Bello, Havana, or Vera Cruz," where demand was higher. On top of the slow sales, in 1719, naval skirmishing in European waters between England and Spain temporarily halted the entire asiento. By 1721, "the Rupture," as company officials dubbed it, was mended, but in the interim, Dudley Woodbridge died in Barbados. The company largely gave up on the island thereafter.[16]

15. SSC instructions to Woodbridge, Jan. 17, 1718, SSC Records, Add. MSS, 25563, 232; SSC to Thompson, Pratter, and Hazelwood, Oct. 31, 1717, ibid., 163–164; "The South Sea Company: Minutes of the Committee of Correspondence," Oct. 22, 1717, in Donnan, ed., *Documents*, II, 219–221 (see also SSC Records, Add. MSS, 25497, 146–149). On the importance of the duty threshold of four thousand slaves delivered annually, see [James Houstoun?], *A True and Impartial Account of the Rise and Progress of the South Sea Company . . .* (London, 1743), 8; [Benjamin Keene?] to SSC, Seville, June 6, 1732, Newcastle Papers, XCII, Additional Manuscripts, 32777, fols. 98–101, British Library, London (hereafter cited as BL, Add. MSS); SSC to Keene, Dec. 5, 1734, ibid., CI, BL, Add. MSS, 32786, fol. 346. "Deficiency of above 1/3": SSC to Rigby and Pratter, Nov. 12, 1724, SSC Records, Add. MSS, 25564, 136–137.

16. Dudley Woodbridge to SSC, Oct. 16, 1717, London, in Donnan, ed., *Documents*, II, 215–219. On halting company operations at Barbados, see also Palmer, *Human Cargoes*, 59.

Meanwhile, Jamaica's importance to the company only grew. Jamaica enjoyed many advantages of geography for Spanish American trade, including prevailing winds that made voyages from the Spanish Main to Barbados difficult; after "the Rupture," company activities focused more on the westernmost British island. By 1722, if not earlier, the South Sea Company built its first sloop explicitly assigned to ferrying Africans between Jamaica and Spanish America. The sloop *Asiento,* under Captain David Greenhill, made at least four such voyages that year, delivering about five hundred Africans to Cartagena and Portobelo. The very name of the vessel implies that transshipment from Jamaica was becoming synonymous with the asiento, and the company built more such sloops. In 1725, when London shipwrights finished constructing the *Prince of Asturias,* the company gave John Cleland command and notified their factors in Jamaica that the new vessel was "to be employ'd between Your Island and the Several Factorys in the Spanish West Indies." The company also empowered the Jamaica factors to hire additional vessels for transshipment, "especially if All Our Own Sloops are otherwise Imployed." Of course, keeping such sloops occupied demanded a regular supply of incoming Africans at Jamaica. After learning that the Jamaica agents resorted to buying Africans for this purpose in 1724, company officials in London assured them, "We are taking and will continue to take the best Care We can to keep you Sufficiently furnished, that as Demands arise from the Several Factorys You may not be at a Loss to give them immediate Supplys." To that end, they noted sending nine ships to Africa in the preceding six months, all with orders to proceed to Jamaica with their human cargoes.[17]

Along with an increased proportion of the trade, the Jamaica agents received greater authority in company affairs. In 1724, company officials shifted the granting of licenses for independent traders from Barbados to Jamaica. They also ordered all returns from the Spanish American factories to be routed to Jamaica and appointed the agents at Jamaica arbiters of any disputes between company factors in Spanish territory. Finally, in 1725, the company officially rendered all of its factors in Spanish America subordinate to

17. SSC to Rigby and Pratter, July 22, 1725, SSC Records, Add. MSS, 25565, 67; see also SSC instructions to "to Capt. Samuel Toft of the Company's Sloop the Don Lewis which is to be Employ'd between Jamaica and the Spanish West Indies in the Service of the Assiento," Mar. 5, 1724, ibid., 25567, 46–50. "If All Our Own Sloops": SSC to Rigby and Pratter, ibid., 25564, 86. "To keep you Sufficiently furnished": SSC to Rigby and Pratter, Nov. 12, 1724, ibid., 135–137. For the *Asiento,* see contaduria 268, Archivo General de Indias, Seville. David Eltis generously shared the information from these records with me from among the shipping records compiled for the *Voyages* website.

the Jamaica agents, explaining, "We have also determined That all the Factorys be made dependant on Jamaica where We Imagine it for the Comp's Service that all their Affairs relating to them should Center." The company's factors on the Spanish mainland might have conducted the actual trade with Spanish colonists, but Jamaica was where instructions, Spanish silver, information about demand, and the Africans themselves flowed in and were rerouted. By the 1730s, in fact, the company largely abandoned trade in Africa to acquire captives, opting instead "to depend on the Jamaica market for the provision of all such negroes." For African people bound to many American destinations, Jamaica was emerging as the primary gateway.[18]

What was the rationale for granting a colony pride of place in the South Sea Company's asiento trade, when the whole point of the asiento was to open Spanish America to British traders? Among the concerns that South Sea Company officials mentioned most when explaining the policy was ensuring that only healthy captives reached Spanish ports. In 1725, Spanish officials threatened to bar deliveries not coming directly from Africa, claiming "That the Negroes by being brought into British Colony's are tainted with Heresy." The British deemed the idea "So ridiculous that it deserves no Answer," yet they were obliged to respond anyway. The company insisted "That a Liberty of refreshing Our Negroes in our own Colonys after a long and sickly Voyage is absolutely necessary and essential to Our . . . Supplying the Spanish West Indies with Sound and healthy Negroes. . . . The refusing this would be very Inhumane and barbarous to them." However disingenuous the company's humanitarian concern for the people it traded, the fact remained that mortality eroded profits; the company did seek to minimize it, ordering the Jamaica agents to hire doctors and give captives herb baths for health. Nonetheless, in practice, the company showed less interest in "refreshing . . . Negroes" in Jamaica than it stated publicly and to Spain. After all, company policy was to sell unhealthy Africans in Jamaica, not nurse them back to health. The goal at the entrepôt was assembling cargoes best suited to Spanish markets, keeping prices high, and ensuring the sale of entire transshipments. Whether fear of heresy was truly foremost in the minds of Spanish opponents of the company's transshipment from Jamaica in 1725 is difficult to gauge. Given the Inquisition, one is hesitant to take Spanish aversion to heresy lightly, but there is

18. SSC to Rigby and Pratter, Nov. 12, 1724, SSC Records, Add. MSS, 25564, 141; SSC to the Cartagena factory, Nov. 19, 1724, ibid., 163; SSC to James Pym, Dec. 12, 1723, ibid., 46; SSC to Rigby and Pratter, Apr. 21, 1725, ibid., 220; SSC to Humphry Morice, 1731, quoted in Palmer, *Human Cargoes*, 62.

little reason to suspect that British traders actually catechized Africans before sending them to Spanish America. Heresy might have been an excuse to block shipments from Jamaica because of suspicions that the British used transshipment to facilitate smuggling contraband goods. Whatever the combination of Spanish motives, the two sides eventually reached a compromise whereby the company sent affidavits with all transshipments guaranteeing that the captives had spent fewer than four months in Jamaica.[19]

Furthermore, as useful as Jamaica was for organizing cargoes of healthy people for transshipment, the company's health concerns alone do not explain the importance of Jamaica as a hub. Its proximity to the primary Spanish American ports also facilitated the timely gathering of information on market conditions, which could change quickly. In June 1718, South Sea Company officials wrote angrily to William Farril, their factor at Havana, about his reports of slow sales of Africans recently transshipped to him from Barbados. Just a month earlier, Farril had reported high demand, claiming that he could easily sell one thousand slaves annually. If officials in London had to make all decisions about supplies of slaves to Cuba, they might have outfitted four vessels to Africa for the necessary captives to fulfill Farril's order before receiving his word that circumstances had changed. Having company agents monitoring demand from greater proximity was prudent, and even Barbados was considerably farther from most Spanish markets than Jamaica. As one observer of the company's Jamaica operation put it, "By being so nearly and happily situated [to Spanish America], the *Assiento* Vessels not only have *quicker Voyages*, but the *Factory* there must of course have *speedier* and *better Intelligence*, than if they were at a greater Distance."[20]

19. "Tainted with Heresy" and "Liberty of refreshing Our Negroes": SSC to Mr. Stratford, June 17, 1725, SSC Records, Add. MSS, 25564, 227–228. The Spanish raised similar concerns about heresy to challenge Dutch transshipment in previous decades; see "Report of the Council of the Inquisition to the King," in Donnan, ed., *Documents*, I, 338–339; Postma, *Dutch Atlantic Slave Trade*, 33–37; Palmer, "The Company Trade," in Lovejoy, ed., *Africans in Bondage*, 28–34. Palmer argues that the primary purpose of routing slave shipments through Jamaica was recuperation before the final passage to Spanish America (he notes the herbal baths ordered for captives), but this assessment overlooks many other factors behind the company's strategy, most notably the integration of slave trading with general commerce (*Human Cargoes*, 61–62, 66–67). In fact, Jamaica was a notoriously unhealthy environment, even for Europeans (Vincent Brown, *The Reaper's Garden: Death and Power in the World of Atlantic Slavery* [Cambridge, Mass., 2008], 13–17, 48–50). On average mortality on transatlantic slavers, see Herbert S. Klein, *The Atlantic Slave Trade* (New York, 1999), 132–142.

20. SSC to Farril, June 5, 1718, SSC Records, Add. MSS, 25563, 343–345; [James Knight], *Some Observations on the Assiento Trade, as It Has Been Exercised by the South-Sea Company: Proving*

Also central to Jamaica's importance was the opportunity to reorganize groups of Africans to match the requirements of destination markets—in terms of size, gender, and, indeed, health. Perhaps most important, the South Sea Company regulated the flow of African migrants to Spanish ports in order to sell as many people as possible without fully sating demand and driving down prices. Thus, when the *Dunwich Merchant* reached Jamaica with 543 Africans in early 1716, the company factors divided these people, splitting the healthy between two sloops—one bound for Cartagena and the other for Portobelo—to avoid saturating either market. The directors approved such attention to demand, constantly reminding their factors in Spanish territory of the importance of "writing to our agents at Jamaica" to keep them informed of "the Quantity and Quality of Negroes your Markett will take off." [21]

The attention to the perceived "Quality" as well as "Quantity" suggests that demand varied across Spanish America not just in terms of the number of Africans wanted but also in terms of the quality of people—as perceived by slaveholders—that they would accept. In 1722, the company's Jamaica factors divided six hundred arriving Africans into three groups for distribution according to health. They sent the healthiest captives to the Spanish Main and transshipped the captives sorted into a middling category to Hispaniola, where the less developed economy prevented buyers from being as discriminating or from affording the most expensive captives. Finally, the factors rejected the least healthy Africans as unsuitable for Spanish markets, opting instead to sell them locally. In some cases, the company sold such ailing captives to independent traders in Jamaica, along with licenses to sell them in marginal Spanish American ports where the company did not have factors. Indeed, one advantage that company officials saw in licensing independent traders was that "this Method has hitherto diverted the Course of a Considerable Number of Refuse Negroes," so that these suffering captives still reached Spanish America and counted toward the company's quota. Unfortunately, the reliance on subcontractors to deliver unhealthy captives to Spanish American backwaters means that little record survives of such ventures' outcomes. Surely these trips were especially dangerous for captives sick from the outset. In other cases, company agents in Jamaica even sorted Africans for transshipment when they were all bound for the same port. In 1725, officials in London

---

the Damage, Which Will Accrue Thereby to the British Commerce and Plantations in America, and Particularly to Jamaica. . . . (London, 1728), 4.

21. "The South Sea Company: Minutes of the Court of Directors," June 15, 1715, in Donnan, ed., *Documents*, II, 195 n. 2; SSC to Charles Reade, June 13, 1718, SSC Records, Add. MSS, 25563, 358.

commended the Jamaica agents for market savvy when they "sent the *Don Carlos* and *Assiento* one after the other to Portobelo . . . sending the Sorts of Negroes least coveted first, You being certainly right, the greater the Demand the fewer objections."[22]

Gender also factored into the sorting at Jamaica. In general, company factors in Spanish America preferred to receive disproportionate numbers of men. Given such gendered considerations, South Sea Company employees in Jamaica might have skewed the enslaved migration more male than the population arriving in Jamaica already was, although this tendency was offset to some degree by the interest in selecting women and girls for transshipment as sex workers. James Knight, an observer of the company's trade in Jamaica, noted that some buyers in wealthy Spanish ports paid exceptionally high prices for female slaves whom company employees called *"clever Girls."* Presumably, the Spanish exploited such women or girls for sex rather than labor, since Knight contrasted "clever girls" with *"working Negroes"* and since "clever" held connotations of comeliness in the eighteenth century. For the women and girls deemed "clever," the leering examinations of merchants in Jamaica must have seemed particularly ominous. If such women became concubines in Spanish colonies, their experience of American slavery might have been more akin to the typical experiences of African women sent to the Middle East in the slave trade. During the same period in which the transatlantic slave trade thrived, sub-Saharan Africa also sent millions of enslaved people to the Middle East; whereas males were overrepresented in the Atlantic trade, women and girls bound for concubinage predominated in the other direction. These women often lived apart from most other Africans and bore mixed-race children who grew up largely divorced from the African culture of their mothers. To the extent that the general traffic to Spanish America overemphasized men, that practice also probably inhibited African cultural survivals. Unbalanced gender roles must have limited family formation in Spanish American slave communities and impeded the transfer of cultural practices associated with women's gender roles.[23]

22. Basnett, Miller, and Mill to Humphry Morice, Kingston, Nov. 9, 1722, SSC Records, Add. MSS, 48590, fols. 29–31; SSC to Rigby and Pratter, Apr. 21, 1725, ibid., 25564, 207, 212.

23. On the general preference for male slaves, see SSC to Thompson, Pratter, and Haselwood, July 12, 1717, ibid., 25563, 106. *"Clever Girls"*: [Knight], *Observations on the Assiento*, 16–17. According to OED, "clever" had connotations of "lithe" and "handsome" in the eighteenth century, including one 1731 example of an author describing "A clever-shaped young woman" (*Oxford English Dictionary* online, s.v. "clever," accessed February 2011, http://www.oed.com /view/Entry/34245 [see esp. definition no. 5]). For another example of the South Sea Company's

Although health and gender were criteria considered in the sorting of captives at Jamaica, company records show less attention paid to ethnicity or African regional background in decisions about dispersal. As such, the British asiento surely added to the diversity of Spanish America's enslaved populations because the forced migration to the British Caribbean drew from a wide array of African regions in the period. As the British transatlantic slave trade ramped up to meet the burgeoning demand in Jamaica and other entrepôts, British Guineamen expanded their range to more African regions. The forced migration to Jamaica included most of the diversity of Atlantic Africa. Akan people (and others) from the Gold Coast held the largest share in the migration, but west central Africans and people from the Bight of Benin each composed sizable portions as well. Enslaved people from these regions were already present in Spanish America (especially west central Africans), but the migration to Jamaica during the British asiento also included groups rarely seen previously in Spanish settlements. Igbos—and perhaps smaller numbers of other people from the Bight of Biafra, such as Ibibios and Efiks—accounted for about one in ten captives disembarking at Jamaica in the period. Spanish slaveholders, like many throughout the Americas, were less fond of exploiting Igbos than some other enslaved African groups, so there is some reason to expect that the South Sea Company avoided them, especially since Spanish buyers often paid in silver, giving them more influence with traders. Nonetheless, to most purchasers, the most important criteria was health, so Igbos who survived the Atlantic crossing to Jamaica in decent condition faced some likelihood of transshipment to Spanish America. In addition, small numbers of people from the Upper Guinea coast also appeared in the slave migration to Jamaica in the British asiento period, and they likely began to appear in Spanish America, as well. These new forced migration streams into Jamaica contributed to an increasingly complex African population in Spanish America (Figures 3 and 7).

Historians of the South Sea Company have portrayed Jamaica as a rehabili-

---

melding sex trafficking and slave trading, see Palmer, *Human Cargoes,* 62–63. For similar use of the slave trade for sex trafficking in the nineteenth-century United States, see Edward E. Baptist, "'Cuffy,' 'Fancy Maids,' and 'One-Eyed Men': Rape, Commodification, and the Domestic Slave Trade in the United States," in Walter Johnson, ed., *The Chattel Principle: Internal Slave Trades in the Americas* (New Haven, Conn., 2004), 165–202. On the importance of women in the diaspora to the transfer of many cultural elements, see Jennifer L. Morgan, *Laboring Women: Reproduction and Gender in New World Slavery* (Philadelphia, 2004), esp. 3–6. On the comparison of the African slave trades to the Atlantic and to the Middle East, see Patrick Manning, *Slavery and African Life: Occidental, Oriental, and African Slave Trades* (New York, 1990).

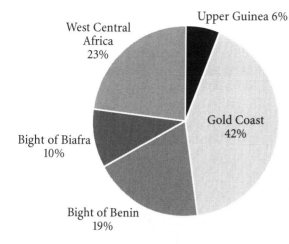

FIGURE 7. Captive Origins in the Transatlantic Slave Trade to Jamaica, 1713–1739

Source: *Voyages: The Trans-Atlantic Slave Trade Database,* accessed January 2013, http://slavevoyages.org/tast/assessment/estimates.faces?yearFrom=1713&yearTo=1739&disembarkation=301

tation center—a place for captives to recuperate before continuing to Spanish America—but given the company's practices of sorting and rerouting people, a better analogy is an airline hub. Jamaica offered a centrally located port where all vessels coming and going could stop, drop off travelers for various destinations, and pick up supplies and passengers headed to that vessel's next port. The system was efficient for the company but disorienting and unpleasant for the passengers, who were temporarily housed in cramped quarters with poor food. Land perhaps offered captives better conditions than aboard ship, but the layover still added to the duress and duration of a trip that travelers surely wanted to end. In addition, the company's handling and sorting of people in Jamaica continued to convey to African migrants their captors' dehumanized view of them. Fear, anger, and sadness were commonplace, as the meanings of traders' choices were imagined or became known through conversations with experienced slaves working the waterfronts or holding pens.

Beyond grouping people for various destinations, centralization of trade in Jamaica offered other advantages to the South Sea Company. Most notably, it facilitated maximum usage of company ships. Vessels bound from London to Spanish America to retrieve the goods factors acquired in exchange for people could stop at Jamaica to obtain Africans for transshipment along the way. In 1716, the South Sea Company sent "the *London* Frygt" to Veracruz to retrieve silver and produce. En route, the company ordered the *London* to stop at Jamaica, instructing the factors on the island "to Ship with all Expedition not Exceed'g 150 Negros" on the *London* for the final leg of the journey to Veracruz. In the same letter, the company also informed the Jamaica factors, "We shall in Less than a Fortnight Dispatch the *Herbert* Gally for Cathagena to bring home the Effects of the *Bedford* Cargo. She will have Orders to touch at your Island to take in not Exceed'g 200 Negros." This option to have vessels from London stop at a Caribbean entrepôt for captives en route to Spanish America was especially important because the asiento contract stipulated that only vessels delivering slaves (and one annual ship with British manufactured goods) would be granted access to Spanish American ports. Hence, the company's instructions to one ship captain departing London for Veracruz ordered him to stop in Jamaica and "apply to Messrs Rigby and Pratter our Agents, for a few Negroes to qualify You for an Assiento Vessel, in order to Your admittance at Vera Cruz." Other business was primary, but enslaved Africans opened the door.[24]

As this venture from England to Spanish America suggests, the South Sea Company was always interested in selling more than African people in Spanish colonies. The company pursued a legal trade in British manufactured goods through the one annual ship the asiento allowed the company to send from England to Spanish America. The high hopes for the annual ship were evident when the company applauded ambassador Benjamin Keene on his success in negotiating a reopening of the asiento after a 1727–1729 stoppage caused by tense Anglo-Spanish relations. The company emphasized that Keene must also ensure a renewed Spanish commitment to the annual ship if the reinstatement was going to mean anything of value. In fact, one former employee estimated the value of goods typically acquired for the "annual ship" at a staggering £250,000, so the interest in using the slave-trading contract to open broader Spanish American trade was powerful. It was also not limited to the legal avenue of the annual ship. The slave trade often served as cover for a broader, illegal trade in British manufactures and other commodities. Particularly suspect in Spanish eyes were the ships that sent company factors provisions and supplies, and company records appear to support such suspicions. The asiento allowed the company to send such material to its factors, but in 1717, the company sent the *Royal Prince* and the *Sarah* from London to Veracruz "with Naval Stores and Provisions." That the six company employees at Veracruz actually needed two transatlantic vessels full of supplies seems highly unlikely, especially considering that local provisions must have been

24. "The South Sea Company to the Jamaica Factors," London, Feb. 6, 1716, in Donnan, ed., *Documents*, II, 206; SSC to John Cleland, July 22, 1725, SSC Records, Add. MSS, 25565, 67. For other examples of vessels from London to Spanish America that stopped at Jamaica for slaves, see SSC to Thompson, Pratter, and Haselwood, July 12, 1717, Jan. 15, 1718, ibid., 25563, 104–105, 212.

cheaper—and much fresher. It is more plausible that the factors in Veracruz sold naval stores and other goods locally.[25]

The company also exploited the clause in the asiento allowing their slave-trading vessels to carry provisions for captives and crew en route to Spanish America and awaiting sale. Often, employees in Jamaica placed extra flour aboard these ships for sale in Spanish markets. In 1717, the company's Jamaica agents sent the sloop *Eagle* to Havana with 132 African captives and 200 barrels of flour; they shipped the *John* to Portobelo with 189 Africans and 200 barrels of flour. That these vessels needed more than a barrel of flour per African for such short journeys is unlikely. Further indication that the company intended the flour for trade comes from their establishing rates of commission for company agents, not only for selling slaves but also for "Flower and Provisions." When the *Royal Prince* reached Cuba in 1717 with forty Africans and fifteen barrels of flour, the company factor reported "having sold the Negroes at 300 [pieces of eight] P head and the Flower at 20 P Barrel." This market for flour from the mid-Atlantic sent illicit profits from the asiento to North America, sometimes in the form of enslaved workers. Surely New York's exports of flour to Jamaica help explain why New York was the biggest market within the empire for Africans transshipped from Jamaica during the British asiento. Even when the company was not smuggling goods aboard their sloops, there were often reports that sailors and agents in the company's employ acted independently to make sure that such smuggling continued—for their own profit instead of the company's. As one Jamaican merchant put it, "Their sloops and vessels being permitted to introduce negroes into the Spanish ports, do at the same time, though not on the company's account, carry on a considerable private trade, which is winked at by the Governors and royal officers, who as it is said generally buy their cargoes by persons they appoint for that purpose."[26]

25. One historian of the company's illicit trade argues, "The slave trade was only a blind which served to give the appearance of legality to the system"; see George H. Nelson, "Contraband Trade under the Asiento, 1730–1739," *American Historical Review,* LI (1945), 57. For Keene, see SSC to Benjamin Keene, Feb. 20, 1730, Newcastle Papers, LXXXIII, BL, Add. MSS, 32768, fols. 46–49; for a similar complaint about needing the annual ship, see SSC to Keene, July 6, 1733, ibid., XCVI, 32781, fols. 303–310. In fact, the concerns were valid, as various obstacles put up by war and the Spanish government limited the company to sending the annual ship just eight times in twenty-five years; see Palmer, *Human Cargoes,* 135. £250,000: [Houstoun?], *Account of the South Sea Company,* 17. The size of the *Royal Prince* was not mentioned, but the *Sarah* measured 150 tons ("Minutes of the Court of Directors," May 24, 1717, SSC Records, Add. MSS, 25497, fol. 75).

26. SSC to Thompson, Pratter, and Hazelwood, Oct. 31, 1717, SSC Records, Add. MSS, 25563, 160; "Minutes of the Court of Directors," May 25, 1716, ibid., 25496, 241–242; SSC to William

The vital importance of Jamaican transshipment to the company's overall operations was never more evident than when Spanish officials opposed the practice, which they often did. In 1718, Spanish officials at Portobelo proclaimed, "Negroes cannot be brought in Sloops from Jamaica but [only] in the vessels that bring them from Africa," and the company immediately (and successfully) appealed to Spain for redress. When a similar disruption halted Jamaica's transshipments to Cartagena in 1723, the company's response was emphatic. Executives in London implored the factors at Cartagena to point out that the right to transship was "very plain by the Convention," insisting that the trade through Jamaica "is so essential to the Carrying on Our Negro Trade that 'tis Impracticable without it." The company once again appealed to Spain, this time with a threat. Company officials instructed their agent in Spain, "You may acquaint his Ex'cy That We have resolved, not to pay one shilling further . . . of the Dutys payable by the Company for these Negroes" until the right to transship from Jamaica was restored. In July 1725, the king of Spain relented enough to create the new policy that largely appeased the company, allowing transshipment of Africans with the limitation of four months in Jamaica. Thus protected by law, Jamaica remained the company's hub until the end of their asiento.[27]

Farril, Oct. 31, 1717, ibid., 25563, 169; see also SSC to Gilbert Grimes, Jan. 2, 1718, SSC to Farril, June 5, 1718, ibid., 191, 343–344. For an example of Spanish officials confiscating flour, see SSC to Pym, Oct. 31, 1717, ibid., 171. For a discussion of the company's flour smuggling to Cuba, see Elena Andrea Schneider, "The Occupation of Havana: War, Trade, and Slavery in Eighteenth-Century Cuba" (Ph.D. diss., Princeton University, 2011), 44. Nelson notes an example in which the *Benjamin* departed Jamaica in 1737 with 30 slaves and "£12,000 in illicit wares" ("Contraband Trade under the Asiento," *AHR*, LI [1945], 59); see also Arthur S. Aiton, "The Asiento Treaty as Reflected in the Papers of Lord Shelburne," *Hispanic American Historical Review*, VIII (1928), 167–168, 174–177; Vera Lee Brown, "The South Sea Company and Contraband Trade," *AHR*, XXXI (1926), 667–668, 671–672. For complaints about private contraband on company ships, see SSC to Rigby and Pratter, Apr. 21, 1725, SSC Records, Add. MSS, 25564, 216, 219. Knight estimated that "a Vessel generally sails from Jamaica to Cartagena or Porto Bello, in three or four Days" (*Observations on the Assiento*, 4). "Their sloops and vessels being permitted": "Observations on the trade and navigation in that part of America which is generally called the trading part of the West Indies," BL, Add. MSS, 32694, fol. 64, quoted in Schneider, "Occupation of Havana," 43. For another example of the South Sea Company's hoping to profit from more than just slave trading in Spanish America, see Kathleen S. Murphy's discussion of company factors engaged in a sort of bio- or agroespionage (Murphy, "Collecting Slave Traders: James Petiver, Natural History, and Slavery in the British Atlantic World," *William and Mary Quarterly*, 3d Ser., LXX [2013], 660–666).

27. SSC to Grimes, Jan. 2, 1718, SSC Records, Add. MSS, 25563, 195; SSC to Pym, Dec. 12, 1723, ibid., 25564, 10–11; SSC to Mr. Stratford, June 17, 1725, ibid., 25564, 228; SSC to Rigby and Pratter, July 29, 1725, ibid., 25565, 78–79.

The South Sea Company's demand for slaves in Jamaica rendered the market attractive to independent slave traders reaching the Americas from Africa. Suppliers to the company became the first transatlantic traders to embrace the role of wholesaler, selling Africans to the company in Jamaica for resale in Spanish America. When planning African ventures, the Jamaican firm Tyndall and Assheton and their partner Isaac Hobhouse of Bristol gave ship captains detailed instructions for acquiring African people of a description most desired in Spanish America. Their vessels, however, were bound for Jamaica. They sold to the company and to interlopers bound for Spanish America with equal enthusiasm. During the 1729 disruption of the asiento, Tyndall and Assheton reported optimistically that an interloper "with 350 Negroes" had recently departed Jamaica for Portobelo. "If she succeeds, as we believe she will," the Jamaica traders predicted, "we may expect a greater demand than ever" for deliveries of enslaved people from Africa. In other words, Tyndall and Assheton did not expect Hobhouse to care whom the buyers in Jamaica were, as long as there were large numbers of them to support his African ventures.[28]

■ As Tyndall and Assheton's sales to interlopers suggest, other traders competed with the company in supplying Africans to Spanish America. In the decades before the South Sea Company asiento, British slave traders had encroached upon the privileges of foreign asientistas, and few felt any more compunction about breaching the South Sea monopoly. Like the company, British freelancers tended to transship Africans from the Caribbean to Spanish America rather than trade directly from Africa because personal connections were vital to trading illegally across borders. Jamaica offered a logical base for several reasons. Owing to the colony's privateering past, many sailors were familiar with the coasts of Spanish America; the island's history of Span-

28. For Africans suitable for Spanish America but bound for Jamaica, see Tyndall and Assheton to Hobhouse, June 8, 1729, Jeffries Coll., XIII, fol. 103; Assheton to Hobhouse, Sept. 7, 1729, ibid., fol. 113. "With 350 Negroes": Tyndall and Assheton to Hobhouse and Tyndall, Kingston, July 18, 1729, ibid., fols. 106–107. Two days later, Tyndall and Assheton noted that interlopers' recent successful ventures to Cuba would also bolster demand; see Tyndall and Assheton to Hobhouse, July 20, 1729, ibid., fol. 107. Hobhouse showed similar willingness to sell wholesale for British America's own markets. In 1730, a friend in Barbados reported to Hobhouse on the sale of slaves from his transatlantic vessel, *Aurora*. Hobhouse's agent, "Mr Harper . . . Sould the Cargo to Mr. Ruddock, who retailed them," the friend reported, "and I hope to good advantage, as they were a good Cargo of Slaves." There is no hint in this correspondence that Hobhouse would be upset his agent sold the slaves to another merchant who might profit from their subsequent sale at higher prices. Hobhouse's friend, himself a merchant, assumed that the convenience of selling the entire group in one transaction would outweigh the discounted prices (ibid., fol. 133).

ish contraband trade meant that many Jamaicans had connections in Spanish America; and, ironically, the South Sea Company's use of Jamaica as a hub for its own trade ensured that a steady stream of captives reached the island from Africa, offering interlopers—as well as the company—frequent opportunities to purchase people for transshipment. As early as 1715, the company heard from its factor in Cartagena that interlopers from Jamaica were selling Africans there. The asiento contract stipulated that Spanish officials should confiscate such ships, surrendering any Africans to the company, but enforcement proved a chronic frustration for South Sea officials. It would also be a bone of contention between the company and Spain, as company officials believed Spanish authorities were lackluster, at best, in stopping the illicit trade—and complicit in it, at worst.[29]

The first step in an interloper's venture was acquiring captives, and some interlopers purchased from the South Sea Company itself. When the company sorted captives at Jamaica, selling off the ill or other "refuse" at a discount, interlopers sat among the buyers scrounging for bargains in the human marketplace. Whether interlopers nursed these suffering migrants back to health (and greater marketability) or simply forced them aboard sloops in their beleaguered state is unclear. Regardless, company factors in Panama caught wind of this purchasing strategy and complained against the policy of selling less marketable Africans in Jamaica. "We are sensible," the directors replied, "of the Inconveniences you mention from Selling the Refuse Negroes at Jamaica by which means they come into the hands of Illicit Traders who carry them to the coast of Portobelo, Carthagena or the Windward Islands in Prejudice to Our Markets." Nonetheless, the policy continued. Six years later, the company was still combating its own sales to illicit traders, cautioning employees in Spanish America against being overly selective with regard to the Africans they accepted from Jamaica. "Extreme Nicety . . . has been a very great Encouragement to the private Traders who find no Difficulty of Furnishing themselves at Jamaica out of what we leave, and at more Easy Rates." Why, the directors wondered, could interlopers sell these Africans to the Spanish, if company factors could not?[30]

Jews in Jamaica—legally barred from many branches of commerce—found a niche in this trade in discounted, debilitated African people. In 1722, the Jamaica merchant house of Basnett, Miller, and Mill served as sales agents

29. SSC to James Stanhope, [May 25, 1715], in Donnan, ed., *Documents*, II, 194–195.

30. SSC to Gilbert Grimes, Oct. 26, 1717, SSC Records, Add. MSS, 25563, 143; SSC to Pym, Oct. 31, 1717, ibid., 173–174; SSC to Pym, Dec. 12, 1723, ibid., 25564, 13.

for a prominent English transatlantic trader, Humphry Morice, and they reported selling most of the healthiest Africans from three of Morice's vessels to the South Sea Company's agents. They struggled "with the Remainder," however, whom the company rejected as unsuitable for the Spanish market. The problem, Basnett, Miller & Mill reported, was that "our Jews, who used to be our best Chaps in that way, are afraid to venture on them," supposedly because they feared reports that the Jamaica Assembly would pass "an Act to prohibit" slave exports. Under normal circumstances, Basnett, Miller, and Mill implied, they counted on Jewish merchants to buy the Africans rejected by the South Sea Company. That such merchants intended these Africans for Spanish America is suggested both by their fear of a law barring slave exports and by an actual confiscation of a vessel near Portobelo. In 1717, a Spanish patrol captured "a Jamaica Sloop, John Stevens Master" that the South Sea Company described as carrying "170 Negros and some Goods belonging Chiefly to Jews of Jamaica." In navigating the perilous waters of illegal trade across imperial boundaries, Jewish merchants likely took advantage of diaspora ties of kinship and religion, which facilitated commercial networking across borders.[31]

31. "With the Remainder": Basnett, Miller, and Mill to Humphry Morice, Kingston, Nov. 9, 1722, BL, Add. MSS, 48590, fols. 29–31. Jamaican merchants Tyndall and Assheton, who were also selling agents for transatlantic traders, also noted selling slaves to Jews who planned to transship them to Cuba (Tyndall and Assheton to Isaac Hobhouse, Kingston, June 8, 1729, Jeffries Coll., XIII, fols.103–105). "A Jamaica Sloop": SSC to Mr. Bowles, June 6, 1717, SSC Records, Add. MSS, 25563, 76–77. Other scholars have noted Jews engaged in such trade in Jamaica at other moments. Trevor Burnard mentions Jews as prominent purchasers of discounted slaves from the Royal African Company in the late seventeenth and early eighteenth centuries (Burnard, "Who Bought Slaves in Early America? Purchasers of Slaves from the Royal African Company in Jamaica, 1674–1708," Slavery and Abolition, XVII, no. 2 [August 1996], 79–80). Likewise, Frances Armytage reports Jews as prominent in the transimperial slave trade from Jamaica in later decades of the eighteenth century; see Armytage, The Free Port System in the British West Indies: A Study in Commercial Policy, 1766–1822 (London, 1953), 7; see also Aiton, "Asiento Treaty," HAHR, VIII (1928), 174. Thomas Clarkson noted in 1789 that, when transatlantic vessels reached the West Indies, "the sickly are generally sold by vendue or public auction, and are bought chiefly on speculation by the Jews" (Clarkson, The Substance of the Evidence of Sundry Persons on the Slave-Trade, Collected in the Course of a Tour Made in the Autumn of the Year 1788 [London, 1789], 45). On the importance of Jewish transnational ties to the building of early modern trade networks more generally, see Jonathan I. Israel, Diasporas within a Diaspora: Jews, Crypto-Jews and the World Maritime Empires (1540–1740) (Leiden, 2002); and Noah L. Gelfand, "A People within and Without: International Jewish Commerce and Community in the Seventeenth and Eighteenth Centuries Dutch Atlantic World" (Ph.D. diss., New York University, 2008). On the legal constraints for Jews entering certain branches of British commerce (and their slightly better position in British colonies than the metropole), see Holly Snyder, "Rules, Rights, and Redemption: The Negotiation of Jewish Status in British Atlantic Port Towns, 1740–1831," Jewish History, XX, no. 2 (2006), 151–156.

One strategy that helped interlopers, both in selling African people deemed not optimal and in avoiding Spanish officials and company factors, was delivering their captives to remote corners of Spain's American empire. In early 1716, the company's Veracruz factors seized "9 Negros Clandestinely introduced from Campeachy"—a smaller port on the Yucatán Peninsula. Pleased as the company was with this confiscation, they must have wondered how many other Africans arrived without crossing the path of the Veracruz factors, housed some five hundred miles away from Campeche (Map 5). A decade later, the company still objected "that an Illicit Trade in Negroes was frequently carried on upon the Coast of Compeachy . . . finding it . . . impossible to prevent it, without . . . a person there to take Care of the Company's Interest." Closer to Portobelo, interlopers apparently had other harbors of choice. In 1723, factors bemoaned "above 600 Negroes Introduced" by interlopers "in the Bastimentos and Places about Chagre in the Space of 2 Months." Isla Bastimentos was more than two hundred miles west of Portobelo, across the Golfo de los Mosquitos. The Chagres River was much nearer Portobelo, but apparently far enough, since the factors failed to confiscate any of the aforementioned Africans. The vast territories that company factors in Spanish America sought to monitor illustrate the nearly impossible task they faced in opposing contraband.[32]

Even the successful confiscations speak to the challenge. In 1717, company officials wrote their Panama factor to "comend yo'r endeavours for Preventing clandestine Importations of Negroes" but added that they were "Sorry you succeeded so ill as out of the 18 you advised us of . . . but one fell into your hands." The same Panama factor had also recently managed to snare just "2 Men and 2 boys . . . of about 100 Landed out of 2 sloops from Jamaica," despite renting "a Bark [a small ship] to observe them." Nonetheless, the company wrote to "comend [the factor's] Diligence herein." The task was simply monumental. To get a better handle on it, Portobelo factors in 1723 requested permission to purchase a small sloop "to Visit the Islands and Ships etc for illicit Negroes." Perhaps anticipating that officials in London would deny the request, the factors offered capitulation as an alternative, suggesting that they buy the Africans that illicit traders delivered at Bastimentos to help the company meet its quota. The company scoffed at both ideas but reserved special vitriol for the latter, insisting that it showed the factors to be "in Correspondence with the Private Traders, at the Expence and Ruin of the Company or

32. "The South Sea Company to the Factors at Vera Cruz," London, Feb. 8, 1716, in Donnan, ed., *Documents*, II, 206; SSC to Rigby and Pratter, Apr. 21, 1725, SSC Records, Add. MSS, 25564, 207; SSC to factors at Portobelo and Panama [1723?], ibid., 30–31.

else . . . Guilty of very Great Ignorance and Folly." Whether the company's factors were guilty of either charge is difficult to assess from existing records, but the exchange certainly suggests that officials in London lacked an understanding of the scale of Spanish American geography and the challenges of patrolling it. That interlopers could navigate these coasts and find buyers without the complicity of company agents seems likely, considering that British interlopers had evaded prior asientistas, too. In avoiding major markets, many independent traders were simply maintaining practices and connections from before the company took over. On the other hand, the company drew employees from among the active slave traders in the Caribbean. Many of these individuals would have participated in clandestine trade in prior decades and probably still had colleagues among the interlopers.[33]

Perhaps because of such connections, some interlopers had the audacity to sail into ports where South Sea Company factors resided, leaving directors in London suspicious of their own employees. In 1716, the company accused its factors at Veracruz of collusion with Jamaican interlopers. A sloop from Jamaica, officially bound for South Carolina with 73 captives, had stopped in Veracruz claiming to need water, and the factors arranged to buy the ship's captives for the asiento. Given that Veracruz is not exactly on the way to South Carolina from Jamaica, officials in England suspected that illicit trade in Spanish America had been the sloop's intention all along and wondered why their factors purchased the Africans instead of pushing Spanish officials to confiscate them. "If you had Studied our Interest," company directors scolded,

> you would have Made the proper Application to have got them seized
> and Condemned pursuant to the Assiento, and not have Consulted
> the Buying them, and thereby given an Encouragem't to carry on that
> Illicit Trade. . . . We have great reason to Believe this Sloop, came in to
> sell her Negros, and Whatever Else she had on Board, And We Cannot
> but Resent it, That you have not thought fit to Acquaint us with
> any thing relating to this affair which together with the Familiarity,
> that seems to be between the Capt. and your Selves gives us no little
> Suspicion, that it was Concerted at Jamaica.

33. SSC to Grimes, Oct. 26, 1717, SSC Records, Add. MSS, 25563, 146–149; SSC to factors at Portobelo and Panama, [1723?], ibid., 25564, 32–34. Houstoun noted a firing of numerous SSC employees from 1733 to 1735 under suspicion of cooperation with interlopers (*Account of the South Sea Company,* 25–26). On the tendency of imperial leaders in Europe to underestimate American geography, see Paul W. Mapp, *The Elusive West and the Contest for Empire, 1713–1763* (Chapel Hill, N.C., 2011).

Partly for this offense, the company soon replaced their chief at Veracruz, but they could not halt the cooperation between factors and interlopers. In 1718, the company actually approved of their Cuba factor's purchasing "127 Negroes of Mr. Wood (who came into the Havanah as was supposed on Clandestine Trade)." The factor explained that Spanish authorities were entirely occupied with a local insurrection among their colonists, leaving the factor no hope of securing a confiscation. Instead, he negotiated to purchase Wood's captives at discounted rates and resold them at a profit. Nonetheless, if the company's own agents participated in or condoned the illicit trade at times, the company had little hope of blocking it. Part of the company's rationale for selling licenses to private traders was to co-opt them into serving the company's interests. As the directors explained to their Jamaica agents, "We observe the Progress you make in the Lycense Trade, and hope . . . that . . . in Time an entire stop may probably be put to the illicit Channel." Selling licenses to independent traders at least ensured that their sales counted toward the company's quota—at least for that trip. With permission to enter a Spanish port, a licensed independent trader had the opportunity to develop connections in Spanish America, or coordinate with existing ones, to facilitate future clandestine trade.[34]

A few of the interlopers' schemes were especially galling to the company. In 1723, officials in London received reports of interlopers' securing convoy from Jamaica to Spanish America with a British naval vessel and even heard rumors that the naval vessel itself carried African captives. Outraged as they were by this "Great Damage to the Company," executives hesitated to act, deeming it "not within Our Province to Complain of it," presumably because the perpetrator was an officer of the Royal Navy. Even more frustrating and costly were the clandestine trades that Edward Sisson and Thomas Ottley operated out of Barbados over a period of several years. In 1718, Sisson and Ottley had together purchased a license from the company for a few slaving voyages from Barbados. Sisson then exploited the connections he forged in that

34. "South Sea Company to Factors at Vera Cruz," in Donnan, ed., *Documents*, II, 206–207 (see also SSC to Charles Reade, July 12, 1717, SSC Records, Add. MSS, 25563, 89); SSC to Thomas, Pratter, and Hazelwood, ibid., 25563, 252; SSC to Rigby and Pratter, [Jamaica,] Apr. 21, 1725, ibid., 25564, 207. In following years, the company became less convinced that their agents in Cuba were not in collusion with interlopers (SSC to Rigby and Pratter, Mar. 31, 1724, ibid., 25564, 87). One critic of the company even accused directors of being in cahoots with their agents in condoning interlopers for private gain at the expense of company shareholders, but the veracity of such charges (by a former company secretary) is difficult to ascertain; see D[aniel] Templeman, *The Secret History of the Late Directors of the South-Sea-Company* . . . (London, 1735), esp. 3–13.

venture to sustain a trade to Caracas for years, "under Colour of the Company's Powers" but without procuring additional licenses. Company attorneys in Barbados succeeded in pressuring Sisson to acknowledge a staggering debt of £13,398, presumably for unpaid fees to license his numerous voyages. With healthy, young African people selling for about £30, this figure suggests a massive trade. Sisson paid the first £1,600 of the debt but then slipped out of the colony, presumably to Caracas, where the Spanish governor had reportedly profited mightily by condoning Sisson's trade. Thereafter, the company only succeeded in obtaining two bills of exchange from Sisson, drawn on a Mr. Newport for £1,000 each, both of which Newport refused to honor.[35]

If Sisson's abuse of the South Sea Company license in Caracas was bold, it still paled in comparison with Ottley's imposture at Puerto Rico. The company discovered in 1724 that Ottley had "proceeded so far as to Settle a Factory at Puerto Rico in the Company's Name." To make matters worse, Ottley had been there "Since the Year 1718," posing as an employee for seven years. The sparsely settled island was not a major outpost for Spain's empire in the eighteenth century, so the real South Sea Company had not bothered to settle agents there, and Ottley filled the void. Exactly how he acquired the African captives he sold in Puerto Rico is unclear, but since the company learned of the ruse from Barbados, Ottley likely traded from there. Upon learning of the scheme, the company's "Attorneys . . . wrote to the Governour of Puerto Rico to undeceive him," but the replies were disappointing, leaving the company to complain that the Spanish governor "Seems Resolved to favour the Interest of these Impostors rather than the Company." Whether the governor of Puerto Rico was simply more inclined to trust his neighbor of seven years than a letter from unknown English attorneys or whether he received compensation (and plausible deniability) from the imposter is uncertain. In either case, it would take letters from Spain at the behest of the company to finally shut Ottley's operation down.[36]

Over the course of the British asiento, the South Sea Company's difficulties in curtailing interlopers such as Sisson and Ottley contributed to rising ten-

35. SSC to Pym, Dec. 12, 1723, SSC Records, Add. MSS, 25564, 31; SSC to Mr. Stratford, Oct. 1, 1724, ibid., 125–126. Presumably, Sisson's debt of £13,398 was rendered in Barbados currency rather than pounds sterling, but in either case, it indicates an extensive trade (SSC to Rigby and Pratter, Nov. 12, 1724, ibid., 145). On the Caracas governor's involvement and rejected bills, see SSC to Rigby and Pratter, Apr. 21, 1725, ibid., 209, 219. For more on Sisson and Ottley, see Palmer, *Human Cargoes*, 78–79.

36. SSC to Mr. Stratford, Oct. 1, 1724, SSC Records, Add. MSS, 25564, 125–126; see also SSC to Rigby and Pratter, Nov. 12, 1724, ibid., 146.

sions between the company and Spain. Company executives suspected Spanish officials of doing far less than their utmost to curb clandestine trade, despite provisions of the asiento that pledged Spain to enforcing the company's monopoly. Officials occasionally saw interlopers captured by Spanish *guarda costas* (coast guard privateering vessels) or royal governors, but even in such cases, the Spanish often sold the seized Africans for their own profit rather than selling them to the company at the discounted rates prescribed by the asiento. In 1717, the company filed suit against Spanish captain George Corres, who had captured the Jamaica interloper that carried Africans "belonging Chiefly to Jews of Jamaica." Instead of processing the prize through official channels and turning the contraband people over to the company, Captain Corres had "Run her [the prize vessel] a Shore and set her on Fire" and "Sold the Negros . . . Directly against the Law." The company won that suit, but only after appealing the matter all the way to courts in Spain. In other cases, the company fared worse, perhaps because the interlopers' captors were wise enough to give a cut of the profits to local officials. When one Spanish captain nabbed an interloper near Panama in 1717, the company's agents in the province reported that the captain bribed a local official for permission to sell the Africans. The company decided not to sue, perhaps deeming it more important to maintain friendly relations with the official than to push this particular case.[37]

In fact, South Sea executives frequently opted for a similar strategy of cutting Spanish officials in on potential prizes to coax them to action. In 1717, hearing reports that Barbados interlopers sold Africans along the "Windward Coast" of northern South America, company directors ordered that more than one-third of the proceeds "may be given to the Governours, Royal Officers or others who may be assisting" in confiscations from interlopers. Despite this policy, the company's frustrations with the Spanish only mounted over the course of its asiento. In 1730, the directors wrote to Benjamin Keene, British ambassador in Madrid, protesting "That these Gov'rs open and shut the Doors against us where and as often as they think fit, [. . . but they are] Friends to Clandestine and illicit Introduction of Negroes for their own ends." In 1733, the company factors at Veracruz finally badgered Spanish officials into confiscating an interloper's cargo of African people and secured a court order that

37. SSC to Mr. Bowles, June 6, 1717, SSC Records, Add. MSS, 25563, 76–77 (for the company's victory in the case, see ibid., 172); SSC to Gilbert Grimes, Oct. 26, 1717, ibid., 147. For another example of the company's filing suit to demand enslaved Africans confiscated by Spanish officials, see "Minutes of the Court of Directors," June 6, 1716, ibid., 25496, 250.

the captives be handed over to the company. But then the commodore of the Spanish ship simply "resisted the Governours authority and refus'd delivering them up." The Spanish sailors sold the Africans for themselves, leaving the South Sea Company no better off than if it had allowed the interlopers to sell them. Keene eventually convinced the Spanish crown to issue new instructions to their governors, stressing the importance of protecting the South Sea Company monopoly, but the problem of interlopers was never solved.[38]

■ British interlopers not only encroached on the South Sea Company's trade to Spanish America in the first half of the eighteenth century but also continued selling Africans illegally in French markets. Especially as Saint-Domingue grew, virtually monopolizing the attention of French slave traders, smaller French colonies faced chronic labor shortages. Guadeloupe relied almost exclusively on transshipments from Martinique and foreign islands from the late seventeenth century until direct imports to the colony boomed in the 1750s and 1760s. Even Martinique, which had received most of French America's African arrivals in the seventeenth century, lost out to Saint-Domingue by the early eighteenth century and resorted to foreign transshipments. Observers on both sides of the imperial divide believed that Britain's clandestine trade played a major role in supplying these French colonies. As trader Richard Harris wrote to the British Board of Trade from Barbados in 1719,

> There is, and allways was, a Clandestine Trade carried on, . . . but for some years past, and particularly the two or three last, Barbados hath been so over supplied, and the price so low, that very great Numbers of Negros have been carryed from thence, both to Martinico, Virginia and all the Leeward Islands.

38. "Minutes of the Court of Directors," Nov. 20, 1717, ibid., Add. MSS, 25497, 161–162; extract of SSC to Keene, May 15, 1730, Newcastle Papers, LXXXIII, BL, Add. MSS, 32768, fols. 50–52; "Transactions of the Vera Cruz Factory," London, May 3, 1736, in Donnan, ed., *Documents*, II, 457; Benjamin Keene to SSC, Mar. 1, 1734, Newcastle Papers, XCIX, BL, Add. MSS, 32784, fols. 112–113. Two years later, the company repeated the complaint to the British secretary of state (SSC to duke of Newcastle, May 10, 1732, ibid., 32777, fols. 42–48). This was probably about Spanish cooperation with Portuguese slave traders for contraband intercolonial deliveries from Brazil to Buenos Aires and other Spanish settlements on the Río de la Plata. Such traders delivered Africans to southern Brazil, the company lamented in 1732, and from there, "Great numbers [are] being annually Clandestinely Convey'd to the Neighbouring [Spanish] Provinces, and We have good Grounds to believe with the Connivance of the Spanish Officers." This Portuguese insurgency so dominated the Río de la Plata market that "our Factors . . . cannot Sell half the Number they us'd formerly, and unless some Care be taken of that Colony, in a little time they [the Portuguese] will have the Whole Negro Trade" (SSC to Keene, Oct. 27, 1732, ibid., XCIV, 32779, fol. 16).

The rupture of the asiento in 1719 had triggered the short-term glut in Barbados by cutting the British off from legal shipments to Spanish America, but the longer-running price discrepancies between French and British colonies owed more to undersupply in French colonies and to British traders' greater efficiency in African trade. Even after the asiento traffic resumed, French officials agreed that the problem of interlopers was growing, warning colonial administrators in 1730 "to be doubly careful that no foreign trade be found to take place" in their jurisdictions.[39]

Looking back from the mid-eighteenth century, Secretary John Pownal of the British Board of Trade argued that a price gap galvanized such British transshipment of Africans to French colonies. The French paid "near 20 p Cent more" for captives on the African coast than British traders did, "and consequently their slaves came proportionally dearer to the market." The differential resulted from Britain's extensive and efficient system of trading posts and forts on the African coast and their consequent speed in acquiring captives, which kept wages and provisioning costs lower. This efficiency was enhanced by their use of smaller ships than French transatlantic traders, which allowed for smaller crews—and hence lower shipping costs—relative to the number of Africans carried. This price differential created an opportunity that British merchants seized eagerly as the volume of their transatlantic trade increased.[40]

39. "Richard Harris to the Secretary of the Board of Trade (?)," London, Sept. 21, 1719, in Donnan, ed., *Documents*, II, 241–242; M. de Clieu to [?], Feb. 26, 1739, Archives Nationales d'Outre-Mer, Aix-en-Provence (hereafter cited as ANOM), C7A, 13, fols. 201–202 ("ordres pour redoubler de soings a ce qu'il ne se fasse aucun commerce éstranger trouvent chez moy"). Slave arrivals in Martinique dwarfed those in other French colonies during the seventeenth century, but in the first quarter of the eighteenth, Saint-Domingue's slave importation outpaced Martinique slightly. During the next quarter century, Saint-Domingue's share doubled Martinique's, and the gap widened thereafter as direct African trade to Martinique declined; see *Voyages*, accessed September 2012 (http://slavevoyages.org/tast/assessment/estimates.faces?yearFrom=1501&yearTo=1866&disembarkation=402.403.401.404.405). See also James Pritchard, *In Search of Empire: The French in the Americas, 1670–1730* (New York, 2004), 215–224; David Geggus, "The French Slave Trade: An Overview," *WMQ*, 3d Ser., LVIII (2001), 119–138.

40. "Mr. Pownal's Account of the Slave Trade," in Donnan, ed., *Documents*, II, 507. In fact, the prices that Pownal quotes suggest that in the French colonies enslaved people were more than "proportionally dearer," if his 20 percent estimate was accurate for the coast of Africa. He cited forty pounds as the price for the finest slaves in British American colonies but asserted that, in French colonies, they sold for the equivalent of more than fifty-four pounds—which is 35 percent higher. On British trade efficiencies versus the French, see David Eltis, *The Rise of African Slavery in the Americas* (New York, 2000), 123–136. French colonial officials agreed that prices for slaves were higher in their territory but tended to blame short supplies from French traders for the problem; see Intendant Mithon of Saint-Domingue to Council of Trade, Leogane, Mar. 10, 1719, ANOM, C9A, 16, fol. 301.

To sneak African captives into French territories, British interlopers and French buyers continued their seventeenth-century practices to avoid prosecution—bribing French officials, cutting them in on trade, or targeting areas away from the administrative centers of French colonies. Intendant Jacques Pannier d'Orgeville of Martinique defended himself against allegations in 1730 that he allowed a "renewal of openly permitted foreign trade," including reports of "15 English ships loaded with sugar for London" from his colony. Unmentioned was the cargo those English ships delivered in exchange for such sugar, but enslaved African men and women were likely possibilities. Furthermore, the word "renewal" in the accusation suggests this was not a new problem. It would also continue. In 1737, Deputy Governor Maisonselle of Guadeloupe denied "with sorrow" the existence of a "pretended foreign trade," only to make similar denials a year later.[41]

Interlopers also devised several new strategies to access French markets from British colonies. In the 1720s, British traders responded to a French crackdown on smuggling by exploiting a loophole in French trade restrictions that allowed foreign ships to enter ports when in need of repairs. French officials in the 1730s complained of vessels from Barbados and Antigua that were regularly selling Africans in their colonies nominally to pay for repairs to temperamental vessels. British smugglers also routed deliveries of captives through neutral territory. Governor William Hart of Saint Christopher reported to the Board of Trade in 1727, "Our British Traders to Affrica have found a way to Rival the Dutch in" the transshipment of Africans to the French. "For as the Island of St Lucia . . . is look'd upon as a Nuteral place," he explained, "the British Ships go into a Harbour there called Petit Carnage, where they sell their Slaves for money or Sugar: This place having the advantage of St. Eustatia [from whence the Dutch traded to the French], being within a few hours Sail of Martinique." This effort to outcompete the Dutch for the French slave trade speaks to British enthusiasm for sales in foreign markets, even outside the asiento arrangement. French officials looked less favorably upon such developments, of course, but in 1731, Intendant d'Orgeville—perhaps still fighting charges of complicity—also acknowledged the role of neutral islands. He complained that Dutch and English ships sold enslaved Africans to French buyers at neighboring Dominica, which was sparsely settled by Europeans at

41. Jacques Pannier d'Orgeville to Council of Trade, Oct. 19, 1730, ANOM, C8A, 41, fols. 73–81, esp. 74 ("renouvellement du commerce Etranger ouvertment permis"; "15 Navires Anglois qui y chargé du Sucre pour Londres"); M. de Maisonselle to Council of Trade, Guadeloupe, May 17, 1737, ibid., C7A, 13, fols. 121–123 ("avec Douleur . . . le prettendû commerce étranger").

that date. Once French buyers acquired Africans at a neutral island, ferrying them home in small vessels via remote coves was relatively easy.[42]

The implications of this illicit commerce for captive experiences changed little from previous decades, but the cultural implications of the traffic grew more significant in the first half of the eighteenth century. The short voyages between English and French territories in the Lesser Antilles continued to minimize the threats of disease and food shortage aboard ships, though these advantages were still partly offset by the risks of clandestine trade. Meanwhile, patterns in the traffic from Africa to British and French colonies diverged, meaning that slave trading between these regions complicated the ethnic mix of forced African immigrants to the French Caribbean, especially Martinique and Guadeloupe. Direct trade from Africa to the French Caribbean still relied on the Bight of Benin for about half its captives, and west central Africa provided one-quarter. The slave trade to the British islands that transshipped to the French looked different. People from the Gold Coast made up more than one-third of the British trade, and captives from the Bight of Biafra—barely present in the French trade—accounted for almost one-quarter of those reaching Britain's Lesser Antilles. As such, the clandestine trade between British and French islands in the eighteenth century likely increased the proportion of Akan and Igbo men and women reaching French territories far beyond what the direct African trade might suggest (Figure 8). Given the longstanding British presence on the Gold Coast and the Bight of Biafra, some of these captives might even have learned some English in Africa before their enslavement—a skill that transfer to a French colony would have devalued.

■ As the scale of the intercolonial slave trade from British to French and Spanish America grew, frustrations mounted among British slaveholders. Plantation owners, especially in Jamaica, redoubled their protestations against mercantile interests and imperial policies that prioritized exploiting Africans for their commodity value instead of their labor. The sales conducted by Jamaican merchants Basnett, Miller, and Mill illustrate the problem from the perspective of planters. In 1722, when four ships belonging to Humphry Morice of London arrived from Africa, Basnett, Miller, and Mill's first inclination was

42. Kenneth J. Banks, "Official Duplicity: The Illicit Slave Trade of Martinique, 1713–1763," in Peter A. Coclanis, ed., *The Atlantic Economy during the Seventeenth and Eighteenth Centuries: Organization, Operation, Practice, and Personnel* (Columbia, S.C., 2005), 235–236, 241; William Hart to Board of Trade, St. Christopher, Feb. 15, 1726/27, in Donnan, ed., *Documents*, II, 336–337; d'Orgeville to Council of Trade, Martinique, June 8, 1731, ANOM, C8A, 42, fols. 210–213.

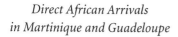

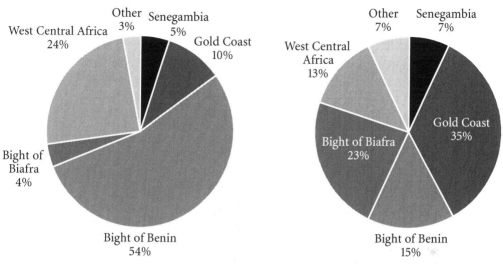

FIGURE 8. Comparison of Captive Origins in the Transatlantic Slave Trades to the French and British Lesser Antilles, 1711–1750

Source: *Voyages: The Trans-Atlantic Slave Trade Database,* accessed January 2013, http://slavevoyages .org/tast/assessment/estimates.faces?yearFrom=1711&yearTo=1750&disembarkation=402.403 and http://slavevoyages.org/tast/assessment/estimates.faces?yearFrom=1711&yearTo=1750 &disembarkation=304.309.302.303.

to sell all the Africans to Edward Pratter, the South Sea Company's Jamaica agent, but Pratter proved unwilling to take everyone. "Mr. Pratter had then three large Sloops returned from the Spanish Factories," the sellers explained, "waiting here for the arrival of Slaves, and capable of takeing our whole Number of 600, w'ch he verry much wanted. But by the bad Condition of them he could pick noe more out of our four Vessells than as follows." Basnett, Miller, and Mill went on to explain that Pratter took 32 people from the first vessel, 57 from the second, 55 from the third, and just 13 from the fourth. Only after the South Sea Company picked out this quarter of the people who appeared strongest did Basnett, Miller, and Mill offer the remainder for sale to the public in Jamaica. The sale went badly, which the agents blamed on a recent hurricane that left planters short of capital. As a result, Basnett, Miller, and Mill subcontracted with the South Sea Company to send the next 150 Africans, in terms of physical condition, to Portobelo on one of Morice's own ships. They then sent the remainder of the marginally fit to Hispaniola, leaving only the worst-off Africans to auction locally. Given that the South Sea Company's own ships from Africa also sorted captives in a similar manner, leaving only the ill and infirm in British territory, it comes as little surprise that Jamaican planters resented the asiento trade. South Sea officials did not misinterpret when lamenting, "We find that the People of Jamaica are set against the Company." [43]

As Kingston emerged as the company's primary asiento hub, the Assembly of Jamaica—dominated by planters—sought to obstruct the company's transshipment of the most desirable slaves from the island, or at least to skim revenue from the trade. In 1714, as it had in the late seventeenth century, the Assembly passed a duty of twenty shillings on each African exported from the island, touching off a conflict between the company and the Assembly that persisted throughout the period of the British asiento. To escape this tax of between 3 and 5 percent, the company immediately appealed to British imperial officials, meeting with the Privy Council, the Board of Trade, the secretary of state, and the king himself over the ensuing months. The fight would continue for years.[44]

In the meantime, the Jamaican Assembly's obstacle led some company vessels from Africa to stop at the cays off Jamaica's coast rather than sail into Kingston's harbor. Such ships gleaned the Jamaican agents' most current information about Spanish demand and perhaps obtained needed provisions while avoiding the duties by not disembarking captives on the island. The problem, as the company quickly discovered, was that this neither protected ships from the elements nor allowed for any repairs. In January 1717, the *John Galley* under Captain Dunkley reached Jamaica with 242 Africans on board. "This ship was by the Pylot brought to at the Cays in order to save the Duty laid on Negroes Exported," the Jamaica factors explained,

> but as it has happened it could not be done. Capt. Dunkley [had previously been] off of Hispaniola in the night Time [and] met a hard Squale of Wind that did a great deal of Damage to his Rudder and Starnpost, so that his Ship [was] not capable to proceed without careening w'ch obliged her to Come into Port.

43. Basnett, Miller, and Mill to Humphry Morice, Kingston, Nov. 9, 1722, BL, Add. MSS, 48590, fols. 29–31; see also Palmer, *Human Cargoes,* 62–64; SSC to Thompson, Pratter, and Hazelwood, Oct. 31, 1717, SSC Records, Add. MSS, 25563, 163–164.

44. "Minutes of the Court of Directors," Apr. 27, 1715, Feb. 22, Mar. 13, 1716, SSC Records, Add. MSS, 25496, 52, 199, 296; Mar. 6, May 15, Aug. 14, Sept. 27, Oct. 23, Oct. 31, Nov. 6, 1717, ibid., 25497, 32, 72, 119, 135, 147, 149, 151. The most valued young, male slaves in the period sold for about thirty pounds, with prices descending from there based on age, gender, and other perceived qualities.

Since the *John* needed repairs, the company "hired a good Sloop to carry his Negroes to Portebelo, so that We shall be obliged to pay Duty for these Negroes." Similarly, the following month, the *Kath Galley* arrived in Jamaica with 464 Africans, and the company factors ordered Captain Heartsease to hold at the cays while awaiting instructions for Spanish America, "but as he broke his Windliss at Jaquine [he] came into the Harbour, and told [the factors that] it was impossible to secure his Ship at the Cays and that his Men were very Refractory so that he did not care to go down in the Ship, but would rather hire Vessels to carry his Slaves." Although avoiding Jamaica's duty, stopping offshore prevented the company from reaping benefits of the transshipment model, such as repairing ships and reorganizing cargoes.[45]

Fortunately for the company, relief came just when they were on the verge of abandoning Jamaica for Barbados. In January 1718, nearly four years after Jamaica passed the duty on exported Africans, the Privy Council declared "That the said Law Shall be repealed, and the same is hereby repealed and declared void." The decision seemed final. The company resumed operations in Jamaica but soon learned that the controversy was far from over. In 1722, the company appealed to the crown again, complaining that Jamaican officials resumed collection of the duty despite the repeal. The crown quickly ordered Jamaica to reimburse the company, but colony representatives were undaunted. In 1724, the Jamaica Assembly levied a new duty on departing Africans, which was, in the company's opinion, "directly Contrary to the Order of Council We formerly Obtain'd." The crown agreed and (after many months' delay) once again ordered repeal, but it was a seemingly endless cycle. The Assembly would introduce a duty; the South Sea Company would appeal to the Board of Trade; the Board of Trade would order repeal; and the Assembly would assent, only to pass the measure again in the next session. Meanwhile, as the relevant paper sailed around the Atlantic, Jamaican officials collected the duty, seemingly content to harass the company even if the crown ordered the duties remitted. The dogged persistence of both sides in the conflict reveals the importance the South Sea Company attached to Jamaica as a hub and the planters' frustration that imperial officials appeared to care more about the slave trade to Spanish America than about the supply of labor to British sugar plantations. At the very least, if the South Sea Company insisted upon whisking exploitable Africans away from labor-hungry Jamaican planters, the duties offered a chance to skim something off the trade for the island.[46]

45. Daniel Wescomb to William Popple, Nov. 15, 1717, in Donnan, ed., *Documents*, II, 225–226.
46. Shift to Barbados: SSC to Thompson, Pratter, and Hazelwood, Oct. 31, 1717, SSC Records,

In fact, Jamaica profited from its role as a slave trade hub in several ways beyond collecting export duties. Although the Assembly, dominated by planters, opposed the transshipment trade, not all Jamaicans were so hostile. For the merchants, sailors, and artisans of Kingston, serving as a base for the asiento offered economic benefits. The South Sea Company was quick to point this out in their appeals to rescind the duty. As company secretary Daniel Wescomb put it, there were "many advantages arising to the Island from the Companys Ships touching there and Refreshing the Negroes and sending them to the Spanish Ports in their own Ships or the Sloops of the Island." The claim was more than just spin, since the company often hired ships in Jamaica for deliveries to Spanish territory. Even the company's own sloops needed captains and sailors, not to mention maintenance, supplies, and longshoremen. Company agents also required facilities in Jamaica, so in 1725, for example, the agents "hired a Penn for the Negroes at the Rent of £200" per year. All these services brought fringe economic benefits to Jamaica. Meanwhile, the "Penn" implied a rudimentary enclosure, designed as much for control as for housing, further impressing dehumanization upon African people. Minimal as such accommodations were, keeping the captives alive and under watch required paying for food, guards, and doctors, with each cost boosting the Jamaican economy and drawing ever more colonists into engagement with the slave trade. More broadly, operating the asiento through Jamaica gave many settlers on the island an opportunity to forge connections in Spanish America that could be exploited in future trading ventures, with or without the company's blessing.[47]

■ Jamaica's role as hub of the asiento brought some profits to local maritime industries, but the South Sea Company grew increasingly disillusioned with the asiento by the end of the 1730s. The company blamed its failures to

Add. MSS, 25563, 163–164. "Law Shall be repealed": SSC copy of a report from the "Office of the Lord High Admiral of Great Britain," in "Minutes of the Court of Directors," ibid., 25562, 77; see also SSC to Thompson, Pratter and Hazelwood, Jan. 15 and Feb. 23, 1718, 25563, 213, 249–250. Jamaica resumes collection 1722: SSC copy of an order from the king and his council, "At the Court of St. James's," Mar. 4, 1721/2, 25562, 186–187. "Directly Contrary": SSC to Rigby and Pratter, Mar. 31, 1724, 25564, 88–89; on the delayed repeal, see SSC to Rigby and Pratter, Nov. 12, 1724, 139. For Jamaica's 1725 duty, see SSC to Rigby and Pratter, Apr. 21, 1725, 214. For additional examples of the controversy, see "The South Sea Company: Minutes of the Court of Directors," Apr. 27, 1715, Wescomb to Popple, and "Order in Council concerning the Jamaica Duty," Dec. 1, 1731, all in Donnan, ed., Documents, II, 194, 225–226, 440.

47. Wescomb to Popple, in Donnan, ed., Documents, II, 224–225; SSC to Rigby and Pratter, Apr. 21, 1725, SSC Records, Add. MSS, 25564, 215.

make the asiento yield all the anticipated profits on the vagaries of trading and negotiating with the Spanish—who were always on the verge of being outright enemies. Indeed, there were two major interruptions of the asiento due to armed conflicts between Britain and Spain: from 1719 to 1721 and again from 1727 to 1729. These were not major wars but were enough to make British ships and company factors unwelcome in Spanish America. The company suffered not only from such halts of trade but also from confiscations thereafter. For instance, when company factors returned to Panama after the 1719–1721 disruption, local officials forced them "to pay a Rent of 800 [pieces of eight] P Annum for Your Negrory"—their combination prison and warehouse for Africans awaiting sale. "Before the Rupture," the company had owned or otherwise controlled the so-called negrory "Rent Free." [48]

The duties paid on imported Africans were another bone of contention. The company asserted that when their ships stopped at multiple ports in Spanish America, Spanish officials charged import duties on all captives on board at every port, regardless of whether they disembarked. As a result, the company paid the import duty multiple times for the same person. Officials repeatedly disagreed over the currency in which duties should be paid and what exchange rate to apply. Ambiguity in the asiento contract itself contributed to this controversy, but even persuading the Spanish to honor provisions explicitly stated in the agreement was a struggle. In 1730, the company complained to the British secretary of state that the king of Spain issued orders to prevent the establishment of a company factor at Panama—which referred to the port on the Pacific side of the isthmus, opposite Portobelo—despite a treaty from the previous year that gave the company explicit permission to do so.[49]

48. SSC to factors at Portobelo and Panama, [1723?], SSC Records, Add. MSS, 25564, 28. Spanish seizures of South Sea Company goods were remembered when some in England advocated war with Spain in 1739; see [Benjamin Robins], *Observations on the Present Convention with Spain* (London, 1739), 10–11. Carl Wennerlind argues that it is unclear whether the South Sea Company was profitable, owing to a lack of accurate accounts, but he nonetheless stresses that the imagined profits of the slave trade were vital for stabilizing the British financial system at the end of the War of the Spanish Succession (Wennerlind, *Casualties of Credit: The English Financial Revolution, 1620–1720* [Cambridge, Mass., 2011], 6, 165–168, 197–199, 223).

49. "The South Sea Company: Representations to the Marquis of Monteleon," [Dec. 7, 1715], in Donnan, ed., *Documents*, II, 201; SSC to Gilbert Grimes, Jul. 12, 1717, SSC Records, Add. MSS, 25563, 102–103. For the currency controversy, see Thomas Geraldino to SSC, Sept. 18, 1733, Newcastle Papers, XCVII, BL, Add. MSS, 32782, fols. 319–320; SSC to Thomas Geraldino, September 1733, ibid., fols. 325–326; SSC to Keene, Oct. 25, 1734, ibid., CI, 32786, fol. 71; [Robins], *Observations on the Convention with Spain*, 15–17. Panama factory: SSC to duke of Newcastle, June 10, 1730, Newcastle Papers, LXXXIII, BL, Add. MSS, 32768, fols. 44–45.

Company officials also complained that Spanish officials stalled the trade with unreasonable standards. In 1717, executives protested against the governor of Santo Domingo for objecting to a shipment of 60 Africans from Barbados, from which, "thro' capriccio, [he] would receive but 20 of them, tho' they were all very good Negroes." To fulfill Santo Domingo's request for one hundred slaves, the company had to send two more transshipments from Barbados with 60 and 80 Africans, respectively, bringing the total to 200. As the company summed up the incident, "We think ourselves very ill used by that Gov'r." Those Africans rejected at Santo Domingo traveled onward to Cuba, which early in the British asiento was something of a market of last resort for selling African people rejected elsewhere—an additional example of how captives deemed undesirable in the marketplace could suffer multi-stage final passages in the purgatory between the Atlantic crossing and American slavery.[50]

The company also faced problems collecting debts from Spanish buyers, an issue that became especially problematic when the Spanish Caribbean became an important market in the 1720s and 1730s. In the islands, silver was less available than on the mainland, forcing company factors to sell on credit, which they had previously avoided. As one company official reported, during a two-month period in late 1730 and early 1731, the company sold 1,549 Africans for 387,250 pieces of eight. Of this amount, the company succeeded in collecting crops worth only 160,384 pieces of eight, or roughly 40 percent of the debt. The solution, he argued, was "to continue the Factorys upon the old footing . . . [under which] no more Negroes are to be sent them from Jamaica, but what can be disposed of for Money." It sounded logical enough, but given the company's problem of never fulfilling its quota, any plan that limited sales carried major costs, so sales on credit continued.[51]

Even where cash was readily available, company factors could not always get their hands on it. Throughout the 1730s, the company decried Spanish officials' using laws designed to control the flow of specie within their colonies to prevent payments to the British. The Spanish crown intended such laws to minimize the amount of silver going into circulation in the colonies,

---

50. SSC to Mr. Bowles, Apr. 18, 1717, SSC Records, Add. MSS, 25563, 59–60. The company also transshipped unsold slaves from Cartagena to Cuba on at least two occasions (see SSC to Pym, June 6, 1717, ibid., 64).

51. "Considerations upon the Trade to Cuba," in Donnan, ed., Documents, II, 438. On the decision against issuing credit early in the asiento, see SSC instructions for Dudley Woodbridge, Jan. 17, 1718, SSC Records, Add. MSS, 25563, 240. The South Sea Company summed up the specie shortage in Cuba in a 1732 letter to Keene: "Money is not to be got at Havana for the Negroes" (Newcastle Papers, XCI, BL, Add. MSS, 32778, fols. 40–42).

in order to reserve more for shipment to Spain and to prevent settlers from illegally purchasing European goods from foreign merchants. The South Sea Company claimed, however, that Spanish officials used the laws to prevent the company from collecting legitimate debts. The company alleged it sold Africans to buyers in possession of specie, only to have Spanish administrators step in at the last minute to bar the transfer of silver or to deny the company permission to export it. As one company leader put it, the asiento promised "a profitable Commerce," but the Spanish "found frequent Means to interrupt the Returns." Such problems required the company to retain Spanish attorneys at each factory—while bemoaning their exorbitant fees.[52]

By the 1730s, tensions over persuading Spanish officials to catch interlopers also built toward crisis. The company's frustration was best expressed by the factors at Cartagena. When instructed to file suit in Spanish courts to gain compensation for Africans confiscated but not turned over to the company, the factors simply retorted that they "must beg leave to inform the Honourable Court [of company directors] that we have no hopes left of Receiving one Ryal of it here." Dismayed by years of futility in their pleas, the factors had apparently given up on seeing this provision of the asiento enforced. The problem was all the more galling because the company occasionally found its own ships confiscated by suddenly zealous Spanish administrators. In 1724, the company complained of frequent shipping disruptions by Spanish guarda costas between Jamaica and Spanish America. They raised similar objections about the waters near Puerto Rico in the early 1730s. Similarly, after the 1727–1729 hiatus, the company factor in Cuba said that Spanish officials confiscated the company's *Anne Galley* in 1731, well after word of peace reached the colony. Neither ship nor cargo was recovered. Even after Spanish American officials reopened their ports to South Sea Company vessels in the early 1730s, independent traders licensed by the company found themselves turned away with new reports that "His C[atholic] M[ajesty] did not approve of that Method" of farming out the trade. Without licensing, "which Method was pursued by all former Assientists," the company insisted that deliveries to "places of less note" in Spanish America would not be viable.[53]

52. SSC to duke of Newcastle, May 10, 1732, Newcastle Papers, XCII, BL, Add. MSS, 32777, fols. 42–48; SSC to Keene, Oct. 27, 1732, ibid., XCIV, 32779, fol. 16; SSC to Keene, Aug. 2, 1734, ibid., XCX, 32785, fol. 318; SSC to Grimes, Oct. 26, 1717, SSC Records, Add. MSS, 25563, 155; [Houstoun?], *Account of the South Sea Company,* 31–32.

53. "No hopes left": extract of letter from SSC agents at Cartagena to SSC, Jan. 16, 1732, Newcastle Papers, XCII, BL, Add. MSS, 32777, fol. 49. Earlier, the company had had some success. A 1717 letter from the South Sea Company to its factors in Santiago de Cuba noted reports of three

In 1733, British annoyance with confiscations and disruptions reached such a height that a British warship seized a Spanish vessel in retaliation, prompting several Spanish governors to halt the asiento temporarily. The *South Carolina Gazette*'s coverage of these events emphasizes the importance of Spanish transshipment to the Jamaican slave trade in the period. "The Market for Negroes . . . is at a stand in that Island," the *Gazette* reported, "by reason of the Trade being stopp'd at the Havvanna and other Places on the Main by the Spanish Governors." Such stoppages were costly, since the company paid import duties each year, regardless of whether they delivered, and such disruptions also left suffering forced migrants in limbo.[54]

The vagaries of commerce with a foreign power made profits elusive for the South Sea Company and caused tensions to escalate despite high slave prices that seemed to promise vast riches. But to highlight the many barriers Spanish officials erected is not to suggest that British traders were innocent victims; indeed, company executives complained nearly as much about British interlopers and schemes of the company's own employees as they did about the Spanish. Furthermore, the company bemoaned Spanish reluctance to enforce some provisions of the asiento while violating other provisions themselves. And Spanish officials matched South Sea Company complaints with ones of their own about the company's duplicity and smuggling. As with other asiento controversies, disputes over British smuggling only escalated with time. The English first received Spanish objections about the company's use of "sloops to stock the Country with Goods" instead of people as early as 1718, but it was in the last decade of the asiento that such conflicts seriously disrupted trade. In the late 1720s, Spanish officials obtained inside information about the South Sea Company's contraband from two disgruntled—or simply bribable—

---

small seizures made by Spanish vessels in Cuba, from which the company acquired the slaves taken according to the contract. See "The South Sea Company: Minutes of the Committee of Correspondence," Oct. 22, 1717, in Donnan, ed., *Documents*, II, 221. For Spanish concerns about specie entering circulation in Spanish America rather than heading to Spain, see Geoffrey J. Walker, *Spanish Politics and Imperial Trade, 1700–1789* (Bloomington, Ind., 1979), 1–15. Guarda costas: SSC to Rigby and Pratter, Nov. 12, 1724, SSC Records, Add. MSS, 25564, 148; extract of SSC to Keene, July 22, 1731, Newcastle Papers, XC, BL, Add. MSS, 32775, fol. 118. *Anne Galley*: Jonathan Dennis to Peter Burrell, Cuba, Nov. 2, 1731, in Donnan, ed., *Documents*, II, 439 n. 2. "His CM did not approve": SSC to Keene, July 6, 1733, Newcastle Papers, XCVI, BL, Add. MSS, 32781, fols. 306–308.

54. "News Item Relating to the Slave Trade," Bristol, Nov. 14, [1733], in Donnan, ed., *Documents,* II, 451. For the controversy over duties for undelivered slaves, see an unsigned letter from Seville: [Keene?] to SSC, June 6, 1732, Newcastle Papers, XC, BL, Add. MSS, 32777, fols. 98–101; and another from October, ibid., XCI, 32778, fols. 210–212.

employees, who detailed how the company used legal slave trading to cover clandestine deliveries of goods and provisions on the same ships. In response, the Spanish ratcheted up antismuggling efforts. In the Treaty of Seville, which ended the 1727–1729 rupture of the asiento, the Spanish insisted on placing their own diplomat on the board of the South Sea Company to monitor smuggling. The company responded by transferring more authority to Jamaica, to keep discussions of smuggling out of directors' meetings. They also made company correspondence increasingly vague for fear of interception. Meanwhile, Spain designed new policies to detect smuggling more easily. In 1733, Spain announced that South Sea Company vessels had to be full of Africans, regardless of demand—with "full" being defined as "4 Blacks to every 5 Tons" of a vessel's capacity. The Spanish hoped that, under this stipulation, enforcement would not require catching the British in the act but only finding records of suspiciously small deliveries of captives.[55]

After 1735, Spanish patrols routinely boarded British ships to search for contraband, and these searches helped trigger the final collapse of Anglo-Spanish relations. Violence in the searches caused protests, with one incident proving especially inflammatory. In 1738, ship captain Robert Jenkins testified in the House of Commons about tensions in the Caribbean. He cut a dramatic figure, missing an ear that he said Spaniards severed when searching his vessel. When Jenkins brandished the detached ear for all to see, he whipped the House into a furor and incited popular outrage. The following year, Britain commenced hostilities in what became known as the War of Jenkins' Ear. Though the South Sea Company's asiento nominally lasted another decade, the outbreak of hostilities blended seamlessly into the broader War of the Austrian Succession that erupted in 1740; it marked the final rupture of the contract. The British did not lose interest in the trade to Spanish (or French) America with the asiento's demise, but after 1739, they would seek alternate ways of using the slave trade to wrench foreign markets open to trade.[56]

55. Nelson, "Contraband Trade under the Asiento," *AHR*, LI (1945), 55–57; SSC to Mr. Bowles, June 1718, SSC Records, Add. MSS, 25563, 394; SSC to Keene, Sept. 14, 1733, Newcastle Papers, XCVII, BL, Add. MSS, 32782, fol. 229.

56. The tensions over Jenkins's ear, British contraband, and Spanish searches in the 1730s were part of a larger debate between the empires over the principle of "freedom of the seas": see Elizabeth Mancke, "Negotiating an Empire: Britain and Its Overseas Peripheries, c. 1550–1780," in Christine Daniels and Michael V. Kennedy, eds., *Negotiated Empires: Centers and Peripheries in the Americas, 1500–1820* (New York, 2002), 248; Eric Williams, *From Columbus to Castro: The History of the Caribbean, 1492–1969* (London, 1970), 93.

7. Entrepôts and Hinterlands

AFRICAN MIGRATION TO THE NORTH AMERICAN
BACKCOUNTRY, CA. 1750–1807

Upwards of two thirds that have been imported have gone backwards.
—Peter Manigault, 1772

By the mid-eighteenth century, as European settlers in North America pushed well away from the Atlantic coast to colonize interior regions, they forced enslaved Africans to move with them. In the Chesapeake, the quest for arable land prompted ever more settlers to venture to the piedmont. By the 1760s, many piedmont counties saw Africans and people of African descent accounting for well over half of their populations, and with more than 100,000 enslaved people in the piedmont by 1782, more black Virginians resided in that region than in the tidewater. Many of these backcountry slaves had previously toiled for years—perhaps since birth—on tidewater plantations, but recently arrived Africans were also prevalent. In the Carolinas and Georgia, planters also ventured inland, especially with the introduction of indigo as the region's companion crop to rice. The enslaved population in South Carolina's backcountry increased from fewer than 2,500 in 1760 to more than 6,500 in 1768, and it continued to grow rapidly thereafter. This explosion led Charleston merchant Peter Manigault to say of arriving Africans in the early 1770s, "Upwards of two thirds that have been imported have gone backwards." In other words, Charleston was an entrepôt that enslaved people passed through on their way inland. The development of the cotton gin toward century's end would only accelerate backcountry development.[1]

1. On the expansion of British colonial settlement away from waterways navigable from the Atlantic, see D. W. Meinig, *The Shaping of America: A Geographical Perspective on 500 Years of History*, I, *Atlantic America, 1492–1800* (New Haven, Conn., 1986), 244–254. The Virginia piedmont slave population grew by nearly one thousand slaves per year between 1760 and the American Revolution (Philip D. Morgan and Michael L. Nicholls, "Slaves in Piedmont Virginia, 1720–1790," *William and Mary Quarterly*, 3d Ser., XLVI [1989], 215–222); likewise, Allan Kulikoff argues for the "Africanization" of the piedmont, asserting that, by the 1760s, "nearly all Africans who arrived in Virginia landed at Bermuda Hundred," the best upriver access point for the overland

Although it is widely understood that slavery expanded outward from coastal population centers in the eighteenth century, little attention has focused on the mechanics of delivering African people to regions distant from their ports of arrival. Study of the Atlantic slave trade tends to end at the water's edge. Scholars of the antebellum period emphasize the overland trade's importance for slavery's expansion, since legal transatlantic importations ceased after 1807, but the antebellum domestic slave trade had an important precursor in the colonial and early national periods, though it was smaller in scale. Enslaved migration to the North American interior can be conceived of in two phases—first, a dispersal of Africans from Atlantic entrepôts between the mid-eighteenth and early nineteenth centuries, and second, the forced migration of American-born slaves from older plantation areas to the burgeoning southwest cotton fields, starting in the late eighteenth century and reaching unprecedented levels in the antebellum period.[2]

Just how eighteenth-century slaves and slaveholders bridged the gap from port to plantation is an important question, given the considerable distances emerging between them by the second half of the eighteenth century. To be sure, some American-born or acculturated slaves migrated inland with plantation owners seeking new lands for themselves (or fleeing the British in the Revolutionary War), but many landless colonists moved westward as a strategy for acquiring land, which was increasingly hard to afford in coastal areas. As such, many backcountry planters owned few slaves, if any, before acquiring interior land. These pioneers often sought so-called "New Negroes," enslaved people just arriving from Africa. For these African immigrants purchased by

---

march (Kulikoff, *Tobacco and Slaves: The Development of Southern Cultures in the Chesapeake, 1600–1800* [Chapel Hill, N.C., 1986], 75, 323–336, esp. 336). See also Richard S. Dunn, "Black Society in the Chesapeake, 1776–1810," in Ira Berlin and Ronald Hoffman, eds., *Slavery and Freedom in the Age of the American Revolution* (Charlottesville, Va., 1983), 54–58. For data on South Carolina in the 1760s, see Rachel N. Klein, *Unification of a Slave State: The Rise of the Planter Class in the South Carolina Backcountry, 1760–1808* (Chapel Hill, N.C., 1990), 19–24, esp. 20 (Manigault quotation); for data on South Carolina in the 1780s and 1790s, see Patrick S. Brady, "The Slave Trade and Sectionalism in South Carolina, 1787–1808," *Journal of Southern History*, XXXVIII (1972), 601–620; see also S. Max Edelson, *Plantation Enterprise in Colonial South Carolina* (Cambridge, Mass., 2006), 255–268.

2. For more on the domestic slave trade in the United States after the abolition of the international trade, see Steven Deyle, *Carry Me Back: The Domestic Slave Trade in American Life* (New York, 2005); Walter Johnson, *Soul by Soul: Life inside the Antebellum Slave Market* (Cambridge, Mass., 1999); Johnson, ed., *The Chattel Principle: Internal Slave Trades in the Americas* (New Haven, Conn., 2004); Michael Tadman, *Speculators and Slaves: Masters, Traders, and Slaves in the Old South* (Madison, Wis., 1989); Robert H. Gudmestad, *A Troublesome Commerce: The Transformation of the Interstate Slave Trade* (Baton Rouge, 2003).

western planters, the forced migration did not end where the sea met the shore. They sailed or paddled up rivers, rode rickety wagons or marched up country roads and trails. These inland movements of captives have received less scholarly attention than the transatlantic trade, which can be more systematically assessed because port officials monitored and documented it. Furthermore, seaborne trade required coordination between merchants on either end of a voyage, leading to extensive correspondence. Newspapers and insurers also recorded the comings and goings of ships. Movements within colonies, by contrast, left far fewer traces in the historical record. As a result, rigorous quantification of African migrations over land in the eighteenth century is not feasible. Only anecdotal sources hint at such trafficking, but careful attention to this fragmentary and unsatisfactory record exposes traders' efforts to profit by delivering exploitable workers to remote areas. It also reveals the elusive experiences of African immigrants between their seagoing voyages and the plantations where they settled.[3]

The journeys would have been rugged. For eighteenth-century settlers in the North American interior, communications and transportation to and from the coastal entrepôts were constant challenges, given the underdeveloped transportation infrastructure, not to mention the spotty postal or shipping services. Backcountry buyers of enslaved people employed an amalgam of methods for acquiring workers. Some traveled to entrepôts to make purchases themselves; others relied on agents to purchase Africans for them and to deliver the captives to the backcountry; still others waited for speculators to arrive in the backcountry with people for sale. As a result, Africans' journeys inland were varied, often makeshift, affairs that posed a range of challenges for captives and, sometimes, presented opportunities.

■ The dealings of Charleston merchant Henry Laurens in the summer of 1764 illustrate the variety of methods for moving incoming Africans from entrepôts to hinterlands. In the wake of the Seven Years' War, demand for slave labor was high throughout South Carolina, and to capitalize on this need, Laurens imported people both directly from Africa and via transshipment from the Caribbean. Recognizing that Charleston and its vicinity accounted for only

3. Richard S. Dunn notes that many Chesapeake planters moved slaves inland during the Revolutionary War to keep them away from British forces ("Black Society in the Chesapeake," in Berlin and Hoffman, eds., *Slavery and Freedom*, 58–59). Tadman has created a rich and detailed quantitative study of the nineteenth-century U.S. domestic slave trade, thanks partly to more detailed merchant accounts but also to the existence of the U.S. census (*Speculators and Slaves*).

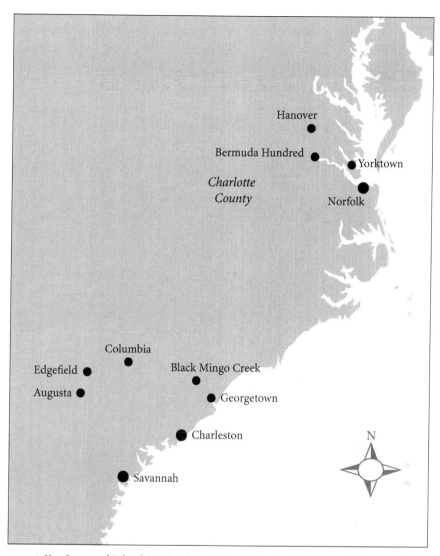

MAP 6. Key Ports and Inland Destinations in North America's Eighteenth-Century Slave Trade. Drawn by the author

part of the region's demand, Laurens sent captives inland through at least five channels (Map 6).

First, Laurens courted remote buyers to sales in Charleston through direct correspondence and advertising. He wrote to William Frierson, in the Williamsburgh Township, sending him broadsides for a sale and asking him "to disperse the Advertisements as quick and as generally as you can and I wish it may suit you and many others of my old friends in your Quarters to attend the Sales." He sent a similar invitation (without extra advertisements) to Daniel Heyward in "Indian Land." Evidently these appeals drew results, as Laurens later noted that "people come from all quarters" to buy Africans.[4]

Second, for those planters who could not travel to Charleston, Laurens fulfilled requests for captives, if the planters were willing to trust his judgment and integrity in making purchases on their behalf. For William Thompson, who lived on Black Mingo Creek in the northern part of the colony, Laurens purchased "two Young Negroes, a Male and a Female," in accord with Thompson's request. The means of transporting these people went unmentioned.[5]

Third, perhaps encouraged by these sales to far-flung customers, Laurens became a buyer on speculation of arriving Africans, sending them to outlying areas for resale to planters who did not travel to the entrepôt. With William Price, a Georgetown merchant, Laurens bought a "parcel of Negroes" imported by other transatlantic traders. Price and Laurens then transferred these people to Georgetown, a smaller port up the coast that rarely received direct shipments from Africa, leading Price and Laurens to expect higher prices. Other merchants also speculated on arriving Africans in the entrepôts in order to sell them in the backcountry.[6]

Fourth, as a selling agent for distant traders who shipped Africans to Charleston, Laurens occasionally sent arriving captives inland for sale. In August, he earned commissions by selling a group of Africans who "came in most wretched plight" from Saint Kitts. From this group, Laurens "sold Three Men and three Women . . . and one Boy" in Charleston, but he explained to the owners in the Caribbean, "As to the other eight I could not get them off here at any . . . tolerable rate." Instead, "I have sent them a little way in the Country where I think there is a better chance of Selling them than here." He later

4. Henry Laurens to William Frierson, June 11, 1764, Laurens to Daniel Heyward, June 11, 1764, both in Philip M. Hamer et al., eds., *The Papers of Henry Laurens*, 16 vols. (Columbia, S.C., 1968–2002), IV, 305–306 (hereafter cited as *Laurens Papers*).

5. Laurens to William Thompson, May 18, June 19, 1764, and Laurens to Joseph Brown, June 29, 1764, in *Laurens Papers*, IV, 281, 314–315, 320–322.

6. Laurens to Paul Trapier, June 25, 1764, Laurens to Brown, June 26, 1764, ibid., 316–318.

reported, "Those 8 Negroes sent into the Country have yielded at least 50 per Cent more than they would here."[7]

Fifth, and finally, investing in as well as trading slaves, Laurens purchased "Eleven New Negroes" for himself and shipped them up the Ashley River to his Mepkin Plantation on the little schooner *Baker,* under Captain John Gray and a crew of enslaved sailors. This wide range of methods that Laurens employed for moving people inland in the summer of 1764 reflected the difficulties of such trade and travel. No merchant in the colony was more knowledgeable or better connected than Laurens, so his varied dealings reveal both the improvised nature of inland trade in the period and the piecemeal manner by which backcountry networks were forged to distribute forced migrants and goods to the growing hinterlands of European settlement in North America.[8]

The most typical arrangement for inland slave migration was probably Africans' traveling in the company of a new purchaser. Buying a slave was a major investment (especially for the less affluent slaveholders who often lived far from major ports), so many remote planters preferred not to delegate selection to friends or merchants. Such an important purchase could draw them to town when other transactions might not. In fact, slave-trading merchants in Charleston considered attracting these remote planters vital to successful sales. In 1756, Laurens (and his partner, George Austin) explained the logic while absolving themselves of blame for the slow sales of fifteen Africans whom Law, Satterthwaite, and Jones of Barbados had transshipped to Charleston for resale. "'Tis much more difficult to run off these small parcells than a Cargo of 3 or 400," Austin and Laurens declared. "When such a [large] Number are for Sale it draws down the People from every part of the Province and one bids upon the other. Very often they in their hurry take hold of very ordinary Slaves as prime overlooking their imperfections which in a small parcell scarse ever escapes notice." Slave traders relied on swarms of distant planters to create a frenzy for purchasing and to generate fear among their peers that hesitation would send them home empty-handed. Fortunately for Law, Satterthwaite, and Jones, their Charleston agents saw an opportunity for such excitement on the horizon. After explaining the slow sales, Austin and Laurens noted, "Yesterday a Brigantine arriv'd to us with 140 [more Africans] from your Island which will bring down our friends from the remote parts of the Country and enable us to run off yours." In 1752, Virginia trader Charles Steuart agreed that backcountry demand was crucial to successful sales, en-

7. Laurens to Day and Welch, Sept. 10, Dec. 17, 1764, ibid., 412–413, 538.
8. Laurens to Timothy Creamer, June 26, 1764, ibid., 319.

couraging a Saint Kitts trader to transship Africans to him in Norfolk with the encouragement that "we have a Letter from our Friends in the Country, advising that negroes are in great demand."[9]

Merchants hoping to attract these "remote" planters actively marketed Africans in the backcountry. Newspapers in the eighteenth century circulated widely, and advertisements reached planters close to town and in outlying areas. To ensure that distant readers had an opportunity to attend sales, merchants generally advertised them well in advance. In Charleston, for example, a quarantine law required all arriving Africans to wait ten days at Sullivan's Island in the harbor to ensure any contagions were under control before entering port. Nonetheless, merchants routinely advertised sales as soon as the ships arrived so that planters could travel to town during the quarantine period. When the brigantine *Two Friends* arrived at the end of October 1752 with Africans transshipped from Barbados, the merchants Glen and Cooper placed an advertisement in the *South-Carolina Gazette*'s October 30 issue, informing readers, "On Thursday the 9th Day of November next, will be sold at Auction at the usual Place in Charles-Town, about Sixty very likely new NEGRO Men, Women, Boys and Girls." Giving potential buyers ten days of warning increased the likelihood that distant planters would attend. In 1772, Edward Blake and Samuel Legaré followed suit, announcing that their "FORTY-FIVE CHOICE SLAVES, JUST arrived from BARBADOS, in GOOD HEALTH, after a short Passage" would also be sold sixteen days from then, on September 25. Charles Steuart also noted that a time lag between a slave ship's arrival and the sale allowed word to spread. In 1752, he wrote to a prospective slave-trading partner in North Carolina, John Campbell, assuring him that, if they collaborated on a venture to Virginia, "an express may be dispatched to you on the arrival of any ship, by which you might attend the Sale before sufficient notice could be given through the Country." In other words, Steuart anticipated enough delay for promoting the sale over a wide area to allow a messenger to reach Campbell in North Carolina and then for Campbell to travel to Virginia to help oversee the sales.[10]

9. Austin and Laurens to Law, Satterthwaite, and Jones, Jan. 12, 1756, ibid., II, 65–66; see also Austin and Laurens to John Knight, Dec. 18, 1755 or Jan. 3, 1756, ibid., 45, 59; Charles Steuart to Thomas Ogilvie, Mar. 9, 1752, Charles Steuart Letter Books, I, 1751–1753, microfilm, M–32, John D. Rockefeller, Jr. Library, Williamsburg, Virginia.

10. Thomas Cooper and David J. McCord, eds., *The Statutes at Large of South Carolina*, 10 vols. (Columbia, S.C., 1837–1841), III, 773–774; *South-Carolina Gazette*, Oct. 30, 1752, Sept. 10, 1772. In the same 1772 issue of the *Gazette*, Edward Fisher and Co. gave their potential customers even more time to travel to Charleston to buy "upwards of One Hundred PRIME SLAVES, (In

Communicating pending sales to remote buyers could require substantial effort, which some slave dealers made directly. In their account for a sale of people from Sierra Leone in July 1756, Austin and Laurens listed a charge of fourteen pounds (South Carolina currency) for "Printed Advertisements, hire of a Man and Horse to disperse them thro' the Country and Expences at the Sale." In this case, Austin and Laurens doubted the effectiveness of their marketing, however, because news of the declaration of war with France had just reached the colony. They were "afraid Our advertisements will Scarce bring a Single person out of the Country to the Sale." Regardless, such attention to drawing planters from afar suggests that, in less volatile times, many attended sales in person, meaning that Africans, after climbing off their ships, made long journeys to backcountry plantations in the company of their new owners.[11]

In other cases, planters chose not to travel to the entrepôts, preferring to appoint an agent to make purchases for them. Given the difficulty and expense of overland travel in the eighteenth century, backcountry planters routinely relied on friends and acquaintances to make smaller purchases for them on visits to larger towns, as Richard Winn of South Carolina's Fairfield District (north of Columbia) did in 1798. He wrote to a neighbor, Mr. S. W. Yongue, having heard that "you are going to Columbia I will take it a favour if you will be so good as to git me One P'd. of Good Tea. At this time I have Not as Much Small Money as will pay for it but Shortly after your Return Shall." Relying on an agent for the purchase of expensive enslaved people could not be undertaken so casually, however, especially when they had to be moved over long distances. In an 1807 bill of sale for a slave, for example, sellers LeRoy Hammond and Charles Goodwyn acknowledged the receipt of four hundred fifty dollars from a Beaufort planter named John Cheney, but Cheney was not actually the buyer. He was the "trustee nominated and appointed for that purpose by Mary Dayley of Edgefield District." It is possible that Dayley engaged

---

GOOD HEALTH) JUST arrived in the Brigantine Lovely Jenny." Fisher and Co. dated their advertisement September 9 but announced the sale for September 25, giving customers sixteen days to plan and to travel. "An express may be dispatched": Steuart to John Campbell, Feb. 27, 1752, Steuart Letter Books, I.

11. "Account of Sale" of slaves from the sloop *Hare* from Sierra Leone, July 17, 1756, in *Laurens Papers*, II, 257–259; Austin and Laurens to Richard Oswald and Co., July 26, 1756, ibid., 270. Merchants also wrote letters to individual planters at times to encourage them to attend sales; see Daniel C. Littlefield, "Charleston and Internal Slave Redistribution," *South Carolina Historical Magazine*, LXXXVII (1986), 94–95; Laurens to Daniel Heyward, June 11, 1764, in *Laurens Papers*, IV, 305–306.

Cheney to buy a slave for her owing more to gender than geography, with a view to having a male agent in the marketplace. On the other hand, given her location in the backcountry Edgefield district (and Cheney's residence in the coastal district of Beaufort), it also seems likely that Dayley employed Cheney because he was closer to the prime markets for African people.[12]

Using an agent made trust vital, underscoring the need for personal ties between planters in the hinterland and people in the entrepôts. In 1786, Joseph Clay of Savannah sent a young man named Mr. Faning to Charleston to purchase "three new Negroes from the Windward Coast" on his behalf because Georgia, devastated by combat, struggled to attract transatlantic shipments in the years immediately following the Revolutionary War. Faning was intimidated by the responsibility, however, so Clay also sent a letter of introduction to Daniel Bourdeaux, a mercantile correspondent in Charleston, stating that Faning "not being willing to depend intirely on his own Judgement in procuring them [slaves] has Requested I wou'd get a Friend to see them before he finally purchased and sent them here in Order to have their Approbation." Clay relied on two agents to purchase Africans on his behalf—perhaps trusting one to keep his interest at heart and the other for experience in trade. Likewise, each of the agents could take comfort that if something went wrong, their concurrence in the decision would minimize suspicions of negligence or fraud.[13]

To cultivate the trust of distant people for whom he made purchases, Henry Laurens sometimes offered clients a selection from among captives he bought both for the clients and for himself. When Elias Ball—a plantation owner

12. Richard Winn to S. W. Yongue, Sept. 4, 1798, Richard Winn Papers, 1786–1798, South Caroliniana Library, Columbia, S.C. (hereafter cited as SCL); Secretary of State, Misc. Records (Columbia Series), S 213006, vol. B, 1776–1875, 457–459, South Carolina Department of Archives and History, Columbia, S.C. (hereafter referred to as SCDAH). Many widows or otherwise independent women quickly adapted to managing financial affairs, considered the proper role of their husbands or fathers; see Mary Beth Norton, *Liberty's Daughters: The Revolutionary Experience of American Women, 1750–1800* (Boston, 1980), 132–138; Suzanne Lebsock, *The Free Women of Petersburg: Status and Culture in a Southern Town, 1784–1860* (New York, 1984), esp. chap. 5.

13. Joseph Clay to Daniel Bourdeaux, Feb. 13, 1786, Joseph Clay Papers, V, Georgia Historical Society, Savannah. On Georgia's struggle to attract slave shipments after the Revolution, see Darold D. Wax, "'New Negroes Are Always in Demand': The Slave Trade in Eighteenth-Century Georgia," *Georgia Historical Quarterly*, LXVIII (1984), 215–216. The slave trade was certainly not the only eighteenth-century trade that required trusted agents in distant ports and towns; the slow pace of travel and communications made the delegation of important decisions a crucial and vexing issue for all long-distance commerce. For a good introduction to the importance of distant agents, see David Hancock, *Citizens of the World: London Merchants and the Integration of the British Atlantic Community, 1735–1785* (New York, 1995), 123–131.

up the Cooper River—asked Laurens to purchase six slaves for him, Laurens purchased eight. He then sent the people to Ball with a letter explaining, "If 8 is more than you want please to draw out two for me and send them when a convenient opportunity offers to Wambaw [one of Laurens's own plantations] or back again to Charles Town. I shall be glad to have them." Through this strategy, Laurens offered his client a degree of choice and perhaps peace of mind from knowing that Laurens was willing to purchase for himself the two captives deemed least desirable. Of course, Laurens also hoped to entice Ball to buy more enslaved Africans than he originally intended.[14]

When agents purchased captives for distant buyers, the Africans presumably traveled from port to plantation either with the purchasing agent or in the company of another traveler who oversaw their delivery for payment or as a favor. Details are sketchy for such arrangements. In a 1794 account, slave sellers James and Edwin Penman and Co. described two Africans as "delivered to John Kendall" but did not explain further. Similar language appears in slave dealer William Ancrum's account book for 1758, which lists the receipt of £260 from Fesch and Guignard on January 14 for "a new Negro Woman Sold and deliver'd to them in September last." Again, precisely what "deliver'd" meant is unclear.[15]

Some owners of backcountry plantations escaped the dilemma of whether to travel to entrepôts for slave sales because they were absentees; they already resided in an entrepôt. Nonetheless, delivering enslaved people to their distant plantations presented a challenge. In the 1770s, William Ancrum resided mainly in Charleston while owning several plantations in the South Carolina backcountry, and the difficulty of moving people, goods, and crops between his plantations and the coast was a constant theme in his letters. Ancrum often noted slave purchases (of both recently arrived Africans and American-born people), and he hinted at varied methods for delivering these captives to the interior. In January 1777, Ancrum wrote to the overseer of his Red Bank plantation near Camden that he was sending him "a Negro Woman named Ruth and her female Child by Mr. Rose's wagon." At times, Ancrum appears to have paid for such transport. In an account for 1778, Ancrum recorded £8,200

14. Laurens to Elias Ball, Jul. 15, 1765, in *Laurens Papers*, IV, 652. For another example, see Laurens to James Cowles, June 30, 1755, ibid., I, 278–279.

15. J. & E. Penman and Co. Daybook and Account Book, 1794, MS, R 498, 10, SCL; William Ancrum Account Book, 1757–1758, 1776–1782, MS, P, ibid. Such notes on delivery might indicate that these merchants paid someone to deliver slaves because the Penmans' other account entries do not list slaves as "delivered," but the record is by no means clear, especially since Kendall's location is not noted.

spent "for 5 Negroes bo't" for his Roundabout plantation on the Congaree River near Columbia, plus an additional £10 for "Carriage up" of the enslaved people.[16]

Ancrum did not always pay for this service, however, since he owned several wagons himself, which were crucial for transporting his indigo to the coast. In December 1777, having just received several loads of indigo from his plantations, Ancrum wrote to Joseph Kershaw, a merchant friend in Camden, to thank him for overseeing the indigo shipment and to report purchasing seven "Negroes to settle at the Congarees" estate. Ancrum noted that he "sent Frank with them as far as Mr. Porckins plant[ation] Amelia." Frank was operating a wagon bound for Ancrum's other plantation at Camden, but the route to the Camden and Congaree plantations would have been the same—along the Cooper River—for the first three-quarters of the journey. Ancrum planned to catch up with Frank and the newly purchased people at Mr. Porckin's plantation in order to take the enslaved the rest of the way to their destination while Frank and the wagon continued to his other estate. (Presumably, Ancrum could outpace the wagon on horseback.) Frank's identity is elusive, but he was likely a slave. In the same letter to Kershaw, Ancrum described arrangements to pay various wagon operators for the delivery of the indigo, stating that he "paid Tomlinson the Carriage of what he brought. Mr. Russley's I shall either settle with him or you." No mention is made, however, of payment to "Frank," and the use of his first name also hints at enslavement. The need to settle an account with Mr. Russley might suggest that another enslaved driver operated his wagon. Experienced slaves often served as wagoners in the era— seen as an elevated position due to the escape from fieldwork—but the task of transporting captives instead of goods exposes a complication to advancement under slavery. Commodified themselves, slave wagoners could be made complicit in the commodification of others. Such transit also offered another site for interaction between veterans of American slavery and newcomers, although the encounter would be profoundly shaped by whether the experienced hand shared a language with the forced immigrants.[17]

Africans' travel inland could be by water as well as overland. Like An-

16. Ancrum to Marlow Pryor, n.d. (between Dec. 23, 1776, and Jan. 16, 1777), William Ancrum Letter Book, SCL; Ancrum Account Book, fol. 24.

17. Ancrum to Joseph Kershaw, Dec. 9, 1777, William Ancrum Letter Book. For more on the growth of wagon traffic between Charleston and the backcountry, see Klein, *Unification of a Slave State*, 13. On slaves as wagoners, see Philip D. Morgan, *Slave Counterpoint: Black Culture in the Eighteenth-Century Chesapeake and Lowcountry* (Chapel Hill, N.C., 1998), 56–57.

crum, Laurens was also an absentee planter, and he shipped recently purchased people upstream to his plantations by riverboat on several occasions. On January 1, 1763, Laurens informed his overseer at Mepkin Plantation, up the Cooper River, "I now send you by Mr. Dick's Schooner 25 Negroes," noting, "They are all well Clothed and I have put a Barrel of ordinary Rice in the Schooner which will serve for provision on the Passage and some time longer." Laurens followed these captives just days later with "Rinah, a Negro Wench big with child in Mr. Broughton's Boat." Peter Broughton was another planter up the Cooper River, so Laurens had clearly arranged for Broughton's vessel to stop at Laurens's plantation on its way. He might have paid for this service or simply called in a neighborly favor. Likewise, in June 1765, Laurens sent 27 "new Negroes" to the overseer of his Wambaw plantation "by a vessel called Wambaw." In later letters, Laurens mentioned owning a schooner by that name, so he apparently used his own ship, crewed by employees or enslaved sailors, to send this group of newly arrived Africans inland.[18]

Another arrangement for slave travel from entrepôt to hinterland was in the company of merchants—either selling agents in the transatlantic trade or colonial speculators who purchased enslaved people for resale in the country. Although most slave traders seemed content to attract backcountry planters to the entrepôts for sales (and let the buyers worry about the logistics of moving captives inland), some traders pursued backcountry sales more directly. Over the course of the 1750s, for example, Charles Steuart shifted away from drawing upland planters to port, turning instead toward sending enslaved Africans inland. At first, he had opted for backcountry sales only as a last resort. In 1751, he wrote to a Barbados merchant, Benjamin Massiah, reporting on sales of enslaved people whom Massiah shipped to him and encouraging Massiah to send more: "We shall always have it in our power to make an immediate sale of any number of Slaves." Steuart preferred to sell Africans upon arrival rather than send them inland where prices were sometimes higher,

18. Laurens to James Lawrence, Jan. 1, 7, 1763, in *Laurens Papers,* III, 203–205; Laurens to Abraham Schad, June 7, 1765, ibid., IV, 634; Laurens to Schad, May 16, 1765, ibid., 625. Ancrum probably sent slaves to his plantations by boat, as well. His letters occasionally mention shipments of corn and other goods down to Charleston, and small boats might have been the primary mode of transport from his Liberty Hill plantation on the Pee Dee River to Charleston. Ancrum's letters include far less about the travel logistics to Liberty Hill, which may reflect the relative ease of water travel, since the lack of discussion about wagons to Liberty Hill is in marked contrast to Ancrum's correspondence with the managers at Red Bank and Roundabout; see Ancrum to Marlow Pryor, Jan. 23, Mar. 5, Dec. 7, 1779, Ancrum to Mr. Gerving, Oct. 17, 1778, and Ancrum to Joshua Ferral, Feb. 6, Nov. 16, 1779, all in William Ancrum Letter Book.

because "it saves great charges and risque which often attends transporting them." Furthermore, if one delayed sales to send captives inland, "while these are sending about the Country, others may arrive" from Africa, giving planters other options and lowering prices. Nonetheless, in 1751 and 1752, he occasionally referred to groups of captives being "sent" or "sent up" to an undisclosed location for sale, possibly to a store on the Potomac River in which he was an investor. In all of these cases, Steuart sent only small numbers of people inland, typically describing them as undesirable human commodities, unsalable in the entrepôt. In July 1751, Steuart noted vending six people off a ship from Saint Kitts, adding, "The old Woman [from the vessel] is sent also for sale, but we have not yet had an Acco't of her." (The slave trade trapped this woman in a tragic limbo, with Steuart lamenting, "We do not think any person will accept of her as a present." Since freedom was not an option, either, this lone, unwanted woman awaited her fate long after her fellow travelers were gone. More than two months later, Steuart would again report, "We have not yet got the Sales of your Negroe Wench.") That same month, Steuart discussed his struggles to sell two "West India Negroes" that another trader had sent from Saint Kitts, explaining that he had placed them with "the Master of the Vessel who carried them up" to a place of sale. In other words, he again sent hard-to-sell people—in this case, undesirable seasoned hands—to more remote markets. On another occasion, Steuart noted a man "in the Country" awaiting sale, and he also referred to a woman sent along with him, who had "died Suddenly" just when traders "thought she was almost well." Given that she had previously been ill, Steuart probably sent her away from port to find a less competitive market.[19]

Steuart's slave trading ebbed during the Seven Years' War (1755–1763), but as his trading revamped in the waning years of the conflict, he was increasingly willing to send even optimal captives into the backcountry for sale. Steuart continued to dispatch small groups inland when he had difficulty selling them at Norfolk; in November 1760, he reported that he "could get no offers here" for the last four captives who had arrived on a vessel from Senegal, so he "sent them to Smithfield, abt. 35 miles from hence up the Ja's River, where they . . . will sell for more than here." But these higher prices began to convince Steuart that even healthy, more marketable people could sell better inland. The fol-

19. See, in Steuart Letter Book, I: Steuart to Benjamin Massiah, July 5, 1751; Steuart, McKenzie, and Co. to Thomas Ogilvie, July 13, 1751; Steuart to Ogilvie, Sept. 23, 1751; Steuart to Anthony Fahie, July 13, 15, 1751; and Steuart to Lewis Brotherson, Feb. 10, 1752. For Steuart's involvement in a store on the Potomac, see Steuart to James Dunlop, June 18, 1753, ibid.

lowing spring, Steuart reflected back on his sales of the full cargo of people from Senegal and lamented not sending all of them toward the piedmont for sale. "The Owner who came w't them was in a hurry to get away, w'ch obliged us to sell here, tho' we could have done better w't them up the Country." By the early 1760s, Steuart had apparently decided that backcountry demand made it worth the risk of transporting enslaved people inland.[20]

Other Virginia merchants found piedmont markets so attractive that they speculated on Africans arriving in the tidewater with an eye to reselling them in western counties. As early as 1751, storekeeper William Jerdone of Yorktown partnered with John Norton and David Anderson to purchase "32 Negroes . . . out of the Ship *Tryall*," just arrived from somewhere in the Congo-Angola region. The trio then "paid James Bowers" three pounds for "the freight of the negroes" some part of the way to Hanover, about seventy-five miles inland, the mode of transit unknown. Perhaps Bowers ferried them up the York as far as the river was navigable, or perhaps he supervised their march overland. Regardless, the three slave dealers made a profit. They had paid just less than £1,040 (Virginia currency) for the 32 west central Africans in Yorktown, and they sold them in Hanover for £1,294. Even after deducting the shipping costs and their "Expences while in Hanover," Jerdone reckoned that each partner cleared more than £65, a nearly 20 percent return on their investment, in only a matter of weeks. In 1772, Paul Carrington—a burgess for Charlotte County in the piedmont—undertook a similar venture, purchasing 50 Angolan people from the slave ship *Polly*, which had delivered 450 captives at Bermuda Hundred, the farthest port up the James River. "Considering the sum large and a Considerable Risque in the health and life of the Slaves," he brought three investors into the scheme and then "convey'd the Slaves to the Country" at his plantation in Charlotte County, from which he "made the Sales and Collected the Debts." Presumably, his customers were piedmont planters from Charlotte and surrounding counties.[21]

Other direct evidence of such speculation in the tidewater for resale in the piedmont proves elusive, but sales records from transatlantic slavers suggest that other Virginia merchants engaged in similar endeavors. When the brigan-

20. Steuart to James Wetherell, Nov. 22, 1760, Steuart to George Spence, Mar. 5, 1761, ibid.

21. William Jerdone Account Book, 1751–1752, ledger B, MS 1929.6.1, esp. fol. 46, Rockefeller Library; *Voyages: The Trans-Atlantic Slave Trade Database,* accessed August 2011, Voyage ID no. 17276; Carrington Family Papers, 1761–1964, sect. 4, MSS, 1, C2358, C5, Virginia Historical Society, Richmond, Va.; see also Morgan and Nicholls, "Slaves in Piedmont Virginia," *WMQ,* 3d Ser., XLVI (1989), 211–212. For more on the *Polly,* see *Voyages,* accessed May 2009, Voyage ID no. 17792.

tine *Eadith* delivered 154 Gambians to the York River in 1761, amid the typical small purchases made by individuals, two mercantile firms bought captives in larger numbers. "Taylor and Snelson" bought 20 people (8 men, 4 women, 4 boys, and 4 girls), and "Samuel Gist and Co." purchased 58 individuals (10 men, 17 women, 15 boys, and 16 girls). Although the records do not indicate buyers' intentions, both the large numbers of slaves and the mercantile designation of the purchasers suggest the buyers were traders rather than planters—at least for these transactions. Such speculation made little sense unless one intended to transport such captives to another market for resale. In Virginia in 1761, the piedmont offered by far the most likely market, and Samuel Gist operated a store in Hanover County, directly inland from the falls of the York River. The overrepresentation of women and children among the group Gist purchased also fits with evidence that piedmont planters purchased more young and female people than other buyers of slaves. Ten years later, large-scale purchasers apparently still abounded, as Norfolk trader William Aitchison exclaimed that at "the falls of James River . . . I had an opportunity of seeing the Sale of ab't 150 negros that sold very high." He was so impressed with the great demand for slaves at this place—the farthest inland point seagoing vessels could reach—that he proposed to a partner in England that they buy "fifty or sixty Slaves or a larger quantity" and some rum and sugar in Barbados or Antigua to send up there. "If the Negroes had a quiet passage here," Aitchison added, "the Mony might be replaced almost as soon as advanced as they will sell for the ready." Realizing that his enthusiasm might seem untoward, Aitchison then added a postscript: "I dare say you'll think me much alter'd both in the Length of this Letter and the contents of it . . . but really the high price of Negros . . . was so striking that I coud not refrain giving you my sentiments." Aitchison did not specify whether the buyers he saw at "the falls" were individual planters or speculators, but presumably a combination of both was driving up prices. That Aitchison courted transshipment from the Caribbean shows how such traders used the slave trade to elaborate commercial networks between the Caribbean and even inland North American regions.[22]

22. Invoice book of the *Eadith,* 1758–1761, DX/169, 23, Merseyside Maritime Museum, Liverpool, U.K. (for more on the *Eadith,* see *Voyages,* accessed May 2009, Voyage ID no. 90873); William Aitchison to Steuart, Mar. 15, 1770, Charles Steuart Papers, 1747–1784 (volume of misc. additions after original collection assembled), microfilm, M–68.9, fols. 91–92. Drawing too stark a line between merchants and planters would be misguided for the eighteenth century, as many individuals held both roles simultaneously or gradually transitioned from trader to landed gentleman. Samuel Gist, for example, owned vast tracts in Hanover County and held dozens of slaves. Nonetheless, that Gist and others made their large purchases from the *Eadith*

South Carolina merchants also organized backcountry ventures in the quest for high prices. In 1765, when transatlantic traders flooded Charleston with African captives, importers Brailsford and Chapman sought to alleviate the glut by sending sixty Angolan and Windward Coast men, women, and children inland to Jacksonburgh for sale, offering an unusually generous eighteen months' credit. Austin, Laurens, and Appleby also advertised inland sales at Jacksonburgh and Dorchester. In 1765, Laurens promised a planter on Black Mingo Creek in the northern part of the colony, "If a proper parcel of good Negroes shall fall in my way I will send them for Sale to Black Mingo," although he cautioned that travel to the area "is so very distant and uncertain that none of my friends can by any means depend upon it." Such distribution of Africans to Charleston's hinterland for sale was not unusual. In the 1750s, Charleston merchants William Woodrop and Paul Douxsaint regularly imported Africans to the colony, and during the same period, they employed John Wilkins to operate a store in Pon Pon. The store's primary purpose was undoubtedly a broader commerce, selling imported goods and buying plantation produce, but given Woodrop and Douxsaint's role as importers of people, backcountry slave sales might also have factored into the operation. The Savannah mercantile firm of Clay, Telfair, and Co. occupied a similar position after the American Revolution. The firm was "concerned with Mr. McLean in a House at Augusta for the purpose of securing the Country and Indian Trading business," and during the same period, these merchants— Joseph Clay, in particular—actively imported enslaved Africans. Direct evidence for transporting captives to their inland trade depot does not exist, but given the growth of the state's interior population in these years, such traffic is plausible.[23]

---

in partnerships or as "companies" suggests mercantile intent. Gist also operated a store in Hanover County and might have intended to sell the Gambians he purchased there. (For more on Gist and his later involvement in the Dismal Swamp Company, see Charles Royster, *The Fabulous History of the Dismal Swamp Company: A Story of George Washington's Times* [New York, 1999], esp. 84–87). Morgan and Nicholls document the overrepresentation of young and female slaves in the piedmont in "Slaves in Piedmont Virginia," *WMQ*, 3d Ser., XLVI (1989), 221–233; see also Jennifer L. Morgan, *Laboring Women: Reproduction and Gender in New World Slavery* (Philadelphia, 2004), 77–92.

23. *South-Carolina Gazette,* Aug. 23, Oct. 11, 26, 1760, July 27, 1765; see also Laurens to John Knight, Dec. 18, 1755, in *Laurens Papers,* III, 43–44, 52; Laurens to David Fulton, May 16, 1765, ibid., IV, 626, 652 n. 9; Joseph Clay to James Seagrove, Apr. 16, 1784, Joseph Clay Papers, III. Other advertisements hint inconclusively at merchants delivering Africans to the backcountry for sale. In 1756, for example, Charleston lawyer James Grindlay advertised "about 25 healthy young slaves" at Jacksonburgh, offering "12 months credit." Grindlay might have been managing

During the Revolutionary War, William Ancrum and Thomas Wade undertook such speculation in human commodities for inland distribution, with Ancrum buying people in Charleston and sending them to Wade in Cheraw—in South Carolina's indigo-producing up-country—for resale. The war hampered their venture; Ancrum complained that he was "sorry to observe the late stoppage of the Circulation of . . . Dollars has frustrated our original plan in regard to the sale of the Negroes and that you [Wade] was under a Necessity of disposing of them on Credit." Nonetheless, despite Ancrum's concern about offering loans "in these troublesome times," the venture was apparently profitable, for Ancrum argued that the "profits likely to be made on the Sale of the Negroes are a sufficient inducem't to have continued the plan, could Negroes have now been purchased at the rate the others were, [but] they are now considerably advanced in price" in Charleston. Ancrum declined to make a further investment. He and Wade probably invested in seasoned people for this overland venture, since African arrivals virtually halted during the peak years of the war, but a similar venture would have been feasible during nonwar years. Mathias Seller, who lived near Stono, might have undertaken such a scheme in 1764 when he purchased three hundred arriving Africans from Henry Laurens on credit. The size of the purchase suggests Seller's intention to resell at least some of these people for profit, but if so, Seller did not live up to his name. Laurens had to threaten legal action for nonpayment the following year.[24]

Regardless of Seller's lack of success, speculations on arriving Africans for distribution to the Carolina backcountry probably only became more common after the American Revolution, when South Carolina reopened the transatlantic slave trade (from 1783 to 1787 and again from 1803 to 1807). Tellingly, up-country planters promoted the reopening, whereas those in the Lowcountry opposed it because they already owned many enslaved people; and limiting

---

an estate sale, but in such cases, advertisements typically specified whom slaves had previously belonged to, and sellers usually avoided selling on credit. Since Grindlay served as a lawyer for English merchant (and slave trader) William Higginson, it would not be surprising if Grindlay used this connection to speculate on slaves for resale in the backcountry. See *South-Carolina Gazette*, Feb. 5, 1756. For Grindlay's connection to Higginson, see *Laurens Papers*, II, 181 n. 7. For Woodrop and Douxsaint as slave importers, see "General Duty Books" of the Public Treasurer, SCDAH; for their store at Pon Pon, see *Laurens Papers*, I, 99 n. 8.

24. Ancrum to Thomas Wade, July 27, 1779, William Ancrum Letter Book (although slave imports stalled during the war, Ancrum implied an interest to import them by including their current prices in a letter to the English merchants Greenwood and Higginson that same year; see Aug. 16, 1779; Ancrum's letter books do not survive for nonwar years); Benjamin Perdriau, Jr., to Mathias Seller, Apr. 23, 1765, *Laurens Papers*, IV, 613.

supply would increase the value of the enslaved already in the state and prevent new competitors from expanding production of the same crops. When the trade was open, especially after 1803, most arriving Africans headed inland. Indeed, with South Carolina the only state to allow African importation and cotton booming—thanks to the spread of the cotton gin—speculators who bought new arrivals in Charleston targeted a hinterland extending well beyond the confines of the state. As British traveler Charles William Janson wrote after visiting South Carolina, "Thousands of these miserable people are dispersed over the adjoining states, through the port of Charleston." With buyers investing in arriving Africans for distribution across the ever-growing backcountry, Janson thought Charleston had become "a greater slave-market than, perhaps, was ever known at one place in the West India islands." [25]

Not all of Charleston's hinterland was inland, however. Merchants had long transshipped Africans from Charleston for sale in the smaller ports up and down the coast where vessels from Africa rarely, if ever, appeared. As a selling agent for slave traders to South Carolina, Henry Laurens often sent small groups of captives to Georgetown. In the fall of 1764, he sent "8 New Negroes" to merchant Samuel Wragg and later explained that for commissions in such cases, he "usually paid only 2 1/2 per Cent and [was] never asked [for] more in the Country for the Sale alone." Since Laurens and other selling agents in Charleston typically received 5 percent commissions on the people they sold for transatlantic traders, the 2.5 percent he offered to Wragg suggests that entrepôt merchants split their commissions with more remote traders when bringing them into the business of dispersing arriving Africans. In the winter of 1765, Francis Stuart purchased "fifty Ebo Slaves" from Laurens in Charleston for transshipment and resale in Beaufort, but the sales might have been sluggish, as Laurens complained the following February and again in May about Stuart's slow remittances. The Africans in this venture had reached South Carolina via Saint Kitts, so they experienced a particularly convoluted journey to American slavery, changing hands at least four times after the Atlantic crossing and enduring at least two subsequent "passages." [26]

25. Deyle, *Carry Me Back,* 19; Charles William Janson, *The Stranger in America: Containing Observations Made during a Long Residence in That Country, on the Genius, Manners and Customs of the People of the United States . . .* (London, 1807), 356.

26. "8 New Negroes": Laurens to Samuel Wragg, Oct. 29, 1764, in *Laurens Papers,* IV, 484–485. "Fifty Ebo Slaves": Laurens to John Knight and Co., Apr. 14, 1764, ibid., 246–247. See also Laurens to Smith and Baillies, Apr. 30, 1764, and Laurens to Francis Stuart, Feb. 6, May 24, 1765, ibid., 255–258, 576, 631. Such internal distribution from major ports to outlying areas within colonies was not limited to the mainland. In 1790, former Jamaican colonist Hercules Ross testi-

This range of possibilities for getting enslaved Africans to remote regions illustrates that interior migration was a varied, often makeshift, enterprise. Africans journeyed inland after the Middle Passage with planters who purchased them, with the agents or creolized slaves of such owners, or with merchants who speculated on their value as commodities—a value they hoped would increase with distance from Atlantic markets. The growth of the colonies ensured increasing demand for enslaved labor in the countryside, away from the Atlantic entrepôts, but the poor transportation infrastructure hindered a systematic overland distribution network from developing. Instead, arriving Africans traveled inland with all manner of people—planters, merchants, slaves, or others who just happened to be going their way. As these inland markets grew, however, both planters and merchants worked to integrate the backcountry with their Atlantic commercial networks. The slave trade proved vital to such elaboration, with planters in the hinterlands desperate for exploitable labor and merchants eager to bring more planters into their webs of trade.

■ What did such inland journeys from Atlantic entrepôts mean for those Africans chosen to undertake them? Fundamentally, Africans selected for labor or sale in remote areas faced yet more travel after they survived seagoing journeys—whether transatlantic or intercolonial. Having endured captivity on deepwater vessels, migrants climbed aboard wagons, boarded riverboats, or simply marched dozens or even hundreds of additional miles to reach the places where their labor was wanted. One interesting wrinkle for the North American slave experience is that, if Henry Laurens was correct in arguing that the largest slave shipments to North America attracted planters from deepest in the interior, it was people arriving directly from Africa who faced the greatest likelihood of an extended inland voyage. Meanwhile, those individuals reaching North America on small transshipments from the Caribbean were more likely to find themselves purchased by slaveholders closer to the entrepôts, for whom the trip to a port town was less of a project. Thus, for African migrants, escaping one form of dispersal after the Middle Passage (seaborne transshipment) increased the likelihood of enduring another (significant overland travel).

---

fied, "There used to be in Kingston many people who bought [arriving Africans] on speculation . . . to carry them to the country, and retail them" (House of Commons of Great Britain, *Abridgment of the Minutes of the Evidence, Taken before a Committee of the Whole House, to Whom It Was Referred to Consider of the Slave-Trade* [London, 1790], IV, 142–143).

More than mere chance condemned Africans to lengthy voyages to interior regions. For instance, the migration to the Virginia piedmont skewed toward both young and female slaves, though the extent to which this trend reflected planter preferences is unclear. On one hand, some backcountry planters might have selected women or children because they cost less than men or could foster the reproduction of their workforce. On the other hand, backcountry planters faced constraints on their choices. In 1755, the Charleston merchants Austin and Laurens struggled to sell a group of recently arrived Africans for Henry Weare and Co. of Bristol, reporting that they were a poor assortment of human commodities, unhealthy and mostly children. Countering allegations that they sold too cheaply, Austin and Laurens insisted that the Africans would have garnered much less, but "We had abundance of poor industrious People [who] attended that Sale which come from 70 to 80 Miles distance who were forced to take such as we had." In another letter, Austin and Laurens noted that planters who traveled long distances to purchase enslaved Africans "are the only ones to raise a Sale for . . . they wont go back empty handed so far." In other words, the cost of travel to Atlantic markets compelled backcountry planters to be less discerning buyers. As such, they might not have purchased disproportionate numbers of women and children by choice. William Aitchison certainly formed the impression that backcountry planters still preferred young adult males when he proposed his scheme for importing enslaved people to "the falls of the James River." In the optimum cargo, "if possible, 2/3'ds shoud be Males." Backcountry planters might have purchased fewer adult males than the wealthy coastal planters simply because they could not afford to be as selective. Whatever the reason, young adult males were underrepresented in the backcountry. And if backcountry buyers could not afford to be choosy, less hale and hearty captives as well as women were likely to be marched (or otherwise transported) into the backcountry.[27]

27. Austin and Laurens to Henry Weare and Co., July 2, Aug. 30, 1755, *Laurens Papers,* I, 281–282, 326–327; Aitchison to Steuart, Mar. 15, 1770, Charles Steuart Papers, 1747–1784, fols. 91–92. Morgan and Nicholls attribute the overrepresentation of young and female slaves to planter concerns about both cost and reproduction ("Slaves in Piedmont Virginia," *WMQ,* 3d Ser., XLVI [1989], 221–233). Morgan argues that planters in developing regions showed particular interest in acquiring enslaved women with an eye to reproduction (*Laboring Women,* 77–92). Jennifer Spear notes a similar preference for women among planters when supplies of arriving Africans were constrained in French Louisiana (Spear, *Race, Sex, and Social Order in Early New Orleans* [Baltimore, 2008], 58). David Geggus also notes that French colonies neglected by transatlantic traders developed more balanced gender ratios (Geggus, "The Demographic Composition of the French Caribbean Slave Trade," *Proceedings of the Thirteenth and Fourteenth Meeting of the French Colonial Historical Society* [Lanham, Md., 1990], 15–17). Ellen Eslinger shows fairly balanced gender

The acutely ill, however, sometimes had their journeys to the backcountry delayed or canceled altogether. In 1775, Savannah merchant Joseph Clay received a shipment of forty or fifty enslaved people bound for the plantation of Benjamin Stead, an absentee planter living in England, but "the Scurvy was among them." Clay reported, "5 that we kept in Town had it to a Violent degree, 2 of whom are Dead; the other three seem likely to do well. We have not made any further attempt to get them on your Land," he continued, "nor shall not till they are all Strong and hearty." As a result, backcountry migrations probably comprised mainly people from the middle of a spectrum of fitness for work and travel. The most coveted slaves (the healthy and strong) and those from the opposite end of the spectrum (those most debilitated from the ocean voyage) tended to remain closer to port, at least initially.[28]

The distances Africans traveled ranged from fifty miles or more to the piedmont in midcentury to hundreds of miles into the interior around the turn of the nineteenth century. In 1755, Austin and Laurens vended a group of Africans in Charleston for Thomas Easton and Co. of Bristol and reported a delay in resolving a dispute with Daniel Heyward, the buyer of several captives, because "He lives near 100 miles distance and writes us there was a mistake of £200 in casting up the Sum total of his Slaves." Austin and Laurens had to wait for Heyward to return his receipt before they could assess whether they had indeed made a mistake. Heyward's plantation was southwest of Charleston on the Combahee River, so the Africans he purchased probably traveled by sea as far as Beaufort and then either up the river by boat or overland to the plantation—a journey of several days by any route. At another sale that year, Austin and Laurens noted, "There were forty or fifty [buyers] that came upwards of Seventy Miles distance." In the 1770s, Peter Manigault reported even more extreme journeys, observing that some backcountry planters "come at the Distance of 300 miles from Chs Town, and will not go back without Negroes, let the Price be what it will." For Africans bound to the Virginia piedmont, the overland journey must also have been considerable. Bermuda Hundred probably served as the most frequent point of disembarkation for piedmont-bound people. From there, the closest and most populous piedmont county, Amelia, was a fifty-mile overland journey. To Charlotte County, where Paul Carrington marched his fifty Angolan captives for resale, the trip was nearly

ratios in Kentucky during the early national period but does not note the presence of recently arrived Africans (Eslinger, "The Shape of Slavery on the Kentucky Frontier, 1775–1800," *Register of the Kentucky Historical Society*, XCII [1994], 14).

28. Clay to Benjamin Stead, Sept. 16, 1775, Clay and Co. Letter Books, 1772–1776, II.

one hundred miles, and these were hard, slow miles on eighteenth-century roads and trails.[29]

Conditions on the journey varied. It is plausible that some people marched in coffles—walking chain gangs, in which at least adult males were shackled to one another. I have found no direct evidence for this practice in eighteenth-century North America, but coffles were common in Africa at the time and were witnessed by English slave traders. In his abolitionist exposé on the slave trade in 1789, Thomas Clarkson recounted an English trader's description of how African slave dealers moved captives overland to the coast:

> They come in droves of three or four hundred at a time. The women and boys are permitted to walk freely. The men, however, are confined; the arms of some of the latter are tied behind them. Two or three others are tied together by means of leathern thongs, or ropes of grass, at the neck. Two others are confined by means of a pole, at each end of which is a crutch to put the neck in. . . . Their two necks being placed in the crutches . . . are confined in them by leather thongs. . . . Such a body of slaves is called a *cauffle*.

Precisely when American slave traders adopted this practice for controlling people on marches is unclear, but coffles certainly appeared in the United States in the nineteenth century. In the eighteenth century, most Africans headed for the interior probably traveled in smaller groups, so if coffles were used, they were probably rare.[30]

For those traveling in small groups with a new owner, or perhaps his emissary, wagon travel was common—and by no means comfortable. Eighteenth-century roads were rough, and wagons were designed for hauling produce and goods, not seating passengers. William Ancrum instructed an overseer to "charge the Waggoner to be particularly careful that [the indigo crop] does not get wet by Rain or the Badness of the Road," suggesting both that the wagons offered poor protection from the elements and that the roads were rutted and potholed enough to risk tossing a load. Such a ride had to be uncomfortable

29. Austin and Laurens to Thomas Easton and Co., July 31, 1755, in *Laurens Papers*, I, 306; Austin and Laurens to Henry Weare and Co., July 2, 1755, ibid., 281–282; *Voyages*, accessed August 2011, Voyage ID no. 17339; Klein, *Unification of a Slave State*, 20.

30. Thomas Clarkson, *The Substance of the Evidence of Sundry Persons on the Slave-Trade, Collected in the Course of a Tour Made in the Autumn of the Year 1788* (London, 1789), 35. For evidence of coffles in the nineteenth-century U.S., see Deyle, *Carry Me Back*, esp. 146–147; Robert H. Gudmestad, "Slave Resistance, Coffles, and the Debates over Slavery in the Nation's Capital," in Johnson, ed., *Chattel Principle*, 72–90; Tadman, *Speculators and Slaves*, 8, 47–48, 71–78.

for any enslaved people on the wagon's return journey. In fact, captives sent overland with wagons might not have been allowed to ride within, as planters often sought space for their goods aboard infrequent wagons headed to the backcountry. Joseph Clay's apology to a backcountry acquaintance was typical when he was "very sorry to inform you the [hogshead of] bottle'd Porter was left behind" by a group of wagons heading out of Savannah. "I try'd all I cou'd to get them to take it but they said 'twas impossible." African people did not travel with this particular caravan, but given the premium for space on such wagons, they often must have been forced to travel on foot.[31]

In any case, journeys to the backcountry could take many days. In 1798, James Sanders Guignard described a trip to Columbia, South Carolina, as "three days Journey from Charleston," but he almost certainly covered the 115 miles on horseback. Furthermore, Columbia was among the largest inland towns, well connected to Charleston by road in 1798. Travel to more remote areas was slower and more arduous. For such journeys of more than one day, little evidence survives with regard to where enslaved people slept, but conditions must have been rugged. Few taverns and inns were available for eighteenth-century travelers in British or early national America, and where such facilities existed, they were surely not afforded for slaves. In 1804, Guignard instructed an employee to assess the logistics of travel between Orangeburg, in the South Carolina backcountry, and Charleston. Guignard's main concern seemed to be finding care for horses along the route, and he made no mention of slaves, but his query suggests a lack of infrastructure for travelers. He complained that "Coburn's old place," the closest site he knew for spending the night, was "rather too far from Charleston," so he instructed his agent to "enquire at Dorchester and at all other Houses on the Road between Dorchester and Charleston" for another lodging option. If this was the situation by 1804, one imagines even scarcer accommodations in the mid-eighteenth century. Wayfarers had to rely on friends and even strangers for lodging, so those traveling with African migrants probably forced them to camp out or found space for them in someone's barn or the slave quarters of a plantation.[32]

When Paul Carrington marched his fifty Angolan captives to the Vir-

31. Ancrum to Marlow Pryor, Oct. 29, 1778, William Ancrum Letter Book; Clay to [?], June 9, 1789, Clay Papers, IV, 341–342.

32. James S. Guignard to "Grandmama" [Sarah S. Sanders?], Dec. 28, 1798, Guignard Family Papers, legal-sized folder 3, SCL; James Sanders Guignard, "Directions for W. M. Jervaine," [April 1804], ibid., letter-sized folder 4. Moncks Corner emerged as a sort of traveler's town in the late eighteenth century, offering accommodations to voyagers to and from the backcountry; see Klein, *Unification of a Slave State*, 19.

ginia piedmont for resale, he housed them at his own plantation while seeking buyers. The process took at least six months, since he made the speculative purchase in May and then bought warm clothing for fourteen Angolans who remained unsold that fall. Lodging recently arrived Africans among seasoned slaves and shipping captives with black wagoners or riverboat sailors brought opportunities for interaction between Africans and African Americans. Through these encounters, one can picture the migrants gleaning much about the geography, the circumstances, and the hierarchical societies they were entering.[33]

Regardless of whether such contacts with African Americans ameliorated conditions for arriving Africans or offered companionship or information, at least some enterprising captives found opportunity in the overland journeys (and waiting periods). Despite the hardship of additional travel after surviving ocean passages, some African immigrants seized the time on land—and perhaps traveling through remote areas—to flee enslavement. Having escaped the confines of the slave ship surrounded by the moat of the ocean, and having possibly had several days of fresh food and drink to recover their strength before sale, many Africans attempted escape shortly after landing. Advertisements for runaways rarely described the circumstances of a person's escape, but a striking number referred to African-born individuals who only recently disembarked from the Middle Passage—especially in the second half of the eighteenth century, when overland journeys grew longer and more common. The *South-Carolina Gazette* frequently published descriptions of captured runaways brought to the "work house" in Charleston, if their owners could not be contacted directly to reclaim them. Among the most common reasons why an owner could not be notified was that the captives were described as speaking no English and not knowing whom their masters were. In 1753, the *Gazette* reported the arrival at the workhouse of "A lusty new negro man, can't tell his master's name, with a white negro cloth jacket, and a new duffil blanket." The following year, the *Gazette* mentioned "A new negro, about 5 feet 2 inches high, cannot tell his own or master's name, has a large bump on his left hand, with his country marks on each side of his temples, above and below his navel." Similar announcements appeared every week or two. Of course, runaways who did speak English might have played dumb in order to avoid return to a particularly abusive master or overseer, but the workhouse cannot have been a pleasant place, and the men placing the announcements in the *Gazette* were probably not fools. Their routine description of captured

33. Morgan and Nicholls, "Slaves in Piedmont Virginia," *WMQ*, 3d Ser., XLVI (1989), 212.

runaways as "new negroes" suggests that many captives spent very little time in the colonies before attempting flight, an impression reinforced by frequent descriptions of their clothing and blankets as "new." Some of these people likely absconded during their journeys from port to plantation.[34]

Slaveholders' advertisements reinforce this picture of Africans escaping shortly after disembarking in North America. Of eighty advertised runaways in the *South Carolina Gazette* in 1760, sixteen (20 percent) were described as "new negroes," who spoke no English and who often did not yet have names assigned by their masters. In 1765, the percentage of "new negroes" among advertised escapees was slightly higher, accounting for eleven of forty-six runaways (24 percent). Most advertisements did not specify precisely where enslaved people were when they made their bid for freedom, but in some cases, the last phase of the slave trade offered the chance. In 1765, William Harris announced, "A New Negro GIRL, about 13 or 14 years of age, was sent on shore at Hobacaw [Hobcaw], out of the ship Elizabeth, Capt. McNeill," which had recently arrived from Africa, "from whence she has either lost herself in the woods, or is taken away, and harboured, by some person or persons." In assuming a teenage girl could not have fled (rather than being lost or stolen), Harris, like many slaveholders, made an infantilizing assumption—that runaways were taken or enticed in their disappearance. Later that same month, Joseph Kershaw placed another advertisement suggesting a possible escape between the Middle Passage and the plantation: "RAN away from the subscriber, on Sunday the 28th of July, four new negro men, lately purchased of Brailsford and Chapman," who were frequent importers of African people. Overall, the ongoing migration of captives after surviving the Middle Passage prolonged their difficult journeys into slavery—full of death, abuse, and coercion—but these advertisements suggest that solid ground and perhaps inland transit provided some forced migrants with a long-awaited opportunity to resist their enslavement.[35]

■ In many ways, the forced migration of enslaved people from Atlantic entrepôts to the North American hinterlands marked the integration of the back-

34. For the particular "work house" announcements mentioned, see *South-Carolina Gazette*, Nov. 16, 1753, Jan. 22–29, 1754.

35. *South-Carolina Gazette*, Aug. 3, 26, 1765. Overall statistics compiled from advertisements cited in Ruth Holmes Whitehead, comp., "Searchable CD-ROM transcription of runaway slave advertisements in Charleston newspapers, 1732–1785," P 900062, SCDAH. On slaveholders' demeaning assumption that runaways had been stolen or lured away rather than fled of their own initiative, see Morgan, *Laboring Women*, 179–180.

country and the Atlantic economy. For the planters settling the up-country, this distribution of African people helped link them to the market economy and the coastal elite (in addition to providing labor for new plantations). The development of a slaveholding class in the backcountry began, not with the advent of the cotton gin in 1793, but in the mid-eighteenth century—a process that gradually unified political interests across the South in a shared commitment to slavery, as opposed to a Jeffersonian backcountry of independent yeomen. The dispersal of Africans to the hinterlands not only provided enslaved labor but also fostered connections between remote planters and elites in and near the mercantile centers. Backcountry planters sought connections to Atlantic markets in order to acquire needed laborers, and their very desire for slaves reflected their commercial orientation—their dream of shifting the North American backcountry to large-scale staple-crop production for the Atlantic marketplace. In recent decades, historians have debated slavery's relationship to capitalism, with some arguing that the eighteenth-century backcountry was "precapitalist—or noncapitalist"—because the backcountry's move to slavery "inhibited the development of a labor market." But this analysis rests on a narrow definition of a labor market. To be sure, slavery stifled the development of free wage labor, but as study of the intercolonial slave trade shows, the slave system created a thoroughgoing labor market. Instead of commodifying labor, Euro-American settlers commodified the laborers themselves in order to maximize production, exchange, and profits. The price of laborers was openly negotiated, and merchants bought, moved, and resold people to capitalize on variations between markets. This was a market logic taken to the extreme, though an extreme that later capitalist thinkers would deem antithetical to "free" market capitalism. Given the experiences of enslaved people in this trade and the vital role that slavery played in the growth of the hinterlands, the dispersal of Africans outward from the Atlantic entrepôts was a crucial stage in the slave trade and an important step in linking the interior of North America to the slave system and the Atlantic marketplace.[36]

Recognizing the connection of Atlantic entrepôts and remote markets in the eighteenth century suggests that slave migration to the backcountry should be

36. Klein argues that the expansion of slavery in the South Carolina was vital for unifying the political interests of backcountry landowners with their counterparts in the Lowcountry (*Unification of a Slave State*), but she also describes the backcountry as "precapitalist" (3–4). My work is more compatible with portrayals of African slavery in the Americas as a capitalist enterprise rather than a precursor to capitalism. See Johnson, *Chattel Principle*, esp. 7–9; Jeffrey Robert Young, *Domesticating Slavery: The Master Class in Georgia and South Carolina, 1670–1837* (Chapel Hill, N.C., 1999), esp. 4–5.

considered in two phases. Just as eighteenth-century traders marched arriving Africans from Atlantic ports to backcountry regions, interstate traders in the nineteenth century would march African American slaves from older Atlantic states to the southwestern frontier of Mississippi, Alabama, and Louisiana. Despite such continuity of a westward migration of enslaved people and the slave system, the pre- and post-1808 migrations differed in a key respect. Until 1808, arriving Africans composed much of this inland migration. Backcountry planters ventured to Atlantic markets to buy laborers, and speculators purchased arriving Africans for resale inland. Only gradually, from the Revolutionary era onward, did American-born slaves overtake Africans as the primary captives in the intra-American slave trade that fed the burgeoning Cotton Kingdom.

8. American Slave Trade, American Free Trade

CLIMAX OF THE INTERCOLONIAL SLAVE TRADE, CA. 1750–1807

[Dominica slave dealers] sell as well to the French and Spaniards . . . as to our Planters of B.Bs. [Barbados] Antigua and Dominica; so that under these circumstances, Dominica seems to bid fairer to render you advantageous sales, than any other Island. —Thomas Lanwarn, 1770

From 1751 to 1800, European and American merchants forced nearly four million Africans across the Atlantic and into American slavery. Those four million captives account for almost one-third of all people who endured the Middle Passage in its entire 350-year history. Plantation economies grew dramatically as the emerging consumer economy in the Atlantic world spurred demand for luxury commodities, such as sugar, tobacco, and coffee. New colonies emerged and old colonies pushed out frontiers, clearing new land for staple-crop production. Enslaved labor powered this growth, which, in turn, fueled demand for more slaves. Traders crossing the Atlantic found steadily increasing numbers of American markets clamoring for human cargoes, and many older markets demanded more captives than ever before.[1]

One might expect such expansion to have undercut the need for intercolonial dispersals since transatlantic traders dealt directly with more American markets than previously, but instead, the growth of transatlantic commerce fostered similar expansion of intercolonial trade. The second half of the eighteenth century was the heyday of the entire American slave trade, transatlantic and intra-American. Several factors ensured that intercolonial trade grew alongside the expanding transatlantic commerce. For one thing, the volatility

1. Estimates of the transatlantic slave trade and the share carried by various nations derived from *Voyages: The Trans-Atlantic Slave Trade Database,* accessed September 2011, http://slave voyages.org/tast/assessment/estimates.faces?yearFrom=1501&yearTo=1866. On sugar's transition from luxury to perceived necessity (and the connection of its rise to the increased consumption of tea, coffee, and chocolate), see Sidney W. Mintz, *Sweetness and Power: The Place of Sugar in Modern History* (New York, 1985), xxix, 37–38, 45, 108–150; Philip D. Curtin, *The Rise and Fall of the Plantation Complex,* 2d ed. (1990; rpt. New York, 1998), 178.

of the Atlantic world in the late eighteenth century made it difficult for traders to keep abreast of changes in imperial borders, market demand, and trade regulations. Within British America, key routes of transshipment shifted as the empire changed shape. The British Caribbean expanded in the Seven Years' War, the French Revolutionary War, and the American War of Independence, with the seizures of new island colonies and territories on the Caribbean littoral, such as Dominica, Grenada, Demerara, Tobago, and Trinidad. As British settlers rushed to claim land in these colonies and to turn them to staple production, intercolonial traders adapted quickly, establishing new routes of transshipment. Intercolonial merchants also adjusted to the shrinking of Britain's empire in North America, where U.S. Independence cut off long-standing routes of intercolonial slave trading not only by severing the mainland colonies' political ties to the British Empire but also by intermittently severing economic ties through trade embargoes. Revolutionary ideology also gave rise to antislavery sentiment in some corners, so most of the new states never revived their slave importation after the War of Independence. Those states that did resume African importation, however, created other opportunities for intra-American traders, who could react more quickly to changing political and ideological winds than their counterparts who sailed from Africa. In an era of upheaval, the ability to adapt gave intercolonial traders—with their shorter lines of trade and communication—some key advantages to offset the African traders' edge in prices paid for enslaved people.

Another circumstance contributing to this expansion of intercolonial slave trading was Britain's ascendancy in the transatlantic trade. As the slave trade grew, British merchants secured a greater proportion of it, spurring the intercolonial trade to foreign colonies. From 1701 to 1750, British (including colonial) traders carried about 39 percent of all Africans delivered to the Americas. From 1751 to 1775, the British share of the transatlantic slave trade increased to about 48 percent—a significantly larger slice of a much larger pie. In just those twenty-five years, British traders transported well over 900,000 African men, women, and children to the New World, versus fewer than 600,000 people in the previous twenty-five-year period. From 1776 to 1800, the British (and U.S.) share of the total transatlantic slave trade fell back to about 41 percent, but this decline owed largely to a major lull during the years of the War of Independence. In the nonwar years, the British share remained larger.[2]

2. Estimates of the transatlantic slave trade and the share carried by various nations derived from *Voyages,* accessed September 2011, http://slavevoyages.org/tast/assessment/estimates.faces

Of course, Britain's stranglehold on transatlantic slaving did not stop planters in foreign empires from seeking exploitable African labor. On the contrary, Spanish and French colonies, especially in the Caribbean, greatly expanded their plantation agriculture in the mid- to late eighteenth century. Cuban slavery grew considerably, especially after the Seven Years' War, although Cuba's enslaved people still worked in a more diversified economy than was typical of other Caribbean colonies. Saint-Domingue's rise was more dramatic—and more plantation oriented. Between the War of the Austrian Succession (1740–1748) and the outbreak of the Haitian Revolution in 1791, the colony emerged from relative obscurity to lead the Caribbean in sugar production. Slave labor, of course, powered the phenomenal growth. By the middle of the eighteenth century, Saint-Domingue often imported more than ten thousand African people annually, and the forced immigration only escalated in the 1770s and 1780s. In 1790, arrivals peaked with more than 40,000 Africans disembarking in the colony in that year alone. As these slave economies blossomed in French and Spanish America, British dominance in the transatlantic trade ensured that Spanish and French slave traders would struggle to meet the burgeoning demand in their colonies. Frustrated French and Spanish planters in ever-greater numbers turned to British suppliers instead, often looking no further than a neighboring British island where a bustling port served as an entrepôt of the slave trade. In this commerce between British traders and French and Spanish buyers, imperial borders, paradoxically, represented obstacles to transatlantic slavers but offered opportunities to intercolonial dealers. Coming from Africa with huge cargoes of enslaved people, transatlantic traders typically considered ventures to foreign colonies too risky, leaving intercolonial merchants a chance for profits if they could navigate the rocky shoals of imperial politics to access nearby foreign markets.[3]

?yearFrom=1501&yearTo=1866; note that estimates of the British Empire's share before 1775 require adding the total for the U.S. to the total for Great Britain on *Voyages,* since the colonies that became the United States were still part of the British Empire.

3. Cuban historiography contains significant disagreement over the timing of the growth of Cuba's plantation sector. Many scholars, especially those studying the nineteenth century and later, depict such growth as a consequence of Spain's loosening restrictions on the foreign slave trade, starting in 1789, partly to capitalize on the collapse of sugar production in Saint-Domingue; see Juan Pérez de la Riva, *El Barracón: Esclavitud y capitalismo en Cuba* (1975; rpt. Barcelona, 1978), 13–14. Likewise, Sherry Johnson describes 1789 as the turning point in the Cuban sugar industry's expansion, although she acknowledges that the island was already home to 90,000 people of African descent by 1792, who presumably worked in ranching, domestic service, and various agricultural tasks (Johnson, *The Social Transformation of Eighteenth-Century*

So crucial to the plantation system was this slave trading across imperial borders that it prompted policy makers on all sides of the divide to reevaluate mercantilist strictures limiting foreign trade. Traditionally opposed to foreign commerce, French and Spanish officials loosened regulations to facilitate the acquisition of African laborers for colonial plantations. Spanish policy for Cuba began to encourage slave importation after the Seven Years' War to spur the colony's growth (and its ability to defend itself) by allowing Cuban settlers limited rights to acquire African people in foreign colonies. African immigration to Cuba especially accelerated (and to Puerto Rico and Santo Domingo, to a lesser degree) after 1789, when Spain eliminated restrictions altogether on purchasing slaves in foreign colonies. With a similar thirst for labor in their booming sugar colonies, French officials also relaxed restrictions on foreign trade in the late eighteenth century. Meanwhile, British policy makers remained keen to sell Africans in Spanish and French America—and remained hopeful such trading could entice foreign colonies into broader trading relationships. In the decades following the 1739 collapse of the South Sea Company's asiento, British policy makers soured on the prospect of another large-scale slave trade agreement with Spain and abandoned the idea of a monopoly joint-stock company managing such commerce. Instead, British policy makers chased the foreign slave trade with new policies. After a wartime lull from the 1740s to the mid-1760s, the British reinvigorated intercolonial slave commerce by declaring several Caribbean ports open to foreign trade in specified commodities, including enslaved African people. Instead of establishing trading houses on foreign soil, British leaders hoped to draw foreign buyers to British

---

Cuba [Gainesville, Fla., 2001], 14, 27, 57, 127). Other scholars see the British occupation of Havana in 1762–1763 as a turning point toward large-scale importation of enslaved Africans; see Dale Tomich, "The Wealth of Empire: Francisco Arango y Parreño, Political Economy, and the Second Slavery in Cuba," *Comparative Studies in Society and History*, XLV (2003), 8; Evelyn Powell Jennings, "War as the 'Forcing House of Change': State Slavery in Late-Eighteenth-Century Cuba," *William and Mary Quarterly*, 3d Ser., LXII (2005), 411–440; Jennings, "In the Eye of the Storm: The Spanish Colonial State and African Enslavement in Havana, 1763–1790," *Historical Reflections*, XXIX (2003), 145–162; Hugh Thomas, *Cuba: The Pursuit of Freedom* (New York, 1971), 52–53. Elena Andrea Schneider argues convincingly for a more gradual rise of the plantation economy, even before 1762, powered by significant (often illegal) slave importation from Jamaica; see Schneider, "The Occupation of Havana: War, Trade, and Slavery in Eighteenth-Century Cuba" (Ph.D. diss., Princeton University, 2011). For estimates of African arrivals in Saint-Domingue, see *Voyages,* accessed September 2011, http://slavevoyages.org/tast/assessment /estimates.faces?yearFrom=1501&yearTo=1866&disembarkation=401. See also David Geggus, "The French Slave Trade: An Overview," *WMQ*, 3d Ser., LVIII (2001), 119–138; Herbert S. Klein, *The Atlantic Slave Trade* (New York, 1999), 30–34.

colonies by removing trade barriers. The resulting "free ports" quickly rose to prominence in slave transshipment, furthering the centralization of slave trading through major American entrepôts from which African men, women, and children endured subsequent intra-American voyages.

The impulse to acquire unfree workers or to profit from their sale was driving Atlantic empires toward free trade. Where earlier policy makers sometimes created ad hoc exemptions to mercantilist policies to facilitate the sale or acquisition of African laborers, late-eighteenth-century imperialists pushed new laws to unfetter trade from bonds limiting the growth of slavery and the plantation economy it supported. The growth of free trade and of the slave trade went hand in hand. But the contrast between free trade and mercantilism should not be rendered too starkly. Mercantilism had always involved exceptions to trade restrictions when foreign commerce seemed advantageous to one government or another. Under mercantilism, empires were never hermetically sealed. Furthermore, "free trade" rarely involves completely deregulated commerce. Just as the freedom that emerged from the American Revolution was granted to some people at the expense of others—most notably, the millions of enslaved people—the freer trade that emerged in the Americas in the late eighteenth century was limited, crafted by rival empires to advance their hegemony over commerce or territory throughout the Atlantic world. The enormous demand for slave labor in the Americas encouraged many Atlantic empires to experiment with trade policies that would eventually become tenets of the new free trade ideology, furthering the paradoxical ties between American slavery and American freedom. Merchants gained greater freedom to trade people they kept in chains.[4]

■ For the intercolonial slave trade from British colonies to foreign territories, the rupture of the asiento (with the outbreak of the War of Jenkins' Ear in 1739) touched off decades of disruption and reorganization, exacerbated by

4. The title of this chapter and this discussion of the links between slavery and freedom is, of course, an homage to Edmund S. Morgan's pioneering work exploring colonial Virginians' seemingly paradoxical embrace of both chattel slavery and a Revolutionary ideology embracing personal liberty (Morgan, *American Slavery, American Freedom: The Ordeal of Colonial Virginia* [New York, 1975]); see also Adam Rothman, *Slave Country: American Expansion and the Origins of the Deep South* (Cambridge, Mass., 2005), xi. Jeremy Adelman notes a link between Spanish Americans' successful lobbying for loosening restrictions on the slave trade from 1789 to 1791 and growing calls in the empire for free trade more generally; see Adelman, *Sovereignty and Revolution in the Iberian Atlantic* (Princeton, 2006), 84–88; see also Tomich, "Wealth of Empire," *Comparative Studies in Society and History*, XLV (2003), 6.

a series of imperial wars for control of the Americas. In the 1740s, during the War of the Austrian Succession, British deliveries of African people across the Atlantic declined by nearly 30 percent from the prior decade. Transshipments of such people to foreign colonies plummeted. The prominence and efficiency of British transatlantic traders and the persistence of labor demand in French and Spanish America ensured that the disruptions of war would not stymie intercolonial trade permanently, but from the 1740s to the early 1760s, war largely distracted the British government from its traditional support for such commerce. From the early 1660s (when the Privy Council first exempted the Navigation Acts to allow exports of enslaved Africans from English colonies) to the Treaty of Utrecht in 1713 (when the British demanded the asiento de negros for the South Sea Company), the British Empire had consistently promoted the slave trade to foreign colonies and seen such trade grow steadily. But during the War of Jenkins' Ear, the War of the Austrian Succession, and then the Seven Years' War, British policy makers were too preoccupied to attend to the slave trade. As a result, the trade across imperial boundaries in these decades was haphazard and localized, with intercolonial traders (and aspiring slaveholders) struggling to navigate the turbulent waters without government support.[5]

After 1739, with the South Sea Company's monopoly derailed, many independent British traders sought to fill the void left by the company in supplying enslaved people to Spanish America. (Some of these traders had likely been interlopers or traders licensed by the company before its demise.) Already in 1740, British merchants Lascelles and Maxwell schemed for a delivery of enslaved people to the Spanish Main, instructing their factor in Barbados that any of their African ships arriving in Barbados should be sent on to Jamaica, where Spanish demand still ensured "that Negroes sell very well." With British "Admiral Vernon having demolished the [Spanish] fortifications at Portobello," intercolonial smugglers, who violated Spanish prohibitions on foreign trade, felt safe to "carry over a number of slaves and other goods and expect to meet with no interruption in trading." The scale of such illegal commerce is difficult to determine, but there were other reports of such clandestine activity in the period. In 1747, during the waning stages of the War of the Austrian Succession, a group of Jamaica merchants even "agreed to supply the Royal Company of the Havannah with Negroes and provisions," leading the Spanish company to send "Don Pedro de Estrada, a Spanish Gentleman to

5. For estimates of various nations' transatlantic slave trades, see *Voyages*, accessed September 2011, http://slavevoyages.org/tast/assessment/estimates.faces?yearFrom=1701&yearTo=1750.

reside [in Kingston] and manage the Affair," despite the ongoing war between Britain and Spain.[6]

Jamaican traders were not alone in capitalizing on the South Sea Company's demise. British traders in the eastern Caribbean also probed for openings to Spanish America. The owners of the snow *Caesar,* bound to Africa to acquire human cargo, probably sought sales to the Spanish (or perhaps the French) when they instructed skipper William Ellery to deliver the captives to British Saint Christopher in 1759. The traders explained that Saint Christopher was "handy to St. Eustatia's," a Dutch entrepôt open to foreign trade that often served as a link between foreign colonies prohibited from trading with one another. Likewise, John Guerard of Charleston hoped to use New Providence—a relative backwater in the British Bahamas—as a similar hub for Spanish trade, having heard that Spanish traders often visited. The scheme he contemplated would have required multiple transshipments. In 1754, he instructed Captain Richard Watts in Barbados that, if no commodities from that island seemed promising for resale in Charleston, Watts should buy Africans for transshipment to New Providence. "In Such Case you may Purchase the full Number of Negroes . . . but Let me beg of you to take none but what is Likely and young, free from Disorders in mind, body, or any Defect whatsoever, all men. The Spaniards are very nice [i.e., picky] in Negroes." To sell from a position of strength, Guerard also suggested, "Should you go to Providence I must further Observe to you that you may perhaps do your Business to more advantage if you were to Feign the want of something and that you put in there rather by Accident than Choice." Under the pretense of a temporarily interrupted journey to some other market, Guerard hoped that Watts could entice the Spanish to offer high prices meant to dissuade him from carrying his African captives elsewhere. This plan was not put to the test, however, because Watts ultimately headed to Charleston from Barbados without slaves.[7]

6. Lascelles and Maxwell to Richard Morecroft, Mar. 28, 1740, Lascelles and Maxwell Letter Books, 1739–1769, microfilm, 97601/2, I, fol. 33, Milton S. Eisenhower Library, Johns Hopkins University, Baltimore, Md.; John Bannister to Hubert Lascelles, Nov. 14, 1747, in Elizabeth Donnan, ed., *Documents Illustrative of the History of the Slave Trade to America,* 4 vols. (Washington, D.C., 1930–1935), III, 141–142; see also Schneider, "Occupation of Havana," 52–55. Trevor Burnard and Kenneth Morgan also note a lull in Jamaica's export slave trade between 1739 and the resumption of large-scale transshipment in the 1760s (Burnard and Morgan, "The Dynamics of the Slave Market and Slave Purchasing Patterns in Jamaica, 1655–1788," *WMQ,* 3d Ser., LVIII [2001], 210).

7. "Instructions to Captain William Ellery," Jan. 14, 1759, in Donnan, ed., *Documents,* III, 68–69 (Dutch islands also served as important neutral sites for trade between the British, French, and Spanish during the imperial wars of the mid-eighteenth century; see Thomas M. Truxes, *De-*

Such routes of transshipment—from Saint Christopher to Saint Eustatius to Spanish America, or from Barbados to the Bahamas to Spanish colonies—were not common, but such convoluted schemes for selling Africans to the Spanish illustrate the difficult, faltering nature of British foreign transshipments at midcentury. With the expansion of British transatlantic trafficking and the removal of the South Sea Company from the largest branch of intercolonial dispersal, private British traders scrambled for access to lucrative Spanish American markets. The trade did not halt altogether, but it was irregular and complicated—and probably especially bewildering and dangerous for captives. To make matters worse for British promoters and practitioners of the slave trade, rival empires also worked to fill the void in the trade to Spanish America. Dutch, French, and Portuguese traders all increased their transatlantic deliveries of Africans during this moment of British regression, and the Dutch entrepôt of Curaçao saw a particular resurgence of commerce with Spanish America in the 1740s and 1750s. Distracted by wars, British policy makers left their slave traders to their own devices in attempting to sustain the Spanish American trade.[8]

The disruption of British commerce to Spanish America also frustrated the potential customers in foreign colonies. By 1761, the governor of Cuba recognized so much desperation for labor in his territory that he sent local merchant Juan de Miralles on a yearlong journey to Jamaica, Barbados, Amsterdam, London, Saint Eustatius, and Martinique, seeking connections that would facilitate a steadier supply of Africans. The Spanish crown rebuked the governor for encouraging such violation of Spanish trade laws, but his willingness to sponsor Miralles's quest for contraband attests to the pent-up demand. Similar zeal for acquiring Africans is indicated by an offer that Philadelphia merchant Thomas Riche received from prospective Cuban slave buyers in 1766. Cubans' contacting Pennsylvania for slaves indicates that in the decades after the collapse of the British asiento, the trade worked to the satisfaction of neither British merchants nor Spanish slaveholders.[9]

———
fying Empire: Trading with the Enemy in Colonial New York [New Haven, Conn., 2008], 2–5); John Guerard to Richard Watts, Mar. 6, 1754, John Guerard Letter Book, 1752–1754, 34/0321 OvrSz, fols. 235–238, South Carolina Historical Society, Charleston.

8. For the resurgence of Curaçao's trade with Spanish America in the 1740s, see Johannes Postma, "The Dispersal of African Slaves in the West by Dutch Slave Traders, 1630–1803," in Joseph E. Inikori and Stanley L. Engerman, eds., *The Atlantic Slave Trade: Effects on Economies, Societies, and Peoples in Africa, the Americas, and Europe* (Durham, N.C., 1992), 292–293.

9. Schneider, "Occupation of Havana," 3–4; Thomas Riche to Henry White, [ca. Aug. 10,

British intercolonial traders enjoyed somewhat more success in shipping enslaved people to French colonies. French officials continued to bar foreign traders, but with the French plantation economy booming, demand for enslaved people was enormous. Plus, French traders to Africa failed to keep pace, probably delivering fewer than half of the forced immigrants around midcentury. As Governor General Maximin de Bompar of Martinique described the situation to France in 1754, "We have 25 to 30,000 negroes fewer than we need in Martinique for manufacturing and for the exploitation of the land." Both French planters and British intercolonial traders worked to evade the restrictive trade laws with slave transshipments across the border.[10]

They devised a variety of strategies to circumvent the restrictions. One method was the continued use of neutral islands, sparsely settled by Europeans, as points of exchange. When asserting their vigilance in suppressing foreign trade to superiors in France—and defending their failures—French colonial officials often noted the difficulty of patrolling the many secluded harbors on nearby islands. As Governor General Bompar explained in 1753, "The foreign trade that is conducted at the contested islands . . . will be impossible to stop . . . unless we occupy them permanently." There were simply too many sites for French administrators to patrol. Some French buyers smuggled captives directly from British territory by avoiding major French harbors, disembarking in hidden backwaters instead. The prevalence of such activity led Bompar and Intendant Charles-Marin Hurson to introduce a regulation in 1754 that outlawed slave sales outside Martinique's primary port town, Saint Pierre, where officials could best monitor trade. As they explained the law's rationale to administrators in France, colonists too readily found "pretext for selling their Negroes in the interior of the island, where they have introduced a great number from foreign sources." Such trade was significant enough that John Guerard complained about its impact on the intercolonial slave trade

---

1764,] Thomas Riche Letter Book, II, 1764–1771, Am 9261, Historical Society of Pennsylvania. On the frustrations of aspiring Cuban slaveholders with the limited slave trade in the wake of the British asiento, see Thomas, *Cuba*, 31.

10. Maximin de Bompar to the Council of Trade, Nov. 29, 1754, Archives Nationales d'Outre-Mer, Aix-en-Provence (hereafter cited as ANOM), C8A, 60, fols. 276–278 ("Nous avons 25 à 30000 nègres demoins a la Martinique qu'il n'en faudrois pour les manufacture et l'exploitation des terres"). See also M. Cazotte to Council of Trade, May 11, 1754, ibid., fol. 295–297. On the scale of the foreign slave trade to French colonies, Robert Louis Stein estimates that French traders carried just 45 percent of slaves imported between 1740 and 1760 (*The French Slave Trade in the Eighteenth Century: An Old Regime Business* [Madison, Wis., 1979], 25–27, 109–110).

within the British Empire. In 1753, he lamented, "There was no Likelywood" that slave prices in Barbados would "fall Considerably" enough to make transshipment to Charleston viable because there was so much demand in Barbados from traders looking "to Supply the French Islands." A decade later, French officials in Guadeloupe also deemed the "very considerable" contraband trade enough of a threat to warrant a proposal for emancipating slaves who offered information on smugglers and their practices. When a slave society contemplated manumitting the enslaved to solve a problem, it was a sure sign that problem was serious.[11]

This surreptitious trade between British and French colonies delivered hundreds of enslaved Africans annually to the French Caribbean around mid-century. As in previous decades, captives ensnared in such illegal commerce endured not only extended and complicated journeys but also the dangers of clandestine trade. The survivors also continued to diversify slave quarters in the French Caribbean, since the French slave trade was becoming increasingly reliant on west central Africa, alongside the Bight of Benin, whereas the nearby British colonies drew nearly half of their captives from the Bight of Biafra, with the Gold Coast a distant second. Given the divergent sources of supply for the French and British African trades, intercolonial trade between the empires surely mingled people of diverse backgrounds together (Figure 9).

11. Bompar and Gurdon to Council of Trade, Dec. 24, 1753, ANOM, C8A, 60, fol. 43–44 ("commerce étranger qui fais dans les isles contentieuses . . . nous ajoutions qu'il en impossible de l'empêcher, es rien n'en place vrai, mais non de le genev [geneo?], es c'est ce dont nous sommes occuper continuellement"); Bompar and Charles-Marin Hurson to Council of Trade, Mar. 6, 1754, ibid., fols. 224–226 ("le prétexte de vendre ces Nègres dans l'intérieur de l'isle, ou en a introduit un grand nombre provenant de l'Étranger"). Smuggling Africans into French colonies was by no means easy, however, as evidenced by Philadelphia merchant Thomas Riche's struggles to open a slave trade to Cayenne (now French Guiana) on the northern coast of South America in the mid-1760s. Riche secured the cooperation of Cayenne merchants and the blessing of Cayenne officials to send shipments of enslaved people, both directly "from the Coast of Africa" and indirectly via British colonies, only to have the arrangement blocked at the last minute by officials in France "to the manifest prejudice and hurt of [his] Intriest"; see Riche to Barnard Gormain, May 8, 1766, Riche Letter Book, 1764–1771, fol. 341. Many of Riche's other letters also refer to his plans for and frustrations with the thwarted Cayenne trade; see especially Riche to William Vernon, Nov. 13, 1764, and Riche to William Stoddart, Nov. 22, 1764. "There was no Likelywood": Guerard to Harrington and Strick, John Guerard Letter Book, fol. 197. Henry Laurens had a similar understanding of the relationship between the trade to French islands and slave prices in the eastern Caribbean; see Henry Laurens to Meyler and Hall, Jan. 20, 1757, in Philip M. Hamer et al., eds., *The Papers of Henry Laurens*, 16 vols. (Columbia, S.C., 1968–2002), II, 422–423 (hereafter cited as *Laurens Papers*). "Very considerable": M. de Bourlamaque to "M. le Duc," Mar. 13, 1764, ANOM, C7A, 24, fol. 50–51.

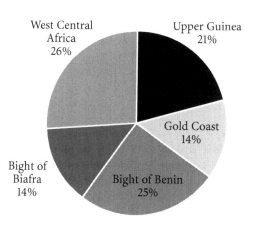

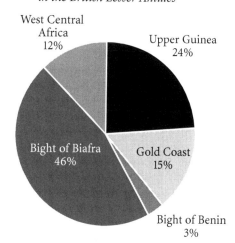

*Direct African Arrivals
in Guadeloupe and Martinique*

West Central
Africa
26%

Upper Guinea
21%

Gold Coast
14%

Bight of Benin
25%

Bight of
Biafra
14%

*Direct African Arrivals
in the British Lesser Antilles*

West Central
Africa
12%

Upper Guinea
24%

Bight of Biafra
46%

Gold Coast
15%

Bight of Benin
3%

FIGURE 9. Comparison of Captive Origins in the Transatlantic Slave Trades to the French and British Lesser Antilles, 1741–1765

Source: Voyages: The Trans-Atlantic Slave Trade Database, accessed September 2012, http://slavevoyages.org/tast/assessment/estimates.faces?yearFrom=1741&yearTo=1765&disembarkation=402.403; http://slavevoyages.org/tast/assessment/estimates.faces?yearFrom=1741&yearTo=1765&disembarkation=304.309.311.302.303.

■ After the midcentury decades dominated by warfare and traders' mixed successes in pursuing the transimperial slave trade, the end of the Seven Years' War brought renewed government attention. With the return of peace in 1763, British officials returned to viewing the slave trade as a great way to siphon colonial resources from rivals. Ironically, what turned Parliament's attention back toward the intercolonial trade was a new policy that unintentionally hampered it. After the war, British authorities—shocked at the expense of defending their American possessions—ratcheted up enforcement of the Navigation Acts to generate revenue from the colonies in the Caribbean as well as on the North American mainland. The new regulations flowing out of Whitehall, in addition to inflaming the mainland colonies, made it increasingly difficult for West Indies officials to bend the rules and allow foreign vessels into British ports for purchases of Africans or British manufactured goods. As an anonymous nineteenth-century author of a history (and endorsement) of the British slave trade described it:

> The late Mr. George Grenville . . . made several Regulations for
> enforcing the Acts of Navigation and thereby greatly obstructed the

Trade beforementioned. He had no Intention to prevent the Slave Trade, and He did the whole thro' mere Ignorance and Inadvertancy. His Conduct however . . . produced a great Clamour among the Merchants of the City of London . . . so that Mr. Grenville determined to legalize the hitherto illicit Trade, between the Spanish Possessions and Our West India Islands, and proposed to Parliament therefore the first free Port Act.

This Free Port Act of 1767 opened a handful of British entrepôts in the Caribbean to foreign commerce.[12]

The impulse to create free ports stemmed not only from the desire to remove unwittingly erected barriers to the slave trade but also from a brief flowering of foreign commerce following Britain's seizures of Guadeloupe and Havana during the Seven Years' War. The Treaty of Paris returned both possessions after the conflict—to France and Spain, respectively—but during the brief British occupations, trade with these territories exploded. British leaders granted the conquered French and Spanish settlers generous terms of surrender, and the settlers rewarded that generosity by spending lavishly on British manufactured goods and on enslaved African men, women, and children. Indeed, some officials in France and Spain alleged that settlers in Guadeloupe and Havana had proffered less than their best defense of their colonies once the British dangled the promise of slave trading in exchange for surrender. And trade slaves they did. African traders from Liverpool alone claimed to deliver more than 12,000 people to Guadeloupe between the British conquest in 1759 and the end of the war in 1763. Likewise, the British occupied Havana for less than a year, 1762–1763, but in that time, British traders sold somewhere between 3,000 and 10,000 enslaved Africans to Cuban colonists. Such fervent demand for British trade in these undersupplied corners of French and Span-

12. An untitled, unsigned, undated draft of a brief (positive) history of the British slave trade, Liverpool Papers, CCXXVII, Papers Relating to the Slave Trade, 1787–1823, British Library, Additional Manuscripts, 38416, fols. 288–292 (hereafter cited as BL, Add. MSS). This brief history of the British slave trade emphasized government sanction and encouragement of the trade in an effort to depict abolitionist proposals in the early nineteenth century as unfair reversals of policy. It focused on British slave trading to foreign colonies because it was written during the debate over a measure to abolish such sales. It is uncredited and undated but was probably written in 1805 or 1806, given the debate it engages. The account also overemphasizes the importance of slave trading to the creation of the free port policy, however, which aimed at stimulating British exports more generally. See Frances Armytage, *The Free Port System in the British West Indies: A Study in Commercial Policy, 1766–1822* (New York, 1953), 24–51.

ish America dazzled British traders and imperial officials. The Free Port Act offered a way to reopen such trade in peacetime.[13]

British policy makers found further inspiration for the Free Port Act in their inability to halt a thriving commerce at various neutral free ports during the Seven Years' War. The Dutch and Danish Empires had long eschewed the mercantilist regulations favored by the larger Euro-American empires, and their Caribbean ports—especially Dutch Saint Eustatius—saw commerce with all the belligerents spike during the Seven Years' War, as colonists of all nations used the neutral ports as outlets for their produce and as sources for scarce European goods and provisions. Even more dramatic was the emergence of Monte Cristi as a bustling free port. During the years of Spanish neutrality before 1762, the sleepy Santo Domingo port grew from a sparsely populated cove to one of the busiest ports in the Americas, largely by serving as an entrepôt for illegal trade between British North American colonies selling provisions and their nominal enemies in French Saint-Domingue. After British officials struggled to stamp out such trade during the Seven Years' War, they understood all too well that free ports could facilitate trade that rival empires deemed illegal. Indeed, colonists of rival or warring empires in the Caribbean had used neutral or sparsely populated harbors as nodes of clandestine exchange for decades.[14]

With the Free Port Act, British policy makers sought not only to shift such trade to British entrepôts but also to regulate and tax it. Unlike the long-standing Dutch and Danish policies, the British Free Port Act of 1767 did not open the British Caribbean entirely to foreign trade. Rather than abandon the restrictions of mercantilism altogether, the Free Port Act opened a few ports to foreign vessels for trade in specified commodities. Enslaved people and British manufactured goods could be exported, and foreigners could deliver colonial produce or specie in exchange. British colonial produce could not be exported from the free ports by foreigners, and foreign manufactured goods (together with a few excluded colonial products) could not be imported. The policy was designed to promote British manufacturing by accessing foreign markets

13. On the seizure of Guadeloupe and the subsequent trade boom, see Richard Pares, *War and Trade in the West Indies, 1739–1763* (Oxford, 1936), 186–195. Estimates for the explosion of British slave trading to Havana vary widely; for the estimate of 10,000 African people delivered, see Jennings, "War as the 'Forcing House of Change,'" *WMQ*, 3d Ser., LXII (2005), 411–440; for the estimate of 3,000 and the Spanish accusations of a half-hearted defense, see Schneider, "Occupation of Havana," 249–266, 303–304.

14. Truxes, *Defying Empire*, 51–64, 72–86.

and to foster British shipping by siphoning off foreign produce for shipment to Europe in British bottoms. The intent was also to bring the rampant inter-colonial exchange occurring in secluded harbors or foreign free ports under British control and to channel it to British aims. Instead of truly freeing trade, the Free Port Act loosened restrictions with an eye to regulating and taxing transimperial commerce for the benefit of the crown and the metropole.[15]

Enslaved Africans entered the act for two reasons. First, increasing British traders' markets for selling people would boost British manufacturing because traders to Africa would need more British goods to exchange for captives. Second, the insatiable demand for African labor in foreign colonies would make enslaved people attractive commodities with which to lure foreign traders to the free ports, where they would hopefully buy British manufactures as well. British policy makers cared more about promoting British industrial development than they did about selling slaves, but in the labor-hungry Americas, human commodities offered the surest way to attract customers. Viewed as human beings (even if just as laborers), enslaved Africans' greatest value would have been within the empire, toiling on British plantations. But in crafting the Free Port Act, Parliament focused only on the exchange value of the enslaved—their unique ability to draw customers to British Caribbean markets. The act created free ports to be centers of the slave trade. For the people exchanged as goods, the policy ensured that tens of thousands of them would travel to slavery in the French or Spanish Caribbean through a British entrepôt.

Parliament chose the free ports for their proximity to foreign colonies. The first were Kingston, Savanna-la-Mar, and Santa Lucea, all in Jamaica (Britain's westernmost island), and Roseau and Prince Rupert's Bay, Dominica, which sat between the two oldest French sugar islands, Martinique and Guadeloupe (see Map 7). Jamaica was an obvious choice, owing to its history as a hub for transshipment. It had merchants experienced in the trade and facilities for housing and confining captives, since colony law required that in the port, they be held on shore rather than aboard ship. Sparsely populated Dominica, on the other hand, had no such trade history or mercantile sector, having been claimed by the British only after the Seven Years' War. But sandwiched

15. To protect British colonial production in Jamaica, imports of sugar, coffee, tobacco, pimento, and ginger were barred at Kingston, where the British hoped to focus the free port trade on Spanish cochineal, cotton, and specie—items that did not compete with Jamaica's produce. Foreign sugar was, however, legal to import to Dominica, where British officials placed more emphasis on courting French traders than on protecting British sugar producers from competition (Armytage, *Free Port System*, 42–43).

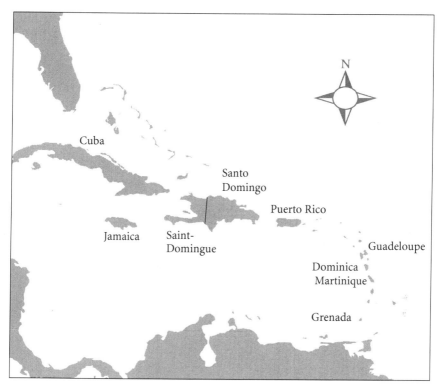

MAP 7. British Colonies with Free Ports and Foreign Colonies with Which They Traded. Drawn by the author

between Martinique and Guadeloupe, both routinely neglected by French traders, Dominica's location was perfect. The French vessel *La Boiteure,* which made repeated voyages between Dominica and Martinique in the late 1780s, illustrated this advantage. The islands were so close together that *La Boiteure* once managed two voyages exporting people from Dominica within two days of each other, departing the free port on June 6 with eighty-nine Africans and again on June 8 with forty-nine more.[16]

16. Armytage, *Free Port System,* 10, 42; "Code Noir of Jamaica, 1788," BL, Add. MSS, 12432, fol. 51; CO 76/4, fol. 9, National Archives, Kew. On Dominica's sparse settlement, mainly by French colonists, before the British claims that followed the Seven Years' War, see Marshall Smelser, *The Campaign for the Sugar Islands, 1759: A Study of Amphibious Warfare* (Chapel Hill, N.C., 1955), 16 n. 6, 118, 182. Dominica also allowed British policy makers to pursue control of Guadeloupe and Martinique's trade without actually retaining possession of either French island after the Seven Years' War; this allowed the British to push the French for other concessions while also appeasing plantation owners in Britain's own sugar-producing colonies, who strongly opposed annexa-

Particularly in its use of Dominica to access French colonies, the Free Port Act—although not truly deregulating trade—marked a significant departure from prior mercantilist restrictions on foreign commerce. British officials had granted previous exceptions to the Navigation Acts primarily to facilitate Spanish American trade because Spanish colonists paid for enslaved Africans (and British manufactured goods) with silver, cochineal, dyewood, and hides—items that British mercantilists and budding industrialists prized and that did not compete with the produce of Britain's own colonies. Slave trading to French colonies had long occurred, as well, but largely at the initiative of individual traders. Before the mid-eighteenth century, British officials tended to see French Caribbean colonies as rival sugar producers to Britain's own tropical possessions. In designating Dominica as the site of two free ports, however, British policy makers explicitly pursued the intercolonial slave trade to French colonies. These colonies still produced sugar, so the shift in policy marks a step toward a philosophy of freer trade. Despite the competition for Britain's own sugar producers, the opportunity to use the slave trade to open French Caribbean markets to exports of British manufactures and to increase British traders' share of the transatlantic carrying trade outweighed the potential damage.[17]

Indeed, the new rules offered numerous benefits. They did not end the efforts of British merchants venturing to foreign colonies for profitable sales of people, but they increased the number of foreign vessels coming to British ports. For British traders lacking connections in foreign colonies, the act allowed them to access foreign markets by selling to French, Spanish, and Dutch traders who came to British territory. The act also eliminated the danger of confiscation, or at least shifted the danger to foreign colonists, who often violated their own laws, if no longer British ones, in buying Africans in Jamaica and Dominica. Furthermore, selling captives to foreign buyers in British ports alleviated the problem of extending credit in foreign colonies, where British traders had often struggled to collect debts. On their own turf, British merchants could more easily demand immediate payment. A final benefit, from the standpoint of the crown, was the potential for generating revenue from such trade. The act included a £1 10s. duty on Africans imported to the free ports. Between 1767 and 1774, Dominica alone collected between £2,000 and

---

tion of Martinique or Guadeloupe, seeing them as competitors (Eric Williams, *From Columbus to Castro: The History of the Caribbean, 1492–1969* [London, 1970], 129–130).

17. On differing attitudes about trade with Spanish America and French America, see Schneider, "Occupation of Havana," 135–138.

£6,000 annually from this duty, and the crown jealously guarded the privilege to tax. By 1787, Saint George, Grenada, had been added as a free port, and local officials there sought their own cut of the tax revenue by placing a duty of 10 s. "for each Negro brought into and carried out of this island." The royal governor blocked the measure, however, because it interfered with the importation of Africans, from which the crown alone hoped to skim profits. Royal officials also confiscated slave trading vessels off the coast of Grenada that sought to sell captives to foreign buyers at sea, avoiding the duties by not entering port.[18]

In Jamaica, the Free Port Act did not immediately spur an acceleration of transshipment, largely because the act's implementation coincided with a fleeting success for British traders in securing the lion's share of the Spanish American slave trade through other channels. In the late 1760s, the Spanish crown granted a monopoly on slave deliveries to a Spanish trading company—La Compañía Gaditana de Negros—that initially used Puerto Rico as its hub for African arrivals. The company placed orders for captives largely from British islands, especially Barbados and Dominica. This trade could rely on Barbados as well as the free ports because the Spanish company could license British traders to enter Puerto Rico from anywhere, free port or not; Barbados was a logical choice, given Jamaica's location downwind and down current from Puerto Rico and given Dominica's lack of economic development immediately after the British takeover. (Britain did not add Bridgetown to the list of free ports, presumably because its location as the easternmost island of the Caribbean made it difficult to sail to from Spanish and French territories.) With British blessing, Spanish merchants transshipped thousands of enslaved people from Barbados, and increasingly from Dominica, to Puerto Rico be-

18. Armytage, *Free Port System,* 42, 45 (Armytage notes similar efforts to avoid duties in Dominica); CO 76/4, fol. 45; William Comp[ton?] to Lord Hawkesbury, June 30, 1791, Liverpool Papers, CCXXVII, BL, Add. MSS, 38416, fols. 256–257. The concern about confiscations was timely, as British imperial officials struggled with Spanish confiscations of their ships in the late 1760s; even those not actually entering Spanish ports could be subject to seizure under suspicion of trading with Spanish colonists (or "under pretense" of such suspicions, as one colonial governor believed); see John Pownal to Robert Wood, Aug. 26, 1769, CO 5/43, fol. 229. For a sample of the challenges of collecting debts in foreign colonies, see the case of Josias de Ponthieu and Edward and Rene Payne (all merchants in London) who attempted to collect from the Larnac brothers (merchants in Martinique). Unfortunately, the goods that had been traded are unspecified, so whether slaves were involved is unknown. When the London merchants appealed to French courts, the Larnac brothers claimed bankruptcy; the London merchants insisted that the Larnacs were prominent merchants with considerable assets. The case involved numerous appeals to both governments, and eventually, Ponthieu headed to Martinique, hoping to disprove the bankruptcy claims. The result of his efforts is not noted. See CO 5/43, fols. 219–220.

TABLE 14. Estimates of Africans Exported from Barbados, Antigua, and Saint Kitts to Foreign Colonies, 1741–1808

Years	Estimated departures	Years	Estimated departures
1741–1745	900	1781–1785	250
1746–1750	2,300	1786–1790	750
1751–1755	5,000	1791–1795	300
1756–1760	350	1796–1800	1,200
1761–1765	1,300	1801–1805	0
1766–1770	10,500	1806–1808	150
1771–1775	10,500	TOTAL	33,500
1776–1780	0		

Note: For the sources and assumptions underlying these estimates, see Appendix, below (especially Table 24). Trade from Barbados probably accounts for about 95 percent of the forced migration estimated in this table, but since some sources (especially in French archives) refer to trade from these islands without differentiating between them, I opted for consolidated estimates of their trade.

tween 1766 and 1772. From Puerto Rico, these captives dispersed across much of Spanish America.[19]

Despite the momentary and significant rise of Barbados as the crucial hub of Spanish transshipment, the British eventually realized their hopes for an escalation of slave trading at the designated free ports. Port records and other government reports from Jamaica show extensive trade with Spanish America and Saint-Domingue after a slow start from 1767 to the first few years of the 1770s. Exports of Africans to foreign colonies boomed starting in 1774, with more than two thousand Africans departing Jamaica annually through 1776. The Compañía Gaditana shifted its center of importation from Puerto Rico to Havana in the 1770s and, according to British ambassador William Eden, "dispatched Spanish vessels in Search of Slaves to the different Foreign Islands but particularly to Jamaica from whence at least three fourths of all the Negroes were supplied." Eden estimated—based on information provided by a British merchant who had resided in both Kingston and Havana—that "The number [of Africans] annually imported into the Havannah was from 2,500 to 3,000, and about half that number was sent to Cartagena and Porto Bello, part of which was sold there and the remainder conveyed by Land to Panama, from whence they were reshipped to Peru etc." This arrangement

19. On the Spanish monopoly slave-trading company from 1766–1772, see Bibiano Torres Ramirez, *La Compañía Gaditana de Negros* (Seville, 1973).

TABLE 15. Estimates of Africans Exported from Jamaica to Foreign Colonies, 1741–1808

Years	Estimated departures	Years	Estimated departures
1741–1745	6,200	1781–1785	13,000
1746–1750	8,400	1786–1790	11,000
1751–1755	5,200	1791–1795	20,000
1756–1760	2,900	1796–1800	8,700
1761–1765	3,800	1801–1805	700
1766–1770	1,400	1806–1808	
1771–1775	6,600	TOTAL	92,000
1776–1780	4,100		

Note: For the sources and assumptions underlying these estimates, see Appendix, below (especially Table 23).

continued until 1779, when the Spanish contract expired. Around the same time, Spanish entry into the U.S. War of Independence—on the side of the rebels—disrupted Anglo-Spanish trade. But the traffic picked up again in 1782, temporarily peaking in 1784, when nearly four thousand Africans reportedly departed Jamaica's free ports for foreign colonies. Then, in the 1790s, the trade to Cuba, in particular, exploded as that colony surged to the forefront in sugar and coffee production, capitalizing on the vacuum created by Saint-Domingue's collapse into slave rebellion and revolution. Several thousand people annually faced redirection from Jamaica to its northern neighbor in first half of the decade. Furthermore, all these numbers reflect only those people lawfully imported and exported at Jamaica, but smuggling to avoid duties at the Free Ports was frequently reported.[20]

20. For reports of the trade's volume, see Liverpool Papers, CCXXVII, BL, Add. MSS, 38416, fol. 179; a second report to the Board of Trade, probably produced in 1793, corroborates the first but breaks the total down after 1774, when Montego Bay, Jamaica, also became a free port and played a significant but lesser role in slave exports. The only discrepancy was a lower total for 1786: the first report showed 3,143 Africans departing, but the second, only 1,918 (ibid., fols. 271–272). On reports of smuggling, see Armytage, Free Port System, 44–51. "Dispatched Spanish vessels": William Eden to first earl of Liverpool, Aranjuez, June 10, 1788, Liverpool Papers, CCXXVII, BL, Add. MSS, 38416, fols. 114–116. According to Donnan, reports circulated in Jamaica in 1773 of an agreement between the Spanish and British crowns for British traders in Kingston to supply Africans at a set price, but Eden makes no mention of such an agreement in his account of the trade in these years. The existence of such an agreement also seems unlikely because the crown no longer had monopoly companies, such as the Royal African Company or

In addition to the importance of Cuba, the Spanish Main, and Saint-Domingue as markets for Jamaica's free ports, the Spanish takeover of Louisiana in the 1770s turned that colony into an important supplementary destination. Under French control in previous decades, Louisiana had relied on direct African shipments for the vast majority of enslaved immigration, but Spain's long-standing exclusion from Africa pushed the colony toward transshipment to obtain laborers. British trade to Louisiana got a brief start in the early 1770s before the War of Independence disrupted it. When peace returned, Louisiana's Caribbean trade resumed with vigor as Spanish officials relaxed duties and restrictions on importing Africans from foreigners. By the end of the 1780s, Louisiana imported more than one thousand Africans from the Caribbean annually, with Jamaica the most important source and hundreds of Africans also arriving from Dominica, Montserrat, Cuba, and Saint-Domingue. In the 1790s, Caribbean transshipments to Louisiana slowed, owing largely to new restrictions from anxious Spanish authorities in the wake of the Saint-Domingue rebellion. In 1796, Louisiana prohibited slave importations altogether. For the enslaved population in Louisiana, there were profound implications in the shift to relying on British colonies for most shipments of enslaved immigrants. Under French rule, the colony had been unique in relying on one African region, Senegambia, for the vast majority of its slave trade. But that region accounted for less than 2 percent of the African immigration to Jamaica in the late eighteenth century. The Bight of Biafra and the Gold Coast together contributed two-thirds of the people forced to Jamaica between 1771 and 1800; the Igbo and Akan peoples from these regions surely began to appear in Louisiana in significant numbers, diversifying the enslaved community.[21]

South Sea Company, to carry out such an agreement. Instead, the crown would have been stuck trying to force independent traders to honor the terms of the agreement, which would have been unpopular and probably untenable. See Donnan, ed., *Documents*, III, 245. See also Torres Ramirez, *La Compañía Gaditana de Negros*.

21. Published findings on slave imports to Louisiana augment the British sources that underpin my research; see Jean-Pierre Leglaunec, "Slave Migrations in Spanish and Early American Louisiana: New Sources and New Estimates," *Louisiana History*, XLVI (2005), 185–209; James A. McMillin, *The Final Victims: Foreign Slave Trade to North America, 1783–1810* (Columbia, S.C., 2004). Works previous to Leglaunec's noted the importance of Caribbean sources for Louisiana's slaves in the Spanish period but did not quantify the traffic; see Paul F. Lachance, "The Politics of Fear: French Louisianans and the Slave Trade, 1786–1809," *Plantation Society in the Americas*, I (1979), 164–165; John G. Clark, *New Orleans, 1718–1812: An Economic History* (Baton Rouge, 1970), 222–225; Daniel H. Usner, Jr., *Indians, Settlers, and Slaves in a Frontier Exchange Economy: The Lower Mississippi Valley before 1783* (Chapel Hill, N.C., 1992), 111; Thomas Marc Fiehrer, "The

As for Dominica's free ports, Barbados eclipsed them in the early years of the policy, but robust trade did quickly emerge. Most was with the neighboring French islands, but Puerto Rico offered a secondary market. Around 1788, the Board of Trade received "An Account of the number of Slaves sold by Kender, Mason and Co.," a British trading partnership in Roseau. The document showed that this firm alone sold thousands of enslaved Africans annually to British and foreign buyers in the free port, occasionally organizing its own shipments to Puerto Rico. In 1768, the first year the act was in effect, Kender, Mason, and Co. reportedly sold 3,710 Africans in Dominica and another 1,713 in Puerto Rico "thro' the medium of Dominica," although some of these deliveries via Dominica were likely continuations of transatlantic voyages, rather than transshipments. A second peak came in 1772, when the firm sold 5,003 Africans, all in Dominica. Slave-trading activities diminished during the War of Independence, but Dominica's exports exceeded prewar levels in the 1780s. The colony's governor stated in 1788 that, of the 27,533 Africans imported from 1783 to 1788, 15,781 (57 percent) were traded away again, within or outside the empire. These estimates significantly exceed those recorded in Dominica's port records, however, so the governor was either suggesting additional smuggling or simply exaggerating.[22]

Despite such possible embellishment, French leaders in Guadeloupe and Martinique echoed English reports that Dominica was a major source of enslaved Africans reaching their territory, continuing to lament the difficulties of quashing contraband foreign commerce. Those on both sides of the imperial divide, then, must have welcomed the news that France decided to open

---

African Presence in Colonial Louisiana: An Essay on the Continuity of Caribbean Culture," in Robert R. Macdonald, John R. Kemp, and Edward F. Haas, eds., *Louisiana's Black Heritage* (New Orleans, 1979), 3–31. Clark, in particular, notes that trade with the French islands was important during the Revolution, when Spain was at war with England (223). On Louisiana's curtailment and abolition of the slave trade, see Lachance, "Politics of Fear," 165–166. See also Gregory E. O'Malley, "Beyond the Middle Passage: Slave Migration from the Caribbean to North America, 1619–1807," *WMQ*, 3d Ser., LXVI (2009), 152–154. On the predominance of Senegambia as the source of Louisiana's African immigrants in the French period, see *Voyages*, accessed February 2013, http://slavevoyages.org/tast/assessment/estimates.faces?yearFrom=1701&yearTo=1765& disembarkation=204; see also Gwendolyn Midlo Hall, *Africans in Colonial Louisiana: The Development of Afro-Creole Culture in the Eighteenth Century* (Baton Rouge, 1992). On African arrivals in Jamaica in the late eighteenth century, see *Voyages*, http://slavevoyages.org/tast/assessment /estimates.faces?yearFrom=1771&yearTo=1 796&disembarkation=301.

22. Armytage, *Free Port System*, 44–45; "Remarks on Gov'r Orde's Statement of the Negroe Population in Dominica" and "An Account of the Number of Slaves Sold by Kender Mason & Co. at the Following Islands in the West Indies," Liverpool Papers, CCXXVII, BL, Add. MSS, 38416, fols. 176, 178.

TABLE 16. Estimates of Africans Exported from Dominica and Grenada to Foreign Colonies, 1761–1808

Years	Estimated departures	Years	Estimated departures
1761–1765	100	1791–1795	7,150
1766–1770	4,250	1796–1800	
1771–1775	4,300	1801–1805	
1776–1780	1,450	1806–1808	
1781–1785	150	TOTAL	26,000
1786–1790	8,600		

Note: For the sources and assumptions underlying these estimates, see Appendix, below (especially Table 25). Dominica and Grenada are treated together here because they both sent enslaved people to some of the same foreign colonies and the records of those colonies did not always differentiate between them. Dominica was by far the more important hub for the slave trade, probably accounting for more than 90 percent of the forced migration described in this table.

Martinique and Guadeloupe to foreign slave traders in 1783. Southern Saint-Domingue—which often complained of the same neglect from French traders that plagued Martinique and Guadeloupe—also opened to foreign slave traders in 1783, though the opening was only temporary, whereas for Martinique and Guadeloupe, it proved lasting. After a century of futility in trying to halt such trade, French officials decided to prioritize a supply of coercible labor over enforcing mercantilist laws. Transshipment from Dominica thrived under the favorable British and French policies. Northern Saint-Domingue monopolized the attention of French traders, and the rest of French Caribbean relied heavily upon British transshipment.[23]

This legalization of a long-running clandestine trade between British and French colonies might have incidentally improved shipboard conditions for captives. Legalization of the Anglo-French trade eliminated the dangers of nighttime landings, hidden coves without port facilities, and secret shipboard compartments. Crossing imperial boundaries still carried the likelihood of cultural alienation, however. In the era of Britain's free port policy, the French

23. On France's opening Martinique and Guadeloupe to foreign slave ships, see Geggus, "French Slave Trade," *WMQ*, 3d Ser., LVIII (2001), 126. For complaints about the lack of French traders in Martinique, Guadeloupe, and southern Saint-Domingue (both before and after the opening to foreign slave traders), see the following correspondence to France in ANOM: Governor General Nolivos, Dec. 9, 1770, C9A, 138; summary report of a petition from Martinique, Jan. 3, 1785, C8A, 84, fols. 381–384; Intendant Faulquier, Nov. 14, 1787, C8A, 87, fols. 195–196; Henry de St. Georges, July 12, 1788, C8A, 88, fol. 143; Faulquier, Oct. 25, 1788, fols. 170–172.

Direct African Arrivals
in the French Caribbean

Direct African Arrivals
in Dominica and Jamaica

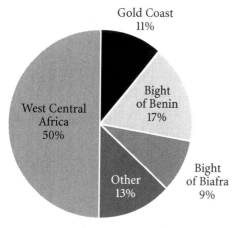

Gold Coast
11%

Bight
of Benin
17%

West Central
Africa
50%

Other
13%

Bight
of Biafra
9%

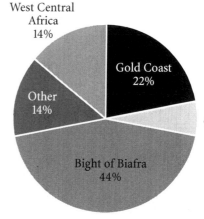

West Central
Africa
14%

Gold Coast
22%

Other
14%

Bight
of Benin
6%

Bight of Biafra
44%

FIGURE 10. Comparison of Captive Origins in the Transatlantic Slave Trades to the French Caribbean and the British Free Ports, 1766–1807

Source: *Voyages: The Trans-Atlantic Slave Trade Database,* accessed January 2013, http://slavevoyages .org/tast/assessment/estimates.faces?yearFrom=1766&yearTo=1807&disembarkation=402.403.401 .404.405; http://slavevoyages.org/tast/assessment/estimates.faces?yearFrom=1766&yearTo=1807 &disembarkation=306.301.

transatlantic trade grew increasingly reliant upon west central Africa, drawing nearly half of its captives there. The Bight of Benin now lagged far behind, as a secondary source, with a smattering of other regions contributing nearly equivalent numbers of enslaved people to the traffic. The British free ports drew captives from different African regions. The Bight of Biafra and the Gold Coast combined to supply about two-thirds of the migrants to Jamaica and Dominica, with the Biafran share the largest. Thus, intercolonial trade continued to bring significant numbers of Igbo and Akan people to the French Caribbean, to settle among the west central Africans who predominated among the direct African arrivals (Figure 10). This influx of Igbo and Akan captives marked an especially significant shift in the migration to Saint-Domingue and Louisiana because those colonies (unlike Martinique and Guadeloupe) had rarely relied on British slave traders in earlier decades. In the migration from British colonies to Spanish America under the Free Port Act, such Igbo and Akan captives also must have predominated, and although they mixed with fewer recent arrivals from foreign parts of Africa, they settled into communities that had historically relied on other sources for captives, meaning that the risks of cultural isolation were similar.

The results of the Free Port Act apparently pleased British officials, because they not only renewed the act repeatedly but also expanded it. In Dominica, the act enjoyed great popularity and broad endorsement for its renewal in the early 1770s. In Jamaica, the act was more controversial, with little acceleration of broader trade alongside the commerce in enslaved people. Vocal opposition came from planters who believed the act facilitated competition from foreign sugar and coffee producers. Only the slave traders benefited, and their support played a large role in renewal of the act for Jamaica. Thereafter, the number of free ports grew. In 1787, Parliament added Saint George, Grenada, and New Providence, Bahamas. In 1792, Bermuda joined. The following year, Antigua and the Caicos Islands received free ports, as well. Finally, in 1805, a consolidated act was passed, pushing the list of islands with free ports to more than a dozen, with several islands harboring more than one. Many of the additional ports developed as significant hubs of transshipment for enslaved Africans, if in some cases only for fleeting moments. Indeed, the vibrant commerce of the free ports might have inspired imperial official Henry Addington's argument in 1797 that Britain should give up its monopoly on trade with its West Indian colonies altogether. He insisted that the exclusivity only provoked hostility from imperial rivals, whereas liberal sharing of trade privileges could give Britain influence with other nations and promote British commerce. In the minds of some British policy makers, trading enslaved people led to advocating freer trade.[24]

Whereas the slave trade was indisputably the crucial instrument of the African Diaspora to the Americas, permanently altering the victims' physical and cultural landscape—the trade's economic importance is contested. Ever since Eric Williams's assertion that the profits of the slave trade provided the capital necessary for Britain's pioneering role in the Industrial Revolution, historiographical debate has raged over the economic significance of the commerce. Some argue that, despite the obvious historical magnitude of the massive unfree migration of African people, trading slaves was an activity of minor economic importance relative to the trades of European manufactured goods and colonial produce that drove the Atlantic economy. Enslaved people, according to this argument, had infinitely greater impact as workers driving plantation economies than as trade goods. Certainly, emphasis belongs on the work enslaved people did. But arguments for the slave trade's relative lack of economic

24. Armytage, *Free Port System*, 50. The forum for Addington's short essay "On Opening British Ports to Free Trade" is unclear, as the paper is mixed in with his correspondence of 1797; see Papers of Henry Addington, First Viscount Sidmouth, 152M/C1797/OT1, Devon Record Office, U.K.

significance view the commerce too narrowly, tending to look at slave trading in isolation, when in reality it was entangled with other branches of commerce. This symbiosis was central to the Free Port Act. British policy makers hoped that Britons would profit not only from sales of enslaved people at the free ports but also from manufacturing the goods that were traded for such people in Africa and from shipping and selling foreign sugars, hides, and silver that were acquired in exchange. By seizing the dominant share of the transatlantic slave trade and facilitating the sale of Africans to foreign colonies through the free ports, British policy makers jockeyed for position in the carrying trade of colonial produce bound for Europe. Given that Britain's dominant position in the transatlantic slave trade predated the free port policy by at least half a century, the opening of free ports was not causal in the commercial might of the British Empire. Instead, the policy marks an effort to use Britain's superior positions in both the slave trade and manufacturing as leverage to expand its markets for both. Making enslaved Africans available for transshipment could bring foreign colonies at least partly into Britain's economic sphere—with British American ports as the entrepôts for foreign traders exchanging staples and specie for Africans and British goods.[25]

In the early days of British slave trading to the Spanish Empire, much of the attention focused on obtaining the jewel of Spanish America: silver. Returns came, however, in produce as well as mineral wealth, with the South Sea Company sending transshipments of people from Jamaica and procuring cochineal and indigo in exchange. Increasingly, merchants recognized the value

25. For some key arguments against the macroeconomic significance of the profits from slave trading, see Stanley L. Engerman, "The Slave Trade and British Capital Formation in the Eighteenth Century: A Comment on the Williams Thesis," *Business History Review*, XLVI (1972), 430–443; Roger Anstey, "The Volume and Profitability of the British Slave Trade, 1761–1807," in Stanley L. Engerman and Eugene D. Genovese, eds., *Race and Slavery in the Western Hemisphere: Quantitative Studies* (Princeton, 1975), 3–31. For arguments more resonant with mine, entangling the profits of the slave trade with broader commerce, see Eric Williams, *Capitalism and Slavery* (Chapel Hill, N.C., 1944); Barbara L. Solow, "Caribbean Slavery and British Growth: The Eric Williams Hypothesis," *Journal of Developmental Economics*, XVII (1985), 99–115; Kenneth Morgan, *Slavery, Atlantic Trade, and the British Economy, 1660–1800* (New York, 2000); David Richardson, "The Slave Trade, Sugar, and British Economic Growth, 1748-1776," in Barbara L. Solow and Stanley L. Engerman, eds., *British Capitalism and Caribbean Slavery: The Legacy of Eric Williams* (New York, 1987) 103-33; Cedric J. Robinson, "Capitalism, Slavery, and Bourgeois Historiography," *History Workshop*, XXIII (1987), 122–140; David Eltis, *The Rise of African Slavery in the Americas* (New York, 2000), chap. 10; Eltis, *Economic Growth and the Ending of the Transatlantic Slave Trade* (New York, 1987); John J. McCusker and Russell R. Menard, *The Economy of British America, 1607-1789* (Chapel Hill, N.C., 1991), 39-46. On mercantilism and the carrying trade, see ibid., 36, 46-50.

of obtaining such commodities, as they offered another chance for profitable trade. Colonial crops were bartered for African people in the New World at lower rates than such crops would bring once transported to Europe. When the free ports opened, British transatlantic traders often directed their ship captains to deliver Africans to the free ports and to acquire foreign produce for the return to Europe. Thomas Leyland ordered Captain Charles Wilson of the ship *Enterprize* in 1787 to carry his cargo of African people to Jamaica and make "Returns in Cotton, Specie, or Bills," noting that "St. Domingo Cotton" was fetching high prices in Liverpool. Leyland saw Jamaica as an advantageous port for selling people, not just for its high demand for Africans but also because the transshipment trade between Jamaica and foreign colonies would give his ship access to a lucrative cargo for Europe. The Board of Trade also considered this movement of foreign produce through the free ports important, gathering reports from the naval officers on the amounts of "several Species of Goods imported . . . pursuant to the Free Port Act," with columns for sugar, coffee, cocoa, ginger, and cotton. Kender, Mason, and Co.'s report to the Board of Trade from Dominica also emphasized the importance of return shipments for Europe. Although the report quantified only sales of Africans from the island, it stated that the "greater part of the Slaves sold at Dominica were purchased by the French and Spaniards, who paid for them in Specie, Bills of Exchange, Cotton, and Coffee: which latter articles gave Freight to a number of British ships for England." To understand the economic importance of the slave trade, such traders and officials implied, one had to understand its connections to other commerce. Profits from shipping Guadeloupe's sugar to London were facilitated by sales of African people.[26]

For some traders, obtaining freights for England was not enough, and in 1792, merchants active in Dominica successfully lobbied for an amendment to the Free Port Act that would allow them to transport foreign colonial produce to mainland Europe, as well. The Privy Council endorsed the plan, arguing

> that a measure of this Nature will not only be advantageous to the
> general Commerce of the Empire, but that . . . it will make the Island of
> Dominica a great Mart and Entrepôt, as well for the Produce of many

26. "Minutes of the Court of Directors," Nov. 16, 1715, in Donnan, ed., *Documents*, II, 196; Letter Book of Thomas Leyland, 1786–1788, 387 MD 59, fol. 316, Liverpool Record Office, U.K.; CO 76/4, fols. 49–50; Liverpool Papers, CCXXVII, BL, Add. MSS, 38416, fol. 178; see also Armytage, *Free Port System*, 35–36. John J. McCusker insists that one of the free port policy's principal aims was the acquisition of raw materials from foreign colonies for British industry ("Introduction," *Business History Review*, LXXIV [2005], 697–713).

of the Foreign Islands, and perhaps of the Spanish Colonies on the Continent of America, as for British Manufactures and other Goods which will be exchanged in Return.

The Privy Council envisioned Dominica becoming a hub where foreign colonial planters or merchants could arrange for British vessels to carry their produce back to their mother country and, while there, shop for British manufactured goods and people imported from Africa. What had started as a mercantilist policy to promote a favorable balance of trade was shifting toward a policy of free trade more generally—a new understanding of commerce itself as profitable, regardless of whether the mother country gained control of the colonial natural resources.[27]

In the minds of those involved in such commerce and those formulating imperial policies, the slave trade and the carrying trade in colonial produce were bound together in ways that made it difficult to assess the value of one without the other. When the Privy Council began to consider the potential impact of ending the slave trade, under pressure from abolitionists, it sent a questionnaire about the trade's economic value to the agents representing several West Indian Islands. The answers do not survive, but the questions reveal contemporary ideas concerning the slave trade's integration in the colonial economy. After several queries about the number and prices of Africans sold to French colonies, the questionnaire asked, "Is not the Price of Freight for a given Quantity of Sugar from the French Islands to Europe greater than the Price of the same Quantity from the British Islands?" The question makes no mention of slaves, yet its inclusion reveals that its writers saw freights for French sugar as an important consideration. In the minds of those who designed British trade policies, the slave trade and the freight of foreign colonial produce were inextricably linked. The slave trade had jump-started British Caribbean free trade, and now abolitionists threatened to kill the engine.[28]

■ As loosening trade regulations fostered a robust intercolonial slave trade across imperial boundaries in the late eighteenth century, ventures ferrying

27. CO 5/36, fols. 448–450. Economic historians refer to profits from freight as an "invisible" commodity in the balance of trade. Typically, mercantilists ignored such invisibles, focusing only on tangible commodities such as sugar. Allowing shipments from British colonies to foreign countries in order to profit from freight charges marks a significant departure from mercantilism. See McCusker and Menard, *Economy of British America,* chap. 2.

28. "Additional Heads of Enquiry Transmitted to the Agents for the West India Islands," Mar. 3, 1788, CO 5/36, fols. 191–192.

enslaved Africans between British colonies prospered, as well. The burgeoning British transatlantic trade served most British colonies' needs, but the intercolonial trade within the empire still surged. Crucial to this development was adaptability and market responsiveness. Transatlantic traders took over some markets that had formerly relied on intercolonial sources, but cycles of war and peace in a volatile age periodically interfered, and British conquests and losses of American territories kept the empire's boundaries in flux. Such conflict and change was disruptive to all traders, but intercolonial merchants sometimes capitalized on the chaos. They enjoyed shorter lines of trade and communication than slave traders crossing the Atlantic, and changes in the shape or policies of the empire created moments of opportunity. Intercolonial traders adapted quickly—rushing captives to emerging markets and abandoning routes of trade that became unfavorable.

One force that disrupted regular trade patterns—and created openings for adaptable traders—was war and the privateering it unleashed across the Atlantic world. Privateers took any and all enemy commercial vessels, but they had a special appetite for slave ships, whose living and breathing commodities packed more monetary value into a ship's hold than just about any other cargo plying the Atlantic. Barbados merchant Charles Bolton reported on successes of British privateers during the War of the Austrian Succession with attention focused on slave ships: "No other trade or voyage is talk [sic] of here, but privateering," Bolton proclaimed;

> Lynch's [ship] took a French Guinea man off our Harbour, 207 Negros, and 3 days ago Mess's Minveiles and Lucky Moll took a Large Snow . . . with 275 choice negro's and Gold, Teeth and other Goods, the vessell and Cargoe supposed to be worth 9 or 10 Thousand Pounds. Within these 2 months past there has been taken off the French vessells and carry'd in to Antigoa and here [Barbados] the number of 30 saill, and some of them very Rich Prizes, [including] two Guineamen carryed into Antegoa with 12 hundred Slaves, and two large Shipps from Marsailes.

In Bolton's eyes, capturing a "Guinea man" was a privateer's surest route to riches. The choice of privateers to take these prizes to Antigua or Barbados was not just a reflection of those islands' robust markets for enslaved African people. To sell their quarry legally, privateers needed an admiralty court to confirm the captured ships and cargoes as lawful prizes, and only a few colonies housed such courts. As such, privateering prizes concentrated in a small number of ports, depressing prices there, and creating opportunities for intercolonial traders to disseminate prize goods—including enslaved people—to other markets.[29]

The scale of such privateering peaked in the Seven Years' War, when British naval ships seized a host of French slavers in the early months of the fighting. In January 1756, when the *Boston Evening-Post* reported the arrival of "His Majesty's Ship the Sphynx" at Jamaica, the paper added that the *Sphynx* "seized a French Guinea Man in his Way." A week later, the *Evening-Post* printed similar accounts from the eastern Caribbean, where "Thomas Frankland, Esq. Commodore, takes every Thing he meets with," including "a Ship and a Snow with upwards of 700 Slaves on board," which he sent to Barbados, and "2 Guinea Men with upwards of 500 Slaves," which he sent to Antigua. As seizures flooded Antigua and Barbados with African captives, intercolonial traders sensed opportunity, especially since prices for Africans had been unusually high in South Carolina during the preceding summer and autumn. In fact, so many traders snapped up the human prizes in Antigua and Barbados for transshipment to Charleston that they glutted the South Carolina market. As Charleston merchants Austin and Laurens explained it, slave sales "went off very dully" because "every Vessell from the West Indias brings down parcells of prize Negroes." Intercolonial traders responded to the glut quickly, however, bringing the markets back into balance. By February 1757, Austin and Laurens once again courted transshipments from the Caribbean, writing to Commodore Frankland that Carolina planters would be in "better spirits to purchase N—s this ensueing Spring . . . if You should have the good luck to take any more."[30]

For the Africans aboard such French vessels seized by British privateers, the hijacking had profound consequences. Of course the danger of a skirmish at sea was considerable, especially for people shackled in the hold, but most slave ships probably opted not to fight against naval vessels that overtook them. The more important implication for captives seized as prizes was long-term and cultural. French slavers in the 1750s and 1760s frequented substantially different African regions than their British counterparts did. British seizures of French vessels reversed the usual patterns of intercolonial commerce that sent Africans from British transatlantic slavers to French colonies, but the transfer from one imperial sphere to another still mixed people of di-

29. Charles Bolton to John Yeates, July 12, 1744, Jasper Yeates Papers, no. 740, Historical Society of Pennsylvania.

30. *Boston Evening-Post*, Jan. 19, 26, 1756; Austin and Laurens to John Knight, Jan. 3, 1756, in *Laurens Papers*, II, 59; Austin and Laurens to Thomas Frankland, Feb. 11, 1757, ibid., 448.

verse backgrounds. Captives aboard French ships taken by British privateers shifted into a distinct branch of the African Diaspora, increasing their risk of cultural isolation while diversifying the slave quarters of British America (Figures 9 and 10).

Meanwhile, intercolonial slave traders seized not only upon the wartime prospects created by privateering but also upon cessations of hostilities and official transfers of territories. As Britain's empire in the Caribbean expanded in various wars, merchants in the intercolonial trade rushed enslaved people to newly acquired territories. One such opportunity emerged after the Seven Years' War, when the Treaty of Paris (1763) handed Britain the so-called Ceded Islands—Grenada, Dominica, Saint Vincent, and Tobago. In the first few years that these islands were in British hands, intercolonial slave traders sent numerous shipments from the older colonies, especially Barbados, carrying several thousand slaves. These deliveries focused primarily on Saint Vincent and Tobago, the last islands to be targeted by transatlantic traders directly from Africa. After the first several years of British occupation, however, transatlantic deliveries to the Ceded Islands accelerated, and this intercolonial trade quickly declined. Intercolonial merchants engaged heavily at the moment when British settlers flocked to the new territories but before transatlantic traders flooded them with enslaved Africans.

The trade from Barbados to Demerara in the 1790s offers another example of the advantage that intercolonial traders enjoyed over their transatlantic counterparts. In 1796, during the warfare associated with the French Revolution, the British wrested control of Demerara, Berbice, and Essequibo—colonies on the northern coast of South America, now Guyana—from the Dutch. British settlers quickly expanded sugar, coffee, and cotton cultivation in these territories, and as the plantation economies grew, demand for enslaved labor surged, as well. Demerara had imported Africans throughout the Dutch era, but the shift to British control saw the slave trade to Demerara increase dramatically, peaking in 1801 with more than 14,000 Africans reportedly arriving. (By 1805, growing British abolitionism would cause an equally dramatic decline.) The transshipment trade to Demerara in these transitional years reveals local traders' responsiveness to changing market conditions. After the transfer of power, transshipments of Africans to the colony spiked in the first full year of British control, only to decline rapidly thereafter, as a steady stream of transatlantic shipments caught up with demand. The ventures of the vessel *Demerara Packet* are particularly revealing of the process. As its name implies, the packet—owned by Barbados merchants—made regular shipments to Demerara from its home colony. In April 1797, owners Robert

TABLE 17. Documented African Migration to Demerara via Transatlantic and Intercolonial Trades, 1797–1801

Year	Africans arriving directly from Africa	Africans sent from Barbados
1797	5,832	1,121
1798	8,035	152
1799	6,045	146
1800	7,974	198
1801	12,532	0

Source: *Voyages: The Trans-Atlantic Slave Trade Database,* accessed January 2012, http://slavevoyages .org/tast/database/search.faces?yearFrom=1797&yearTo=1801&mjslptimp=35304.35305; Naval Office Shipping Lists for Barbados, CO 33/21, National Archives, Kew. Unfortunately, Barbados shipping lists from 1796 and the first quarter of 1797 do not survive.

Reed and Stephen Holman added 15 people, recently imported to Barbados from Africa, to the *Demerara Packet*'s mixed cargo of provisions and European manufactured goods. Apparently these captives met with a favorable market because the ship's owners included even more people in the *Demerara Packet*'s following voyages—50 in May, 130 in June, 50 in July, 95 in August, and 130 in November. Other vessels exhibited a similar response to the favorable market.[31]

All told, merchants exported well over one thousand Africans from Barbados to Demerara in 1797, accounting for at least 18 percent of the documented African arrivals in Demerara that year (Table 17). (Furthermore, these transshipped people accounted for more than one-third of the year's African arrivals in Barbados.) And even these numbers may underestimate the importance of transshipment in supplying Demerara with African labor: enslaved people likely arrived from other islands, such as Antigua, which had shipped several cargoes to Demerara in the 1780s—even before the British takeover. Regardless of the total number of transshipments, when demand and prices were highest in Demerara, transatlantic traders must have envied the *Demerara Packet*'s one-month turnaround time from Barbados with fur-

31. Alvin O. Thompson argues for a major increase in the scale of the slave trade to Demerara after the British takeover in his *Colonialism and Underdevelopment in Guyana, 1580–1803* (Bridgetown, Barbados, 1987), 65, 92. *Demerara Packet:* CO 33/21, fols. 3, 3a, 5, 8–9, 13a. For instance, the *Governor Ricketts* left Barbados for Demerara with 28 Africans in May 1797, only to repeat the voyage in July with 118 slaves; see ibid., fols. 3a, 8.

ther supplies. Once transatlantic deliveries to the colony stepped up, the inter-colonial deliveries dropped precipitously.[32]

Wars and conquests of new territories were not the only changes that altered trade routes in the second half of the eighteenth century and created short-term opportunities for intercolonial slave trading. Given the fairly autono-mous governance of Britain's myriad territories across the Americas, changes of policy in individual colonies or groups of colonies could also alter patterns in the slave trade, providing openings for those who adapted quickly. For in-stance, localized intercolonial trades formed across borders between colonies that developed discrepancies in taxation. In the late 1750s and 1760s, Virginia imposed much higher duties on imports of enslaved Africans than Maryland did. As a result, Virginia merchants and planters often purchased captives in Maryland and ferried them back to the Old Dominion. A loophole in the Virginia law made such imports legal—without paying the duty—if the en-slaved people were for one's personal use, but many merchants engaged in such transshipment with the intent to resell. In fact, a young George Wash-ington asked a trader to purchase slaves for him in Maryland. One merchant reported in 1759 that more than two thousand Africans had reached Virginia via Maryland in the previous year alone, but that figure is surely hyperbole as it vastly exceeds the number of Africans who arrived in the region that year. Port records from the Potomac do not survive (and smugglers avoided port officials anyway), but this traffic more likely moved a few hundred people annually.[33]

Similar tax-evasion routes emerged from New Jersey to both New York and Pennsylvania in the same period, because New Jersey, unlike these neighbors, imposed no duty on imported slaves. The New Jersey Assembly attempted to discourage such trading in 1762 by levying its own duty on Africans, but the Board of Trade vetoed the bill. Colony governor Josiah Hardy informed the board of the New Jersey Assembly's willingness to comply with the veto—whereas New York and Pennsylvania defied the board's wish for colonies to leave the slave trade unobstructed—but Hardy also reminded the board of "the inconvenience the Province is exposed to in lying open to the free impor-tation of Negros, when the Provinces on each side have laid duties on them;

32. For Barbados's export records, see CO 33/21, fols. 20–58. Demerara's import records and many colonies' export records do not survive for the period, so precise figures remain elusive.

33. Donald M. Sweig, "The Importation of African Slaves to the Potomac River, 1732–1772," *WMQ*, 3d Ser., XLII (1985), 507–524. For African arrivals in the Chesapeake, see *Voyages*, ac-cessed December 2013, http://slavevoyages.org/tast/assessment/estimates.faces?yearFrom=1755 &yearTo=1761&disembarkation=202.

for which reason great Numbers of Negros are landed in this Province every Year in order to be run into New York and Pensylvania."[34]

The most dramatic examples of shifting political winds' spurring intercolonial slave trading came with the imperial crisis preceding the American Revolution, which prompted North American colonies to embargo British imports—including shipments of enslaved people from Africa. Despite largely disrupting the slave trade, such interdictions also spurred localized intercolonial trades in more ways than one. First, intercolonial trading could emerge to smuggle enslaved people into the areas prohibiting the traffic. As with the illegal trade across imperial boundaries, intercolonial traders enjoyed an advantage for smuggling, thanks to shorter lines of communication and the ability to operate profitably on a smaller scale, alleviating risk. During the Townshend Duties controversy (1767–1770), clandestine trading emerged between Georgia and South Carolina. Like most other North American colonies, South Carolina signed on to the trade embargoes, but Georgia demurred until 1775. Having legalized slavery only in 1750 and still struggling to attract African shipments, Georgia saw the nonimportation elsewhere as a rare opportunity to entice slave traders away from wealthier northern neighbors. Thus, Georgia kept the trade open. In addition to providing enslaved labor for Georgia's fledgling plantations, some slave traders sought to exploit Georgia's openness to use the colony as a base for smuggling Africans to South Carolina planters who were willing to flout the Sons of Liberty. When Charleston officials turned away several slaving vessels in 1770 in compliance with the embargo, the *South-Carolina Gazette* reported concerns that the vessels were headed south to sell their captives to "the unfeeling Merchants of Georgia ([who will] counter-act our Resolutions, and remain dead to every Thing but their own Interest) by purchasing Slaves in That Province, and introducing them over Land into This." Indeed, two months later, the paper noted confiscations of African people illegally transshipped from Georgia to outlying South Carolina ports, such as Beaufort and Port Royal.[35]

34. Josiah Hardy to Board of Trade, Perth Amboy, Jan. 20, 1762, in Donnan, ed., *Documents*, III, 456. In 1731, the Board of Trade ordered all import duties on the slave trade repealed, but a number of colonies refused to comply; see Darold D. Wax, "Preferences for Slaves in Colonial America," *Journal of Negro History*, LVIII (1973), 387.

35. "News Items Relating to Slave Trade, 1770," in Donnan, ed., *Documents*, IV, 436. On Georgia's struggles to attract slave shipments during the first years after legalizing the institution, and on Georgia's delayed entry into the Continental Association, see Darold D. Wax, "'New Negroes Are Always in Demand': The Slave Trade in Eighteenth-Century Georgia," *Georgia Historical Quarterly*, LXVIII (1984), 196–197, 213.

Intercolonial traders also pounced (legally) on the moments just before and after such blockades took effect, when great opportunities emerged for slave traders who acted quickly. Some planters would be desperate to acquire laborers before and after nonimportation. As the biggest slave market in North America, with the most robust demand for exploitable labor, Charleston offered the best prospect for merchants to capitalize on planters' fear of a pending closure or on their relief when trade reopened. In the window from 1771 to 1774, between the Townshend Duties embargo and the crisis over the Coercive Acts, Carolina plantation owners scrambled to import as many African people as they could afford, fearing further cessation of trade. In 1772, Nathaniel Russell of Charleston described the clamor for slave labor: "Their [sic] has been a Great many negroes imported here this Summer and many more Expected; they continue at very Great Prices . . . , the highest ever known here, they are at Least £10 Stlg. higher here than in the West Indies." Russell was not alone in noting the discrepancy between Caribbean and Carolina markets after the Townshend embargo ended. Intercolonial arrivals in Charleston surged in the early 1770s as the high prices attracted merchants from all over British America. Levinius Clarkson's letter to a partner in New York requesting "any New Negroes who have not been Six Months in any of his Majesty's Colonies" was part of a frenzy to draw Africans to Charleston. Some merchants were so eager to capitalize on Charleston's high prices that they sent seasoned slaves, hoping to find a way around the prohibitive duty on them. In July 1773, Nathaniel Russell scolded Christopher Champlin, one of his Rhode Island correspondents, for sending a seasoned "Negro fellow" to Charleston under the expectation that Russell would smuggle him in for sale without paying the duty. Most transshipments, however, carried people who had recently arrived in the Caribbean from Africa. Between 1771 and 1774, Charleston received more than three thousand people from the islands, accounting for more than 15 percent of enslaved arrivals in the period. Through most of the eighteenth century, transshipments accounted for far less of the migration to Charleston—typically about 5 percent.[36]

36. Nathaniel Russell to Aaron Lopez, Charleston, July 14, 1772, in Donnan, ed., *Documents*, IV, 450; Levinius Clarkson to David Van Horne, Charleston, Feb. 23, 1773, ibid., 456; Russell to Christopher Champlin, Charleston, July 28, 1773, ibid., 464–465. For transatlantic shipments, see *Voyages*, accessed January 2013, http://slavevoyages.org/tast/database/search.faces?yearFrom=1701&yearTo=1808&mjslptimp=21300. For a comparison of the transatlantic and intercolonial trades to South Carolina, see O'Malley, "Beyond the Middle Passage," *WMQ*, 3d Ser., LXVI (2009), 140–155, 165–166; see also O'Malley, "Diversity in the Slave Trade to the Colonial Caro-

Such brisk intercolonial trade to Charleston illustrates that, when demand was high enough in one colony to drive up prices, intra-American merchants were willing to compete with transatlantic traders. In fact, "compete" may be a misleading term. What intercolonial merchants actually did was identify moments at which demand was high enough to allow transshipments to supplement direct African arrivals. Rather than compete with transatlantic traders, whose costs were lower, intercolonial traders simply sold additional people in markets where demand for African laborers exceeded transatlantic supply.

When such commerce bridged the Caribbean and the North American mainland, it tangled distinct lines of migration from Africa to the Americas, diversifying enslaved communities. The slave trade to the British Caribbean in the second half of the eighteenth century drew captives primarily from the Bight of Biafra, with the Gold Coast as the most important supplemental region, so Igbo and Akan people together probably accounted for more than half of the captives in the intercolonial traffic from the Caribbean to North America. By contrast, captives bound directly across the Atlantic to North America primarily embarked from the Upper Guinea coast, comprising Senegambia, the Windward Coast, and Sierra Leone. West central Africa was the secondary region of origin for the mainland (with the Gold Coast close behind). As such, the ongoing intercolonial commerce between the Caribbean and North America forced the integration of Igbo people into a migration composed of many Upper Guineans (Figure 11).[37]

■ One effect of the increasing scale of intercolonial slave trading in the mid- to late eighteenth century—both within the British Empire and across imperial boundaries to French and Spanish territory—was that more transatlantic traders embraced roles as wholesalers of African people, eagerly selling to American traders in bulk rather than seeking out the end consumers. Such merchants counted on intercolonial trade to create reliable markets in key American entrepôts. Owners of vessels carrying enslaved people from Africa

linas," in Michelle LeMaster and Bradford J. Wood, eds., *Creating and Contesting Carolina: Proprietary Era Histories* (Columbia, S.C., 2013), 234–255.

37. For the regions of embarkation in the slave trade to the British Caribbean from 1751 to 1800, see *Voyages,* accessed December 2012, http://slavevoyages.org/tast/assessment/estimates.faces ?yearFrom=1751&yearTo=1800&disembarkation=305.304.307.306.309.308.311.310.301.302.303; for the regions of embarkation in the slave trade to North America, see ibid., http://slavevoyages .org/tast/assessment/estimates.faces?yearFrom=1751&yearTo=1800&disembarkation=205.204 .201.203.202.

Direct African Arrivals
in the British Caribbean

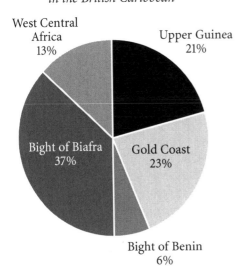

West Central
Africa
13%

Upper Guinea
21%

Bight of Biafra
37%

Gold Coast
23%

Bight of Benin
6%

Direct African Arrivals
in North America

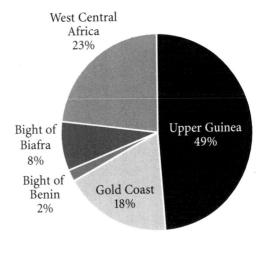

West Central
Africa
23%

Upper Guinea
49%

Bight of
Biafra
8%

Bight of
Benin
2%

Gold Coast
18%

FIGURE 11. Comparison of Captive Origins in the Transatlantic Slave Trades to the British Caribbean and North America, 1751–1807

Source: Voyages: The Trans-Atlantic Slave Trade Database, accessed January 2013, http://slavevoyages .org/tast/assessment/estimates.faces?yearFrom=1751&yearTo=1807&disembarkation=305.304.307 .306.309.308.311.310.301.302.303; http://slavevoyages.org/tast/assessment/estimates.faces?yearFrom =1751&yearTo=1807&disembarkation=205.204.201.203.202.

increasingly recognized (and welcomed) the fact that bulk purchasers for distribution and resale made a few American markets into dependable ports of entry for slave sales. Some earlier transatlantic traders had given their ship captains lists of American markets to try when seeking the highest prices. Isaac Hobhouse, Noblet Ruddock, and William Baker of Bristol organized a slaving voyage in 1725 and instructed Captain William Barry to proceed from Africa in their ship *Dispatch* to Antigua but, if favorable terms were not offered there, to try Nevis and then Charleston as a last resort. Captain Anthony Overstall received similar directions for the *Judith* in 1728, suggesting that he try Barbados, Antigua, Saint Christopher, Jamaica, and then possibly Spanish America in the hunt for high prices—although the ship's owner did encourage Overstall to sell all his captives at one port, once chosen.[38]

38. Isaac Hobhouse, Noblet Ruddock, and William Baker, to the captain of the brig *Dispatch,* Oct. 7, 1725, Jeffries Collection, XIII, fol. 3, Bristol Central Library, U.K.; "The Slave Trade," London, July 8, in Donnan, ed., *Documents,* II, 366–371. For instructions suggesting a balance of

TABLE 18. Estimates of Africans Reaching British North American Colonies from the Caribbean, 1751–1808

Years	Estimated arrivals	Years	Estimated arrivals
1751–1755	4,100	1786–1790	1,600
1756–1760	2,100	1791–1795	700
1761–1765	4,600	1796–1800	600
1766–1770	3,200	1801–1805	1,400
1771–1775	5,900	1806–1808	1,100
1776–1780	100	TOTAL	27,500
1781–1785	2,100		

Note: For the sources and assumptions underlying these estimates, see Gregory E. O'Malley, "Beyond the Middle Passage: Slave Migration from the Caribbean to North America, 1619–1807," *William and Mary Quarterly*, 3d Ser., LXVI (2009), esp. tables I–V, VII–X.

After midcentury, owners of transatlantic slaving ventures increasingly mentioned only a single port in their instructions for selling Africans. In 1765, Aaron Lopez of Rhode Island warned the captain of his ship *Betsey* about the dangers of shipboard mortality and port fees when instructing him to head directly from Africa to Jamaica. "We would not have you put into any port in the West Indies if it Can be avoided," Lopez cautioned. "We have no need of recommending to you that in the persuit of your Voyages, you use the greatest dispatch, as Such a Small Vessel cannot Support any great Expen[se]." But even large ships faced concerns about the port costs of multiple stopovers. As such, many slave merchants ordered ships from Africa to head directly to a single port for all sales or instructed ships to stop only once for information (usually at Barbados, the first island en route from Africa) before proceeding to a final port of sale. Henry Trafford typified this trend when routinely cautioning ship captains that "dispatch is the life of the African Trade." Trafford, like many other merchants, valued speed over finding the absolute highest price. This shift away from port-hopping for prices likely contributed to the declining mortality in the transatlantic trade over the eighteenth century by shortening the duration of the average voyage.[39]

---

speedy sale and high prices, see also "Instructions to Captain William Atkinson," Boston, Dec. 28, 1728, ibid., III, 37; Wilkinson and Ayrault to David Lindsay, Newport, R.I., June 19, 1754, ibid., 148; or Matthew Strong and Co.'s instructions for the *Corsican Hero* in 1771, Tuohy Papers, part 4, 380, TUO 4, letter 4, Liverpool Record Office.

39. Aaron Lopez to Nathaniel Briggs, Newport, R.I., July 22, 1765, in Donnan, ed., *Documents,*

Selling hundreds of African men, women, and children at one place and time, however, required strong demand, making markets where intercolonial traders purchased slaves attractive to many transatlantic traders. Rather than cutting out the middleman by figuring out where and how intercolonial merchants dispersed people for profitable resale, many transatlantic traders trusted that American slave distributors would keep demand stable and prices high enough at the major entrepôts. When Thomas Lanwarn suggested Dominica as a market to Aaron Lopez in 1770, he insisted that merchants there "sell as well to the French and Spaniards, for whom they have large orders to execute, as to our Planters of B.Bs. [Barbados] Antigua and Dominica; so that under these circumstances, Dominica seems to bid fairer to render you advantageous sales, than any other Island." Lanwarn did not recommend a transatlantic voyage to the ultimate consumers of enslaved labor in foreign colonies or even on other British islands. He suggested targeting the busiest hub of transshipment.[40]

The difficulty merchants faced in collecting debts in foreign colonies also convinced British transatlantic traders to sell as wholesalers. In 1788, Liverpool merchant Thomas Leyland warned a partner in the slave trade that sending their ship from Africa directly to Saint-Domingue posed problems, despite the French repeal of laws barring foreign traders, because "the only people who made trial of the St. Domingue market are disappointed, for it is two years ago [and] they have not received their own money." Leyland was aware that intercolonial traders often transshipped arriving Africans from Jamaica to Saint-Domingue, but he preferred security in the sale of his transatlantic

---

III, 211–212 (see also "Instructions to Captain William Ellery," Jan. 14, 1759, 68–69). Rhode Island traders often used smaller ships than was typical of the transatlantic slave trade; see Jay Coughtry, *The Notorious Triangle: Rhode Island and the African Slave Trade, 1700–1807* (Philadelphia, 1981). Writing about early-nineteenth-century trade more generally, Richard Pares argues that port costs and duties were too high in the West Indies to allow trading ventures with numerous ports of call to remain profitable (Pares, *West-India Fortune* [New York, 1950], 226). Trafford reiterated this statement in multiple letters in the 1770s; see Tuohy Papers, part 4, 380 TUO 4, letters 6, 7, Liverpool Record Office. See also Thomas Leyland to Charles Wilson, Dec. 9, 1786, Letter Book of Thomas Leyland, 387 MD 59, 199, ibid. On declining mortality in the eighteenth-century trade, see Herbert S. Klein et al., "Transoceanic Mortality: The Slave Trade in Comparative Perspective," *WMQ*, 3d Ser., LVIII (2001), 93–117.

40. Thomas Lanwarn to Aaron Lopez, Jan. 12, 1770, in Donnan, ed., *Documents*, III, 245. For additional examples of foreign traders' buying slaves in the free ports, see Account Book of the Schooner *Mongovo George*, 1785–1787, BL, Add. MSS, 43841, fols. 29–34; Liverpool Papers, CCXXVII, ibid., 38416, fol. 172; Sales Account Book of Case and Southworth, 1763–1769, Case and Southworth Papers, 380 MD 36, fols. 122–124, Liverpool Record Office.

human cargo. From Liverpool, the logistics of foreign trade and debt collection in the Caribbean were too difficult.[41]

The increased specialization of some transatlantic slave traders as wholesalers (and some American merchants as retailers or distributors) is revealed by two related trends evident in sales of Africans after the Middle Passage. Smaller numbers of buyers purchased larger numbers of people, and increasingly, these buyers were merchants. This trend emerged in the largest British slave market in the Americas—Kingston, Jamaica—even in the late seventeenth and early eighteenth centuries, but it grew more pronounced thereafter and reached other ports. For example, the Kingston branch of the Case and Southworth merchant house routinely sold arriving Africans in large groups during the mid-eighteenth century. Of the 204 captives who arrived on the *Buckley* in 1755, Benjamin Perreira purchased 75 and Jasper Hall bought 47, accounting for more than 60 percent of the shipment between just the two of them. At the sale of the *Adlington*'s cargo later that year, Case and Southworth sold 14 people to the Grant and Lesslie merchant house, while Aaron Barrah Lousada purchased 47. A few months later, Jasper Hall returned to Case and Southworth for the sale of Africans from the *Judith* and purchased 117, whereas Bayley, Ellworthy, and Co. bought 14. For these three shipments combined, Case and Southworth sold more than half the arriving Africans in groups of 45 or more.[42]

The ultimate destinations of these Africans are not documented with certainty, but other records suggest that many of these buyers transshipped Africans to foreign colonies. Jasper Hall sent enslaved people to Curaçao in 1753 and to Havana in 1762, and he also invested in transatlantic slaving voyages that touched at Jamaica before proceeding to Spanish colonies. A "Grant and Co." owned two small transshipments of Africans leaving Kingston in 1755, and these might have been the people that "Grant and Lesslie" purchased from the *Adlington*. Aaron Barrah Lousada made large purchases at all three sales in

41. Leyland to Cornelius Donovan, Aug. 8, 1788, Letter Book of Thomas Leyland, 1786–1788, 387 MD 59, fol. 724–725.

42. On the early rise of bulk purchases in Kingston, see Trevor Burnard, "Who Bought Slaves in Early America? Purchasers of Slaves from the Royal African Company in Jamaica, 1674–1708," *Slavery and Abolition*, XVII, no. 2 (August 1996), 72. Case and Southworth sales: Journal of Case and Southworth, Kingston, 1754–1757, Case and Southworth Papers, 380 MD 33, fols. 120–132, 143–177, 190–216. See also Burnard and Morgan, "Dynamics of the Slave Market," *WMQ*, 3d Ser., LVIII (2001), 214; the authors highlight the prominent role of Jamaica merchants in bulk purchases of arriving African people but seem to assume that these traders purchased people for resale within Jamaica rather than for transshipment.

the Case and Southworth records, and although he does not appear as a ship owner in Jamaica's export records, he and a partner named Samuel Pereira Mendez made their payments to Case and Southworth in "Heavy Money," making it likely that they traded to Spanish America, where hard currency was much more prevalent than in British colonies. Whether these Africans faced transshipment to foreign colonies or not, the consistent prominence of merchants purchasing large groups of arriving Africans suggests that Case and Southworth's suppliers were aware that distributors of Africans formed a large share of their market. They continued to sell African people in Jamaica because intercolonial merchants kept demand and prices steady, allowing Case and Southworth—and other transatlantic traders—to sell captives quickly.[43]

In some cases, intercolonial merchants apparently negotiated discounts for such bulk purchases of people. At the sale of the *Elizabeth*'s cargo at Kingston in 1754, the firm Dias and Gutteres purchased 44 arriving Africans, whereas other purchasers bought just one or two people each. The small purchasers paid an average of £43.75 for adults; Dias and Gutteres paid £35 each (though that rate was for a mix of men and women, whereas the small purchasers bought only men). Similarly, small purchasers on average paid just more than £35 for boys and just less than £35 for girls; Dias and Gutteres paid just £20 each for boys and girls. Some of this discount may be explained by the timing of their purchase late in the sale. The selling agent described the whole group of beleaguered immigrants as "no better than refuse," and, buying late in the

43. Naval Office Shipping Lists for Kingston, Jamaica, CO 142/15, fol. 62, and 142/16, fol. 176; "The Case of the *Africa*," Mar. 27, 1769, in Donnan, ed., *Documents*, II, 533–536; CO 142/16, fols. 73, 83; Journal of Case and Southworth, 380 MD 33, fols. 189–190. Several problems impede tracking slaves by the owners given in the shipping lists even where the lists survive. First, the owner named usually possessed the vessel, but if a merchant paid freight charges to ship goods or slaves aboard a vessel he did not own, his name will not appear in the lists. Second, for ships owned by several people, often only one individual is recorded in the shipping lists; this is apparent from numerous inconsistencies where departure records give one owner but arrival records at another port list a different owner for the same vessel. Perhaps most important, vessels owned by foreigners did not appear in the shipping lists at all before passage of the Free Port Act, and thereafter, foreign ships were recorded in a separate register that did not offer information on ownership. For additional examples of bulk sales in Jamaica, see the records of the slaving ship *Harlequin* from 1782, "Records of Ships Engaged in the Slave Trade from Liverpool: *Harlequin*," Dumbell Papers, MS 10.46, Special Collections and Archives, University of Liverpool Library, U.K.; and three voyages of the ship *Earl of Liverpool*, from 1797–1799, ibid., MS 10.50. See also Burnard and Morgan, "Dynamics of the Slave Market," *WMQ*, 3d Ser., LVIII (2001). For examples from Barbados, see Sales Account Book of Case and Southworth, 1763–1769, 380 MD 36, fols. 120–121; "Accounts of the *Adventure*," 1773, in Donnan, ed., *Documents*, III, 266–267.

sale, Dias and Gutteres might have purchased mainly ill captives. Nonetheless, the price differential is striking.[44]

Not all transatlantic traders were convinced that bulk sales to American merchants worked to their advantage. In 1768, one group of Liverpool merchants—James Clemens, Matthew Stronge, Follicott Powell, and Henry Hardwar—specifically cautioned the captain of their transatlantic vessel *Sally*, bound for Barbados, that intercolonial traders would try to slash prices. The Liverpool traders advised against selling Africans for less than thirty-two pounds each, "for you know they [Barbados traders] Buy Slaves there to make an Advantage of them by sending them to another Markett." Instead, they insisted "that Advantage we may Avail Ourselves of, as well as they, provided the Cargo be healthy, and the Ship in condition to proceed elsewhere." The suspicious Liverpool traders even feared collusion between their own selling agents and intercolonial traders. In 1767, James Clemens and Co. warned the captain of their transatlantic ship *Ranger* that his work would not end once he found a selling agent in the West Indies. Though Clemens recommended specific agents in Barbados, Grenada, Dominica, or Saint Christopher, he urged Captain Speers to monitor these agents during the sale, "allways observing that a large lott of the Slaves be not Sold to some friend or intimate under the price" for which most of the Africans sold. The problem, according to Clemens, was that some agents "Sell off some [slaves] at a tolerable price and let a very large Lott go much under [that price] to their friends, which are sent to other Islands for Sale at an Advance price." Clemens believed the agents "will endeavour to persuade you they are Sold . . . at that low price rather than risque Mortality or detain the Ship," when, in actuality, the selling agents were partners with those who purchased captives for transshipment. Liverpool slave traders Leyland, Penny and Co. revealed a similar concern, telling Captain Charles Wilson in 1788, "Its now become too much the Custom among the Factors to be both buyers and sellers of Slaves." Regardless of such concerns, bulk purchases by intercolonial merchants had become common by the late eighteenth century, and most transatlantic traders welcomed the role of wholesaler for the speedy sales it allowed.[45]

44. "Sale of the Cargo of the *Elizabeth*, 1754," in Donnan, ed., *Documents*, III, 145.

45. Tuohy Papers, part 4, 380 TUO 4, letters 2, 3; "*Madampookata*," 1783, Dumbell Papers, MS.10.47. For another example, see Francis Ingram and Co.'s instructions to Capt. George McMinn of the *Ingram*, bound to Africa and the West Indies, Liverpool, Dec. 31, 1783, Tuohy Papers, part 4, 380 TUO 4, letter 10.

■ Owing to the growth of entrepôts, the free port policy, and the continued expansion of plantation economies, intercolonial slave transshipment reached new heights in the second half of the eighteenth century, but by the century's close, transshipment faced a variety of countervailing pressures, as well. Most notable among these was abolitionism. With strong ties to the spread of new, evangelical forms of Christianity, the abolition movement achieved one of the more dramatic changes of sentiment in human history. The slave trade went relatively unquestioned for centuries; little inkling of future abolitionism can be found in records from the first half of the eighteenth century or earlier. Yet, by the early nineteenth century, passionate and organized abolitionists held the upper hand in both Great Britain and the United States. On the North American mainland, Revolutionary ideology gave rise to significant abolitionist sentiment from the 1770s onward, particularly north of the Carolinas. The constitutional compromise of 1787 prevented federal abolition of the slave trade until 1807, but most states independently maintained prohibitions on African arrivals even after the various nonimportation agreements of the American Revolution had expired. The Carolinas and Georgia offered key exceptions at times, and when they allowed the trade, these states saw robust African arrivals (including transshipments from the Caribbean that approached prewar levels), highlighting the ambiguous relationship between the American Revolution and the slave trade. Nonetheless, elsewhere in the United States, abolitionism halted the importation of Africans—via direct or intercolonial trade—after 1775.[46]

In Britain, as well, abolitionism was on the rise in the late eighteenth century, and discussions of British trade policy at the turn of the nineteenth were full of speculations about the potential economic impact. The practical implications of this moral and economic debate first emerged in legislation to regulate the transatlantic slave trade—policies to standardize sanitation, food, and crowding aboard ship—but they had little effect on transshipment. By contrast, the first major British act curtailing the trade in slaves affected the

46. Winthrop D. Jordan, *White over Black: American Attitudes toward the Negro, 1550–1812* (Chapel Hill, N.C., 1968), 44. It is critical to note that opposition to the slave trade in the Revolutionary era often did not include opposition to slavery more generally, nor egalitarianism with regard to Africans or African Americans; see David Brion Davis, *The Problem of Slavery in the Age of Revolution, 1770–1823* (Ithaca, N.Y., 1975), esp. chaps. 6 and 7. On the slave trade to the early Republic and federal policies toward it, see McMillin, *Final Victims*; Don E. Fehrenbacher, *The Slaveholding Republic: An Account of the United States Government's Relations to Slavery* (New York, 2001); Jed Handelsman Shugerman, "The Louisiana Purchase and South Carolina's Reopening of the Slave Trade," *Journal of the Early Republic*, XXII (2002), 263–290.

intercolonial trade at least as much as the transatlantic one. In 1806, Parliament passed An Act to Prevent the Importation of Slaves, by Any of His Majesty's Subjects, into Any Islands, Colonies, Plantations, or Territories Belonging to Any Foreign Sovereign, State, or Power. The act applied to both direct African shipments and intercolonial ones, but given the prevalence of transshipment as a strategy for selling captives abroad, the act was a huge blow to the intercolonial trade. Distribution from one British colony to another could continue, but the largest branch of the intercolonial slave trade was finished, at least legally. The next major blow came just one year later, when both Parliament and Congress approved abolition of the transatlantic slave trade altogether, effective January 1, 1808. Movements of enslaved people within and between British colonies and between American states would continue until slavery itself was abolished, but these internal migrations would be quite different—no longer final passages of journeys from Africa. The intercolonial and interstate slave trades after 1808 mainly involved movements of people who had worked for years or their entire lives on New World plantations.[47]

Though abolitionism posed the most powerful challenge to the intercolonial slave trade, it was not the only pressure against transshipment at the close of the eighteenth century. Paradoxically, the broader phenomenon that produced the Free Port Act also undercut the intercolonial trade. The act was part of a trend toward less restricted international trade—a movement away from mercantilism and toward free-market capitalism. As imperial regulations and confiscations in foreign ports diminished, the need to route the slave trade through colonial hubs declined. To attract slave shipments to French colonies,

47. Copy of "A Bill Intituled, An Act to Prevent the Importation of Slaves, by Any of His Majesty's Subjects, into Any Islands, Colonies, Plantations, or Territories Belonging to Any Foreign Sovereign, State, or Power . . . ," Dropmore Papers, CDLI, BL, Add. MSS, 59305, fols. 42–51. On British debates over abolition, see, for starters, Davis, *Problem of Slavery in the Age of Revolution;* Christopher Leslie Brown, *Moral Capital: Foundations of British Abolitionism* (Chapel Hill, N.C., 2006); Seymour Drescher, *Econocide: British Slavery in the Era of Abolition* (1977; rpt. Chapel Hill, N.C., 2010); David Beck Ryden, *West Indian Slavery and British Abolition, 1783–1807* (New York, 2009). For the intra-Caribbean trade after 1807, see D[avid] Eltis, "The Traffic in Slaves between the British West Indian Colonies, 1807–1833," *Economic History Review,* XXV (1972), 55–64; Hilary McD. Beckles, "'An Unfeeling Traffick': The Intercolonial Movement of Slaves in the British Caribbean, 1807–1833," in Walter Johnson, ed., *The Chattel Principle: Internal Slave Trades in the Americas* (New Haven, Conn., 2004), 256–274. For the internal U.S. trade, see Johnson, ed., *Chattel Principle;* Walter Johnson, *Soul by Soul: Life inside the Antebellum Slave Market* (Cambridge, Mass., 1999); Michael Tadman, *Speculators and Slaves: Masters, Traders, and Slaves in the Old South* (Madison, Wis., 1989); Steven Deyle, *Carry Me Back: The Domestic Slave Trade in American Life* (New York, 2005).

for example, French officials went so far as to place a bounty on all deliveries in the 1780s, adding to the profits available for slave traders. The bounty was officially for French merchants, but administrators in France liberally granted British slave traders the right to sail directly from Africa under the French flag in order to supply labor to French colonies and collect the bounty. As a British ambassador in France reported to a Liverpool merchant in 1788, "The advanced Prices which slaves fetch at St. Domingo have induc'd many English Houses to send their Vessels there in preference to the other Islands." Sailing under the French flag, such traders had little cause to stop in the British Caribbean. British officials condoned the practice because it bolstered their slave trade, increased their exports of manufactured goods to Africa, and routed more French Caribbean produce to England. The intercolonial slave trade might have jump-started Caribbean free trade, but now free trade was running just fine on its own.[48]

The story of Liverpool transatlantic trader Thomas Leyland illustrates both the pressure against transshipment due to loosening trade restrictions and the reason why British slave traders had employed transshipment for so long. In the last two decades of the eighteenth century, Leyland organized numerous transatlantic voyages that delivered African people to various British entrepôts. He consistently instructed captains to buy people in Africa who would suit Spanish markets but then sent them to British ports for sale. Unlike many fellow wholesalers in the transatlantic trade, Leyland was not satisfied selling slaves in Kingston when he knew these people resold in Spanish America at higher prices. Leyland sent letters to merchants and officials far and wide, seeking information on how to proceed directly to Spanish America without having his ship and cargo confiscated. He wrote to Moses Benson of London, inquiring whether bribing Spanish officials was the best strategy, and shortly thereafter, he wrote to a Spanish ambassador in London, promising to pay "whatever may be required as an equivalent" for a license to trade in Cuba. Nonetheless, his voyages continued to sell Africans in Barbados, Jamaica, and Dominica. The most exasperating might have been his shipment of people to Dominica in 1786, where a Mr. Blair purchased them all—and then proceeded to hire Leyland's own ship to deliver the human cargo to Cuba. In 1803, how-

48. Frank J. Nephews to Joseph Ingram, Bordeaux, Jun. 9, 1788, Liverpool Papers, CCXXVII, BL, Add. MSS, 38416, fol. 111. In the early nineteenth century, the Dutch started allowing British traders to ship slaves under the Dutch flag to attract direct shipments to their colonies as well. Spanish trade barriers also eased. See ibid., 38416, fols. 315–316. See also Geggus, "French Slave Trade," 126; Ryden, *West Indian Slavery and British Abolition*, 6–7; Stein, *French Slave Trade*, 39.

ever, Leyland finally managed to send a transatlantic vessel directly to Spanish America. He instructed his ship *Enterprize* to head to Barbados for information, but its account of sales is from Havana. Apparently, Spain's loosening restrictions offered Leyland a way in. As trade barriers fell, more transatlantic traders were able to head directly to foreign markets. Nonetheless, Leyland's prior struggles to circumvent transshipment for direct deliveries to Spanish America underscore the crucial role it played in extending commercial networks and spreading African slavery. Intercolonial traders had capitalized on their proximity to foreign territories to acquire timely information and build foreign connections, opening routes of commerce that had remained stubbornly closed to transatlantic traders based in Europe. In the process, they had extended the reach and duration of the transatlantic slave trade, adding final passages for hundreds of thousands of captives who spread the African Diaspora across the Americas.[49]

49. For the thwarted desire to trade to Spanish America, see Letter Book of Thomas Leyland, 1786–1788, 387 MD 59, esp. fols. 19–20. For the voyage directly to Cuba, see Account Book of the *Enterprize*, 1803, in Account Books of the Ships of Thomas Leyland and Co., 387 MD 43.

epilogue
Defending the Human Commodity; or, Diversity and Diaspora

A trade to [the] Spanish main for British manufactures and Indian goods, is cover'd wholly by a few slaves, and the Trade dependant altogether on that share in the assortment. — George Rose, 1806

Dey talk all kind of Country. — 'Sibell, 1799

In 1806, frustrated by a recent string of defeats, British abolitionists developed a strategy to neutralize two key arguments for the slave trade, changing the debate in a way that forced defenders of the commerce to articulate the value of the intercolonial branch of the trade. In the late eighteenth and early nineteenth centuries, momentum for abolishing the slave trade had surged in the British Empire (and in the newly independent United States), but in 1804 and 1805, not to mention several times in preceding decades, abolitionists had tried and failed to push bills for total slave trade abolition through Britain's Parliament. Slave trade proponents had employed two key arguments to keep parliamentary opinion on their side: that colonial economies would collapse without steady supplies of enslaved labor, and that the transatlantic slave trade—far from harming Africans—rescued them from a backward and heathen "Dark Continent" by delivering them into the light of Christian civilization. As Robert Bisset summed up the second point when opposing the total abolition bill of 1805, "By the Slave trade, humanity was essentially promoted, instead of being violated."[1]

Abolitionists refuted such arguments, citing evidence of horrific disease on slave ships and brutality on American plantations, but having failed to win the parliamentary battles in 1804 or 1805, they decided to exploit a different

---

1. Robert Bisset, *The History of the Negro Slave Trade, in Its Connection with the Commerce and Prosperity of the West Indies, and the Wealth and Power of the British Empire* (London, 1805), I, ix. For an overview of the pro–slave trade arguments, see David Beck Ryden, *West Indian Slavery and British Abolition, 1783–1807* (New York, 2009), chap. 8.

weakness in 1806. The logic of the pro–slave trade arguments only applied to deliveries of Africans to British colonies. If settlements would collapse without slave labor, abolitionists asked, why were British slave traders propping up the economies of French and Spanish America? If Africans benefited from being introduced to civility and Christianity in the Americas, then how could slave traders from Britain justify their sales of innocent, impressionable Africans to the colonies of backward, Catholic France and Spain? In 1806, abolitionists compelled slave trade supporters to confront such questions by pushing Parliament to consider a partial abolition that would bar traders only from selling Africans in foreign colonies. This penultimate act to outlawing the slave trade has been overshadowed in historical memory by the more thorough-going abolition of the following year, but the partial abolition held particular significance for the intercolonial trade, since slave dealers preferred to access foreign markets via transshipment. As such, the debate surrounding the 1806 act highlighted the intercolonial slave trade's significance — or perceived significance — to British commerce.[2]

Focused solely on the slave trade to French and Spanish America, the 1806 debate forced defenders of the slave trade to emphasize the profitability of selling commodified people, since arguments about a workforce for British

2. On the abolitionists' strategy in 1806, see [William Grenville?], "Observations in Answer to the Question 'Whether a General Abolition Bill Should Now Be Brought into Parliament,' May 19, 1806," Dropmore Papers, CDLI, Additional Manuscripts, 59305, fol. 60, British Library, London (hereafter cited as BL, Add. MSS). Seymour Drescher argues that abolitionists' critique of the foreign trade in 1806 was especially resonant in the context of the Napoleonic Wars, given the strong anti-French (and Spanish) sentiments in Britain (Drescher, *Abolition: A History of Slavery and Antislavery* [New York, 2009], 226). Abolitionists in the U.S. had actually made a similar argument about American involvement in slave trading to foreign territories a decade earlier. In a petition to Congress in 1790, Connecticut abolitionists argued "That the principle, 'that the labor of slaves is necessary to the due cultivation of our land,' has introduced a commerce in the human race far beyond the pretended necessities of our country, and has led the citizens of these States into a very extensive trade for the supply of other nations with slaves — a trade, in the end, generally unproductive to the adventurers, always destructive to the lives and morals of the seamen, and, as relative to the victims devoted to slavery, most inhuman, not only with respect to their subsequent situation, but especially during their passage." Congress agreed, barring the U.S. slave trade to foreign territories. In this case, however, separately targeting the foreign branch of the trade had more to do with the Constitution's protection of slave importation to the U.S. (until 1808) than it did with abolitionist strategy, see *Memorials Presented to the Congress of the United States of America, by the Different Societies Instituted for Promoting the Abolition of Slavery, etc. etc. in the States of Rhode-Island, Connecticut, New-York, Pennsylvania, Mary-Land, and Virginia* (Philadelphia, 1792), 8; see also Hugh Thomas, *The Slave Trade: The Story of the Atlantic Slave Trade, 1440–1870* (New York, 1997), 518–519.

colonies and about introducing Africans to Protestantism were now irrelevant. Public claims about the profitability of selling people to rival empires were not new; they had appeared, for instance, in the debate over Dolben's Act in 1788, which limited the number of captives each vessel could carry. Anti-abolitionists had protested that Dolben's Act threatened the foreign slave trade, since that branch depended on British merchants' having competitive prices relative to imperial rivals. As Henry Ellis explained, "If those Restraints [on the number of people carried] should . . . discourage the Merchants, or considerably . . . raise the Price of Slaves in the West Indies, the Consequences, must necessarily be fatal; for then, we shall lose the Advantage of supplying other Nations with them, which we have hitherto done to a very large Amount." Former slave ship captain and merchant Thomas King articulated a similar point in testimony before the House of Commons in 1790, insisting the British "West India islands . . . would be very materially affected" by any limits on the slave trade "by losing that most valuable branch of the trade, the exportation to foreigners of a large proportion of the negroes imported in British ships." [3]

Although arguments like Ellis's and King's had been made before 1806, the more limited abolition bill of that year compelled slave trade proponents to rely almost entirely on such economic logic. Their resulting statements were particularly revealing of the value that slave traders and some imperial thinkers perceived in the intercolonial slave trade to French and Spanish America. To defenders of the slave trade, supplying enslaved Africans to foreign colonies was inextricably linked to all other British commerce with these territories. As George Rose put it, "A trade to [the] Spanish main for British manufactures and [East] Indian goods, is cover'd wholly by a few slaves and the Trade dependant altogether on that share in the assortment." An anonymous slave trade advocate agreed:

> If the Bill now depending in the House of Commons for preventing
> the Importation of Slaves by British Subjects into foreign Colonies
> should pass into a Law, it would . . . much injure one important Trade
> to Spanish America, and annihilate another. The first alluded to is the
> Trade carried on from the Free Ports in the British West Indies to the
> . . . Settlements of the Spaniards . . . as that is considerably facilitated

3. Henry Ellis to Lord Hawkesbury, Apr. 12, 1788, BL, Add. MSS, 38416, fol. 162; *Abridgment of the Minutes of the Evidence, Taken before [a] Committee of the Whole House, to Whom It Was Referred to Consider of the Slave-Trade* ([London], 1789), I, 72.

and extended by the Vessels carrying cargoes of British Manufactures
. . . having a few Negroes on board; without which in some Instances
they would hardly obtain Admittance.[4]

Abolitionists countered with examples of British ventures to foreign colonies without enslaved people—but in many ways, the debate was already won. Refuting that the slave trade opened other branches of commerce was unnecessary. With pro–slave trade arguments about British colonial labor needs and the conversion of Africans to Protestantism now immaterial, abolitionists had obliged defenders of the slave trade to assert the value of enslaved people as goods. For it was only when viewing Africans as commodities—not as laborers or candidates for conversion—that selling Africans to rival, Catholic empires made sense. Abolitionists had spent the two preceding decades persuading the British populace to see enslaved Africans as people, humanizing them through stories of families torn asunder and powerful firsthand accounts like Olaudah Equiano's. Now, supporters of the slave trade were stuck insisting that Africans were living trade goods in such high demand that the markets of French and Spanish America would open to traders who sold them.

In a speech in the House of Lords, anti-abolitionist Edward Law epitomized this view of slaves while describing the long history of government support for the slave trade to foreign colonies. The crown "recommends the Trade in this Article" and "made Jamaica a Mart for the same Commodity, for other Nations" with the Free Port Act. With his use of "article" and "commodity," Law sought to dehumanize enslaved people for his audience, but the language played right into the hands of his opponents. In the context of the early nineteenth century, with Enlightenment ideals of equality—and evangelical zeal for the equality of all souls—on the rise, defenders of the slave trade struggled to make purely economic arguments resonate with the British populace. Arguments defending slavery as a civilizing institution for supposedly benighted Africans—or even casting Africans as essential laborers for Britain's colonies—continued to carry some force in Anglo-Atlantic arguments, but the insistence that African people were valuable "articles" that facilitated trade in other items simply abstracted enslaved Africans from their humanity more thoroughly than most early-nineteenth-century Britons would bear. The 1806 bill for abolishing the slave trade to foreign colonies passed easily, and the

4. George Rose is quoted in William Young's 1806 notes on a report on imports and exports of slaves in British Caribbean colonies; see BL, Add. MSS, 59305, fol. 56; "May 1806, Observations on the Bill for Preventing British Ships Supplying Foreign Colonies with Slaves and on the Trade to South America," in Dropmore Papers, CDLI, ibid., fols. 67–68.

abolitionist momentum carried over to the following year, when the termination of Britain's transatlantic slave trade finally pushed through Parliament. A similar bill passed through the U.S. Congress, resulting in both powers' outlawing the trade as of January 1, 1808.[5]

In addition to being on the wrong side of history, anti-abolitionists were also incorrect about the slave trade's necessity for opening commerce with foreign colonies by the early nineteenth century. Britain's trade with French, Spanish, and even Portuguese America would grow, rather than decline, with the slave trade banned. It was no longer necessary. In preceding centuries, most empires had espoused policies that limited international commerce with their colonies, and slave trading had provided a key to the closed gates of foreign markets. Some colonies had exhibited such insatiable demand for enslaved workers that colonists and colonial officials—induced by need or bribes—had been convinced to evade or to ignore imperial laws in order to allow British slave traders to enter. Once inside, traders sold both slaves and goods at great profits. The slave trade proponent's notion that the trade in other merchandise was "facilitated and extended by the Vessels . . . having a few Negroes on board" accurately described the seventeenth- and eighteenth-century commerce across imperial boundaries.

But circumstances were changing. In part to ensure supplies of slave labor or to profit by being the suppliers, the French, Spanish, and British Empires all relaxed restrictions on foreign trade over the final decades of the eighteenth century. By the early nineteenth century, enough barriers had fallen that traders no longer needed slaves to facilitate a broader foreign commerce. As abolitionist William Young argued in the 1806 debates, records from the British "free port" of Grenada from the first years of the nineteenth century showed "Mr. George Rose to be wholly unfounded in his assertion," about foreign trade's dependence on human trafficking. Though Grenada had formerly been a thriving port of the British slave trade to Spanish America, Young noted that in 1802 and 1803 Grenada still possessed "a very considerable share" of the trade to Spanish America of "print'd Cottons, and hardware, etc," despite having "Exported only 4 Slaves" in those two years. Young insisted the slave trade could be abolished without cutting British traders out of such commerce. Indeed, British merchants would remain prominent throughout the Americas long after abolition. The slave trade had been central to loosen-

---

5. Speech of Edward Law in the House of Lords, BL, Add. MSS, 12433, fol. 11. The vote on the Foreign Abolition Bill was 35 to 13 in the House of Commons and 43 to 18 in the House of Lords (Thomas, *Slave Trade*, 553).

ing trade restrictions, but was no longer needed in the era of freer trade. The commercial networks that slave traders had established across borders could be maintained without continuing that gateway commerce. The British government accordingly heeded abolitionist calls and barred British traders from selling African people in foreign colonies. For intercolonial merchants, the trade in newly arrived Africans was over.[6]

■ But, of course, the end of the slave trade for merchants was not an ending for their captives. Additional enslaved people would not legally enter the trade, but those Africans who had survived the journeys and the seasoning to new environments lived on in the communities where the slave trade left them. Many reared children in these new lands as well. Since the slave trade was always two things at once, commerce and migration, we need a second conclusion to reflect on the implications of the intercolonial slave trade as diaspora. The most important legacy of this forced migration was its dispersal of African people—with their diverse languages, folkways, and foodways—from the entrepôts of the slave trade to the broad swaths of the Americas where slavery abounded. By shuttling people between American colonies, the intercolonial slave trade added a degree of complexity to the dispersal of people and cultures to various American communities.

Henry Laurens captured something of this complexity when he courted slave shipments from the Caribbean in the summer of 1755, reminding merchants in the islands to recognize the diversity of captives arriving from Africa. All slaves were not created equal. For the South Carolina market, "There must not be a Callabar amongst them. Gold Coast or Gambias are best; next to them the Windward Coast are prefer'd to Angolas." That Laurens felt compelled to include a list of alternates to his top choices captured an important truth about the Atlantic slave trade. An array of African peoples populated the traffic, and although plantation owners had preferences for their captives' backgrounds, they could not count on having those preferences met. Even a prominent merchant like Laurens, in the biggest slave market in British North America, saw that he might have to settle for third, fourth, or fifth choices. In fact, despite his emphatic rejection of "Callabars" (captives from the Bight of Biafra) as unsuitable for the South Carolina market, Laurens repeatedly managed to sell people of just that description to labor-hungry planters.[7]

6. See William Young's notes, BL, Add. MSS, 59305, fol. 56.

7. Henry Laurens to Smith and Clifton, July 17, 1755, in Philip M. Hamer et al., eds., *The Papers of Henry Laurens,* 16 vols. (Columbia, S.C., 1968–2002), I, 294–295. For examples of Laurens's

This range of regions from which traders drew their human commodities led to diversity in the enslaved populations on the ground in American colonies. Although patterns in the transatlantic slave trade linked particular African regions to single colonial places to some degree, the intercolonial slave trade tangled those lines of connection. People from all the far-flung African regions that Laurens ranked in his list (and a few others) ended up in individual American colonies. As a result, diversity shaped life in the slave quarters of colonial America. Even planters and merchants recognized that men and women from the Gold Coast were quite different from those from the Bight of Biafra; people from Angola were not like those from Senegambia. For the captives, these differences were profound.

In Olaudah Equiano's account of captivity in the slave trade, he described not only a Middle Passage from the Bight of Biafra to Barbados but also an intercolonial journey from Barbados to Virginia, and his narration of arrival and dispersal in America emphasized a series of separations. Each stage of the journey, each transaction, left him more alienated from his shipmates and farther from all that was familiar. After the initial sale of captives from his transatlantic vessel in Barbados, during which Equiano went unsold, he explained, "I now totally lost the small remains of comfort I had enjoyed in conversing with my countrymen," as most of them were purchased and taken away. His estrangement was not yet quite total, however, because after several days, he and a few other unsold captives were transshipped to Virginia. After the intercolonial voyage, Equiano's alienation deepened. He described his sloop's being "landed up a river a good way from the sea . . . where we saw few or none of our native Africans, and not one soul who could talk to me." After "a few weeks" in this new land, Equiano's "companions were distributed different ways, and only myself was left. I was now exceedingly miserable, and thought myself worse off than any of the rest of my companions; for they could talk to each other." Again and again, Equiano noted the partings and parsings of shipmates and his growing inability to speak to those around him. This isolation did not result from being the only enslaved person in his vicinity; he referred to a few others explicitly, and he described the place he toiled as a "plantation" and an "estate," implying the presence of numerous enslaved people. Equiano's loneliness owed, rather, to his separation from

---

selling so-called Calabars in South Carolina despite his oft-repeated preferences against merchants' sending them, see ibid., I, 257–259, II, 493, IV, 246–247, 320–322. On colonists' general inability to compel slave traders to meet their preferences, see David Eltis, Philip Morgan, and David Richardson, "Agency and Diaspora in Atlantic History: Reassessing the African Contribution to Rice Cultivation in the Americas," *American Historical Review,* CXII (2007), esp. 1345.

the "countrymen" with whom he had crossed the Atlantic and with whom he shared language and culture. He described no bond that he felt with the American-born slaves or people from foreign parts of Africa that populated his new plantation home. Just like his European captors, the other enslaved people were strangers to Equiano, leaving him with "no person to speak to that I could understand." [8]

Whether this segment of Equiano's *Interesting Narrative* presented his lived experience or a composite account based on scenes he witnessed or heard described in the Americas, his description of growing disaffection as the vagaries of American slave markets separated shipmates reflects the intercolonial slave trade's impact on captives. An astonishing array of people crossed the Atlantic from Africa. Even though many traversed the ocean on ships with people of a similar background, the intercolonial trade increased the mixing of peoples from various African regions. As the routes of the slave trade—transatlantic and intercolonial—overlapped and meandered through time, they scattered and blended African peoples from a smattering of different regions across the American landscape in myriad combinations.

Furthermore, the broad African regions to which scholars typically refer to impose order on the slave trade do not correlate directly to discrete or unified African cultures. Ports on the Bight of Benin or the Gold Coast or in west central Africa served as gateways for the departure of captive African people from broad hinterlands. Such people did not necessarily share languages, beliefs, or any sense of solidarity just because they departed Africa from the same stretch of coast—at least, not at the outset. As 'Sibell put it when remembering her confinement at an African port before crossing the Atlantic, she was placed in

> a long House full of new negurs talking and making sing—but veddy few of dem bin of my Country. . . . De sailors keep me in dere a long time and bring down two, tree ebbery day 'till de long house bin full— dere bin many Black people dere reddy bad man, dey talk all kind of Country and tell we all dat we going to a good Massah yonder yonder.

8. "The Interesting Narrative of the Life of Olaudah Equiano, or Gustavus Vassa, the African, Written by Himself," in Vincent Carretta, ed., *The Interesting Narrative and Other Writings* (New York, 2003), 62. This challenge for a young Igbo in the slave trade would have been compounded by the fact that many dialects of Igbo existed, which were only mutually intelligible with skill and effort (Alexander X. Byrd, *Captives and Voyagers: Black Migrants across the Eighteenth-Century British Atlantic World* [Baton Rouge, 2008], 18–19, 30). For a rich discussion of this section of Equiano's narrative and of the importance of shared language to captives in the slave trade, see also Byrd, "Eboe, Country, Nation, and Gustavus Vassa's *Interesting Narrative*," *WMQ*, 3d Ser., LXIII (2006), 132–133.

The full meaning of 'Sibell's story is unclear at times—owing, at least in part, to the phonetic transcription of her words by a British traveler—but at several points, 'Sibell indicates her sense of isolation from fellow captives. "Veddy few of dem bin of my Country," she notes, and when she refers to the communication between her captors and her fellow captives with the phrase "dey talk all kind of Country," she suggests that many languages were spoken. Before even departing Africa, 'Sibell found herself thrust among people incomprehensible to her. It is unknown from which African port or region she departed, but it could have been any of them. Survivors like 'Sibell encountered new people at every stage of the journey from interior Africa to New World slavery, and the intercolonial branch of the trade added yet another layer of separation, sortings, and thrusting together of diverse peoples.[9]

This emphasis on diversity in the slave trade, however, should not obscure things all survivors of the forced migration shared—the experience of being wrenched from one's homeland, surviving torturous confinement aboard a slave ship (or ships), and settling in a strange, new land under the harsh regime of chattel slavery. These survivors' backgrounds varied, but the seeds of co-operation and adaptation were sown in their shared experiences and predicament. Survivors of the slave trade would bridge their diversity to create new, vibrant cultures grounded in both new soil and myriad old traditions. Adaptation to new environments and to new, multicultural comrades-in-chains was central to the experience of the Atlantic slave trade—transatlantic and intercolonial. To preserve elements of their African pasts, survivors of the Atlantic slave trade shared with one another, sought common ground where possible, and embraced adaptation.[10]

The Gullah language is a fundamental example of enslaved people's adjusting to their new environment in order to communicate. For enslaved immigrants to the South Carolina and Georgia Lowcountry, Gullah offered the means by which they bridged linguistic barriers to communicate, negotiate,

9. 'Sibell's account, transcribed by John Ford in Barbados in 1799, is reprinted in Stephanie E. Smallwood, *Saltwater Slavery: A Middle Passage from Africa to American Diaspora* (Cambridge, Mass., 2007), 203–204; see also Jerome S. Handler, "Survivors of the Middle Passage: Life Histories of Enslaved Africans in British America," *Slavery and Abolition,* XXIII, no. 1 (April 2002), 32–33, 46.

10. On Africans' forging new, broader identities based on the shared experience of enslavement, see Byrd, "Eboe, Country, Nation," *WMQ,* 3d Ser., LXIII (2006), 139–141; Michael A. Gomez, *Exchanging Our Country Marks: The Transformation of African Identities in the Colonial and Antebellum South* (Chapel Hill, N.C., 1998), esp. chaps. 8–10; Michael Mullin, *Africa in America: Slave Acculturation and Resistance in the American South and the British Caribbean, 1736–1831* (Urbana, Ill., 1992).

and cooperate with one another—without simply adopting the language of those who held them in bondage. Gullah was no one African language transplanted but had roots in Wolof, Ibo, Ga, Yoruba, Ewe, Fante, Kikongo, Kimbundu, Mandinka, Twi, and probably others. Spoken nowhere in Africa, Gullah nonetheless injected America with African culture and offered enslaved people a social and cultural sphere that colonists of European descent could not readily penetrate. Gullah thus offers one example of how diverse African settlers both adapted to one another and their new surroundings while transplanting vital elements of African culture and seeing them flower in new hybrid forms.[11]

Music offered another sphere in which enslaved Africans in the Americas could transplant elements of their cultures while also forging links with one another. When the British naturalist and physician Hans Sloane and a French musician named Baptiste visited a Jamaica plantation in 1688, they enjoyed a rare opportunity to observe the enslaved inhabitants in an evening of music and dance. That the music these European visitors heard had African roots was clear. For one thing, the instruments were foreign to Europeans— including an eight-stringed harp, "several sorts . . . in imitation of Lutes, made of small Gourds fitted with Necks," and "Rattles" the performers "ty'd to their Legs" while dancing. The rhythms and melodies were also exotic to European ears. Sloane found some of the music dissonant at first, although he gradually succumbed to its allure. Not only was this music different from anything the European visitors had heard, but it also varied from song to song. A first piece emphasized percussion and group vocals, with dozens of dancers singing and pounding out a rhythm upon makeshift percussion instruments of many sorts: sticks, hoe blades, and drums. A second song was instrumental, with a repetitive tune over a hypnotic beat. Another piece struck the observers as more melodic, with a single vocalist accompanied softly by an unrecognized instrument. When the music ended, an overseer questioned the musicians in a pidgin language on behalf of Sloane and Baptiste; he learned that the musical styles came from varied parts of Africa. The first song, he believed the slaves told him, was Angolan; the second, Papaw; and the last, Koromanti. The enslaved inhabitants of this single Jamaican plantation were re-creating and adapting musical traditions carried from west central Africa, the Bight of Benin, and the Gold Coast. And people of all of these backgrounds sat and danced around one fire sharing these musical traditions, suggesting an inevi-

11. Charles Joyner, *Down by the Riverside: A South Carolina Slave Community* (Urbana, Ill., 1984), chap. 7, esp. 197.

table melding of styles, traditions, and influences. Percussion banged out on hoe blades suggests that the new American plantation environment influenced this music, as well. It was both traditionally African and something new under the sun—a product of the pan-West African slave quarters of America.[12]

The unwilling passengers in the slave trade—transatlantic and intercolonial—were wrenched from the cultures of their birth but could never be stripped of those cultures entirely. Wherever they settled, enslaved Africans in the Americas were sure to meet fellow slaves who clung to different elements of different African pasts. This diversity limited opportunities for preserving any one African culture intact in an American colony, but the creation of new hybrid languages, rituals, and musical styles attests to the flowering of new African American cultures and to the resilience of the human spirit.

■ Discussion of the slave trade often treats it as a trade apart. Because this peculiar commerce involved the buying and selling of human beings rather than things, most people cordon it off as distinct from the trade in pottery, cloth, or sugar. The great accomplishment of abolitionists was to convince people to see the slave trade in this way—as a brutal removal of people from families and homelands, not just a series of purchases, shipments, and profitable sales. That shift in perception was a humanitarian triumph that rendered slave trading unseemly, brutal, and unacceptable in the eyes of many who had previously tolerated it without much thought. This truth that the commodities of the slave trade were people who suffered unspeakable hardship and degradation made the old view of the slave trade obsolete. In many ways, abolitionists' success was predicated on redefining slaves as captive people rather than commodities and redefining the slave trade as a forced migration rather than commerce. Once most people in London or Philadelphia empathized with captive human commodities, they stopped caring as much about what slave traders' accounting ledgers said about the profitability of the commerce in African people—or its utility for enabling other trades. Many who once had been blind to slaves' humanity developed a new aversion to seeing slaves as commodities.

Laudable as that awakening is, the troubling reality is that understanding the full significance of the slave trade requires reckoning not only with

12. Sloan and Baptiste's encounter (Hans Sloane, *A Voyage to the Islands of Madera, Barbados, Nieves, St. Christopher, and Jamaica* . . . , I [London, 1707], xlviii–xlix, liii) is analyzed and quoted in Richard Cullen Rath, "African Music in Seventeenth-Century Jamaica: Cultural Transit and Transition," *WMQ*, 3d Ser., L (1993), 700–726, esp. 712; for Sloane's illustration of the instruments, see 704.

the abolitionists' truth but also with the traders'. The extensive intercolonial slave trade from British colonies to those of France and Spain and the British Empire's aggressive pursuit of this commerce (a branch often omitted from studies of the transatlantic slave trade) was grounded in the traders' and policy makers' disconcerting view of Africans as trade goods, rather than laborers. To understand why slave traders transshipped so many Africans from one colony to another when the initial port had plenty of demand for enslaved labor, to understand why British traders provided laborers to the colonies of supposed rivals and enemies, and to appreciate fully the profits that slave-exploiting societies generated on the backs of African people, one must reckon not only with the labor value of the enslaved toiling on American plantations but also with their commodity value in the Atlantic marketplace.

Only that commodity value explains British traders' and imperial policy makers' aggressive pursuit of slave sales to rival empires. It made little sense to provide workers to one's rivals, but it made perfect sense to sell commodities to rivals at inflated prices. A similar logic applied to the intercolonial trade within the British Empire. When intercolonial merchants purchased enslaved people in labor-hungry Barbados for transshipment to labor-hungry South Carolina, the needs of either colony interested the traders only insofar as those needs affected prices. If prices in the two colonies did not support slave transshipment, such traders would deal in rum, sugar, or European manufactured goods instead. Such treatment of African people as items for exchange offered a vital source of profit in the slave system, alongside the obvious benefits of exploiting enslaved people for work. In fact, the potential exchange value persisted even after Africans settled on American plantations; the enslaved faced not only toil in the New World but also the persistent threat that a master might choose to capitalize on their exchange value, severing whatever personal ties they managed to develop. This exploitation of African people as trade goods exposed chattel slavery at its most dehumanizing, which is why the slave trade proved more vulnerable to abolitionist critique than slavery itself on the plantations of America.

In one of the most poignant passages of his narrative of life as an enslaved sailor working in the slave trade, Olaudah Equiano appealed to the emotions of his readers by describing the heartbreak of captives separated from loved ones. "It was not uncommon," Equiano noted, "to see negroes taken from their wives . . . and children from their parents." Although abolitionists often highlighted such rending of families to humanize the victims and to invite readers to empathize, Equiano's story was distinct because it did not occur in Africa, with a captive's initial enslavement. Equiano's tale of separation took place on an American pier, "at or after a sale," as some arriving African men, women, and children headed back out to sea. Equiano described "the friends of the departed [who] have been at the water side, and, with sighs and tears, have kept their eyes fixed on the vessel till it went out of sight." Abolitionists like Equiano, by adding "sighs and tears" to public awareness of the slave trade, recast it as a forced migration with unspeakable consequences. But to understand why so many arriving Africans were "sent off to other islands" in the first place, we must also consider the perspective of the less sympathetic characters in this drama—men like George Rose, who were unmoved by "sighs and tears" but who were moved instead by an understanding that "a trade to [the] Spanish main for British manufactures and [East] Indian goods, is cover'd wholly by a few slaves." That commodity logic entangled the profits of slave trading with the profits of broader commerce and dictated that, in the American entrepôts of the slave trade, men would be "taken from their wives . . . and children from their parents" so that some could be "sent off to other islands." The human drama of the victims and the cold calculus of the traders went hand in hand. Only by comprehending both of these aspects of the exploitative trade can we begin to fathom what was gained through the final passage—and what it cost.[13]

13. "The Interesting Narrative of the Life of Olaudah Equiano, or Gustavus Vassa, the African, Written by Himself" (1789), rpt. in William L. Andrews and Henry Louis Gates, Jr., eds., *Slave Narratives* (New York, 2002), 126 (this version is based on a different eighteenth-century edition of Equiano's text than the one cited elsewhere in the present work); BL, Add. MSS, 59305, fol. 56.

appendix
Estimating the Scale of the Intercolonial Slave Trade

All estimates of the volume of the intercolonial slave trade in the present work derive primarily from a database, compiled by the author, of individual shipments carrying African people between American colonies. This database is modeled on the website *Voyages: The Trans-Atlantic Slave Trade Database* (www.slavevoyages.org), but whereas the *Voyages* site only includes shipments that carried enslaved people across the Atlantic, the intercolonial database includes only shipments originating in one American colony and delivering African people to another. All intercolonial voyages were checked against *Voyages* before being added to the intercolonial database to ensure that they truly originated in the colonies rather than being continuations of transatlantic voyages that stopped in multiple American ports. The principal sources for the intercolonial database are the Naval Office Shipping Lists (port records) for all British colonies in North America and the Caribbean for which they survive. Those records are supplemented with references to specific shipments in merchant correspondence, newspapers, and government documents and with information that David Eltis and the other compilers of *Voyages* shared regarding intercolonial voyages; their information was especially valuable for helping me document arrivals in Spanish American ports. All told, this intercolonial database contains information on 7,685 individual shipments that carried Africans between American colonies between 1616 and 1818.[1]

No data set of this type can ever be complete, so developing estimates of total migration calls for extrapolation from the documented voyages to account for gaps in the records. Two levels of estimation are required. First, one must account for docu-

---

1. Naval Office Shipping Lists in Britain's National Archives and on microfilm (Walter E. Minchinton, ed., *The Naval Office Shipping Lists, in the Public Record Office, London* [Wakefield, 1966–1981]): for Antigua, T 1/498, CO 10/2, T 1/502, T 1/512; for the Bahamas, CO 27/12–15; for Barbados, CO 33/13–23, T 64/47–49; for Bermuda, CO 41/6–8; for Demerara, CO 116/17; for Dominica, CO 76/4–8; for Florida, CO 5/573; for Georgia, CO 5/709–710; for Grenada, CO 106/1–5; for Jamaica, CO 142/13–29, T 1/507, T 1/512; for Martinique, CO 166/6–7; for Maryland, CO 5/749–750; for Massachusetts, CO 5/848–851; for Montserrat, T 1/489, T 1/498, T 1/507, T 1/512; for Nevis, CO 187/1–2, T 1/489, T 1/498, T 1/507, T 1/512; for New Hampshire, CO 5/967–969; for New Jersey, CO 5/1035–1036; for New York, CO 5/1222–1228; for Saint Kitts, CO 33/18, CO 243/1, T 1/489, T 1/498; for Saint Vincent, CO 265/1–2; for South Carolina, CO 5/508–510; for Surinam, CO 278/8–9; for Tobago, CO 290/1–3; for Tortola, CO 317/1; for Trinidad, CO 300/16; for Virginia, CO 5/1441–1450.

mented shipments of people for which the exact number of captives went unrecorded. Most port records specified the number of people aboard each shipment, but newspaper accounts and some less thorough port records failed to give specific data, noting only that a ship carried "Negroes" or "a parcel of Negroes." In such cases, I imputed a figure for the number of people carried by calculating the average number of captives aboard other vessels. Of course, averages varied considerably across space and time, so I calculated these numbers from similar voyages where possible, looking only at other voyages in the same time period that delivered Africans to the same port—but I defined the time period narrowly or broadly, depending on the number of relevant cases available. If there were at least ten other documented slave deliveries to that port in the same year, I used the average for that year only. If there were fewer than ten cases in that specific year, I expanded the time frame to a five-year period for the calculation. If that still failed to furnish ten cases, I expanded to a ten-year period, then a twenty-five-year period, then a fifty-year period, and then the entire time period covered in the database. If there were not ten documented cases for the port of disembarkation in the entire database, I then assumed that the port was a marginal destination for enslaved Africans, inserting an estimate of three people on board.

A second, more problematic, level of estimation accounts for times and places where adequate port records or other data on slave shipments is simply unavailable. Small gaps in the documentary record are addressed with some confidence by calculating averages from more complete data for preceding and subsequent years, and considering other historical factors—such as wars or fluctuations in the transatlantic slave trade—that might have made the period in question anomalous. Larger gaps require more guesswork and result in more tentative conclusions. This is a particular problem for the seventeenth and early eighteenth centuries because shipping lists for this early period are less abundant, and those lists that exist often fail to document shipments of enslaved people, reporting only on trade goods specified for monitoring by British trade laws. To estimate the volume of intercolonial slave trading in such cases requires attention to other available data for the colonies in question, such as the scale of the transatlantic slave trade to the region, estimates of the African population in the colony, and anecdotal references from colony officials and plantation owners on the sources of their slaves. From such sources, rough estimates can be forged, but they must be viewed as tentative and applied judiciously. Fortunately, eighteenth-century records are more complete for most colonies, making for less guesswork.

These two levels of inference are separated in the tables that follow to make the estimates more transparent and to invite revision as new information comes to light. The first column in each table, "Documented departures," presents the number of African captives actually recorded in port records or other documents as shipped to a given colony. The second column, "Documented and imputed departures in documented shipments," adds the estimate of captives delivered aboard documented voyages for which the precise number of people on board went unspecified. Where the figure in column two is the same as the figure in column one, this means that data exists on the number of people carried aboard all the relevant documented shipments in the database. The third column in each table, "Estimated total departures," presents my attempt to estimate the total volume of the intercolonial slave trade to or from a given port by making some accounting for missing records. The text that accompanies these tables seeks to elucidate the evidence and assumptions that governed my development of the estimates in this third column. The correlation between the figures in the third column and the first two columns of each table will reflect the degree of certainty for the estimates. Where the figures in the third column are similar to the figures in the other columns, they are supported by fairly comprehensive shipping data; where numbers in the third column are substantially larger than numbers in the other columns, hard data is scarce and the estimates of forced migration are more tentative. (Because the figures in the third column are estimates, they are rounded; since the data in the first two columns is derived from documented voyages, the sums are not rounded.) All of these tables present data and estimates in five-year windows out of concern for space, not because those five-year windows have historical significance. In fact, short-term peaks and troughs in the commerce are sometimes obscured by the five-year windows, but presenting data for individual years in a study covering most of two centuries proved untenable. Since this study marks the first attempt to systematically document and estimate the scale of the intercolonial slave trade of British America, future research will surely enhance the findings presented here. I welcome the revisions and improvements with the simple hope that these estimates offer a strong foundation for future research.

ESTIMATES IN CHAPTER THREE

Estimates in Chapter 3 are discussed in detail in Gregory E. O'Malley, "Beyond the Middle Passage: Slave Migration from the Caribbean to North America, 1619–1807," *William and Mary Quarterly*, 3d Ser., LXVI (2009), 125–172.

ESTIMATES IN CHAPTER FOUR

Jamaica export records do not survive for this period, with the exception of records covering just more than a year in the early eighteenth century. As such, the estimates for Jamaica in Chapter 4 derive more from educated guesswork drawing on anecdotal sources than from calculations based on firm data. Reports of Spaniards coming to the island seeking slaves began in 1661, and virtually all of Jamaica's foreign trade in

TABLE 19. Africans Sent from Jamaica to Foreign Colonies, 1661–1715

Years	Documented departures	Documented and imputed departures in documented shipments	Estimated total departures
1661–1665	797	797	2,000
1666–1670	5	5	1,200
1671–1675			130
1676–1680			350
1681–1685	300	300	3,500
1686–1690	300	300	3,500
1691–1695			2,100
1696–1700	1,211	1,211	2,910
1701–1705	112	112	1,810
1706–1710	516	672	3,840
1711–1715	803	851	7,210
TOTAL	4,044	4,248	28,550

Sources: See accompanying text.

this period was with Spanish America.[2] For the 1660s, documented shipments in the database only include two legal shipments to Portobelo in 1665 and one legal shipment to Cartagena in 1666. They appeared in Spanish import records because they were transshipments organized by the asientistas Grillo and Lomelin, who purchased African captives from England's Company of Royal Adventurers Trading to Africa. That company never fulfilled its subcontract (active 1663 to 1671) to deliver 3,500 slaves annually to Grillo and Lomelin in Jamaica for transshipment to Spanish America, but it did deliver more people than accounted for in the three documented shipments. The estimate in Table 19 assumes 100 Africans sent from Jamaica to Spanish America annually in the 1660s, except for the following aberrant years: In 1665, the Royal Adventurers reportedly delivered 1,600 captives to the asientistas, probably their largest delivery. In 1666, the Royal Adventurers again delivered large numbers of captives to the asientistas at Jamaica, perhaps 1,000 people.[3] In 1667 and 1668, the Royal Adven-

2. George Frederick Zook, *The Company of Royal Adventurers Trading into Africa* (Lancaster, Pa., 1919), 84; Charles Lyttelton, "A Proclamaçon," Sept. 21, 1662, HCA 49/59, fol. 12, National Archives; "The Privy Council to Francis Lord Willoughby," Whitehall, Mar. 11, 1663, in Elizabeth Donnan, ed., *Documents Illustrative of the History of the Slave Trade to America*, 4 vols. (Washington, D.C., 1930–1935), I, 161–164.

3. Nuala Zahedieh, "The Merchants of Port Royal, Jamaica, and the Spanish Contraband

turers collapsed, and African arrivals in Jamaica plummeted, presumably interrupting the Spanish trade.[4]

From the 1670s, fewer anecdotal records refer to Spaniards venturing to Jamaica. Likewise, Henry Morgan served as governor for much of the decade and was less encouraging of Spanish trade than his successors would be. Trade did not halt entirely. In fact, in 1677, citing labor shortages, Spanish American officials gave permission for colonists to venture to Jamaica to buy slaves outside the asiento.[5] The estimate here assumes twenty-five Africans departing Jamaica annually from 1671 to 1676, and one hundred departing annually thereafter.

For the 1680s, only two shipments are documented in the database. The first (described by Jamaica governor Thomas Lynch) carried three hundred Africans to Cartagena in 1684; the other (recorded in Spanish import records because Dutch asientista Balthasar Coymans legally transshipped people purchased in Jamaica) carried three hundred Africans to Veracruz in 1686. Other sources suggest extensive, if somewhat sporadic, trade. First, direct imports to Jamaica from Africa increased dramatically in the 1680s, and Jamaica became an important source for Dutch holders of the asiento. Asientistas even settled agents in Port Royal, Jamaica, to buy arriving Africans from British traders (James de Castillo in 1684; Diego Maget in 1686).[6] Nuala Zahedieh estimates that the Royal African Company sold between 25 and 50 percent of the Africans they delivered to Jamaica during the decade to buyers trading to Spanish America. Likewise, the Jamaica Assembly's repeated attempts to tax the trade exporting slaves from the island suggests that such commerce was frequent.[7] The estimates presented here assume five hundred departures annually from 1681 to 1683; one thousand annually from 1684 to 1687; and five hundred annually from 1688 to 1690.

The database's twelve documented shipments carrying Africans from Jamaica in the 1690s all derive from Cartagena import records between 1698 and 1700, when a Portuguese asientista legally transshipped numerous Africans from Jamaica. Before that date, the clandestine trade still likely thrived, since, in 1691, Governor Inchiquin of Jamaica declared that it was "trade and the *asiento* which are the life of this place."[8]

Trade, 1655–1692," *William and Mary Quarterly*, 3rd Ser., XLIII (1986), 589; K. G. Davies, *The Royal African Company* (London, 1957), 43, 327; Zook, *Company of Royal Adventurers*, 93–95.

4. *Voyages: The Trans-Atlantic Slave Trade Database,* accessed January 2011, http://slavevoyages .org/tast/assessment/estimates.faces?yearFrom=1661&yearTo=1670&disembarkation=301.

5. Zahedieh, "Merchants of Port Royal," WMQ, 3rd Ser., XLIII (1986), 590.

6. *Voyages,* accessed January 2011, http://slavevoyages.org/tast/assessment/estimates.faces ?yearFrom=1681&yearTo=1690&disembarkation=301; Zahedieh, "Merchants of Port Royal," WMQ, 3rd Ser., XLIII (1986), 590.

7. Zahedieh, "Merchants of Port Royal," WMQ, 3rd Ser., XLIII (1986), 590–592.

8. Quoted ibid., 593.

Likewise, arrivals of captives directly from Africa accelerated in the decade—apart from a considerable dip from 1695 to 1698—as Jamaica blossomed as the most prominent port for the English slave trade by the end of the century.[9] The trade from Jamaica to Spanish America received a particular boost after 1697 because the French sack of Cartagena (and the War of the Spanish Succession, 1701-1714) considerably disrupted Spain's convoy trade to Spanish America, pushing Spanish American settlers to increase dealings with interlopers for all manner of commerce.[10] The estimates here presume five hundred departures annually from 1691 to 1694 and one hundred annually from 1695 to 1697. From 1698 to 1700, the estimate assumes a clandestine trade of five hundred Africans annually in addition to the asiento traffic documented at Cartagena.

For the period from 1701 to 1715, the first Jamaica export records survive, but they document only 1709 to 1711. The database also includes import records for Santiago de Cuba showing shipments from Jamaica in 1702 and 1703, from whence the new French asientistas acquired captives. Other sales to asientistas in the period were likely but sporadic, since the French preferred to cut the English out of the trade when enough enslaved Africans arrived from other traders. The War of the Spanish Succession partially disrupted Atlantic commerce for much of this period, but because England was allied with a key Spanish faction, channels to Spanish America remained open. Furthermore, arrivals in Jamaica from Africa averaged about 5,000 captives per year in the period, making substantial Spanish trade possible.[11] The spotty Jamaican export records demonstrate that such trading continued, with 380 Africans leaving Jamaica for Spanish America aboard seven shipments in 1710, the only year for which records are complete. The problem with extrapolating from Jamaica's export records is that port officials only recorded the movements of British vessels, despite allowing foreign vessels to enter for certain types of trade, including the export of enslaved people. Thus, one possible method for estimating the trade in the period is to inflate the 1710 figure from Jamaican records to compensate for foreign vessels, then assume that year's trade was representative of the surrounding period. For instance, taking the documented figure from 1710 (380) and doubling it to account for foreign vessels yields an estimated figure of 760 Africans departing Jamaica that year. If that figure was constant over the fifteen-year period, 11,400 Africans would have departed Jamaica for Spanish America. But the many layers of assumption built into that figure make it problematic. Another estimate of the trade in this period came from Stephen

9. *Voyages,* accessed January 2011, http://slavevoyages.org/tast/assessment/estimates.faces?yearFrom=1691&yearTo=1700&disembarkation=301.

10. See, for example, Robert Allen, *An Essay on the Nature and Methods of Carrying on a Trade to the South-Sea* (London, 1712), 20.

11. *Voyages,* accessed June 2011, http://slavevoyages.org/tast/assessment/estimates.faces?yearFrom=1701&yearTo=1715&disembarkation=301.

Fuller, a London-based agent for Jamaica who presented data on the slave trade to Parliament in 1788, having purportedly compiled it from export records then extant in Jamaica. Fuller reported a steadily growing trade from 1701 to 1715, with a total of about 19,000 Africans leaving the island. The trick with Fuller's estimate is that he did not differentiate by destination. Only some of the Africans he notes leaving the island would have headed to foreign colonies. I have assumed that about two-thirds of the Africans Fuller described departing Jamaica were headed to foreign territory. Since Fuller claimed to compile his figures from no longer extant port records, working from his estimates seems to offer the best guess.[12]

■ Few Barbados shipping returns for the seventeenth century survive either, and those existing from the first few decades of the eighteenth century did not document slave trading because they only reported exports of goods that faced an export duty or were "enumerated goods" in the Navigation Acts; enslaved Africans fit neither criterion. This leaves historians to estimate the scale of the forced migration based on the few shipping returns that do survive and anecdotal reports and comments made by merchants of the day. All of these documents point to a significant export trade to Spanish America and the French islands of the eastern Caribbean. Spanish import records provide some information, but the French nearly always prohibited such trade by law, so it went largely undocumented. The following paragraphs attempt to develop estimates from this admittedly unsatisfactory record.

Reports of Spaniards coming to Barbados seeking slaves begin in 1661, but Barbados governors turned them away, viewing such trade as a violation of the Navigation Act. In 1663, however, the Privy Council decreed that exports of slaves to Spanish America should not be interpreted as flouting the act.[13] Documented shipments in the database for the 1660s only include one legal shipment to Veracruz in 1664 and two legal shipments to Cartagena in 1666, both of which appeared in Spanish import records because they were part of the asiento—transshipments of people Grillo and Lomelin purchased from the Company of Royal Adventurers Trading to Africa.[14]

12. Fuller's estimates are reprinted in Orlando Patterson, *The Sociology of Slavery: An Analysis of the Origins, Development, and Structure of Negro Slave Society in Jamaica* (Rutherford, N.J., 1969), 289–292. In addition to failing to distinguish between trade within the empire and exports to foreign colonies, another problem with Fuller's figures is that they do not always mesh with surviving port records, leading one to question what records he truly used (or how careful he was). Although somewhat problematic, where other information is lacking, his numbers offer some guidance.

13. Zook, *Company of Royal Adventurers,* 84; "Privy Council to Willoughby," in Donnan, ed., *Documents,* I, 161–164.

14. Davies, *Royal African Company,* 43, 327; Zook, *Company of Royal Adventurers,* 93–95.

TABLE 20. Africans Sent from Barbados to Foreign Colonies, 1661–1715

Years	Documented departures	Documented and imputed departures in documented shipments	Estimated total departures
1661–1665	666	666	820
1666–1670	255	713	1,110
1671–1675	1	1	330
1676–1680			330
1681–1685			1,150
1686–1690			1,150
1691–1695			570
1696–1700	264	264	1,560
1701–1705			1,750
1706–1710			1,750
1711–1715	35	135	2,050
TOTAL	1,221	1,779	12,570

Sources: See accompanying text.

Nonetheless, in comparison with Jamaica, Barbados's much greater distance from the major ports of Spanish America inhibited extensive contraband trade, especially since winds and currents impeded sailing from Spanish America to Barbados. Imperial correspondence and other anecdotal accounts contain far fewer references to Barbados's Spanish American trade than is the case for Jamaica. As such, there is little reason to assume major trade beyond the few documented, large asiento shipments.

Unlike Jamaica, however, Barbados also transshipped African people to the French Caribbean in the seventeenth century. By the end of the 1660s at the latest, French imperial officials discussed the challenges of preventing contraband trade with their Caribbean colonies (for slaves and various commodities). The Dutch played an important role during this period, but Barbados also shipped captives to Martinique and Guadeloupe. Based on demographic data from French colonies and transatlantic slave trade data for the French, Dutch, and English, Pritchard, Eltis, and Richardson estimate that English colonies exported 9,000 Africans to the French Caribbean by 1715. That estimate is accepted here (in the third column of Table 20), with 350 people from that total attributed to the 1660s.[15] As such, the estimate presented here assumes 50

15. James Pritchard, David Eltis, and David Richardson, "The Significance of the French Slave Trade to the Evolution of the French Atlantic World before 1716," in Eltis and Richardson,

Africans per year sent from Barbados to French colonies and another 50 to Spanish territories from 1664 (the first year after the English Privy Council declared the foreign slave trade legal) to the end of the decade, except for the aberrant years (1664 and 1666), when the large, documented transshipments in the asiento have been interpreted as those years' total trade with Spanish America. In 1670, the slave trade from Africa to Barbados slowed, presumably slowing the foreign trade, in turn.[16]

For the 1670s and 1680s, the only documented shipment from Barbados in the database (noted in a French letter) carried a solitary African woman from Barbados to Martinique, along with assorted provisions. There are several reasons to expect this shipment was only the tip of the iceberg of Barbados's clandestine slave trade to the French Caribbean. First, French imperial correspondence describes illegal foreign trade as rampant in the period, though pointing to the Dutch as the main suppliers. (By contrast, anecdotal records include fewer references to Spaniards' venturing to Barbados in this period.) Furthermore, the 1680s saw direct immigration to Barbados from Africa grow rapidly.[17] As such, from Pritchard, Eltis, and Richardson's estimate, of 9,000 Africans exported from the English colonies to the French Caribbean, 500 people are attributed to the 1670s and 2,000 to the 1680s.[18] The estimates in column three of Table 20 assume 15 Africans departing Barbados annually for Spanish colonies and 50 departing annually for the French Caribbean from 1671 to 1680. In the 1680s, the estimate increases to 30 Africans departing annually for Spanish America and 200 annually bound to the French.

Arrivals of Africans in Barbados were slower in the first half of the 1690s than in preceding and following periods, suggesting a slower transshipment traffic from the island, as well.[19] The three documented shipments in the database for the 1690s all appeared in Cartagena import records from 1699 and 1700, when a Portuguese asientista legally transshipped numerous Africans from Barbados (to supplement the steadier traffic from Jamaica). The French trade was surely still Barbados's most significant foreign commerce, and from Pritchard, Eltis, and Richardson's estimate of 9,000 Africans sent to the French Caribbean by 1715, I assume that 1,650 people made the voyage in

eds., *Extending the Frontiers: Essays on the New Transatlantic Slave Trade Database* (New Haven, Conn., 2008), 213–214.

16. *Voyages,* accessed January 2011, http://slavevoyages.org/tast/assessment/estimates.faces ?yearFrom=1661&yearTo=1670&disembarkation=302.

17. *Voyages,* accessed January 2011, http://slavevoyages.org/tast/assessment/estimates.faces ?yearFrom=1671&yearTo=1690&disembarkation=302.

18. Pritchard, Eltis, and Richardson, "Significance of the French Slave Trade," in Eltis and Richardson, eds., *Extending the Frontiers,* 213–214.

19. *Voyages,* accessed January 2011, http://slavevoyages.org/tast/assessment/estimates.faces ?yearFrom=1690&yearTo=1700&disembarkation=302.

this decade.[20] The estimates in Table 20 presume 15 departures for Spanish America annually from 1691 to 1695, with 100 departures annually to the French in the same period. From 1696 to 1700, the estimate to Spanish America rises to 30 annually, plus the documented traffic of the asiento in 1699 and 1700. For French America, the estimate is 1,150 Africans departing Barbados from 1696 to 1700.

From 1701 to 1715, the database includes just two foreign shipments from Barbados. The first, in 1713, departed for French territory but was seized by Spanish pirates or privateers and rerouted to Santo Domingo. The other appeared in import records for Havana in 1715, documenting the new British asientistas transshipping captives from Barbados. Since France and Britain were enemies in the War of the Spanish Succession, one might expect the war to have particularly disrupted Barbados's slave trade with foreigners in the early eighteenth century, but English merchants (such as Richard Harris) noted accelerating exports of enslaved people from Barbados. Meanwhile, French complaints about foreign commerce did not decrease.[21] As such, half of Pritchard, Eltis, and Richardson's estimate of 9,000 Africans sent from the English to the French Caribbean before 1715 is attributed to this fifteen-year period.[22] The estimates in Table 20 assume 350 slaves exported to foreign territories annually from 1701 to 1710 (300 of them sent to the French Caribbean). For 1711 to 1715, the estimate is modified because the British asiento began in 1713, although the South Sea Company's operations were tentative until 1716. (See Chapter 6, above, and further explanation below at Table 22.)

ESTIMATES IN CHAPTER FIVE

Estimates in Chapter 5 are discussed in detail in Gregory E. O'Malley, "Beyond the Middle Passage: Slave Migration from the Caribbean to North America, 1619-1807," *William and Mary Quarterly,* 3d Ser., LXVI (2009), 125-172.

ESTIMATES IN CHAPTER SIX

Africans departing Jamaica for foreign colonies during the asiento period (1713-1739) headed almost exclusively to Spanish America, though a single voyage from Jamaica

20. Pritchard, Eltis, and Richardson, "Significance of the French Slave Trade," in Eltis and Richardson, eds., *Extending the Frontiers,* 213-214.

21. "Richard Harris to the Secretary of the Board of Trade (?)," London, Sept. 21, 1719, in Donnan, ed., *Documents,* II, 241-242. See also *Voyages,* accessed January 2011, http://slavevoyages .org/tast/assessment/estimates.faces?yearFrom=1700&yearTo=1715&disembarkation=302.

22. Pritchard, Eltis, and Richardson, "Significance of the French Slave Trade," in Eltis and Richardson, eds., *Extending the Frontiers,* 213-214.

TABLE 21. Africans Sent from Jamaica to Foreign Colonies, 1716–1740

Years	Documented departures	Documented and imputed departures in documented shipments	Estimated total departures
1716–1720	4,500	4,677	5,610
1721–1725	11,422	11,422	13,960
1726–1730	6,009	6,470	8,010
1731–1735	16,175	16,175	19,660
1736–1740	3,856	3,856	4,830
TOTAL	41,962	42,600	52,070

Sources: See accompanying text.

to Saint-Domingue is documented in the 1711–1715 figures. Although Jamaican export records are missing for this period, Spanish import records offer good coverage for the major ports of arrival. Figures from these records have been accepted as an estimate of the South Sea Company's total Jamaican export trade in the period, with the exception of the trade to the northern coast of South America (i.e., Venezuela), for which Spanish records are inadequate. In the 1720s, the company began licensing traders to that region out of Jamaica, so I estimate fifty captives annually (1721–1739) leaving Jamaica in addition to the documented total.

Interlopers on the South Sea Company's monopoly also used Jamaica as a hub for transshipment, and their clandestine activities were hidden from Spanish port officials for fear of confiscation. Accounting for this clandestine trade is extremely difficult, but for most years, a tentative estimate of 20 percent has been added to the documented South Sea Company trade to arrive at the total estimates in Table 21.

■ The data for Barbados is far less satisfactory than the data for Jamaica in the period of the British asiento. First, Barbados port records do not survive. Second, Barbados supplied African captives for the South Sea Company's trade to more remote corners of Spain's American empire than Jamaica did, and Spanish records were less carefully kept in such regions. Third, Barbados engaged much more extensively in the trade to French colonies, which was illegal and thus under- or undocumented. Fourth, there were reports of substantial operations from Barbados to Spanish America by interlopers on the South Sea Company monopoly. As a result, the gap between documented departures and estimated departures is quite wide in Table 22. The estimates must be considered tentative. Saint Kitts, Montserrat, and Antigua are treated with Barbados here because reports of the clandestine French trade mention shipments from all of

TABLE 22. Africans Sent from the British Lesser Antilles to Foreign Colonies, 1716–1740

Years	Documented departures	Documented and imputed departures in documented shipments	Estimated total departures
1716–1720	923	1,003	3,200
1721–1725	54	54	2,050
1726–1730	529	529	2,530
1731–1735	646	727	2,730
1736–1740	245	392	2,390
TOTAL	2,397	2,705	12,900

Note: See accompanying text.

those islands, but with so few records, it is difficult to discern between them in estimating the forced migration. The South Sea Company also occasionally purchased African captives for transshipment from Saint Kitts.

For the South Sea Company trade from these colonies, the documented totals have been accepted as the total trade, with the exception of the traffic to the "Wild Coast," or modern-day Venezuela, for which Spanish records are inadequate. Company correspondence suggests a small but considerable trade from Barbados of merchants licensed by the company for trade to the region. I have added 50 Africans per year to the documented totals for the company's forced migration to this region until 1719, to reach the estimates presented in Table 22. Thereafter, the company moved licensing to Jamaica, so no further estimates are made for such traffic from Barbados. Company records also suggest interlopers on the company's monopoly operating from Barbados to the "Wild Coast" and Puerto Rico. To account for this illegal trade to Spanish settlements, I have added another 100 Africans departing the island annually through the asiento period to develop the total estimates. To factor in trade to French colonies, I have presumed that the trafficking suggested by Pritchard, Eltis, and Richardson's analysis of French Caribbean before 1715 persisted. Since British and French reports on the clandestine trade for the ensuing decades mesh well with the Pritchard, Eltis, and Richardson estimates and suggest no decline in the commerce, I have assumed a similar rate of transshipment—300 African captives per year—heading from Barbados and Saint Kitts to French territory from 1716 to 1740.[23]

23. Ibid.

By the second half of the eighteenth century, Jamaica exported enslaved people to a host of foreign territories—the Spanish Main, the Spanish Caribbean, Saint-Domingue, Louisiana—in addition to the British colonies that relied on Kingston as an entrepôt. Fortunately, documentation of Jamaica's extensive export slave trade in the mid- to late eighteenth century is fairly good. Jamaican export records exist for much of the eighteenth century (though British records often failed to document foreign vessels entering and clearing, at least before the Free Port Act). Records from Jamaica can also be supplemented periodically by Spanish colonial import records to fill some of the holes.[24]

The period covered by Table 23 starts, however, with an exception to the good coverage in surviving records. Port records from 1741, three-quarters of 1742, and three-quarters of 1743 do not survive. Trade was hampered by war in the period, but surviving records from the last quarter of 1742 and 1743 nonetheless show numerous vessels departing Jamaica for Spanish America with enslaved Africans. Enslaved people continued to arrive in Jamaica during the war, and trade with the enemy did not halt. To account for the missing records, I have assumed that the surviving three months of records from both 1742 and 1743 accounted for half of the trade in those years. I have also estimated that trade in 1741 matched the trade of 1742, since Jamaica received an equivalent number of enslaved people from Africa in those years.[25]

Jamaican export records are then quite good for most of the remaining 1740s, the 1750s, and the 1760s. These show robust Jamaican exports to the Spanish, with shipments increasingly focused on the Spanish Caribbean rather than the mainland. Where holes exist in these records, the solid documentation of surrounding years allows for fairly reliable extrapolation (presented in column 3 of Table 23). To account for a gap in the records from mid-1749 through 1751, I calculated an annual average from the documented departures of Africans in the two years preceding and the two years following the gap, which yielded an estimate of 1,656 people exported annually. However, African arrivals in Jamaica were down in the period from 1749 to 1751, so to develop an

24. For more on the Spanish end of the trade, see Herbert S. Klein, comp., "Slave Trade to Havana, Cuba, 1790–1820," a dataset of slave imports on file at the University of Wisconsin Data and Information Services Center, Madison, accessed October 2013, http://www.disc.wisc.edu/archive/slave/slave09_index.html; Jean-Pierre Leglaunec, "Slave Migrations in Spanish and Early American Louisiana: New Sources and New Estimates," *Louisiana History*, XLVI (2005), 185–209.

25. For estimates of African arrivals in Jamaica from 1741 to 1808, see *Voyages*, accessed October 2011, http://slavevoyages.org/tast/assessment/estimates.faces?yearFrom=1741&yearTo=1810&disembarkation=301.

TABLE 23. Africans Sent from Jamaica to Foreign Colonies, 1741–1808

Years	Documented departures	Documented and imputed departures in documented shipments	Estimated total departures
1741–1745	3,101	4,377	6,200
1746–1750	7,174	7,189	8,400
1751–1755	4,201	4,355	5,200
1756–1760	1,894	2,296	2,900
1761–1765	3,566	3,566	3,800
1766–1770	951	951	1,400
1771–1775	2,621	2,621	6,600
1776–1780			4,100
1781–1785	8,975	8,980	13,000
1786–1790	6,461	6,461	11,000
1791–1795	1,986	2,034	20,000
1796–1800	3,559	3,559	8,700
1801–1805	393	432	700
1806–1808			
TOTAL	44,882	46,821	92,000

Sources: See accompanying text.

estimate for the years with missing (or partially missing) data, I assumed a reduction in trade by 50 percent from the average of the preceding and following years. A gap in Jamaica's export records from 1758 to 1761 is slightly more problematic, since the Seven Years' War was raging. What records do survive suggest slowed but not halted trade. Complete export records from 1762, for example, show 240 Africans leaving the island for foreign colonies aboard three separate shipments. Furthermore, isolated Spanish records show two vessels carrying African people from Jamaica to the Spanish Main in January of 1760, so I have estimated that this was an average during the war (African arrivals in Jamaica were fairly steady) and applied that figure to the missing years.

In 1767, Parliament declared Kingston, Jamaica, officially a free port, allowing foreign vessels in to acquire enslaved people (and British manufactured goods) for export, but records of this trade in its early years are inadequate to estimate it with precision. From 1770 to 1782, no Jamaican export records survive, but in the mid-1770s, African imports to Jamaica soared, with more than 22,000 Africans reaching the island in 1774 alone—the highest total up until that time. The totals were nearly as high for the next two years.[26] It is highly likely that a considerable proportion of these forced African migrants found themselves transshipped to foreign colonies. Scattered Spanish records and British government reports on the Free Port Act suggest that this was the case. One such report to the British Board of Trade in 1793 gave annual totals for exports from Jamaica under the Free Port Act showing nearly 3,000 captives leaving the island in the peak year of 1775.[27] Since the report's findings for the 1780s mesh with surviving shipping lists from that period, I have accepted the report's estimates for the years from 1774 to 1782. From 1767 to 1773, however, the report shows only a negligible slave trade departing Jamaica, which does not fit with surviving port records from 1767 to 1769. For 1770 to 1773, I estimate that the traffic continued at the level documented for 1769. This still marks a conservative estimate, since African arrivals in Jamaica were considerably higher from 1770 to 1773 than they were from 1767 to 1769.

Jamaican export records then survive from late 1783 through half of 1788, showing a brisk trade in enslaved people from Kingston to foreign colonies. For this period of coverage, the documented numbers of people leaving the island have been accepted as the total forced migration. A gap in the records from 1788 to 1795, however, is a difficult one to account for. The last fully documented year before the gap, 1787, suggests a slowing of the trade, with just 1,242 captives leaving the island, but the prior year had seen nearly double that number of people sent off, whereas the first half of 1788 alone saw 1,001 enslaved people listed as exported. After the gap in the records, departures of enslaved people were again robust, with 1,994 captives leaving in the portion of 1796 for which records survive. One might expect a slowing of the trade in these years owing to the slave rebellion in Saint-Domingue, since that colony was a major destination for Jamaican exports in the 1780s, but surprisingly, the 1796 records show continued exports to Saint-Domingue, though at lower volume. Surviving import records from Havana from 1793 to 1795 also show extensive trade from Jamaica to Cuba, with about 700 African people traveling that route annually. Arrivals in Jamaica from Africa were extraordinarily high in the 1790s, with more than 30,000 enslaved people disembarking at the island in 1793 alone, making it the single biggest year for Jamaica's slave trade. (In 1787, by contrast, Jamaica only imported slightly more than 7,000 people.) It is hard to imagine that exports of enslaved people from the Jamaican free ports were

26. For direct arrivals in Jamaica from Africa, see ibid., accessed January 2012, http://slave voyages.org/tast/assessment/estimates.faces?yearFrom=1651&yearTo=1808&disembarkation =301.

27. Liverpool Papers, CCXXVII, Additional Manuscripts, 38416, fols. 271–272, British Library, London (hereafter cited as BL, Add. MSS). A different report giving the same figures is cited in Frances Armytage, *The Free Port System in the British West Indies: A Study in Commercial Policy, 1766–1822* (New York, 1953), 150.

not heavy in these undocumented years. Given these scraps of information, an estimate of 2,000 African people exported annually from 1788 to 1790 is plausible, whereas the years of excessive importation from Africa from 1791 to 1795 probably saw at least 4,000 people per year exported. With more than 100,000 Africans arriving in that five-year period, this estimate may be too conservative, but without more detailed records, caution seems advisable.

The years after 1796 are also tricky to account for. Partial Jamaican port records survive from 1796 to 1798, but the records of foreign vessels entering and clearing survive for only part of 1796. From 1798 to late 1801, even the registers of British ships are missing. In 1802, records resume. Despite the gaps, surviving records do suggest a pattern, with British vessels exporting many Africans in the mid-1790s, but few when records commence in 1802. Arriving at tabulations remains difficult, however, because the surviving records only list British vessels, failing to record foreign shipments from the free port. Faced with this paucity of data, I have added 500 people exported to the documented totals for 1796 and 1797, which show British ships carrying more than 1,500 Africans from Jamaica to foreign colonies (mainly Cuba) in the documented portion of each year. The partial records from 1798 suggest slower trade, so I have only rounded that year's count to 500 to account for missing records. Since 1799 and 1800 saw heavy importation from Africa (with over 40,000 enslaved people arriving in the two-year period), these years likely saw a bit of a resurgence, so I have estimated exports of 2,000 of these arriving Africans in each. In 1801, with African arrivals in Jamaica dropping dramatically, I have estimated just 300 people exported. From 1802 onward, I have relied on the figures recorded in export records; foreign registers are missing, but the exports carried in British vessels are small enough to suggest the trade was on the wane. In 1806, the British abolished slave sales to foreign colonies as the first legislative step toward abolition of the transatlantic slave trade in 1807 (effective 1808). Jamaican export records show a last vessel carrying four enslaved people to Cuba in 1809. All told, approximately 170,000 (more than 15 percent) of the African men, women, and children who disembarked from the Middle Passage at Jamaica boarded other vessels that whisked them to foreign colonies.

■ Barbados, Antigua, and Saint Kitts are treated together in Table 24 because they share similar profiles with regard to assessing their transshipment of enslaved Africans to foreign colonies in the late eighteenth century. Surviving port records for all of them are inadequate; none became slave-trading "free ports" under the British Free Port Act, but all engaged in some intercolonial slave trading with foreign colonies in the Lesser Antilles. (Britain's other long-standing colonies there—Montserrat and Nevis—also share the criteria of spotty records and a lack of free ports, but there are

TABLE 24. Africans Sent from Barbados, Antigua, and Saint Kitts to Foreign Colonies, 1741–1808

Years	Documented departures	Documented and imputed departures in documented shipments	Estimated total departures
1741–1745			900
1746–1750			2,300
1751–1755	640	640	5,000
1756–1760			350
1761–1765	105	105	1,300
1766–1770	7,167	7,167	10,500
1771–1775	3,326	3,326	10,500
1776–1780			0
1781–1785	205	205	250
1786–1790	576	576	750
1791–1795	66	66	300
1796–1800	921	921	1,200
1801–1805			0
1806–1808	125	125	150
TOTAL	13,131	13,131	33,500

Sources: See accompanying text.

Note: These estimates include shipments to Demerara until the British takeover in 1796, but not thereafter.

no documented transshipments of Africans from either island to foreign colonies from other sources, so no estimates are made for such trade.) Antigua and Saint Kitts were minor players in this commerce, with Barbados accounting for about 95 percent of the documented traffic in the table above, but since a fair amount of educated guesswork is required for assessing the trade for all three islands, it simplifies matters to consolidate that guesswork in one table. Including Antigua and Saint Kitts here also helps complete a picture of the total slave trade from British colonies to foreign settlements.

Port records are almost entirely missing for Barbados, Antigua, and Saint Kitts from 1740 to 1773, so estimates for these islands are inherently less precise than those for Jamaica. There is little reason to suspect much trade during the war years from 1739 to 1748, when only about 1,000 Africans per year arrived in Barbados, with the exception of 1740 and 1741, when close to 10,000 people arrived over the two years. African arrivals in Saint Kitts and Antigua were also inconsistent.[28] Some transshipment to the French and Dutch islands of the Lesser Antilles likely continued but probably only amounted to 100 people transshipped annually, except for the peak year of importation to Barbados during the war, 1741, when 500 of the over 6,000 African people arriving likely left the island. When peace returned to the Caribbean after 1748, anecdotal sources make clear that Barbados exported many more enslaved people to the French. French colonial officials in the 1750s bemoaned their inability to block slave imports from Barbados (and other British territories), and South Carolina merchant John Guerard reported in 1754 that such trade with the French drove slave prices too high in Barbados to make transshipment to South Carolina profitable.[29] This French demand for British slaves is also suggested by the barrage of transatlantic shipments Guadeloupe received during the brief years that the British controlled that colony during the Seven Years' War. Only five months of Barbados export records survive from the 1750s—from late 1752 and early 1753—but these also show numerous large transshipments from Barbados, totaling 640 enslaved people. Nearly all these shipments are listed as bound to the Dutch island of Saint Eustatius, but since that island was mainly an entrepôt for foreign trade rather than a site of slave labor, the French (or Spanish) islands were probably the final destination for the captives caught up in this convoluted trade. Since the French crown barred foreign imports to French colonies, Saint Eustatius (and other neutral or unoccupied islands) provided safe locations for British slave dealers and French colonists to trade, leaving the French to smuggle, bribe, or finesse their way home again with African laborers. Regardless of the logistics, or whether the captives headed to French, Dutch, or neutral islands, the fragmentary export records suggest transshipments of 1,000 African people annually from Barbados (with Antigua and Saint Kitts as minor sources) during the years of peace from 1749 to 1755. Four to five thousand African people reached Barbados annually during the period, with Antigua and Saint Kitts receiving somewhat smaller numbers.

The Seven Years' War disrupted the trade from 1756 to 1763, as French and British forces clashed and privateers from both sides made trade of all kinds dangerous. Illegal trade between French and British colonists continued during the war to no inconsiderable degree, but such contraband commerce focused primarily on provisions (for which the French Caribbean was desperate).[30] The British seizures of Guadeloupe in

28. For estimates of African arrivals in Barbados, Antigua, and Saint Kitts from 1741 to 1808, see *Voyages,* accessed October 2010, http://slavevoyages.org/tast/assessment/estimates.faces ?yearFrom=1741&yearTo=1808&disembarkation=304.302.303.

29. John Guerard Letter Book, 1752–1754, 34/0321 OvrSz, fol. 197, South Carolina Historical Society, Charleston. For assorted French reports of this commerce, see Chapter 8, above.

30. Thomas M. Truxes, *Defying Empire: Trading with the Enemy in Colonial New York* (New Haven, Conn., 2008).

1759 and Martinique in 1762 temporarily opened those markets to British traders, but vessels coming directly from Africa quickly stepped into that trade, so there is little reason to suspect more than fifty Africans departing Barbados, Antigua, and Saint Kitts for foreign colonies annually from 1756 to 1758, or one hundred Africans exported annually thereafter.

After the war, Barbados export records survive for only the first quarter of 1764, documenting two slave shipments leaving the colony for foreign territory—the sloop *Philis,* carrying ninety-nine captives for Dutch Curaçao, and the sloop *Mary,* shipping six Africans to Essequibo, a Dutch settlement on the northern coast of South America. Port records from British Grenada later in the decade also show a Barbados vessel stopping at that island with an enslaved cargo, before continuing to the French Caribbean.[31] Such records offer a tiny sample from which to generalize, but taken with the fact that arrivals of people directly from Africa spiked in Barbados after the war, they indicate that traders to foreign colonies operated from Barbados on a significant scale with the return of peace, suggesting a conservative estimate of five hundred Africans transshipped from the colony annually in 1764 and 1765.

Starting in 1766, Barbados found a new outlet for the export slave trade. The Spanish crown granted a new slave trade monopoly to a Spanish company that centered its importations in Puerto Rico. From there, the company distributed African people to the other Spanish territories.[32] Import records from Puerto Rico show that Barbados served as the company's major source for human commodities. Thousands of Africans annually faced transshipment from Barbados to Puerto Rico between 1766 and 1772, mainly in Spanish vessels. These arrivals are documented in Puerto Rico import records and counted in the first two columns of Table 24. Since Barbados export records do not survive for the period, it is difficult to determine whether the Puerto Rico trade accounted for all of the island's exports of people. With more than 5,000 Africans reaching Barbados in the transatlantic trade in most of these years, more exports were possible, and both Antigua and Saint Kitts imported thousands of Africans annually in the period as well. Partial export records do survive from Barbados for 1772 to 1774, and these show the emergence of other important markets for Barbados transshipments, with several hundred Africans sent to Dutch Demerara. Some records from Saint Kitts also survive from the early 1770s, showing more occasional foreign exports—one vessel to Demerara and another bound for Louisiana. Finally, import records from Cuba in 1774 show extensive importation to that island from Barbados, with 1,178 Africans arriving in that year alone. (These shipments do not appear in the Barbados export records because they were made in Spanish vessels; Barbados records

31. See the import and export records of the sloop *Jenny,* in CO 106/1, fols. 26–27.
32. Bibiano Torres Ramirez, *La Compañía Gaditana de Negros* (Seville, 1973).

only listed the movements of British ships.) Given this conglomeration of partial data, the Barbados export trade appears to have been considerable between the Seven Years' War and the American Revolutionary War. Documented exports topped 1,000 people in most years, despite coming from fragmentary records. Actual exports must have been higher, so I have adopted a tentative estimate of 2,000 enslaved people leaving the colony annually from 1766 to 1775, though this surely flattens out a more sporadic trade, since transatlantic imports to Barbados fluctuated significantly from year to year. Another 100 African captives are presumed to have departed annually from Antigua and Saint Kitts combined in the same period.

From 1776 to 1783, the American Revolutionary War severely hampered the transatlantic slave trade to Barbados, Antigua, and Saint Kitts, curtailing intercolonial dispersals, if not entirely, then nearly so. Even the return of peace did not restore the slave trade to its former ignominious glory. Export records from Barbados survive for the first few years of peace but do not show resumption of slave transshipment at prewar levels; most of the roughly 350 Africans shipped abroad from 1784 to 1786 were bound for Dutch Demerara. These documented departures have been accepted unadjusted. The next ten years of Barbados port records are missing, but arrivals from Africa were not robust in the period, so departures are presumed to have averaged only 50 people annually. The booming free port trade at Kingston and Roseau in these years might have caused the decline of Barbados's trade relative to the prewar years. Export records survive from Saint Kitts and Antigua for the years immediately following the Revolutionary War, and they document a slightly divergent pattern, showing small but considerable transshipments of enslaved Africans to Demerara and French Cayenne (also on the northern coast of South America), as well as isolated shipments to Saint Eustatius and Louisiana. From 1784 to 1787, the documented totals from export records are assumed to represent the total trade. Thereafter, African arrivals severely declined in Saint Kitts and Antigua for the remainder of the slave trade era. No further transshipments are presumed beyond a few very small ventures noted in Puerto Rican and Cuban import records from the early 1790s.

In the second half of the 1790s, forced African immigration to Barbados revived, and surviving export records reveal that transshipments of enslaved people resurged, as well. Demerara emerged as the most important destination, but since the British seized that colony from the Dutch in 1796, such transshipments are not counted as part of the trade to foreign colonies in Table 24. Martinique and Saint Croix, however, became important secondary destinations, thanks (in Martinique's case) to a French relaxation of the strictures against foreign trade. To account for a few gaps in the mostly complete Barbados export records from 1796 to 1800, I have added 25 percent to the documented numbers of enslaved people departing. Thereafter, export records

TABLE 25. Africans Sent from Dominica and Grenada to Foreign Colonies, 1761–1808

Years	Documented departures	Documented and imputed departures in documented shipments	Estimated total departures
1761–1765	99	99	100
1766–1770	482	482	4,250
1771–1775			4,300
1776–1780			1,450
1781–1785	105	105	150
1786–1790	8,105	8,105	8,600
1791–1795	2,756	2,756	7,150
1796–1800			
1801–1805			
1806–1808			
TOTAL	11,547	11,547	26,000

Sources: See accompanying text.
Note: Includes Demerara until the British takeover in 1796, but not thereafter.

are far less complete, but African arrivals in Barbados declined severely, so there is little reason to presume significant trade beyond the documented totals after 1801.

■ Dominica and Grenada are treated together in Table 25 because both shared similar histories in relation to the intercolonial slave trade with foreign colonies and with incorporation into the British Empire more generally. Britain secured claim to both colonies in the treaty ending the Seven Years' War in 1763, and the empire established free ports at both islands, although Dominica's was established first and became far more important for the slave trade. Transshipments of enslaved Africans from Grenada account for less than 10 percent of forced migration described in Table 25.

Although the British established free ports at Dominica before enacting the policy in Grenada, the latter island appears to have engaged in transshipments of enslaved Africans to foreign colonies first. Surviving records from Grenada from late 1764 to mid-1767 show the island gradually emerging as a small-scale exporter of enslaved people in the first years after the British takeover (and before passage of the Free Port Act). After exporting no Africans in the first documented year, 1764, Grenada sent a few shipments to unspecified destinations in "Spanish America" in late 1765 — amounting to 129 captives. In the following year, port records reveal Grenada exporting more than 400 Africans to Spanish America and to French Saint Lucia. Partial records from 1767 suggest that such trade continued to be significant, despite the Free Port Act's omitting the colony that year. Unfortunately, export records for Grenada do not survive from then to the American Revolutionary War. The letters of a local merchant, however, indicate that such trading continued into the 1770s. In correspondence from the late 1770s and early 1780s, Charles Bell complained of ongoing struggles to collect payment for Africans sold in Spanish Tobago in 1775 or 1776, while Bell was a merchant in Grenada. It is not entirely clear that Bell transshipped these people from Grenada rather than managed the sale of transatlantic cargoes in Tobago, but given his residence in Grenada and the records of exports to the Spanish in the 1760s, transshipment is likely, especially since direct African arrivals in Grenada numbered several thousand annually.[33] To account for such trade, I have estimated 150 Africans exported annually from 1768 to 1776, when war disrupted Caribbean trade.

After the Revolution, patchy records exist for Grenada, showing minor slave exports in the mid-1780s—not surprising, given the prominence that nearby Dominica achieved under the Free Port Act. No trade, beyond the few hundred people documented in port records as leaving the island, is estimated for the period from 1783 to 1788. In 1788, Saint George's, Grenada, was added as a free port, but port records do not document the trade. An initial report from Grenada's governor about the free port trade notes successful export of British manufactured goods in the late 1780s but ignores enslaved people, suggesting that trade was minimal.[34] From the early 1790s, however, reports survive of extensive slave trading at the Grenada free port, or perhaps more accurately, near the free port. Slave traders reportedly traded clandestinely at anchor just outside Saint George's harbor to avoid export duties. One report estimated more than 1,000 African people exported from Grenada annually through such trade. The report was part of a proslavery argument for the economic necessity of keeping the slave trade legal, and its claims about the trade's scale must be taken with a grain of salt. Nonetheless, the early 1790s did see Grenada's most extensive importation from Africa in its slave-trading history, with about 25,000 Africans reaching the island in just three years from 1791 to 1793.[35] Exports of 1,000 people annually in those three years and of 500 in 1790, 1794, and 1795 are likely. In 1795, Liverpool slave trader

33. Correspondence and Papers of Charles Bell, MSS, 30189, letters no. 3, 33, 43, Bristol Record Office, U.K. For estimates of African arrivals in Grenada, see *Voyages*, accessed October 2011, http://slavevoyages.org/tast/assessment/estimates.faces?yearFrom=1761&yearTo=1808&disembarkation=305.

34. Edward Matthews to Lord Sydney, Feb. 12, 1788, CO 5/2, fols. 33–34.

35. Liverpool Papers, CCXXVII, BL, Add. MSS, 38416, fols. 256–257, 288–292; see also Armytage, *Free Port System*.

Thomas Leyland even instructed one of his ship captains bound for Africa to buy slaves that would suit Spanish buyers and deliver them to Grenada. Clearly, the island was a known point of transshipment.[36] Soon thereafter, the Grenada trade appears to have quickly dried up. Port records do not document the trade (or lack thereof), but imports from Africa plummeted. Imperial correspondence about the colony describes negligible slave exports by the end of the century, with one series of letters in 1805 discussing ways to revive the transshipment trade from Grenada to the Spanish, implying that it had recently been dormant. The next year, however, Parliament abolished the slave trade to foreign colonies, so such a revival never occurred.[37]

Like Grenada, the British also claimed sparsely settled Dominica after the Seven Years' War, but the island saw little trade—in enslaved Africans or otherwise—for the first few years as a British territory. The island's economy received a boost in 1767 when Parliament included Roseau and Prince Rupert Bay in the Free Port Act. The colony was relatively undeveloped but benefited from its proximity to Martinique and Guadeloupe, which were perennially undersupplied by French slave traders. Dominica quickly became an important entrepôt. Having received fewer than 1,000 enslaved Africans annually in its first years as a British colony, Dominica imported more than 3,000 Africans in 1767 and averaged more than 4,000 arrivals over the ten-year period from 1767 to 1776.[38] Surely British settlers put some of these forced immigrants to work locally, but Dominica is a mountainous, fairly arid island that never developed a strong plantation sector. Mainly, the colony served as an entrepôt. Most Africans arriving at the island quickly boarded vessels for transshipment. Export records do not survive to document the first years of Roseau's free-port trade, but a 1785 report on the Free Port Act suggests that slave exports quickly reached several hundred annually, with 984 people leaving the island in 1768 (not including some of Kender, Mason, and Co.'s transatlantic ventures that merely stopped in Dominica before obtaining permission to continue to Puerto Rico).[39] In lieu of other evidence, I have adopted this report's totals for the years it covers between 1766 and 1778, but the report inexplicably skips the years 1770 to 1776. Possibly no Africans were transshipped, but the

36. Records of the *Spitfire*, 1795, Dumbell Papers, MS, 10.49, Special Collections and Archives, University of Liverpool Library, U.K.

37. For negligible trade, see Dropmore Papers, CDLI, BL, Add. MSS, 59305, fol. 56; for efforts to revive the trade, see CO 5/2, fols. 72–89.

38. For estimates of African arrivals in Dominica from 1761 to 1808, see *Voyages*, accessed October 2011, http://slavevoyages.org/tast/assessment/estimates.faces?yearFrom=1761&yearTo=1808&disembarkation=306.

39. Naval Officer's Shipping Lists for Dominica, CO 76/4, fol. 49. For estimates of African arrivals in Dominica, see *Voyages*, accessed October 2011, http://slavevoyages.org/tast/assessment/estimates.faces?yearFrom=1761&yearTo=1808&disembarkation=306.

abundant transatlantic arrivals in these years make this unlikely. Furthermore, other accounts suggest transshipments remained significant, such as Thomas Lanwarn's recommendation in 1770 that colonial merchants in Dominica "sell as well to the French and Spaniards, for whom they have large orders to execute."[40] For the undocumented years, I have thus estimated steady trade, taking an average of the report's figures for 1767–1769 and for 1777 and applying that figure (715) to the years in between. The American Revolutionary War then disrupted African arrivals, and hence departures, almost entirely from 1778 to 1782.

Luckily, port records survive for the period after the war. They document a slow resumption of the trade in the first years of peace, but by the late 1780s, transshipments of Africans soared with more than 1,000 captives leaving Dominica annually—mainly for Martinique and Guadeloupe, but occasionally for Dutch and Spanish islands as well. These records are solid for the 1780s but broken by periodic gaps in the 1790s. The latter half of 1792 is undocumented, but the first half of the year saw 1,116 people exported. Since the latter half of the year was usually a slower time for the trade, I estimate an additional 500 departures. Dominica's trade apparently ended suddenly. Records for 1793 show a dramatic decline, with fewer than 100 people exported, probably owing to the French Revolution's prohibition of slavery in the empire. The patchy records for later years show no Africans departing for foreign colonies. As such, despite the gaps in this record, no revisions seem necessary to augment the meager documented totals. After 1793, Dominica rarely imported 1,000 enslaved Africans in a year.

OTHER ESTIMATES

Tables 19, 21, and 23 (with the text that accompanies them) present estimates of the number of African people departing Jamaica for foreign colonies from 1661 to 1808, but in order to estimate the total departures from Jamaica for all destinations, intercolonial trade within the British Empire must also be considered. Chapters 3 and 5 present data and estimates on the traffic from the Caribbean as a whole to various British North American destinations, but since Jamaica was the most active entrepôt in British America, Table 26 singles the island out to assess how many arriving Africans departed via transshipment to North America or British Caribbean colonies. Taken

---

40. Thomas Lanwarn to Aaron Lopez, Jan. 12, 1770, in Donnan, ed., *Documents,* III, 245. Another report on the slave sales of one merchant firm in Dominica suggests far more slave purchases "by the French and Spaniards" at Roseau, with that firm alone selling thousands each year, but the report is likely bogus. It was part of a collection of papers designed to show the economic importance of the slave trade to counter abolitionist arguments, and the total supposedly exported in some years exceed the known totals of slaves to have arrived from Africa. See Liverpool Papers, CCXXVII, BL, Add. MSS, 38416, fol. 178.

TABLE 26. Estimates of Slaves Departing Jamaica for Other British Colonies, 1661–1808

Years	Documented departures	Documented and imputed departures in documented shipments	Estimated total departures
1676–1680			100
1681–1685			250
1686–1690	105	105	250
1691–1695			250
1696–1700			500
1701–1705	4	22	500
1706–1710	170	177	525
1711–1715	233	233	1,100
1716–1720	575	575	1,225
1721–1725	186	193	1,250
1726–1730	673	678	1,250
1731–1735	916	952	1,250
1736–1740	215	228	1,050
1741–1745	74	176	250
1746–1750	280	297	450
1751–1755	273	383	450
1756–1760	161	161	375
1761–1765	2,192	2,329	2,400
1766–1770	932	1,017	1,450
1771–1775	176	437	1,800
1776–1780		7	450
1781–1785	1,296	1,301	1,550
1786–1790	1,465	1,465	1,900
1791–1795	150	150	1,550
1796–1800	521	521	1,300
1801–1805	2,112	2,151	2,450
1806–1808	679	679	700
TOTAL	13,388	14,237	26,575

Sources: See accompanying text.

with Tables 19, 21, and 23, this allows for an overall sense of how many Africans arriving in Jamaica left again rather than settling. The other British Caribbean destinations include some territories that were not formally claimed by the British, such as Salt Tortuga and the Turks and Caicos Islands, but that British colonists occupied seasonally to harvest various resources, such as salt and logwood. Since British colonists were presumably the intended customers of these slave-trading ventures, it makes sense to treat this small branch of the trade alongside the ventures from Jamaica to formal British possessions.[41]

In the first decades after the English takeover of Jamaica in 1655, Jamaica was not a significant supplier of enslaved Africans to other parts of the empire. In fact, during these early years, Jamaica supplemented direct arrivals of enslaved people from Africa with a small intercolonial migration from Barbados. Few seventeenth-century port records survive to document precisely when Jamaica emerged as an important supplier for other British colonies. (Those records that do survive only documented shipments of "enumerated goods" specified for scrutiny by the British Navigation Acts, and since enslaved people were not so "enumerated," the port records omitted them.) The one exception in Jamaica's seventeenth-century export records is the vessel *Margaritt*, which carried 105 enslaved people from the island in 1688, bound for New York. The large scale of the venture may explain why customs officials recorded it. Regardless, there are other hints that Jamaica had begun to transship enslaved people to other British colonies with some regularity by the last quarter of the seventeenth century. As early as 1676, the Royal African Company clarified for colonial traders that the company did not consider private merchants' transshipments of enslaved people from Barbados or Jamaica to be a violation of the company's monopoly on African trade—implying that intercolonial merchants were at least interested in such shipments from Jamaica.[42]

Certainly, by the early eighteenth century, observers all across North America referred to Jamaica as a vital source of enslaved laborers. A visitor to Virginia in 1702 reported, "Negroes are brought annually in large numbers from Guiné and Jamaica." When the British Board of Trade, in 1708, asked colonial governors for information on their supplies of slaves, imperial officials in other North American territories (South Carolina, Maryland, and Massachusetts) agreed on the importance of Jamaica. Estimates of the scale of such trade remain tentative, but from 1676 to 1710, Jamaica secured an increasing share of a growing trade between the British Caribbean and the

41. For the British use of such territories and the exploitation of slaves there, see Michael J. Jarvis, *In the Eye of All Trade: Bermuda, Bermudians, and the Maritime Atlantic World, 1680–1783* (Chapel Hill, N.C., 2010), 185–208.

42. CO 142/13, fol. 192; John Werden to William Dyer, Nov. 30, 1676, in Donnan, ed., *Documents*, III, 435.

British mainland—from perhaps twenty people exported annually from 1676 to 1680, to fifty people per year from 1681 to 1695, and one hundred enslaved people transshipped annually from 1696 to 1708.[43]

For the two-year period between mid-1709 and mid-1711, the first reliable export records from Jamaica survive to document this British colonial traffic, and they show twenty-five vessels removing 309 enslaved people from the island for other British American destinations (primarily South Carolina). All but one of these voyages headed to the North American mainland while the outlier headed to Montserrat. Ventures from Jamaica to other British Caribbean destinations were infrequent in this period, probably because of Jamaica's western location relative to Britain's other Caribbean territories: sailing eastward demanded beating into the trade winds and against prevailing currents, which swirl clockwise through the Caribbean, making it fairly easy to sail to the north from Jamaica—following the Gulf Stream up the North American coast—but difficult to sail to the Lesser Antilles.

From late 1711 through most of 1718, Jamaican export records are again missing, but there is little reason to expect less intercolonial trade than was documented for the 1709–1711 period. After 1713, the South Sea Company's asiento commerce claimed many of the enslaved people arriving in Jamaica for transshipment to Spanish America, but assorted records from North America suggest that Jamaica's transshipments in that direction continued unabated. Philadelphia merchant Jonathan Dickinson received several Jamaican shipments in the 1710s carrying one, two, or three people. Some New York and South Carolina import records from the period also survive and show frequent arrivals of small shipments from Jamaica. Furthermore, Jamaican export records from part of 1718 and all of 1719 show 444 enslaved people shipped to British North America. As such, 225 African people are assumed to have endured transshipment from Jamaica to other British colonies annually through the period of missing port records from late 1711 to late 1718.[44]

Unfortunately, a major gap in Jamaica's export ledgers partly obscures the intercolonial slave trade from the island from 1720 to 1743, but here again, scattered North American records show a considerable trade. New York's import records alone—which provide the only fairly complete coverage for the period—document 181 ven-

43. "Journey of Franz Ludwig Michel to Virginia," April 1702, in Donnan, ed., *Documents,* IV, 68; Governor and Council of South Carolina to the Board of Trade, Sept. 17, 1709, ibid., 256; John Seymour to Board of Trade, 1708, ibid., 21–23; Governor Dudley to Board of Trade, Boston, Oct. 1, 1708, ibid., III, 23–25.

44. Jonathan Dickinson to John Besswick, Apr. 26, 1715, in Jonathan Dickinson Letter Book, 1715–1721, Yi 2/1628, alcove 4, shelf 12, fol. 12, Library Company of Philadelphia; see also Dickinson to [Isaac Gale?], May 2, 1715, and to John Lewis, May 2, 1715, Aug. 15, 1716, ibid., fols. 13–14, 21–22, 92.

tures carrying typically small groups from Jamaica from 1720 to 1740, which amounted to more than 1,300 people transported in total, for an average of about 65 captives per year. Pennsylvania newspapers also suggest frequent arrivals from Jamaica, though they offer less systematic coverage. Meanwhile, Virginia and South Carolina records also survive for parts of the period and document considerable trade, though it varies significantly from year to year. For instance, Virginia imported as many as 207 enslaved people from Jamaica in the peak year of 1733 but received only 8 people from Jamaica the prior year. The spotty South Carolina records suggest a similar story of significant, but sporadic, trade. Given these scraps of information, there is no reason to expect a decline between 1720 and 1739 from the well-documented period in 1718 and 1719. The total estimates in Table 26 assume that Jamaica exported 250 African captives to other British colonies annually from 1720 to 1739.

Between 1739 and 1748, however, war significantly disrupted the traffic. The War of Jenkins' Ear (1739–1748) and the overlapping (and larger) War of the Austrian Succession (King George's War, 1740–1748) disrupted Caribbean trade generally but also affected the slave trade specifically in several ways. By ending the South Sea Company's asiento with Spanish America, the wars temporarily diminished Jamaica's role as the major British slave-trading entrepôt. The wars also proved disruptive to the trade between mid-Atlantic colonies and Jamaica because North American flour-producers had exported grain to Jamaica in significant quantities for the South Sea Company's smuggling trade to Spanish America. The mid-Atlantic colonies now had less business with Jamaica, meaning that fewer enslaved Africans boarded ships returning from Jamaica to New York, Pennsylvania, and their neighbors. From 1744 to 1748, Jamaica export records are largely complete and show only about fifty captives departing Jamaica annually for North America. This lower average is assumed to have prevailed in the earlier years of war, 1740 to 1743.

With the return of peace in 1749, the port records went missing again until 1751, but the good records from 1752 and subsequent years suggest the pattern of trade between the War of the Austrian Succession and the Seven Years' War. It was not particularly strong. From 1752 to 1754, Jamaican export records show only an average of about seventy-five enslaved people departing the island annually, bound for other British American territories. That rate of forced migration is assumed to have held for the period from 1749 to 1751. The entire slave trade to Jamaica from Africa was curtailed owing to the rupture of the asiento commerce, and that seems to have had a ripple effect even on Jamaica's trade within the British Empire, underscoring the importance of the asiento trade to Jamaica's overall economic growth. In any case, from 1752 to 1757, Jamaican records are complete enough for one to accept their documented total as an accurate reflection of the total slave trade off the island. During the middle years of the Seven Years' War, from 1758 to 1761, port records are again lacking, but there is little reason to expect robust trade, given the disruptions of combat. However, partial records from South Carolina and Georgia during the war do indicate that Jamaica continued to transship some of the Africans who reached the island. Those two colonies alone received fifty-five enslaved people from Jamaica in 1760, so a continuation of the average of seventy-five people exported from Jamaica to other British colonies during the war seems to be a reasonable assumption, especially considering the explosion of trade upon the return of peace.

From 1762 to 1769, Jamaica's export records are quite complete and show a boom in the intercolonial slave trade starting in 1763, as the war burned itself out. In addition to the familiar North American destinations, new Caribbean markets emerged as important ancillary markets for Jamaican transshipments. Britain's small Bahamas colony—easily reached from Jamaica by vessels heading toward North America or Europe via the Straits of Florida—relied almost entirely on Jamaica for its small enslaved population. Britain's dyewood and timber harvesting operations in Honduras also received numerous small transshipments of enslaved laborers. From 1770 to 1783, Jamaica records are again missing, but there is little reason to expect much variation from the pattern set in previous years until the imperial crisis in British North America disrupted regular trade patterns, starting in 1774 and especially 1775 with the trade embargoes that preceded the Revolutionary War. Surviving records from North and South Carolina, in particular, show a continuation of strong Jamaican trade in the early 1770s. Since Jamaica sent an average of about 425 enslaved people to other British colonies annually from 1763 to 1769, that rate of transshipment is presumed to have held from 1770 to 1774. This may be an overly conservative estimate, considering that nearly twice as many enslaved Africans arrived in Jamaica between 1771 and 1775 as had arrived between 1766 and 1770. From 1775 onward, nonimportation pacts and war stifled Jamaica's intercolonial slave trade along the most significant routes within the empire—those to North America. Trade to other British Caribbean regions continued, however. Olaudah Equiano describes purchasing arriving Africans in Jamaica in 1775 or 1776 for transshipment to a plantation he oversaw in Honduras. Since that commerce moved an average of about 90 enslaved Africans annually out of Jamaica from 1764 to 1769, that rate of forced migration is presumed to have held through the years of the revolutionary conflict. This is likely, since African arrivals in Jamaica remained robust and since this traffic to other British Caribbean possessions would grow to even higher rates in the 1780s.[45]

The years following the American Revolutionary War show a revival of Jamaica's

45. "The Interesting Narrative of the Life of Olaudah Equiano, or Gustavus Vassa, the African, Written by Himself," in Vincent Carretta, ed., *The Interesting Narrative and Other Writings* (New York, 2003), 213.

trade to other British colonies (and to the newly independent states) but not quite to prewar levels. This incomplete recovery is unsurprising, given that most of the American states did not reopen the slave trade after the war, permanently closing some old markets for Jamaican slave transshipments. From 1784 to 1788, surviving Jamaica export records document this trade well. South Carolina, Georgia, North Carolina, the Bahamas, and Honduras were the primary markets, in descending order of importance. From 1789 to 1795, the port records are again missing, but one cannot assume that trade continued at previous levels, because Jamaica's most significant British or U.S. market—South Carolina—temporarily abolished the slave trade in 1787, keeping it closed until 1803. North Carolina and Georgia records help fill in the gap, at least for 1789 and part of 1790, so the only estimate required for those years is that of the trade to other British Caribbean possessions and North Carolina in 1790. Since the traffic to other British Caribbean territories transported an average of about 200 people annually away from Jamaica for 1785 to 1788, that commerce is assumed to have continued on a similar scale from 1789 to 1795. North Carolina received an average of 35 people from Jamaica annually between 1787 and 1789, so that rate of immigration is presumed to have held until the colony closed its slave trade in 1794. Finally, since Georgia imported about 25 enslaved people from Jamaica annually between 1787 and 1790 but an average of 105 annually from 1795 to 1796, a rate of 65 is presumed to have held from 1791 to 1794. From 1796 to 1798, partial records survive, but for 1797 and 1798, half of each year is undocumented; the average rate for the documented portions of the years is used to estimate the traffic for the undocumented months.

The period from 1799 to 1801 is also undocumented in the Jamaican records but was probably a slow time, since none of the United States allowed slave importation (although at least one ship carrying enslaved people from Jamaica was captured in South Carolina).[46] Only shipments to British Caribbean territories need to be accounted for. Since such trade carried an average of 80 Africans per year from Jamaica in the preceding documented years and 550 per year in the two-year period from 1802 to 1803 (when records are good again), it is assumed that 315 people departed Jamaica annually for other British Caribbean destinations from 1799–1801. From 1802 until British abolition of the transatlantic slave trade in 1808, Jamaican export records provide thorough coverage and record a brisk traffic in forced migrants from the island—especially after 1803, when South Carolina reopened its slave trade to stock up on exploitable laborers before the U.S. federal abolition of the international slave trade took effect in 1808.

All told, these estimates suggest that more than 26,000 African people were swept into the slave trade from Jamaica to other destinations in British America (or the

46. William Read to Jacob Read, Mar. 21, 1800, William Read Papers, 1800–1804, South Caroliniana Library, Columbia, S.C.

United States) between the late seventeenth century and 1808. Taken together with the even larger intercolonial trade that carried slaves from Jamaica to French, Dutch, and Spanish America, out of more than one million African men, women, and children who survived the Middle Passage to Jamaica, nearly two hundred thousand of them—about one in five—quickly embarked on a final passage to some other American destination.

index

Cayenne (French Guiana), 300 n. 11, 370
Champlin, Christopher, 324
Charles II (king of England), 142
Charleston, S.C., 1–6, 23, 34 n. 6, 36, 48,
    101, 105, 112, 171, 189, 264, 266–270,
    273–274, 280–281, 286, 297, 300, 323,
    326; quarantine in, 35 n. 7; slave sales
    in, 44–45, 59, 283–284; slaves exported
    from, 51, 54, 59, 197–198, 200–201, 207,
    209, 211, 272, 281; Caribbean shipments
    to, 55, 59, 74, 77–78, 80, 111, 173, 181,
    184, 319, 324–325; transatlantic slave
    trade to, 103, 171, 187–188, 279; run-
    aways in, 287. See also South Carolina;
    Slaves: demand for; Slaves: prices of
Cheney, John, 271–272
Chesapeake, 11, 17 n. 19, 22 n. 22, 115–118,
    129–133, 137, 172, 174–177, 187–188,
    206, 264, 266 n. 3. See also Maryland;
    Virginia
Children: trade of, 23, 37, 43, 45–46, 55,
    59–62, 74–75, 78, 88, 94, 100, 114, 126,
    128–130, 171, 173, 197–199, 201, 204,
    207, 209–212, 215, 237, 246, 268, 270,
    273, 275, 278, 283, 285, 288, 330, 343–
    344, 348–349
Clarke, Gedney, 1–2
Clarkson, Levinius, 23, 324
Clarkson, Thomas, 37–38, 42–44, 245
    n. 31, 285
Clay, Joseph, 48 n. 25, 59–60, 73 n. 52,
    272, 279, 284, 286
Clemens, James, 331–332
Cochineal, 143, 304 n. 15, 306, 315
Coffles, 285
Commodification: of African people,
    5–6, 11–12, 15–16, 20–21, 24–29, 60, 67,
    75–76, 79, 83–84, 86, 90, 94, 100, 110,
    126, 131, 143, 162–163, 170, 181, 183, 197,
    210, 217–220, 254, 274, 276, 282, 289,
    304, 318, 338–340, 347–349
Compañía Gaditana de Negros, 307–309
Company of Royal Adventurers Trading
    to Africa, 123 n. 9, 146, 354–355, 357
Coor, Henry, 38–39

Cornell, Samuel, 216
Corres, George, 250
Cotton: trade of, 59, 104 n. 29, 304 n. 15,
    316, 341; production of, 264–265, 281,
    289–290, 320
Cranston, Samuel, 119
Credit, 7, 121 n. 7, 148, 165, 168–169,
    183–184, 188, 192, 196, 227, 260, 279–
    280, 306
Creoles. See Slaves: seasoned
Cresswell, Nicholas, 37–38
Crews. See Sailors
Cuba, 37, 41, 56, 65, 67, 70, 82, 91–92, 94,
    104, 140, 147, 212 n. 46, 218, 224 n. 6,
    228, 230–232, 235, 241, 243 n. 28, 245
    n. 31, 248, 260–262, 293–294, 298, 302,
    305, 308–310, 329, 334–335, 356, 360,
    365–366, 369–370
Curaçao, 57, 93, 97, 146, 149–151, 225,
    298, 329, 369

Dalrymple, John, 198
Danish Empire, 98, 303; slave trade of,
    15, 96, 154, 158, 225. See also individual
    colonies
Dayley, Mary, 271–272
Delaware, 201–202, 206–207, 215–216
Demerara, 292, 320–322, 367, 369–371
Dias and Gutteres, 330–331
Dickinson, Jonathan, 24, 206, 210–211,
    377
Doctors: treating of slaves by, 3, 35, 38,
    42, 66, 73, 230 n. 14, 234, 258
Dolben's Act, 64, 339
Dominica, 5–6, 30–31, 41, 56, 64, 87, 115,
    253, 291–292, 310, 320, 328, 331, 334;
    free ports in, 304–307, 311–314, 316–
    317, 370–374
Douxsaint, Paul, 279–280
Downing, Emanuel, 128
Dry goods trade, 65, 83, 130–131, 165–166
Dudley, Joseph, 119
Dutch Empire, 86, 89, 95, 320; slave
    trade of, 8, 13, 15–16, 88, 90, 93, 96–98,
    107 n. 33, 122, 128–130, 144, 146–147,

Malmaison, Hermon Coinard de la, 155, 158

Manigault, Peter, 264, 284

Manufactured goods. *See* Great Britain: manufacturing of

Margarett (slave), 210

Martinique, 5, 64, 97, 101, 153–160, 225, 251–255, 298–299, 301, 304–307, 311–313, 358–359, 369–370, 373–374

Maryland, 56, 121, 137, 174, 177, 206, 218, 322, 376. *See also* Chesapeake

Massachusetts, 7, 59, 73, 100, 105, 119, 128–129, 135, 171, 194, 201, 203, 206 n. 7, 215, 319, 376. *See also* New England

Massiah, Benjamin, 275–276

Mercantilism, 12–13, 139–140, 143, 153, 162–163, 295, 303, 315–317, 333

Merchants: strategies of, 2–8, 11, 19, 23, 54, 58–59, 63, 65, 73–74, 114, 124–127, 130–131, 165–166, 178–185, 187–198, 203–208, 215–216, 226–246, 253–255, 297–300, 326–327, 330–331, 334–335; and comments on slave mortality, 3, 65–67, 75–76, 222, 234, 327, 331; and views of slavery, 25–26. *See also* Agents

Mexico, 68, 88, 92, 142 n. 3, 230. *See also* Campeche; Veracruz

Middle East: slave trade to, 237

Middle Passage, 1, 3, 5, 40, 291; recovery from, 2, 37, 41–42, 62, 68 n. 48, 72–74, 184–185, 222, 226; as part of longer migrations, 8–9, 14, 21, 30, 32, 60, 83, 90, 211, 235, 282, 343, 381; conditions in, 53–57, 62, 64. *See also* Transatlantic slave trade

Miralles, Juan de, 298

Molesworth, Hender, 149

Monopolies, 42, 66, 86, 95–98, 106, 108, 112, 114–115, 123, 132–133, 137–138, 148, 150, 157–158, 168, 213, 214 n. 48, 224, 232, 243, 250–251, 294, 296, 307, 361–362, 369, 376. *See also* Interlopers

Montesdoco, Don Gaspar de, 147

Montserrat, 34 n. 6, 76, 93, 96–97, 106, 117, 122, 222, 310, 361, 366, 377

Morgan, Henry, 91–92, 147, 161 n. 27, 355

Morice, Humphry, 75 n. 54, 245, 254–255

Mortality: in intercolonial trade, 2–3, 10, 28, 48, 57, 65–75, 78, 80, 82–83, 91, 100, 105, 110, 135, 159, 200, 222, 234, 288; in transatlantic trade, 14, 53, 65, 71–72, 75–76, 100 n. 23, 106, 125, 135, 187, 190–191, 228–229, 327, 331; after surviving passage, 22, 48, 57, 67, 74–75, 117–118, 159 n. 26, 179, 276; of sailors, 81 n. 61

Moses, Captain, 2–3

Murray, James, 51, 182, 194–200

Native Americans: European perceptions of, compared to Africans, 29 n. 30; as captives in intercolonial slave trade, 120, 127–128; European exploitation of, for labor, 142 n. 3, 144

Navigation Acts, 121 n. 7, 129–130, 139–143, 145, 296, 301–302, 306, 357, 376

Negrories, 66–67, 259

Nevis, 53, 94, 96–97, 106, 117, 122, 124–126, 208, 326, 366

New Amsterdam, 57, 88, 90, 127

New England, 57, 85, 91, 102, 107, 121, 128, 137, 166, 172, 201–204, 213; merchants of, 28. *See also individual colonies*

New Hampshire, 213

New Jersey, 24 n. 25, 58, 107, 118 n. 3, 121, 201–202, 209, 213, 215–216, 322

Newport, Christopher, 87

Newport, Mr. (merchant), 249

Newton, John, 43

New York, 23 n. 23, 24, 31, 82, 100, 106, 119–121, 178, 195 n. 23, 201–202, 204–205, 211, 213, 215, 241, 322–324, 376–378. *See also* New Amsterdam

North America: as destination for slaves, 7, 21 n. 22, 24 n. 25, 42, 57–60, 75, 115, 121, 135–136, 171–218, 264–290, 292, 323–327, 332, 342, 374, 376–379; ori-

Royal African Company, 19, 53, 55 n. 34, 95–98, 106, 108, 112, 115, 119–126, 129–133, 137, 147–150, 161–162, 191 n. 20, 214 n. 48, 226, 228, 245 n. 31, 309 n. 20, 355, 376

Rum. *See* Sugar (and sugar products)

Runaway slaves, 40–41, 68, 287–288. *See also* Rebellion; Slaves

Russell, Nathaniel, 324

Ruth (slave), 273

Rutherford, James, 198

Ryan, John, 207

Sailors: oversight of slaves by, 2, 33, 37, 42, 76, 81–82, 167, 216–217, 275, 344; enslaved people working as, 2, 33–34, 45, 57, 76, 81, 210, 269, 287, 348; conditions for, 52 n. 30, 54, 159, 263; average numbers of, aboard slave ships, 56–57, 81–82, 99, 167; mortality of, 70, 72, 81, 252; abuse of slaves by, 70, 75–80, 100, 106; of African descent, 79–81; firing of, after Middle Passage, 99; employment of, 187, 223, 243, 258; smuggling of, 241

Saint Christopher. *See* Saint Kitts

Saint Croix, 74–75, 100, 155, 206, 370

Saint-Domingue, 1, 92, 153, 156, 158, 251, 293, 303, *305*, 308–310, 312–313, 316, 328, 334, 360, 363, 365. *See also* Haiti

Saint Eustatius, 96–98, 253, 297–298, 303, 368, 370

Saint George. *See* Grenada

Saint Kitts, 23, 43–44, 50, 59, 75, 93, 96–97, 117, 122, 156, 180, 207, 222, 253, 268, 270, 276, 281, 297–298, 308, 326, 331, 361–362, 366–370

Saint Lucia, 253, 372

Saint Martin, 79

Saint Thomas, *97*–98, 154, 158, 225

Saint Vincent, 40, 101 n. 24, 320

Saltonstall, Gurdon, 119

Sampson (slave), 209

Santo Domingo, 87, 97, 140, 228, *230*, 236, 255, 260, 294, 303, *305*, 360

Savannah. *See* Georgia

Scarborough, Edmund, 127–128

Seller, Matthias, 280

Senegambia, 1–2, *47*, 55; captives from, 1, 20, 109–110, 134, 150–152, 160, 180, 184–188, 255, 278, 310, 325, 342–343. *See also* Upper Guinea: captives from

Seven Years' War, 1–2, 192, 197 n. 25, 214, 266, 276, 292–294, 296, 301–305, 319–320, 364, 368, 370–371, 373, 378

Seymour, John, 137

Shackles, 55–56, 285

Shipmates (enslaved), 10, 46, 48–49, 53, 61, 63, 67, 74–75, 108, 222, 343–344

Ships. *See* Vessel types

'Sibell (slave), 45, 337, 344–345

Sierra Leone, *47*, 195; captives from, 40, 82, 151, 215, 271, 325. *See also* Upper Guinea: captives from

Silver, 86, 104 n. 29, 139–145, 149–150, 161–163, 165, 234, 238–239, 260–261, 306, 315, 330

Sisson, Edward, 248–249

Slaves: shipboard experiences of, 1–3, 8–10, 19–20, 25, 30–31, 33, 35–36, 46–58, 60, 62–65, 69–84, 86, 102–103, 108, 110–112, 135, 173, 216–217, 254, 281, 311, 319, 337, 345; sicknesses of, 2–5, 8, 10, 22, 28, 35, 38–39, 41–42, 56–58, 60–61, 65–67, 71–75, 80–81, 83, 95, 125–126, 135, 138, 159, 190–191, 198, 216, 222, 226, 229, 234, 236, 245, 254, 283–284, 337; sales of, 3–5, 23, 25, 27, 29, 35, 38–39, 43–44, 58–62, 65–68, 75, 123, 126, 180, 183, 205–209, 217, 254–256, 268–271, 276–281, 283–284, 299, 319, 329–331, 343, 349; separations of, 4, 10, 42–46, 49, 60–63, 67, 83, 92, 108–109, 135, 151, 173, 179, 203, 207, 209, 211–212, 229, 236, 311–312, 343–345, 348–349; overland migrations of, 4, 8–9, 19, 68, 95, 193–194, 206, 216, 266, 282–288, 308; domestic service of, 24, 142, 209–212; cultures of, 44, 46, 108, 135, 187, 199–200, 212,

237, 342–347; "refuse," 73, 102, 124–127, 129–130, 139, 157–158, 162, 171, 197, 200, 206, 216–217, 226, 229, 236, 244–246, 255–256, 276, 283, 330; in Spanish America, 237. *See also* Commodification: of African people; Mortality: in intercolonial trade; Rebellion; Runaway slaves; Sailors: enslaved people working as
—demand for, 6–7, 10, 59, 95–96, 102, 124, 127, 137, 171–172, 178–179, 187, 192, 204, 212, 282, 291, 295, 304, 320–321, 328, 340–341, 343; in South Carolina, 1–2, 4–5, 23, 78, 178–181, 183, 266–269, 271, 279–281, 324–325; in Barbados, 2, 252, 296, 300; in French colonies, 8, 11–13, 153, 156–159, 293–294, 296, 299–300, 302, 368; in Spanish colonies, 11–13, 142–144, 147, 163–164, 167, 227–228, 232–237, 243, 293–294, 296, 298, 302; in Pennsylvania, 24, 205–207, 210–211, 214, 217–218; in Jamaica, 37, 147, 223, 238, 243–244, 316, 330; in North Carolina, 102, 182, 196; in Virginia, 131, 181, 269–270, 275–278; in Maryland, 137; in New York, 213, 215; in Dominica, 328
—prices of, 2, 6–7, 28, 42, 45, 73, 86, 103, 126, 129, 184, 187–191, 200, 228, 289, 318, 326–331, 348; in South Carolina, 2, 4, 59, 78, 178–182, 268–269, 279–280, 284, 324–325; for seasoned slaves, 22–23, 210; in Barbados, 112–113, 180–181, 229, 251, 300, 318–319, 368; in French colonies, 156–157, 159, 251–252, 300, 334, 339, 368; in Jamaica, 162, 166 n. 35; for women and children, 173, 211, 237; in Africa, 174, 292; in North Carolina, 195–197; in northern colonies, 211, 215, 218; in Spanish America, 227, 234, 236–237, 262, 339; in Virginia, 251, 275–278; in Antigua, 319; in Demerara, 321
—seasoned: rarity of, in intercolonial trade, 21–24; and encounters with arriving Africans, 36, 39, 239, 274, 282, 287; resistance of, to sales, 46 n. 24; in intercolonial trade, 72, 204, 208–210, 276, 280, 324

Slave trade: seasonality of, 2, 179–180, 183; layovers in, 2, 35–46, 58–62, 162, 173, 221–222, 234, 238–239, 244–245; duration of, 5, 8–10, 66, 74, 83, 88, 90, 173, 191, 206, 221–222, 281, 326–327; within the United States, 15 n. 17, 27 n. 28, 79, 265–266, 285, 333; unsold captives in, 59–60. *See also* Africa: slave trade in; Intercolonial slave trade; Middle Passage; Slaves; Transatlantic slave trade

Sloane, Hans, 346

Smallpox, 2, 38, 41, 65–66, 72–73, 229

Smith, Venture, 53, 203

Smuggling. *See* Interlopers

South Carolina, 32, 98–99, 103, 115; intercolonial slave trade to, 1–3, 11, 22–24, 55, 59, 92, 112, 120–121, 174, 176, 178–186, 247, 270, 281, 319, 323, 342, 348, 368, 376–380; transatlantic slave trade to, 1–2, 106, 174, 176, 178–180, 184–186, 189, 192, 271, 279–281, 283–284, 342; and dispersal of captives, 5, 102, 193, 195, 207, 264, 266–275, 279–281, 286; slave culture in, 345–346. *See also* Slaves: demand for, in South Carolina; *individual towns*

South-Carolina Gazette, 3, 178, 183, 262, 270, 287–288, 323

South Sea Company, 19, 36, 40, 42, 61–62, 65–67, 74, 78 n. 57, 104, 164, 219–251, 254–263, 294, 296–298, 315, 360–362, 377–378; creation of, 168–170; smuggling of, 213, 222, 239–242, 247–248, 262–263

Spain. *See* Spanish Empire

Spanish Empire, 86–93, 116, 158, 302–303; British trade to, 6–8, 11–13, 36–37, 40, 42, 48, 61–67, 74, 98, 139–153, 160–170, 213, 219–251, 254–263, 293–294, 296–298, 302–304, 306–310, 313, 315–

317, 325–326, 329–330, 334–335, 337–341, 348–349, 351, 353–365, 368–369, 371–374, 377–378, 381; and reliance on foreign trade, 8, 16, 143–144, 163–164, 293, 310, 356; Portuguese trade to, 8, 87–90, 100, 145, 152; Dutch trade to, 8, 13, 96 n. 16, 144, 146–147, 297–298; trade policies of, 12–13, 142–144, 163, 260–261, 263, 293–294, 303, 310, 335, 341, 355; slave trade within, 67–69, 82–83, 142; French trade to, 94, 156; slave regimes within, 151–152. *See also Asiento de negros; individual regions and towns*

Spotswood, Alexander, 101–102
Spriggs, Francis, 104–105
Stapleton, William, 106, 125
Stead, Benjamin, 284
Stede, Edwin, 53, 74, 124–126, 134, 167
Steuart, Charles, 23, 50, 75, 181, 183, 269–270, 275–277
Stuart, Francis, 59, 281
Sugar (and sugar products): production of, 1, 11, 89, 96 n. 16, 116, 130, 132, 135–136, 150, 153, 160, 171–173, 211, 257, 293–294, 304–306, 309, 314, 320; trade of, 11, 27, 46, 51, 59, 83, 97, 99, 104, 111, 130–132, 137, 139–140, 143, 158, 172, 181–182, 189, 195, 201, 204, 253, 278, 306, 314–317, 347–348; consumption of, 291
Suicide, 80

Taylor and Snelson, 278
Teach, Edward (Blackbeard), 101–103, 108
Thompson, William, 268
Timber trade, 11, 27, 139, 172, 204, 306, 376, 379
Tobacco: trade of, 11, 99, 129–131, 139–140, 183; production of, 172, 178, 304; consumption of, 291
Tobago, 40, 115, 292, 320, 372
Trafford, Henry, 327
Transatlantic slave trade: organization of, 2, 8; British traders in, 6, 10–11, 15,

112, 114–115, 137–138, 142, 147–148, 150, 156, 223–224, 238, 252, 292–293, 296, 298, 315; scale of, 6–7, 11, 13–14, 99, 114, 122–123, 133, 137–138, 171, 174–177, 201, 218, 223, 279, 291–292, 296, 298, 311, 317, 320–322, 352, 358, 364–370, 374; Portuguese traders in, 6, 8, 87–90, 100, 145, 152, 298; Brazilian traders in, 6; cargo sizes in, 7, 10, 167; concentration of deliveries in, 7, 9, 95, 115–124, 171–172, 187–192, 203, 222, 227–228, 243, 272, 291, 293, 316, 320, 325–331, 334–335; historiography of, 13–15, 18, 265–266, 314–315, 348, 351; sales after, 35–39, 41–46, 58, 62, 126–127, 187, 244–245, 268, 275, 277, 281, 329; vessel sizes in, 46, 49, 192, 252; embarkation regions in, 47, 108–110, 152, 159–160, 185–188, 238–239, 254–255, 300–301, 312–313, 325–326; shipboard conditions in, 52–55, 64–65, 184; crews in, 56; rebellion in, 81, 99; Dutch traders in, 93, 298; French traders in, 156, 252, 298. *See also* Abolitionism; Intercolonial slave trade; Mortality; Slave trade
Treaty of Madrid, 89, 91–92, 147
Treaty of Paris, 302, 320, 371
Treaty of Tordesillas, 143–144
Treaty of Utrecht, 169–170, 296
Trinidad, 40, 232, 292
Tucker, Samuel, 58–59, 215–216
Tullideph, David, 194
Turks and Caicos Islands, 98–99, 314, 376
Tyndall and Assheton, 42, 190–191, 243, 245 n. 31

Upper Guinea: captives from, 238–239, 301, 325–326. *See also* Senegambia; Sierra Leone; Windward Coast (Africa)

Vane, Charles, 103
Vaucresson, Nicolas François Arnoul de, 154

Venezuela, *69*, 87, *97*, *230*, 232, 249, 361–362

Veracruz, 66, 68, 92, 149, 221, 225, 228, *230*, 232, 239–241, 246–248, 250, 355, 357. *See also* Mexico

Vessel types, 49–50, 63–64; brigs (or brigantines), 2, 46, 50–51, 72, 82, 100–101, 105, 215, 269–270, 277; schooners, 5, 49–51, 56, 62–64, 81–82, 215–216, 269, 275; sloops, 42, 49–52, 55–56, 59, 61–66, 70, 76, 79, 94, 100, 103–104, 111–112, 137, 164–167, 170, 224, 227, 230, 232–233, 236, 241–242, 244–247, 255, 257–258, 262, 343, 369

Virginia, 140, 264; intercolonial slave trade to, 23, 32–33, 39, 50, 54, 57, 75, 88–93, 102, 121, 127, 129–133, 137–138, 174–175, 181, 183, 185, 215, 251, 322, 343, 376, 378; transatlantic slave trade to, 101, 129–133, 137–138, 171, 174–175, 189, 192, 200, 215, 269, 277–278, 376; and dispersal of captives, 102, 178, 192–193, 200, 269–270, 276–278, 283–284, 286–287; African culture in, 135. *See also* Chesapeake

Wade, Thomas, 280

War of Jenkins' Ear, 213, 263, 295–296, 378

War of the Austrian Succession, 263, 293, 296, 318, 378. *See also* King George's War

War of the Spanish Succession, 154, 165, 168–170, 259 n. 48, 356, 360. *See also* Queen Anne's War

Washington, George, 322

Watson, John, 192

Watts, John, 215

Watts, Richard, 55, 181–182, 185 n. 15, 297

Weare, Henry, 283

West central Africa, *47*, 93; captives from, 90, 109–110, 134, 150–152, 160, 186–188, 238–239, 254–255, 277, 300–301, 313, 325–326, 344, 346. *See also* Angola: captives from

Wheatley, Phillis, 212

Wheat trade. *See* Flour trade

Williams, Eric, 12 n. 14, 314–315

Windward Coast (Africa), *47*; captives from, 40, 272, 279, 325, 342. *See also* Upper Guinea: captives from

Windward ("Wild") Coast (South America), *230*, 250

Winthrop, John, 90, 128

Women: and nursing of slaves, 3; as captives, 3, 5, 37, 43–46, 48, 55, 58–62, 74–75, 78–79, 91, 111, 114, 128–129, 136, 173, 197–200, 204, 206, 208, 210, 215, 237, 268, 270, 273, 276, 278, 283, 285, 330, 359; as pirates, 103; as overseers, 204–205; as buyers, 271–272

Woodbe, Emanuel, 204–205

Woodbridge, Dudley, 220 n. 1, 228, *231–232*

Woodrop, William, 279–280

Wragg, Samuel, 281

Wright, Thomas, 196

Yaws, 38, 60, 66, 72–74

Yeates, John, 210

Young, William, 341

Zong (slave ship), 75–76